the Valuation

of Business Interests

Ian R. Campbell
Howard E. Johnson

National Library of Canada Cataloguing in Publication Data

Campbell, Ian R.
  Valuation of business interests

Includes bibliographical references and index.
ISBN 0-88800-614-4 (bound)   ISBN 0-88800-624-1 (pbk.)

1. Business enterprises — Valuation. I. Johnson, Howard E., 1966- .
II. Canadian Institute of Chartered Accountants. III. Title.

HG4028.V3C36 2001   658.15   C2001-930063-8

Copyright © 2001
Ian R. Campbell
Howard E. Johnson

Printed and bound in Canada

Disclaimer

The income tax, corporations law, Family Law and other legal references contained in this book are included for information and general guidance only. Because the specific facts related to each business transaction may lead to different interpretations or application of the relevant law, no commercial transaction should be consummated without seeking the advice of legal and tax counsel.

Authors

Ian R. Campbell, FCA, FCBV

Ian R. Campbell is a graduate of the University of Western Ontario School of Business Administration, a Fellow of the Canadian Institute of Chartered Accountants and a Fellow and founding member of the Canadian Institute of Chartered Business Valuators. He is the author of the previous business valuation texts *The Principles and Practice of Business Valuation* (1975), Richard De Boo Limited, Toronto, *Business Valuation for Business People* (1981), Richmond House Publishing Limited, Toronto, *Business Valuation, A Non-Technical Guide for Business People* (1984), The Canadian Institute of Chartered Accountants, Toronto and *The Valuation and Pricing of Privately Held Business Interests* (1990), The Canadian Institute of Chartered Accountants, Toronto. Mr. Campbell is Editor-in-Chief, *Canada Valuation Service* (a loose-leaf periodical), Carswell Publishing Limited, Toronto. He is a Director and past Director of several publicly held and privately held Canadian corporations.

Howard E. Johnson, CA, CMA, MBA, CBV, CPA

Howard E. Johnson holds a Bachelor of Commerce Degree from Concordia University (Governor General's Award, 1988), a Graduate Diploma in Public Accountancy from McGill University (Kenneth F. Byrd Prize, 1989) and a Masters degree in Business Administration from McMaster University (D.M. Heddon Gold Medal, 1992). Mr. Johnson is a member of the Institute of Chartered Accountants of Ontario, the Society of Management Accountants of Ontario, the Canadian Institute of Chartered Business Valuators, and the American Institute of Certified Public Accountants. He received national honours standing in each of the Chartered Accountancy (1989), Certified Management Accountancy (1990) and Chartered Business Valuator (1998) membership examinations. He is a Contributing Editor for *Canada Valuation Service* and has written several articles on business valuation and related topics. Mr. Johnson has held senior management positions in industry, including Chief Financial Officer of a mid-sized equipment manufacturing company, and Corporate Planning Manager of a multi-national food company.

Messrs. Campbell and Johnson are Principals in **Campbell Valuation Partners Limited** (www.campbellvaluation.com), one of Canada's leading consulting firms dealing exclusively in business valuation and related acquisition, divestiture, financial litigation, and advisory services.

Preface

The manuscript for this book was delivered to the publisher in the fall of the year 2000 – a particularly interesting time from the point of view of business valuation. In the past seven years we have lived in a heated growth economy in North America, and have seen the emergence and continuing development of the Internet and resultant 'information age'. Mature so-called 'Old Economy' companies have fallen out of favour with public stock market participants, many of whom seem caught up in a short-term trading speculative maelstrom. Seemingly, shares in any public company that is involved, or peripherally involved, in technology and e-commerce trade at prices based on what appears in many cases to be long-term promises of economically unviable results. Many of these companies have little or no revenue, no EBIT-DA or EBIT, and have monthly 'cash burn rates' that defy what always has been thought to be reality. Stock market analysts seemingly more heavily weigh than they have in the past ratio relationships such as multiples of revenue, forecasted revenue, and forecasted 'growth relationships' to support the stock market pricing of many of these 'New Economy' businesses. Much of this type of stock market activity seems on its face to be inconsistent with traditional views of business value and the application of business value models. Following from this, it is important to understand that this book largely has been written in the context of the valuation and pricing of all of the outstanding shares (or all of the 'net assets') of a business viewed 'en bloc'. In this regard, it is assumed that notional or real purchasers have both a detailed knowledge of the business and a long term investment time horizon – circumstances which we believe are in many cases in direct contrast with the underlying dynamics of the current stock market environment. In the end, logic typically prevails over emotion. With this in mind, we believe the principles, concepts, and valuation methodologies set out in this book will continue to be relevant over time.

With the help of our colleagues, we have written this book for both professionals and business owners. It is a consolidation of our current knowledge and experience. As such, it represents our best effort to explain the meaning, significance, and applications of the principles, concepts and methodologies we believe applicable in the year 2000 to the valuation of Canadian business interests in an increasingly complex environment with constantly changing dynamics. We believe the time we have spent on this book will be worthwhile if each reader gains even one useful point of information or knowledge by reading it.

Ian R. Campbell
Howard E. Johnson

Toronto, Canada
November 19, 2000

Acknowledgements

We express our gratitude to the many people who contributed to this book. In particular, we would like to recognize the contributions of the following individuals:

- Chapters 2 and 12 – Mr. Larry Lowenstein and Ms. Jeanie DeMarco of the legal firm Osler, Hoskin and Harcourt in Toronto;
- Chapter 6 (Real Estate Valuation) – Mr. John Davies of the firm Fish, Marks and Associates;
- Chapter 6 (Equipment Valuation) Mr. Gilles Moss; and
- Chapter 14 – Mr. Colin Campbell of the legal firm of Davies Ward & Beck in Toronto.

In addition, we would like to recognize the efforts of:

- Messrs. H. Christopher Nobes, Tom A. Tsiokos and Darrin R. Pickett of Campbell Valuation Partners Limited, who contributed to the development of this text;
- Ms. Lynn Smith of Campbell Valuation Partners Limited and Ms. Shannon Brooks for the diligent research they conducted;
- Wayne P. Albo of Calcap Corporate Finance Limited, who made a contribution to the development of the principles and concepts discussed throughout;
- Ms. Jodie Price for her administrative assistance; and
- Mr. Peter Hoult and Ms. Maggie Tyson of the Canadian Institute of Chartered Accountants for coordinating this book's publication.

Ian R. Campbell
Howard E. Johnson

Toronto, Canada
November 19, 2000

Glossary of Defined Terms

Absolute risk

The difference between *going concern value* and *liquidation value* at the valuation date.

Acquisition date

In the context of an open market transaction, the date of closing.

Adjusted cost base

An income tax term relating to capital property, generally meaning the amount from which capital gains and losses are measured. See paragraph 54(a) of the Income Tax Act.

Adjusted net book value

The amount by which the *fair market value* of the tangible and identifiable intangible assets (where these are separately quantifiable) of a business, determined on the basis of their value in continued use (adjusted for income tax considerations where appropriate), exceeds the *fair market value* of the liabilities of the business. When used in the context of risk measurement, this amount often is referred to as *tangible asset backing*.

Amalgamation

The statutory joining or merging of two or more previously separate corporate entities.

Amortization

The systematic assignment of the cost of intangible assets to expense.

Appraisal

The act or process of determining the value of something. See *Valuation*.

Appraisal date

The date as of which it is necessary to determine the value of something. See *Valuation date*.

Appraisal remedy

See *Dissent right.*

Asset transaction

A term used to describe the acquisition of a business entity pursuant to the direct purchase of its tangible and intangible operating assets. The operating liabilities of the acquired business often are assumed as satisfaction of a portion of the transaction price. Contrast with *share transaction.*

Associated corporations

Pursuant to the Income Tax Act (Canada), two or more corporations are associated if they are owned or controlled by the same individual or group of individuals.

Base rate of return

An *unlevered return on equity* that reflects the starting point for establishing a *discount rate* or *capitalization rate* pursuant to an en bloc equity investment.

Benchmark analysis

The comparison of an indicated performance measure of a business to a standard, expected, or average measure.

Blockage discount

The decrease in market price resulting from the imbalance of supply and demand that results when market supply is increased pursuant to unusual market activity. In the context of the public stock markets, the decrease in stock market trading price created by the forces of supply and demand when a block of shares larger than normal trading lots is exposed for sale at one time.

Business risk

That portion of total risk arising due to the uncertainty associated with the *unlevered prospective discretionary cash flow* of a business.

Business valuation

The act of determining the value of, or the estimated value of, a business enterprise, or an interest therein.

Buy-sell agreement

See *Shareholder's Agreement*.

Canadian Controlled Private Corporation (CCPC)

A term defined in the Income Tax Act (Canada) to mean a privately held corporation that is not majority-owned by non-residents of Canada.

Capital asset pricing model (CAPM)

A theoretical comparative risk model that relates risk and return.

Capital cost allowance (CCA)

An income tax term generally meaning the amount of depreciation deducted by a business for income tax purposes. Capital cost allowance rates are set out in Part XI of the Income Tax Regulations. See also *tax shield* and *undepreciated capital cost*.

Capital dividend account

An account established under the Income Tax Act (Canada) that applies to qualifying privately held corporations whereby certain amounts, including that portion of a capital gain not subject to taxation, can be distributed on a tax free basis to shareholders. See subsection 83(2) of the Income Tax Act (Canada).

Capital intensive business

A business requiring significant capital investment, with resultant comparatively low labour cost per unit of output relative to capital investment per unit of production.

Capital structure

The mix of debt and equity used to finance a business.

Capitalized cash flow

The present value of a perpetuity determined by dividing a point estimate of cash flow (normally *discretionary cash flow*) by a *capitalization rate,* or multiplying (*discretionary*) *cash flow* by a *multiple.*

Capitalization rate

The rate of return (usually expressed as a percentage) that is used to convert a point estimate of cash flow into value. The inverse of the capitalization rate is referred to as the *multiple.* Alternately, a divisor used to convert a uniform (or constant) stream of cash flow to a capital amount, or value.

Closely held corporation

A term used to describe a corporation whose shares are neither listed for trading on a recognized *stock exchange* nor traded in an *over-the-counter market.* Technically, *a closely-held corporation* has less than fifty-one shareholders, excluding employees (Canada). See *privately-held company.*

Coattail provision (or coattail right)

The right afforded to a *minority shareholder* of a business entitling him or her to sell with the controlling interest in the business at *ratable value.* Synonymous with *tagalong right.*

Compulsory sale provision

See *mandatory sale provision.*

Confidential information memorandum

A compilation of corporate information used in connection with the sale of a business concern in the private sector. A confidential information memorandum is to some degree similar to a prospectus prepared in a public market context.

Conglomerate

A business that is comprised of two or more distinct operating segments or divisions, each of which is a material component of the overall operations.

Control premium

See *premium for control*.

Controlling interest

An equity interest in either a *public company* or a *privately-held company* that by itself is one which carries sufficient votes to be able to elect all (or at least a majority) of the members of the Board of Directors and, through them, to govern the company's business. A controlling interest can be comprised of either the outstanding voting shares that collectively represent more than 50% of the outstanding votes (*de jure control*) or, in some circumstances 50% or less of the outstanding votes (*de facto control*).

De Facto control

A term used to describe the situation where one person beneficially owns or holds proxies for the outstanding voting shares of a corporation that collectively do not represent more than 50% of the outstanding votes, but nonetheless effectively controls the corporation, either by virtue of diffusion of ownership, or by indirect means, such as economic control or control by agreement.

De Jure control

A term used to describe the situation where one person beneficially owns or holds proxies for outstanding voting shares of a corporation that collectively represent more than 50% of the outstanding votes.

Debt servicing costs

Annual interest payments and changes in debt principal pursuant to interest bearing debt obligations.

Depreciation

The systematic assignment of the cost of tangible assets to expense.

Depreciated replacement value

A term used by real estate and equipment appraisers to describe the amount determined by estimating the *replacement cost (new)* of buildings and equipment less an amount for depreciation and obsolescence to equate the replacement cost (new) to the depreciated assets being appraised.

Derivative securities

A financial instrument whose value is a function of another instrument. Examples include stock options and warrants.

Dilutive securities

A financial instrument that could result in a reduction in the *ratable value* of the common shares of a company.

Discount for illiquidity

The amount by which the *en bloc value* of a business or *ratable value* of an interest therein is reduced in recognition of the expectation that a ready market for the disposition of said interest does not exist. Synonymous with *marketability discount*.

Discount for non-control

The amount by which an interest in a business is reduced from its *ratable* portion of *en bloc value* in recognition of the inability to unilaterally control the business.

Discount rate

A rate of return used to convert a monetary sum, payable or receivable in the future, into present value. Alternately, a rate of return used to convert a series of future anticipated cash flow to a present value.

Discretionary cash flow

Cash flow from operations less income taxes thereon, *net trade working capital* requirements, *sustaining capital reinvestment* and other capital additions, net of the related income *tax shield*. Normally, discretionary cash flow is determined prior to *debt servicing costs*.

Dissent right

Where provided in the incorporating statute of a company, a statutory right enabling a minority shareholder in specified circumstances to cause the corporation in which he or she beneficially owns shares to purchase his or her shareholding at *fair value*. Synonymous with *appraisal remedy*.

Earnout

A term used to describe a method of structuring a purchase and sale transaction whereby the quantum of the purchase price is established in part by the future performance of the business being acquired, and a portion of the purchase price is conveyed or paid at a specified date(s) subsequent to the closing of the transaction.

EBIT

Earnings before interest and taxes.

EBIT-DA

Earnings before interest, taxes, depreciation and amortization. A measure of the operating cash flows of a business before changes in net *working capital*.

Economic life

The period over which property may be profitably used, a product may be profitably manufactured and marketed, or a service rendered.

Economies of scale

The decreases in combined operating expenses and/or increases in combined revenues which result following the merging of two or more business operations. See *Synergy, Post-Acquisition Net Economic Value Added (or Benefits)*, and *Strategic Advantage*.

En bloc value

The value of the assets or ownership interests of a business viewed as a whole.

Enterprise value

The total value of a business including both its interest bearing debt and equity components.

Equity value

The value of a business to all of its shareholders.

Externally financed transaction

A term used to describe the purchase of a business interest where the funding for the acquisition is provided by the purchaser through sources external to the business being acquired. Contrast with *internally financed transaction*.

Fair market value

The highest price available in an open and unrestricted market between informed and prudent parties, acting at arm's length and under no compulsion to act, expressed in terms of cash.

Fair value

A value term commonly used in connection with minority shareholder *dissent* and *oppression* remedy rights, describing the basis upon which the acquisition price for the minority shares is to be determined.

Family control

A term used to describe that circumstance where family members, who collectively own sufficient voting shares in a company to control it, are presumed to act in concert to exercise control over the economic direction and *liquidity* of their collective investment. In Canada, the concept of family control principally has been put forward in the context of *fair market value* determinations required for income tax purposes.

Financial leverage

The use of interest bearing debt or other fixed payment financial obligations in the *capital structure* of a business.

Financial risk

The portion of total risk associated with the use of *financial leverage* in the *capital structure* of a business.

Financial synergies

That portion of total post-acquisition *synergies* relating to the benefits associated with a more efficient *capital structure* or lower cost financing.

Forced liquidation

The sale of the assets where an immediate cessation of the business and disposition of assets is assumed on an 'as is/where is' basis. In the context of equipment *appraisal*, forced *liquidation value* contemplates the sale of equipment assets at auction. Contrast with *voluntary liquidation*.

Going concern

A business enterprise that is both conducting operations at a given date, and has every reasonable expectation of doing so for the foreseeable future after that date.

Going concern risk

The difference at the date of valuation/acquisition between *going concern value* and *tangible asset backing (adjusted net book value)*.

Going concern value

The present value of all future benefits expected to accrue from ownership, where a business operation is expected to continue to operate (usually) indefinitely into the future.

Goodwill

The difference between *going concern value* and the sum of the net tangible assets and *identifiable intangible assets* (where these can be separately quantified). See also *individual goodwill, personal goodwill* and *value to owner*.

Group control

A term used to describe that circumstance where a group of shareholders, who otherwise deal on an arm's length basis, collectively own sufficient voting shares in a *privately-held company* to control it, are presumed to act in concert to exercise control over the economic direction and *liquidity* of their collective investment. In Canada, the concept of group control principally has been put forward in the context of *fair market value* determinations required for income tax purposes.

Hard right of first refusal

A *right of first refusal* whereby the shareholder wishing to divest of his or her interest solicits third party offers, the highest of which is presented to the other shareholder(s) who are given the opportunity to acquire the offering shareholders interest on the same price and terms as those offered by the third party. Contrast with *soft right of first refusal*.

Holding company

A company with (usually) no active business operations, owning passive investments in assets such as *real property*, shares in *publicly-held companies*, and shares in *privately-held* operating companies. The earnings generated by a holding company (in the form of rent or dividends, for example) normally are of less significance from a value standpoint than is the appreciating value of the underlying investments themselves.

Horizontal analysis

The process of comparing actual or projected results of a business, normally with the objective of detecting trends or anomalies.

Hurdle rate of return

See *Threshold rate of return*.

Identifiable intangible assets

Assets that can be transferred separate from the business that owns them and which have *intrinsic value* in a going concern scenario. Contrast with *goodwill*.

Individual goodwill

The economic advantage that accrues to a business by virtue of its employment of a given individual who has abilities, business contacts, good name and reputation that could be, or would be, harmful to the economic well-being of the business should he or she leave the employ of the business and compete with it. In contrast with *personal goodwill*, individual goodwill does not expire at the time of the loss of interest, retirement, or death of said individual. Rather, the business has the capacity to substitute another individual to fill the role played by said individual prior to his retirement or death. In an open market context, it is *non-competition agreements* that result in individual goodwill having commercial value.

Industry specific activity ratios

Commonly used criteria within a specific industry used to gauge an element of business value. Industry specific activity ratios often are referred to as *rules of thumb*.

Insolvency

The inability of an individual or corporation to pay debt obligations as they become due.

Intangible operating synergies

That portion of total post-acquisition *synergies* relating to *strategic advantage* or other benefits that cannot be readily segregated and analyzed on an individual basis.

Intermediaries

External advisors involved in the sale and purchase of business interests.

Internal rate of return (IRR)

That *discount rate* which reduces to equality the present value of expected cash outflows to the present value of expected cash inflows. Stated in the context of a return on *invested equity*, an internal rate of return is the aggregate after tax *return on levered equity* expected over the life of the investment.

Internally financed transaction

A transaction pursuant to which all or part of the outstanding shares or assets of a business are sold to a purchaser who requires the business being purchased to fund all, or part of, the purchase price out of funds it generates subsequent to purchase. Contrast with *externally financed transaction*.

Intrinsic value

A *notional market value*, based upon rates of return required by investors given economic and business conditions existing at the valuation date, without consideration of possible *synergies or economies of scale* that might accrue in differing degrees to arm's-length purchasers. Synonymous with *stand-alone value*.

Invested equity

See *levered equity*.

Leverage

The relationship between interest bearing debt and equity in a business (*financial leverage*). Alternately, the effect of fixed charges on after tax earnings and/or *discretionary cash flow* (*operating leverage*).

Leveraged buyout

A transaction pursuant to which an acquirer borrows against the assets of the acquired business to fund all, or part of, the purchase price.

Levered equity

That portion of an aggregate value determination (or purchase price) represented by the difference between the aggregate value determination and the amount of interest bearing debt deemed appropriate for the business interest being valued (or acquired). Synonymous with *invested equity*.

Liquidation

The process of converting assets into cash.

Liquidation value

The net amount of money, if any, available to equity owners following a *voluntary liquidation*, a reorganization of a business pursuant either to a proposal to creditors, or a liquidation of a business pursuant to a receivership or other proceeding under The Bankruptcy Act *(forced liquidation)*.

Liquidity

The ability to readily convert non-cash assets into cash for reasonably certain proceeds.

Maintainable after tax earnings from operations

After tax earnings from operations that reasonably can be expected on a year-in year-out basis prospectively from the valuation date, expressed in dollars current to the valuation date.

Management agreement

An agreement made between two parties pursuant to which one of the parties agrees to offer either general or specific management services to the other for a specified period of time.

Marketability discount

See *Discount for illiquidity*.

Minority discount

The reduction from the *pro rata* portion of the *en bloc value* of the assets or ownership interests of a business as a whole to reflect the disadvantages of owning a *minority shareholding*. A minority interest may suffer a discount for reasons of:

- the absence of the power of control and the resultant inability to dictate such matters as the future direction of the corporation, the election of Directors, the performance of the investment because of the inability to dictate dividend payments, or the sale of the shareholding where there are legal or contractual restrictions with respect to such a sale and a sale of all of the shares of the corporation (i.e. a *discount for non-control*); and/or
- the inherent lack of *liquidity* or marketability of the investment (i.e. a *discount for illiquidity*).

Minority shareholding (shareholder)

Any shareholding in either a *public company* or a *privately-held company* that is not a *control shareholding*.

Multiple

The reciprocal of the *capitalization rate*.

Negative redundancy

A term used to describe the equity amount required to be injected into a given business entity in order to 'normalize' its balance sheet, such that following said equity injection the business interest owes an 'appropriate' amount of interest bearing debt vis a vis its revised equity balance.

Net book value

- with respect to individual assets or liabilities, the capitalized cost, or otherwise determined book value, of an asset or liability less accumulated *depreciation* or *amortization* as it appears on the books of account of the enterprise; or
- with respect to a business enterprise, the difference between total assets (net of *depreciation* and *amortization*), and total liabilities of an enterprise as they appear on the balance sheet.

Depending on what is referred to, this term is synonymous with the terms book value, net worth and *shareholders' equity*.

Net income (loss)

The amount remaining when all expenses, (including income tax), incurred and accrued during an accounting period, are deducted from all revenues received and accrued during that same period.

Net realizable value

The net proceeds obtainable upon the sale of an asset, after providing for all costs of disposition, including income taxes.

Net trade working capital

The amount by which current assets related to the principal operating activities of the business (e.g. accounts receivable and inventories) exceed current liabilities that have arisen from the business' operating activities (e.g. accounts payable and accrued liabilities). Contrast with *working capital* that includes all current assets and current liabilities.

Nominal rate of return

A *discount rate* that includes both an inflation component and a '*real rate of return*', as contrasted with a '*real rate of return*', which does not include an inflation component.

Non-competition agreement

An agreement made between two parties pursuant to which one of the parties agrees not to compete with the other party for a specified period of time, usually within a specified geographic area and within identified parameters of product or service. See *individual goodwill*.

Non-identifiable intangible assets

Those intangible assets that cannot be readily segregated from the operations of a business that is a going concern. Examples include deferred charges and *goodwill*. Contrast with *identifiable intangible asset*.

Notional market

A term used to describe circumstances where it is necessary to determine *fair market value, fair value,* or some other value in the absence of *open market* negotiations.

Open market

A term used to describe the market in which arm's length, negotiated transactions take place.

Operating leverage

The use of fixed costs in the operations of the business. Contrast with *financial leverage*.

Opportunity cost

The value of benefits sacrificed in selecting a course of action among alternatives. In relation to value determination, the value of alternative investments not made.

Oppression remedy

Where provided in the incorporating statute of a company, a statutory right enabling a *minority shareholder* to claim that the corporation in which he or she is a shareholder has acted in a manner he or she believes contrary to the best interest of his or her shareholding.

Over-the-counter market

The trading of securities or commodities not listed on an established stock exchange.

Partnership

A form of business organization where persons carry on a business in common with a view to profit. This term does not apply to the relationship which exists between owners of a corporation.

Personal goodwill

The unique advantage enjoyed by a given individual which arises from his or her particular abilities, personal characteristics, good name and reputation, and which is not transferable by contract or otherwise. The term personal goodwill can be used to describe either economic advantage, non-economic advantage, or a combination of both. In this book, the term is used only in the context of economic advantage.

Post-acquisition net economic value-added (or benefits)

The capitalized value of *economies of scale* and/or *strategic advantages* that a prospective purchaser of a business interest perceives may accrue from its acquisition. This sometimes is referred to in this book as post-acquisition value-added. See *purchaser perceived net economic value-added (or benefits), strategic advantages,* and *synergies.*

Premium for control

The amount by which the value or price of a share that forms part of a *controlling interest* exceeds the value or price of a share of a non-controlling interest where it is determined that the excess is attributable to the benefits associated with a *controlling interest.*

Price

The consideration paid in a negotiated *open market* transaction involving the purchase and sale of an asset.

Price earnings ratio

The reciprocal of the *capitalization rate,* commonly referred to as the *multiple.*

Primary offering

The offering for sale of treasury share capital. A primary offering results in the proceeds accruing to the issuer with a simultaneous dilution of the percentage ownership interest of pre-offering business owners.

Privately held business interest

An en bloc, *controlling interest*, or *minority shareholding* in a *privately-held company*, or all or part of the business of a privately-held company represented by its net operating assets or all or one or more partnership interests in a *partnership*, or part of the business of a *partnership*.

Privately held company (or corporation)

Technically, a business that is incorporated, has less than fifty-one shareholders excluding employees (Canada), and does not offer its shares to the public. For purposes of this book, a privately-held company simply is defined as one that does not offer its shares to the public. See *closely-held corporation*.

Pro-forma

A term applied to a document or statement which indicates the anticipated effects of stated assumptions or contractual commitments which have not yet been completed.

Pro-rata value

See *ratable value*.

Proposal to creditors

A scheme for extension of time, and/or reduction or rearrangement of debt, put forward to creditors by a debtor.

Proprietorship

A form of business organization where one individual owns an unincorporated business concern.

Purchaser-perceived net economic value added

See *post-acquisition net economic value-added*, and *strategic advantages*.

Public company

A company whose equity shares and/or issued debt are traded on an established *stock exchange* or in an *over-the-counter* market. Alternately, a company that is not *privately-held* or *closely-held* as defined in Corporations and Income Tax statutes.

Rate of return

An amount of income realized or expected on an investment, expressed as a percentage of that investment. See *Capitalization Rate* and *Discount Rate*.

Rate of return on levered (invested) equity

The rate of return that results when an annual actual or expected (after tax) operating result is divided by *shareholder's equity* at a given point in time, expressed as a percentage. In this context, the term 'operating result' can mean *net income* or *discretionary cash flow*. In this book, the term 'operating result' is taken to mean *discretionary cash flow* unless otherwise stated.

Ratable value

That portion of the *en bloc value* represented by each ownership percentage. Synonymous with *pro-rata value*.

Real estate

An identified parcel or tract of land, including improvements, if any.

Real property

The interests, benefits, and rights inherent in the ownership of real estate.

Real rate of return

A *discount rate*, or *capitalization rate*, that excludes consideration of inflation, as contrasted with a *nominal rate of return*, which includes both an inflation component and a real rate of return.

Recaptured depreciation (recapture)

This term usually is used in an income tax context although it is not specifically found in the Income Tax Act. Recaptured depreciation is measured as the excess of the proceeds of disposition of depreciable property of a prescribed class (to the extent of original cost) over the undepreciated capital cost of assets in the class. If no further assets of that class are purchased in the year, then the excess is added to income. See section 13 of the Income Tax Act (Canada).

Receivership

The legal status of a debtor for whom a receiver has been appointed.

Redundant assets

Assets which are excess to (and which therefore do not influence) the *going concern value* of the operating assets of a business. Redundant assets sometimes are referred to as non-operating assets.

Refundable dividend tax on hand (RDTOH)

A tax account applicable to *Canadian Controlled Private Corporations* intended to create an integrated income tax system such that an individual taxpayer essentially is in the same net after tax position regardless of whether investment income is earned directly or through a corporate entity.

Replacement value (new)

The current cost of a similar new item having the nearest equivalent utility as the item being appraised.

Reproduction cost (new)

The current cost of an identical new item.

Right of first refusal

The right afforded to a shareholder in a company whereby he or she can elect to acquire another shareholder's interest before it is sold to another party. See also *hard right of first refusal* and *soft right of first refusal*.

Risk free rate of return

The prevailing rate of return on money market investments such as long term government bonds, being investments which are generally free from substantial credit risk, are priced to reflect a relatively long term holding period, and hence, aside from inflation related purchasing power risk, put the investor in a position that in all practical respects is risk-free. These securities typically are fixed in income as well as in principal and, hence, generally do not offer any potential for capital growth.

Rollover

An income tax term used to describe a tax-deferred transfer of assets among related parties.

Rules of thumb

See *Industry specific activity ratios.*

Safe income

This term is not defined in the Income Tax Act, but is generally taken to mean the amount of post-1971 retained earnings in a Canadian corporation that has already been taxed and from which a tax-free dividend can be paid to shareholders.

Secondary offering

The offering of previously issued share capital for sale by the present owner.

Security analysis

The analysis of the publicly traded securities of a business based on financial models and utilizing publicly available market data.

Share for share exchange

A *share transaction* whereby the consideration received is in the form of shares of the acquiring company.

Share transaction

The sale of a business interest through the purchase and sale of the share capital of the corporation overlying it. Contrast with *Asset transaction*.

Shareholder's Agreement

A contract between the equity holders of a corporation that defines the rights, privileges and obligations of those individuals.

Shareholder's equity

The aggregation of a company's paid-in capital, retained earnings, and contributed, appraisal and other surpluses. Alternately, the result obtained when the net book value of all liabilities of a company are subtracted from the book value of all that company's assets. See *net book value*.

Shotgun clause

An agreement whereby one shareholder of a corporation offers to purchase the shares of another, and the shareholder receiving the offer must either sell to the offering shareholder on the price and terms presented in the offer, or must acquire the shares of the offering shareholder on the same price and terms as those offered.

Small business deduction

A reduction in the tax rate applicable to *Canadian Controlled Private Corporations* on the first $200,000 (Federal) of income earned on active business carried on in Canada. The deduction must be shared among *associated corporations*.

Soft right of first refusal

A *right of first refusal* whereby the shareholder wishing to divest of his or her interest first offers that interest to the other shareholder(s). If the other shareholder(s) choose not to accept the offer, the offering shareholder is free to divest of his or her interest to third party acquirers at a price and on terms no less favourable to the offering shareholder than those offered to the other shareholder(s). Contrast with *hard right of first refusal*.

Special interest purchaser

A purchaser who can, or believes it can, enjoy *post-acquisition economies of scale (or synergies)* or *strategic advantages* by combining the acquired business interest with its own. See *post-acquisition net economic value added (or benefits), and strategic advantages.*

Squeeze-out

A corporate action taken pursuant to applicable corporate law by a controlling shareholder with 90% or more of the voting shares of the company to remove the *minority shareholders*. In such circumstances, the minority shareholders are able to exercise an *Appraisal Remedy*.

Stand-alone value

The value of a business interest determined without reference to prices that might be paid by purchasers who perceive *post-acquisition net economic value-added*. Synonymous with *intrinsic value*.

Stock exchange

A facility where members can trade, on their own behalf or on behalf of clients, corporate equity shares, debt or other financial instruments.

Strategic advantage

In the context of *purchaser perceived post-acquisition net economic value-added*, those things that it is believed will result in short-term risk reduction, or possible economies of scale that are not immediately available but may be realized over the long term.

Sustaining capital reinvestment

The capital outlay required each year to maintain operations at existing levels.

S.W.O.T. analysis

The process of assessing the strengths, weaknesses, opportunities and threats of a given business.

Synergy

The effect created by *economies of scale* or other *post-acquisition benefits*. The realization of increased *discretionary cash flow* (as a result of the combination of two or more business operations over and above the aggregate *discretionary cash flow* of the two businesses viewed separately), or reduced risk in attaining same.

Tag-along provision (rights)

See *coattail provision*.

Tangible asset backing

See *adjusted net book value*.

Tangible operating synergies

That portion of total post-acquisition *synergies* related to those benefits that can be readily segregated and analyzed in isolation.

Tax shield

The present value of the anticipated tax savings which will accrue in the future as a result of the owner of capital (depreciable) assets claiming *capital cost allowance* in respect of them.

Threshold rate of return

A benchmark predetermined *rate of return* on equity (or *discount rate*) criteria that is applied to a projected cash flow (generally *discretionary cash flow*) that includes both inflation and a *real rate of return*, where *financial leverage* and *debt servicing costs* are excluded, and where *purchaser perceived net economic value-added* (generally) is taken into account. Synonymous with *hurdle rate*.

Undepreciated capital cost (UCC)

The remaining balance of depreciable capital assets used as the base for future *capital cost allowance* claims.

Unlevered rate of return on equity

A *discount rate*, or *capitalization rate*, that assumes a debt-free *capital structure* for a given business.

Valuation

The act or process of determining the value of something. See *appraisal*.

Valuation date

The specific point in time at which a value or price determination is made. See *appraisal date*.

Value

A return or equivalent in goods, services, or money for something exchanged.

Value in exchange

The worth of an asset, or pool of assets, if sold in the open market.

Value in use (or value in continued use)

The value of the tangible assets of an operating business, viewed as a pool of assets in a specific use. Value in use is determined referable to the contribution of that asset pool to the ongoing business.

Value to owner

The value of an asset to the owner of it. The term value to the owner can be used to describe either owner-perceived economic advantage, non-economic advantage, or a combination of both. In this book, the term is used only in the context of economic advantage. Viewed solely in an economic context value to the owner may be equal to, or greater than, *fair market value*. It is never less than *fair market value*. Where value to the owner is greater than *fair market value*, the increment over *fair market value* often is attributable to *personal goodwill*.

Vendor take-back

Where the vendor finances all or part of the acquisition *price* in an *open market* transaction pursuant to accepting non-cash consideration that defers payment (e.g. a note payable or preferred shares of the acquirer).

Vertical analysis

The process of analyzing the financial statements (normally) with the purpose of understanding financial relationships and detecting anomalies.

Voluntary liquidation

The sale of the assets and wind-up of operations that is controlled by the owners of the business, and where residual value normally is expected to be realized by the owners. Contrast with *forced liquidation*.

Weighted average cost of capital (WACC)

A *rate of return* determined as the weighted average of the after-tax cost of debt and *levered equity*. WACC assumes an ability to deduct interest expense when calculating taxable income and can be used either as a *discount rate* (inclusive or exclusive of inflation) or a *capitalization rate*. When applied to a stream of cash flows, the result is *enterprise value*.

Widely held corporation

See *public company*.

Wind-up

The process of discontinuing the operations of a corporate entity.

Working capital

The amount by which current assets exceed current liabilities. Working capital incorporates all assets and liabilities of a current nature, contrasted with *net trade working capital* that reflects only those current assets and liabilities arising from the operations of the business.

Table of Contents

TABLE OF CONTENTS

Disclaimer		iii
Authors		v
Preface		vii
Acknowledgements		ix
Glossary of Defined Terms		xi
CHAPTER 1	**Business Valuation and Pricing**	1
	Introduction	3
	Business Valuation vs. Security Analysis	4
	Determining the 'En Bloc' Value of the Shares of Public vs. Private Companies	8
	Open Market Transactions vs. Notional Market Valuations	11
	The Market for Business Interests	13
	Overview	13
	Vendors	14
	Corporate Acquirers	15
	Intermediaries	18
	Components of Price	21
	Overview of Business Valuation	23
	Overview of this Book	27
CHAPTER 2	**Valuation Terms and Principles**	29
	Introduction	31
	Value Terms	31
	Fair Market Value	31
	Fair Market Value vs. Open Market Price	38
	Fair Value	40
	Value to Owner	43
	Value in Family Law Acts	44

Other Important Valuation Concepts 50
    Intangible Value 50
    Goodwill 51
    Non-Competition and Management
       Agreements 53
    Internal vs. External Financing. 57
    Assets vs. Shares. 60

Principles of Business Valuation. 60

Summary 72

CHAPTER 3 **Business Analysis** 73

Introduction. 75

The Information Base. 75

Internal Analysis 79
    General Business Review 80
    Financial Analysis 81
    Marketing 87
    Operations 88

Industry Analysis. 89

Economic Analysis 90

S.W.O.T. Analysis 91

Redundant Assets 92
    Overview. 92
    Identifying Redundant Assets 93
    Working Capital Redundancies
       (Deficiencies). 97
    Identifying Redundancies (Deficiencies)
       in Non-Current Accounts. 102
    Redundant Assets and Risk Assessment . . . 103
    Financial Redundancies (Deficiencies) 105
    Example of a Redundant Asset
       Calculation. 106

Summary 110

CHAPTER 4   **Capitalization of Discretionary Cash Flow Methodology** 111

    Introduction. 113
    Components of the Capitalization of Discretionary Cash Flow Methodology 114
        Overview............................. 114
        Estimating Maintainable Earnings Before Interest, Taxes, Depreciation and Amortization (EBIT-DA) 118
        Income Taxes......................... 124
        Sustaining Capital Reinvestment 125
        Net Trade Working Capital Requirements. 130
        Discretionary (or 'Free') Cash Flow....... 131
        Capitalization Rates 132
        Existing Income Tax Pools 134
        Other Adjustments 138
        Redundant Assets 139
        Interest Bearing Debt and Equivalents 142
        Adjustments to En Bloc Equity Value 144
        Example of the Capitalization of Discretionary Cash Flow Methodology 145
        Alternate Calculation 150
    Preferred Shares............................. 151
        Overview............................. 151
        Convertible Preferred Shares 152
        Retractable Preferred Shares 153
        Redeemable Preferred Shares 154
        Preferred Share Liquidation Premiums.... 154
        Preferred Share Valuation Based on Dividend Yield 155
        Participating Preferred Shares............ 156
    Different Classes of Common Shares............. 157
    Primary and Secondary Offerings................. 157

Dilutive Securities 159
    Convertible Securities................... 159
    Options and Warrants 162
The Valuation of Outstanding Shares vs. the
    Valuation of Net Assets 164
Multi-Divisional Businesses 169
    Head Office Costs 169
    Income Taxes........................... 171
Summary 172

CHAPTER 5   **Discounted Cash Flow Methodology 173**

Introduction..................................... 175
    Use of the Discounted Cash
        Flow Methodology 175
Components of the Discounted Cash Flow
    Methodology 177
    Overview............................... 177
    Analyzing Forecasts 180
    Cash Flow from Operations 186
    Income Taxes........................... 186
    Capital Investment 189
    Net Trade Working Capital
        Requirements 190
    Terminal or Residual Value.............. 194
    Discount and Capitalization Rates........ 195
    Existing Tax Pools...................... 196
    Redundant Assets 197
    Interest Bearing Debt 197
    Example of the Discounted Cash Flow
        Methodology 198
    Assets vs. Shares........................ 204
    Start-up and High Growth Businesses 205
Summary 209

CHAPTER 6	Asset Valuation Methodologies 211	
	Introduction.................................. 213	
	Adjusted Net Book Value........................ 214	
	Overview............................... 214	
	Current Assets 216	
	Fixed Assets 216	
	Intangible Assets 216	
	Liabilities............................. 217	
	Deferred Income Taxes 218	
	Income Tax Considerations 218	
	Example of the Adjusted Net Book Value Methodology 220	
	Real Estate Valuation 223	
	Overview............................... 223	
	Depreciated Replacement Cost Methodology 226	
	Direct Comparison Methodology 228	
	Cash Flow Real Estate Valuation Methodologies...................... 229	
	Real Estate Valuation Example........... 230	
	Apportionment Between Land and Building 231	
	Equipment Valuation........................... 232	
	Holding Companies 235	
	Overview.............................. 235	
	Marketable Securities 235	
	Investments in Operating Companies or Divisions 236	
	Real Estate Assets 238	
	Summary 240	
CHAPTER 7	Capital Structure 241	
	Introduction.................................. 243	
	Enterprise Value vs. Equity Value................. 244	
	Financial Leverage............................. 246	

Weighted Average Cost of Capital 254
    Overview. 254
    The Cost of Debt. 255
    The Cost of Equity 256
    The Cost of Preferred Shares. 256
    WACC Calculation Example. 258
    Alternative WACC Calculation 260

Determinants of Capital Structure 261
    The Theory of Capital Structure. 261
    Employing Capital Structure Estimates in
        Valuation and Pricing Analysis 262
    Factors Influencing Capital Structure 264
    Short Term vs. Long Term Debt. 267
    Capital Structure Estimation Example 267

Summary 275

CHAPTER 8   **Discount and Capitalization Rates 277**

Introduction. 279

Discount Rates vs. Capitalization Rates. 279

Underlying Principles of Discount and
    Capitalization Rate Determination. 280

Discount Rate Determination 283
    Overview. 283
    Base Rate of Return Components 288
    Adjustments to the Base Rate of Return . . 296
    Financial Leverage Adjustment. 301
    Additional Adjustments to the
        Discount Rate 302
    Adjustment for Post-Acquisition
        Strategic Advantage 303
    Other Considerations. 304

Capitalization Rate Determination. 305
    Overview. 305
    Inflation Adjustment 307
    Real Growth 308
    Terminal Value Risk Adjustment. 310
    Other Adjustments 311

	Discount and Capitalization Rate Example......... 311
	The Capital Asset Pricing Model 315
	Overview............................. 315
	The CAPM Methodology................ 316
	Interpreting CAPM Results.............. 317
	Adjustments to the Basic CAPM Model ... 318
	Difficulties Inherent in CAPM 319
	Comparable Data 322
	Summary 322
CHAPTER 9	**Comparative Analysis.......................... 325**
	Introduction................................... 327
	Application of Comparative Analysis.............. 328
	Comparative Analysis in the United States 329
	Identifying 'Comparable' Companies 330
	Factors to Consider..................... 330
	Comparability Adjustments 334
	Benchmark Analysis 336
	Public Equity Market Multiples 337
	Applications and Limitations 337
	Application of Public Equity Market
	Data to Privately Held Businesses 341
	Initial Public Offerings.................. 343
	Purchaser's or Vendor's Stock Price 343
	Industry Transactions.......................... 344
	Acquisition of Control of 'Comparable'
	Companies......................... 344
	Acquisitions of Minority Interests
	in 'Comparable' Businesses 346
	Transactions Involving Equity in
	the Subject Business.................. 347
	Summary 349

CHAPTER 10	**Other Valuation Methodologies**	**351**

Introduction................................353
Capitalization of Maintainable Earnings
  Methodology.............................353
    Overview.............................353
    Components of the Capitalization of
      Maintainable Earnings Methodology ... 356
    Example of the Capitalization of
      Maintainable Earnings Methodology ... 360
The Dual Capitalization of Earnings Methodology .. 365
Operating Multiples 369
    Multiple of Maintainable or
      Trailing EBIT......................369
    Multiple of Maintainable or Trailing
      EBIT-DA 371
Liquidation Value 372
    Overview............................372
    Approaches to Determining
      Liquidation Value..................372
    Liquidation Value Methodology 374
    Example of Liquidation Value
      Calculation........................385
Summary 392

CHAPTER 11	**Business Pricing**	**393**

Introduction................................395
Differences Between Notional Fair Market
  Value and Open Market Price 395
Notional Market Valuations 396
Open Market Transactions 398
Post-Acquisition Net Economic Value Added 402
    Identifying Special Interest Purchasers 402
    Identifying Post-acquisition Net
      Economic Value Added...............403
    Transaction Costs 406
    Quantifying Post-acquisition
      Net Economic Value Added...........409

	Industry Research 417
	Business Pricing Example 418
	Additional Factors Influencing Price 424
	Form of Consideration................... 424
	Negotiations.......................... 426
	Other Factors 427
	Share for Share Exchanges..................... 428
	Overview............................ 428
	Acquisition for Shares 428
	Amalgamations 430
	Summary 431
CHAPTER 12	**Controlling and Minority Interests** 433
	Introduction................................ 435
	The Valuation of Controlling and Minority Interests........................... 436
	Controlling Interests.................... 436
	Minority Interests 437
	Determinants of Control 438
	Types of Control 438
	Means of Control 439
	Group Control........................ 442
	The Canada Customs and Revenue Agency and Control 443
	Rights of Controlling and Minority Shareholders ... 444
	Overview............................ 444
	Corporations Legislation 445
	Dissent Remedy 449
	Oppression Remedies................... 451
	Articles of Incorporation and By-laws..... 453
	Shareholder's Agreements 454
	Types of Shareholder's Agreements....... 454
	Purpose 454
	Triggering Events 456
	Reciprocal Buy/Sell Provisions 463
	Right of First Refusal 463
	Mandatory Sale and 'Coattail' Provisions........................... 465

Restrictions on Share Transfer 465
Value Terms in Shareholder's
    Agreements 466
Alternative Ways to Derive 'Value'
    Pursuant to Shareholder's
    Agreements 467
Summary 470

CHAPTER 13 Discounts for Non-Control and Illiquidity 471

Introduction................................... 473
Types of Discounts 474
    Discounts for Non-Control and
        Discounts for Illiquidity 474
    Basis of En Bloc Value Determination 476
Discounts for Non-Control..................... 478
Quantifying Discounts for Non-Control.......... 479
    Minority Interests 479
    Controlling Interests................... 487
Discounts for Illiquidity......................... 490
Quantifying Discounts for Illiquidity............. 492
    Overview............................. 492
    Minority Interests 493
    Controlling Interest 500
The Position of the Canada Customs
    and Revenue Agency 500
Summary 501

CHAPTER 14 Income Tax Considerations 503

Introduction................................... 505
Taxation and Fair Market Value.................. 505
    Acquisition of Property 506
    Disposition of Property 507
    Eligible Capital Property 508
    Becoming or Ceasing to be a
        Resident of Canada.................. 509

Corporate Restructuring 510
    Transfers to a Corporation 510
    Share Capital Reorganizations 511
    Price Adjustment Clauses 512
    Amalgamation 513
    Winding Up of a 90% Subsidiary......... 514
    Section 88(2) Winding Up 514
    Share for Share Exchange................ 515
Assets vs. Shares............................... 515
    Overview............................... 515
    Comparison of Purchaser's and
        Vendor's Positions 517
    Income Tax Loss Carry-Forwards 522
    Capital Gains Exemption and Reserves.... 523
    Proposed Capital Gains Rollover 524
    Section 22 Election 525
    Earn-outs 525
Private Corporations 526
    Capital Dividend Account ('CDA') 527
    Refundable Dividend Tax on Hand
        ('RDTOH') 528
    Small Business Deduction 528
Tax Avoidance Provisions 529
    Arm's Length Disposition to
        Obtain Tax Benefits 529
    Dividend Stripping Sections 84.1
        and 212.1 530
    Capital Gains Strips (Section 55)
        and Safe Income 531
    General Anti-Avoidance Rule ('GAAR')... 532
Other Taxation Issues........................... 532
    Transfer Pricing........................ 532
    Corporate Owned Life Insurance......... 533
    Interest Deductibility 534
    Scientific Research and Experimental
        Development ('SR&ED') Tax Credits... 535
Summary 536

Appendix A	**Table of Selected Court Decisions**............... 537	
Appendix B	**Selected Financial Ratios** 565	
Bibliography	 575	
Topical Index	 583	

Chapter 1
Business Valuation and Pricing

Introduction

This book is intended to provide an in-depth understanding of the valuation principles, concepts and methodologies employed when determining the value of business interests, where:

- 'business interests' are taken to mean en bloc, controlling and minority ownership interests in privately held companies, publicly held companies, sole proprietorships and partnerships; and
- there is a presumption the owner is intent on satisfying long term financial objectives.

For simplicity, reference is made throughout to the value or price of 'a business'. In fact, what typically is valued in a notional market valuation or priced in an open market transaction is not a business per se, but rather an ownership interest in the overlying shares or underlying net assets of a business. As discussed herein, value or price can vary significantly depending on whether it is the outstanding shares or net assets of a business that are being valued.

> Unless otherwise specified, where reference to the value or price of 'a business' are made, it should be taken to mean the en bloc value or price of the outstanding shares of the business.

This book does not deal with security analysis per se. Although the underlying principles essentially are the same, there are important differences between business valuation in the context of business interests as set out in this book, and security analysis in respect of 'normal' or 'usual' daily public company security trades.

Every valuation and pricing exercise is unique. In the end, the valuation and pricing of a given business interest is a comprehensive task that requires rigorous analysis and judgement. This book seeks to familiarize the reader with the underlying concepts and principles that generally apply in business valuation and pricing. As such, there are no general business analysis, valuation methodology, rate of return, legal, income tax or other guidelines that can be said to apply in every circumstance. Generally it is advisable to retain competent valuation, legal and tax advisors in each fact specific circumstance.

Business Valuation vs. Security Analysis

There are fundamental differences between the 'en bloc' valuation of the equity in a business and the analysis of daily trading prices of public companies whose shares are listed on an organized securities exchange. In summary, these differences principally relate to:

- information availability;
- liquidity;
- risk and return assessment, including different investment time horizons; and
- the valuation of controlling as contrasted to minority interests.

This book examines the 'en bloc' valuation and pricing of business equity from a long-term investment perspective, and should not be taken to be directly applicable to the pricing of securities in a public market context. This is because:

- the analysis undertaken and methodologies adopted by stock market analysts and other public market investors generally differs to some degree from that applied by corporate acquirers;
- daily trading prices of publicly held securities and resultant rates of return implied by the public market rarely can be directly applied as a principal valuation methodology in the en bloc valuation of a given privately-held or publicly-held business; and
- where 'comparative' public market data is considered when determining 'en bloc' privately held and publicly held business value, comparability differences must be accounted for.

Information Availability

In the public stock markets, buyers and sellers generally act on a limited amount of available information. Such information normally includes quarterly and annual financial reports, press releases, annual information returns, and analyst reports. Investment bankers, large financial investors, and some individual buyers and sellers may be able to obtain additional information through discussions with company management and industry knowledgeable people. However, the information obtained pursuant to such inquiries seldom is of the same depth and quality as that available pursuant to an open market pricing or notional market valuation exercise. This principally is because of legislative restrictions against disclosure of sensitive 'inside information', which information is available through an open 'due diligence' process.

A corporate acquirer or a business valuator seeking to determine 'en bloc' price or notional value of the outstanding shares of a given public or private company in either an open or notional market context typically has access to a greater amount and better quality of information than is available to 'normal course traders' of publicly held company securities. This additional information:

- typically includes detailed financial and operating data, details of strategic plans, long-term forecasts, and open access to management and key operating personnel; and
- normally is subject to either implicit or explicit confidentiality agreements that prevent it from being used except in either the notional context in which the valuation is required, or in the consummation of an open market transaction.

It follows that the corporate acquirer or valuer generally is in a better position to assess the prospective cash flows and the risks and opportunities for the subject business than are stock market analysts.

Liquidity

Liquidity can be viewed in the context of the number of willing acquirers for a particular asset at any given time, and the resultant ability of a seller to convert an asset into cash at a known price within a very short time frame. Most widely and actively traded publicly traded securities offer holders of 'normal sized' trading lots a high degree of liquidity due to the organization and regulation of public securities markets. The holder typically can crystallize that value in a very short period of time (within minutes for many widely held companies) at a relatively minor cost (broker's commissions). The same degree of liquidity:

- generally is not be afforded to thinly traded securities (including most of those listed on so-called 'third markets', also referred to as over the counter markets); and
- typically will not be available to public company shares that are escrowed, or otherwise restricted as to sale pursuant to Securities Acts or Stock Exchange Regulations.

A purchaser acquiring either a publicly or privately held business 'en bloc' accepts a different and normally greater degree of liquidity risk than does a purchaser of a normal sized trading block in a widely held public company whose shares are actively traded. This is because:

- a business purchased 'en bloc' cannot be disposed of with the ease that normally is attributed to the sale of normal sized blocks of widely held publicly traded shares. For a business to be sold 'en bloc', the typical divestiture process may take several months or sometimes years, during which time significant events (either positive or negative) affecting the value of the business may occur;
- the divestiture of a business en bloc (particularly in the case of small private companies) may be more costly (viewed as a percentage of the sale price) than the disposition of normal sized trading blocks in the public markets. This is because a corporate divestiture normally is a major undertaking requiring significant advisory and intermediary expenditures and management time at (possibly material) opportunity cost;
- there usually is a degree of uncertainty regarding the ultimate price that will be fetched in an open market transaction. This is because there are numerous reasons why the value of a business interest as determined in a notional market context may be significantly different from open market price. Until a business is exposed for sale, negotiations with prospective purchasers are held, and the ultimate proceeds and form of consideration are known, price is uncertain;
- as a general rule, due to the relative size of the financial commitment and nature of the investment there are fewer potential buyers for a business 'en bloc' than there are for normal sized trading blocks in publicly held companies;
- in circumstances of the required commitment of financial (and management) resources and legal documentation related to a purchase and sale of 100% or control of the outstanding shares or net assets of a business:
  — a purchaser generally conducts more detailed due diligence than does a buyer of a normal sized block of publicly traded shares,
  — a vendor typically is required to provide indemnifications and warranties related to the financial position and underlying assets and liabilities of the business being sold, which a vendor of a normal sized trading block in a publicly held company does not do; and
  — as a general rule, most corporate acquirers do not purchase businesses 'en bloc' with the intent of selling them in the near term. Rather, they purchase them pursuant to long term objectives.

Risk and Return Assessment

There are three principal broad investor categories, being:

- stock market investors, including mutual fund companies and pension funds, who typically seek a return on capital in the form of dividends and capital gains. Most pursue a diversified portfolio strategy, whereby the risk of losses in any particular security held is reduced pursuant to holding a portfolio of securities in a variety of industries and geographies. As such, stock market investors typically are more focused on the performance of their portfolio as a whole rather than with gains or losses on any particular security. The prices of normal sized trading blocks of publicly traded securities are known at any point in time. Accordingly, stock market investors can determine their return on investment on an intra-day or daily basis;
- financial investors, including venture capital and 'mezzanine' funds, who invest debt and equity with a pre-determined investment horizon which generally ranges from five to ten years. These investors generally anticipate that their target return on invested capital will be realized pursuant to either a subsequent en bloc sale of the business, or in the public markets following an initial public offering; and
- corporate acquirers who, for the most part, purchase businesses 'en bloc' for their strategic value where post-acquisition returns are expected to include both the returns generated by the acquired company on a stand alone basis, and incremental returns expected from the business combination. Corporate acquirers typically seek to satisfy long term financial objectives, and measure returns in terms of monthly, quarterly and annual financial performance. Where an acquisition is motivated in part by anticipated synergies, significant capital or other expenditures may be required in order to realize those anticipated synergies over several months or years.

Given the differences in investment horizons, the risk perceptions and target rates of return of the three different types of investors typically will be different for a given investment opportunity.

Controlling vs. Minority Shareholdings

Trades of publicly held securities typically reflect small blocks of shares, each of which constitutes a small minority shareholding. As such, the individual (external) shareholders of a public company usually have little or no direct influence on the management of the business.

Conversely, the acquisition (or valuation) of a business en bloc, or of a controlling interest therein, offers the purchaser the benefits of control. A controlling shareholder has the ability to elect the majority of the Board of Directors and, subject to possible limitations pursuant to Shareholder's Agreements and legislative authority, to:

- establish or change the strategic direction or key operating decisions of the business, thereby altering the degree of operating and financial risk in the business;
- determine the quantum and timing of dividend distributions or other returns to shareholders;
- appoint themselves as management of the business; and
- decide whether to sell or wind up all or part of the business.

Although a minority shareholder is not in a position to determine one or more of these things, the risk associated with non-control is significantly mitigated in circumstances where the security is freely traded in the open market. Simply put, if the individual shareholder is not satisfied with the company's direction, management, dividend policy, and so on, and holds only a normal sized trading block, then the shareholding can be readily sold. This often is not the case where the shareholder is in a minority position in a privately held company.

Publicly traded securities do not necessarily trade at prices that reflect 'minority discounts', nor do purchasers of a controlling interest in publicly held companies necessarily pay a 'premium for control'. In most cases where an acquisition premium over market price is paid, the premium is based on the purchaser's analysis of post-acquisition results. Accordingly, whereas control of the subject business is necessary in order for the acquirer to realize post-acquisition net economic value added (synergies), it typically is perceived post-transaction economic advantage that commands the premium price and not 'control' per se.

Determining the 'En Bloc' Value of the Shares of Public vs. Private Companies

The valuation methodologies discussed in this book can be applied equally to both publicly held companies and privately held businesses. However, the 'en bloc' valuation of the shares of publicly held companies may be influenced by the:

- nature, quantum and quality of information available, which may in some instances differ from that available in the case of privately held businesses; and
- market price at which the shares trade prior to and at the valuation date.

Information Availability

Most publicly held companies are analyzed and reported on by stock market analysts and bond rating services. Some analysts compile their own set of projected operating results for the company being analyzed. Where available and believed relevant, such reports normally should be considered when estimating value. However, when reviewing such reports, one should bear in mind that:

- the analyst who prepared the report projections and conclusions may have done so based on less than complete information with respect to the company due to an understandable inability to obtain 'insider' and other information that typically is obtained pursuant to a full due diligence process; and
- for many industries, stock market analysts employ earnings-based valuation techniques based on actual or projected earnings per share as a principal valuation methodology. Further, the multiples used generally are based on so-called 'comparable' public companies, which most often are at best only 'broadly' comparable. Such analysis often is based on the 'Capital Asset Pricing Model', which in turn is based on what is referred to as the 'efficient market theory' – see Chapter 8. Appropriately applied, the Capital Asset Pricing Model is theoretically meaningful when used in the analysis of investments in normal sized public market trading lots. However, direct application of the Capital Asset Pricing Model in the rate of return determination when developing en bloc value is problematic. Where 'comparable' public company information is utilized, it is important to consider the degree of comparability between the subject business and the 'comparables' adopted.

Market Prices

The price at which a public company's shares trade in the open market provides a point in time consensus of the view of stock market participants as to the value of a 'normal sized' trading block of shares in that company. Canadian Courts generally have recognized that where a market price exists for a given company's stock depending on circumstances it should be accepted, weighted or rejected as meaningful when determining the 'en bloc' value of the outstanding shares of a public company or the value of a specific public company shareholding. In this context, the following important things must be taken into account:

- public equity market prices typically reflect 'normal' sized minority trading blocks where buyers and sellers have varying amounts of information, knowledge and sophistication, and a multiplicity of investment time horizons. While this has always been the case, these variables have been exacerbated in recent years by the proliferation of information available on the Internet, and by the recent rapid escalation of so-called 'day trading'. Where a public company is acquired pursuant to a take-over bid, the acquisition price per share typically exceeds the market price per share prior to the transaction. However:
  — the price paid by a corporate acquirer pursuant to a take-over bid may (and likely does) include economies of scale or other post-acquisition synergies anticipated to be realized. As a result, the purchase price may not be indicative of the 'en bloc' value of the outstanding shares viewed on an intrinsic (or stand-alone) basis, and
  — such evidence pertains to transactions that have occurred, and should not be taken to mean that the en bloc value of the outstanding shares of every public company is in excess of its prevailing stock market price. The prevailing share price of many public companies is such that point in time analysis does not support a takeover bid in excess of said stock market price. In such instances bids are not made, and takeovers do not occur;
- large blocks of shares in publicly traded companies may face discounts from prevailing stock market prices when liquidated, particularly in circumstances where:
  — securities are thinly traded,
  — there is little interest in the company shown by financial institutions, pension funds, equity funds, and so on, and
  — public companies have comparatively small market capitalizations;
- in some cases, 'normal' trading lots of publicly listed company shares may incorporate a 'minority discount' due to the inability of minority shareholders to unilaterally exercise control of the company (although this generally is not the case, particularly for normal sized trading lots in public companies whose shares are widely held and actively traded); and
- market prices can be subject to considerable volatility. Prices can fluctuate significantly in a short time frame due to news releases, euphoria in the markets, a sudden general market 'crash', and so on. Therefore, considera-

tion must be given to the level of stability in the trading price of the public company's stock and the historic range in market price when assessing its comparability to current value conclusions and to the market prices of so-called 'comparables'.

As discussed in Chapter 2, there are important differences between the 'en bloc' valuation of the outstanding shares of a public company and the price at which that company's shares trade in the open market. These differences may result in an 'en bloc' value/price (expressed on a pro-rata 'per share' basis) being different, perhaps significantly so, from the prevailing trading price.

Open Market Transactions vs. Notional Market Valuations

There are two distinct circumstances where the en bloc value of the equity in a business must be determined:

- first, where an open market transaction is contemplated, and price is negotiated between a vendor and a purchaser acting at arm's length. For a transaction to occur, the vendor and purchaser must agree on a price and terms where each perceives economic advantage; and
- second, where it is necessary to determine fair market value, fair value, or some other legislated or agreed defined value in the absence of open market negotiations for either all or part of the outstanding shares or net assets of:
  — a privately held business, or
  — a publicly held company where the public market price is not representative of such values.

Valuations conducted for the latter case are referred to as notional market valuations. Situations where business value determinations are required in a notional market context include:

- where transactions occur between 'non-arm's length' parties as that term is defined in the Income Tax Act (Canada). Such transactions typically must be consummated at fair market value in order to satisfy the provisions of the Income Tax Act;
- those pursuant to income tax reorganizations (typically fair market value), Provincial Family Law Acts (generally either value or fair market value), the Federal Divorce Act (value), and the Federal and various Provincial Expropriations Acts;

- so-called 'fairness opinions' required pursuant to Provincial Securities Acts;
- the exercise by shareholders of minority appraisal remedies and oppression remedies pursuant to Federal and Provincial Corporations Acts (typically fair value);
- those pursuant to the 'value' provisions of Shareholder's Agreements;
- the sale of shares in privately-held companies to employees, including establishing share ownership plans and prices;
- business value requirements pursuant to commercial litigation and business interruption claims; and
- negotiation of financing with banks and other lenders.

The value term most frequently encountered in notional market valuations is fair market value. There may be important differences between fair market value and other value terms, such as fair value or simply value. Various definitions of value and differences between them are addressed in Chapter 2. There are numerous Court Decisions dealing with the definition and interpretation of value terms and definitions, particularly with respect to fair market value and fair value. Selected Canadian Court Decisions are summarized by topic in Appendix A.

Although the title of this book does not include the word 'pricing', the underlying concepts of valuation also apply to the pricing of a business in an open market transaction. It is important to note that there may be significant differences between fair market value (or some other value term) as determined in a notional market context and price as determined in an open market transaction. As discussed in Chapter 2, this difference may be attributable to factors such as:

- the negotiating skills of the buyer, seller and their respective advisors;
- the knowledge of each party with respect to the business interest itself and the industry(ies) in which it participates;
- the amount of competition for the acquisition of a given business interest; and
- the possible fact-specific impact of so-called 'special interest purchaser' analysis in price determination.

The Market for Business Interests

Overview

There are important differences between publicly held and privately held business interests that impact upon the open market price of each. These include:

- the level of awareness surrounding a divestiture. Unlike the public stock markets, or other organized regulated exchanges, the market for privately held business interests is not regulated, nor is it organized in any formal way. As a result, particularly where privately held business interests are not effectively (i.e. widely) marketed, transactions involving privately-held business interests are characterized by prices being struck where:
  - generally there is no 'benchmark' price against which to measure them,
  - generally there is no wide-spread knowledge of the transaction prior to its closing,
  - when negotiating with only one (or a limited number of) possible purchaser(s), a vendor seldom can be certain that other possible purchasers will surface if negotiations are terminated,
  - vendors can never be certain that all possible purchasers have been canvassed, and hence that they have achieved the highest possible price,
  - potential purchasers may only hear about a transaction on a post-closing basis, and
  - as a rule, purchasers can never be certain during the negotiation process if there is an alternate bidder for a given acquisition, or what price that other bidder(s) might be willing or able to pay;
- the fact that transactions involving publicly traded companies have a benchmark price, being the recent trading prices of the company's shares, which private companies do not. The shareholders and Board of Directors of the target public company typically review any price offered at least in part in relation to those trading prices;
- as contrasted to the market for privately held business interests, a bid for an en bloc, controlling, or significant or strategic minority interest in a public company is characterized by public transaction publicity. In many cases, such publicity brings forth prospective purchasers who only express an interest when they learn that the outstanding shares of a company are 'in play'. This in turn may place upward pressure on the transaction price; and
- the fact that in public company takeovers, there is an overriding emphasis on economic interests. That is, shareholders typically are focused on short-term capital gain maximization. Conversely, vendors of privately held businesses may be acting out of both economic and non-economic in-

terests, including satisfaction of personal income tax planning objectives, continuity of corporate culture, paternalistic sentiment toward both family and employees, and personal employment continuity after the transaction.

Vendors

Vendors generally can be categorized as:

- a private or public company that is selling only part of its business enterprise; or
- individuals or corporations where what is being sold comprises all or part of the vendor's ownership interest in the underlying business enterprise.

Generally, the reasons a vendor divests only a portion of its operations are economic, contractually or legislatively driven. These reasons may include one or more of the following:

- the business interest to be sold is not generating a sufficient return on either net assets employed or investment, and is not expected to do so in the foreseeable future;
- the business interest to be sold is 'off-strategy' relative to the vendor's long-range planning;
- the vendor is in financial difficulty, and looks to sale proceeds from the business interest to be sold as a total or partial remedy;
- the vendor is required to sell pursuant to legislation or Court or government direction;
- the vendor perceives prospective:
  — negative changes in the market position for the products or services of the business, or
  — significant sustaining capital expenditures, often related to technological change issues; and
- in the case of a public company vendor, a public market perception that the business interest to be sold is:
  — either a negative influence on the price at which the public company's shares trade; or
  — not as valuable as in fact it is, and hence is 'spun out' so as to increase overall shareholder wealth.

In the case of privately held businesses, reasons for divestments of entire business operations may include one or more of the aforementioned reasons in combination with one or more of the following:

- the age or health of the owner/manager;
- a reduction in, or loss of, interest in the business on the part of the owner/manager that is either emotionally-driven, or driven by changed personal or business interests or circumstances;
- familial or partner pressure to sell based on dissention among owners;
- a desire to reduce the risk resulting from having a disproportion of one's personal wealth in a single asset;
- a desire to be released from continued exposure to risk of personal guarantees; and
- lack of management depth, and an inability to change management readily.

Corporate Acquirers

There are at least four identifiable categories of corporate acquirers. Within each category each purchaser has its, or their, individual motivations and investment philosophies. These four purchaser categories are:

- publicly held companies;
- privately held companies;
- financial buyers; and
- company management.

Publicly Held Companies

Publicly held companies typically have access to larger capital bases than do privately held companies. Moreover, in some circumstances and at their option, public company acquirers are able to use their own stock as 'currency' in a transaction. Management of publicly held companies answer to the company's Board of Directors, the lending institutions it deals with, and (generally) a widely based shareholder group to whom it has a fiduciary duty.

While not always the case, management of publicly held companies tend to perceive post-acquisition economies of scale and/or strategic advantage in a combination of their own business operations and those of acquisition candidates. Publicly held companies tend to acquire other publicly held or large privately held businesses, and tend to be long term investors who intend to integrate the purchased operations with little or no intent of re-selling them. When analyzing potential acquisitions they focus on:

- how the business(es) of the acquisition candidate will advance their long-term corporate strategy;

- the motivations of other potential acquirers (i.e. competitors for the acquisition);
- rates of return on investment that consider their long term financing costs, the risks they perceive associated with the business(es) of the acquisition candidate, and the multiples (implied rates of return) of EBIT-DA, EBIT, after tax discretionary cash flow and after tax earnings implied in their purchase offer; and
- the amount of intangible value implied in the final purchase price, and the period over which it will be required to be amortized pursuant to applicable Generally Accepted Accounting Principles ('GAAP'), and as a result:
  – whether they will suffer near-term post-acquisition dilution in consolidated earnings per share, and if so
  – at what point in time the acquisition is expected to have an accretive affect on post-acquisition consolidated earnings per share.

There is a motivation to acquire business interests at prices that result in little or no near-term post-acquisition dilution of the acquirer's consolidated earnings per share, and near term positive (accretive) contribution to consolidated earnings per share. Accordingly, public company rate of return objectives in acquisitions often are higher than the rates of return implied by prevailing stock market prices for their own shares. Stated differently, as a general rule public companies set target acquisition multiples of prospective (including consideration of expected post-acquisition 'synergies') incremental discretionary cash flows and after tax earnings that are no higher than the prevailing and prospective multiples paid by stock market participants for minority shareholdings in the acquirer company. The target acquisition multiples are then adjusted (typically) upward (i.e. target rates of return typically are adjusted downward) to account for such things as scarcity value, strategic value, and so on.

Privately Held Businesses

Privately held businesses principally purchase other privately held businesses but may also acquire publicly held companies. In the case of the latter:

- the private company acquirer can use the acquiree as a vehicle to become public itself. Such transactions commonly are completed pursuant to 'share for share exchanges', and are referred to as 'reverse takeovers'; or
- where 100% of the outstanding shares are not purchased in the first instance, the public company acquiree subsequently may be taken private, in which case any remaining public minority shareholders are bought out; or

- where public minority shareholders remain, the acquiree continues as a publicly traded company.

Managements of privately held corporate acquirers typically answer to no one but the lending institutions they deal with, and to their own, generally close-knit, shareholder group. Frequently the owners comprise the management group. While at any given point in time they must be aware of the motivations of other potential acquirers, they tend to look to rates of return that combine consideration of both their long term financing costs and the risks they perceive associated with the business of a particular acquisition candidate. They tend to be less concerned with near term accretive earnings per share, but are concerned with near and long-term accretive discretionary cash flows. Similar to publicly held companies, privately held business acquirers generally anticipate post-acquisition net economic value added.

Financial Buyers

Financial buyers are purchasers who view acquisitions of business interests essentially as financial transactions. These purchasers tend to be financially sophisticated, rely on professional managers, and do not necessarily purchase to hold for the long term. They tend to have a substantive appetite for post-acquisition debt in relation to underlying assets and equity, frequently resulting in so-called 'leveraged buyouts'. Often the price they are willing to pay is strongly influenced, and in some cases dictated by, the amount, terms, and conditions of capital available from credit sources. Unless fact specific circumstances dictate otherwise, post-acquisition net economic value added generally is not available to financial buyers. Accordingly, as a general rule financial buyers do not factor post-acquisition net economic value added into their transaction prices.

Company Management

Company management in this context refers to those individuals who comprise all or part of the management group of the business interest that is acquired. So-called management buyouts typically are perceived as long-term investments by the purchasers. Such purchasers generally are more informed as to the detail of the operations of the business that is acquired than are other categories of purchasers, although they may suffer from a narrower outlook relative to external business influences. They also tend to borrow more heavily than do the first two categories of purchaser, again often pursuant to a so-called leveraged buyout. These transactions tend to be 'internally-financed', and often are influenced by circumstances particular to the management group and the business itself. These transactions usually by themselves result in no significant post-acquisition net economic value-added. The price paid often is strongly influenced by the amount, terms, and conditions of capital available from their credit sources, and tends to be lower than that which the other categories of purchaser might pay.

Intermediaries

Few transactions involving the sale and purchase of business interests are completed without the input of external advisors, or 'intermediaries'. Intermediaries generally do not take a neutral role in the transaction process, and as a result typically play either a constructive or destructive role. They frequently influence open market price, sometimes to a significant degree. Of particular importance in this regard, are:

- the timing of intermediary involvement in the transaction. As a general rule, the later an intermediary gets involved in a transaction, the more disruptive to the process he or she may be;
- the understanding and execution by each intermediary of his or her role in the negotiation process leading to the structure of the transaction, and the price agreed;
- the understanding and execution by each intermediary of his or her role in the process leading to the final documentation of the transaction;
- the intermediary's level of understanding as to the respective motivations and objectives of the vendor and the purchaser;
- the ability of the intermediary to 'set the tone' in negotiations and to meaningfully assist in crucial decisions;
- the experience, ability, and negotiating skill of each intermediary; and
- the basis of remuneration of each intermediary, and the related degree of possible intermediary 'vested interest' and resultant degree of non-objectivity in pushing the transaction to close.

Essentially, intermediaries fall into one of three categories:

- financial intermediaries (investment bankers, business brokers, merger/acquisition specialists, public accountants, and so on);
- legal advisors; and
- income tax advisors (usually either lawyers or public accountants).

Financial Intermediaries

In Canada, the low end of the transactions market for privately-held business interests is served principally by business brokers (and real estate brokers where the interest involves real property). Transactions involving publicly held companies and the middle and high-end market (measured by business size) for privately held companies is served by any number of intermediaries of widely diverse backgrounds, business experience and knowledge, abilities, resources, and negotiating skills. As a result, different intermediaries contribute varying amounts of either 'value added' or 'negative value' to a given open market transaction.

Financial intermediaries generally provide a full range of services to both vendors and purchasers. Often the potential remuneration accruing to them from a transaction is all or in part contingent upon the successful completion of the transaction, and the way it is structured. In such circumstances, depending upon the terms and conditions of the fee arrangement, they are to some degree direct participants in the transaction. Importantly, financial intermediaries acting in the sale and purchase of business interests frequently have a vested interest in a transaction closing. In such circumstances they are in a conflict of interest position, albeit one that their client(s) presumably finds acceptable. Thoughtful structuring of the financial intermediaries fee arrangement can assist in mitigating this 'negative influence' issue.

The role played by a financial intermediary in any given transaction can include:

- assisting in the identification of possible purchasers or vendors;
- coordinating the preparation and circulation of an 'information package' with respect to the business of a vendor;
- ranking possible purchasers or vendors as to possible business 'fit' from greatest to least, and resultant possible post-transaction net economic value-added perceived to accrue to each;
- making an initial contact with possible purchasers or vendors;
- coordinating the collection and analysis of information required to assess the possible post-transaction economies of scale and/or strategic advantages to each possible purchaser or vendor;
- fulfilling an intermediary role between the vendor and those who respond to a vendor 'information package';
- acting as a 'sounding board' for ideas of the purchaser and/or vendor and reviewing the analysis of each;

- acting to deflect and resolve conflict between purchaser and vendor where it arises;
- functioning as part of the acquisition or divestiture team, thereby providing transaction planning and analysis expertise not otherwise available to the vendor or purchaser;
- assisting in the negotiation and structuring of the transaction;
- arranging or assisting in the arrangement of some or all of the financing for the transaction; and
- completing 'due diligence' reviews prior to closing.

Often it is the ability of the financial intermediary to bring creative solutions to bear on seemingly irreconcilable positions that determines the ultimate success of the sale and purchase of a business. However, not all financial intermediaries bring the same experience, capability and objectivity to a transaction. For this reason, the highest open market price may not be achieved in the sale of a given business interest. However, careful selection of a financial intermediary, including an assessment of personality fit between the intermediary and his or her client, can assist in the maximization of sale proceeds to a vendor or price minimization to a purchaser.

Legal and Income Tax Advisors

It is common practice for lawyers to actively participate in the negotiation process, in particular to deal with corporate law issues that relate to transaction structuring and with issues surrounding representations and warranties that survive the closing of the transaction. Likewise, it is common practice for income tax advisors to actively participate in the negotiation process, in particular to deal with income tax issues relating to transaction structuring.

As is the case with financial intermediaries, individual lawyers and income tax advisors bring different levels of experience, business knowledge and judgement, ability, and negotiating skills to the bargaining table. However, their respective fees generally are not contingent, at least to a substantive degree, on whether or not a transaction is completed. Accordingly, as a rule, lawyers and income tax advisors generally do not have expressed or implied conflicts of interest relative to such transactions.

Components of Price

When dealing with 100% of the outstanding shares or net assets of, or a control shareholding in, a business that is valued on the assumption that it will continue to operate as a going concern, and where post-acquisition synergies are expected, the two possible components that comprise any given open market price are:

- that reflective of the value of all of the outstanding shares, or net operating assets of the business viewed on a stand-alone basis. That is, the value of the business interest assuming the business will continue to operate 'as is' absent a divestiture of all or part of it. This value component often is referred to as intrinsic (or 'stand-alone') value. Intrinsic value is comprised of three distinct components. These are:
  — tangible operating assets, net of liabilities, required to carry on the business;
  — identifiable intangible assets (if any), which may include brand names, patents, copyrights, franchise agreements, trademarks, and so on, the value of such assets which seldom is quantified separately. Rather, the global perceived value of such assets normally is included as part of generic 'intangible value', or 'goodwill'; and
  — where applicable, intangible value (which often is generically referred to as goodwill), being the aggregation of non-identifiable (or 'non-specific') intangible assets (which in theory is the 'goodwill' component of intangible value), and identifiable intangible assets not otherwise accounted for; and
- an incremental value over stand-alone, or intrinsic, value perceived by a purchaser at the time of acquisition comprised of purchaser-perceived post-acquisition economies of scale and/or strategic advantages. The quantification of this incremental value is unique to each potential purchaser. Examples of post-acquisition economies of scale include incremental revenue opportunities, cost savings and overall risk reduction that the purchaser expects will result from combining the acquired business with its existing operations, and so on. Examples of purchaser-perceived strategic advantages include post-acquisition business combination opportunities that otherwise would be unavailable to the purchaser, scarcity value perceived by the purchaser, enhanced post-acquisition management depth and critical mass, and so on. These benefits are collectively referred to as either 'post-acquisition net economic value-added', or simply 'synergies'. Purchasers who anticipate synergies often are referred to as 'special interest

purchasers'. The combination of 'intrinsic value' and 'post-acquisition net economic value added' sometimes is referred to as 'special interest purchaser price'.

The components of 'intrinsic value' and 'special interest purchaser price' can be summarized as follows:

CHART 1.1

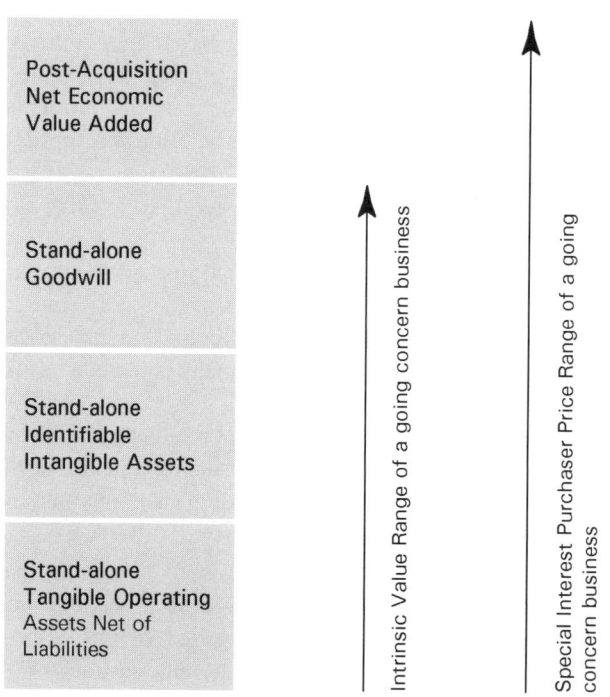

Although the tangible assets of a business often can be valued separately, it is considerably more difficult to assess the value of a particular identifiable intangible asset. Further, intangible value rarely can be quantified in isolation. As a result, when reference is made to the specific amount or quantification of intangible value or goodwill inherent in a business, that amount normally is derived by deducting the 'value in use' of the net tangible assets from overall 'going concern value'. In practice values for identifiable intangibles and goodwill seldom are segregated, but rather are aggregated and together referred to as 'intangible value' or 'goodwill'.

When determining fair market value in a notional market context, it is necessary to address the question of possible open market prices that might be paid by so-called special interest purchasers. Since open market negotiations current to the required date of value typically have not taken place, it often is difficult:

- to identify possible purchasers who might be interested in acquiring a given business interest;
- where such possible purchasers are identified, to determine which of them would be considered to be 'qualified' purchasers who have both the appetite for, and the financial capability to effect, a transaction;
- to identify post-acquisition value-added benefits each 'qualified' purchaser might enjoy;
- importantly, to quantify the identified post-acquisition value-added benefits that might be realized in different degrees by each 'qualified purchaser'; and
- to assign a probability to the likelihood of the business interest being sold at a price which would include some or all of said possible post-acquisition value-added benefits.

Further, where values are determined pursuant to business re-organizations, estate planning, Family Law requirements and so on, and an attempt is made to quantify an incremental amount over intrinsic value to account for possible purchaser-perceived post-acquisition net economic value-added, the potential exists for significant business disruption. This is particularly the case where monies to fund an acquisition must be extracted from the operating assets of a business. This is sometimes referred to as an 'internal vs. external financing issue' — see Chapter 2.

Overview of Business Valuation

When determining the value of a particular business, an assessment must be made as to whether a liquidation or going concern approach should be the primary method of valuation. The primary method that should be adopted is the one that yields the greatest net contribution to the equity owners. This can be measured by comparing:

- the present value of the estimated prospective discretionary after-tax cash flows to be generated by the business; and

- the estimated net proceeds which could be attained by disposing of the underlying net assets of the business, where both amounts are income tax effected in a consistent manner.

Where a business prospectively is economically viable on a stand-alone basis, a going concern approach normally yields the higher value. In some cases the going concern assumption is self-evident, whereas in other cases a thorough analysis must be undertaken to determine whether the business in question is viable as a going concern and hence will continue to operate. Where a business is forecast to incur continuous negative operating cash flow, it may be worth more pursuant to a liquidation assumption than it is pursuant to a going concern assumption. For the most part, this book has been written on the assumption that the business being valued or priced is a viable going concern. Chapter 10 is dedicated in part to the liquidation-based valuation methodology.

As previously noted, the en bloc intrinsic value of the outstanding shares or net assets of a business that is a going concern may include the net tangible assets required to operate the business, identifiable intangible assets (where they exist), and where applicable, non-identifiable intangible assets. Going concern value generally is determined on a composite basis, rather than by individual component. The most common going concern methodologies include the capitalization of discretionary cash flow and discounted cash flow methodologies. Often these are supplemented by alternative 'test' methodologies, including multiples of revenue, multiples of EBIT-DA (earnings before interest, taxes, depreciation and amortization), and multiples of EBIT (earnings before interest and taxes). Business valuation methodologies are not mutually exclusive. Accordingly, consideration generally should be given to comparing the conclusions derived by various methodologies as a test of the reasonableness of any value determination.

As a practical matter, generally corporate acquirers primarily are interested in perceived prospective discretionary cash flows that a business may generate. Having said that, going concern value sometimes is best determined utilizing an asset-based valuation technique as a primary valuation methodology. However, the use of asset-based valuation techniques as a primary valuation methodology generally is restricted to circumstances where the business being valued is a holding company that has no active operations of its own. Where the underlying assets of a holding company are represented by operating businesses, the value of each of those businesses typically is derived pursuant to going concern methodologies. Their respective values are then adopted to derive the value of the outstanding shares of the holding company.

CHART 1.2

DETERMINATION OF PRIMARY VALUATION APPROACH

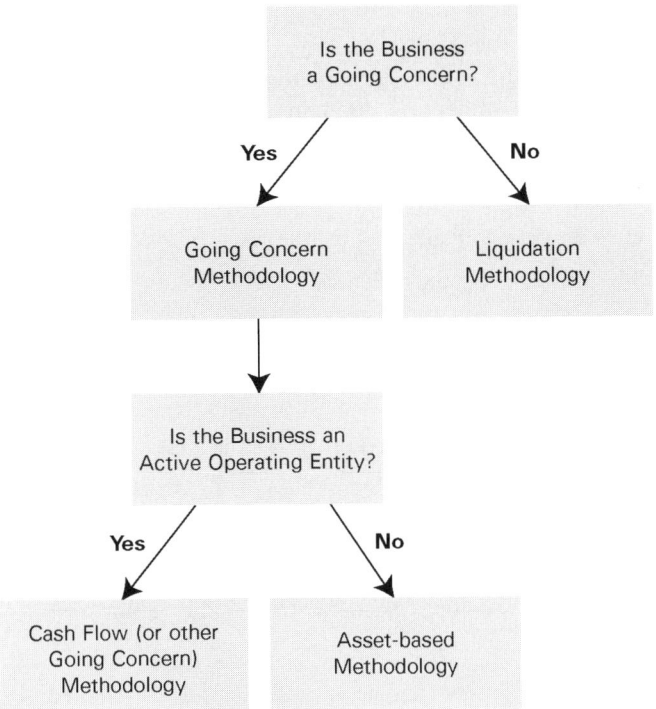

The determination of going concern value where the business is an active operating entity normally is best developed pursuant to a cash flow based methodology. Various cash flow and other going concern valuation methodologies exist, but all require:

- an assessment of the future prospects of the business be made. This normally is taken to be the amount of discretionary cash flow which the business prospectively is expected to generate based on its operating assets and perceived prospects;
- an assessment of the risk of achieving those prospects. That is, the discount or capitalization rate, as the case may be, which is applied to the estimated discretionary cash flows; and

- that redundant assets be identified and segregated. Redundant assets are those not required to generate the prospective discretionary cash flow of the business. Redundant assets are assumed to be liquidated, and their net realizable value at the corporate level is added to the going concern value of the business.

Simplistically, if a business has redundant assets valued at $2 million, is expected to generate $1 million in discretionary after-tax cash flow each year, and a 10% rate of return is considered appropriate, then the 'value' of the business would determined as follows:

Prospective discretionary after-tax cash flows	$ 1 million
Divided by the required rate of return	10%
Equals the going concern value of the underlying operations of the business	10 million
Add the net realizable value of redundant assets	2 million
Equals the en bloc value of the equity of the business	$12 million

Importantly, the prospective discretionary after-tax cash flows and the rate of return applied thereto are interdependent. That is, if the 'correct value' of the going concern value of the underlying operations of the business was thought to be $10 million (i.e. before consideration of redundant assets), that figure could be derived by:

- capitalizing discretionary after-tax cash flows of $1.5 million at a 15% return;
- capitalizing discretionary after-tax cash flows of $800,000 at an 8% rate of return; or
- an infinite number of other combinations.

Simply stated, as a practical matter, the en bloc value or price of the equity in a business is what it is at any given point in time. Accordingly, as a general rule, the more aggressive the discretionary cash flow assumptions, the greater is the risk in achieving them and the higher should be the targeted rate of return. In the end, selection of these key variables must recognize their reciprocal relationship, and must be based on experience and judgement resulting in a 'value' or 'price' determination that is not merely arithmetic.

For the most part, in a given business valuation or open market pricing exercise, emphasis is placed on determining the level of prospective discretionary cash flows and the rate of return to apply thereto. The theories, valuation methodologies, and commentary presented in this book are intended to assist the reader in understanding, developing, and applying these variables to result in a 'reasoned' value or price for any given business interest. Having said that, there is no substitute for thorough analysis and judgement in what is inherently a subjective exercise.

Importantly, the going concern methodologies discussed in this book apply to the 'en bloc' valuation of the shares of both publicly held and privately held companies. Where the net assets of a business are being valued, adjustments are necessary to 'en bloc' share values. As a general rule, the value of a pool of net assets that collectively comprises a business typically is greater than the value of all of the outstanding shares of the company that owns that net asset pool. This is because an arm's length purchaser of:

- assets that are depreciable for income tax purposes is able to claim capital cost allowance (tax depreciation) based on the portion of the gross purchase price allocated to such depreciable assets. In most instances, the amount allocated to depreciable assets exceeds the tax base of those assets. In such circumstances, due to resultant incremental 'income tax shelter', the post-acquisition after tax cash flow to a purchaser of such assets would exceed the after tax cash flow to a purchaser of the shares of the business that owns such assets; and
- net assets, as a rule, does not assume the contingent liabilities that may accrue to the vendor corporation.

Having said that, there are exceptions to the general rule that the value of net assets is greater than the value of outstanding shares, particularly if noncapital income tax losses exist. The valuation of 'net assets vs. shares' is addressed in Chapter 4.

Overview of this Book

Chapter 2 outlines the underlying principles, concepts and definitions used in business valuation, including important distinctions between fair market value, fair value, price, and other value terms.

Chapter 3 focuses on business analysis. A thorough and objective analysis of the business is a critical element in any notional market valuation or open market pricing determination.

Chapter 4 addresses the capitalization of discretionary cash flow methodology. Chapter 5 expands on those concepts when addressing the discounted cash flow methodology. As noted throughout this book, cash flow based methodologies generally are the preferred basis by which to value a business. Empirical evidence suggests that most corporate acquirers utilize a discounted cash flow approach as an important component of their pricing decisions.

Chapter 6 addresses asset based valuation methodologies. The adjusted net book value methodology normally is restricted to businesses that do not have active operations, and sometimes is used as a risk assessment tool in the determination of going concern value.

Chapters 7 and 8 discuss the interrelated topics of capital structure and discount and capitalization rates. The determination of 'appropriate' capital structure and rates of return is one of the most difficult and judgmental elements of any business valuation or pricing exercise.

Chapter 9 addresses the topic of comparative analysis. While an analysis of so-called 'comparable companies' sometimes is undertaken in determining the value or price of a particular business interest, meaningful 'comparables' rarely exist from which value conclusions can be directly derived. It is important to understand the limitations of comparative analysis and the context in which it should be used.

Chapter 10 provides an overview of other valuation methodologies, including capitalization of earnings, multiples of EBIT and EBIT-DA, and the liquidation approach.

Chapter 11 addresses business pricing. There may be a considerable difference between the value of a business interest pursuant to a notional market valuation, and the price fetched for all of the outstanding shares or underlying net assets of a business when exposed for sale in the open market. So-called 'special interest purchasers' and post-acquisition net economic value added are discussed.

Chapters 12 and 13 deal with the topics of controlling and minority interests, including so-called 'premiums for control' and minority discounts.

Finally, Chapter 14 provides an overview of the income tax considerations in business valuation, and in business acquisitions and divestitures.

Chapter 2
Valuation Terms and Principles

Introduction

Whether the equity value of a business interest is determined in a notional market context or is crystallized as price in a purchase and sale agreement, its determination is a subjective exercise. Moreover, there often is a significant difference between the value of a business interest determined based on a 'stand-alone' (or 'intrinsic value') basis in a notional market context and the price at which a transaction is consummated in the open market. As a consequence, any well-reasoned value or price determination must be based on a well-defined and applied theoretical foundation, in combination with the application of experience and informed judgement.

This Chapter examines various value terms, including fair market value, price, fair value, value to owner, and the differences between them. This is followed by a discussion of issues essential to valuation theory and practice. These include various forms of goodwill, management and non-competition agreement terms, the implications of internal vs. external financing on value, and the impact of valuing the equity in underlying net assets of a business as contrasted with valuing overlying share equity. The Chapter concludes with a discussion of the fundamental principles underlying business valuation and pricing.

Value Terms

Where value is determined in a notional market context it is important that what is meant by 'value' be clearly defined. The most common definitions of value include 'fair market value', 'fair value', and 'value to owner'.

Fair Market Value

In a notional market context, the definition of fair market value generally accepted by Canadian Courts has been:

> 'the highest price available in an open and unrestricted market between informed and prudent parties, acting at arm's length and under no compulsion to act, expressed in terms of cash'.

This definition postulates a market that exists neither in an open market arm's length negotiation context, nor generally as a practical matter in a notional market context. As a practical matter, in a notional market context, fair market value is quantified pursuant to what can be described as a 'best efforts' basis. This is because no information base is ever 'perfect', and because the degree of subjectivity in the value determination is a function of numerous factors influencing both the business interest being valued and the industry in which the business operates. An analysis of each of the components of fair market value follows — see Appendix A for a summary of related Court Decisions.

Highest Price Available

Determination of the 'highest price available' must consider that each of the vendor and purchaser would transact only at a price and on terms deemed fair by each. Technically, it is necessary to identify the purchaser that will pay the highest price, being the one with the greatest justifiable economic rationale to consummate a transaction. As a practical matter, a 'price' negotiated following well researched, wide market exposure is the ultimate determinant of value at a point in time. Even then, the 'real world' market for any business interest is not a systematic and consistent one when contrasted with, for example, a regulated stock exchange where normal sized trading lots in public companies are transacted. As a result, even open market exposure of all of the outstanding shares or net assets of a business does not ensure realization of the highest possible price.

A notional market valuation requirement arises where no open market arm's length sale is contemplated or likely. Accordingly, without testing the market or having meaningful discussions with potential purchasers, the highest price available can never be ascertained in any notional market valuation with certainty due to the possible existence of 'special interest purchasers' and their respective and individual 'pricing quantifications' that become evident through a 'marketing process', or for other fact-specific reasons.

As discussed in Chapter 11, a special interest purchaser is a purchaser who expects to achieve post-acquisition net economic value added (or 'synergies') by combining the acquired business interest with its own. The anticipated synergies may be in the form of economies of scale (such as cost reductions and operating efficiencies) or perceived strategic advantage (such as risk reduction, enhanced market share, and incremental growth opportunities). Every potential purchaser can, and likely will, pay a price unique to it given individually perceived post-acquisition synergies. Only in negotiation with each prospective purchaser can the perceived economies of scale and strategic advantages of each be quantified. Even then, they typically can not be quantified with certainty.

In a notional market context, the ability to identify special interest purchasers varies depending on the characteristics of the business itself and on the industry in which it competes. Further, the ability to meaningfully quantify the net economic value-added perceived by, or available to, each possible purchaser, and to determine whether such purchasers can be enticed to pay for some or all of it varies in each case. As a practical matter, one or more special interest purchasers generally exist for any sizeable business interest. However, absent open market negotiations it seldom is possible to reasonably quantify the post-acquisition net economic value added each would be willing to pay. Accordingly, in a notional market context business interests often are valued based on their stand-alone or 'intrinsic' values. Such notional market value determinations generally are qualified with regard to the inability to identify and quantify the effect on value of possible purchasers who might perceive economies of scale or strategic advantage. Having said that, where there are no extenuating circumstances such as Shareholder's Agreements that dictate or suggest value definitions that exclude consideration of special interest purchasers, where:

- likely purchasers are readily identifiable; and
- post-acquisition net economic value added can be credibly quantified; and
- there is believed to be a high probability that one or more prospective purchasers would pay for some or all of those benefits,

then notional fair market value determinations may be made inclusive of all or part of such assumed synergies.

Open Market

The term 'open market' refers to the assumption that no potential purchasers are to be excluded from participation in the notional market for the business interest being valued. It is assumed that the business interest is exposed to all potential purchasers with the will and resources to buy, notwithstanding that this rarely occurs during the course of a business sale. On the other hand, neither the vendor nor the purchaser is assumed to possess personal characteristics that as a practical matter may influence value, either positive or negative. Both vendor and purchaser are expected to evidence both a deemed desire and a full facility to transact for the business interest in the open market at the highest price obtainable having regard to all circumstances attendant to ownership. The term 'personal characteristics':

- pertains to those things that are inherent in, and unique to, individual persons such as physical characteristics, unique personal abilities, non-transferable personal contacts, and so on — see discussion dealing with 'individual goodwill' in this Chapter; and
- does not pertain to those things that inherently directly or indirectly attach to the business or asset itself, and which hence would influence the decision of either or both the vendor or purchaser when establishing the price and terms at which a transaction would be consummated, which also relates to the concept of prudence on the part of both vendor and purchaser (see commentary following under the heading 'Between Prudent Parties'). For example, in an open market context (although to date this has not been addressed in a notional context in such specific terms by Canadian Courts) consequences to:
  - the vendor beyond, and arising from, the isolated sale of a particular asset should be considered when determining both the price and terms pursuant to which the vendor would be prepared to sell. Such consequences could arise, for example, where the sale of a particular asset would influence or affect the value of other assets owned by the vendor; and
  - a purchaser beyond, and arising from, the isolated purchase of a particular asset should be considered when determining both the price and terms pursuant to which a purchaser would be prepared to purchase. Such consequences could arise, for example, where the purchase of a particular asset would result in the purchaser being fettered in its ability to deal with the asset as a result of terms imposed by the vendor at closing.

Unrestricted Market

An unrestricted market refers to an assumption that any statutory, contractual, or other restrictions influencing the marketability of a business interest are momentarily lifted in order to facilitate a sale in the notional market. Restrictions on ownership transfer commonly are specified in Shareholder's Agreements and in the Articles of Incorporation of privately held companies, and may be found in prevailing contracts executed by the business interest itself. Such restrictions generally require the approval of the company's Board of Directors or other shareholders. Usually these issues bear on the question of the illiquidity that often attaches to minority shareholdings of privately held businesses. As a practical matter, where all of the outstanding shares of a company are sold together, such restrictions have little bearing on the price received. On the other hand, if a minority block (or in some unusual instances a control block) of shares is sold by itself, such restrictions may have a significant downward influence on price. In the latter instance, absent the existence of a Shareholder's Agreement that sets out 'valuation rules and procedures', this often depends on the relationships among shareholders prevailing at any given point in time.

Prevailing jurisprudence suggests (see Appendix A) that in a notional market context the assumption of an unrestricted market does not extend to the complete disregard of the existence of either technical or practical restrictions on the sale or transfer of a business interest. Rather, hypothetical purchasers are assumed to assess the value of the business interest such that prevailing restrictions are accounted for by considering, and if deemed appropriate, adopting an appropriate discount from the value otherwise determined on the basis that they will be subject to those same prevailing restrictions following acquisition. It is necessary to assume that transfer approval is not withheld, but there would be no assurance that approvals for subsequent transfers would be granted. Accordingly, both technical and practical restrictions on transfer should be weighed when reaching notional value conclusions, with appropriate consideration being given to the nature and extent of such restrictions, and the likelihood that they might prove to be an impediment to a subsequent transfer of the acquired shares.

Between Informed Parties

The phrase 'between informed parties' relates to the inherent assumption that both the vendor and purchaser are informed with respect to all facts important to value determination. In an open market context a vendor typically is 'reasonably' but may not be 'fully' informed with respect to its financial position, management, product strengths and weaknesses, competitive issues, general and specific risk issues, stand-alone strategy, its near-term prospects, and other value-related matters. Concurrently, the vendor frequently either does not know or is unable to meaningfully quantify the purchaser's perceived post-acquisition synergies and strategy. The purchaser generally has a better idea of post-acquisition business opportunities than does the vendor. As a result, it is not uncommon for open market transactions to be consummated at prices less than a purchaser would in fact be willing to pay. On the other hand, the purchaser likely will not have the same depth of information with respect to the specifics of the business interest being sold as will the vendor, and often the purchaser will not understand all the reasons (financial and other) that have motivated the vendor to sell.

Canadian jurisprudence supports the proposition that full and open disclosure of information relevant to a purchase and sale that was available at the date of value is to be assumed in notional market value determinations. In essence, all information that would or should have been available in an open market context generally should be assumed to be available on a 'best efforts' basis in a notional market context.

The information gathering process in a notional market context in many respects parallels an 'open market' purchaser's due diligence process where, prior to closing, a purchaser gleans as much information as possible with respect to the business being acquired. Notwithstanding, seldom (if ever) in either the notional or open market are value/price decisions based on 'full' or 'perfect' information. Having said that, the following (often significant) differences exist between the information gathering process that occurs pursuant to a notional market value determination as contrasted to that completed pursuant to an open market pricing exercise:

- in the open market, purchasers may have an advantage in information gathering – certainly from the point of view of their perception of post-acquisition business strategy and forecasted combined operating results;
- in a notional market context, there theoretically is an equal information gathering opportunity to all parties and their respective advisors. However, particularly where matters are acrimonious or litigious, as a practical matter an equal information gathering (and hence information assessment) opportunity may not exist. Accordingly, in such circumstances one group often begins and ends with a greater information and knowledge base than the other;
- in the open market, people who have worked in the type of business that is subject to negotiation generally gather information. Accordingly, they bring an 'operational' industry and business knowledge and focus to bear when requesting and analyzing information that often is greater than that of professionals generating notional value determinations in circumstances where the latter have comparatively little, or less, 'operational' industry and business knowledge; and
- in the open market, a large part of the cost of information gathering frequently is absorbed in the existing infrastructure of the purchaser. In a notional market context, information gathering typically is expensive. Accordingly, practical cost/benefit factors come into play in the development of notional market values that may result in an incomplete information base being used to develop appropriately qualified notional market value determinations.

Because the achievement of a perfect and complete information base seldom is possible in either an open or notional market context, differences of opinion as to price or value based on somewhat different databases and analysis and conclusions drawn from them may result.

Between Prudent Parties

The phrase 'between prudent parties' relates to the contemplation of a marketplace where both vendor and purchaser exercise reasonable and appropriate diligence and care when assessing issues relevant to their respective sale and purchase decisions. A distinction clearly can be drawn between acting without what is believed to be adequate information, which itself may be imprudent, and acting in an imprudent manner referable to known information.

Acting at Arm's Length

The phrase 'acting at arm's length' relates to the contemplation of negotiation between parties with opposing interests, each of whom has only an economic interest in the outcome. The notion of 'acting at arm's length' is a matter of fact. In other words, it is not necessarily the case that related parties always act on a non-arm's length basis, or that non-related parties always act on an arm's length basis.

Under No Compulsion to Act

The phrase 'under no compulsion to act' relates to the contemplation of negotiation between parties where neither is forced to transact nor is constrained from acting with full choice. This clearly is not the case in many open market transactions. For example, where a business is in financial difficulty that threatens its continuity, but otherwise is viable as a going concern, its owner(s) may be compelled to sell. In such circumstances:

- in an open market context the purchaser often will attempt to take advantage of the vendor's weakened financial position in its negotiations; and
- in a notional market context, unless it is assumed that a purchaser can and will refinance an over-levered business without accounting for said over-leverage in the purchase price, a determination of fair market value normally should consider the fact that the business is in an adverse financial position, but should not reflect a discount for vendor lack of knowledge of financing and financing sources and other alternative business solutions.

While the notional market contemplates a circumstance where neither vendor nor purchaser is influenced pursuant to a compulsive force to sell and buy respectively, it is assumed that each is willing to sell and buy at a fair price and on terms that ensure that.

Expressed in Terms of Cash

Open market transactions frequently are consummated in circumstances where a portion or all of the price is not in the form of cash or equivalent. Examples of 'non-cash consideration' include shares of the acquiring corporation, vendor take-backs (e.g. a note or preferred shares which may or may not be reflective of prevailing commercial terms) and so-called 'earn-out' arrangements. Notional market valuations are expressed on a cash equivalent basis and assume an unequivocal transfer of the risks and rights associated with the property. The assumption of a cash based notional market transaction avoids interpretations of value that otherwise would result from assumptions as to non-cash terms and conditions.

Fair Market Value vs. Open Market Price

Importantly, there can be a significant difference between fair market value or other value term as defined and determined in a notional market context on one hand, and price as determined in an open market transaction on the other. If the components of fair market value are interpreted literally, at least the following differences exist between the determination of fair market value in a notional market context and price in an open market context:

Notional fair market value	Open market price
Hypothetical vendors and purchasers are assumed to have equal knowledge, negotiating abilities, and financial strength. Transactions are assumed to be consummated at the highest available price, but not at an unrealistically high, non-economic, price.	Typically, prices are negotiated between parties with differing knowledge, negotiating abilities, and financial strength. Accordingly, transactions may or may not be consummated at the highest available prices and indeed may be consummated at unrealistically high, non-economic, prices. Further, there is no assurance that all potential purchasers have been canvassed. Finally, even if canvassed, a potential purchaser may be unable or unwilling to transact due to lack of interest, or financial or other constraints.
Legal and contractual restrictions that prevent an unfettered sale are momentarily disregarded. However, existing restrictions are considered when formulating the value conclusion.	Legal and contractual restrictions that prevent an unfettered sale usually are enforceable. These issues typically have to do with the illiquidity that may attach to minority shareholdings. As a practical matter, where all of the outstanding shares of a company are sold together such restrictions have little bearing on the price received by each shareholder. However, if a minority share block (or in some instances a control block) of shares is sold by itself, such restrictions may have a significant downward influence on price. In the latter instance this typically depends on the relationship among shareholders at the date of sale.

Notional fair market value	Open market price
The possibility of imprudent actions is not considered.	Open market price may be struck as a result of imprudent decisions by the vendor, the purchaser, or by both.
Although as a practical matter not realistic (see previous commentary) it is assumed the hypothetical vendor and purchaser are apprised of all information and factors relevant to the valuation determination at the valuation date.	Either the vendor, the purchaser, or both may not be apprised of relevant information or factors concerning the business that might influence price.
The hypothetical vendor and purchaser are assumed to be dealing at arm's length.	The vendor and purchaser may not be dealing at arm's length.
Forced or compulsive acts are not considered.	Open market price may be struck as a result of forced or compulsive acts by the vendor, the purchaser, or both.
The transaction is assumed to be consummated for cash.	The price paid may not be all cash, but may all or in part be comprised of non-cash consideration.

Fair Value

The Canada Business Corporations Act and various Provincial Corporations Acts contain what generally are termed:

- minority shareholder appraisal remedies. In specified circumstances these remedies enable minority shareholders to require the issuer corporation to purchase their shares at 'fair value'; and
- oppression remedies. Pursuant to these, shareholders that believe they are being unfairly treated can petition the Courts to require the Issuer Corporation to be wound-up or to purchase their shares at 'fair value'.

Fair value is not specifically defined in any of the Corporations Acts. To date, 'fair value' generally has been interpreted by Canadian Courts to mean fair market value without the application of a discount to reflect the fact the shareholding(s) in question is a minority shareholding (i.e. a 'minority discount'). In addition, as subsequently discussed, Canadian Courts have addressed other possible adjustments to fair market value otherwise determined, including post-amalgamation benefits, premiums for forcible taking, and the weighing of public market trading prices where the defendant company whose shares require valuation is publicly owned. Appendix A sets out a list of Court Decisions dealing with the determination of fair value.

Minority Discounts

A reduction from the pro rata portion of the en bloc value of the assets or ownership interests of a business as a whole to reflect minority shareholding disadvantages related to non-control and where applicable, related illiquidity is referred to as a minority discount — see Chapter 13. Control of a business typically is thought of as the ability to elect the majority of the Board of Directors and hence direct the strategy and operations of the business, and ultimately dictate the timing of liquidity related to it. Control of the Board, subject to proper Corporate Governance, generally enables the controlling shareholder to control, or as a minimum significantly influence, the:

- economic direction of the business; and
- timing and quantum of dividend payments.

A controlling shareholder generally is in a position to dictate the election of Board members, the timing of the sale of the outstanding shares of the business, and in the case of an individual, personal employment and remuneration.

The en bloc valuation and pricing of the shares or net assets of a business implicitly incorporates all of these things. Absent an agreement that provides otherwise, a minority shareholder typically does not have the ability to exercise control of the company, or to readily liquidate his or her ownership interest. Therefore, depending on prevailing fact specific circumstances (for example, whether a minority shareholder has grounds for commencing an appraisal or oppression remedy action, the existence and terms of a Shareholder's Agreement, and so on) a minority shareholding may be worth less than a ratable portion of the en bloc value of all the outstanding shares. Stated differently, absent appraisal and oppression remedies that lead to 'fair value' determinations, valuation pricing and theory suggests the value of a minority shareholding may be less than the value of a control shareholding where each is expressed on a 'per share' basis.

As previously noted, to date, minority discounts generally have not been applied in circumstances where Canadian Courts have determined 'fair value'. Accordingly, exercise of appraisal or oppression remedies in some circumstances may enable minority shareholders to realize liquidity in respect of their investment where it otherwise may not be available to them.

Post-amalgamation Benefits

Post-amalgamation synergies or other benefits often are expected following amalgamation of the vendors and purchasers businesses. Accordingly, where an appraisal remedy is triggered pursuant to an amalgamation the question of whether some or all of such benefits should be considered in the determination of fair value arises. Although Canadian Court Decisions have varied with respect to this issue, the general principles that have been applied to date by Canadian Courts are that:

- consideration of post-amalgamation benefits is unlikely where the dissenting shareholders are not being 'forced out' but rather voluntarily decide to discontinue their investment in the company. That is, Canadian Courts generally have held that a minority shareholder cannot elect to receive a portion of the post-amalgamation benefits while foregoing the risk that such benefits might not materialize; and
- dissenting shareholders may receive some consideration for post-amalgamation benefits where specific synergies are anticipated and the dissenting shareholders are 'forced out' of the combined firm. That is, Canadian Courts generally have held that where the dissenting shareholders wanted to retain their interest in the combined firm and participate in the anticipated post-amalgamation benefits, consideration should be given to their opportunity to do so.

Premium for Forcible Taking

On occasion Canadian Courts have concluded that a 'force out' of a minority shareholder is analogous to the interest of the minority shareholder being expropriated and have awarded the minority a 'premium for forcible taking'. Having said that, the award of a premium for forcible taking rarely has been recognized by Canadian Courts.

Public Equity Market Prices

Where a company is publicly traded, the relevance of the company's historic share trading prices prior to the valuation date often is at issue in the determination of 'fair value'. In general, Canadian Courts have:

- recognized that where trading was thin or sporadic trading prices may not be, and generally are not, indicative of fair value;
- considered whether the impact of the transaction giving rise to the appraisal remedy may already be incorporated in the share price; and
- generally concluded that historic trading prices, if appropriately considered at all, in most instances should be only one factor to be considered in the determination of fair value.

Value to Owner

The term 'value to owner' refers to all of the economic and non-economic benefits that accrue from business ownership that are incremental to the fair market value of the business interest owned. In this regard, the value to its owner of an ownership interest in a business may be significantly different than its fair market value or fair value for several reasons. In particular:

- the business might provide its owner with benefits not quantified as part of a fair market value determination. These might include economic benefits (e.g. employment income, generous expense accounts, and so on) and non-economic benefits (status, prestige, lifestyle, and so on). Where an owner draws remuneration from a business that does not approximate arm's length equivalents, such remuneration typically is 'normalized' in the determination of fair market value. The quantification of non-economic returns is highly subjective, and rarely is meaningful given that such benefits vary considerably based on the owner's personal value system;
- the owner might be able to cause the business to generate excess returns in the business due to his or her non-transferable personal knowledge, abilities, contacts, and so on, that would be lost in the event that the owner was no longer actively involved. As subsequently discussed in this Chapter, the ability to generate such excess returns that cannot be transferred to a third party purchaser does not constitute a component of fair market value in a notional market context; and
- where a shareholder controls a corporation through ownership of voting shares and also beneficially owns redeemable, but not retractable, preference shares or non-voting participating shares, those preference and non-

voting participating shares may have value to the controlling shareholder beyond the price that could be realized for them in a sale to an arm's length third party where only the preference and non-voting participating shares were sold.

In a notional market context, the aforementioned factors might result in the value to the owner of a business being greater than fair market value. From both a theoretical and practical standpoint, 'value to owner' can never be less than 'fair market value'.

Value in Family Law Acts

In Canada, divorce and related matters (such as custody of children and support payments) are Federally legislated. However, property rights are a Provincial jurisdiction. Accordingly, each Province has its own legislation governing the division of assets upon the termination of marriage. In all Provinces except Quebec, individuals retain their respective property ownership rights throughout the marriage. On the occurrence of a specified triggering event such as divorce, annulment, separation, or death of one spouse, a spouse may acquire a right to an interest in the property of the other spouse generally evidenced by what is referred to as an 'equalization payment'.

When structuring their affairs, business owners should consider the potential impact of Family Law on their business in the event of marriage breakdown. Not only does the possibility of marriage breakdown become a factor, but since several Provinces have extended the availability of equalization rights to the death of a spouse in priority to will provisions, Family Law can also affect estate plans and other business succession arrangements. Business assets receive different treatment in the various Provinces, ranging from specific exclusion from division, to availability for sharing at the discretion of the Courts, to mandatory equal division. Further, family legislation varies by jurisdiction as to what events trigger rights of property division, the relevant valuation date, and the basis of valuation. In Quebec, property rights are determined pursuant to the Civil Code. The Civil Code provides for full community of property. That is, all property acquired during a marriage is deemed to be held jointly by both spouses. Each Province specifies various assets excluded from division.

A Provincial comparison of the legislative treatment of various key matters follows:

CHART 2.1[1]

Legislation	Alberta	British Columbia	Manitoba	New Brunswick	Nfld.	Nova Scotia	Ontario	P.E.I.	Quebec	Sask.
Property Rights Triggered by										
Separation	Yes	No	No	Yes	Yes	Yes	Yes	Yes	Yes	No
Divorce	Yes	Yes	No	Yes	Yes	Yes	Yes	Yes	Yes	No
Dissipation of Property	Yes	No	No	No	No	No	Yes	Yes	No	Yes
Nullity	Yes	Yes	No	Yes	Yes	Yes	Yes	Yes	Yes	No
Death of spouse	No	No	No	Yes	Yes	Yes	Yes	No	Yes	Yes
Upon Application	No	Yes	Yes	Yes	No	Yes	No	No	No	Yes
Value Basis	Market Value	Not Stated	Fair Market Value	Not Stated	Not Stated	Not Stated	Value	Not Stated	Not Stated	Fair Market Value
Valuation Date	Date of Adjudication	Date of Adjudication	As Agreed or Date of Last Cohabitation or Application	Not Stated	Not Stated	Not Stated	Earliest of Triggering Events	Earliest of Triggering Events	Date of Application or Adjudication	Date of Application or Adjudication
Property Specifically Exempted										
Business assets	No	No	No	Yes	Yes	Yes	No	No	No	No
Pre-marriage assets	Yes	No	Yes	No	Yes*	No	Yes*	Yes	Yes	Yes*
Post-separation assets	No	Yes	Yes	No	No	Yes	Yes	Yes	Yes	No
Gifts and inheritances	Yes	No	Yes	Yes	Yes	Yes	Yes*	Yes	Yes	No
Gifts made by spouse	No	No	No	Yes	No	No	No	No	No	No
Personal injury awards	Yes	Yes	Yes	No	Yes	Yes	Yes	Yes	Yes	Yes
Insurance proceeds	Yes	Yes	Yes	No	No	Yes	Yes	Yes	Yes	Yes
Property traceable from exempt property	Yes	Yes	Yes	No	No	No	Yes	Yes	Yes	Yes*
Family heirlooms	No	No	No	No	Yes	No	No	No	No	No
Personal effects	No	No	No	No	Yes	Yes	No	No	Yes	No

* except Matrimonial home

In the context of matrimonial disputes, the business assets at issue usually are transacted between the separating spouses in a notional market context. That is, infrequently are they sold in the open market. As a result, notwithstanding the lack of uniformity in Provincial matrimonial property legislation, certain issues regularly surface to complicate the process of dividing property on marriage breakdown.

The Definition of Value

Most Provincial legislation does not specifically define value. Presumably this is intentional, following from the general intent to provide in law for the orderly and perceived equitable settlement of the affairs of the spouses. Where value is not specifically defined an assessment must be made as to what value term (fair market value, fair value, value to owner, etc) is appropriate in each fact-specific circumstance.

Of particular importance in those jurisdictions which do not define the term 'value' is the concept of 'value to owner'. This issue arises where either one or both spouses hold an interest in a business in which one spouse is actively involved and is essential on a personal basis to the continuation of the business as a going concern. In such circumstances one spouse may be able to generate considerable income as a result of his or her personal knowledge, abilities, reputation and business contacts. As a result, the business may be worth much more to the spouse who operates the business than would be generated if the business were sold in an arm's length transaction.

Where value is required for transactions pursuant to Family Law legislation, the following factors may be significant to the determination thereof:

- 'value to owner' generally does not have commercial value and typically does not form a component of fair market value in Family Law matters;
- in those jurisdictions where fair market value is not specifically prescribed as the basis of valuation, there may be opportunity to consider alternate value concepts in the interest of achieving an equitable outcome;
- if a Court believes an equalization payment based on agreed or adjudicated asset values does not result in an equitable 'final' settlement between spouses, it may make adjustments it deems appropriate by dictating ongoing spousal support payments;

- unless the sale of a business interest appears imminent, the existence of purchasers who perceive net economic value-added is highly likely, and the quantum of 'premium' inherent in prices such purchasers might be prepared to pay can be estimated with a reasonable degree of certainty, stand-alone value tends to be taken as the basis by which 'value' is determined;
- consideration should be given to whether a notional transaction would be consummated by way of financial resources that are internal or external to the business being valued – see discussion in this Chapter. In this context, in some circumstances it may be appropriate for the Courts to consider the ramifications of the value determinations to parties other than the spouses (i.e. employees, creditors, and so on); and
- where spouses together own all of the outstanding shares of a corporation, or where spouses together control a corporation, their respective ownership interests generally are dealt with on a ratable (non-discounted) basis for equalization purposes, provided that equal liquidity is ensured to both spouses in the context of the final asset equalization agreement.

Valuation Date

Some Provinces specify the relevant date(s) value must be determined, in some instances even specifying the appropriate time of day, while others are silent. Several Provinces have extended the availability of division or equalization rights upon the death of a spouse, in which case the death of a spouse is considered to be a triggering event for purposes of dividing marital assets.

Minority Discounts

Where spouses collectively control a corporation and have a continuing marriage, it is logical to expect that they will share a common pool of wealth and income, and generally each act in their mutual best interest. As a result, so long as a marriage is intact, when valuing minority interests held by spouses that collectively comprise either all of the outstanding shares or a control shareholding, in Family Law matters, a discount from a ratable portion of en bloc value seldom is applied.

Upon the breakdown of marriage, the shareholding relationship typically changes to an adversarial one. Should one spouse retain a minority interest post-equalization, as a continuing minority shareholder he or she would have available the protection of the appraisal and oppression remedies of the applicable corporations statute. Notwithstanding, assuming the overall objective of family legislation is to attempt to ensure an equitable distribution of assets, the acquisition of the minority interest by the majority or a separation of equity interests pursuant to a corporate reorganization (a so-called 'structured settlement') generally should be a priority in matrimonial settlements.

Financing the Equalization Payment or Spousal Buyout

When addressing 'value' in a matrimonial context, as in shareholder disputes a determination must be made as to how the payment (whether it is an equalization payment, a buyout, or a combination of both) is to be financed. The specific issue that must be addressed is whether:

- the required funds are available external to any operating business assets, or
- it will be necessary to look to operating business assets within the familial 'asset pool' for all or part of the required funds.

Where shareholding interests in a privately held company represent the only asset of any significance other than the matrimonial home, equalization payments often must be, and are, funded through those businesses. Where the equalization payment amount is based on stand-alone value and is financed directly or indirectly by the business, undue financial hardship may be placed on the business. This eventually could force a sale of the business or cause its insolvency, which in turn would affect the:

- spouse whose shares were re-organized or sold in circumstances where the equalization payment was not fully paid;
- spouse who continued as a shareholder; and
- all other 'non-spouse' shareholders of the business,

and in the end might threaten the jobs of employees and expose suppliers and other stakeholders to losses. Stated differently, the issue arises as to whether the 're-structuring plan' or purchase will require an operating business within the familial 'asset pool' to provide funds to satisfy at least a portion of the required funds (a so-called 'internal financing'). Internally financed transactions sometimes result in an operating business assuming additional debt or foregoing necessary expenditures, each of which prospectively may reduce the business' prospective discretionary cash flow from the level otherwise expected on a stand-alone basis, and unduly increase the financing-related risk of the business. In such cases, a lower 'en bloc' value invariably results from that which might otherwise be determined — see discussion later in this Chapter.

As a result, in order to achieve equity in a family dispute situation, it is necessary to look to all of the assets comprising each spouse's Net Family Property and determine the extent to which internal financing of the equalization payment might be required. This analysis should then consider whether 'en bloc' value should be established on a stand-alone basis, under an assumption of internal financing, or on some other assumption.

Extended and favourable equalization payment terms may aid in reducing hardship where stand-alone (or 'intrinsic') value is used as the basis of 'en bloc' value. Where an open market price inclusive of assumed purchaser perceived synergies is taken as 'value', it may be that an arm's length sale of the shares owned by the spouse(s) is the only means of effecting the equalization payment without unduly impairing the underlying and future value of the business. Although a 'forced sale' (if that is the result) generally is undesirable from the standpoint of equitable treatment and otherwise, extended and favourable payment terms may provide the only means of avoiding this.

Income Taxes and Disposition Costs

Most Provincial legislation is silent with respect to the treatment of tax costs and other expenses which should be accounted for where specific assets notionally are disposed of pursuant to 'equalization' determination. This then becomes an extension of question of appropriate 'value' definition. Where business interests are sold, typically disposition costs as well as underlying tax liabilities are incurred. The magnitude of underlying contingent disposition costs and (in particular) income tax liabilities can be significant in the case of business assets. Where income tax treatment is not legislatively specified, in Family Law matters Canadian Courts have accepted taxes on notional disposition as either:

- full disposal and income tax costs;
- no disposal or income tax costs; or
- some discounted amount representing the deferral and/or uncertainty associated with the existing contingent disposal costs and income tax liabilities.

When determining the treatment and quantum of income taxes and disposition costs on notional disposition in Family Law matters, at least the following factors should be considered:

- the appropriate assumption(s) as to business continuity following the equalization payment, including consideration of the plans for the business vis-à-vis expansion, diversification, succession planning, and so on;

- the basis on which 'value' was determined and the likely timing of sale. Where, based on current market conditions, a premium that a special interest purchaser might pay has been incorporated in the value conclusion, the likely only means of extracting that additional value may be pursuant to a near term sale;
- the age, health and personal interests of the majority shareholder(s);
- income tax planning opportunities known or likely to exist; and
- where the business requires additional capital, the ability of the owner(s) to provide same from personal resources.

Finally, no guidance is provided in Provincial Family Law Legislation as to the appropriate treatment of personal guarantees (bank guarantees, lease guarantees and so on) that often are inherent in business ownership.

Other Important Valuation Concepts

Intangible Value

Fundamental to an understanding of valuation and pricing of a business is an understanding of the concept of intangible value. In financial terms, intangible value represents the amount by which the going concern value (or price) of a business interest exceeds the value of its underlying net tangible assets restated to their respective 'going concern values', which generally are determined based on their respective 'values in use'.

For example, assume that a business was expected to generate discretionary (after-tax) cash flow of $750,000 per annum and that a capitalization rate of 15% was appropriate. Further assume that the business had net tangible assets with an aggregate going concern value of $3 million. Intangible value then would be determined as:

Going concern value $750,000/15%	$5,000,000
Going concern value of underlying net tangible assets	3,000,000
Intangible value	$2,000,000

That portion of the going concern value of a business attributed to intangible value at a given point in time sometimes is referred to as 'going concern risk'. It is the amount not supported by the underlying net tangible assets of the business.

As a practical matter, determining the value in use of the net tangible assets of a business is itself a subjective task, particularly where the asset base of a business consists of a large fixed asset component. As a result, in a notional market context intangible value may be better viewed as a value range. Further, where intangible value is computed to be a negative amount, it does not necessarily mean that no goodwill exists. Rather, it may indicate that certain tangible assets are not fully productive, or that the 'value in use' estimates made for the net tangible assets are overly optimistic. When analyzing a business with apparent intangible value, it is important to consider what it appropriately is attributed to. That is, specifically why the business is worth more than the sum of the going concern value of its underlying net tangible assets.

Goodwill

Intangible value, which is more fully discussed in Chapter 6, can consist of the value of identifiable assets such as patents, copyrights, licences, and so on, and of non-identifiable assets which, as a general rule, collectively are referred to as 'goodwill'. Further, it is common not to distinguish between identifiable and non-identifiable intangible assets and to generically refer to all intangible value as 'goodwill'. Goodwill viewed in isolation can be broadly characterized as commercial, personal or individual.

Commercial Goodwill

Commercial goodwill accrues to a business by virtue of its products, services offered, location, and other features that are not dependent upon, or particular to, individual employees of the business. Commercial goodwill can be readily transferred upon the sale of the business. Specific examples include:

- goodwill of product due to product identity and acceptance the business enjoys in the minds of its customers and potential customers. This is evidenced by its installed product base, market share, brand name recognition, and so on;
- goodwill of service that accrues to a business by virtue of the identity and acceptance of its service in the minds of its customers and potential customers;
- goodwill of location that accrues to a business by virtue of a strategic or otherwise advantageous physical location; and

- fact-specific goodwill that accrues to a business by virtue of such things as opportunity cost and time value to replicate, scarcity value related to previously approved and non-replicable environmental site approvals, and so on.

Commercial goodwill is transferable upon the sale of the shares or underlying net assets of the business. Therefore, where commercial goodwill exists, it is reflected in en bloc business value.

Personal Goodwill

Personal goodwill is goodwill that accrues to a specific person. It arises from his or her personal characteristics and attributes as evidenced by particular abilities, physical characteristics, good name and reputation. Such personal characteristics are not transferable by contract or otherwise. Personal goodwill that is measured solely in economic terms expires at the time the person who enjoys it loses interest in the business, retires as a result of either personal choice, age, or disability, or dies. While personal goodwill may be all or in part secured through management and non-competition contracts in the near-term, it generally is accepted both in an open market context and by the Courts in a notional market context that personal goodwill is not transferable, and hence that:

- unless adequately secured by contracts that ensure and secure its near term benefits, in an open market context little if any commercial value attaches to it; and
- as a general rule it is not included when determining 'fair market value' in a notional market context.

Individual Goodwill

Individual goodwill accrues to a business by virtue of its employment of one or more individuals who have the abilities, business contacts, good name and reputation that could be, or would be, harmful to the economic well-being of the business should those individuals leave the employ of the business and compete with it. However, in contrast with personal goodwill, at the time of retirement or death of said individuals, individual goodwill does not expire in so far as the business is concerned where:

- the business has the capacity to substitute other people to fill the role played by those individuals who cease to be employed by the business; and

- those individuals who cease to be employed by the business are precluded from competing with it. In an open market context, it is non-competition agreements either separate from or combined with practical considerations related to business size, required capital investment, market share related practicalities, and so on, that would preclude competitive start-up, that result in individual goodwill having commercial value.

Non-Competition and Management Agreements

Non-competition agreements typically are a condition precedent to the acquisition of a business where a selling shareholder is active in the operation of the business and is believed by the purchaser, absent such an agreement, to be in a position to negatively affect the purchased business post-acquisition. Non-competition agreements specify the parameters of agreed non-competition, including geographic area, nature of non-permissible activities, and period of time (typically two to five years).

Management agreements generally are offered to selling shareholders where the purchaser believes their business acumen, knowledge, contacts and abilities will be beneficial during the transition period following acquisition. Management contracts commonly are of one to three years' duration, and vary considerably in terms of responsibility, authority and remuneration.

Both non-competition and management agreements typically come into existence on the closing of an open market transaction. In Canada a portion of the aggregate purchase price seldom in the past has been allocated to the non-competition agreement during the negotiation process. However, this has changed in recent years based on the view that if specific compensation is given for the non-compete that non-competition will prove to be more enforceable than it otherwise would be. On the other hand, management contracts often result from the negotiation process. This is because payments received by the vendor pursuant to such a contract typically can be written off by the purchaser for income tax purposes against the post-acquisition income of the acquired company. As a result, different views as to open market price often are 'bridged' by reducing the purchase price, but increasing what otherwise would be the amount payable to the vendor(s) pursuant to a post-closing management contract(s). Generally the Canada Customs and Revenue Agency (formerly Revenue Canada) does not take exception to this bridging because the transactions are negotiated at arm's length and hence are difficult to dispute, and in any event pursuant to Canada's largely integrated income tax system such arrangements generally have comparative little long term 'net taxes paid' consequences.

The valuation of a non-competition agreement is a highly subjective exercise. In a notional market context, it generally is assumed in en bloc value determinations that a non-competition agreement will be struck as necessary in order to consummate a transaction, and a specific amount to account for it generally is not separated from the en bloc value in which it is embedded. In order to effectively deal with that component of fair market value or price that might reasonably be attributed to an assumption of the execution of a non-competition agreement, it is necessary to have a clear understanding of the various types of 'goodwill' that exist in an economic context.

Valuing Non-Competition Agreements in a Notional Market Context

Where the value of a non-competition agreement must be isolated in a notional market context, it generally is not practical to hypothesize the terms and conditions that would be agreed by the vendor and purchaser. Accordingly, emphasis should be placed on determining that individual goodwill indeed does exist, and the ability of the individual(s) in whom it resides to compete effectively with the business absent a non-competition agreement. This requires consideration of the individual business owner(s), the business itself and the nature of the industry in which the business participates. In general, the potential value attributed to a non-competition agreement increases:

- where the business owner(s):
  - is relatively young and not expected to retire from daily business activity in the near term,
  - enjoys good physical health,
  - is expected to have a high level of interest in continuing the business or a similar business following closing,
  - possesses valuable personal knowledge and inter-personal relationships with employees, suppliers and customers that are important to the prospective viability of the business that can not be readily past on, and that will continue to reside with the business owner following closing,
  - has the financial ability to compete following closing, and
  - has in-depth knowledge of the near term plans and longer term strategies of the business;
- where the business itself:
  - is relatively small in size,
  - is less capital intensive than more capital intensive,
  - sells products that are non-proprietary, or is service related, and
  - sells products that are in the earlier stages of the product life-cycle;
- where the industry in which the business competes:

- is such that the business owner's options to compete would include a ready opportunity to start a new competitive business, enter into a joint venture or other participating equity relationship with an existing competitor, or enter into a contract of employment with a competitor,
- is subject to a comparatively weak competitive environment, and
- has the potential for, or would allow for, a comparatively rapid near term expansion.

Non-Competition Agreements in Open Market Transactions

Where a non-competition agreement is executed in conjunction with an open market transaction, its terms and conditions become important when determining that portion of 'effective' price, if any, that should be allocated to the non-competition agreement. In addition to the general factors noted above, consideration also should be given to:

- the terms of payment. For example, if a significant portion of the ultimate purchase price will be determined pursuant to an 'earn-out' arrangement (i.e. where a portion of the price is paid dependant on achievement of agreed post-closing objectives by the acquired company), it is likely that less value will be attributed to non-competition agreements than otherwise would be the case;
- the specific terms of the agreement itself, including the definition of the specific business(es) from which the vendor is prohibited from competing, and the geographic area in which, and length of time over which, competition is restricted. In theory, there should be a direct relationship between the compensation paid to a vendor related to non-competition and the magnitude and scope of the agreed competitive restrictions; and
- judicial interpretations with respect to non-competition agreements, and non-competition itself. It is necessary to make an assessment of and assumptions as to the enforceability of an assumed non-competition agreement — the greater the ability to legally enforce, the greater the potential value of an agreement to a purchaser.

In the United States arm's length purchasers are able to amortize for U.S. Federal Income Tax purposes that portion of the purchase price properly attributable to a non-competition agreement. In general, U.S. Courts have applied four tests when adjudicating whether an amount attributed to a non-competition agreement can be amortized. These are:

- whether the compensation paid for the agreement is severable from the price paid for acquired goodwill. Pursuant to this test, the purchaser must demonstrate that the vendor possessed a probable and viable means of competition;
- whether either party to the contract is attempting to repudiate an amount knowingly fixed by both the purchaser and the vendor as allocable to the non-competition agreement;
- whether proof exists that both parties actually intended, when they signed the sale agreement, that some portion of the price be assigned to the non-competition agreement; and
- whether the non-competition agreement is economically real and meaningful.

Estimating the portion of value to attribute to a non-competition agreement normally is done by notionally determining the value of the given business interest assuming a non-competition agreement is not executed. The result then is compared with the value otherwise determined in a notional market context or the price paid in an open market transaction. This is an extremely subjective process.

Apportioning Value to a Management Agreement

In a notional market context there is no basis for ascertaining whether the parties would enter into a post-closing management agreement and what its terms would be. As a result, in a notional market context it generally is assumed that appropriate management agreements are struck on commercial terms and at market rates. Because fair market value is defined in terms of cash or cash equivalents, it would be inconsistent to assume that a portion of that fair market value related to an extraordinary management agreement.

In an open market transaction, a portion of the stated price seldom is attributed to a management agreement executed on closing. As previously noted, management agreements often provide for remuneration greater than the value of the services provided in order to bridge a price gap between vendor and purchaser. However, payments pursuant to such agreements typically are not guaranteed in the event of the vendor's death, and any incremental remuneration over what would be viewed as 'market commercial' generally would represent a comparatively small portion of the overall purchase price.

In exceptional cases, where the remuneration set out in a management contract includes a significant premium to the value of services performed which in turn represents a material portion of the purchase price, it may be appropriate to allocate a portion of the purchase price to the management agreement. In such circumstances the analysis would parallel that undertaken when determining that portion of price appropriately assigned to a non-competition agreement.

Internal vs. External Financing

In an open market context many factors, including the specific characteristics of the transacting parties, influence the price of a business interest at a given point in time. One factor that can be isolated for consideration is funding sources available to any specific purchaser, which typically will affect the price each purchaser will offer. Depending on the reason value determination is necessary, one important aspect of this financing issue has to do with whether the purchaser:

- has access to funds external to the business interest being acquired to complete the purchase; or
- must utilize what would otherwise be all or a portion of the post-acquisition cash flow of the acquired business to pay for it.

A transaction where all or part of the outstanding shares or net assets of a business are sold to a purchaser who:

- does not require all or part of the purchase price to be funded from the post-acquisition cash flow of the acquired business is referred to as an 'externally financed' transaction; and
- requires all or part of the purchase price to be funded from the post-acquisition cash flow of the acquired business is referred to as an 'internally financed' transaction.

In an internally financed transaction the purchase price may be funded by:

- excess cash or cash equivalents that are 'redundant assets' of the acquired business;
- incremental funds borrowed at arm's length by the acquired business at or following closing; or
- post-acquisition cash flows of the acquired business that are paid to the vendor over an agreed period of time.

The distinction between externally and internally financed transactions arises where:

- privately-held business interests are sold to employees pursuant to a so-called 'management buyout' or otherwise;
- privately-held company shareholdings are bought and sold among existing shareholders, either during their respective lifetimes or on the death of one of them. In the latter circumstance, insurance funding often is used to avoid the necessity of:
  - utilizing the post-death cash flow of the business to acquire the deceased's ownership interest, or
  - selling the business in circumstances where the risk of funding the purchase of the deceased's shareholding from internally generated cash flow is untenable;
- the value of a privately-held business interest must be determined in circumstances where there are parties in dispute, it is unlikely that an 'en bloc' open market sale will occur, but where a value determination likely will influence the quantum and terms of a financial arrangement between the parties. Examples arise in litigation, including the quantification of payments to equalize the value of net assets accumulated by separating spouses pursuant to Family Law requirements, and in shareholder disputes (including minority shareholder appraisal and oppression remedy actions); and
- price is determined in open market transactions involving a high utilization of debt, such as leveraged buyouts.

In circumstances of transactions among shareholders, the concept of 'fairness' may be viewed as a notional value or transaction price pursuant to which no individual stakeholder is better or worse off relative to the intrinsic value of the ownership interest of each before and after such transaction takes place. For example, assume that the en bloc 'intrinsic' value of Company B's equity is $2 million and that there are 4 equal shareholders. It follows that the pro-rata value of each shareholders' interest is $500,000. Further assume that one of the 4 shareholders retires and the remaining shareholders agree to purchase the one quarter interest held by the retiring shareholder at its ratable value. If this transaction was to be financed internally, this might be accomplished by:

- Company B borrowing $500,000 and paying it to the departing shareholder. This results in Company B having to repay the debt and, all other things being equal, will result in a reduction in the 'en bloc' value of Company B's equity by that amount;
- paying the departing shareholder over time (including commercial rates of interest) from what otherwise would be the discretionary (or 'free') cash flows of Company B. This theoretically would reduce the discretionary cash flows of Company B by $500,000 on a present value basis; or

- paying the departing shareholder a sum of $500,000 from redundant cash or cash equivalents held by Company B.

In each case, in theory, the 'en bloc' value of Company B's equity would decline from $2 million to $1.5 million. However, the remaining shareholders would now have a one third interest with a ratable value of $500,000. Accordingly, the value of each of their economic interests has not changed relative to the 'intrinsic value' of Company B's equity. As a result, 'fairness', defined in terms of pro-rata value, is preserved. However, in practice this does not always result.

In the case of a going concern, the value of any business asset largely is a function of prospective discretionary cash flows that accrue to it and the risk attached to those discretionary cash flows. Accordingly, depending on fact-specific circumstances an internally financed 'value' or 'price' determined in the context of 'stand-alone' or 'intrinsic' value theoretically might be less for any particular shareholding than the intrinsic value determined pursuant to an assumption of an externally financed transaction. This is because in order to finance the payout required pursuant to an internally financed transaction the business may have to:

- forego necessary expenditures to maintain its operations at present levels;
- forego anticipated growth opportunities; or
- obtain incremental financing and thereby incur incremental financial risk beyond what could be regarded as 'acceptable' for the business.

As a result, the impact of internal financing may be that the post-acquisition en bloc 'intrinsic' value of the business declines by more than the pre-acquisition ratable 'intrinsic' value of the interest being acquired. In such circumstances the post-acquisition pro-rata interest held by each remaining stakeholder declines. Further, as a practical matter in an open market transaction, the fact that internal funds are required to finance an acquisition often enters into negotiations and places downward pressure on the departing shareholder(s) with respect to price.

To the extent purchaser perceived synergies would result in an open market sale price exceeding en bloc 'intrinsic value', the 'remaindermen' following an internally financed transaction could be benefited by what would be their comparative respective equity interest in any incremental open market price over 'intrinsic value'. Where such incremental open market price is likely, as a practical matter this would tend to offset the risk associated with the remaindermen assuming any perceived near-term negative economic connotations resulting from the internally financed transaction.

Assets vs. Shares

As a general rule, an arm's length purchaser will pay a higher price for all of the underlying net assets of a going concern than it will for the outstanding shares of the company that operates that going concern. This is because following the acquisition of net assets the purchaser:

- typically enjoys greater post-acquisition cash flows related to Canadian Income Tax Laws that enable:
  - a step up in the cost base of the underlying depreciable assets, and hence enhanced post-acquisition capital cost allowance claims, and
  - the ability to amortize the amount paid for intangibles (in Canadian Income Tax parlance 'eligible capital property'); and
- generally does not assume any liabilities other than those specifically agreed to.

Conversely, the vendor generally prefers to sell the company's outstanding shares. This is because such a sale results in realization of capital gains (or losses) which, depending on fact-specific circumstances, may be taxed at a more favourable net income tax rate than income generated pursuant to a sale of net tangible and intangible assets. An exception to this general rule sometimes occurs where the business being sold has substantial non-capital loss carried forwards for income tax purposes available only to a prospective purchaser of shares.

The impact of valuing assets vs. shares is illustrated in Chapter 4. The income tax consequences of selling net assets as contrasted to selling shares are discussed in Chapter 14.

Principles of Business Valuation[2]

The following principles are the foundation of business valuation theory. As a general rule, they are applicable in both a notional and open market valuation context. These principles are founded in a combination of economic theory, common sense, open market reality, and jurisprudential authority.

Principle # 1 – Value is Point in Time Specific

> *Value is determined at a specific point in time. It is a function of facts known and expectations made only at that point in time.*

Value is determined at a specific point in time. By way of simple example, prices of normal sized trading lots of public company shares typically fluctuate daily. Businesses themselves are constantly in a state of flux as a result of acquisitions or sale of business segments or changes in product lines, management, financing arrangements, market conditions, general and business specific economic conditions, industry and competitive conditions, and so on. Such changes may be dictated by things within the control of management, or be imposed by circumstances external to the business over which management has no control. Under any circumstance, internal and external changes that affect the prospects of the business typically lead to changes in value. Hence, value is time-specific.

Commensurate with the notion of time-specific value, it generally is accepted in notional market valuations, and a fact in open market transactions, that hindsight or retrospective evidence should not be considered. When negotiating open market transactions, neither the vendor nor the purchaser has the benefit of knowledge of events that will take place at a future date. Rather, they can only utilize informed judgement, and as a result, hypothesize such events. Canadian Courts generally have found that hindsight evidence is inadmissible when determining value in a notional market context, except to the extent it is utilized to determine whether or not subsequent actual events were generally consistent with the assumptions made and conclusions reached at the relevant value date. In this latter regard, where projections were prepared prior to the valuation date and utilized in the value determination, Canadian Courts sometimes have permitted the limited use of hindsight when reviewing those financial projections. Thus in a notional market context, hindsight is simply one factor that may be considered in post-valuation date evidence, not in the actual value determination.

Principle # 2 – Value is Principally a Function of Prospective Discretionary Cash Flow

> *Value principally varies directly with the ability of a business to generate prospective discretionary cash flow, except in unusual circumstances where net asset liquidation results in a higher value.*

As discussed in Chapter 4, discretionary cash flow normally is determined as cash flow from operations less income taxes thereon, net trade working capital requirements, and capital investment requirements net of the related income tax shield. In open market transactions, corporate acquirers typically assess acquisition candidates on the basis of their apparent ability to generate post-acquisition discretionary cash flows. To some extent, historic results to the date of valuation are useful as a guide to future prospects. However, it is necessary to carefully analyze and understand the significant factors that gave rise to those historic results to determine whether such factors – both internal to the business and therefore to some large degree controllable, and external to the business and therefore generally less controllable – are likely to continue in the manner consistent with their historic behavior patterns.

Forecasting prospective results is by any measure a difficult and subjective task. However, the better the historic data base the greater the ability to identify and assess assumptions that underlie the forecast. As a general rule, the higher the perceived uncertainty associated with the prospects of a business interest at a point in time, the greater will be the perceived risk and the lower will be the price or value.

Principle # 3 – The Market Dictates the Appropriate Rate of Return

> *While market rates of return are constantly in a state of flux, they provide important benchmark indicators at any given point in time, and over the long term influence rates of return sought by individual corporate acquirers.*

At any given point in time, market forces work to dictate prescribed rates of return to be applied in the determination of the value of all of the outstanding shares or net assets of a business. These market forces include:

- general economic conditions, but in particular short and long-term borrowing rates, which influence both acquisition and divestiture activity level, and the rates of return purchasers require. Given that the acquisition of a business generally is viewed by a purchaser as a long-term investment, short-term borrowing rates tend to influence activity level, whereas anticipated long-term borrowing rates tend to influence required rates of return;
- the types of purchasers in the market, and the motivations and investment philosophy of each. As discussed in Chapter 1, there are four identifiable categories of corporate purchasers. These are:
  — publicly-held companies;
  — privately held operating companies;
  — purchasers that see acquisitions as financial transactions (i.e. often 'leveraged buyouts'); and
  — purchasers that comprise the management group of the acquired business.

In an open market context, only when all these possible purchaser groups have been canvassed and their respective sources and costs of funds have been surveyed can an appropriate rate of return be determined at a point in time. In a notional market context canvassing of potential purchaser groups typically does not occur. Accordingly, publicly available information and the experience and judgement of those determining value must be substituted for open market exposure and negotiation.

As discussed in Chapter 1, the prospective discretionary cash flows of a business and the rate of return applied to those cash flows are interdependent in a business value context. All other things equal, the greater the risk of realizing the anticipated prospective discretionary cash flows, the higher will be the required rate of return. The value of a business interest cannot be altered by changing either the prospective discretionary cash flows or the rates of return applied thereto in isolation from one another.

Principle # 4 – Value is, or may be, Influenced by Underlying Net Tangible Assets

> *In theory, the underlying net tangible asset value of a business will, or may, influence the going concern value of that business.*

As a general (albeit not an absolute) statement, all other things equal (and subject to the following discussion), within reasonable parameters the existence of higher underlying net tangible asset value (measured in terms of both value in use (i.e. going concern value) and liquidation value) lends support to a higher going concern value than would otherwise be the case. 'Within reasonable parameters' means that tangible asset backing differences likely would have to be material (i.e. very large) to have an impact on going concern value as a result of tangible asset backing being adopted as a risk measurement tool. For example, assume going concern value was determined in a notional market context pursuant to a discounted cash flow valuation methodology to be $10 million, and tangible asset backing was determined (depending on assumptions) to be either $7 million or $6 million. Depending on circumstances, going concern value might reasonably be concluded to be $10 million pursuant to either assumed tangible asset backing scenario. However, and again depending on circumstances, this might not be the case if tangible asset backing was determined to be $1 million.

This finds conceptual support on two bases:

- first, going concern value presumes perpetuation of the business entity that is being valued. For example, tangible assets such as single use real estate and manufacturing equipment often have a greater 'value in use' than liquidation value. In theory, where each business asset and liability is restated to its depreciated replacement value (or 'value-in-use'), the greater the dollar value of the aggregation of the net tangible assets of a business, the greater is the investment amount required to enter the industry in which the business operates. All other things equal, it follows that the higher the cost of industry entry, the lower the probability of new competition, and the lower will be the purchaser's required rate of return at the time of acquisition; and
- second, on the date a business is acquired, the net assets of the acquired business have an underlying liquidation value. In theory, the greater the acquisition date liquidation value of said underlying net assets, the lower is the downside risk of the purchaser at that point in time, and hence the lower will be the purchaser's required implied rate of return at the time of the acquisition. Having said that, as a practical matter absent unusual circumstances, purchasers acquiring what they believe to be a viable going concern with a long prospective life typically do not weight liquidation value heavily, if at all, when pricing an acquisition.

As a practical matter, in buoyant economic times and times of industry consolidation (as experienced in North America through the 1990's) risk comparisons based on tangible asset backing tend to be emphasized to a lesser degree than they are in less buoyant times. Concurrently, through the 1990's (and continuing) there is ever increasing emphasis on, and analysis of, forecasts and related utilization of 'forward looking' valuation methodologies (in particular, the discounted cash flow methodology) as the 'methodology of choice'. This in turn has led through the 1990's to less emphasis being placed on risk relationships based on tangible asset backing and liquidation value comparisons, particularly where larger businesses are the subject of analysis. Having said that, the comparison (in particular) of estimated tangible asset backing and liquidation value with apparent going concern value may surface risk related issues (such as implied evidence of technologically obsolete equipment) which in turn may result in necessary adjustments to prospective discretionary cash flows that might otherwise be missed.

In theory, and setting aside the possible influence of liquidation values, at the date of acquisition or valuation of a business that is a going concern, the prospective discretionary cash flow of that business can be thought of as having two 'layers':

- a first layer, being a return at an appropriate rate on the 'tangible asset backing', being the net tangible asset value of the business based on 'value in use' values (which value in use determinations in themselves may be a highly subjective estimate); and
- a second layer, to the extent there is incremental cash flow over and above that required to service the first layer, being a return at an appropriate rate on the intangible assets, in turn being the difference between the aggregate purchase price of the business interest and the 'tangible asset backing'. The theoretical required rate of return applied to this second layer would be higher than that applied to the first layer, since the risk attaching to the second layer theoretically is greater than the risk attaching to the first.

The following example will serve to illustrate this point. Companies M and N are competitors in the same industry. Both companies generate discretionary cash flow of $100,000, and are otherwise identical in all respects except that the tangible asset backing of Company M's net assets is $300,000, whereas the tangible asset backing of Company N's net assets is $500,000.

Where the outstanding shares of each of Company M and N are to be valued on an en bloc basis, and the required rates of return to be applied to the discretionary cash flows are taken to be on:

- tangible asset backing – 12.0%; and
- the intangible assets (the difference between aggregate price and tangible asset backing) – 20%,

it follows given the perceived rates of return that in theory the value of the outstanding shares of Companies M and N would be calculated as follows:

	Company M	Company N
Discretionary cash flow	$100,000	$100,000
Return on tangible asset backing		
$300,000 @ 12%	36,000	
$500,000 @ 12%		60,000
By deduction, discretionary cash flow related to intangible assets	$ 64,000	$ 40,000

Summary of Value

Tangible asset backing	$300,000	$500,000
Capitalization of discretionary cash flow associated with intangible assets		
$64,000 @ 20% (5X)	320,000	
$40,000 @ 20% (5X)		200,000
En bloc value of outstanding shares	$620,000	$700,000

In this example, both Companies M and N are assumed to have an identical discretionary cash flow, that is, $100,000. The one composite rate of return that would have to be derived to determine the en bloc value of the outstanding shares of Company M to be $620,000 would be 16.13% ($100,000/$620,000). The one composite rate of return that would have to be derived to determine the en bloc value of the outstanding shares of Company N to be $700,000 would be 14.28% ($100,000/$700,000).

As a practical matter, there may be reasons that when viewing Companies M and N on a going concern basis the fact that their different underlying tangible asset backing values are different may not result in their respective going concern values being different, particularly where the determination of tangible asset backing involves a high degree of subjectivity. At the same time, a review of underlying tangible asset backing, especially where value is being determined for smaller non-capital intensive businesses with significant dependence on the personal characteristics and contacts of the owner, may assist in sounder risk analysis and hence result in better based value conclusions.

In the end, the significance (if any) of comparisons of imputed going concern value with either or both tangible asset backing and liquidation value when concluding on going concern value is fact specific, and must be based on experience and informed judgment.

Principle # 5 – Commercial and Non-Commercial Value are Distinct Concepts

> Where the value of a business is based on its prospective discretionary cash flows, it may have two distinct components: commercial (or transferable) value and non-commercial (or value-to-owner) value.

The prospective discretionary cash flows of a business may be generated irrespective of the involvement of specific individuals, or all or in part may accrue directly as a result of the non-transferable talents of specific characteristics or abilities. Where prospective discretionary cash flows accrue:

- irrespective of the involvement of specific individuals, value generally may be said to be commercial, or transferable; and
- all or in part directly as a result of the non-transferable characteristics or abilities of specific individuals, value generally may be said to be non-commercial in nature. In such circumstances, all or part of value determined pursuant to a valuation methodology employing prospective discretionary cash flows may represent 'value to owner' that is not commercially transferable. While this concept is not difficult to articulate, often it is very difficult to quantify. This is particularly so when it is confused with apparent value consolidated in an open market purchase price pursuant to post-acquisition management and non-competition agreements. As discussed earlier in this Chapter, Canadian Courts generally have adopted the position that 'fair market value' in a notional market context does not encompass personal goodwill since it does not constitute a component of commercial value.

For example, assume Company D is in the creative design business, and that all of the outstanding shares of Company D are owned by one person. Further assume that:

- whereas Company D employs eight other people, it is dependent on the owner to generate virtually all sales;
- with few exceptions, Company D's projects are of a 'one-of' non-repetitive nature; and
- Company D shows very little growth from year to year.

An extremely creative person, the owner also is highly independent. Business accrues to Company D as a result of his personal contacts, his reputation for creativity, his selling abilities, and his high level of personal time commitment. The owner generates a much higher personal income each year from Company D than he could earn elsewhere in an employee capacity.

Even if the owner was agreeable to signing a long-term management and non-competition agreement in conjunction with the sale of his Company D shares, absent unusual circumstances it is unlikely a purchaser would pay more than the value in use of the underlying net tangible assets of Company D. This is because the business of Company D essentially is a function of the owner's interest in, and ongoing involvement with, Company D. Accordingly, so long as the owner:

- continues to have the same degree of interest in operating the business of Company D as he has had in the past;
- does not become disabled such that he is unable to continue to operate Company D; or
- does not die,

the outstanding shares of Company D have a value to the owner that exceeds the commercial value of those same shares.

Principle # 6 – Value is Influenced by Liquidity

> *In both a notional valuation and open market context, as a general rule the greater the liquidity of a business interest, defined in terms of the number of prospective purchasers, the greater the value of the business interest.*

The value of a business interest is influenced by the liquidity of that interest. All other things being equal, greater liquidity decreases risk, which in turn leads to higher value. This is commonly observed in the public equity markets where heavily traded broadly held securities often trade at higher multiples of historical earnings when contrasted with securities of thinly traded companies.

Where a business is being sold 'en bloc' in an open market transaction, the vendor(s) typically maximize proceeds by canvassing as many prospective purchasers as possible as opposed to notifying only one or a few possibly interested parties. By soliciting numerous prospective purchasers, the price fetched for the business is likely to be greater where:

- one or more prospective purchasers is identified that might enjoy significant post-acquisition net economic value added; and
- given more than one interested party, the vendor typically is in an improved negotiating position.

In both a notional and open market context it is important to identify whether or not one or more such purchasers exist. In theory, absent consideration of a so-called 'middle-market' of speculators who might buy to immediately resell:

- if there is only one purchaser with a special interest in acquiring a business interest, that purchaser will pay only a nominal amount more than purchasers without such special acquisition interest. Having said that, where only one such purchaser exists, as a practical matter open market negotiations with that purchaser may result in price concessions related to perceived synergies due to the negotiating skill of the vendor, scarcity of acquisition opportunities available to the purchaser, and so on; and
- where there are two or more purchasers with special interests in acquiring, purchasers without such special acquisition interests may be excluded from the market by economic conditions beyond their control. This would be the case where purchasers with special interests bid the price up, thereby creating a market in which only they participate.

It is important that open market vendors understand this principle, as it is fundamental to price maximization. This is becoming ever more important as businesses are being marketed on an increasingly sophisticated basis, and where industry consolidation occurs. An understanding of this principle also is important when determining fair market value, or other value, in a notional market context. Finally, in limited circumstances it may be appropriate to consider the aforementioned 'middle market' of hypothetical speculators who in theory might be prepared to bid against one another in anticipation of an immediate resale to a single purchaser with a special interest.

Principle # 7 – The Value of a Minority Interest may be Worth Less than the Value of a Controlling Interest where Each is Viewed on a 'Per Share' Basis.

> *Absent a Shareholder's or other Ownership Agreement, or legislation or adjudicated legislative intent that dictates otherwise, the value of a controlling interest in a business may have a greater value per share than does a minority-interest in that same business when each is viewed in isolation.*

In either a notional or open market context it is important to distinguish between the determination of the en bloc value of the outstanding shares of a company and the determination of the value of an individual shareholding that comprises less than all of those outstanding shares. Individual shareholdings essentially fall into two classes, those that control and those that do not. A controlling interest can be represented by either an individual shareholding, a combination of shareholdings of different outstanding share classes beneficially owned by the same owner which together constitute control, or a grouping of shareholdings each of which by itself would not constitute a control position. Simply stated, a controlling interest is one that carries sufficient votes to be able to elect at least a majority of the members of the Board of Directors and, through them, to govern the business. All other individual shareholdings typically are referred to as minority interests.

Agreements among shareholders can fetter the ability of a controlling interest to unilaterally control business operations, business strategy, and to dictate either a return on investment or the timing of sale. Absent such agreements or Court intervention, the owner of a controlling interest typically can dictate the timing of an offer to sell his or her shareholding. As previously discussed, the essential reason that a minority interest viewed in isolation may have less value per share than does a controlling interest has to do with the minority shareholder's inability to be guaranteed influence over business strategy, business operations, and the timing and quantum of return on investment. When determining the value of a minority interest in either a notional or open market context, these factors often result in discounts from what otherwise would be the per share value of the shareholding. Broadly, such discounts are referred to as 'minority discounts' – see Chapter 13.

Commensurate with this principle is the notion that the sum of the values of individual shareholdings that comprise the entire business may be less than the value of total ownership viewed 'en bloc'. Where all of the outstanding shares of a business are sold in the open market, an appropriate portion of the sale proceeds typically is allocated to each share class. Each shareholder typically then receives his or her pro rata portion of the aggregate sale proceeds allocated to the class of shares of which his or her shareholding comprises a part. When dealing with business interests in an open market context, infrequently is a value determined for a control shareholding viewed in isolation. This is because most often when business interests are sold, all of the outstanding shares are sold, or there is a contractual commitment on the part of the purchaser ultimately to buy them all. Further, where value is determined for a controlling interest in a notional market context, typically it is perceived to be equal to a pro rata portion of the en bloc value of all of the outstanding participating shares of the company that it controls. Rarely in a notional market context is a controlling interest afforded a value in excess of said pro-rata value. This is because:

- there are legislative fetters governing the behavior of controlling shareholders that preclude them, certainly in theory and generally in practice, from economically abusing minority shareholders;
- although the controlling shareholder can dictate the quantum and timing of return on investment by causing dividends to be declared and paid, such dividends are shared pro-rata with all other shareholders of a particular share class; and
- in the event of an open market sale of all of the outstanding shares, it is assumed each shareholder would receive his pro rata share of that portion of the proceeds attributed to each outstanding share class.

Where controlling and minority interests are valued in isolation from one another and are accorded different values per share, it follows that it would be an unusual circumstance where the aggregation of those separate values was equal to the en bloc value of all of the outstanding shares.

Consider the following example. Company A has one class of shares outstanding. The en bloc value of its outstanding shares is $3,000,000. There are two shareholders, one owns 60% of the outstanding shares, and the other 40%. Where the two shareholdings are valued independent of one another, it is determined that the 60% shareholding has a value of $1,800,000 ($3,000,000 X 60%), and that the 40% shareholding has a value of $840,000 ($3,000,000 X 40% = $1,200,000 less a minority discount of, say, 30% = $840,000). The sum of the parts valued separately is $2,640,000, being $360,000 less than the en bloc value of the outstanding shares.

Summary

Fair market value or fair value are the value terms most often adopted in a notional market context. These concepts are distinct from value to owner, which may reflect economic and non-economic benefits, including 'personal goodwill', generally not incorporated as an element of either fair market value or fair value. In addition, 'value' as determined in a notional market context may be different from price as negotiated pursuant to an open market transaction.

The underlying principles of business valuation generally apply in both a notional market and open market context. That being said, every notional market valuation and every open market pricing exercise is unique, and in each case the specific relevant facts must be considered.

NOTES

1 Chart 2.1 is provided only as a general guideline. There are many exceptions that have not been addressed herein, given that details of Family Law matters are beyond the scope of this book. Legal advice should be obtained in each fact-specific situation.

2 In previous writings, eleven valuation principles were defined. In this text, those eleven valuation principles have been consolidated into seven underlying principles as set out herein.

Chapter 3
Business Analysis

Introduction

Whether the outstanding shares or net assets of a business are being valued pursuant to a notional market valuation or an open market transaction, detailed analysis of the business itself, the industry in which it operates, and prevailing economic factors must be completed. A comprehensive and objective assessment of the quantitative and qualitative elements of the business and its environment is important in order to assess prospective operating results and the risks attaching thereto.

The three principal variables influencing the value of a business interest in valuation or pricing exercises are the:

- amount and timing of future discretionary cash flows;
- level of risk perceived referable to realizing those discretionary cash flows; and
- net realizable value of redundant assets, if any.

The information gathering process and analysis should be conducted in a manner that will provide insight into, and an objective assessment of, these key variables.

This Chapter begins with an overview of what generally is included in a business analysis ('internal analysis'), followed by an overview of industry and general economic factor analysis ('external analysis'). The latter part of this Chapter addresses the identification of redundant assets. Subsequent Chapters address the topics of discretionary cash flow estimation, risk assessment (i.e. rate of return determination), and redundant asset quantification.

The Information Base

The initial steps in a value determination are to identify the purpose for which the value is required, to identify the shares or assets to be valued or priced, and to assemble an information base. Where a notional market value is required, it also is necessary to know whether the determination is to be made as at a current date or at some prior date. Where a notional valuation is to be made at a prior date, care must be taken to focus and rely only on information available at that time.

The information base is assembled as several interrelated components:

- facts contained in the documents and records of the business;

- facts, opinions, and observations obtained from interviews with the owners and management of the business;
- if believed useful and appropriate, facts, opinions and observations obtained from:
  - interviews with advisors to the owners and management of the business;
  - real estate valuers, equipment valuers, environmental engineers, and others with relevant expertise;
  - outside parties knowledgeable in the industry in which the business operates; and
- published information concerning the industry and the general business and economic environment.

A useful strategy for accumulating an information base is to assemble and review financial and contractual documents of the business and general industry information prior to conducting in-depth interviews with management and others. A list of information obtained in the preliminary stages of a price or value assessment may include:

General Corporate Information

- incorporation documents and amendments thereto;
- listing of key management personnel, Directors, shareholders (including their respective ownership interests) and the relationships, familial or otherwise, between those parties;
- minutes of meetings of shareholders, Directors, the audit committee, and other relevant Board committees;
- organization charts;
- product and service catalogues, brochures, and other marketing materials;
- brokerage research reports covering the business and the industry in which it operates;
- relevant consulting studies commissioned by the business; and
- names of auditors, legal counsel, and other outside advisors.

Financial Information

- prior year's financial statements (preferably audited);
- interim financial statements and supporting trial balance, where applicable;
- detailed internal financial statements for the same periods where these contain necessary additional detail;

- projections, including details of underlying assumptions, accompanying narrative and, where computerized, a copy of the program and worksheets;
- capital budgets, including details of all underlying assumptions and all accompanying narrative;
- business plans, marketing plans and related qualitative analyses;
- Federal and Provincial corporate income tax returns and supporting schedules for the most recent fiscal years;
- analyses of historic and projected sales and production volumes, geographic breakdowns, customer profiles, product lines, and so on;
- financial filings made to regulatory and other bodies;
- banking agreements and terms of any outstanding debt obligations;
- previous valuations of the outstanding shares or net assets of the business;
- details of offers previously received for the business; and
- details (including price and terms and conditions) of past share ownership transfers.

Contractual Documents

- Shareholder's Agreements and other contracts affecting ownership of, or assets of, the business being valued;
- significant lease contracts;
- franchise agreements and licenses;
- patents and copyrights;
- significant customer and supplier contracts;
- special permits or licenses required by the business;
- collective agreements;
- pension plan documentation and actuarial valuations;
- insurance coverages, including summaries of insured values of fixed assets and life insurance policies on the lives of key managers and business owners;
- legal claims;
- stock option agreements;
- documentation supporting recent acquisitions or divestitures of operating divisions; and
- other contracts important to business continuity.

Operational Information

- details with respect to size, location, ownership and other important characteristics of operating facilities. If leased, details with respect to the terms and conditions of the lease agreement(s);
- key employees, their functions and reporting relationships;
- flowcharts or diagrams of significant operating processes and quality control procedures;
- a copy of any environmental assessments, management consulting, market research or engineering studies completed for the business in the previous (say) five years; and
- a summary of historic and prospective key operating statistics (units produced, number of service calls, and so on) and operational indicators considered important.

Industry Information

- annual and quarterly reports for publicly traded companies in the same industry. If these companies are also listed in the U.S., S.E.C. filings (10-K, 8-K, and so on);
- recent filings of public offering documents and prospectuses for companies in the same industry;
- information regarding transactions involving businesses in the same industry in recent years;
- information from industry or trade associations, or independent industry statistics regarding industry size, identifiable market segments, and so on;
- relevant published information concerning the industry, the business, and its competitors derived from sources such as Internet searches, business newspapers, and trade journals;
- a copy of any significant industry-specific regulations, including recent and proposed amendments thereto;
- a listing of principal competitors, including (where available) their respective scope of operations, estimated market share, strengths and weaknesses; and
- research reports regarding the industry or various participants, prepared by financial analysts, economists or other external parties.

General checklists or questionnaires (where used in the information gathering process) should not be taken to be all-inclusive summaries of required information. Every business interest has its own unique characteristics. A generic document cannot contemplate all of the peculiarities of all industries and business situations. In the end, the terms of reference specific to a given value/pricing exercise combined with experience and judgement are required to determine an appropriate scope of review and analysis.

An analysis of the information collected generally should be incorporated in discussions with management regarding the historic, current, and anticipated future operating results of the business. This is necessary to ensure that the views and opinions of management factually are supported, and that the facts are correctly interpreted. In most circumstances, the inability to interview key management personnel would pose a sufficient limitation on the review, usually rendering any value determination subject to qualification, and as a result less reliable than it otherwise would be. When conducting interviews with the owners and managers of a business each likely will bring his or her own biases and objectives to the discussion. Accordingly, the interests of those individuals in the outcome of the value determination, whether direct or indirect, must be understood. Depending on the size and complexity of the business, consideration should be given to interviewing one or more managers from each key operating area. The reliance placed on such discussions will vary depending on their knowledge of the business and the industry, length of service, possible bias, and so on. Where believed necessary and if possible, key information obtained from inside sources should be externally confirmed.

Internal Analysis

When performing an operational and financial review of the business, it is important to develop an understanding of the key variables and critical success factors which influence operating cash flows. Cash flows can be significantly influenced by both non-controllable external factors such as foreign exchange rates, commodity prices, market demand, and by factors under some degree of the business' control, such as quality of management, production scheduling, marketing, and risk management.

General Business Review

A general business review typically includes:

- a review of the share structure of the business, including classes and numbers of shares authorized, issued and outstanding, the characteristics of each class of shares, including voting rights, conversion features, participation in dissolution, dividend rights (cumulative or non-cumulative), and whether shares are retractable, redeemable, and so on;
- determining whether transactions have taken place involving some or all of the shares or net assets of the business;
- developing an understanding of:
  - the history of the business, and significant developments that have shaped the business over time. This is important when assessing the relevance of historic information. For example, where the business acquired a major division or significant production capacity has been added in recent years, consolidated financial results prior to that period likely will not be indicative of post-valuation date expectations,
  - the nature and general structure of the business, including product lines, markets served, physical locations, and so on,
  - the key managers, their area of responsibility, experience, knowledge and level of authority. An understanding should also be obtained as to how key operating and financial decisions are made,
  - the organizational structure, including whether or not employees are unionized, turnover of key employees, ability to replace or find new workers, compensation structure (e.g. fixed, variable, bonuses, and so on), the use of part-time or seasonal workers, and the status of management-employee relations,
  - in conjunction with historical and prospective financial data, how seasonal or cyclical the business is, and where the business is in relation to that cycle at the valuation date, and
  - understanding the long range strategic plans for the business, and what the key variables and assumptions are;
- identifying (particularly in the case of small businesses) key employees whose knowledge, abilities or business contacts are important to business continuity;
- assessing the quality of the financial information systems and operational reporting. An understanding should be obtained of the reports and key operating indicators management relies upon and why;
- identifying and analyzing material non-arm's length transactions between shareholders, affiliates, and related businesses;

- with the assistance of legal counsel, identifying and assessing any outstanding legal matters and the likely outcome thereof; and
- identifying (to the extent possible) who the most likely acquirers for the business are, and what synergies each might realize by combining the subject business with their own.

Financial Analysis

A detailed analysis of historic and projected financial statements is a critical step in any value determination. The objective of the analysis is to understand the future prospects of the business in terms of discretionary cash flows, and the risks attached to achieving them.

Financial Analysis – Historic and Current

Financial analysis typically should begin with historic and current balance sheets. Specifically, this analysis should include consideration of:

- whether redundant assets exist. A redundant asset is defined as one that is not required to generate the prospective operating cash flows of the business. Identification and treatment of redundant assets is addressed later in this Chapter;
- the business' current capital structure, being the blend of debt and equity used in financing the business operations, and whether that represents an appropriate mix given the business itself and industry in which it competes. This requires analysis of the current balance sheet, the business' operations, and the industry in general. Capital structure is an important consideration in the derivation of appropriate discount and capitalization rates. The topic of capital structure is addressed in Chapter 7;
- historic working capital requirements and how key working capital items (receivables, payables, inventory, and so on) vary in relation to sales. It is also important to assess whether any working capital deficiency (or surplus) exists at the valuation date;
- the operating cash cycle of the business (generally defined as days in inventory plus days in receivables less days in payables) and trends therein; and
- historic capital asset additions and the reasons therefor (i.e.; replacement, sales growth, technological advancements, and so on).

An analysis of historic operating results should be undertaken in order both to understand past performance, and as a starting point in the assessment of prospective operating results. Where there are seasonal fluctuations in the business, this analysis should not necessarily be limited to annual financial information. Depending on the nature of the business, it may be appropriate to complete a review of monthly or quarterly financial data.

It is important in historic financial analysis to recognize that:

- where the operations of the business or dynamics of the industry have changed significantly over the review period, historic operating results may not be indicative of prospective financial performance. Significant change may result from the acquisition or divestiture of an operating division, fundamental change in the competitive landscape or change in the strategic direction of the business, changes in production capacity, and so on;
- where the business has more than one operating division, analysis of divisional income statements, cash flow statements, and balance sheets (where available) generally is required;
- unusual or non-recurring items may be included in historic financial results. Because the objective is to assess the quantum and quality of prospective discretionary cash flows, such items should be segregated. Importantly, simply because an income or expense item was reported as an 'unusual' or 'extraordinary' item in the financial statements does not necessarily mean it should be assumed to be non-recurring when assessing prospective discretionary cash flows; and
- where they are material, non-arm's length transactions should be identified and assessed separately. Non-arm's length transactions might include remuneration to owners or their family members, rental payments on premises owned by related persons, or transactions between businesses under common control. As discussed in subsequent Chapters, where non-arm's length transactions are material and are conducted at other than market rates they should be adjusted to reflect market rates.

Utilizing historic results and forecasts, sensitivity and break-even analysis may be helpful in understanding the risks inherent in the business. This normally requires the segregation of operating costs into their variable and fixed components, and determining the key variables (such as sales, gross margin, and so on) that result in significant discretionary cash flow and earnings variations.

Financial analysis also should include an assessment of the tax status of the business. Specifically:

- the income tax rates applicable to the business, and whether it is associated with other companies for income tax purposes;

- whether the business qualifies for reduced tax rates or credits such as the small business deduction, manufacturing and processing profits deduction, scientific research and experimental development (SR&ED) tax credit, investment tax credits, and so on;
- whether there are any income tax net capital or non-capital losses available, including expiry dates and restrictions on use;
- the balance in any undepreciated capital cost allowance and eligible capital expenditure tax pools;
- a review of historic income tax returns and pending income tax returns (where available); and
- for private companies, whether there is a balance in the refundable dividend tax on hand account or capital dividend account — see Chapter 14. Such accounts typically are relevant in open market transactions.

Financial Analysis – Business Plans and Forecasts

A thorough and objective assessment of the reasonableness and credibility of available business plans and forecasts is an essential component of business analysis. Where business plans and forecasts are available, they usually form the starting point in determining prospective discretionary cash flows, which in turn are utilized as one component in the determination of the value of the shares or net assets of the business (see Chapters 4 and 5). When reviewing business plans and forecasts, the following things typically should be considered and addressed:

- the business plan and forecast preparation process. In some organizations, the forecasting process is well established and forecasts pass through a series of reviews and approvals. Conversely, other organizations develop only cursory top-line revenue and expense forecasts with little underlying analysis or support;
- the level of detail employed in forecast preparation. A forecast that is prepared on a line by line basis with careful consideration as to what drives each income and expense item typically is more credible than a forecast that is based on the philosophy of 'last year plus X%'. In many cases, where longer term forecasts are compiled, the first year forecast is prepared in detail, with subsequent year forecasts being less detailed;
- the individuals involved in preparing the forecast and the reason it was prepared. This is important for two reasons. First, the level of knowledge and experience of those preparing the forecast will influence its credibility. Second, in many cases the persons preparing the forecast may have some de-

gree of bias. For example, a forecast prepared by the owners of a business to secure bank financing may present an optimistic view of the business. Conversely, a forecast prepared by management that will be used to establish targets for their performance reviews and bonuses likely will reflect a more conservative scenario. Forecasts prepared in contemplation of the sale of a business tend to be optimistic. If follows that it is important to recognize bias in the forecast and to make adjustments, as necessary, either to the forecast itself or to the rates of return applied to the forecast;

- the accuracy of historic forecasts. A comparison of historic forecasts to actual operating results and analysis of the reasons for variations between them may assist in assessing the credibility of prospective forecasts;
- the underlying assumptions by which the forecasts were prepared. When reviewing these assumptions, it is important to assess whether they are credible, and whether they have been applied to the forecasts on an internally consistent basis;
- analysis segregating revenue by product or location, identifying cost of sales adjustments and inventory turns, and segregating fixed and variable costs all assist in assessing risks associated with the generation of forecasted cash flows. The nature and extent of such analysis will vary depending on the fact-specific situation;
- the nature of the business' revenue and expense streams. Where long term contracts and supplier and customer relationships exist, the associated revenues and expenses generally are more predictable as contrasted to, for example, businesses that generate revenues through a competitive bidding process on each project undertaken;
- the capital investment requirements to meet forecasted operating results. These should be segregated into sustaining capital and growth capital. Capital requirements should take into account the condition of existing equipment, existing and prospective capacity levels, the impact of technological change, and other factors that necessarily influence business investment; and
- incremental working capital requirements should be reviewed to ensure they are credible, and are consistent with historical results.

Financial Analysis Tools

Common tools used when analyzing financial data (both historical and prospective) include ratio analysis, trend analysis and common size financial statements.

Ratio analysis assists in the assessment of a business' liquidity, the identification of redundant assets, and the development and understanding of historic and prospective revenue and expense relationships. The nature and extent of ratio analysis completed depends on the fact-specific situation. Ratio analysis can be useful, but always must be combined with careful interpretation of the economic, industry and business specific factors affecting each component and ratio. Ratios are clues to questions and assessments that collectively contribute to a basis for informed judgement. Ratios calculated from a business' financial statements for only one year generally are of limited value. However, they take on meaning when compared with other ratios either internally (with a series of similar ratios of the same business over a period), or externally (with comparable ratios of meaningfully similar companies, or with meaningful industry averages). Where believed useful in a particular analysis, ratios generally should be calculated for at least three to five years. If the operating cycle of the company is longer than five years, then it may be appropriate to review ratios for a longer period of time.

Ratios commonly used in business analysis can be categorized as follows:

- liquidity ratios (such as the current ratio and quick ratio), which measure short term solvency;
- profitability ratios (such as gross profit margin, operating profit margin and return on equity), which measure expense control and shareholder returns;
- efficiency ratios (such as asset turnover, inventory turnover and average accounts receivable collection period), which measure business productivity;
- leverage ratios (such as debt to equity, interest coverage and debt serviceability), which are used to assess financial risk; and
- industry-specific or business specific ratios such as sales per square foot and price per ton of output.

Selected financial ratios commonly used in financial statement analysis and business valuation can be found in Appendix B.

Trend analysis normally should be performed to understand changes in the business' key operating indicators. This may include analysis of trends in sales, operating margins, capacity utilization, and so on. To assess relative performance, it often is helpful to compare trends for the business with those of the overall industry during the same time period.

Common size financial statements are those that express each account group as a percentage of the total. For example, for the income statement this would entail expressing each line item as a percentage of sales. Similarly, each balance sheet line item would be expressed as a percentage of total assets. Common size financial statements prepared over time can provide insight into segregating fixed and variable costs, and can assist in identifying unusual or non-recurring expenditures. Common size financial statements also may be helpful when comparing businesses of different size, and may provide insight into questions such as normal expense ratios, working capital requirements, capital structure and fixed asset additions.

Difficulties Inherent in Financial Analysis

When undertaking financial analysis, it is not sufficient to calculate a myriad of ratios, trends and other indicators. Rather, it is important to select those indicators that are useful in the circumstances, calculate them correctly and in context, and interpret them meaningfully. Difficulties encountered in financial information analysis typically include:

- subjectivity employed in the application of underlying Generally Accepted Accounting Principles. For example, alternate methods of calculating depreciation on the same or similar assets, alternate bases of valuing both tangible and intangible assets, and the manner in which lease commitments are classified for financial accounting purposes (i.e. either operating leases or capital leases) all are subject to some element of subjectivity;
- the extent of judgement and estimates adopted when preparing financial statements. For example, the estimation of an allowance for bad debts or provision for inventory obsolescence;
- the fact that the balance sheet typically is neither a reflection of the current worth of the underlying capital assets of a business nor of the net equity of the business. Balance sheet items usually are stated at historical cost, inherently distorting the comparison of a particular business to an industry average; and
- annual financial statements may be too summarized and aggregated. That is, they may be a consolidation of different operating entities and hence reflective of different risks inherent in those different operating entities. Further, annual financial statements often do not provide sufficient detail to permit the analysis of operating results generally on more than an overview basis. Detailed internal management financial statements should be requested in order to carry out the necessary review.

Marketing

It is important to have an understanding of the key marketing and sales elements in a business, as these will drive future revenues and profitability. This normally includes a review of the business' marketing and sales strategy, and an assessment of whether cash flow projections are reasonable and consistent based on the businesses' sales plans and production capacity. Marketing strategy and plans may address the following areas:

- the products and services offered by the business, and whether they are proprietary. Where thought to be useful, a breakdown of sales by major product and service line should be completed. An assessment normally should be made as to where various principal products are in their respective life cycles (introduction, maturity or decline). Plans for new product/service introductions and product line rationalization should be considered. New products can be classified as to whether they represent extensions of existing lines or new lines altogether. There usually is a greater degree of risk associated with the latter. It may also be insightful from the point of view of risk assessment to analyze the percentage of future revenues expected to be derived from new products or services;
- the primary and secondary target markets, including market niches the business focuses on, and principal demographic, geographic and other relevant characteristics;
- the customer base, including such things as the number of customers, the portion of revenues generated through repeat business, whether individual customer(s) account for a significant portion of total revenues, whether there are significant long term customer contracts or purchase commitments, and so on;
- the sales force and distribution channels, including whether intermediaries are used and if so the contractual relationship with, and commitments to, those parties, the number of distribution locations, and so on;
- the pricing structure, including price sensitivity (elasticity of demand), volatility, discounts and rebates; and
- the methods of advertising, including reliance on general media, direct marketing and promotional tools, and any meaningful trend relationships between advertising expenditures and revenues.

Operations

The analysis of a business' operations usually involves a tour of the facilities and discussions with those involved in said operations. Specific relevant considerations may include:

- for manufacturers, the source and reliability of raw material supply and an analysis of key suppliers. Particular attention should be given to the issue of supplier dependence and whether alternative sources of supply exist. The terms of any significant contracts or commitments that exist with any suppliers should be considered. Historical and projected fluctuations in the prices of key inputs typically are important;
- production and operating capacity and the cost to increase capacity. A business that is operating at or near its practical operating capacity normally will have to incur fixed 'step' costs to increase capacity if it is planning revenue growth. Where a business operates from more than one location, an analysis of each location (profitability, capacity utilization, and so on) often is necessary. Such analysis typically includes a review of significant lease commitments and expiry dates, where applicable;
- the age, condition and expected life of production and service equipment. This will assist in estimating sustaining capital requirements, and in assessing whether near term equipment upgrades are necessary for technological or other reasons. An analysis of prior years repairs and maintenance expenses often is important in this regard. In the period prior to sale, a vendor may defer equipment upgrades and maintenance, which in turn might result in a significant unexpected post-acquisition cost to the purchaser if those things are not quantified and accounted for in the purchase price;
- research and development (R&D), including the importance of R&D activities to the business and the history of success with new products;
- the identification of environmental liabilities or potential environmental liabilities, including estimated clean-up costs. Where the nature of the business is such that environmental liabilities might be significant, legal and engineering or other expertise in environmental matters may be required;
- the degree to which the operations are capital or labour intensive, whether or not the labour force is unionized, the terms of any collective agreement(s), and history of labour relations;
- quality control procedures, and whether or not the business conforms to quality standards such as ISO 9000; and
- where the business is subject to government regulation, confirmation of compliance therewith.

Industry Analysis

A comprehensive review of the industry(ies) in which the business competes is important when identifying its prospects and risks. Industry analysis normally should include an assessment of the market for the products or services, the competitive environment, and other factors that affect all businesses in a given industry.

Industry Overview

An industry overview can be helpful both in understanding the nature of the operations of a business and in assessing from a macro perspective the reasonableness of, and hence risk related to, its projections. In general terms, the following things typically should be reviewed:

- the industry in terms of size, maturity, fragmentation, rate of change, and perceived growth potential of distinct market segments;
- the market for the products and services offered, including possible substitute and complimentary products, product and service trends, and recent developments;
- the importance of technology and the apparent speed and impact of technological change on industry participants;
- key success factors. Most industries have one or more key economic drivers on which every business in that industry focuses. Common industry drivers include price, product quality, product features, delivery time, and so on;
- the ability of the industry as a whole, and the business in particular, to control pricing and cost structure;
- social attitudes toward the industry; and
- government policies and regulations with respect to the industry.

Competitive Environment

An important element of industry analysis is the assessment of the competitive landscape including recent and pending changes. Subject to meaningful information availability, the businesses of principal competitors should be reviewed to the extent practical, including their comparative size (typically measured by revenue and net asset base), comparative product offerings, estimated market share, known strengths and weaknesses, production capability, geographic coverage, and so on. The ease of entry of new competitors and the threat of competition from other industries (e.g. substitute products) also should be considered.

For competitors that are publicly held companies, copies of their most recent annual reports and regulatory filings should be obtained and analyzed. Where industry or stock market analysts report on public company competitors, consideration should be given to obtaining copies of their most recent research reports.

Consideration generally should be given to completing a comparative analysis of key operating ratios, financial ratios and pertinent statistics for the business with those of competitors where relevant and detailed segmented competitor information can be obtained. In this regard, publicly available composite industry ratio and operating data generally is not particularly useful other than as broad guidelines. There usually are significant limitations to the generation of meaningful, directly comparative analysis.

Information available with respect to recent industry open market transactions should be reviewed. In some cases it may be possible to interview industry representatives and analysts with respect to industry value criteria and acquisition practices. However, in the absence of direct involvement with a particular industry transaction it generally is difficult, if not impossible, to draw well founded conclusions and to relate the value of a particular business interest to one or more open market transactions in a meaningful way.

Economic Analysis

Economic analysis focuses on the relevant historic and prospective economic factors that affect the business community as a whole, and on those specific historic and prospective economic factors that bear directly on the business being analyzed. It generally takes the form of trend analysis as contrasted with focusing on a specific point in time. Where historic performance is being used as an indicator of anticipated future results, the economic conditions under which historic results were achieved must be reviewed in order to assist in predicting prospective results. It also is helpful to review the impact of past economic conditions on the business in order to assess management's ability to cope through changing economic cycles.

The amount of economic information obtained and depth of review conducted depends on the degree to which such factors influence the business interest being valued. Examples of the type of economic information that normally are reviewed include historic and prospective:

- investment interest rates (for example Treasury-Bills, term deposits, long term government bonds, long term investment grade corporate bonds, and other securities that generally are believed to be relatively risk free investments);
- borrowing rates (bank prime rates, mortgage rates);
- stock market performance both in general (including the availability of, and demand for, funds in capital markets) and specific to the industry in which the business competes. The limitations on the application of stock market multiples in business valuation and pricing are discussed in Chapter 9;
- economic indicators such as unemployment rates, general wage levels, price index and gross domestic product (GDP) levels;
- economic factors specifically related to the business under review;
- if applicable, historic and prospective price trends in commodities associated with the sales or cost of sales of the business;
- changes in import/export tariffs and foreign trade relations with respect to specific goods, services, and markets; and
- relevant changes in government fiscal policies (taxation and government expenditures).

SWOT Analysis

After obtaining, organizing and analyzing data regarding the prevailing economic environment, the industry and the business, and following discussions with management and other relevant parties, conclusions should be drawn with respect to the business' strengths, weaknesses, opportunities and threats ('SWOT').

The strengths and weaknesses components of the SWOT analysis largely relate to the business itself. They arise from the business' particular advantages or disadvantages in several areas including management, products, financial position, market position, operating practices, and so on. The opportunities and threats components of the SWOT analysis largely relate to the industry in which the business operates. Opportunities and threats may arise from competitive or market developments, changing industry regulation, specific economic factors, and so on. An objective and comprehensive SWOT analysis generally is important in the assessment of risk attaching to achievement of prospective discretionary cash flows, and as a result typically forms an important component in the determination of appropriate rates of return.

Redundant Assets

Overview

Redundant assets are defined as tangible and identifiable intangible assets (such as brand names, patents, licenses, and so on) that are not required by a business to generate the operating cash flows as projected. Where redundant assets exist, their value (typically net realizable value) is added to the going concern value of the shares or net assets of the business determined pursuant to a cash flow based or other valuation methodology. Therefore, the net realizable value of redundant assets directly increases the value of a business interest otherwise determined.

The two principal reasons for identifying and segregating redundant assets are:

- redundant assets may not contribute cash flow to the business, or may contribute cash flow that is at different risk than is cash flow generated by the operating assets of the business. In such circumstances cash flow based valuation techniques would not attribute appropriate economic value to these assets, even though these assets almost always would have a realizable value in and of themselves. It could be argued that the different risk levels related to redundant assets could be factored into the overall determination of a discount or capitalization rate, and that this would result in 'full' value being attributed to all of the assets of the business. However, the selection of discount and capitalization rates is sufficiently complex and subjective without incorporating further subjectivity into them; and
- where it is believed meaningful, to enable appropriate comparisons of value or price conclusions with respect to the operations of a business with the underlying net operating tangible assets employed – which latter amount appropriately would be developed net of any redundant assets. This is discussed under the heading 'Redundant Assets and Risk Assessment'.

For notional market valuation purposes, identification and segregation of redundant assets is important in order to satisfy the 'highest price available' requirement. In open market transactions, the identification of redundant assets normally will allow a vendor to realize a higher overall price. No prudent vendor would sell a going concern without either first extracting redundant assets from the business, or alternately adding the net realizable value of redundant assets to the value of the operating assets. Extracting redundant assets from the business prior to sale usually is preferable in the open market because:

- the purchase price is then lower; and
- an acquirer may not want the redundant assets, and hence either may discount their value for the nuisance factor and liquidation risk related to acquiring them or not fully recognize their value as loan collateral.

The balance of this Chapter addresses the identification of redundant assets. The valuation of redundant assets is discussed in Chapter 4.

Identifying Redundant Assets

Identification and segregation of redundant assets requires a detailed review of the balance sheet in conjunction with an understanding of the business' operations, prospects, and the industry in which it operates.

Fundamentally, redundant assets fall into two basic categories:

- surplus net assets. Examples include marketable securities, vacant land, unused operating licenses, and other assets that are in excess of the business' ongoing operating requirements; and
- underutilized financial leverage (or so-called 'hidden redundancy') which can be realized through use of a more appropriate capital structure (i.e. mix of debt and equity) in the business.

The two forms of redundant assets are interrelated. An appropriate capital structure in part depends on the composition of the underlying net assets of the business. Therefore, a determination should first be made of which assets (if any) can be withdrawn from the business. An assessment of capital structure then can be conducted based on the net operating assets remaining.

To qualify as a redundant asset, two criteria must be met:

- the asset must represent an operating asset or financial asset (including hidden redundancy) in excess of the current and prospective operating or financing requirements of a business; and
- there must be an ability to liquidate the excess asset, or to utilize it in the business to generate incremental value to the business owners beyond what otherwise is the going concern value of the outstanding shares or net operating assets of the business.

To satisfy the first criteria, the asset must not contribute to the operating cash flow projections of the business. In this context 'operating cash flow projections' refers to what are taken to be maintainable (or 'indicated') discretionary cash flows in a capitalization of cash flow methodology (Chapter 4), and to projected discretionary cash flows in a discounted cash flow methodology (Chapter 5). Therefore, assessing whether or not a particular asset is redundant requires an understanding of the business' operations and future plans and prospects.

Incremental value pursuant to the second criteria might be realized by:

- liquidating the asset and paying a dividend to the owners without affecting either the risk or return attached to the underlying going concern;
- transferring the asset to another business without affecting either the risk or return attached to the underlying going concern;
- liquidating the asset and reinvesting the proceeds in the business, thereby generating growth in excess of what otherwise is forecast;
- using proceeds from the sale of the asset to reduce the level of debt in the business. This would result in a greater proportion of the resultant enterprise value (being the total value of the business, including its debt and equity components) accruing to the 'en bloc' equity value of the business operations. As an example:

	A	B
Going concern value of operating assets	$ 900	$ 900
Redundant assets	100	0
Enterprise Value	1,000	900
Debt outstanding	(400)	(300)
Equity Value	$ 600	$ 600
Equity Value to Enterprise Value	60%	67%

- where underutilized financial leverage exists, by borrowing money against the business and using those proceeds to finance a payment to the business' owners, or to invest in growth assets within the business; and
- selling the shares or the underlying assets of the business at a price the vendor is satisfied includes equivalent value for the redundant asset.

Redundant assets are characterized by 'permanence of their redundancy'. Accordingly this excludes from consideration those assets that are temporarily idle or underutilized. For example:

- excess working capital might include excess cash, marketable securities, or high levels of accounts receivable or inventory that result from seasonality and hence are temporary. When considering whether there is excess working capital, consideration must be given to the date of valuation in relationship to the annual business cycle. A determination then can be made of whether excess (or deficient) working capital is consistent over the entire annual business cycle; and
- a business may own vacant land required in the near term for expansion. To the extent the benefits of the expansion program have been integrated in the determination of going concern value, the excess land would not be redundant.

Redundant asset adjustments affect both projected cash flows and rate of return assessments. In order to avoid double counting, prospective cash flow must be adjusted to account for the notional removal of redundant assets or the notional increase or decrease in financial leverage. That is, where an asset has been assessed as redundant, any income generated from that asset (for example, dividends on portfolio investments) must be eliminated from the discretionary cash flow stream being capitalized or discounted in the determination of going concern value. Additionally, assumptions with respect to an appropriate amount of financial leverage should be integrated into capitalization or discounted cash flow valuation methodologies, and be should be reconcilable on both a levered and an unlevered basis.

Care must be taken when assessing how the redundant asset proceeds would be employed. For example:

- where redundant assets have been pledged as collateral for business debt, the net proceeds realized therefrom would be first applied to the outstanding debt so collateralized. The residue, if any, would then be available for withdrawal or used to finance incremental growth within the business. In such a case, care must be taken to ensure that withdrawal of such security would not result in a higher borrowing cost, a reduced credit line, or an inability to borrow. If any of these things would result, the assets thought to be redundant might not be so, or appropriate adjustments to prospective discretionary cash flow and risk rates would be required; or

- a high debt/equity ratio may suggest business solvency to be at risk. In such circumstances, the funds assumed to be realized from the disposition or assumed disposition of redundant assets typically should be applied to outstanding debt principal to the point where a more appropriate debt/equity ratio prevails. The residue, if any, would then be available for withdrawal or be used to finance incremental growth within the business.

Theoretically, where a business is viewed in isolation redundant funds should be applied to outstanding debt to the point where the value of the shares or net assets is maximized. Such value maximization is premised upon the financial principle of optimal leverage. Optimal leverage occurs at the point where the debt/equity ratio and related risk assessment viewed in combination optimize shareholder value — see Chapter 7. In a notional market context where buyers are assumed with the capability to 'optimally finance' the business following acquisition, redundant assets are added to enterprise value otherwise determined – resulting in the same net equity value as if redundant assets are offset against outstanding debt (see previous example).

Just as it is important to identify and segregate redundant assets, it is equally important to evaluate whether negative redundancies exist. Examples of negative redundancies include working capital deficiencies and excessive debt employed in a business' capital structure. Where negative redundancy exists, it serves to effectively reduce the going concern value of the shares or net assets of the business.

Redundant assets, hidden redundancies and negative redundancies can be found either in working capital accounts or non-current accounts. Identification of redundant assets and negative redundancies normally follows from:

- an analysis of the balance sheet at the valuation/pricing date. In this regard, it is important to have an understanding of the composition of balance sheet accounts, since redundant assets sometimes are combined with other assets for financial statement presentation purposes;
- inquiries of management, who may (should) be aware of underutilized assets;
- ratio analysis. As discussed previously in this Chapter, ratio analysis is a tool used to detect trends and anomalies in key operating ratios over time, and in comparison with industry norms. Importantly, because a ratio suggests that an asset account is high relative to the norms of the business and the industry, that does not necessarily mean that a redundant asset exists. Further investigation and analysis must be undertaken; and

- developing a thorough understanding of the nature of the business, the business' plans, and key economic drivers. In so doing, it is important to address the issue of whether the business is subject to seasonal or longer term cyclical trends. Although a particular asset may be temporarily underutilized, if it is required over the forecast period to enable the business to meet its cash flow projections that asset likely is not redundant.

Where redundant assets exist, said assets should be segregated and their net realizable value should be added to the going concern value of the shares or assets of the business. Conversely, where a working capital infusion is required, this may result in an additional carrying cost (interest expense) if additional debt is obtained to fill this gap. On the other hand, an infusion of additional equity capital may be required in order to reduce financial risk. Such additional equity infusion is in fact a 'negative redundancy'. Where a notional capital infusion is required to normalize financial risk, the amount of assumed capital infusion should be deducted from what otherwise would be the going concern value of the outstanding shares or net assets where going concern value has been determined assuming the business to be 'appropriately financed'.

Where redundant assets, hidden redundancies, or negative redundancies exist, it may be helpful to construct a notional balance sheet segregating the operating assets from non-operating assets and reflecting notional leverage adjustments to test the overall reasonableness of the estimated level of net redundant assets and business' resultant capital structure.

Working Capital Redundancies (Deficiencies)

For any business, there generally is a range of net working capital that should be maintained to appropriately support its operations. Where actual net working capital is above this range, a portion thereof may be redundant, or may provide incremental borrowing capacity. Conversely, where actual net working capital is below this range, a deficiency may be indicated which must be remedied by liquidating redundant non-current assets, or by infusing capital.

Determining an appropriate range of net working capital requires analysis and judgement. For the purpose of redundant asset identification, working capital can be viewed as being comprised of net trade working capital, operating cash requirements, and short term debt, the collective analysis of which may lead to a conclusion that there is either a net working capital surplus or deficiency.

Net Trade Working Capital

Trade working capital items are those which arise from a business' normal ongoing operating activities. Trade working capital assets generally include accounts receivable, inventories and, in some cases, prepaid expenses. Trade working capital liabilities generally include accounts payable, taxes payable, accruals and, in some cases, short term reserves (e.g. warranties) and deferred revenues. Net trade working capital represents the amount by which trade current assets exceed trade current liabilities. For most businesses over the long run, variations in net trade working capital tend to correlate with changes in revenues.

The assessment of net trade working capital requirements of a particular business is important not only from the standpoint of assessing whether redundant assets exist, but also in the determination of discretionary cash flows pursuant to a capitalization of discretionary cash flow and discounted cash flow valuation methodology. An evaluation of a business' net trade working capital requirements typically includes:

- the computation and comparison of key operating ratios over time; and
- if available and meaningful, comparisons with companies in the same industry.

Where believed to be relevant, financial ratios that are computed in the analysis of net trade working capital requirements may include (see Appendix B):

- days sales in accounts receivable;
- days purchases in accounts payable;
- inventory turnover;
- operating cash cycle; and
- average net trade working capital as a percentage of revenues.

Although an analysis of these and other operating statistics may indicate that a business is becoming more or less efficient over time or is more or less efficient than its competitors, it does not necessarily mean that redundant assets exist. For example, where:

- accounts receivable are comparatively high, one or more of a poor collection record, inadequate allowance for doubtful accounts, or the impact of seasonality might be indicated;
- inventories are comparatively high, one or more of a possible obsolescence problem, poor inventory management practices, or the impact of seasonality might be indicated; and

- accounts payable are comparatively low, that may suggest the business has credit problems and suppliers are demanding cash on delivery, or that the business takes advantage of supplier discounts for early payment. In the latter case, the impact of supplier discounts should appropriately be reflected in the determination of discretionary cash flows.

Where excess receivables or inventory that is not considered redundant exists, incremental financing capacity may be available. This is addressed below.

In some cases, management may argue that a portion of net trade working capital is effectively redundant because of plans to better manage inventories, receivables, and so on, which will lead to an overall reduction in those accounts. Caution should be exercised when adding any such projected redundancy to the going concern value of the shares or assets of the business. As a practical matter, management expectations as to the amount of working capital that can be freed up pursuant to more efficient operating practices often are overstated. Incremental value from net trade working capital should only be considered when the benefits of realization are highly likely based on both reasonable expectations and a sound strategy for achieving the result.

An unusually high or low net trade working capital balance should not be dismissed without adequate investigation. It generally is advisable to determine the underlying composition of balance sheet accounts to determine whether any redundant assets are contained therein. For example:

- accounts receivable may include non-trade receivables such as loans to Directors, shareholders and affiliated companies;
- inventories may include an obsolete component which has not been factored into projected cash flows, and which can be readily sold;
- prepaid expenses and other current assets may include items which are not required in the ongoing operations of the business, and which have not been segregated for financial statement presentation purposes; and
- accounts payable and accrued liabilities may include amounts which should be reclassified such as non-interest bearing loans payable to related parties.

Operating Cash Requirements

Most businesses require a cash balance on hand in order to meet their current obligations as they come due. In particular, where trade accounts receivable are less than the aggregate of accounts payable, accruals, and near term debt obligations, a business usually requires cash to compensate for the difference. An appropriate range of operating cash requirements normally should be estimated based on consideration of:

- net trade working capital, both in absolute dollars and expressed as a percentage of sales. The sum of the operating cash balance plus the net trade working capital requirements should be at a level that allows the business to maintain its operations. Where net trade working capital is low, a notional cash injection (or alternately a risk adjustment) may be required to compensate for the perceived shortfall;
- the nature of the business. For example, service businesses whose expenses primarily consist of labour costs may require an operating cash balance to satisfy payroll;
- the composition of current liabilities. For example, current liabilities might include deferred revenues which in part will be brought into income in the normal course of business;
- ratio analysis, particularly the quick ratio, number of days sales in accounts receivable, and number of days sales in accounts payable – see Appendix B; and
- operating cash balances and balance sheet relationships of so-called 'comparable businesses'. Although the cash needs of each business are unique, an analysis of companies in the same industry may provide insight with respect to an appropriate range of operating cash balance for the business being valued.

In a notional market context, cash on hand often is netted against interest bearing debt and equivalents when determining the amount of debt outstanding. This implies that the business could use cash on hand to reduce outstanding debt, and that its cash management philosophy is irrelevant to the en bloc equity value of the business. This approach requires consideration of the fact-specific circumstances of the business being valued, and in many cases may be overly simplistic with a resultant over-statement of equity value by the amount of the cash on hand.

In open market transactions where assets are purchased, the price paid often is reduced by the target business' existing cash on hand at the transaction date as cash on hand usually is not acquired. However, post-acquisition the purchaser may be required to make a capital injection (or make financing arrangements) to replace that cash in order to maintain the operations of the business.

Short Term Interest Bearing Debt and Equivalents

Short term interest bearing debt and equivalents normally includes a bank line of credit and may include advances from related parties, whether or not such advances include a stated interest rate. In some cases, short term interest bearing debt equivalents include accrued bonuses to owner managers unpaid at the valuation date.

Utilization of short term interest bearing debt is a function of working capital requirements and management decisions with respect to capital structure. The determination of an appropriate level of short term interest bearing debt should be based on the net amount and nature of trade working capital notionally adjusted for existing redundancies or deficiencies. Again, a business might have a temporary excess of trade working capital assets due to the seasonal nature of its business, which excess might be offset by a seasonally high amount outstanding on the business' bank operating line. A more detailed discussion of short term interest bearing debt is included in Chapter 7.

Excess (Deficient) Net Working Capital

The sum of net trade working capital, operating cash requirements, and an appropriate amount of short term interest bearing debt and equivalents should be within what is considered to be an 'appropriate' range of working capital for the business. Where actual working capital is greater than or less than this range, it may indicate a redundancy or deficiency. However, before concluding that a redundancy or deficiency exists, the following things should be considered:

- whether there are any debt covenants specifying minimum working capital requirements;
- the nature of what are perceived to be excess assets. Where these are in the form of marketable securities, loans to related parties, or otherwise can be readily converted to cash, they are more likely to be redundant. As noted above, where the excess is attributable to accounts receivable or inventories which cannot be extracted from the business and converted easily to cash, a redundant asset may not exist;
- whether the excess or deficiency is temporary due to the seasonal nature of the business; and
- whether there are any non-current redundant assets that could be used to compensate for a perceived working capital deficiency. In this regard, because redundant assets generally can be readily converted into cash, non-

current assets and liabilities such as deferred income taxes, deferred pension obligations, deferred charges, and so on typically would not be considered redundant.

When valuing a business pursuant to a discounted cash flow methodology, changes in working capital may already be incorporated in the projected discretionary cash flows. Where this has been done, redundant (or deficient) working capital likely already has been accounted for, and should not be double counted pursuant to an adjustment to 'en bloc' value of the shares or assets of the business otherwise determined.

Identifying Redundancies (Deficiencies) in Non-Current Accounts

Non-current assets typically include fixed assets, long term receivables and investments, intangible assets, and other assets that will not be realized by a business within one year. Redundant assets may exist within these accounts, and may include:

- long term loans to affiliated and related businesses, shareholders, Directors or other parties that arose outside the normal course of business;
- long term investments, such as an equity investment in another business;
- redundant fixed assets, including holdings of vacant land, rental buildings, and excess equipment. Again, it is important to ensure that these items are not temporarily idle and awaiting the implementation of a planned expansion program to be put into use; and
- unutilized or underutilized licenses, franchises, copyrights and patents.

Sometimes redundant fixed assets are not obvious. For example, a business may own land and buildings that are worth more in the open market than the value they contribute to going concern value functioning as operating assets. For example, a manufacturer owning premises in the downtown core of a major city might maximize value by selling the property and moving, or by entering into a sale-leaseback arrangement for the property on favourable terms. In such a case, redundancy would exist to the extent after tax proceeds arising from the sale would be greater than the after-tax cost of relocating or leasing the premises.

Redundant Assets and Risk Assessment

When assessing and contrasting the components of a business' going concern value, care must be taken to recognize and properly deal with redundant assets. This is because it is foremost the business' operations that are being valued. Where ratios and multiples are being calculated based on inferred valuation conclusions, those calculations should exclude redundant assets. For example, the ratio of enterprise value to revenues, enterprise value to EBITDA and price to after-tax earnings or after-tax discretionary cash flow should exclude the impact of redundant assets in both the numerator and the denominator.

Example

Company A is a manufacturer of specialty plastic products. At the date of valuation, its aggregate tangible asset backing and liquidation value are $600,000 and $400,000, respectively. Included in both of these aggregate values is the net realizable value of a redundant marketable securities portfolio in the amount of $200,000. The aggregate fair market value of the outstanding shares of Company A is $800,000, comprised of net tangible operating assets of $400,000, goodwill of $200,000 and net redundant assets of $200,000.

It is possible to compare the relative values of the components of Company A's going concern value on either of the following mathematical bases:

	Comparing all Assets	Comparing only Operating Assets
Total Value	$800,000	$800,000
Going Concern Value		$600,000
Tangible asset backing	$600,000	$400,000
Goodwill	$200,000	$200,000
Liquidation value	$400,000	$200,000
Tangible asset backing of all assets as a % of total value	75.0%	
Tangible asset backing of operating assets as a % of going concern value		66.7%
Goodwill as a % of total value	25.0%	
Goodwill as a % of going concern value		33.3%
Liquidation value of all assets as a % of total value	50.0%	
Liquidation value as a % of going concern value		33.3%

Since little if any risk generally attaches to net redundant assets (in this case, a marketable securities portfolio), comparisons should be made referable only to the operating assets of the business. In this example, it is the manufacturing business of Company A that is being valued. Accordingly, any risk assessment based on underlying net tangible asset values should be made referable only to the net tangible assets required in Company A's manufacturing business. If the redundant assets are included in the tangible asset base for comparative purposes, the amount of goodwill in Company A's manufacturing business may be perceived to be less than it really is on a percentage basis.

Financial Redundancies (Deficiencies)

Financial redundancies (deficiencies) are created when a business has under utilized (over utilized) its debt capacity compared to what is believed to be an 'appropriate' level of debt given the nature of its operations and the industry in which it competes. When determining whether financial redundancies or deficiencies exist at least the following things should be considered:

- where a business is under-levered, incremental equity value often can be created by borrowing incrementally and either paying out the proceeds to the business' owners or, assuming an adequate return on incremental invested capital can be generated in the business, by reinvesting the proceeds in growth assets within the business. The resultant increase in leverage (and hence financial risk) to the business may be more than offset by the increase in en bloc value (before distribution of the incremental funds, or after reinvestment of the incremental funds, as the case may be); and
- where a business is over-levered, the equity value otherwise determined is reduced by the amount of incremental capital injection required to compensate for the deficiency.

Where a cash flow based valuation methodology is employed, a weighed average cost of capital normally is used to discount or capitalize discretionary cash flows before debt servicing costs, thereby determining 'enterprise value' (i.e. the total value of a business including its debt and equity components). The amount of interest bearing debt outstanding is then deducted from enterprise value to arrive at the value of the equity component. In such cases, an 'appropriate' (or 'normalized') capital structure is incorporated into the discount or capitalization rate adopted and generally no further 'financial leverage related' adjustments are necessary.

Example of a Redundant Asset Calculation

Goodbrew Coffee Ltd. (GCL) is a privately held producer of ground coffee that is sold to coffee shops and supermarkets under retailer private label brands. GCL's balance sheet at December 31, 2000 is as follows:

SCHEDULE 3.1

Goodbrew Coffee Ltd.
Balance Sheet
At December 31, 2000
($000)'s

Cash	0
Trade current assets	1,044
Advances to shareholder	477
Total current assets	1,521
Capital assets (net)	725
Investment property	555
Total assets	2,801
Bank loans	763
Trade current liabilities	499
Current portion of mortgage	36
Total current liabilities	1,298
Mortgage on property	404
Total liabilities	1,702
Shareholder equity	1,099
Total liabilities & equity	2,801

Additional information:

- an appropriate current ratio for the business is considered to be 1.2:1.0 and a normal interest bearing debt to equity ratio is estimated at 0.5:1.0 at book value;
- based on industry analysis and a review and assessment of the company's operations, a normal ratio of net trade working capital to net sales is estimated at 30%. GCL's net sales have been fairly consistent over the past few years at approximately $2.2 million per annum;
- the investment property is an industrial building (the underlying land is leased by GCL) which is rented to third parties. The property was purchased during 1996 for $600,000. There is a mortgage outstanding of $440,000. The market value of the building at December 31, 2000 was estimated at $800,000. The undepreciated capital cost on the building is equal to its book value. Disposition costs are estimated at 5%; and
- income taxes are paid at a rate of 40% on business income and at an effective rate of 25% on capital gains.

Redundant Asset Determination

On the surface, GCL seems to have significant redundant assets. Specifically, the advances to shareholder and market value of the investment property total $1,277,000. However, adding this amount to going concern value would be misleading because it cannot be readily withdrawn from the company. Rather, net redundant assets available for withdrawal are estimated at $329,000, as explained below.

SCHEDULE 3.2

Goodbrew Coffee Ltd.
Balance Sheet
At December 31, 2000
($000)'s

	As Stated	Adjustments	Restated Redundant	Operating
Cash	0	110		110
Trade current assets	1,044			1,044
Advances to shareholder	477	(410)	67	0
Total current assets	1,521			1,154
Capital assets (net)	725			725
Investment property	555	147	702	0
Total assets	2,801	(153)	769	1,879
Bank loans	763	(300)		463
Trade current liabilities	499			499
Current portion of mortgage	36		36	0
Total current liabilities	1,298			962
Mortgage on property	404		404	0
Total liabilities	1,702			962
Shareholder equity	1,099	147	329	917
Total liabilities & equity	2,801	(153)	769	1,879
Financial Ratios				
Current ratio	1.17:1.0			1.20:1.0
Interest bearing debt to equity (at book value)	1.09:1.0			0.50:1.0
Net trade working capital to sales	25%			30%

The following notional adjustments are made to the balance sheet:

- the advances to shareholder are assumed to be liquidated, generating gross proceeds of $477,000. The proceeds are assumed to be applied as follows:
  — $110,000 to provide an operating cash balance. This is considered appropriate in order to produce a current ratio within a 'normal' range (of 1.20:1.0) and to compensate for the estimated shortfall in net trade working capital to sales (25% as indicated vs 30% 'appropriate');
  — $300,000 to reduce the bank loan. This allows for a more appropriate current ratio (1.2:1.0) and debt to equity ratio (0.5:1.0) based on the information provided. (As a result, the $410,000 in the adjustments column for advances to shareholder is comprised of the $300,000 bank loan and $110,000 of operating cash requirements); and
  — the balance of $67,000 is assumed to be redundant, and hence available for distribution or reinvestment in the business; and
- for simplicity, the investment property is assumed to be liquidated, although as a practical matter other alternatives may exist. This generates net proceeds of $702,000, determined as follows:

Market value of property		$800,000
Less: 5% disposition costs		(40,000)
Proceeds before taxes		$760,000
Income taxes:		
Recapture (40% x [$600,000 - $555,000])	(18,000)	
Capital gains (25% x [$760,000 - $600,000])	(40,000)	(58,000)
Net proceeds		$702,000

The net proceeds:

— include a gain of $147,000 (being net proceeds of $702,000 less book value of $555,000 which is added to retained earnings in the adjustments column; and
— are first applied to eliminate the mortgage on the property of $440,000 (including the current portion of $36,000 and long term portion of $404,000). The balance of $262,000 is available for either distribution or reinvestment in the business.

It follows that net redundant assets aggregate $329,000 (comprised of $67,000 available from the shareholder loan and $262,000 available from the investment property), and that is the amount which should be added to going concern value of the shares or net assets of GCL.

If the going concern value of the shares or net assets of GCL was determined pursuant to an 'enterprise value' approach based on an 'appropriate' level of debt, the actual amount of debt outstanding (1,203,000, comprised of the bank loan of $763,000 and mortgage of $440,000) would be deducted to determine the amount of going concern value attributable to equity. The gross amount of redundant assets (1,179,000, comprised of the advances to shareholder of $477,000 and net proceeds on investment property of $702,000) then would be added to the equity value. The resultant equity value, including redundant assets, would be the same.

Summary

A thorough analysis of the business being valued or priced, the industry in which it operates, and economic factors in general are all important to the formulation of reasoned value conclusions. The nature and extent of the information gathering process and analysis thereof (including ratio analysis and trend analysis) should be tailored as appropriate in each specific instance.

In most cases, the principal variables influencing the value of a given business interest are the discretionary cash flows the business prospectively is expected to generate, the level of risk perceived in realizing those discretionary cash flows, and any redundant assets that the business owns. Redundant assets are those that are not required for the business to generate projected cash flows from operations, and that can be disposed of without impairing the operating value of the business. The net realizable value of redundant assets is added to going concern value, thereby increasing the en bloc equity value of the business. The quantification of redundant assets is addressed in the following Chapter.

Chapter 4
Capitalization of Discretionary Cash Flow Methodology

Introduction

When determining value or price, the discretionary (or 'free') after-tax cash flow that a business is expected to generate is of primary importance. After-tax earnings (or profit after tax) determined pursuant to Generally Accepted Accounting Principles generally is less important, although forecasted post-acquisition consolidated after tax earnings does play a role in acquisitions by public companies. This is because public company acquirers estimate post-acquisition consolidated earnings per share to determine whether the acquisition is expected to be accretive or dilutive to their reported earnings per share in the near term following closing.

The aggregate after-tax cash flow generated by a business typically has both a non-discretionary and a discretionary component. Non-discretionary after-tax cash flow is defined as that component of the aggregate after-tax cash flow that must be reinvested to sustain the existing business volumes, competitive abilities, and so on at current levels of cash flow generation. Because this cash flow component must be reinvested to enable the business to sustain itself, in both theory and practice it does not provide the business owner(s) with a return on investment. The business owner's return on investment comes from the remainder, or discretionary component, of the aggregate after-tax cash flow. The discretionary cash flow component can be withdrawn from the business without impairing prospective operating results, or alternatively can be reinvested in the business to generate growth and incremental financial returns.

As a general rule, when valuing or pricing the outstanding shares or net assets of a business the 'discounted cash flow methodology' (Chapter 5) should be adopted. Pursuant to this methodology, a forecast of revenues and expenses is developed, the resultant discretionary (after-tax) cash flow is then discounted back to a present value, and a terminal value is developed at the end of the forecast period and likewise discounted to present value. Terminal value typically represents a significant portion of the total value developed pursuant to the 'discounted cash flow methodology'. Terminal value generally is developed pursuant to a 'capitalization of discretionary cash flow methodology'. In some cases, the capitalization of discretionary cash flow methodology is used on its own to develop business value. This Chapter discusses the 'capitalization of discretionary cash flow methodology'. It has been written assuming an 'en bloc' valuation of the outstanding shares of a company is mandated. Where it is mandated that net assets be valued on a going concern basis, additional considerations must be taken into account. These are discussed separately in this Chapter.

Components of the Capitalization of Discretionary Cash Flow Methodology

Overview

The mechanics of a capitalization of discretionary cash flow methodology involve estimating a range of maintainable (or 'indicated') discretionary (after-tax) cash flow, and capitalizing that amount by a rate of return (a capitalization rate). Adjustments are then made for redundant assets, the present value of existing tax pools, one time costs (net of tax), and outstanding interest bearing debt and equivalents to derive en bloc equity value. Where net assets and not shares are being valued further adjustments typically are required.

The capitalization of discretionary cash flow methodology can be used as a stand-alone valuation methodology based on estimated maintainable discretionary cash flows, or as the 'terminal value' component of the discounted cash flow methodology. Importantly, the capitalization of discretionary cash flow methodology assumes relatively stable discretionary cash flows into perpetuity. As such, its application generally is appropriate in circumstances:

- of mature businesses with relatively consistent discretionary cash flows;
- of businesses where average discretionary cash flows through a business cycle can be reasonably estimated;
- when forecasts are not available or are not believed meaningful; and
- when the terminal value component in a discounted cash flow methodology is determined at the time discretionary cash flows are expected to be relatively stable.

The components of the capitalization of discretionary cash flow methodology are as follows:

- an estimated range of maintainable (or 'indicated') cash flow from operations is determined. This normally is defined as earnings before interest, income taxes, depreciation and amortization (EBIT-DA). This estimate generally is based on an analysis of current, historical and (where available) projected operating results, and consideration of company, industry and economic factors that are believed to impact on the prospective ability of the business to generate cash flow;
- interest on outstanding debt is not deducted where the capitalization rate adopted is a 'weighted average cost of capital'. Interest on outstanding debt is deducted where the capitalization rate adopted is a 'return on equity';

- income taxes are applied against maintainable EBIT-DA at the prevailing cash tax rate to derive net operating cash flow (before capital reinvestment);
- the net amount of sustaining capital reinvestment is determined. Sustaining capital reinvestment represents the dollar amount of fixed assets that must be acquired on average each year in order to sustain EBIT-DA at the levels projected. Where real perpetual growth (that is, perpetual growth excluding an inflation component) is reflected in the capitalization rate, capital reinvestment should include the amount necessary to realize that growth. Sustaining capital reinvestment is determined net of the present value of its related capital cost allowance (CCA) tax shield;
- where real perpetual growth is reflected in the capitalization rate, expected annual incremental net trade working capital requirements resulting from prospective growth assumptions must be considered;
- the resultant net amount of sustaining capital reinvestment and annual incremental net trade working capital requirements (if any) are deducted from the after tax cash flow from operations to derive discretionary cash flow;
- a capitalization rate is derived, the inverse of which is referred to as a 'cash flow multiple' or simply a 'multiple'. The capitalization rate is a function of general economic conditions, the nature of the industry, company-specific factors, anticipated future discretionary cash flow growth to the extent that is not reflected in estimated maintainable discretionary cash flow, and the level of risk believed inherent in the maintainable discretionary cash flow estimate. Where discretionary cash flows are determined before interest expense (which normally is the case), the capitalization rate will reflect a weighted average cost of capital (a blend of debt and equity — see Chapter 7);
- the estimated maintainable discretionary cash flow is divided by the capitalization rate (or multiplied by the cash flow multiple) to derive 'capitalized discretionary cash flow';
- the present value of existing income tax pools is added to the capitalized cash flows. Existing income tax pools normally include the undepreciated capital cost for assets in place at the valuation date, and may also include available tax losses and other prospective tax benefits not accounted for as a component of discretionary cash flows;
- where redundant assets exist, their net realizable value is added to capitalized discretionary cash flow;

- where appropriate, other adjustments are made to capitalized discretionary cash flow. These may include one time (generally after-tax) costs or benefits that have not been included in the determination of maintainable discretionary cash flow;
- the capitalized discretionary cash flow plus and minus the present value of existing tax pools, redundant assets, and other adjustments is then taken to be the enterprise value (being the aggregate value of the business, including its debt and equity components, measured on a share, as contrasted to net asset, basis) of the business; and
- the outstanding interest bearing debt and interest bearing debt equivalents are deducted from enterprise value to determine the en bloc fair market value of the outstanding shares.

The mechanics of the capitalization of discretionary cash flow methodology where the capitalization rate is a weighted average cost of capital is summarized in Exhibit 4.1

EXHIBIT 4.1

Estimated maintainable operating cash flow *(EBIT-DA)*

Less

Income taxes on maintainable EBIT-DA

Equals

Net operating after-tax cash flow

Less

Sustaining capital reinvestment net of present value of CCA shield

Less

Annual incremental net trade working capital requirements (where applicable)

Equals

CAPITALIZATION OF DISCRETIONARY CASH FLOW METHODOLOGY

Estimated maintainable discretionary cash flow

Divided by

Capitalization rate developed as a weighted average cost of capital

Equals

Capitalized discretionary cash flow

Add

Present value of existing income tax pools

Add

Net realizable value (to corporation) of redundant assets

Add (deduct)

Other adjustments, generally being one time after-tax prospective benefits or costs

Equals

Enterprise value

Deduct

Outstanding interest bearing debt and 'interest bearing debt equivalents'

Equals

En bloc fair market value of all issued and outstanding shares

Estimating Maintainable Earnings Before Interest, Taxes, Depreciation and Amortization (EBIT-DA)

Maintainable EBIT-DA represents the amount of operating cash flow the business prospectively is expected to generate consistently (or on average) year over year. The capitalization of discretionary cash flow methodology assumes either a:

- constant level of EBIT-DA is generated each year into perpetuity; or
- base level of EBIT-DA that grows at a consistent rate into perpetuity where growth is incorporated in the capitalization rate adopted.

Although absolute consistency is not a plausible assumption, maintainable EBIT-DA represents the point estimate (or range) that is reflective of average operating cash flow expectations. As a result, this valuation methodology does not account for timing differences that prospectively may result from 'average' but 'uneven' future cash flows.

A reasoned estimate of maintainable EBIT-DA requires an understanding of prevailing and prospective relevant economic, industry and business factors, and a thorough and objective assessment of the historical, current and prospective financial position and operating results of the business.

Historic Operating Results

In virtually all circumstances, historic operating results should be analyzed to help assess both general and specific business trends, and management's ability to adapt to change. Historic operating results frequently form an effective data base from which to assess prospective operating results.

When adopting (adjusted) historical results to estimate maintainable EBIT-DA, there should be reasonable assurance that historical results likely are reflective of future maintainable results. In particular, where significant changes have occurred in past years, historical results may not be indicative of prospective operating cash flows. This may be the case where there have been:

- major changes in the industry (such as substantial consolidation of companies, the entrance of new competitors, a significant change in consumer behavior, and so on); or
- significant changes in the business' principal operations (such as the addition or disposition of a major division, substantial changes in management personnel or philosophy, capital (capacity) expansion, and so on).

Adjustments to historic operating results commonly are required to reflect unusual, non-recurring and non-arm's length transactions. Examples of such adjustments include:

- owners of privately-held businesses frequently draw compensation and benefits disproportionate to the time and effort they expend in the business. Excessive drawings are a form of return on investment. On the other hand, inappropriately low drawings contribute to profit overstatement. Economic compensation for services performed must be segregated from return on investment. Accordingly, EBIT-DA should be adjusted up or down to reflect appropriate owner/management salaries;
- where a business has recently introduced new product lines or undergone capacity or other operating changes, EBIT-DA might have to be adjusted upward to eliminate non-recurring start-up or transition costs;
- there may be other non-recurring revenue and expense items which require an adjustment of historic EBIT-DA. These could include things such as moving expenses, losses caused by labour problems, pension plan past service liabilities, and so on;
- where a business deals on a non-arm's length basis with others, it often is difficult to ascertain whether costs and revenues equivalent to arm's length costs and revenues are being paid and received. Where non-arm's length transactions are being consummated at non-commercial rates, appropriate cash flow (and possibly asset) adjustments are necessary. These adjustments are particularly important in situations where the business interest on only one side of the non-commercial transaction is being valued, or where two business interests are at materially different risk. A skewing of the operating income to one or the other would result in erroneous value/price conclusions;
- it is important to be aware of the classification of income and expense items. For example, 'other income and expense' line items may include both non-recurring items and normal operating items. Therefore, a thorough analysis of the financial statements, and where deemed appropriate supporting working papers, is essential when determining whether or not adjustments are necessary; and
- revenues and expenses related to redundant assets should be removed from historical results. Because the net realizable value of redundant assets is added to determine the enterprise value of the business it is assumed the revenue and expense streams associated with them will terminate.

When making adjustments to historical data for so-called 'unusual' items, consideration must be given to whether said items are expected to recur. For example, a business may experience periodic labour disputes, and classify the related cost as an 'unusual' item. However, if labour disputes are expected to recur with regularity, then an allowance should be made for such costs either in the estimation of maintainable EBIT-DA, or alternatively in the capitalization rate adopted.

Finally, because historical results are stated in nominal dollars (i.e. inclusive of inflation), it generally is appropriate to adjust historical (normalized) EBIT-DA for the effects of inflation. Either the consumer price index, the GDP deflator or other relevant inflation indicator may be used for this purpose.

Current Operating Results

An evaluation of current operating results is essential. This includes not only the income statement, but also the balance sheet and statement of cash flows. It is important to understand the drivers behind the current (annual or trailing twelve months) operating results, which operating results sometimes are accepted as the most appropriate measure of maintainable EBIT-DA. Where meaningful financial projections are not available and the business has:

- recently changed its products or services;
- experienced a drastic change in operating cash flow which is expected to continue;
- matured in terms of its development in recent past; or
- experienced a constant upward trend in cash flow which is expected to continue after the valuation date,

then current operating results may be most indicative of future expectations.

Care must be taken to ensure that current operating results are representative of what are believed to be prospective cash flows. Analysis must be made to ensure that adequate consideration has been given to cyclicality, results of most recent months, short-term product line changes, and so on. In unusual circumstances it may be appropriate to adopt EBIT-DA levels not previously achieved where there exists great potential for rapid cash flow growth. As is the case with historical operating results, adjustments to current operating results may be necessary to derive a maintainable EBIT-DA estimate.

Prospective Operating Results

Management of many businesses annually prepare 'business plans' which represent their 'best forecast' of operating and financial results for the next fiscal year, and longer term forecasts (usually for not more than an additional four years) beyond the next fiscal year. During the ensuing fiscal year management often 're-forecasts' monthly or quarterly for the balance of that fiscal year. In this book reference to 'forecasts' or 'projections' means 'annual forecasts' or 'annual projections' for one or more years prepared in advance of an ensuing fiscal year, whether or not included in business plans.

The selection of maintainable EBIT-DA levels typically is aided by thoughtfully developed financial projections. The use of forecasted cash flows in large measure is a prospective refinement of current cash flow. Where discretionary cash flows vary significantly from year to year and meaningful projections are available it usually is appropriate to employ a *discounted* (discretionary) cash flow methodology. The *capitalization* of discretionary cash flow methodology normally is appropriately applied as a stand-alone valuation methodology where meaningful projections are not available. This most often is the case where there is an absence of forecast detail, or there is a high degree of subjectivity incorporated in projections.

Regardless of whether historic cash flows are believed to provide a reliable indication of future expectations, a review of prior year management forecasts measured against comparative year historic operating results often is useful. A review of prior years' forecasts and business plans, coupled with the assumptions that underlie them, can provide valuable insight into management's forecasting abilities. It may also highlight unusual risks or opportunities that have been anticipated in the past, and generally may assist in assessing the probability of achieving current forecasts.

When assessing forecasted EBIT-DA, care must be taken to ensure that expected operating cash flows are plausible, and that the assumptions underlying the forecasts have been consistently applied. For example, an assumption of a doubling of sales without provision for required increases in manufacturing capacity, increased overheads, changes in gross margins, or market demand and competitive reaction would result in a meaningless arithmetic exercise.

Averaging Results

Where current or forecasted cash flows viewed in isolation are not appropriate as a guide to prospective cash flows, an averaging (trend) analysis of historic, current, and forecast results may be warranted. These methods simply are aids to the exercise of informed judgement which results in the selection of maintainable EBIT-DA.

A simple average of adjusted EBIT-DA may be appropriate where adjusted cash flow from operations has been relatively stable and a future change in the cash flow generation pattern of the business is unlikely. For a simple average of adjusted EBIT-DA to be a fair reflection of the prospective cash flow of a business, industry conditions, operating capacities, and overall business operations all generally must be consistent over the review period and must be expected to remain so beyond the valuation date. The review period must reflect an appropriate number of years' operations, and prospects for the business must be reflected in historic or 'adjusted historic' activity.

A second technique sometimes utilized to develop maintainable EBIT-DA entails adopting a weighted average of adjusted historical, current and projected results. Each prior year's adjusted EBIT-DA is multiplied by a weighting factor. The sum of the results then is divided by the sum of the weighting factors to derive a weighted average. A weighted average of historic inflation impacted adjusted EBIT-DA may be appropriate where cash flows have been inconsistent from year to year but have shown an overall upward or downward trend. The weighting factors adopted are a matter of judgement, reflecting the overall rate of earnings growth or decline and future expectations. Again, for a weighted average result to be meaningful, the nature of the operations of the business generally must be consistent over the period reviewed, and it must be expected that prospective operations will not be materially affected by the changing business environment, technological change, operating capacity changes within the business, and so on.

Other Considerations

When estimating maintainable EBIT-DA it sometimes is necessary to look beyond adjustments normally encountered. Such considerations include circumstances where:

- distinct divisions or subsidiaries operate under one corporate umbrella. Difficult issues may arise in the valuation/pricing of one division in isolation because it may not be possible to specifically allocate all costs by division or subsidiary. Common overhead costs, including management costs, often are allocated arbitrarily. Further, there may be economies of scale reflected in consolidated earnings due to the integration of operations. For example, divisional management charges generally would be less if several divisions enjoyed common centralized management than would be the case where each division was autonomous. Similarly, if two divisions manufacture complementary goods that can be sold by the same sales force, selling costs per unit typically would be less than if each division operated separately. This economy of scale issue tends to be magnified where fixed costs are high and excess capacity exists. In such circumstances, any increase in capacity utilization often results in large incremental profits if the original level of fixed costs is maintained. Such factors need to be considered where the valuation of only one division is required, and that division then is valued in isolation from the others;

- a business interest consists of different divisions or subsidiaries and where the risk attaching to the cash flows of each differs. In such circumstances it is necessary to estimate the maintainable EBIT-DA for each division or subsidiary. Where such risk variations occur, depending upon other variables such as perceived prospective growth rates, different capitalization rates typically are assigned to the estimated discretionary cash flows of each division or subsidiary to reflect the different risks related to those cash flows; and

- there is clear evidence of purchasers who perceive post-acquisition net economic value-added. In such circumstances it may be important to consider the incremental post-acquisition EBIT-DA said purchasers may be able to generate. It generally is appropriate to segregate such incremental post-acquisition EBIT-DA, and apply a higher capitalization rate to it to reflect its higher level of risk (or alternatively, to probabilize the incremental EBIT-DA and apply a 'market driven' capitalization rate). This is in contrast to the presumed lower risk related to the generation of maintainable discretionary cash flow expected from the business viewed on a stand-alone basis.

Where operating results have demonstrated a growth trend that is expected to continue, and annual projections beyond a one-year forecast period are not available, the growth in maintainable EBIT-DA can be accounted for either by:

- applying a growth factor to maintainable EBIT-DA based on current or forecasted operating results. This technique is most appropriate where a business is expected to experience modest near-term growth, and EBIT-DA thereafter is expected to stabilize or continue to grow at relatively low rates; or
- adopting current or projected operating results as maintainable EBIT-DA and reducing what otherwise would be the selected capitalization rate for a growth factor that reflects expected long term real growth. This technique tends to be more appropriate where the business is expected to grow at a modest rate for the foreseeable future. See Chapter 8 for discussion of such adjustments.

Finally, it generally is useful to perform an analysis of the sensitivity of the estimated maintainable EBIT-DA to variations in each of the principal key economic drivers, both in isolation and in combination. This will provide a measure of the degree to which cash flows are at risk. The impact of an optimistic scenario, a pessimistic scenario, and a most likely case prospective cash flow scenario then can be considered when selecting an appropriate capitalization rate.

Income Taxes

Income taxes are deducted from EBIT-DA to determine estimated maintainable operating after tax cash flow. The tax rate utilized normally should be the effective corporate cash tax rate on active business income. Where EBIT-DA does not approximate taxable income before consideration of 'capital cost allowance' ('CCA', being the term used in the Canadian Income Tax Act for depreciation and amortization allowed for income tax purposes), a more detailed income tax calculation may be required. In particular, estimated maintainable EBIT-DA may include certain items that are not fully deductible for income tax purposes (such as meals and entertainment expenses), or where there is a timing difference between an expense for financial accounting purposes and an allowable deduction for income tax purposes (such as warranty reserves). It is important that income tax rate considerations be consistent with estimated EBIT-DA levels. The Canadian corporate income tax system provides for fact specific income tax rates, including tax reduction opportunities such as the 'Small Business Deduction' (available to Canadian Controlled Private Corporations) and the 'Manufacturing and Processing Profits Deduction'. Whether or not to incorporate these or other tax-rate adjustments when determining notional market value or open market price depends on the particular facts of each case. A detailed discussion of these and other income tax matters is addressed in Chapter 14.

Sustaining Capital Reinvestment

Sustaining capital reinvestment represents the expected annual investment in fixed assets that a business must make to enable it to generate estimated maintainable EBIT-DA. Estimation of an appropriate level of sustaining capital reinvestment, which necessarily involves an understanding of the business' operations combined with thorough analysis of its historic and prospective capital and repair and maintenance spending in relation to its operating capacity is an important (and often material) consideration in many valuations.

Determining the appropriate level of sustaining capital reinvestment must be done on a basis that is internally consistent with the derivation of EBIT-DA and the capitalization rate. Moreover, as discussed below, where the capitalization rate incorporates a perpetual real growth element, sustaining capital reinvestment must include an appropriate amount to achieve that growth.

Developing a realistic estimate of sustaining capital reinvestment generally requires the following:

- an analysis of past and prospective repair and maintenance expense. In this regard, privately owned businesses (which tend to be driven by income tax minimization as opposed to enhancing earnings per share) are prone to expense what a public company (whose managers are driven in part to report enhanced earnings) is prone to capitalize;
- a review of past and prospective fixed asset additions and, where practicable, a segregation of the amounts expended and planned to be spent on maintaining existing practical capacity from those expenditures related to real growth in capacity. This requires judgement where specific capital expenditures combine both replacement capital and incremental capacity;
- inquiring and analyzing industry developments vis-à-vis capital spending. Where competitors are undertaking aggressive capital expansion programs, the business being valued may have to increase capital spending to maintain market share and generate prospective estimated EBIT-DA at the levels estimated;
- assessing the current condition and technology of the businesses' existing operating equipment, and prospective changes in equipment technology; and

- discussing future required sustaining and growth capital investment with management, and where considered necessary with industry equipment and related technology experts.

The estimate of sustaining capital reinvestment generally is stated as a constant level of expected annual fixed asset additions. Where this is the case, it should exclude any near-term one time upgrades that may be required by the business. For example, where the business will be undertaking a one-time plant expansion project in order to expand its operations and generate the projected levels of EBIT-DA, capitalized discretionary cash flows should be adjusted to account for that investment net of the related tax shield as subsequently discussed.

In most cases, over the long term, subject to inflationary and deflationary issues, in theory annual sustaining capital reinvestment should approximate depreciation expense on that sustaining capital investment, subject only to the differences that arise due the timing of capital expenditures and depreciation expense claims. Some difference between depreciation expense and sustaining capital may arise due to the impact of inflation. That is, depreciation expense is calculated based on historical cost, whereas sustaining capital typically is estimated on a current dollar basis.

The Impact of Technological Change

As a rule it is difficult to segregate the amount of capital required to maintain operations from that invested to expand capacity or to realize operating efficiencies. This is because sustaining capital reinvestment reflects only the annual capital cost over and above normal repair and maintenance costs required to be spent by a business to maintain its competitive position so that estimated maintainable EBIT-DA is not eroded. Specific capital additions frequently embody sustaining, improvement and growth elements. Further complicating the segregation issue is that capital additions containing an element of 'improvement' may be required by a business just to maintain its competitive position, and therefore may be better classified as 'sustaining'.

The prospective impact of technological change on a business is fundamental to a meaningful analysis of its discretionary cash flow. Significant improvements in the productivity of conventional machinery continue to result from increased computerization and automation. Computer Aided Design (CAD), Computer Aided Manufacturing (CAM), robotics, and flexible manufacturing systems continually change business efficiency and operations. To the extent that capital additions are required to remain competitive in the face of new technological developments, the non-growth portion of such expenditures should be considered sustaining.

If a business has not been properly maintaining its equipment, or if the equipment is technologically obsolete, the future security of lender's loans or the businesses' equity could be permanently impaired. Such impairment would relate to the fact that the business would be required to utilize a greater portion of its future cash flows to fund the maintenance of its market position and business viability, and hence reduce the going concern value of its shares. In such circumstances, the ability of the business to invest in growth assets, pay dividends, repay debt obligations, and so on, would be less than it would be if equipment had been well maintained and kept up to date technologically.

Equipment and related technology utilized by a business may change, or may be expected to change. Where this is the case, analysis of the current condition and state of repair of existing equipment and prospective equipment requirements may be important to the analysis of prospective sustaining capital reinvestment, and hence to prospective discretionary cash flow. In some cases, equipment valuers and equipment manufacturers can assist by analyzing and commenting on existing equipment referable both to existing technology and to the historic, current, and prospective rate of change in technology related to equipment utilized by a particular business.

Real Growth

As discussed in Chapter 8, the capitalization rate used in a capitalization of discretionary cash flow methodology in some circumstances might consider, over and above a potential for nominal growth, an element of real growth (that is, growth in excess of inflation) beyond the valuation date. In order to generate real growth, annual capital expenditures beyond those accrued to maintain existing EBIT-DA levels may be required. Therefore, estimated annual capital requirements not only will include an amount for 'sustaining' capital but should also reflect an amount for capital acquisitions necessary to generate the anticipated real growth rate. Any estimate of incremental capital requirements should take into account factors such as the rate of compound growth anticipated, practical capacity limitations of the existing facilities and equipment, when additional capacity will be required, and what the cost will be.

It often is necessary to segregate capital requirements between that portion that is 'sustaining' and that portion required for growth in order to ensure that each is reasonable. As previously noted, as a practical matter, capital asset additions often combine 'sustaining capital', technological advances, and greater capacity where segregation of these elements is difficult and subjective.

Tax Shield Considerations

The term 'capital cost allowance tax shield' is defined as '*the sum of the present values of anticipated tax savings which will accrue as a result of the owner of capital (depreciable) assets claiming capital cost allowance in respect of them*'. Pursuant to the Canadian Income Tax Act, depreciation and amortization in any fiscal period is determined by:

- adding the cost of capital assets acquired in a taxation year to the previous taxation year-end balance of a 'like' asset 'class'; and
- calculating capital cost allowance ('CCA'), being depreciation and amortization allowed for income tax purposes, on the balance existing in that class at prescribed rates.

Accordingly, the final determination of sustaining capital reinvestment should consider the benefit of income tax savings arising from the future CCA tax shield resulting from sustaining capital reinvestment expenditures.

The determination of the present value of the CCA tax shield generally is calculated pursuant to the following formula:

FORMULA 4.1

$$\frac{C \times D \times T}{(K+D)} \times \frac{[1+(0.5 \times K)]}{(1+K)}$$

where:

C = the investment cost. That is, the adjusted cost base for income tax purposes, including all costs that are capitalized for tax purposes, including transportation, installation, and so on;

D = the CCA rate, as prescribed in the Canadian Income Tax Act;

T = the effective income tax rate at which capital cost allowance would reduce taxable income; and

K = the cost of capital.

Formula 4.1 incorporates the so-called 'half year rule' whereby only 50% of the CCA eligible can be deducted in the year of acquisition. Where the half-year rule is not applicable, the formula can be simplified to:

FORMULA 4.2

$$\frac{C \times D \times T}{(K+D)}$$

The above formula applies to assets for which CCA is calculated on a declining balance basis, which is the case with most capital assets acquired in Canada. However, certain capital assets are eligible for CCA calculated on a straight-line basis. Examples include leasehold improvements, and intangibles such as patents and licenses. Where this is the case, the annual calculation of CCA is determined as:

FORMULA 4.3

$$C \times D \times T \times \text{PVIFA},n,k \times \left[(1+0.5 \times K)/(1+K)\right]$$

where (PVIFA,n,k) is the present value of an annuity calculated for the number of years (n) over which tax depreciation is allowed, calculated at the appropriate cost of capital (k).

Formula 4.3 takes into account the 'half year rule'. Where the 'half year rule' is not applicable (for example, on Class 14 assets such as licenses), the equation can be simplified to:

FORMULA 4.4

$$C \times D \times T \times \text{PVIFA},n,k.$$

In theory it is arguable that the cost of capital (K) adopted in the calculation of the CCA tax shield should reflect the weighted average cost of capital determined on a nominal basis (i.e. including inflation) because:

- it reflects the 'appropriate' basis by which capital additions will be financed; and

- the annual tax deduction is calculated using the cost of the asset in circumstances where the tax shield is being calculated on a cost base that is being continuously eroded in real dollars due to inflation.

It also is arguable that a risk rate lower than a melded weighted average cost of capital should be adopted in the tax shield calculation because capital cost allowance is applied to the first dollars of available discretionary cash flow. In practice, the capitalization rate used to capitalize discretionary cash flows (a real weighted average cost of capital, as discussed below) frequently is adopted as the cost of capital (K) in the CCA tax shield calculation.

Generally, the estimate of sustaining capital reinvestment encapsulates various types of assets, which, according to the Income Tax Act, are eligible for CCA at differing rates. Sometimes a blended CCA rate is adopted. However, where annual sustaining capital reinvestment is significant, or CCA rates on the additions differ significantly, when calculating the CCA tax shield consideration should be given to segregating the assets into groups with similar CCA rates.

Net Trade Working Capital Requirements

As explained in Chapter 3, net trade working capital generally comprises accounts receivable and inventories net of accounts payable and accrued liabilities. Where the capitalization rate used in a capitalization of discretionary cash flow methodology reflects a real (i.e. net of inflation) weighted average cost of capital, an adjustment for annual net trade working capital normally is not required. This is based on the assumption that net trade working capital will remain stable, and will increase at the rate of inflation included in the determination of the capitalization rate.

However, where the capitalization rate incorporates an element of real growth (i.e. growth in excess of inflation), incremental net trade working capital to finance that growth normally is required during the period real growth is assumed. That portion of after-tax operating cash flow required to finance incremental net trade working capital requirements is not discretionary, and should be accounted for in the determination of discretionary cash flows.

Example

Company X has net trade working capital of $1 million, and is expected to generate annual after-tax operating cash flows of $500,000 on sales of $10 million. Based on general economic, industry and business analysis, real growth in revenue is estimated at 1% per annum to perpetuity (however, see discussion of perpetual growth rates elsewhere). Annual capital investment is estimated for purposes of this example at $90,000, including both a sustaining and growth component, net of the associated capital cost allowance tax shield. Assuming that the ratio of net trade working capital to sales will remain constant, it is further assumed Company X will require a 1% real increase in its annual net trade working capital (or $10,000) to support the underlying perpetual real growth assumption. Therefore, Company X's discretionary cash flow would be determined as:

After tax operating cash flow	$500,000
Less: capital investment (net of related tax shield)	90,000
Less: annual incremental net trade working capital requirements	10,000
Estimated discretionary cash flow	$400,000

The above example illustrates the impact of real (in this example 'perpetual') growth on annual trade working capital requirements. However, in some cases a business may have a working capital deficiency that requires a one-time capital injection. Where the working capital adjustment is a one-time occurrence, it should not be capitalized. Rather, the adjustment should be made to the capitalized discretionary cash flows otherwise determined. Because working capital calculations are expressed on an after-tax basis, no further tax adjustment is required.

Discretionary (or 'Free') Cash Flow

Discretionary cash flow (sometimes referred to as 'free cash flow') is determined by subtracting income taxes, sustaining capital reinvestment (net of the associated CCA tax shield), and annual net trade working capital requirements (where applicable) from maintainable EBIT-DA. Where discretionary cash flow has been determined before debt servicing costs (which normally is the case), a portion of that discretionary cash flow will be required to pay loan interest (net of related income tax) and debt principal repayment. Pursuant to any valuation methodology that adopts a 'weighted average cost of capital' ('WACC') as a capitalization rate (and hence where discretionary cash flow is determined before consideration of debt servicing costs) discretionary cash flow represents the amount of cash available to the providers of capital to the business. Once the holders of the business' interest bearing debt and equivalents have been satisfied, the remaining discretionary cash flow represents the amount of 'free' cash that can be:

- withdrawn by the owners (through dividends, remuneration or other distributions) without impairing the prospective operating results of a business, thereby generating a return on investment;
- reinvested in the business, thereby creating incremental discretionary cash flow in excess of the amount projected;
- applied against the interest bearing debt of a business, thereby enhancing the equity component of its enterprise value;
- retained in the business as a redundant asset, which would be expected to result in incremental value over what otherwise would be the en bloc value of the business (either shares or net assets); or
- a combination of these things.

In any valuation methodology that adopts a 'return on levered equity' as a capitalization rate, discretionary cash flow must be determined after debt servicing cost – both interest expense (net of related taxes) and required principal payments. To do otherwise would result in an 'overstatement of value' in circumstances where there is financial leverage in the business.

Capitalization Rates

Where maintainable discretionary cash flows have been determined before interest expense, the capitalization rate (or 'rate of return') adopted represents a weighted average cost of capital ('WACC'). That is, a rate of return on the blended capital of the business, including its debt and equity components. As discussed in Chapter 7, WACC is a function of three variables:

- the unlevered return on equity. That is, the rate of return required by equity holders assuming no debt in the business. Stated another way, the unlevered return on equity is a function of the business' operating risks and not its financial risk;
- the debt to equity ratio. That is, the extent to which the capital structure of the business includes interest bearing debt or other financial leverage (excluding trade payables and similar non-interest bearing trade or 'normal course' debt). The debt to equity ratio used in calculating WACC should be reflective of a long term capital structure that is considered 'appropriate' given the circumstances and prospects for both the business and the indus-

try in which it competes. This ratio may be different than the actual existing debt to equity ratio of the business whose outstanding shares or net assets are being valued or priced; and

- the income tax rate. The tax rate used should be the marginal rate at which interest expense is deducted. This is because the WACC formula assumes the tax deductibility of interest expense.

These three variables can be incorporated into the following formula to compute WACC:

FORMULA 4.5

$$WACC = K_U \times \left\{1 - \left[T \times D/(D+E)\right]\right\}$$

where:

K_U = the unlevered rate of return on equity;

T = the marginal income tax rate; and

$D / (D+E)$ = the proportion of debt to enterprise value (i.e. debt plus equity at current market value).

In most cases, the income tax rate (T) is readily determinable, but the appropriate capital structure (D / [D+E]) and the unlevered rate of return on equity (K_U) require analysis and judgement. WACC normally is first determined on a nominal basis, using an unlevered rate of return on equity that incorporates an element of inflation. Where a real WACC is required, inflation then is deducted from nominal WACC.

Pursuant to a capitalization of discretionary cash flow methodology, the capitalization rate normally is expressed in real terms (i.e. net of inflation). Further, it may include a real growth component where a modest level of sustainable annual real growth is expected. Alternately, where near-term growth is expected to be significant, with subsequently sustainable annual real growth either being maintained at modest (or non-existent) levels, it generally would be preferable to adopt a discounted cash flow methodology as contrasted to adopting a capitalization of discretionary cash flow methodology using a 'blended' capitalization rate comprising a high short term real growth component and a low (or non-existent) long term real growth component.

As a general rule, under any circumstance the discounted cash flow methodology normally is preferable over the capitalization of discretionary cash flow methodology because the former inherently considers the specific near-term real growth in discretionary cash flows expected at the valuation date.

By way of example of the application of the foregoing in a capitalization of discretionary cash flow methodology, assume that analysis of Company N suggests an appropriate unlevered return on equity to apply against estimated maintainable discretionary cash flows is 14%, which return on equity includes 2% inflation. Further assume that an appropriate debt to equity ratio for Company N is 25% debt and 75% equity, and the applicable income tax rate is 45%. The 'real' (i.e. inflation excluded) WACC would be determined as follows:

$$\text{Nominal WACC} = 14\% \times [1 - (45\% \times 25\%)] = 12.4\%$$
$$\text{Real WACC} = 12.4\% - 2\% = 10.4\%$$

In the end, the integration of the components of the capitalization of estimated maintainable discretionary cash flow methodology must be internally consistent. Because risk varies in direct proportion to the quality of estimated discretionary cash flow, the selection of an appropriate capitalization rate is interdependent with its determination. Capitalization rates often are expressed in a range, and applied to a range of estimated discretionary cash flows. The higher capitalization rate typically is applied to the higher cash flow estimate to reflect the added degree of risk in that estimate, and vise versa. The discretionary cash flows are divided by the capitalization rates (or multiplied by the 'reciprocal' multiples generated from the capitalization rates) resulting in capitalized maintainable discretionary cash flow. The determination of capitalization rates and discount rates is addressed in greater detail in Chapter 8.

Existing Income Tax Pools

Pursuant to the capitalization of maintainable discretionary cash flow methodology as described herein, the present value of future tax savings that may arise from existing 'tax pools' generally represents incremental 'point in time' business value of the outstanding shares assuming likely (or in the case of notional market value determinations hypothetical) buyers are taxable entities. Existing tax pools in Canada may include balances in the following tax accounts:

- undepreciated capital cost (UCC);

- cumulative eligible capital (CEC);
- non-capital income tax losses carried forward;
- net capital income tax losses carried forward;
- allowable business investment losses (ABIL) carried forward; and
- other tax pools.

The present value of existing tax pools represents incremental value only where outstanding shares are being valued, and *does not represent incremental value where net assets are being valued*. This is because where net assets are purchased, the existing tax pools do not flow to the acquirer. Rather, in Canada an acquirer of net assets is able to claim capital cost allowance on the 'stepped up' value of the assets acquired, subject to the so-called half year rule. The subject of net asset vs. share value/price is addressed later in this Chapter.

Undepreciated Capital Cost (UCC)

At any given point in time, businesses usually have an undepreciated capital cost (or 'undepreciated tax balance') on hand referable to their existing depreciable asset base. These UCC balances (by income tax 'asset class') typically can be determined by reference to the UCC schedule included in the income tax returns of the business for its latest fiscal year, combined with capital additions made since the end of its latest fiscal year. Pursuant to the prevailing Canadian Income Tax Act, each income tax 'asset class' is depreciated for income tax purposes at prescribed rates.

For income tax asset classes that prescribe both a declining balance methodology for determining capital cost allowance (depreciation and amortization for Canadian income tax purposes) and a capital cost allowance rate, the appropriate tax shield formula is:

FORMULA 4.6

$$\frac{U \times D \times T}{(K+D)}$$

where:

- U = the undepreciated capital cost at the valuation date;
- D = the CCA rate as prescribed in the Income Tax Act;
- T = the effective income tax rate; and
- K = the cost of capital.

This formula reflects the fact that there is no 'half-year rule' on existing UCC balances. Where significant capital additions have been made after the previous fiscal year end up to the valuation date and are included in the UCC balance for purposes of the foregoing calculation, an adjustment may be required to take into account the so-called 'half-year' rule on those acquisitions. Pursuant to that rule the year capital assets are acquired only 50% of what otherwise would be the UCC on those capital additions is allowed for income tax purposes (see Formula 4.1).

Some classes of assets (Class 12, 13, 14) are eligible for CCA on a straight-line basis. The present value of the CCA tax shield on these classes is determined as follows:

FORMULA 4.7

$$U \times D \times T \times (PVIFA, n, k)$$

where (PVIFA, k,n) represents the present value interest factor of an annuity for n years at the cost of capital (K).

As previously noted, in practice the same capitalization rate adopted when capitalizing discretionary cash flows (typically a real weighted average cost of capital) often is utilized when determining the present value of existing UCC balances. The present value of the UCC tax shield then is added to capitalized maintainable discretionary cash flows.

Cumulative Eligible Capital (CEC)

Cumulative eligible capital for income tax purposes exists where a business has unamortized 'eligible capital property' (in simple terms, 'acquired goodwill') and where there have been incorporation costs or transactions other than the acquisition of goodwill that have resulted in an incremental CEC balance. Where a CEC balance exists, the present value of the related capital cost allowance should be added to the value of the capitalized discretionary cash flows. The formula to apply is the same as that for the determination of the present value of the existing UCC tax shield (Formula 4.6).

Income Tax Losses Carried Forward

The present value of available income tax loss carry forwards should be added to capitalized discretionary cash flows. These losses represent incremental value pursuant to the fact that income taxes are deducted when deriving maintainable discretionary cash flows. When applying income tax loss carry forwards in the valuation of the shares of a business, consideration must be given to:

- whether the tax loss(es) carry forward is a capital, non-capital, or allowable business investment loss carry forward. Generally, net capital losses are not considered as part of the business' value because net capital loss carry forwards can be applied only against net capital gains, and maintainable discretionary cash flow rarely includes capital gains against which capital losses can be utilized. Moreover, in Canada net capital loss carry forwards generally expire upon a change of control of the business. However, capital losses may have value where they are assumed to be applied to reduce a capital gain arising on an assumed disposition of redundant assets prior to a change in control, or where the circumstances of the valuation assume no change in control;
- the amount(s) of the tax loss(es) and time over which it (they) likely will be utilized. For example, in circumstances where a company has non-capital loss carry forwards of $5 million and maintainable pretax income (EBITDA less interest expense and annual CCA claims) is estimated at $1.25 million, the aggregate loss carry forward would take approximately 4 years to be absorbed. In such circumstances its value should be discounted to present value to account for this timing difference. The discount rate adopted in determining the present value of tax losses generally should be the same as the discount rate applied to prospective discretionary cash flows;

- the date(s) the losses expire for income tax purposes. Any portion of the losses that cannot be used before expiry generally are of no value; and
- the appropriate income tax rate(s) to apply. For example, where a business is eligible for the Small Business Deduction, consideration may be given to maximizing the present value of non-capital loss carry forwards by applying them against taxable income only to the so-called 'small business limit' in any fiscal period. Residual non-capital loss carry forwards would then be carried forward to ensuing fiscal periods. This then becomes a timing issue in loss carry forward utilization.

Other Income Tax Pools

Some Canadian companies have additional income tax 'pools' available such as unused investment tax credits, scientific research and development (SR&ED) tax credits, unamortized resource exploration pools, and large corporation tax balances which can be applied against the Federal surtax. Where they exist, each should be analyzed to determine:

- whether there are restrictions on utilization following transfer to an arm's length acquirer;
- the likelihood and timing of their utilization; and
- whether each expires, and if so when.

Where appropriate, the present value of the benefit from these tax pools should be added to the value of the capitalized discretionary cash flows.

Other Adjustments

Where the business is expected to experience one-time non-recurring future cash inflows or outflows, they should not form part of maintainable discretionary cash flow, but rather should be accounted for separately. Examples of such items include:

- legal claims of a non-recurring nature;
- one-time property or other tax refunds;
- significant capital additions required to generate the estimated maintainable EBIT-DA levels adopted; and
- a working capital deficiency that necessitates a one time capital injection.

Where one time adjustments exist, their after-tax present value should be deducted (or added) to the value of capitalized discretionary cash flows. For capital additions, this means calculating the present value of the CCA tax shield. Where the one-time occurrence is not expected in the near-term, it should be discounted from the time of its expected receipt or expenditure to its present value.

Redundant Assets

Because redundant assets may be disposed of following a transaction, they generally are included in aggregate business value at their respective net realizable values. In this context, net realizable value generally is taken to mean the market value of the redundant assets at the valuation date, less disposition costs and income taxes that then would be incurred at the corporate level. Specifically:

- where it is assumed a redundant asset is disposed of, market value generally is determined as the 'value in exchange' of a given asset as contrasted with its 'value in continued use'. In some cases market values may be readily available (e.g. marketable securities), whereas in other cases estimates must be made (e.g. vacant land);
- disposition costs should reflect all costs incurred to convert the redundant asset to cash. These costs may include commissions on the disposition of marketable securities or real estate properties, legal and consulting fees on the disposition of non-productive patents, and so on;
- where income taxes at the corporate level may arise on gains realized on the notional or actual disposition of redundant assets, it is important that the tax rates applied reflect the nature of the income. For example, 'recapture of tax depreciation' on the sale of a redundant building will give rise to business income, taxed at operating income tax rates, whereas a capital gain on the disposition of capital property effectively is taxed at a lower tax rate. Where the business is a privately held company that qualifies for refundable dividend tax treatment, the effective tax rate used normally should incorporate the refundable dividend tax portion where taxes are computed only at the corporate level — see Chapter 14. If a capital loss is incurred, and no capital gains are available against which to apply it, the value of the capital loss may be nominal if it is unlikely to be utilized in the foreseeable future; and
- where redundant assets are not readily liquid, it may be appropriate to consider uncertainty with respect to the timing of their sale when developing their net realizable value.

As a general rule, in notional market valuations the net realizable value of redundant assets is determined at the corporate level and not at the shareholder level. This is because:

- the Canadian Income Tax Act generally allows shareholders in one Canadian corporation to transfer assets to another Canadian corporation on a tax deferred basis. For example, prior to a sale of the outstanding shares of a corporation, marketable securities owned by it can be transferred without income tax to a second corporation. Alternatively, after disposition of the operating business, marketable securities in a corporation can either be retained for investment purposes or sold with the resulting net proceeds used for other investment activity within the corporation. In essence, so long as the marketable securities or cash proceeds arising from their sale is not distributed to the corporation's shareholder(s), income taxes at the individual level can be deferred indefinitely; and
- post-valuation date discretionary cash flow calculated pursuant to a cash-based going concern valuation methodology represents cash which can be withdrawn from the business without affecting business risk. Stated differently, post-valuation date discretionary cash flow, if not distributed, will constitute a post-valuation date redundant asset. The capitalization or discounting of discretionary cash flows is based on taxation only at the corporate level and not at the personal level. Accordingly, to apply personal income taxes to redundant assets existing at the valuation date would be inconsistent.

In an open market transaction, it generally is advisable for the vendor to remove any redundant asset(s) from the business prior to sale. Doing so often simplifies the transaction, and reduces the purchase price to an acquirer. Having said that, in some open market transactions redundant assets may not be extracted prior to a sale of corporate shares. Where this occurs vendors typically consider the net cash available to them after they pay income tax on the distribution of the net proceeds from redundant asset liquidation to be the minimum acceptable price for that component of the total transaction price represented by the redundant assets. Such a vendor then would reject a price for the shares of the company which included redundant assets which would not, after paying tax on capital gains, net at least equivalent after tax proceeds related to the redundant asset component of the share sale. Conversely, where redundant assets are not extracted by the vendor prior to sale, a purchaser might pay a share price reflecting the full market value of the redundant asset if the purchaser had a use for the asset that was not contemplated by the vendor. For example, the purchaser might be able to use vacant land for the expansion of its own business that the vendor could not use effectively. It follows that in an open market context, the price received for the shares of a company in respect of a retained redundant asset component normally would reflect an amount ranging from:

- at the low end, the net realizable value of the redundant asset, net of the full amount of disposition costs and income taxes incurred at the corporate level; and
- at the high end, the market value of the redundant asset before any disposition costs or income taxes.

As a result, when estimating the value of redundant assets as a component of en bloc share value in a notional market context, depending on their nature it may be appropriate to discount disposition costs and income taxes on their assumed notional disposition to reflect the fact that in an open market transaction:

- depending on their nature, it may be possible to extract redundant assets from the business on a tax deferred basis prior to a sale of shares; or
- the buyer and seller may agree on a price for redundant assets included in the transaction that is between their net realizable value and their market value. The purchaser then can hold the redundant assets, dispose of them, or employ them (or the net proceeds generated from them) in its other operations.

Valuation of Excess Net Assets

In some cases, a business has assets that are not immediately required in its ongoing operations but which cannot be withdrawn due to seasonal fluctuations, bank covenants, expansion plans, and so on. These assets do not qualify as redundant. Rather, they can be viewed as 'excess net assets' that may contribute to the value of the outstanding shares of the business beyond what otherwise would be their value.

Where such excess net assets generate income (interest, dividends, rents, and so on), that income stream should be segregated from operating cash flows and valued separately. It generally would be appropriate to apply a lower capitalization rate to that income stream where the risk pertaining to it is lower than the risk attributable to the businesses' operations. The capitalized value of the after tax income stream should be added to the capitalized discretionary cash flows of the businesses' operations. The value of these excess net assets to the business determined pursuant to a capitalization of discretionary cash flow or discounted cash flow valuation methodology should not exceed their market value.

Excess net assets sometimes do not generate income. For example, a seasonal business might make interest free loans to affiliated companies during times where surplus funds are available. Where non-income generating excess net assets are significant, consideration should be given to assuming that such funds are invested at a risk-free rate of return during the time they are available and capitalizing that income stream – concurrently assuring no double counting of value occurs.

Interest Bearing Debt and Equivalents

Where discretionary cash flows are determined before interest expense and the capitalization rate adopted is a weighted average cost of capital (which in these circumstances it must be to ensure internal consistency in the valuation model), the enterprise value (i.e. the aggregate value of the debt and equity components of the business) is derived. Accordingly, the amount of interest bearing debt (and equivalents) outstanding at the valuation date must be deducted to determine en bloc equity value.

For the purpose of determining en bloc equity value, the interest bearing debt deduction may be comprised of one or more of the following three components:

- short term interest bearing debt;
- long term interest bearing debt; and
- interest bearing debt equivalents.

Short Term Interest Bearing Debt

Most businesses have a short term operating credit facility with a financial institution that they can draw on as required principally to finance trade current assets (accounts receivable and inventory). Because of its current nature, and the fact that interest rates on short term operating debt typically 'floats' (or 'adjusts') with financial institution lending rate fluctuations, the face value of short term debt seldom is adjusted. The extent to which short term interest bearing debt obligations are deducted from enterprise value when determining going concern equity value is fact specific. As a general rule:

- where short term operating debt is relatively stable throughout the year, the amount outstanding at the valuation date normally is deducted from enterprise value; and
- where short term interest bearing debt fluctuates significantly during the course of a given year (e.g., in the case of a seasonal business), then typically either:
  — an average amount of short term interest bearing debt over the year is deducted from enterprise value; or
  — short term interest bearing debt is not deducted. In this case, discretionary cash flow should reflect the after-tax cost of interest expense on the operating line expected to be incurred over the course of a given year.

The deduction for short term interest bearing debt should be considered in conjunction with appropriate levels of trade working capital and net working capital — see Chapter 3. That is, while the short-term operating debt of a business may be high at a particular point in time, that in part may be due to higher than usual trade working capital assets. Therefore, at that point in time the deduction from enterprise value for short term interest bearing debt all or in part may be offset by a trade working capital surplus. Further, any cash balance on hand at the valuation date normally is applied against the amount of short term interest bearing debt outstanding.

Long Term Interest Bearing Debt

Long term interest bearing debt commonly includes term debt, mortgages payable, bonds payable, capital lease obligations, and so on. Generally, both the long term and current portion of such debt obligations are described as long term debt. In most cases, the value of long term interest bearing debt is taken to be its face value. However, where the rate of interest on long term debt is not reflective of market rates prevailing at the valuation date given the risks and characteristics of the debt, it may be appropriate to determine the market value of the debt obligation and deduct that amount (as contrasted with the face amount of the long term debt) from enterprise value.

In addition, it is necessary to determine (pursuant to a detailed assessment of the financial statements and accompanying notes, or otherwise) if there is any 'off balance sheet financing' or other debt obligations that should properly be included as part of either short term or long term interest bearing debt. Such amounts might include operating lease obligations, guarantees of other companies that may be called, and so on. It is important that consistency be applied when determining both enterprise value and equity value. For example, if a company has an operating lease that is reclassified as a capital lease for valuation purposes (thereby increasing both the assets and debt of the business), the capital lease obligation should be deducted from the enterprise value of the business. However, in these circumstances the operating lease payments should not be deducted when determining maintainable discretionary cash flows as to do so would result in a 'double discount' to equity value.

Interest Bearing Debt Equivalents

The liabilities of a business (particularly privately held businesses) sometimes include non-interest bearing advances from shareholders, Directors, affiliated organizations, governments, and so on. These may be classified for financial statement presentation purposes as being either of a short term or long term nature.

Interest bearing debt equivalents normally are deducted from enterprise value since they represent a source of non-operational financing. As a practical matter, in an open market transaction advances from shareholders generally are either repaid when the shares of the business are sold or (infrequently) left in place on commercial terms. In either case, such advances represent a financial obligation which diminishes what otherwise would be equity value. In most cases, accrued bonuses payable to owner-managers at the valuation date also represent a form of non-interest bearing debt, and should be deducted accordingly. This is because, in most cases, a selling shareholder to whom the business owes a bonus will insist on the bonus being paid at the close of the transaction, which similar to other interest bearing debt equivalents, results in a near-term cash outflow or the need to obtain external funds to finance the bonus payment.

Adjustments to En Bloc Equity Value

En bloc equity value is derived by deducting interest bearing debt and equivalents from enterprise value. However, further adjustments are required if only a portion of the equity is being valued. For example, where:

- less than 100% of the outstanding shares are being valued, it is not necessarily correct to assume it appropriate to value a particular shareholding at a ratable portion of en bloc equity value. In such circumstances a discount for either non-control or illiquidity might be warranted — see Chapter 13;
- the share capital includes preference shares, en bloc equity value typically first is attributed to those preference shares with the balance being attributed to the outstanding common shares. The valuation of preference shares is addressed later in this Chapter; and

- the business has more than one class of common shares, en bloc equity value attributed to all common share classes must be apportioned among the common share classes. (See — 'Different Classes of Common Shares').

Example of the Capitalization of Discretionary Cash Flow Methodology

Crunchy Cracker Limited (CCL), based in Halifax, N.S. is a wholly owned subsidiary of Mega Corporation (Mega), a U.S. conglomerate. CCL produces a variety of soda crackers that are sold in supermarkets and other food retailers throughout the Atlantic Provinces.

CCL began operations in 1996 when Mega decided to expand into Canada. CCL invested substantial amounts in 1996 and 1997 to build a new facility in Halifax, to get its operations up and running, to obtain listings in retail accounts, and to promote public awareness of the company's products. Since start-up, growth has stabilized, and CCL is now operating at about 80% of capacity. CCL's most recent financial statements follow:

SCHEDULE 4.1

Crunchy Crackers Limited
Balance Sheets
At December 31st
($000)

	Actual	
	2000	**1999**
Trade current assets	8,671	7,605
Fixed assets (net)	13,094	14,089
Total assets	21,765	21,694
Trade current liabilities	3,032	2,966
Due to Mega	6,152	7,234
Current portion of long term debt	790	750
Total current liabilities	9,974	10,950
Long term debt	7,190	7,940
Total liabilities	17,164	18,890
Shareholder equity	4,601	2,804
Total liabilities & equity	21,765	21,694

SCHEDULE 4.2

Crunchy Crackers Limited
Income Statements
For the Fiscal Years Ending December 31st
($000)

	Budget	Actual			
	2001	2000	1999	1998	1997
Sales	43,000	41,663	38,996	32,698	27,949
Cost of sales	17,200	16,874	15,949	13,668	16,895
Gross profit	25,800	24,789	23,047	19,030	11,054
Selling & administration	19,610	19,574	18,821	16,886	13,410
Depreciation	2,000	1,937	1,742	1,614	1,242
Loss (gain) on asset sales	0	(370)	211	0	0
Interest expense	650	750	812	874	560
Total expenses	22,260	21,891	21,586	19,374	15,212
Income before taxes	3,540	2,898	1,461	(344)	(4,158)
Income taxes (current & deferred)	1,345	1,101	555	(131)	(1,580)
Net income	2,195	1,797	906	(213)	(2,578)

CCL's operations are expected to remain relatively stable for the foreseeable future. The company invests approximately $2 million each year in new fixed assets that give rise to a corresponding CCA tax shield, the present value of which is estimated at $500,000 per annum. In addition, at December 31, 2000, CCL had undepreciated capital cost of $2,000,000 in present value terms. All income tax losses had been utilized.

Mega is undergoing a corporate reorganization whereby all of its food subsidiaries, including CCL, will be transferred to a newly formed entity, Mega Foods Corporation. Accordingly, Mega requires a valuation of CCL for income tax purposes.

Assume that:

- the effective corporate income tax rate is 38%;
- there are no redundant assets;
- an appropriate capitalization rate (*real*, as contrasted with *nominal*, weighted average cost of capital) is 8% to 10%; and
- net trade working capital is at 'appropriate' levels.

Valuation Determination

The fair market value of the shares of CCL is determined to be in the range of $8 million to $10 million, as follows:

SCHEDULE 4.3

Crunchy Cracker Limited
Determination of en bloc fair market value
At December 31, 2000
($000)

	Low	High
Estimated maintainable EBIT – DA (Schedule 4.4)	$ 5,000	$ 6,000
Income taxes @ 38%	(1,900)	(2,280)
Net operating cash flow	3,100	3,720
deduct: sustaining capital reinvestment net of CCA tax shield	(1,500)	(1,500)
Estimated maintainable discretionary cash flow	1,600	2,220
Capitalization rate	8.0%	10.0%
Capitalized discretionary cash flow	20,000	22,200
Add: present value of existing CCA shield	2,000	2,000
Add: redundant assets	0	0
Enterprise value	22,000	24,200
Less: interest bearing debt & equivalents	(14,132)	(14,132)
Estimated en bloc fair market value of equity	7,868	10,068
Say,	$ 8,000	$ 10,000

Maintainable EBIT-DA is estimated at $5 million to $6 million based on a simple average and weighted average of the actual results for fiscal 1999 and 2000, and budgeted results for fiscal 2001. In this case, more emphasis was placed on the weighted average to reflect the growth that CCL has realized in recent years, and which it expects will continue. Results prior to 1999 were not considered in the estimation of maintainable EBIT-DA because they were reflective of CCL's start-up years, and believed not indicative of prospective operating cash flows. In estimating maintainable EBIT-DA, pre-tax earnings are increased by the amount of interest expense, depreciation and the loss (gain) on asset sales (which are not operating cash flows). The range of $5 million to $6 million is reflective of the 2000 actual EBIT-DA and the 2001 budgeted EBIT-DA, respectively.

SCHEDULE 4.4

Crunchy Crackers Limited
Estimation of Maintainable EBIT-DA
For the Fiscal Years Ending December 31
($000)

	Budget 2001	Actual 2000	Actual 1999
Pretax income as reported	$3,540	$2,898	$1,461
Adjustments			
Interest expense	650	750	812
Depreciation	2,000	1,937	1,742
Loss (gain) on asset sales	0	(370)	211
Adjusted EBIT - DA	$6,190	$5,215	$4,226
Simple average	$5,210		
Weighted average (weights of 3, 2, 1 to fiscal 2001, 2000 and 1999, respectively)	$5,538		

	Low	High
Range, say	$5,000	$6,000

Income taxes are deducted from EBIT-DA at a rate of 38% to derive net operating cash flow after-tax. Net sustaining capital reinvestment is deducted at $1.5 million per annum, being the gross sustaining capital amount of $2 million less the related CCA tax shield of $500,000. Maintainable discretionary cash flow so determined is $1,600,000 to $2,220,000 which, divided by capitalization rates of 8% and 10% respectively yield capitalized discretionary cash flows of $20,000,000 to $22,200,000. The higher capitalization rate is applied to the higher estimate of discretionary cash flow to reflect the greater risk of maintaining cash flows at that level. The present value of the existing undepreciated cost allowance tax shield of $2,000,000 is added to the capitalized cash flows to derive an enterprise value of $22 million to $24.2 million. CCL has no redundant assets. If CCL had redundant assets, their net realizable value would have been added to enterprise value as derived.

Because the capitalization rate adopted reflects a weighted average cost of capital, enterprise value represents the aggregate of its debt and equity value. The aggregate amount of interest bearing debt and equivalents is $14,132,000, comprised of long term interest bearing debt, including the current portion thereof, and the amount due to Mega. This amount of interest bearing debt and equivalents outstanding at the valuation date is deducted to determine the en bloc fair market value of the equity of $8 million to $10 million, rounded.

Alternate Calculation

The foregoing example illustrates the capitalization of discretionary cash flow based on what is commonly referred to as an 'unlevered' or 'enterprise value' methodology. That is, discretionary cash flows before interest expense are capitalized by a weighted average cost of capital, adjustments are made thereto to determine 'enterprise value', and interest bearing debt and equivalents outstanding are deducted to derive en bloc equity value.

The capitalization of discretionary cash flow methodology can be adjusted and applied on a levered basis, although this requires additional steps. The procedure is the same as that previously described except that:

- discretionary cash flows are reduced by interest expense, net of the related tax shield. The amount of interest expense deducted is based on current rates and an 'appropriate' level of debt, which may be different from the amount of debt actually outstanding. In theory, the interest rate used should be the real rate, net of inflation, consistent with the basis the capitalization rate is established. Where appropriate (generally based on industry and business norms), the balance sheet should be notionally adjusted to reflect the increase or decrease in debt to 'appropriate' or 'normalized' levels;
- where the capitalization rate incorporates an element of real long term growth, discretionary cash flows include the anticipated annual benefits of interest bearing debt financing;
- the capitalization rate adopted then *reflects a return on 'levered equity'* as contrasted with a weighted average cost of capital. Again, the rate of return is based on an 'appropriate' debt to equity structure. The derivation of a return on levered equity is addressed in Chapter 8; and
- the resultant en bloc equity value is adjusted to reflect the assumed notional increase or decrease in the amount of outstanding interest bearing debt.

The only differences in the levered approach pertains to the manner in which outstanding debt and related interest expense are treated. In theory, the conclusion as to en bloc equity value should be the same under either a levered or unlevered methodology.

CAPITALIZATION OF DISCRETIONARY CASH FLOW METHODOLOGY

Although both approaches are theoretically acceptable, the calculations are simplified when the capitalization of discretionary cash flow methodology is completed on an unlevered basis. In the levered calculation, the notional debt adjustment becomes an iterative calculation. As a practical matter, corporate acquirers typically use the unlevered approach.

> Unless otherwise indicated, the unlevered (or 'enterprise value') approach is used throughout this book.

Preferred Shares

Overview

Where a corporation's capital structure includes preferred shares, their value must be deducted from aggregate en bloc equity value to derive en bloc common share value. For example, if en bloc equity value is $10 million and there are preferred shares outstanding with an aggregate value of $2 million, the en bloc common share value would be $8 million. Having said that:

- it is not necessarily correct to assume that the value of preferred shares is equal to their stated or redemption value (i.e. redeemable at the option of the company); and
- where preferred shares are *retractable* at the option of the holder and the en bloc equity value exceeds the aggregate retraction amount they generally are taken to have a value equal to said retraction amount.

The valuation of preferred shares should be determined based on their ownership and specific attributes. In particular, the following normally should be taken into account:

- ownership of the preferred shares irrespective of preferred share attributes. For example, in circumstances where redeemable preferred shares that are not retractable are owned by a common shareholder who controls the company, it would be unlikely those preferred shares would be worth less than their stated redemption amount (also see Chapter 2 — 'Value to Owner');
- whether the preferred shares enjoy voting rights at all times or only in special circumstances and, in the case of the latter, the likelihood of a triggering event occurring giving rise to voting rights;

- whether the preferred shares are convertible into common shares, the conversion price or terms, and what the dilutive impact on the existing outstanding common shares would be;
- whether the shares are retractable at the holder's option, are redeemable at the company's option, or both, and the retraction and redemption price(s) and timing related thereto;
- the quantum of premium, if any, to be paid to preferred shareholders on the dissolution of the company;
- where there is more than one class of preferred shares, their ranking in terms of dividend payments and proceeds on dissolution;
- the quantum of annual dividends, including whether they are fixed or variable rate and cumulative or non-cumulative;
- whether and to what extent the preferred shares are participating (i.e. whether they share in the residual earnings available to all shareholders after payment of preferred dividends); and
- restrictions on transfer found in corporate law and agreements among shareholders.

Convertible Preferred Shares

Where preferred shares are convertible into common shares, the provisions of the conversion feature must be considered. As a general rule, where:

- preferred shares are convertible at any time at the option of the holder, they are valued at the greater of their conversion value and their value based on other features including (where applicable), retraction value and dividend yield. Where conversion value is higher, no reduction in the en bloc equity value of the business is made in respect of the convertible preferred shares. In these circumstances the convertible preferred shares are assumed to be converted, and assuming no other class of shares outstanding, the entire equity value accrues to the then notionally outstanding common shares. The pre-conversion ratable common share value declines as a result of conversion and resultant dilution of the pre-conversion common shares. Conversely, where the value of the convertible preferred shares based on their features is less than conversion value, the value determined for the preferred shares is deducted from en bloc equity value and the pre-conversion common shares suffer no dilution;
- preferred shares are convertible at any time at the option of the issuer, they typically are valued at the lower of their conversion value and their value based on other features. Where conversion value is lower the convertible

preferred shares are assumed to be converted, and assuming no other class of shares outstanding the entire equity value accrues to the then notionally outstanding common shares. In these circumstances the pre-conversion ratable common share value increases as a result of conversion and resultant dilution of the pre-conversion common shares. Where convertible preferred share value based on other features is less than conversion value, the estimated value of the preferred shares is deducted from aggregate en bloc equity value, with the remaining en bloc equity value accruing to the undiluted outstanding common shares; and

- where the conversion rights held by either the holder or issuer of the preferred shares (or both) are deferred on a time specific basis, then the value assigned to the conversion option should be discounted accordingly.

When estimating the value of convertible preferred shares, it is important to consider other features attaching to those shares that might affect the conversion option. For example, where:

- the preferred shares are redeemable at the option of the issuer on pre-emptive notice, the value of the conversion feature might be impaired where the shares can be redeemed prior to the time conversion rights vest; and
- conversion rights are triggered by an event such as non-payment of dividends it is necessary to consider the probability of that event taking place, and the resultant value of the conversion feature should that occur.

In the end, when determining the value of preferred shares and their value implications with respect to other equity share classes, their conversion feature as well as any other feature attaching to them must be considered in light of all of their characteristics and attributes.

Retractable Preferred Shares

Where the preferred shares are retractable at any time at the option of the holder, they normally should be valued at their retraction value plus any cumulative dividends in arrears, assuming a good covenant on the part of the issuer. Consideration of the issuer's covenant typically includes consideration of whether the en bloc value of the company's equity exceeds the stated retraction price and the issuer's financial position at the relevant point in time. Where the issuer's covenant is inadequate, a discount from the stated retraction price may be warranted. Where the retraction right vests only at a future date, a discount from the stated retraction price may be warranted. However, the discounted amount typically would be not less than the value ascribed to the retractable preferred shares absent the retraction feature.

Redeemable Preferred Shares

Where preferred shares are redeemable at the issuer's option, at any given point in time the redemption price plus cumulative dividends in arrears generally sets a ceiling on the value of the preferred shares. However, depending on their terms, conditions and attributes, the state of the issuer's covenant, and the probability of redemption and timing thereof, their value may be less than their redemption price. Considerations include:

- cross-ownership of redeemable preferred and common voting shares. Where redeemable preference shares are held by the owner of a majority of the common voting shares, the likelihood of valuing the preference shares at their redemption value is greater than where the owner of the redeemable preferred shares does not control the issuer;
- whether the redeemable preferred shares impair the ability of the common shareholders to manage the company;
- the current dividend yield and whether it is cumulative. Assuming dividends are cumulative, the higher the yield, the greater the likelihood of redemption;
- the availability of funds to redeem the preferred shares; and
- whether the redeemable preferred shares carry conversion rights that would cause a dilution in common share ownership. Depending on circumstances, the issuer may be incented to redeem the preferred shares when the redemption price is less than their post-conversion common share value.

Preferred Share Liquidation Premiums

In some cases, preferred shareholders are entitled to a premium over stated or par value on liquidation of the issuer. Where the issuer's business is valued as a going concern, such a premium typically would not be accounted for in the value of the preferred shares. Where the business is valued on a liquidation basis, any such liquidation premium normally would be considered a component of preferred share value. However, where estimated net after tax proceeds on liquidation at the corporate level are less than the liquidation value of the preferred shares, a discount from the liquidation value of the preferred shares would be applied to reflect this.

Preferred Share Valuation Based on Dividend Yield

In simple terms, the annual dividend on a well covenanted non-term, non-retractable, non-redeemable *cumulative* preferred share is akin to an annuity where preferred share value normally can be determined pursuant to:

FORMULA 4.8

Annual Dividend Payment / Required Rate of Return.

For example, if a cumulative preferred share pays a quarterly dividend of $1 per share and an appropriate rate of return is estimated to be 8% after tax, then the value of each preferred share would be $50 (i.e. $4 dividend per annum divided by 8% rate of return).

Dividend payments on preferred shares (be they cumulative or non-cumulative) can be at either fixed or variable rates (tied in the latter case to a benchmark such as the prime lending rate), but generally are known or capable of estimation. Greater uncertainty typically is associated with the determination of an appropriate rate of return, which requires consideration of:

- whether dividends are cumulative. Where cumulative, risk tends to be related to timing of payment rather than whether payment will be made;
- the financial stability of the issuer, including the size of its business and risk related thereto, and financial risk related to both dividend payments and preferred share redemption. In this context:
  - business risk relates to the issuer's operating activities, and
  - financial risk related to preferred shares relates to the overhang and prioritization of issuer obligations (generally being debt and priority preferred shares) ranking ahead of them;
- whether preferred shares have voting rights, or voting rights triggered when dividends are in arrears or by some other event. Where preferred shares have voting rights or conditional voting rights, there may be (depending on the significance of the preferred share vote) an incentive for the Board of Directors to declare the preferred dividend;
- the issuer's preferred dividend payment history. Where regular dividend payments have been made, lower risk likely is implied than where dividend payments have been missed;
- the dividend yield paid by companies reasonably similar to the issuer (where they can be identified) whose preferred shares are publicly traded and have like terms and conditions to those of the issuer; and

- general economic conditions, in particular short and long term interest rates, including prevailing 'risk free' rates of return.

Where dividends are cumulative and in arrears, and where the issuer's covenant ensures ultimate payment, unpaid cumulative dividends (discounted where appropriate) normally should be added to the value of the preferred shares otherwise determined. In unusual circumstances where the company's en bloc equity value is less than the combined value of the preferred shares and cumulative dividends in arrears, a discount from that amount would be warranted.

Participating Preferred Shares

Participating preferred shares are those entitled to receive incremental dividends beyond their stated dividend rate in circumstances where dividends beyond prescribed dividend amounts per common share are paid. The valuation of participating preferred shares is an extension of the dividend yield valuation where the elements of the participation feature are appropriately incorporated. Factors to consider normally would include:

- the history of participating preferred and common share dividend payments;
- operating projections of the issuer, including prospective cash reinvestment requirements and discretionary cash flows;
- participating preferred and common share ownership. Where the common shares and participating preferred shares are held by the same person(s), there generally is a greater likelihood of participating dividend payments; and
- other features attaching to the participating preferred shares, such as redemption, retraction and conversion rights that might encourage or discourage a company's Board of Directors from declaring common share dividends that give rise to participation rights.

In theory, the value of participating preferred shares is never less than their value absent the participation feature. Accordingly, the value of participating preferred shares can be valued as the sum of two components – the value of the preferred shares absent the participation feature and, where appropriate, a premium over that value to account for the participation rights.

Different Classes of Common Shares

Where more than one class of common shares is outstanding it may be necessary to apportion the en bloc value of the common equity among them. Such apportionment is a relative valuation exercise that requires consideration of:

- the specific attributes of the common share classes, including:
  — voting rights (non-voting, voting or multiple voting),
  — the circumstances in which otherwise non-voting shares would become voting, and the likelihood of a triggering event occurring giving rise to voting rights,
  — ranking on proceeds of distribution in the event of a windup,
  — rights with respect to dividend distributions,
- the ownership structure of all classes of common shares. For example, where four shareholders each own 25% of both outstanding voting and non-voting common shares and each is expected to vote so as to protect their respective equity interests, the non-voting common shares owned by each likely would be valued identically with their respective voting common shares;
- whether an organized market for any or all of the common share classes exists;
- recent transactions involving any of the outstanding common shares, be they non-voting or voting; and
- the dividend history of all classes of common shares.

Canadian Jurisprudence dealing with the apportionment of value among various common share classes is listed in Appendix A. When analyzing these cases it should be noted that most have arisen in an income tax context.

Primary and Secondary Offerings

A factor which influences the value (as evidenced by the price) of a given business interest is whether the transaction involves previously issued share capital or newly issued share capital. A sale of a company's treasury shares which results in 'new' capital being received by the company commonly is termed a 'primary offering' of shares, whereas a sale of previously issued shares by a shareholder to another party commonly is termed a 'secondary offering' of shares.

Primary Offerings

In the case of a primary offering, the share sale proceeds accrue to the company that issues the shares, and thus enhance the en bloc value of the issued shares of the company. The percentage interest of existing shareholders is diluted by the newly-issued share capital. However, the net funds raised through the sale of the newly outstanding share capital accrues to the company, thereby enhancing pre-issue en bloc equity value by at least the amount of the proceeds received from the offering as a result of:

- a reduction in the amount of debt outstanding;
- providing financing to undertake expansion plans;
- favourably changing the risk profile of the business; or
- remaining in the company as a redundant asset.

Example

Company H has reached a stage where it requires additional equity funds to finance growth. Company H's current operations (excluding any new growth achievable with additional equity) are valued at $8,000,000. Pro-rata value per common share, based 1,000,000 common shares outstanding is $8.00 per share.

Shareholder A owns 150,000 of the 1,000,000 outstanding shares. Prior to a primary (treasury) common share offering, these shares represent a 15% interest in Company H, and are valued on a ratable basis at $1,200,000 (150,000 x $8.00).

Assume that Shareholder B purchases 200,000 treasury shares in Company H at a price of $8.00 per share. If this cash was not invested in operating assets and therefore considered to be a redundancy, the following results:

Value of existing operations	$8,000,000
Add proceeds from share issue	1,600,000
Value after issue of shares	$9,600,000
Value per share, based on 1,200,000 shares outstanding	$8.00

Shareholder A continues to own 150,000 shares. Following the primary share issue, his percentage interest declines from 15% to 12.5%. However, his shareholding is still valued at $1,200,000 (150,000 X $8.00) on a ratable basis.

Secondary Offerings

In the case of a secondary offering, the share sale proceeds accrue to the vending shareholder, and as such have no effect on the en bloc value of the issued shares of the company. No dilution of any share interest takes place, and no funds accrue to the company.

Referring to the preceding example, assume that Company H has not identified a need for additional equity funds. Accordingly, it does not intend to issue treasury shares. Shareholder B wishes to own equity in Company H and agrees to purchase Shareholder A's interest at $8.00 per share. This transaction occurs between Shareholder A and Shareholder B, without affecting Company H. The vendor receives the net proceeds of the sale rather than the Company. There is no dilution of any shareholding interest as no new shares are issued.

Sometimes a secondary distribution of shares is coupled with a primary offering. For example, where a privately-held company goes public pursuant to an initial public offering, for reasons related to post-issue public market liquidity, personal liquidity, or portfolio diversification shareholders in the private company may offer some of their pre-IPO shareholdings concurrent with a treasury share offering. In such circumstances share sale proceeds are allocated to the shareholders and the company in proportion to the shares given up by each, and the value of the company is enhanced only to the extent of the funds that accrue to it.

Dilutive Securities

Convertible Securities

When the capital structure of a business includes securities with a conversion feature (usually convertible debt or preferred shares), the potential impact on the en bloc value of the common shares must be addressed.

In theory, the value of an asset with a conversion feature is equal to the value of that asset absent the conversion feature plus the value of the conversion feature. In public financial markets, the value of the conversion feature typically is determined akin to a call option. The conversion feature normally is offered by the issuer in exchange for more favourable financial instrument terms than otherwise would be available to it.

In a business valuation context, convertible securities normally should be valued at the greater of their face value or their conversion value. This is because in determining intrinsic en bloc equity value, it generally is the inflows and outflows of cash from the company's perspective that are considered. For example, assume the following:

Face value of debt:	$20,000,000
Market value of debt:	$18,000,000 excluding conversion feature. The value of the conversion feature is estimated at $2 million at time of issue based on the company's enterprise value of $40 million
Convertible into:	5,000,000 common shares at any time for 5 years after issue date
Common shares outstanding prior to conversion:	10,000,000

The value of the debt and the existing common shares is dependent upon the enterprise value of the business. Assume the following scenarios:

	At issue date	Two years after issue Scenario 1	Two years after issue Scenario 2
Enterprise value	$40,000,000	$30,000,000	$80,000,000
Value of debt:			
Excluding conversion feature	18,000,000	18,000,000	n/a
Conversion feature	2,000,000	0	n/a
Total	$20,000,000	$18,000,000	n/a
Value attributed to equity	$20,000,000	$12,000,000	$80,000,000
Equivalent shares outstanding	10,000,000	10,000,000	15,000,000
Pro-rata value per share	$2.00	$1.20	$5.33

In this example, at the time the convertible debentures are issued the enterprise value of the company is $40 million. $20 million was paid for debentures with a fair market value of $18 million absent the conversion feature. The remaining $2 million is the estimated value of the conversion feature. At time of issue, an immediate conversion would result in a value of approximately $13.3 million ($40 million x 5,000,000/15,000,000) which is less than the amount paid. Therefore, the conversion rights only have value pursuant to their upside potential. Whether or not that potential is realized depends on the company's financial performance and prospects subsequent to the issue date. The conversion feature is 'in the money' at a price in excess of $4 per share.

In scenario 1, two years after issue enterprise value has declined to $30 million. The conversion option has no underlying value at that date. In a public market context, the debentures may trade at a premium to face value due to the conversion option and pursuant to a public market option pricing model. However, at the valuation date, where conversion would result in lower proceeds to the security holders, the option has no stand-alone value. Accordingly, the value attributed to the common equity is $12 million, or $1.20 per share.

In scenario 2, enterprise value two years after issue has risen to $80 million. The value of the conversion feature has increased as well, and is now 'in the money' based on 15 million shares prospectively outstanding. The debentures have a value of $26.7 million based on 5 million shares at $5.33 per share. Therefore, the value attributed to the pre-conversion common shares (10 million shares) is approximately $53.3 million.

The value of the debentures is based on its conversion value with no premium for upside potential. Again, although public market option pricing models may afford a premium to such potential, at any particular time that is not a component of its value to the company. Stated differently for purposes of calculating equity value, any premium afforded to the conversion feature in the public markets would constitute a transaction among third parties, and would not directly impact the intrinsic en bloc value of the company's equity (see 'Primary and Secondary Offerings').

Options and Warrants

Some companies offer stock options to their Directors or employees as performance incentives. Warrants normally are offered in conjunction with the issue of debt or shares as an incentive to prospective purchasers of those instruments, usually in exchange for a reduction in the interest or dividends that otherwise would be paid on those securities. In the context of business valuation, only outstanding treasury options and warrants are considered (i.e. those that, en bloc when exercised, require the issuer to issue new shares from its treasury). Trades in public company common share options represent contracts between parties external to the company, and hence are not relevant from a business valuation perspective given that:

- shares and proceeds are transferred between third parties; and
- no change in the number of outstanding shares occurs.

The underlying value of a warrant or option is the amount, if any, by which the pro-rata valuation date price per share exceeds the exercise price. Where an option or warrant has positive underlying value it is commonly referred to as being 'in the money'. A warrant or option issued by the company may trade for an amount in excess of its intrinsic value. Where the shares are publicly traded, placing a value on the warrant or option normally is done pursuant to an 'option pricing model'. However, application of such models generally is not practical for privately held company options and warrants.

When options or warrants are exercised in respect of common shares, the number of shares outstanding increases, thereby reducing the pro-rata value of each common share. However, the exercise price is paid to the issuer which then can:

- invest the proceeds in growth assets;
- reduce the amount of outstanding interest bearing debt (or equivalents), thereby increasing the en bloc value attributable to all common shares;
- redeem outstanding preferred shares, or purchase for cancellation outstanding common shares. Where the exercise price of a warrant or option is lower than the current common share value when the warrants or options are exercised (which typically is the case), there is a net increase in the number of common shares outstanding; or
- hold the proceeds as a redundancy, thereby increasing the enterprise value of the business and the en bloc value attributable to all outstanding common shares.

It follows that the net exercise price (net proceeds received by the issuer) militates against the dilutive impact of an option or warrant. The assumption as to how the net proceeds are used normally is dependent on such factors as:

- whether their utilization is specified in advance (e.g. warrants sometimes specify that net proceeds will be applied against debt, or will be used to purchase outstanding shares for cancellation);
- the financial condition of the issuer and its pre-issue financial leverage both in absolute terms and having regard to an 'appropriate' capital structure; and
- if and when the cash will be required to meet operating requirements or expansion plans.

In either a notional market valuation or open market pricing exercise the implications of options and warrants are as follows:

- where the options and warrants are 'out of the money' (i.e. the exercise price exceeds the pro rata value per share) there is no impact; and
- where the options and warrants are 'in the money', (i.e. the pro-rata value per share exceeds the exercise price) then:

- the en bloc value of the company's equity is increased by the proceeds of the exercise price; and
- the number of shares outstanding is increased, which in turn typically decreases the pro-rata value per share.

Example

The en bloc value of Company G's common shares is estimated at $20 million. There are 10 million common shares outstanding. The pro-rata value per share is $2.00. Company G has issued 2 million common share options to its senior managers at an exercise price of $1.50 per common share. Therefore, assuming exercise:

- the en bloc value of Company G's outstanding shares increases by $3 million ($1.50 x 2 million shares) to $23 million; and
- the pro-rata value per share declines to $1.92 ($23 million/12 million shares).

The Valuation of Outstanding Shares vs. the Valuation of Net Assets

The capitalization of discretionary cash flow methodology as discussed in this Chapter assumes the en bloc valuation or pricing of outstanding shares. When the net assets of a business are being valued, some modifications must be made to this methodology to recognize that:

- in Canada an arm's length purchaser of net assets:
  - is entitled to claim capital cost allowance on the 'stepped up' values assigned to the depreciable assets acquired in an arm's length transaction, subject to the so-called 'half year rule',
  - does not receive the flow-through of existing tax pools, including undepreciated capital cost, cumulative eligible capital, any non-capital loss carry-forwards and other tax pools at the valuation date; and
- to the extent that the purchase price exceeds the amounts allocated to the net tangible assets acquired that excess is deductible from income for Canadian income tax purposes. For Canadian Income Tax Purposes this excess amount is referred to as 'eligible capital property'. At the time of writing, 75% of eligible capital property is deductible at a rate of 7% computed on a declining balance basis.

Subject to other adjustments to price in an open market context that might arise from the different indemnifications, representations, and warranties required in a share transaction vs. a (net) asset transaction, the essential differences between the en bloc fair market value of share equity vs. underlying net assets can be reconciled as follows:

EXHIBIT 4.2

> En bloc fair market value of shares

Deduct

> Present value of existing tax pools, including UCC tax shield, non capital loss carry-forwards, and so on

Add

> Present value of CCA tax shield based on purchase price of acquired assets – incorporating the '½ year rule' where appropriate

Add

> Present value of tax shield arising from 'eligible capital property'

Equals

> En bloc fair market value of underlying net assets

When determining the en bloc fair market value of equity pursuant to a purchase of net assets, two specific issues arise:

- in a purchase of net assets the buyer and seller normally agree on an allocation of the total value among tangible and identifiable intangible assets. When determining notional fair market value in the absence of actual negotiations, the determination of goodwill as a residual value necessitates a determination of the market value of the underlying net tangible and identifiable intangible assets. Book values may not be indicative of market val-

ues for many assets, particularly those of a non-current nature. Estimates of underlying net asset values normally are completed pursuant to a determination of tangible asset backing — see Chapter 6; and
- given the tax deductibility of eligible capital property (i.e., goodwill), the determination of the notional fair market value of net assets which collectively constitute going concern value becomes a circular calculation. This is because a greater 'en bloc' fair market value leads to a greater notional eligible capital property amount which in turn generates a greater tax shield. This in turn leads to higher fair market value, and so on.

Due to the CCA and goodwill write-off advantages that accrue to a purchaser of net assets:

- where non-capital loss carry-forwards do not exist; and
- depreciable capital assets and eligible capital property do exist,

the en bloc fair market value and price of underlying net assets typically is greater than is the fair market value of the overlying shares.

Example

The en bloc fair market value of the shares of Company Z is estimated at $12 million as follows ($000):

Estimated maintainable discretionary cash flow	$ 1,500
Capitalization rate (real WACC)	10%
Capitalized discretionary cash flow	15,000
Add: Present value of existing UCC tax shield	2,000
Add: Net realizable value of redundant assets	0
Equals: Enterprise value	17,000
Deduct: Interest bearing debt and equivalents	(5,000)
Equals: en bloc equity value of shares	$12,000

CAPITALIZATION OF DISCRETIONARY CASH FLOW METHODOLOGY

The balance sheet of Company Z at the valuation date is as follows ($000):

Trade current assets	$ 6,000
Fixed assets (net)	8,000
Total assets	14,000
Trade current liabilities	3,000
Long term debt (including current portion)	5,000
Total liabilities	8,000
Shareholders equity	6,000
Total liabilities and equity	$14,000

Other information:

- the estimated market value of Company Z's net fixed assets is $10 million, all of which are subject to a prescribed 30% CCA rate and subject to the half-year rule. The market value of all other assets and liabilities approximates their book values; and
- Company Z's income tax rate is 40%, and it has no loss carry-forwards available.

Based on this information, the en bloc fair market value of Company Z's net assets would be estimated as follows:

En bloc fair market value of shares (above)	$12,000
Deduct: present value of existing UCC shield	(2,000)
Add: present value of CCA on fixed asset additions	2,864
Add: present value of CEC tax shield on goodwill	650
Equals: en bloc fair market value of net assets	$13,514

The present value of the existing UCC shield is deducted from the en bloc fair market value of the shares given that existing tax pools do not flow through to the purchaser. However, a taxable acquirer will be able to claim CCA on the stepped up value of the fixed assets acquired, estimated (pursuant to Formula 4.1) as follows ($000):

$$\frac{\$10,000 \times 30\% \times 40\%}{(10\% + 30\%)} \times \frac{[1 + (0.5 \times 10\%)]}{(1 + 10\%)} = \$2,864$$

In addition, in Canada a taxable acquirer of the net assets will be entitled to claim cumulative eligible capital ('CEC') allowance on the goodwill created for income tax purposes. The amount of goodwill acquired (before consideration of the iterative calculation, discussed below) is estimated as follows ($000):

Fair market value of the shares		$12,000
Deduct: present value of existing UCC tax shield		(2,000)
Add: present value of CCA on assets acquired		2,864
Value of the net assets before tax shield on goodwill		$12,864
Net assets acquired:		
Book value of Company Z	6,000	
Add: market value of fixed assets	10,000	
Deduct: net book value of fixed assets	(8,000)	
Net tangible assets acquired		8,000
Goodwill, before consideration of related income tax shield		$ 4,864

Therefore, the goodwill created on the transaction is $4,864,000. At the time of writing, 75% of this amount is deductible for income tax purposes at a rate of 7% per annum on a declining balance basis (and subject to the half-year rule). This suggests a present value of the income tax shield on goodwill equal to ($000):

$$\frac{(\$4,864 \times 75\%) \times 7\% \times 40\%}{(10\% + 7\%)} \times \frac{[1 + (.05 \times 10\%)]}{(1 + 10\%)} = \$574$$

Therefore, rather than paying $12,864,000 for the net assets, an acquirer might pay an additional $574,000 in recognition of the value of the income tax shield on goodwill, for a total of $13,438,000. At this amount, the goodwill created increases from $4,864,000 to $5,438,000. This in turn increases the income tax shield on the goodwill, and hence, as previously explained, results in an iterative calculation. Solving the calculation results in a present value of the tax shield on goodwill being approximately $650,000.

Therefore, the fair market value of the net assets of Company Z is estimated at $13,514,000, which includes goodwill with a value of $5,514,000 (including the value of the tax shield on said goodwill of $650,000). As a result, the en bloc fair market value of the net assets of Company Z is approximately $1.5 million more than the en bloc fair market value of its underlying shares.

Multi-Divisional Businesses

For the purpose of this discussion, a multi-divisional business is defined as a business with two or more distinct operating segments of material size. The legal structure of the business might include a corporate entity with segregated or partially segregated unincorporated divisions, parent/subsidiary relationships, or a holding company that owns a controlling interest in two or more subsidiaries. (Holding companies are discussed in more detail in Chapter 6). When valuing a multi-divisional business where the nature of each of those businesses, the industries in which they operate, and appropriate rates of return and other valuation factors are distinct, it may be appropriate to separately value one or more such divisions or subsidiaries. When valuing a multi-divisional business, issues that often arise include:

- the treatment of 'head office costs'; and
- the treatment of income taxes in circumstances where the disposition of one or more divisions is assumed.

Head Office Costs

In many multi-divisional businesses, the operating businesses are centrally managed. Combined with support staff and general administrative expenses involved in business management, such costs often are referred to as 'head office costs'. Often it is impossible to allocate head office costs to specific divisions or operating entities in a meaningful way. Accordingly, where a multi-divisional business is being valued en bloc, the usual treatment of head office costs is to capitalize the annual normalized net head office expenses, and to deduct that amount from the sum of the values determined for the divisions. Net head office expenses would consist of normalized head office costs, including sustaining capital, net of income taxes. The capitalization rate and income tax rate adopted normally should be the blended weighted average rates applied to the divisions overseen by head office personnel. Finally, one time costs (net of income taxes) prospectively to be incurred at the head office level should be separately deducted.

Example

Q Limited has 3 distinct operating divisions – A, B and C. The valuation of each of these divisions is as follows:

Division	Capitalization Rate (WACC)	En bloc fair market value
A	9%	$ 20 million
B	10%	$ 80 million
C	12%	$ 50 million
Total		$150 million

Q Limited has a head office administrative staff that oversees all of its operations at a cost of $1 million per annum after income taxes. Adopting a blended rate of return, the capitalized amount of these head office costs would be determined as $1 million / 10.5% = $9.5 million. The 10.5% capitalization rate is the blended weighted average capitalization rate of the operating divisions. Therefore, the en bloc fair market value of Q Limited (before consideration of income taxes, discussed below) would be $140.5 million ($150 million en bloc fair market value less $9.5 million in capitalized head office costs).

Where it becomes necessary to determine the value of a particular operating division(s) or subsidiary(s) on a stand-alone basis, an allocation of head office costs may be required. Such an allocation typically should be made in consideration of head office management time spent by division – gauged through discussions with management, and based on factors such as the complexity, size and strategic importance of the division relative to the company as a whole.

Due to administrative economies of scale that a multi-divisional business may enjoy, head office costs so allocated might be less than actually would be incurred on a stand-alone basis. Where this is the case, the amount of normalized head office costs included in each division should consider:

- the nature, size and complexity of the division; and
- the amount of administrative costs incurred in businesses of a similar nature, both in absolute terms and expressed as a percentage of sales.

Income Taxes

Acquirers of a multi-divisional business may only be interested in purchasing specific divisions or subsidiaries. In such circumstances in order to maximize net proceeds on sale, a multi-divisional business might have to:

- sell each underlying operating division/subsidiary to different purchasers who perceive the greatest ability to generate post-acquisition net economic value added; or
- dispose of all of the operating businesses en bloc to one purchaser who then would divest of those operating businesses it did not wish to retain. Since disposal costs and income taxes would be incurred on the subsequent divestiture, the purchaser normally would seek to be compensated therefor pursuant to a reduced en bloc purchase price for the collective operating companies.

It follows that for a multi-divisional business, in some circumstances it may be appropriate to deduct some amount in respect of income taxes. An adjustment for income taxes would be unusual where the multi-divisional business is operationally integrated, is valued on a stand-alone basis, and it is assumed it will continue to operate 'as is'. Where it is deemed appropriate to reflect all or part of the income taxes that would arise on the sale of the underlying net assets or shares of divisions/subsidiaries (respectively) they usually are discounted having regard to:

- the amount of 'safe income' on hand (see Chapter 14);
- the basis of determining the fair market value of the operating entities, specifically the extent to which 'special interest purchaser premiums' are reflected therein (see Chapter 11);
- the plausibility of combining one or more operating divisions to reduce the number of dispositions;
- the extent to which income tax planning opportunities are perceived to exist that could reduce the overall tax liability; and
- the expected timing, as to when, if ever, the underlying operating businesses would be sold.

Summary

The capitalization of discretionary cash flow methodology has applications both as a stand-alone valuation methodology and as the terminal value component of the discounted cash flow methodology. The capitalization of discretionary cash flow methodology is premised on estimating maintainable discretionary cash flows of the business' operations, normally defined as EBIT-DA, less income taxes, capital investment (net of the related CCA tax shield) and incremental net trade working capital requirements. Discretionary cash flows normally are determined before debt servicing costs (comprised of interest expense net of tax, and changes in debt principal outstanding). Accordingly, the rate of return adopted generally is a weighted average cost of capital – being a blend of debt and equity, which yields capitalized (unlevered) discretionary cash flows. Adjustments then are made to capitalized discretionary cash flows for the value of existing tax pools, prospective non-recurring revenues and expenses (net of tax), and the net realizable value of redundant assets to derive the enterprise value of the overlying shares of the business. Interest bearing debt and equivalents are deducted from enterprise value to determine the en bloc equity value of the shares of the business. Further adjustments are necessary if the underlying assets, and not the shares of the business, are being valued, or if the business' capital structure includes preferred shares or dilutive securities. Finally, in some circumstances the valuation determination may require adjustment where the actual or notional transaction represents a primary as opposed to a secondary offering of shares, or where the business has more than one operating division and it assumed they are to be disposed of individually.

Chapter 5
Discounted Cash Flow Methodology

Introduction

The Discounted Cash Flow ('DCF') Valuation Methodology arguably is the most theoretically sound of the valuation methodologies currently utilized. In recent years it has become a preferred valuation methodology. This is because it forces detailed analysis of key forecast and valuation variables and hence facilitates an understanding of important external and internal business drivers, revenue and expense behavior, and business risks. Accordingly, where meaningful financial projections are available, the DCF methodology generally should be adopted, either by itself or in conjunction with other valuation methodologies.

The DCF methodology, in many respects an extension of the capitalization of discretionary cash flow methodology, is premised on:

- an assumed realization of redundant assets on hand at the beginning of the cash flow period;
- a forecast of the prospective discretionary cash flows. Discretionary cash flows are determined as cash flows from operations (EBIT-DA), less income taxes, capital expenditure requirements (net of the related tax shield), and net trade working capital requirements, and represent the amount of 'free' cash that can be withdrawn from the business (after recognizing debt servicing) without impairing its income generating ability;
- the application of a discount rate to those cash flows to determine their present value; and
- an assumed realization of the residual value of the business in the last year of the cash flow forecast based on a terminal value calculation using the capitalization of discretionary cash flow methodology.

This Chapter has been written from the standpoint of en bloc share valuation. Additional factors must be taken into account where the net assets of a business are valued — see Chapter 4.

Use of the Discounted Cash Flow Methodology

When utilizing the DCF methodology, it is important that discretionary cash flows are believed to be neither overly aggressive nor overly conservative, assumptions are applied consistently within the DCF model, and that the discount rates (i.e. rates of return) adopted are internally consistent within the DCF model.

The DCF methodology is premised on:

- continuing and increasing recognition that discretionary (after-tax) cash flow based analysis typically is more meaningful than earnings based analysis;
- recognition that DCF analysis forces separate and detailed analysis of variables that collectively dictate value (e.g. multiple year forecasts of revenues, gross margin, operating expenses, capital expenditures (both sustaining and growth), working capital requirements, and resultant operating and invested capital returns. It is the rigor of this analysis that makes the DCF methodology particularly useful when developing en bloc fair market value in either a notional or open market context;
- recognition that where the discount rate used is a weighted average cost of capital, 'financial risk' related to interest bearing debt is either largely or entirely accounted for in the valuation model. That is to say, the implications of financial risk arising from an existing over-levered financial structure are largely or entirely disregarded. Accordingly, when determining en bloc fair market value in a notional market context generally it is assumed that:
  - purchasers are able to ensure that following the acquisition the business will operate with what is believed to be an appropriate amount of debt, and
  - in circumstances of existing excess leverage, vendors are not disadvantaged in negotiations.

These assumptions are consistent with that portion of the 'fair market value' definition which prescribes that fair market value is to be determined on the assumption that neither the vendor or the purchaser is 'under compulsion to transact'. In an open market transaction where a purchaser believes a target business is over-levered, and as a result it has a negotiating advantage, the purchaser normally will consider this in its pricing decision. As a practical matter, the ability of an acquirer to exploit such perceived negotiating advantage depends on, among other things, the number of prospective acquirers interested in the target business, and the alternatives available to the target business.

The validity of the value determinations developed from the application of the DCF methodology, as with all other business valuation methodologies, is dependent upon the objectivity, quality of analysis, thought process, experience and judgement of those completing the analysis.

Components of the Discounted Cash Flow Methodology

Overview

The mechanics of the discounted cash flow methodology are similar in many respects to those of the capitalization of discretionary cash flow methodology. However, more variables typically are considered. In summary, the steps are as follows:

- annual prospective cash flow from operations (EBIT-DA) is estimated, generally for a period of three to seven years;
- income taxes at applicable rates are applied against annual EBIT-DA to derive net operating cash flows (before financing costs). Income tax loss carry-forwards (where they exist) are applied in the year they are expected to be utilized;
- capital investment (net of the present value of the related CCA income tax shield) is deducted on an annual basis. When used in the discounted cash flow methodology, capital investment during the forecast period includes both sustaining capital and growth capital required to meet operating projections;
- annual increases (decreases) during the forecast period in net trade working capital are deducted from (added to) net operating cash flows;
- the resultant annual forecasted net operating cash flow less capital investment (net of taxes) and the changes in net trade working capital represents the (unlevered) annual discretionary cash flow;
- the value of cash flows beyond the forecast period are estimated using the capitalization of discretionary cash flow methodology. The resultant capitalized discretionary cash flow commonly is referred to as the 'terminal value'. Alternatively, where the business will be discontinued after the projection period, an estimate of the residual value of the business' underlying net assets is made;
- the annual discretionary cash flows and terminal (or residual) value are discounted to present value at a rate which reflects an appropriate weighted average cost of capital. The discounted cash flows are then aggregated to determine total net present value;
- where not accounted for during the forecast period, the present value of the tax shield on tax pools in existence at the valuation date is determined and added to the discounted discretionary cash flow;

- the net realizable value of redundant assets (if any) is added to the discounted discretionary cash flow. The total net present value of the cash flows during the forecast period and terminal value, plus the present value of the tax shield and redundant assets, results in the 'enterprise value' of the business; and
- because discretionary cash flows have been determined before debt servicing costs, and the discount and capitalization rates reflect a weighted average cost of capital (being a blended rate of return on debt and equity), the amount of interest bearing debt and equivalents outstanding is deducted to determine the en bloc value of the equity (i.e. outstanding shares) of the business.

A schematic overview of the DCF methodology is illustrated in Exhibit 5.1.

EXHIBIT 5.1

> Present Value of Discretionary Cash Flows during Forecast Period

Plus

> Present Value of Terminal Value

Equals

> Present value of All Prospective Discretionary Cash Flows

Plus

> Present Value of Existing Tax Shields Not Included in Discretionary Cash Flows

Plus

> Net Realizable Value of Redundant Assets

Equals

> Enterprise Value

Less

> Interest Bearing Debt and Equivalents Outstanding

Equals

> En bloc Equity Value

Analyzing Forecasts

An objective and detailed assessment of forecasted income statements, cash flow statements and balance sheets is important. These forecasts are fundamental to the DCF methodology. When analyzing a long range forecast, consideration should be given to the following:

- who prepared the forecast and for what purpose;
- the time period of the forecast;
- the key variables and underlying economic drivers;
- underlying assumptions and internal consistency; and
- whether inflation has been built into the forecast.

Who Prepared the Forecast and for what Purpose

It is important to determine who prepared the forecast, the extent of their experience, biases they may have had or that may have been imposed upon them when developing the forecast, and the process they adopted when developing, reviewing and finalizing the forecast. Ideally, those involved will have developed prior years forecasts, the forecasting accuracy of which should be used as one benchmark to assess the probability of achievement of the most recent forecast.

The degree of input received from various disciplines within the organization (sales, marketing, manufacturing, personnel, and so on) is an important consideration in forecast analysis. Some management groups have a formal strategic planning process while others employ less vigor when preparing forecasts. Where a forecast goes through a detailed review and approval process by several levels in an organization, it likely will better reflect management's consensus expectations for the business than otherwise will be the case.

The Forecast Period

Forecasts typically are prepared for a three to ten year time frame, with a period of three to seven years most often being adopted. In both the preparation and evaluation of longer range forecasts, each successive forecast year is subject to an ever increasing degree of uncertainty.

Because uncertainty increases with the number of years forecast, and is exacerbated in a rapidly changing economic and business environment, a cash flow forecast period may be as short as one year or as long as ten years. Forecasting beyond ten years would be unusual. Depending on circumstances, reliability of forecasted cash flow may diminish significantly beyond a short time frame. Business prospects beyond the forecast period then are an integral component of terminal value in the DCF methodology.

The determination of the length of the forecast period generally stems from the circumstances of the business. The forecast period may be dictated by the finite, or term certain, nature of the business. Examples are:

- single project ventures, such as construction of a commercial building, where value would relate to the cash flow to be derived over the term of the project;
- business ventures limited in life to the remaining term of a contract or agreement where there is no right of renewal, or where following the remaining term of a premises lease, business relocation is not feasible; and
- resource extraction businesses, where the depletion of a non-renewable resource is expected to occur over a predicable time period without replacement.

However, most businesses are presumed to have an infinite life. Therefore, the forecast period for each will depend upon specific circumstances. In general, the forecast period should be sufficiently long enough to consider:

- the likely reactions of the business to known or prospective economic, technological and industry changes, including the likely effects on discretionary cash flow of planned plant expansion, product line changes, or changes in the competitive environment faced by the business. For example, if a capital expansion program is planned over the next four years, and it takes three years after the capital expenditure period to fully realize the benefits of the expansion, then it may be appropriate to extend the forecast period to seven years.
- the reliability and likely effect of trends affecting cash flow. The forecast period should include anticipated revenue growth reflecting market maturation during the forecast period, and the effects of a changing cost of sales structure or other cost components;
- where the business historically has been, and prospectively is expected to be, subject to cyclicality, the forecast period should be sufficiently long to demonstrate cash flow trends during an entire business cycle, and the forecast utilized in the terminal value calculation should reflect what are expected to be trend operating results; and
- in acquisition analysis (as contrasted with stand-alone market value analysis) the prospective net economic value-added anticipated to be derived from an acquisition. Some expected synergies, such as administrative effi-

ciencies, may be realized quickly. Conversely, other expected synergies, such as benefits from plant and product integration and rationalization, may take longer to materialize if they are realized at all. Similarly, perceived post-acquisition strategic advantage may occur immediately, may be realized over an extended time period, or may not materialize.

Key Variables and Economic 'Drivers'

Every industry and business has a set of economic 'drivers' that collectively influence business risk at a given point in time. Key drivers normally have a direct impact on revenues, operating costs and capital employed. When reviewing financial forecasts particular attention should be devoted to these key variables. As a general guideline, such a review generally would include consideration of:

- in respect of revenues:
  - assumptions regarding selling prices and prospective selling prices. It often is helpful to review historic trends to determine when and why selling price changes have occurred in the past, and their impact on revenues (i.e. as an assessment of price elasticity). Where significant increases in unit selling prices are anticipated in a forecast, the reasons and justification of the resultant forecasted revenues should be clearly set out,
  - unit sales. Growth in unit sales normally should be segregated between industry growth, growth due to market share changes, and so on. Further, the underlying reasons for growth, be it growth due to product line extensions, new products, new markets, and so on, require analysis. This is because the source of anticipated growth may directly impact risk inherent in the projections, and
  - it is not uncommon for longer term projections to be aggressive in anticipation that planned expenditures will generate exceptional returns. Consideration should be given to whether those returns are reasonable in light of economic and industry projections, and anticipated competitive reaction;
- in respect of operating costs:
  - the cost structure and the degree of operating leverage (i.e. based on the fixed and variable cost mix). Cost structure relates both to cost of sales and other operating costs, excluding depreciation, amortization and interest. The greater the comparative fixed cost component as a percentage of total cost, the greater the sensitivity of the operating results to revenue change and vice versa,

— where revenue growth is anticipated, an assessment should be made as to which costs will increase, and to what degree. For example, where revenue growth is expected, the number of sales and support staff may have to be increased. Additional marketing and advertising costs may also be necessary, and
— whether one time costs prospectively will be incurred with respect to new product line introductions, facilities start-up costs, and so on; and
- in respect of capital requirements:
  — capital expenditures representing both sustaining capital and growth capital requirements,
  — working capital to meet growth expectations. In particular, revenue growth generally necessitates increased working capital requirements. To the extent that cash has to be used to finance accounts receivable, inventories or other working capital requirements, it is not available for distribution to owner(s) or to be reinvested in the business. Accordingly, it must be deducted when determining annual discretionary cash flow, and
  — the projections must be assessed in light of the business' production capacities. Specifically, the practical operating capacity of the plant facilities, production equipment and so on must be considered to determine whether capacity constraints exist. Where capacity additions or additional work shifts (including related costs) are required, these should be accounted for in the capital expenditure projections.

It often is useful to conduct sensitivity analysis on the forecast. Frequently several scenarios may be prepared reflecting pessimistic, most likely, and optimistic assumptions with respect to key economic drivers. These sensitivity tests not only may assist in meaningful forecast development, but also may contribute significantly to risk assessment, and hence to the determination of appropriate discount rate(s).

Underlying Assumptions

Forecasts are premised on assumptions regarding revenues, cost behavior, capital requirements, and so on. Thorough, objective analysis of those assumptions is important. In particular, it is important that assumptions are complete, reasonable, and internally consistent within the forecast.

Completeness refers to ensuring that the forecast assumptions encompass all key variables believed to impact prospective discretionary cash flows. All sources of revenues, operating costs, fixed asset additions and working capital requirements should be accounted for. Completeness also addresses whether all material relevant factors, including the variables that influence economic trends, market growth, competitive behavior, and so on, have been considered in the forecasts.

An internal consistency review should be completed to assess the validity of the forecast as a whole. It should address issues such as:

- whether forecasted marketing and selling expenses increases are consistent with increased revenue forecasts;
- whether existing and planned production capacities are consistent with increased revenue forecasts; and
- whether forecasted labour, equipment and other production costs are consistent with forecasted capacity increases.

Inclusion (Exclusion) of Inflation

It is important to consider whether inflation has been incorporated in the forecast and, if it has, the basis on which it has been included. This is because discount rates applied to forecasted cash flows are either 'nominal rates of return' which include an inflation component, or are 'real rates of return' which do not. As a result, if a forecast that:

- did not include an inflation component was discounted by a nominal rate of return, the resultant value determination would be understated (i.e. the discount rate would be overstated by the inflation component included in it); and
- included an inflation component was discounted by a real rate of return, the resultant value determination would be overstated (i.e. the discount rate would be understated by the inflation component excluded from it).

Regardless of whether inflation has been included in forecasts it is important to consider the relative inflationary impact between cost and revenue components. For example:

- businesses that operate in highly price sensitive industries may have difficulty passing on cost increases to customers. Where this is the case, the forecast should contemplate that the business may experience an erosion of its profit margin in real terms;

- where a business' key manufacturing input is a commodity (such as steel, wheat, oil, and so on) the near term and long term selling price and raw material cost trend forecasts (either in real or nominal terms consistent with the inclusion or exclusion of inflation in the forecast) of the commodity should be considered;
- where a business has long term fixed price contracts (with either suppliers or customers), the forecast should be consistent with their terms;
- certain expenses, rent for example, are fixed for a period of time. Where such expenses increase upon contract renewal or over time, that should be reflected in the forecast; and
- for those businesses with collective bargaining agreements, the terms of the agreement should be considered when forecasting labour costs.

It follows that the rate of inflation employed in forecasted revenue and expense streams may be different. Accordingly, it is important that there be internal consistency in forecasted revenues and expenses on one hand, and in risk (and hence discount rate) assessment on the other.

Adjusting for Unreasonable Forecasts

A forecast thought to be unreasonably optimistic or pessimistic can be dealt with by:

- revising the forecasts to levels believed reasonable so as to develop forecasts that then can be discounted by unadjusted 'market dictated' discount and capitalization rates;
- increasing or decreasing the discount rate(s) and terminal value capitalization rate(s) to reflect the resultant high or low level of risk perceived in the forecasts; or
- applying probability factors to forecasted revenues and expenses, or discretionary cash flows, so as to develop forecasts that then can be discounted by unadjusted 'market dictated' discount and capitalization rates.

As a practical matter, where the forecasts are believed to be only slightly optimistic or pessimistic, it normally is easier to adjust the discount and capitalization rates up or down from 'market dictated' rates that otherwise would have been adopted. However, where it is perceived there is a significant degree of optimism or pessimism in the forecasts, revising or probabilizing the forecasts is preferred since that then enables adoption of perceived appropriate unadjusted 'market dictated' discount and capitalization rates. Again, there is a direct interrelationship and interdependency between the discretionary cash flow projections and the discount/capitalization rates adopted and applied to them. As a result, a determination of appropriate rates of return requires a thorough and unbiased assessment of the forecasts themselves.

Cash Flow from Operations

The cash flow from operations (generally taken to be EBIT-DA) should be projected for each year of the forecast period and in the final year of the forecast, in the latter case for purposes of terminal value determination. Importantly, any prospective one time benefits or costs should be reflected in the EBIT-DA projections in the year they are expected to be realized or incurred.

Where an expected event has a significantly different level of risk attached to it than do other operating cash flows, it may be appropriate to segregate that event and make a one time adjustment (net of applicable income taxes) to enterprise value otherwise determined. For example, if the outcome of an outstanding lawsuit cannot reasonably be estimated, it may be preferable to show the impact of a range of possible outcomes as an adjustment to enterprise value, rather than speculate within the forecast itself as to when and on what terms a final determination will occur.

Finally, EBIT-DA should be adjusted where necessary to exclude any income and expenses from redundant assets that are added to enterprise value otherwise determined.

Income Taxes

Where projections are based on EBIT-DA, the tax rate applied should be a cash tax rate, being the effective income tax rate incurred by the business, without consideration of deferred income taxes. EBIT-DA less 'cash equivalent' income tax thereon yields after-tax (or 'net') operating cash flows. Income tax savings applicable to prior and prospective capital investment, loss carry forwards, and other non-operating realizable amounts are considered separately. Net capital loss carry forwards normally are not considered because capital gains usually are not a component of cash flow from operations. However, net capital loss carry-forwards may have value, and as such require separate consideration.

Where the business has existing non-capital losses at the valuation date, or where a non-capital loss is projected during the forecast period, consideration should be given to the timing of the income tax recovery. Non-capital losses (which in Canada at the time of writing can be carried forward seven years and back three years from the year incurred) are applied against taxes otherwise payable during the forecast year in which they first can be absorbed. The timing of forecasted recovery of non-capital losses depends in part on whether those losses can be carried back to recover previous years' taxes paid. If the aggregate taxable income in the three years preceding the loss year is sufficient to enable a full immediate recovery by carrying a loss back, the operating cash flow loss giving rise to the income tax loss should be reduced in the year the income tax loss arises. Where aggregate taxable income in the preceding three years is less than the current year loss, a portion of the related tax recovery should be reflected in future years as appropriate.

When determining the amount of non-capital losses that can be absorbed in any given year, consideration also should be given to the capital cost allowance inherently projected through both the tax shield on existing UCC and on prospective fixed asset additions. That is, for purposes of analyzing the timing of income tax loss utilization, EBIT-DA in any given year should be reduced by the amount of CCA for that year to determine the amount of non-capital losses which can be utilized. Where annual CCA is significant, an adjustment to the timing of income tax recovery may be necessary. Additionally, where pre-tax operating cash flows have been determined on an unlevered basis (i.e. before interest expense) consideration should be given to what the prospective annual interest expense will be based on 'appropriate' debt levels. This may reduce the amount of the non-capital losses otherwise recoverable in a given year. In summary, where non-capital losses exist, it generally is necessary to calculate forecasted taxable income and then forecast the timing of tax loss utilization.

Example

ABC Limited, a company in a cyclical industry, has non-capital losses of $800,000 at its fiscal year ending September 30, 2000. The losses expire in fiscal 2003. EBIT-DA is projected as follows:

Fiscal Year	EBIT-DA ($000)
2001	$600
2002	$1,000
2003	$400
2004	($500)
2005	$200
2006	$700
2007	$1,200

ABC's effective income tax rate is 40%. Assuming an appropriate level of forecasted interest expense is $100,000 per annum, and that forecasted capital cost allowance is $200,000 per year, the calculation of forecasted income taxes payable each year would be as follows ($000):

	2001	2002	2003	2004	2005	2006	2007
EBIT-DA as projected	600	1,000	400	(500)	200	700	1,200
Less: interest expense	(100)	(100)	(100)	(100)	(100)	(100)	(100)
Less: capital cost allowance	(200)	(200)	(200)	(200)	(200)	(200)	(200)
Net	300	700	100	(800)	(100)	400	900
Non-capital loss carry-forward used	(300)	(500)	0	0	0	(400)	(200)
Non-capital loss carried back				(300)			
Taxable income	0	200	100	(300)	0	0	700
Taxes payable (recoverable)	0	80	40	(120)	0	0	280
Non-capital losses available at:							
Beginning of year	800	500	0	0	500	600	200
End of year	500	0	0	500	600	200	0

The existing non-capital loss of $800,000 is applied against pre-tax earnings in fiscal 2001 up to the maximum of $300,000. The balance of $500,000 is carried forward to fiscal 2002. The loss of $800,000 forecast for fiscal 2004 is not fully recoverable in that year. Taxes can be recovered only to the extent of taxes paid in the previous three years. In this case, it is 40% of $300,000, or $120,000. The remaining $500,000 is carried forward. The $100,000 loss forecast for fiscal 2005 is not recoverable in that year because the previous three years have no taxable income after the application of the loss forecast for fiscal 2004. The unused losses from fiscal 2004 and 2005 are carried forward to fiscal 2006 up to the pre-tax income in that year. The remainder of $200,000 is carried over to fiscal 2007, and applied in that year.

In this example, it is assumed that the company claims CCA prior to the application of income tax losses. This is not always the case. However, where non-capital losses are not expected to expire before utilization, it generally is advantageous to claim the full amount of CCA tax shield each year.

Capital Investment

The timing and quantum of capital expenditures is particularly relevant when applying the discounted cash flow methodology. Again, there must be internal consistency between the cash flow projection and the capital investment required to achieve it. In any given forecast year, capital investment should consider:

- the required amount of sustaining capital reinvestment, i.e. the annual fixed asset additions required to maintain operations at the level projected each year. This should take into account changes in technology, industry developments, and so on — see Chapter 4. It should be noted that as operating cash flows are projected to increase, there may be an associated increase in the level of sustaining capital investment required to maintain forecasted cash flows at those levels; and
- the incremental capital investment required for planned capacity additions to generate incremental forecasted revenues and operating cash flows. This may include new machinery and equipment for expansion (growth in revenues), for operating efficiencies (reduction in costs), or both.

As previously noted, where incremental capital expenditures are forecast to increase revenues or to realize operating efficiencies, the forecast period should be of sufficient length to fully reflect the benefits attributable to the capital expenditure – thereby ensuring both capital expenditures and resultant cash flows are properly integrated.

The amount of annual capital expenditures required should be reduced by the present value of the capital cost allowance ('tax shield') arising from those expenditures — see formulae in Chapter 4. Again, in Canada the 'half-year rule' (that is, where one half of the allowable CCA is taken in the year of acquisition) should be taken into account where applicable.

Net Trade Working Capital Requirements

Most businesses require a net trade working capital balance in order to sustain operations. Net trade working capital is defined as the operational working capital balances required to sustain business operations, and normally includes accounts receivable, inventories, accounts payable, accrued liabilities, taxes payable and other accounts associated with the normal operations of the business. An operating cash balance may be required depending on the 'normal' practices of the particular business (see Chapter 3). Net trade working capital specifically excludes:

- short-term interest bearing debt (i.e. bank operating facilities) and current non-interest bearing equivalents;
- non-operating assets, such as advances to shareholders, non-trade receivables, and so on. These items normally are dealt with as redundant assets, which are segregated and valued separately;
- deferred income tax balances included in current assets or current liabilities. This is because deferred income taxes do not relate to cash flow from operations; and
- excess cash balances. Changes in cash (and interest bearing debt) normally represent discretionary cash flow that is subject to discounting. Therefore, in many cases the entire change in net cash (cash less interest bearing debt) is considered discretionary. To the extent that some or all of that cash is not discretionary (i.e. where the business requires an 'operating cash balance'), it should not form part of discretionary cash flow and should be segregated for the purpose of the DCF calculation.

Where a business forecasts that revenues will increase, that growth generally necessitates corresponding increases in accounts receivable, inventories, and other current assets of a non-cash nature. This increase in non-cash current assets usually in part (or sometimes all) is offset by an increase in accounts payable and other current liabilities. However, the net result often is an increase in net trade working capital requirements. Where cash is required to finance incremental net trade working capital requirements in any forecast year, that cash requirement should be deducted from the forecast when determining discretionary cash flows.

Where income and cash flow forecasts are compiled, corresponding balance sheets may or may not be prepared. Where pro-forma balance sheets for the projection period have been prepared, the change in net trade working capital can be computed. However, it is important to determine whether the assumptions underlying prospective working capital requirements are reasonable. Sometimes a net trade working capital decrease is projected on the assumption of prospective improved management of receivables, inventories and accounts payable. Where such assumptions are made, they should be closely scrutinized to determine whether or not they are well founded. If not, adjustments may be necessary.

Where projected balance sheets do not accompany cash flow projections, an estimate of net trade working capital requirements should be made. This usually can be done pursuant to analysis of historic relationships between revenues, operating results, current assets, and current liabilities. In particular, it may be appropriate to calculate historic ratios such as:

- the current ratio and quick ratio;
- net trade working capital as a percentage of sales;
- days sales in accounts receivable;
- inventory turnover; and
- days purchases in accounts payable.

If these ratios (see Appendix B) are consistent and are expected to remain so, they can be used to assist in estimating working capital requirements. Where appropriate, the ratio of non-cash working capital to sales can be used to estimate the changes in net trade working capital resulting from a change in sales.

*Example of a Calculation of Prospective
Net Trade Working Capital Requirements*

XYZ Inc. ('XYZ') has compiled a three year financial projection which includes the following working capital balances:

SCHEDULE 5.1

**XYZ Inc.
Projected Working Capital
At November 30
($000)**

	Actual	Forecast		
	2000	2001	2002	2003
Cash	0	0	303	898
Accounts receivable	1,830	2,013	2,214	2,435
Loan to affiliated company	300	250	200	150
Inventories	775	853	938	1,032
Deferred income taxes	113	124	136	150
Prepaids and other assets	80	80	80	80
Total current assets	3,098	3,320	3,871	4,745
Bank loan	360	145	0	0
Accounts payable & accruals	1,292	1,421	1,564	1,720
Taxes & other payables	261	287	316	347
Current portion of long term debt	150	150	150	150
Total current liabilities	2,063	2,003	2,030	2,217
Net working capital	1,035	1,317	1,841	2,528

Assuming that XYZ does not require an operating cash balance, net trade working capital requirements would be calculated as follows:

SCHEDULE 5.2

XYZ Inc.
Estimated Net Trade Working Capital Requirements
($000)

	Forecast		
	2001	2002	2003
Cash required to finance increase in:			
Accounts receivable	183	201	221
Inventories	78	85	94
Prepaids and other assets	0	0	0
	261	286	315
Less: portion of increase financed by:			
Accounts payable and accruals	129	143	156
Taxes and other payables	26	29	31
	155	172	187
Net trade working capital requirements	106	114	128

On the asset side, only changes in accounts receivable, inventories and prepaids and other assets are considered. The loan to the affiliated company is assumed to be a redundant asset, and would be valued separately. Changes in the deferred income tax asset are not part of operating cash flows. On the liability side, only changes in the accounts payable and accruals and taxes and other payables are considered. The bank loan and current portion of long term debt are part of XYZ's financial structure. This is separately addressed in the DCF methodology.

The above calculation assumes the entire net change in cash (debt reduction) is discretionary in nature. Where appropriate, an adjustment should be made to reflect that portion of the change in cash required to sustain the operations of the business (which was assumed not to be the case for XYZ), and which therefore is not discretionary.

Terminal or Residual Value

Usually businesses are not perceived to have a finite life. However, where they do, they nonetheless may have residual value including net working capital, fixed assets, and other miscellaneous assets. When calculating the net residual proceeds of a business with a finite life all assets should be valued at net realizable value, and all costs must be taken into account. For example, when operations terminate there may be ongoing liabilities, such as product warranties and environmental clean-up. The expected net residual proceeds then are discounted to present value.

Where a business is expected to continue as a going concern for an indefinite period the value of the business beyond the projection period, commonly referred to as a 'terminal value' or less commonly as a 'residual value', must be determined. The terminal value represents the value of discretionary cash flows expected to be generated from the end of the forecast period to perpetuity. In a discounted cash flow valuation methodology 'terminal value' typically is determined at the end of the forecast period pursuant to the capitalization of discretionary cash flow methodology. It then is discounted to the valuation date using the discount rates employed in the DCF calculation. That is:

- maintainable annual EBIT-DA beyond the forecast period is estimated. It is generally based on analysis of historic and forecasted EBIT-DA's. Maintainable annual EBIT-DA adopted for purposes of developing terminal value normally is expressed as a range of prospective operating results;
- income taxes are deducted at the appropriate cash tax rate to yield net operating (after-tax) cash flows before consideration of interest expense;
- sustaining capital reinvestment, net of its related tax shield, is deducted from net operating cash flow. The quantum of sustaining capital reinvestment must be consistent with estimated maintainable net operating cash flow adopted in the terminal value determination;
- where perpetual real growth is assumed in the capitalization rate adopted to develop terminal value – which practice is questionable, see Chapter 8 — an appropriate amount of 'growth' capital investment, net of its related tax shield, should be deducted from net operating cash flow when developing terminal value — see Chapter 4; and
- incremental working capital requirements generally are not considered in the terminal value calculation, except where perpetual real growth is assumed in the capitalization rate adopted to develop terminal value. In these circumstances it is appropriate to deduct an amount required for incremental net trade working capital to support said perpetual real growth.

Net (after-tax) operating cash flows less the aggregate of net sustaining capital reinvestment, net growth capital investment (if any) and net trade working capital requirements (if any) yields discretionary cash flows for purposes of developing terminal value. The resultant discretionary cash flows are capitalized at an appropriate capitalization rate reflective of a real weighted average cost of capital where discretionary cash flows have been determined before interest expense and in real dollar terms (i.e. without an inflation component). The capitalization rates adopted must consider the risk inherent in the level of maintainable discretionary cash flow adopted in the terminal value determination.

As a practical matter, the present value of the terminal value often accounts for the largest portion of overall present value in a DCF calculation. Accordingly, well founded analysis is important in the development of the key terminal value calculation components. It often is beneficial to perform sensitivity analysis on the terminal value components to better assess the underlying risks.

Finally, the present value of the terminal value should be determined using a present value factor that is the same as the last year of the forecast period. This is because the capitalization rate inherently assumes a perpetual stream of discretionary cash flows beginning one year forward.

Discount and Capitalization Rates

A discount rate is a rate of return that converts a series of forecasted cash flows to present value. Conversely, a capitalization rate is a rate of return that converts a point estimate of continuing cash flows to value. A discount rate is applied to forecasted annual discretionary cash flows in a DCF calculation. A capitalization rate is applied to estimated maintainable discretionary cash flows beyond the forecast period when deriving terminal value. Because terminal value at that point is expressed in a future dollar amount it must be discounted to the valuation date at the discount rate used in the DCF analysis to derive its present value. It bears repeating that the rates of return used in a DCF analysis (both discount and capitalization rates) and the discretionary cash flows to which they are applied are interrelated.

The discount rate applied to determine the present value of the annual cash flows and to discount terminal value must be determined consistent with the determination of the cash flows. That is, where:

- inflation has been incorporated into the determination of discretionary cash flows throughout the forecast period, the discount rate selected to be applied to the those forecasted cash flows should reflect a nominal rate, inclusive of inflation;
- inflation has not been incorporated into the determination of discretionary cash flows throughout the forecast period, the discount rate selected to be applied to those forecasted cash flows should reflect a real rate, exclusive of inflation;
- discretionary cash flows have been determined before consideration of interest expense (which typically is the case), the discount rate should reflect a weighted average cost of capital, including both an appropriate debt and equity component; and
- discretionary cash flows have been determined net of interest expense (which, as explained in Chapter 4, is a theoretically acceptable approach but generally not practical), the discount rate should reflect a return on levered equity.

The timing of annual cash flows should be considered in the discounting process. Where cash flows evenly accrue to a business, mid-year discount rates would be appropriate. Where cash flows accrue primarily at the beginning or end of a business' fiscal year, the calculation theoretically should be adjusted to reflect this, although in practice this is not always done.

In some cases, a business has two or more distinct sources of revenues each of which is subject to different risks. For example, a business might have certain revenues that are divisional, fixed by contract, or that are highly volatile. In such circumstances either:

- the discretionary cash flows should be segregated by revenue stream and appropriate risk-adjusted rates of return should be applied to each. This generally is the preferred approach; or
- a blended rate of return should be applied to aggregate discretionary cash flows to account for the different risk profiles of the different revenue streams.

Existing Tax Pools

Where not accounted for in the discretionary cash flow projections, the present value of Undepreciated Capital Cost Allowance (and other tax pools) on hand at the valuation date is added to the present value of the forecasted discretionary cash flows and the present value of the terminal value, consistent with the capitalization of discretionary cash flow methodology. It is also important to note that the present value of the existing UCC calculation is premised on the assumption that a business will claim the maximum allowable CCA each year. Where this is not the case (for example where a company chooses to defer its CCA claim to use non-capital losses which would otherwise expire), the present value of the existing UCC calculation should be adjusted accordingly.

Unlike the capitalization of discretionary cash flow methodology, pursuant to the discounted cash flow methodology non-capital income tax losses normally are not considered separately as a possible addition to value otherwise determined. This is because they normally are reflected as a reduction of the cash income taxes otherwise payable in the cash flow forecasts. Any non-capital income tax losses (and other tax shields) not accounted for as part of discretionary cash flows are adjusted for separately.

Redundant Assets

As with other valuation methodologies, pursuant to the discounted cash flow valuation methodology redundant assets are assumed to be realized at the valuation date, and their estimated net realizable value is added to the present value of the cash flows. Again, any income or expense stream associated with redundant assets is removed from projected EBIT-DA. As discussed in Chapter 4, when determining the net realizable value of redundant costs at the corporate level, disposition costs and income taxes often are discounted in recognition of tax deferral opportunities that might exist.

Interest Bearing Debt

Since enterprise value reflects the aggregate of the debt and equity components of a business, the amount of interest bearing debt outstanding at the valuation date must be deducted from enterprise value to determine the going concern value of the equity owners interest in the business. In this context, interest bearing debt outstanding includes short term and long term interest bearing debt, and equivalents such as interest free loans. As discussed in Chapter 4, where short term operating debt is not deducted (due to seasonality issues, for example), the after tax cost of that credit facility must be reflected in the projected discretionary cash flows.

Example of the Discounted Cash Flow Methodology

Assumed Facts

Control Dynamics Limited ('CDL') is a manufacturer of equipment used to control the production processes of food, chemical, pharmaceutical and similar non-durable goods producers. CDL was established in 1985 by four engineers who are equal shareholders. The Company operates out of owned premises in Montreal. In addition to its equipment manufacturing business, CDL owns a 20% interest in Clean-All Inc., an office cleaning company, which it accounts for using the equity method. CDL's most recent balance sheet is presented below.

SCHEDULE 5.3

Control Dynamics Limited
Balance Sheet
At December 31, 2000
($000)

Cash	1,866
Trade current assets	12,578
Total current assets	14,444
Investment in Clean-All Ltd.	595
Fixed assets (net)	17,472
Total assets	32,511
Bank loans	2,400
Trade current liabilities	3,294
Current portion of long term debt	1,885
Total current liabilities	7,579
Deferred income taxes	1,695
Long term debt	10,405
Total liabilities	19,679
Shareholder equity	12,832
Total liabilities & equity	32,511

The manufacture of control equipment is capital intensive, and CDL has a large capital asset balance. In this regard, CDL has recently developed and patented a new line of process control technology which is believed to be revolutionary. Trial runs with customers have proven successful and CDL, following purchase of specialized machinery, is planning to actively market equipment based on the new technology. CDL intends to finance most of the new machinery through debt, and has prepared a five year strategic plan for its bank which includes the following financial forecasts.

SCHEDULE 5.4

Control Dynamics Limited
Earnings Forecast
Fiscal Years Ending December 31
($000)

	Actual	Forecast				
	2000	2001	2002	2003	2004	2005
Sales	38,472	45,000	60,000	80,000	90,000	100,000
Cost of sales	20,005	22,500	30,000	40,000	45,000	50,000
Gross margin	18,467	22,500	30,000	40,000	45,000	50,000
Selling and administration	12,915	15,950	17,600	22,800	25,400	28,000
Equity earnings in Clean-All	(36)	(50)	(50)	(50)	(50)	(50)
Interest	1,370	3,000	3,000	3,000	3,000	3,000
Depreciation	1,822	3,400	5,000	5,700	5,600	5,500
Total expenses	16,071	22,300	25,550	31,450	33,950	36,450
Earnings before tax	2,396	200	4,450	8,550	11,050	13,550
Income tax (current & deferred)	767	64	1,424	2,736	3,536	4,336
Net income	1,629	136	3,026	5,814	7,514	9,214
Capital investment net of CCA shield		8,000	6,000	4,000	4,000	4,000

The forecasts were prepared in real dollars (i.e. net of inflation). Accompanying balance sheets and cash flow statements were not prepared.

In January 2001 one of the shareholders of CDL was killed in a car accident. Pursuant to an enforceable Shareholder's Agreement, in the event of the death of one of the shareholders the remaining shareholders are entitled to purchase the deceased's shareholding. The agreement specifies the price, determined at CDL's most recent fiscal year end, to be a pro-rata share of the 'en bloc' 'intrinsic' (i.e., 'stand-alone') fair market value of CDL's outstanding shares. The purchase of the deceased's shares will be funded by proceeds from a corporate life insurance policy, which is not considered in determining en bloc fair market value, in accordance with the terms of CDL's Shareholder's Agreement.

When calculating the en bloc intrinsic fair market value of CDL's outstanding shares it is assumed that the:

- tax rate on operating income is 32%;
- ratio of net trade working capital (i.e. excluding cash) to sales is expected to be 25%. Operating cash requirements for the company are negligible;
- book value of the investment in Clean-All approximates its net realizable value;
- opening balance of undepreciated capital cost is $15 million, and the present value of the CCA shield is $2.7 million;
- company expects that beyond fiscal 2005 discretionary cash flows will stabilize to within +/- 10% of fiscal 2005 discretionary cash flows;
- appropriate discount rate to apply to discretionary cash flows for fiscal 2001 through 2005 is 12%, being a real weighted average cost of capital as the forecasts exclude inflation. Mid-year discount rates are adopted; and
- appropriate multiple to apply in the calculation of terminal value is 7x to 8x (i.e. a real weighted average cost of capital of 14.3% and 12.5%, respectively) to account for what is believed to be greater risk beyond the forecast period due to the uncertainty of continued patent protection.

Valuation Determination

The 'en bloc' fair market value of the common shares of CDL is estimated in the range of $42 million to $48 million, determined as follows:

SCHEDULE 5.5

Control Dynamics Limited
Estimate of Fair Market Value
At December 31, 2000
($000)

	Low	High
Present value of discretionary cash flows:		
Fiscal 2001 through 2005	$ 5,699	$ 5,699
Terminal value	45,466	52,360
	51,165	58,059
Add: present value of existing CCA tax shield	2,700	2,700
Add: net realizable value of redundant asset	595	595
Enterprise value	54,460	61,354
Less: interest bearing debt outstanding (net of cash)	(12,824)	(12,824)
En bloc fair market value of shares	41,636	48,530
Say,	$ 42,000	$ 48,000

The present value of discretionary cash flows is segregated between those expected to be realized from fiscal 2001 through 2005, and maintainable discretionary cash flows adopted when determining terminal value. Because the required investment in fixed assets and working capital in the first year of the forecast period is significant, the majority of the present value of cash flows is generated from terminal value. Discretionary cash flows were determined as follows:

SCHEDULE 5.6

Control Dynamics Limited
Fiscal Years Ending December 31
($000)

	2001	2002	2003	2004	2005	Thereafter Low	Thereafter High
Forecasted pretax income	200	4,450	8,550	11,050	13,550		
Adjustments							
Equity earnings in Clean-All	(50)	(50)	(50)	(50)	(50)		
Depreciation	3,400	5,000	5,700	5,600	5,500		
Interest	3,000	3,000	3,000	3,000	3,000		
EBIT-DA	6,550	12,400	17,200	19,600	22,000	19,800	24,200
Income taxes at 32%	(2,096)	(3,968)	(5,504)	(6,272)	(7,040)	(6,336)	(7,744)
Cash flow from operations	4,454	8,432	11,696	13,328	14,960	13,464	16,456
Capital investment (net)	(8,000)	(6,000)	(4,000)	(4,000)	(4,000)	(4,000)	(4,000)
Working capital	(1,632)	(3,750)	(5,000)	(2,500)	(2,500)	0	0
Discretionary cash flow	(5,178)	(1,318)	2,696	6,828	8,460	9,464	12,456
Terminal multiple						8x	7x
Terminal Value						75,712	87,192
Discounted at 12% (mid-year)	(4,893)	(1,111)	2,031	4,592	5,080	45,466	52,360

Forecast pre-tax income for fiscal 2001 through 2005 is adjusted to reflect non-cash items. Specifically, the equity earnings in Clean-All Ltd. are deducted and depreciation is added back. Interest expense is added back because the discount and capitalization rates used are based on a weighted average cost of capital. Operating cash flows beyond fiscal 2005 are estimated at +/- 10% of fiscal 2005 levels. The resultant earnings before interest taxes and depreciation (EBIT-DA) is subjected to income taxes at 32% to derive net cash flow from operations.

Capital investment is deducted at the amount specified, net of the related capital cost allowance tax shield. In addition, working capital is deducted at 25% of incremental revenues. Because changes to operating cash requirements are assumed to be insignificant no adjustment to discretionary cash flows has been made to account for this. No incremental working capital requirements are accounted for beyond fiscal 2005 on the assumption that sales and working capital requirements remain relatively stable after fiscal 2005.

The sum of after-tax cash flow from operations less net capital investment and working capital yields the discretionary cash flow. The discretionary cash flow from fiscal 2001 through 2005 is discounted at a real weighted average cost of capital of 12%, the sum of the present values being $5,699,000. Mid-year discount rates are assumed.

Maintainable discretionary cash flows beyond 2005 are capitalized at real risk-adjusted weighted average costs of capital of 12.5% to 14.3% (multiples of 8x and 7x) resulting in a terminal value in the range of approximately $75 million to $87 million. This terminal value range is discounted at 12% resulting in a present terminal value range of $45,466,000 to $52,360,000. Therefore, the present capital value of all discretionary cash flows is approximately $51 million to $58 million. Enterprise value then is determined by adding the:

- present value of the capital cost allowance tax shield of $2,700,000;
- investment in Clean-All, which is treated as a redundant asset, and is assumed to have a net realizable value equal to its book value. As discussed in Chapter 4, the valuation of a redundant asset should take into account numerous factors. In this case, it would be prudent to review the financial statements of Clean-All, the Shareholder's Agreement for that company (if one exists), recent equity transactions in that company, and so on.

The result is an enterprise value for CDL (for purposes of a valuation of shares, and not for purposes of a valuation of net assets) in the range of approximately $54 million to $61 million.

As a weighted average cost of capital has been adopted for discount and capitalization rate purposes, the enterprise value represents the aggregate value of the interest bearing debt, interest bearing debt equivalents, and share equity of CDL. Therefore, to determine the en bloc value of the outstanding shares of CDL the amount of interest bearing debt and interest bearing debt equivalents must be deducted from enterprise value. This deduction is in aggregate $12,824,000 comprised of the bank loan and long term debt, including the current portion, net of cash on hand. The cash balance is deducted from interest bearing debt outstanding on the assumption that it could be used to reduce the amount of debt on hand at the valuation date.

The resultant 'en bloc' fair market value of the shares of CDL is approximately $42 million to $48 million. Therefore, the pro-rata value of the deceased's 25% shareholding is $10,500,000 to $12,000,000. In this example no consideration has been given to the impact on CDL of a buyout of the minority interest using company funds (an internally financed transaction), based on the assumption that 'external' life insurance proceeds are available — see Chapter 2. Finally, it is important to note that this conclusion represents the intrinsic value of the shares, without consideration of purchaser synergies.

Assets vs. Shares

The determination of 'en bloc' equity value as outlined above assumes a valuation of outstanding share capital as contrasted with a valuation of net assets. Where the underlying net assets of a business are valued, additional adjustments are required to reflect the after-tax cash flows resulting from the tax treatment afforded a purchaser of assets as opposed to that afforded a purchaser of shares — also see Chapter 4. Specifically, where net assets are valued in Canada:

- a purchaser of net assets is able to claim capital cost allowance (or equivalents) on the negotiated values of depreciable tangible and intangible assets, as contrasted with a purchaser of shares who 'inherits' the existing 'undepreciated capital cost' and 'eligible capital property' (goodwill) balances of the company whose shares are acquired. Accordingly, where net assets are valued, the tax shield inherent in the (usually) 'stepped up' asset balances depreciable for income tax purposes is added to the capital value of the discretionary cash flows, subject to, the 'half year rule' where applicable; and

- non-capital income tax losses do not flow through to a purchaser of net assets. Therefore, whereas such losses are properly incorporated in the determination of discretionary cash flows where shares are valued, they are not so incorporated where net assets are valued.

Start-up and High Growth Businesses

Start-up and high growth businesses are:

- defined as those that do not have a long operating history and are generating revenues and (perhaps negative) discretionary cash flows significantly below future expectations;
- often associated with the biopharmaceutical, technology, information and telecommunication industries, but can include any business where significant growth in near term revenue and discretionary cash flow is expected; and
- normally valued pursuant to a discounted cash flow methodology.

In most cases, value determinations necessarily are more subjective in start-up and high growth businesses due to the absence of quality historical data and uncertainty regarding the assumptions underlying the projections. Accordingly, the valuation of such business is discussed here to focus in circumstances of their valuation on the:

- assessment of the reasonableness of their forecasted cash flows; and
- determination of appropriate rates of return to apply to those forecasted cash flows.

Forecasted Discretionary Cash Flows

Long term cash flow forecasts are fundamental to the valuation of start-up and high growth businesses. As a practical matter, such forecasts often reflect an overly optimistic outlook for the business due to:

- management's incentive to present the business in a positive light in order to obtain financing;
- failure to account for all of the costs associated with revenue growth; and
- insufficient recognition of the risks associated with a start-up or high growth ventures attributable to factors such as:
  — being by-passed in technology,
  — increased competition from larger and better financed competitors, and
  — reliance on one or a few key personnel.

As with any business, assessing the reasonableness of the cash flow forecasts necessitates an understanding of the business itself and the industry in which it operates. A careful, objective analysis of the assumptions underlying the projections is essential. In particular, emphasis should be placed on the reasonableness of:

- the business plan, which normally accompanies the revenue and cash flow forecast. Business plans typically set out important details regarding the business, including its target market, competition, personnel, strategic advantages, strengths and weaknesses, and so on;
- revenue forecasts. Normally revenues should be analyzed by product, customer, territory and so on in order to determine precisely what the driving forces are behind anticipated revenue growth. Both quantity and pricing assumptions should be set out; and
- cost forecasts. In particular, costs should be analyzed in the context of consistency with revenue assumptions and completeness. With respect to completeness, consideration should be given to fixed 'step' costs, capital spending requirements, working capital requirements, and all other cash outlays required to generate forecasted revenues.

In many cases, it will be appropriate to probabilize the projected discretionary cash flows by some factor or otherwise adjust the projections in recognition of the uncertainty related thereto. In most cases, the probability factor applied will be greater for longer term vs. shorter term projections given that uncertainty will increase over time. Finally, as a practical matter, where a start-up or high growth business is valued pursuant to a discounted cash flow methodology, virtually all of the en bloc value generally is attributed to the terminal value component.

Rates of Return

The risks associated with achieving forecasts generally are perceived to be greater in start-up or high growth businesses than is the case with mature businesses. As a result, the rates of return utilized in valuing start-up or high growth businesses normally are greater than those utilized in the case of mature businesses. In the context of start-up or high growth businesses rates of return on equity utilized are often reflective of those sought by venture capitalists, which are commonly in the pre-tax range of 30% to 40% or greater.

Because rates of return and the prospective discretionary cash flows to which they are applied are interrelated, care must be exercised to appropriately reflect the degree of risk attached to the forecasts in the rates of return adopted.

Just as to adopt over-conservative forecasts and apply an inappropriately high rate of return to them would understate value, so to would adopting over-optimistic forecasts and applying an inappropriately low rate of return to them overstate value.

As discussed in Chapter 7, the capital structure decision is an integral component of the discount and capitalization rate determination. In the context of a start up or high growth business, the ability to use financial leverage often is thwarted due to the inability of such businesses to finance operations conventionally through non-participating interest bearing debt. Many traditional lenders are wary of start-up and high growth companies because of the degree of subjectivity required when assessing forecast risk, potential near term cash flow volatility, and what often is an absence of underlying net tangible assets. As a result, it may be appropriate to assume that little or no conventional debt financing is reflective of an 'appropriate' capital structure.

The Valuation Conclusion

As with all notional market valuation and open market pricing exercises, the conclusion reached for a start-up or high growth business must be objectively assessed for overall reasonableness. Because the level of subjectivity in value determinations related to start-up and high growth businesses normally is greater than it is in the case of mature businesses, it may be beneficial to consider the following when concluding on value:

- ratios of enterprise value to revenues, EBIT-DA, EBIT and equity value to net income and net tangible assets. Importantly, a comparison of these ratios to stock market multiples alone may lead to an unsupportable valuation conclusion — see Chapter 9. As a practical matter, such ratios often are meaningless due to operating losses or very low income levels at the valuation date;
- so-called rules of thumb. In some start-up and high growth businesses, rules of thumb are used as a guideline to value. For example, for certain technology businesses rules of thumb based on number of computer programmers employed have been cited. A rule of thumb in isolation rarely will provide an appropriate base for a well founded valuation conclusion;
- cost of reproduction. For start-up companies in particular, a purchaser may have the option of purchasing an existing business or starting one. A 'cost of reproduction' analysis also may help identify those components that are not readily replaceable (proprietary technology, for example) that might properly influence value; and

- the implied rate of perpetual real growth, if any, adopted in the rates of return utilized. Where discretionary cash flows are positive at the valuation date, the valuation or pricing conclusion derived pursuant to a discounted cash flow methodology can be computed by 'interpolating' or 'forcing out' an equivalent capitalization rate against what are perceived at the valuation date then to be maintainable discretionary cash flows. As discussed in Chapter 8, in the discounted cash flow methodology the capitalization rate adopted to develop terminal value is based on the discount rate applied against discretionary cash flows during the forecast period adjusted, where appropriate, for growth. Knowing the discount rate applied, it may be possible to 'force out' the real perpetual growth rate implied by the value conclusion. Where the resultant perpetual growth rate appears unreasonable, further analysis of the valuation conclusion would be required.

For example, assume that ABC Limited generated discretionary cash flows of $1 million in its most recent fiscal year ending June 30, 2000, and that it had compiled the following annual discretionary cash flow projections in real dollar terms ($000):

Fiscal year	$000
2001	1,500
2002	2,000
2003	2,500
2004	3,000
2005	3,500
Thereafter	4,000

It is further assumed that a 15% real weighed average cost of capital is an appropriate real discount rate (based on 100% equity financing) and capitalization rate, and that the business has no interest bearing debt or equivalents, and no redundant assets. It follows that the en bloc fair market value of its shares would be estimated at $21,174,000, pursuant to a discounted cash flow methodology. Alternatively, the same result could be obtained based on the reciprocal of the en bloc equity value to actual discretionary cash flows for fiscal 2000:

$$= 1 / (21{,}174{,}000 / 1{,}000{,}000) = 4.7\%$$

Given that the capitalization rate equals the discount rate less growth — see Chapter 8 — and assuming a real discount rate of 15% to be appropriate, the equivalent implied rate of perpetual growth is 15% - 4.7% = 10.3%. The implied rate of perpetual real growth then would be assessed for reasonableness in light of the nature of the industry and business-specific facts of each case.

In the end, the valuation conclusion derived for any business must comprise a carefully considered synthesis of the specific economic, industry and business facts that affect each.

Summary

The discounted cash flow methodology is a preferred valuation methodology, both in theory and practice. The in-depth analysis and projections that accompany a discounted cash flow methodology usually contribute to a more comprehensive understanding of the risks and opportunities faced by a business, and hence a more supportable valuation conclusion.

The discretionary cash flows that are discounted pursuant to the discounted cash flow methodology normally are forecast for a period of 3 to 7 years, with a terminal value component capturing the value of discretionary cash flows beyond the forecast period. Discretionary cash flows normally are defined as EBIT-DA less income taxes, capital investment (sustaining and growth capital, net of the related CCA tax shield) and net trade working capital requirements necessary to generate the projected cash flows. The capitalization of discretionary cash flow methodology typically is adopted for the terminal value component. Discretionary cash flows usually are determined before debt servicing costs. Accordingly, the discounted value of the prospective discretionary cash flows and terminal value in aggregate represents the 'enterprise value' of the shares of the business. Interest bearing debt and equivalents are deducted, and the net realizable value of redundant assets and the present value of existing tax pools not accounted for in the projections are added to enterprise value, to arrive at the equity value of the shares of the business, en bloc.

While the mechanics of the discounted cash flow methodology are the same for both mature and high-growth and start-up businesses, there generally is an increased level of subjectivity in the case of the latter two.

Chapter 6
Asset Valuation Methodologies

Introduction

Through the 1990's increasingly less emphasis has been placed on underlying net tangible asset values than was the case in the past, and ever increasing emphasis has been placed on the perceived ability of a business to generate cash flows in accord with forecasts. This trend has arisen largely out of ongoing technological change, and the resultant technology driven evolution of the corporate mosaic in recent years from one substantively comprised of 'bricks and mortar', to a greater representation of service and technology companies where human capital plays a comparatively greater role.

Having said that, financial statements for most businesses are prepared based on historic cost, as required pursuant to Generally Accepted Accounting Principles. As a result, equity as stated in financial statements may be considerably different than equity based on the current market values of the underlying net assets of the business. In open market transactions purchasers and vendors typically weight the current market values of underlying net tangible net assets (i.e. tangible assets less liabilities) when negotiating the price of the outstanding shares of a business or its net assets. In a notional market context the balance sheet of the business at the valuation date generally should be adjusted to reflect the market values in use (i.e. going concern values) of the underlying tangible assets and liabilities of the business. The result derived commonly is referred to as the adjusted net book value or the net tangible asset backing of the business. In some circumstances, net tangible asset backing serves as a risk measurement tool. The difference between going concern value determined pursuant to a cash flow (or earnings) based valuation methodology and net tangible asset backing often is referred to as going concern risk. Frequently where a business has substantial assets of a non-current nature, adjusted net book value estimates are subject to wide variation depending on the assumptions adopted and analysis with respect to the respective fair market values of the individual underlying assets.

Occasionally adjusted net book value is used as a primary basis of determining business value. As a practical matter, the use of the adjusted net book value methodology as the principal determinant of value generally is restricted to holding companies whose value is comprised of a 'collection of individual assets'. Holding companies are those that do not carry on an active business themselves, but rather invest in various assets and businesses that may include income producing real estate, shares of privately held or publicly held companies, and so on. In such circumstances a holding company's adjusted net book value indirectly may include intangible value pursuant to the valuation of a subsidiary.

This Chapter discusses the derivation of adjusted net book value (or net tangible asset backing). It also discusses the valuation of commercial real estate and equipment. The Chapter concludes with a discussion of the application of the adjusted net book value valuation methodology in holding company valuation.

Adjusted Net Book Value

Overview

The adjusted net book value (or net tangible asset backing) underlying the outstanding equity of a business is determined by adjusting shareholder's equity as stated in the financial statements as follows:

- add (deduct) the amount by which the greater of the market value or depreciated replacement value (or 'value in use' if different from depreciated replacement value) of each of the business' tangible asset pools exceeds (is less than) their respective book values;
- deduct (add) the amount by which the market value of the business' liabilities exceeds (is less than) their respective book values;
- deduct the book value of intangible assets;
- add (deduct) the portion of deferred income tax credits (debits) that appropriately should be reclassified as business equity; and
- deduct (add) the present value of the capital cost allowance tax shield not available to a purchaser of shares (as contrasted to that available to a purchaser of the underlying net assets of the business).

ASSET VALUATION METHODOLOGIES

Schematically, the calculation is as follows:

EXHIBIT 6.1

> Shareholder's Equity per Financial Statements

Add

> Greater of Market Value or Depreciated Replacement Value (or Value in Use if Different from Depreciated Replacement Value) of Tangible Assets

Add

> Book Value of Liabilities

Add (Deduct)

> Deferred Income Tax Credits (Debits) Appropriately Reclassified as Equity

Deduct

> - Net Book Value of Tangible Assets
> - Net Book Value of Intangible Assets
> - Market Value of Liabilities
> - Present Value of CCA Tax Shield not Available to a Purchaser of Shares

Equals

> Adjusted Net Book Value

Asset values in an adjusted net book value calculation are premised on a going concern assumption. That is, their values are determined based on their net contribution to the business assuming continued use as opposed to value in exchange. The essential difference between value in use and value in exchange in this context is that value in use:

- reflects the net cash inflows accruing from asset utilization; and
- includes all installation and start-up costs.

In the context of adjusted net book value, value in use is never less than value in exchange.

Current Assets

At any given point in time adjustments to the book value of current assets may be required where:

- marketable securities are included in current assets and their book value is greater or less than their aggregate current market value;
- book value represents a significant overstatement or understatement of the going concern value of accounts receivable or inventories; and
- the book value of other current assets (such as mortgages receivable, notes receivable, and so on) are materially different than their market values when considered in terms of payment and collectibility.

Fixed Assets

When determining the going concern value of fixed assets such as land, building, machinery and equipment, it may be necessary to obtain the opinions of real estate and equipment valuers. In a notional market context these assets typically are valued as follows:

- market value for vacant land;
- the greater of market value and value in use for land and buildings which form part of the business' operations. Value in use for the building often is taken to be depreciated replacement value; and
- the greater of value in use. (generally taken as depreciated replacement value plus installation costs), or market value for equipment and other fixed assets employed in the business.

The valuation of real estate and equipment is discussed later in this Chapter.

Intangible Assets

Where a business accounts for intangible assets resulting from goodwill, deferred charges, and so on that are not separately identifiable from the business itself, such intangibles are assigned a nil value for the purpose of computing adjusted net book value.

Where a business has identifiable intangible assets resulting from royalty agreements, patents, licenses, and so on, these may form part of adjusted net book value where a value can be meaningfully developed for these assets in isolation. Where separately valued, identifiable intangible assets normally are valued using a discounted cash flow methodology, based on the discretionary cash flows that arise pursuant to the use of that asset, that are believed incremental to the discretionary cash flows the business would generate in the absence of that asset.

As a practical matter, it seldom is possible to isolate the discretionary cash flows that arise due to the use of a particular intangible asset. Therefore, in most cases, identifiable intangible assets are not reflected as a component of adjusted net book value, rather their value is incorporated in the catch-all category of 'goodwill'.

Liabilities

Liabilities other than deferred liabilities generally are taken at face value, although in circumstances where interest rates on existing debt differ from interest rates prevailing at the valuation date a compensating adjustment to debt principal may be required.

Deferred revenues represent liabilities for future goods or services and, assuming a continuing going concern, normally will be earned in due course. Accordingly, deferred revenue accounts usually are not adjusted where the goods and services have not yet been provided.

Deferred pension liabilities may exist where there is defined benefit pension plan for employees. The deferred liability represents a non-identifiable intangible which should be assigned a nil value. However, adjusted net book value should be increased (decreased) by the tax effected excess (deficiency) of the market value of the pension fund assets over the estimated present value of the actuarial liabilities of the pension plan. This information normally is disclosed in the notes to the financial statements. Pursuant to a going concern assumption, a pension surplus represents the approximate present value of the pension contribution savings. The net surplus (deficiency) should be tax-effected where contributions to a pension plan are deductible for income tax purposes. In addition, the business may offer other post-employment benefits to is former employees that also should be considered when determining the completeness of its liabilities.

Finally, the notes to the financial statements should be reviewed for off-balance sheet financing, contingencies, commitments, and other 'hidden' liabilities. The adjusted net book value methodology should incorporate a reduction for those 'hidden' liabilities (or should be increased for 'hidden assets') where appropriate.

Deferred Income Taxes

Analysis of deferred tax credits (or debits) is required to determine the:

- basis for the deferred tax account, which typically relates to differences in timing between reporting revenue and claiming expenses for accounting and income tax purposes; and
- probability of the deferred tax account reversing in the foreseeable future.

In general, where all or part of the deferred tax liability (asset) is not expected to reverse in the foreseeable future, some or all of it may represent an 'equity equivalent' for purposes of adjusted net book value determination. In theory, the amount of 'equity equivalent' should be determined as the book value of the deferred income tax credit less the present value of future income taxes calculated on the basis of when the timing differences that gave rise to it are expected to reverse. Where adjusted net book value is reduced by the present value of the CCA tax shield not available to an acquirer of shares, the deferred income taxes relating to those assets should be added to adjusted net book value.

Income Tax Considerations

In most cases, when calculating the market value or value in use of assets within a business when determining net tangible asset value or otherwise, no deduction is made for income taxes that might arise due to income tax 'recapture of depreciation' or tax on capital gains on their notional disposition. However:

- as discussed later in this Chapter, in some circumstances income taxes appropriately may be considered where a business interest is held by a holding company;
- where assets are deemed redundant, an adjustment for income taxes may be appropriate; and

- an adjustment for income taxes generally is required when value is ascribed to the underlying net assets and not the outstanding shares of a business. This adjustment largely is attributable to income tax considerations related to undepreciated capital cost allowance balances.

An adjusted net book value determination used to aid in share valuation must consider the existing income tax cost base of depreciable assets underlying the shares. Assets depreciable for income tax purposes (e.g. buildings, machinery and equipment) typically are appraised on a free and clear basis without consideration of either debt registered against the asset or particulars of the overlying corporate ownership structure. Accordingly, such appraised values implicitly assume an undepreciated capital cost allowance equivalent to the appraised value. This is the case because the real estate or equipment appraiser's value conclusions inherently assume it is the asset that will be sold, including all future ownership benefits, which includes the ability to claim capital cost allowance on the purchase price. While this assumption generally is correct where the underlying net assets of a corporation are acquired directly, it is not correct where the shares of a corporation are acquired and:

- the existing tax pools, including the balances of undepreciated capital cost, 'flow through' to the acquirer; and
- post-acquisition capital cost allowance claims are based on the existing tax values at the date of acquisition.

It follows that where shares are valued, when determining adjusted net book value an adjustment may be necessary to reflect the value of the capital cost allowance tax shield inherent in fixed asset appraisals that would not be available to an acquirer of shares.

Example of the Adjusted Net Book Value Methodology

Assumed Facts

Esco Construction Limited (ECL) is a construction and roadwork contractor. ECL contracts on both government and private jobs. Competition is intense, and the contract is almost always awarded to the lowest bidder. ECL's balance sheet and asset values for its most recent fiscal year ending October 31, 2000 are as follows:

SCHEDULE 6.1

Esco Construction Limited
Balance Sheet at October 31, 2000
($000)

Current assets	8,524
Fixed assets (schedule)	4,553
Goodwill	783
Total assets	13,860
Current liabilities	5,811
Deferred income taxes	711
Long term debt	3,450
Total liabilities	9,972
Shareholder equity	3,888
Total liabilities & equity	13,860

Additional information related to ECL's fixed assets, goodwill and liabilities, including estimated current market value and value in use, is as follows:

SCHEDULE 6.2

Esco Construction Limited
Asset Valuation Schedule
At October 31, 2000
($000)

	Original Cost	Accum. Dep'n	Net Book Value	Undep. Capital Cost	CCA Rate	Estimated Market Value	Estimated Value in Use
Land	245		245	n/a		500	400
Building	420	(222)	198	217	4%	450	300
Construction equipment	8,432	(4,650)	3,782	2,266	30%	5,000	6,500
Office furniture	461	(133)	328	246	20%	300	300
	9,558	(5,005)	4,553	2,729		6,250	7,500

In addition, ECL's cumulative eligible capital (CEC) balance relating to 'acquired' goodwill is $727,000.

ECL's tax rate is 45%. An appropriate after-tax weighted average cost of capital is 10%. The entire deferred income tax balance is related to timing differences between CCA and accounting depreciation.

Adjusted Net Book Value Determination

The adjusted net book value of the shares of ECL then would be determined as follows:

SCHEDULE 6.3

Esco Construction Limited
Adjusted Net Book Value Calculation
At October 31, 2000
$(000)

	Current Value	Book Value	Gross Increment	CCA Rate	CCA tax shield	Net Increment
Land	500	245	255			255
Building	450	198	252	4%	(27)	225
Construction equipment	6,500	3,782	2,718	30%	(1,329)	1,389
Office furniture	300	328	(28)	20%	(12)	(40)
Goodwill	0	783	(783)	7%	101	(682)
Deferred income taxes						711
						1,858
Add: book value of equity						3,888
Estimated adjusted net book value						5,746

Adjusted net book value is determined by first analyzing the assets and liabilities which have a current value that is different from their respective book values. For the fixed assets, current value is the greater of market value or value in use, without consideration of disposition costs. Goodwill is assigned a nil value because it is a non-identifiable intangible asset. Deferred income taxes are added back because tax and accounting timing differences are accounted for as part of the income tax shield calculation. The amount by which the current values exceed the book values of the tangible assets and liabilities is the aggregate net tangible asset value restatement.

Because it is shares and not net assets that are being valued, an adjustment for the capital cost allowance tax shield not available to an acquirer of shares is made for the depreciable fixed assets — see Chapter 4. For example, in the case of construction equipment, this is determined as ($000):

$$\boxed{\text{CCA to an acquirer of assets}} \quad \text{less} \quad \boxed{\text{CCA to an acquirer of shares}}$$

$$\frac{6{,}500 \times 45\% \times 30\%}{(10\% + 30\%)} \times \frac{[1 + (0.5 \times 10\%)]}{(1 + 10\%)} - \frac{2{,}266 \times 45\% \times 30\%}{(10\% + 30\%)} \text{ equals } \$1{,}329$$

Note that the 'half-year rule' is incorporated in this calculation on the assumption that an acquirer of assets would be subject to one half of the CCA claim in the year of acquisition. Conversely, an acquirer of shares is not subject to that restriction. The $101,000 adjustment for goodwill reflects the present value of the tax shield of the existing CEC balance ($727,000) that would be available to an acquirer of shares.

The gross increment less the CCA tax shield not available to an acquirer of shares plus the present value of the CEC tax shield results in the net incremental value of those depreciable assets. The sum of the net incremental values is $1,858,000. The net value increment is added to the book value of ECL's equity. This implies that all other assets have market values which approximate their book values. The result is an estimated adjusted net book value for ECL of $5,746,000.

Real Estate Valuation

Overview

Real estate values commonly are required in the valuation of business interests in the context of the development of adjusted net book value, value in use values, adjusted net book value and liquidation value. The valuation of real estate assets often requires the assistance of a qualified real estate valuer. When accredited real estate valuers determine real estate values in a notional market context they typically:

- adopt a pre-tax rate of return which represents a blend of debt and equity and is applied to the unlevered pre-tax cash flow of the property, as contrasted with an after-tax weighted average cost of capital applied to discretionary (after-tax) cash flow, in their discounted cash flow or capitalization of cash flow value methodologies. In the context of real estate valuation, the

pretax rate of return adopted normally is influenced to some degree by the observed rates of return believed applicable to so-called 'comparable' real estate properties; and
- assume value in the context of an asset transaction, as contrasted with a share transaction. That is, inherent in most notional market real estate opinions is a stated or implied assumption of a 'step-up' in undepreciated capital cost of the depreciable portion of the real estate asset to current market value.

The assessment of real estate properties held by a particular business can sometimes lead to the identification of redundant assets not previously identified. For example, assume that Company P operates a commercial printing business. It owns the land and buildings utilized by it in its operations. The market value of the land and building is $1,500,000. Company A is interested in acquiring all of the outstanding shares of Company P. Management of Company A assesses potential acquisitions based on a 12% after tax rate of return requirement. When determining the price it is prepared to offer for the outstanding shares of Company P, management of Company A has not distinguished between the lower risk attaching to the real estate component of Company P's assets, and the higher risk attaching to the non-real estate assets. The shareholders of Company P feel the price offered is inadequate, and suggest that they would be prepared to remove Company P's real estate assets from Company P prior to sale and lease them to Company P at an annual net rental of $175,000 pursuant to a long term lease. Such a rental expense would reduce Company P's prospective annual operating cash flow by $105,000, assuming a corporate income tax rate of 40% ($175,000 x [1-40%]). Assuming management of Company A does not adjust its required rate of return to compensate for non-ownership of the real estate assets, Company A's offering price would be reduced by approximately $875,000 ($105,000 capitalized at a 12% capitalization rate). Aside from possible personal income tax deferral advantages the vendor shareholders collectively would have succeeded in increasing price by approximately $625,000 ($1,500,000 - $875,000), assuming that income taxes and disposition costs on the property are deferred indefinitely.

In this example it is assumed the acquirer did not recognize the relatively low after tax return relative to an investment in real estate versus the rate of return applicable to the business operations. In theory it should do this, and adjust its composite rate of return accordingly. However, in the open market, this segregation of 'business' and real estate assets often results in a higher aggregate 'price' paid to the vendor. This particularly is the case where the vendor is able to utilize a tax-free rollover to segregate the real estate assets, thereby deferring the income tax consequences and retaining an inflation hedge.

The determination of the going concern value of real estate generally is satisfied through an estimate of either market value or 'value in use'. The Appraisal Institute of Canada defines market value as:

> 'The most probable price which a property should bring in a competitive and open market under all conditions requisite to a fair sale, the buyer and seller each acting prudently and knowledgeably, and assuming the price is not affected by undue stimulus.'

Implicit in this definition is the assumption of a sale and passing of title at the valuation date under conditions whereby:

- neither the buyer nor seller are unusually motivated;
- the buyer and seller both are well informed, well advised, and acting in their respective best interests;
- the property has been exposed to the market for a reasonable time; and
- payment is made in cash or cash equivalent.

The market value of real estate generally is taken to mean the greater of 'value in exchange' or 'depreciated replacement value' where incorporated in business value being developed pursuant to a going concern assumption. Where such real estate has special characteristics and is an important part in the operation of the business, a going concern value measure may involve an estimate of 'value in use' or 'special use value'. For example, a business that manufactures hazardous materials might be required to ensure that its manufacturing facilities conform to applicable standards set for explosion-proofing, and may incur significant costs to upgrade its facilities to those standards. Such improvements would have value to the hazardous materials manufacturer, but not to a manufacturer of non-hazardous products.

'Value in use' generally is determined pursuant to a cash flow based valuation methodology. As a practical matter, it often is difficult to segregate the cash flows associated with a special use property from those of the business as a whole. As a result, depreciated replacement cost often is adopted as the appropriate measure of 'value' for special use properties.

Where the business being valued is not a going concern, value in exchange (or market value) normally is adopted as the appropriate measure of real estate value. Market value typically is determined based on the 'highest and best use' of the property. Market value usually is determined on the assumption that the property is free and clear of all encumbrances and possible encumbrances, including unidentified contingent environmental liabilities. Where there are known environmental liabilities these either are considered in the value determination, or the value determination is qualified in that regard.

Three methodologies are commonly employed when determining the market value or 'value in use' of real property. These are the:

- depreciated replacement cost methodology;
- direct comparison methodology; and
- capitalization of cash flow methodology (often referred to as the 'income approach' by real estate valuers).

Varying valuation estimates can result from application of each methodology. In practice, real estate valuers often use all three methodologies concurrently and compare, and sometimes blend, the results when reaching notional real estate value conclusions. The nature of the property and purpose of the valuation should govern the selection of the approach(es) to be relied upon. As a general rule, for income producing properties the capitalization of cash flow methodology is preferred. On the other hand, the depreciated replacement cost methodology may be appropriate to develop the going concern value of a special use property utilized in the operation of a viable ongoing business. The direct comparison methodology is useful as a primary methodology for non-income producing properties where there is significant commonality of property characteristics and numerous transactions (such as single family dwellings). However, in the valuation of commercial and industrial properties the direct comparison methodology typically is best used to test values determined pursuant to the capitalization of cash flow methodology, and to a lesser extent the depreciated replacement cost methodology.

Depreciated Replacement Cost Methodology

Depreciation theory referable to buildings and other improvements is founded on the general concept that there is a loss or decrease in the present worth of physical building and improvements with the passage of time. In this sense, it is different from the accounting concept of depreciation which allocates costs rather than estimating value. The three main depreciation categories are:

- physical deterioration, which is a reduction in utility resulting from an impairment of physical conditions (i.e. 'wear-and-tear');

- economic (locational) obsolescence, which is the loss in the value in use of a property arising from factors external to the property, such as economic forces or environment changes, which affect market supply/demand relationships; and
- functional (or technological) obsolescence, which is the loss in value brought about by such factors as inefficiency, inadequacy, and other changes that affect the property, or the ability of a structure to adequately perform its function. Functional obsolescence may result from structural deficiencies, or over-building that a purchaser or owner would not be justified in replacing, adding, or removing.

Having said that, the depreciated replacement cost methodology is comprised of four steps:

- the value of the site (i.e. the land) is estimated as though vacant. This normally is completed pursuant to the direct comparison methodology;
- an estimate is made of the cost of replacing the building and site improvements (sewer system, paving, fencing, and so on) with a new identical building and site improvements;
- a depreciation factor is deducted from the replacement cost of the new identical building and site improvements to reflect the current condition and status of the building and site improvements on the subject property. In this regard, the depreciation factor normally is comprised of physical depreciation, economic obsolescence, and functional depreciation; and
- the estimated vacant site value then is added to the estimated depreciated replacement cost of the property to derive depreciated replacement value.

Physical and economic depreciation estimates are based to a considerable degree on judgement. Accordingly, an estimate of depreciated replacement cost may require the assistance of qualified experts in real estate, construction and engineering, particularly where special use properties are involved.

The depreciated replacement cost methodology often is the only method available for valuing single use or special use properties. However, because costs constantly change, building cost estimates may not be accurate. Further, due to building age and quality of estimates, depreciation cannot be precisely measured, especially as buildings get older. Finally, as a practical matter there may be circumstances where the depreciated replacement cost approach may not adequately reflect market conditions.

Direct Comparison Methodology

The direct comparison methodology involves comparing sales and listings of properties believed similar enough to the property being valued to make comparisons meaningful. The principal difficulties encountered in this approach are identifying properties that in fact are comparable in a meaningful way, assessing the degree of their respective comparability, and adjusting for the differences, if any, which exist. The basic elements of comparison that normally are relevant in direct comparison analysis include:

- real property rights conveyed;
- financing terms;
- conditions of sale (i.e. whether special motivation exists);
- market conditions (time);
- location;
- physical characteristics;
- economic characteristics;
- environmental contaminants;
- use (zoning); and
- non-realty components of value.

Advantages of the direct sales comparison methodology are that it is easily understood, publicly available market data generally is readily available, it is an approach accepted by many Courts, and, depending on the specific property being valued, to varying degrees it may reflect actual market behaviour. The primary disadvantage of this methodology is the difficulty in finding meaningfully comparable property transactions given:

- variations in the way the buyer and seller may have weighted the above-noted factors; and
- what generally is a lack of fact specific transaction knowledge with respect to those factors, as well as the specific factors that influenced negotiations between the purchaser and the vendor. As a rule, any attempt to adjust for such differences necessarily involves what are often uninformed and subjective estimates.

The direct comparison methodology may be of assistance when valuing houses and vacant land in larger urban centres where there is an active market and numerous transactions involving a multiplicity of broadly similar properties. It generally is less useful when determining the value of special use properties, properties located in areas where few comparables are available, and commercial and industrial properties traded for their income producing capabilities. Where there are special interest purchasers for a subject property, the applicability of the direct comparison methodology generally is limited. Notwithstanding, in many instances use of this methodology enables 'benchmarking', or 'testing' of value for all types of property, and may assist in identifying relevant considerations not readily apparent – thereby assisting in developing sounder value conclusions pursuant to other methodologies.

Cash Flow Real Estate Valuation Methodologies

Pursuant to the cash flow methodology utilized to develop value for real estate, value is determined as the present value of all future expected net cash flows. As is the case with business valuation, the valuation of income producing real estate normally is best assessed based on discretionary cash flow rather than income. If adopted at all, an income-based methodology should be utilized only where prospective income for accounting purposes approximates prospective discretionary cash flow.

The two principal methods employed in the valuation of income-producing real estate are the operating cash flow capitalization methodology and the discounted cash flow methodology. The basic elements of these two approaches are similar to the capitalization of discretionary cash flow methodology and the discounted cash flow methodology adopted in business valuation. However, real estate industry practice, particularly in a notional market context, generally has been to value income producing real estate utilizing pre-tax cash flow, where pre-tax cash flows are subjected to pre-tax discount and capitalization rates. The principal rationale for adopting a pre-tax approach in a notional market context is that the market for real estate properties is comprised of purchasers subject to varying, and generally unknown, income tax rates. In an actual real estate market context, purchasers make purchase offer decisions based on their perceptions of both the prospective discretionary cash flow they anticipate from the real estate property, and their expected future income tax rates.

When estimating the quantum of pre-tax cash flows to capitalize (or discount) for an income producing property the following things should be considered:

- historic operating results, including non-recurring and unusual revenues and expenses;

- the physical condition and general attractiveness of the property. This includes consideration of the amount of sustaining capital reinvestment, lease inducements, and whether any one time improvements are required. An estimate of sustaining capital normally is deducted when determining discretionary cash flow or pretax cash flow;
- the composition of the tenant base. For retail, industrial and office premises, this includes the type of tenants, their financial stability, the amount of space they occupy, the duration and terms of the lease, and expected vacancy rates. For residential properties, considerations may include the demographics of the tenant base (age, income, marital status), tenant turnover, and expected vacancy rates; and
- prospective property management fees appropriately deducted when determining discretionary cash flow.

When determining appropriate capitalization or discount rates for an income producing property, the following things should be considered:

- the ability to finance the acquisition with debt, and to what degree;
- the rates of return imputed from recent sales of what are believed to be 'comparable' properties;
- the age, location and physical condition of the property;
- relevant legal considerations (rent control, zoning, and so on);
- the stability of prospective cash flows; and
- general and local economic conditions prevailing at the valuation date.

Real Estate Valuation Example

Palace Place is a 200 unit, one and two bedroom apartment complex located in Regina, Saskatchewan. The property enjoys an attractive location and a stable tenant base. The building is 15 years old. Its electrical, heating, ventilating and air conditioning systems have been kept up to date and are well maintained, as has been and are the building structure, lobbies, elevators and common areas. The roof is in need of repair, which is expected to cost $500,000 (in present value terms) over the next two years. Other facts are:

- the average rental rate is $700 per month;
- the historical vacancy rate is 5%, which is expected to continue at that level;
- operating expenses are approximately $700,000 per annum;
- annual required refurbishments (painting, appliances, and so on) average $300 per unit;

- a management fee of 4% of gross income is considered appropriate; and
- inflation is expected to be in the order of 2% for the foreseeable future.

A potential buyer, Residential Realty Inc. (RRI) has a pre-tax nominal hurdle rate of 13% (being a real pre-tax hurdle rate of 11%) for this type of property. Based on the foregoing, RRI would estimate the market value of Palace Place at approximately $6,500,000 as follows:

SCHEDULE 6.4

Palace Place
Estimate of Market Value
(figures rounded)

Gross potential income	200 suites @ $700 / month	$1,680,000
less: vacancy allowance	5% of gross potential income	84,000
Effective gross income		1,596,000
Operating expenses	Fixed	700,000
Refurbishments	$300 / unit / annum	60,000
Management fee	4% of effective gross income	64,000
Net operating income		772,000
Capitalization rate		11%
Capitalized value	Rounded	7,000,000
less: one time costs	Roof repairs (present value)	500,000
Estimated market value		$6,500,000

Apportionment Between Land and Building

When the property being valued includes both land and building (or some other physical structure) because the building portion is eligible for capital cost allowance and the land portion is not, it generally is necessary to apportion the aggregate property value between the two components. The allocation of aggregate property value between land and building necessarily involves analysis and judgement. In general, the allocation should be determined based on considerations including:

- recent sales of 'comparable' vacant land in the area, where meaningful;

- alternate uses available for the land, based on its size, zoning and prospective or possible zoning;
- the estimated depreciated replacement cost of the facilities, excluding the land component; and
- insured values, where it is believed the property and insurance risk managers have objectively valued the building component for insurance purposes.

Where both purchaser and vendor are taxable entities, the purchaser generally seeks to have a greater portion of value assigned to the building component in order to claim higher capital cost allowance. On the other hand, the vendor generally seeks a greater apportionment to the land component in order to convert recapture of tax depreciation to capital gains, thereby reducing income tax that otherwise would be payable.

Equipment Valuation

When valuing business interests, independent assessment of equipment values sometimes is required pursuant to the development of sustaining capital reinvestment, adjusted net book value, value in use value, and liquidation value. The various bases for valuing equipment include:

- replacement cost new, defined as:
  - for non-custom built assets, the cost of an equivalent new asset of similar capacity, utility and current technology as available from manufacturers, suppliers and distributors, on a lowest available price basis, plus installation costs, and
  - for custom-build assets, the current cost to replace similar or reasonably similar assets of equivalent utility, as obtained from custom designers and cost engineers or as established utilizing quantitative valuation procedures, plus installation costs;
- depreciated replacement cost, defined as replacement cost new, less an allowance for accumulated depreciation evidenced by the observed condition of the asset compared with new like units having regard to existing physical and functional (technological) deterioration;
- value in use, normally defined as the present value of discretionary cash flows expected to accrue from use of the equipment. An estimate of value in use normally is restricted to special use equipment essential to the ongoing business operations. Value in use may exceed the replacement cost new

of identical equipment. As a practical matter, it generally is difficult to segregate discretionary cash flows that accrue from specific special use equipment from the business' aggregate discretionary cash flows; and
- liquidation value, defined as the aggregate gross sales proceeds expected from the sale of the assets at auction, where it is assumed:
  — the assets are sold on an assembled 'as is, where is' basis,
  — the assets are removed for offsite use,
  — sales are completed within a short time period (normally three to twelve months) from the valuation date; and
  — market conditions will remain constant during the liquidation period.

Liquidation value can be further categorized as being either a 'forced' liquidation or an 'orderly' liquidation. A forced liquidation generally occurs pursuant to a Court Order (or some other order) that arises on the insolvency of a business, and is overseen by a trustee. An orderly liquidation normally is presumed to take place under more favourable circumstances, such as the voluntary wind-up and dissolution of a business. It generally is assumed that the net proceeds generated on an orderly liquidation will exceed those of a forced liquidation, although this is not always the case. Liquidation value is further discussed in Chapter 10.

Generally, where:

- adjusted net book value is determined, equipment values are based on replacement cost new or depreciated replacement cost; and
- the liquidation value of a business is determined, orderly and forced liquidation values generally are most applicable.

When determining liquidation value, equipment valuers normally consider:

- prospective market prices for similar used equipment;
- the time value of money over the liquidation period;
- continuing operating costs, including overhead costs that may be incurred during the liquidation period;
- bulk sales or other taxes, and broker's and dealer's fees, that will arise on the sale of the assets; and
- additional costs to remove, dismantle and transport the assets that will be incurred by the vendor.

In addition, liquidation value normally takes into account corporate income tax consequences (including recapture, capital gains, terminal losses, and so on) that will arise on disposition of the assets (see Chapter 10). Both orderly and forced liquidation values are estimated on the basis of value in exchange, where assets are sold on an 'as is, where is' basis. Where the assets are not in working order, they may have to be sold at a combination of:

- salvage value, for those parts that can be salvaged; and
- scrap value, where the remainder of the assets that can be sold only for their material component.

The various equipment valuation methodologies and their application in business valuation can be summarized as follows:

EXHIBIT 6.2

Equipment Valued Based On

Liquidation		Going Concern Value	
		Replacement Cost New	or
			Value In Use
		Depreciated Replacement Cost	
	Orderly Liquidation Value		
Forced Liquidation	or		

Holding Companies

Overview

A holding company generally is thought of as one that carries on no active business of its own, but whose principal activity is investment in various other assets. Alternately, a company that operates two or more businesses as divisions (which it might do for business risk hedge or income tax purposes) might be referred to as a holding company. As such, the assets of holding companies may include:

- marketable securities including publicly traded shares and fixed income securities;
- two or more distinct operating divisions (see Chapter 4 — 'Multi-divisional Businesses');
- a controlling or minority interest in one or more privately or publicly held companies; and
- real estate assets, which might include income properties (apartment buildings, hotels, shopping centres, office buildings), vacant land, or land under development.

Earnings generated by a holding company (in the form of rent or dividends for example) normally are less significant from a value perspective than is the appreciating value of the underlying investments themselves. Accordingly, holding companies typically are valued pursuant to the adjusted net book value methodology where each asset, investment, or division separately is valued on a market or going concern value basis as appropriate. As a result, holding companies generally are valued as a 'collection of individual assets' such that no intangible value (or goodwill) exists within the holding company itself. However, the en bloc value of the outstanding shares of a holding company indirectly may incorporate intangible value where it exists in one or more of its investee companies or divisions.

Marketable Securities

In a holding company context, non-controlling marketable securities generally are valued in a manner similar to that adopted for redundant assets in an operating company. That is, the gross value of marketable securities is based on the prevailing market price at the valuation date. From this amount, notional disposition costs (which from a practical standpoint normally are not significant) and income taxes on notional capital gains and losses generally are accounted for. Where a holding company controls a public company, the en bloc value of the outstanding shares of that public company typically must be valued, with the value of the holding company's shareholding in turn being determined. Depending on circumstances, disposition and income tax costs may be discounted to reflect the uncertainty as to the timing of sale — see Chapter 4. Where the market value of securities exceeds their adjusted cost base, some amount for income tax on the notional capital gain normally is deducted at the corporate level. However, whether or not the income tax recovery related to a notional capital loss is used to reduce a shortfall of market value from the cost base of an asset is fact specific. Normally a marketable securities portfolio is considered as a whole, and losses on individual securities serve to offset gains on others. Income tax recoveries related to net capital losses also are recognized where offsetting capital gains from other sources (such as a business investment or real estate property) exist. Where capital losses exceed capital gains, value normally is not attributed to the excess given that capital losses can only be applied against capital gains without carry back.

The income tax rate used to calculate the notional tax liability normally should be the corporate income tax rate on capital gains, inclusive of any refundable tax component. As explained in Chapter 14, Canada has an 'integrated income tax system' which is intended to provide shareholders of a Canadian Controlled Private Corporation ('CCPC') the same after tax amounts whether investments are held directly or through a holding company. At the time of writing, refundable income taxes are 20% of the corporate base rate plus an additional 6 2/3% in respect of 'additional refundable tax'. Refundable taxes of $1 paid by a CCPC are returned to it for every $3 in dividends paid to its shareholders. However, because income taxes are calculated only at the corporate level in a business valuation or pricing exercise, the pre-refund rate (normally in excess of 50%) is used in the income tax calculation. Where a Canadian holding company does not qualify as a CCPC, the refundable tax system does not apply.

Investments in Operating Companies or Divisions

Where a holding company owns a controlling interest in one or more operating companies or owns operating divisions, those investment(s) normally should be valued using a cash flow based (or other) going concern valuation methodology. This generally also is the case where a holding company owns a minority interest in a privately held company, although fact specific circumstances may dictate otherwise. In the case of minority interests, a discount for non-control or discount for illiquidity may be appropriate — see Chapter 13.

When the estimated value of such business interest(s) exceeds the tax cost base thereof, a notional capital gain results. Whether or not income taxes are deducted depends on the prevailing circumstances. As a general rule, where a holding company owns 90% or more of the outstanding common shares of an operating business income taxes are not deducted. This is because a holding company is able to wind-up the subsidiary operating company on a tax-deferred basis, and subsequently operate the business as an unincorporated division of the parent company. However, whether an indefinite tax deferral is assumed is fact specific and dependent on:

- whether the holding company is expected to operate 'as is' for the foreseeable future;
- the other assets and liabilities owned by the holding company. Where these are immaterial, a wind-up into the holding company may be practical;
- whether the holding company or operating company has litigation outstanding that upon wind-up of the subsidiary into the holding company would expose other assets to litigation risk; and
- the practicality of wind-up given factors such as minority shareholder appraisal and oppression rights — see Chapter 12.

Where a holding company owns a minority interest in one or more operating companies, or where a tax-free wind-up of a 90% or more owned operating business is not practical, income taxes normally are deducted on any notional capital gain amount. Income taxes payable frequently are discounted having regard to:

- the uncertainty as to the timing of the disposition of the underlying operating businesses, which reduces the income tax burden on a present value basis;
- the amount of 'safe income' available in the operating business to the holding company. As explained in Chapter 14, safe income can serve to defer a gain on the sale of a subsidiary company by payment of a tax free dividend to the holding company up to the amount of the subsidiary's safe income, thereby reducing the subsequent sale price of the operating business; and
- other tax planning opportunities, such as unused capital losses at the holding company level.

Real Estate Assets

Income Properties

As discussed earlier in this Chapter, income properties (such as apartment buildings, shopping centres, hotels, office buildings, and so on) held by a holding company for investment purposes typically are valued using cash flow methodologies supplemented by asset based methodologies. Income taxes may be deducted depending on fact specific circumstances including the number of income properties held, and whether other operating businesses are owned directly or indirectly by the holding company.

Where income properties held for investment are not of material value in comparison to the holding company's interest in operating businesses, the income property likely would be valued as if redundant. In such circumstances, income tax typically is deducted at the corporate level based on the notional amount of recapture of capital cost allowance previously taken and tax on capital gains that would result on disposition. Disposition costs and income taxes may be discounted where there is uncertainty as to the timing of disposition. Where such a holding company is a Canadian Controlled Private Corporation and a notional capital gain is realized, the refundable tax component should be incorporated into the effective income tax rate.

A complication arises where the income property derives a significant portion of its rental revenues from a related business. In such circumstances:

- where rental amounts are not reflective of market rates they should be restated, with appropriate adjustments being made when valuing both the income property and the operating business; and
- whether the income property is viewed as a redundant asset depends on factors such as:
  - to what extent the premises are occupied by arm's length third parties; and
  - whether the property is integral to the operating business.

Where income properties are valued on the assumption of an asset sale and represent the holding company's principal assets, an adjustment for income taxes normally is made to account for the capital cost allowance tax shield not available to an acquirer of shares — see Chapter 4. However, income taxes normally are not deducted on the notional disposition of the property (properties) as a whole.

Where a holding company owns a portfolio of investment properties, consideration should be given to whether they would be sold en bloc. Where the portfolio of assets is diverse (either due to the nature of the properties or geographic location) a purchaser may be interested in only one or a subset of the properties. Where this likely is the case, consideration should be given to income taxes that would be incurred pursuant to a sale of the investment properties to different purchasers. Specifically:

- if one or more of the underlying real estate assets is sold, recapture and capital gains or losses might result; or
- if one or more of the properties is spun off on a tax-deferred basis to a newly incorporated subsidiary of the holding company, then:
  — the value of the shares of the newly formed subsidiary would have to reflect the flow through of the existing tax base of said property(ies), and
  — a capital gain may result on the disposition of the shares of the newly formed subsidiary.

The income tax liability otherwise determined pursuant to the sale of a diverse portfolio of properties normally would be discounted to reflect the uncertainty as to the timing of disposition of the properties, and other tax planning opportunities where available. The quantification of this discount, if any, will vary depending on the fact specific circumstances.

Vacant Land

Where a holding company owns vacant land, the market value of the land usually is estimated based on benchmarks such as recent sales and listings of similar properties, adjusted for the unique characteristics of the particular parcel(s) of land held. In a holding company context, vacant land normally is viewed as a redundant asset. As such, disposition costs and income taxes (at the corporate level) typically are calculated and deducted on a similar basis as for marketable securities. Where specific development plans for the land exist, the amount of income tax deducted on any imputed income or capital gain should consider this.

Summary

The adjusted net book value (or net tangible asset backing) methodology consists of adjusting the equity of the business, as stated for accounting purposes, to reflect the market values of the business' underlying assets and liabilities. In this regard, assets and liabilities are valued based on their value in continued use (or market value, if greater), and adjustments are made where appropriate for income taxes where the overlying shares of the business are being valued as opposed to a valuation of net assets. Non-identifiable intangible assets such as deferred charges and accounting goodwill are assigned a nil value.

The importance attaching to the underlying net tangible and identifiable intangible assets of a business vis-à-vis the valuation conclusion varies in each case. Corporate acquirers typically place greater emphasis on the prospective discretionary cash flows a business is expected to generate as opposed to the value in use of its underlying net assets. Accordingly, the application of the adjusted net book value methodology as a principal valuation methodology normally is restricted to non-operating businesses (such as holding companies). The difference between going concern value developed pursuant to a cash flow based valuation methodology, and the net tangible assets of a business (including its identifiable intangible assets, where in unusual circumstances these can be quantified in isolation) sometimes is referred to as 'going concern risk', or more commonly, 'goodwill'.

Chapter 7
Capital Structure

Introduction

This Chapter discusses the factors generally considered when determining an 'appropriate' capital structure for the business being valued. This is a fundamental consideration in rate of return determination. The concepts of unlevered equity, levered equity and weighted average cost of capital are addressed in detail. Chapter 8 discusses the factors considered when developing an appropriate cost of equity, a principal component in the determination of discount and capitalization rates.

Determining the optimal capital structure for a given business has long been a topic of debate. In theory, the optimal capital structure of a business occurs at the point where the weighted average cost of capital (mix of debt and equity) of the business is minimized and reciprocally, shareholder value is maximized. In practice, it generally is impossible to determine that 'balance point' with certainty. As a result, most businesses have a range of debt/equity mix believed to represent a satisfactory balance between financial risk and shareholder wealth maximization.

In the context of a notional market valuation or open market transaction, it is always necessary to consider whether the existing capital structure is 'appropriate' based on the nature of both the business being valued, and the industry in which it competes. This task necessarily is subjective. However, where the existing capital structure of a business appears to be outside appropriate limits, adjustments should be made to 'normalize' the level of financial risk. This generally is accomplished by applying a weighted average cost of capital ('WACC') to discretionary cash flows determined before debt servicing costs, thereby developing 'enterprise value' from which existing interest bearing debt and equivalents are deducted to derive en bloc 'equity value'. This 'normalization' also can be achieved by making a notional adjustment to the balance sheet, although this approach is not commonly done. Pursuant to either approach, the levered cost of equity is affected.

Debt and equity assume various forms, including secured debt, unsecured debt, subordinated debt, convertible debt, participating debt, term preferred shares, and different classes of preferred and common shares. Each inherently embodies a unique combination of risk and return. For simplicity the capital structure discussion set out in this Chapter is for the most part restricted to conventional interest bearing debt and common share equity.

Enterprise Value v. Equity Value

The enterprise value of a business (also known as the 'debt-free' value) generally is defined as the market value of the equity of the business plus the market value of its interest bearing debt, net of cash. Enterprise value is determined by applying a capitalization or discount rate to discretionary cash flows determined before debt servicing costs. In this context debt servicing costs generally are defined as interest expense net of its related tax shield and changes (increases and decreases) in debt principal outstanding. The capitalization or discount rate applied is a weighted average cost of capital comprised of an 'appropriate' mix of debt and equity. The value so determined represents the aggregate value of the interest bearing debt (and equivalents) and equity of the business. The actual interest bearing debt outstanding at the valuation date (net of available cash) is then deducted from the enterprise value to determine the 'en bloc' value of the equity.

In the equity value approach (also known as the 'net of debt' approach) the balance sheet of the business notionally is adjusted to reflect an 'appropriate' level of interest bearing debt. A capitalization or discount rate is applied to the discretionary cash flow determined after deducting debt servicing costs. The amount of interest expense (net of tax) deducted and changes to debt principal included in the derivation of discretionary cash flows is based on what is taken to be an 'appropriate' level and mix of short and long term debt at prevailing interest rates. In this case, the capitalization or discount rate reflects only the return on levered equity. The value determined represents the 'en bloc' value of the equity of the business, subject to an adjustment for the notional increase or decrease in the amount of debt outstanding at the valuation date. Although theoretically valid, this approach necessitates lengthy iterative calculations. As a result it seldom is adopted.

EXHIBIT 7.1

APPROACHES TO DETERMINING VALUE

Enterprise Value Approach	*Equity Value Approach*
Discretionary cash flows before debt servicing costs	Discretionary cash flows net of debt servicing costs based on an 'appropriate' capital structure
Divided by	Divided by
Weighted average cost of capital based on an 'appropriate' capital structure	Levered return on equity based on an 'appropriate' capital structure
Equals	Equals
Capitalized unlevered discretionary cash flows	Capitalized levered discretionary cash flows
Add / deduct	Add / deduct
Redundant assets, present value of tax pools and other operating adjustments	Redundant assets, present value of tax pools and other operating adjustments
Equals	Equals
Enterprise value	Unadjusted equity value
Deduct	Add / deduct
Interest bearing debt and equivalents outstanding	Notional debt adjustment made to reflect an 'appropriate' capital structure
Equals	Equals
En bloc equity value of shares	En bloc equity value of shares

Financial Leverage

A rate of return on unlevered equity is a capitalization or discount rate that assumes a debt-free capital structure. As discussed in Chapter 8, the cost of unlevered equity is a function of the operating risks (as contrasted with financial risk) given the nature of the business, the industry in which it competes, and prevailing economic factors. The most appropriate financing structure (i.e. the appropriate mix of debt and equity) is the essence of the capital structure decision, and is distinct from the operating risk faced by the business. Accordingly, the appropriate unlevered return on equity should first be determined, and where applicable that rate should be adjusted to reflect the impact of financial risk.

Regardless of whether enterprise value or equity value is being determined, the cost of equity viewed either in isolation or as a component of the weighted average cost of capital should be the levered cost of equity. Stated differently, the cost of equity should reflect the risk of financial leverage (debt) in the capital structure because debt holders rank ahead of equity holders in claims against cash flows and net assets. It is axiomatic that the greater the amount of debt in the capital structure the greater is the financial risk and, all other things equal, the greater must be the cost of equity.

Modern finance theory[1] postulates that where profits are subject to tax, the value of a levered firm (i.e. a firm that uses debt in its capital structure) is equal to the value of an unlevered firm plus the present value of the tax shield from interest expense on tax-deductible interest bearing debt. Mathematically this is expressed as:

FORMULA 7.1

$$V_L = V_U + [T \times D]$$

where:

V_L = the value of a levered firm;

V_U = the value of an unlevered firm;

T = the marginal corporate income tax rate; and

D = the market value of interest bearing debt.

The following example serves to illustrate the impact of interest bearing debt on the enterprise value and equity value of a business. Assume that Company R can prospectively generate (in real terms) $1 million in EBIT (which is assumed for purposes of this example to approximate pretax discretionary cash flows) based on current trade assets of $2 million and fixed assets of $4 million. Further assume that trade creditors (e.g. accounts payable) normally are owed $1 million, leaving $5 million of net assets to be financed. If Company R were financed entirely through equity (say, 500,000 shares at $10 per share), its balance sheet would appear as follows ($000):

Current trade assets	2,000
Fixed assets	4,000
Total assets	6,000
Current trade liabilities	1,000
Interest bearing debt	0
Total liabilities	1,000
Equity (500,000 shares @ $10)	5,000
Total liabilities & equity	6,000

At $1 million EBIT, the unlevered pretax return on equity is 20% ($1 million/$5 million), or 12% after tax, in real terms, assuming a 40% income tax rate. Alternatively, the unlevered value of the equity in Company R would be determined as follows ($000):

EBIT	$1,000
Less: interest expense	0
Earnings before tax	1,000
Less: income tax @ 40%	(400)
Discretionary cash flows	600
Divided by unlevered return on equity	12%
Equals: unlevered equity value	$5,000

In this case, the $5 million would represent both Company R's enterprise value and its equity value since there is no interest bearing debt.

Further assume that management of Company R can finance up to $2 million of its net asset requirements with interest bearing debt at a nominal interest rate of 8%, equating to a real interest rate of 5%. The remaining $3 million would be financed through equity (300,000 shares at $10). The balance sheet of Company R then would appear as follows ($000):

Current trade assets	2,000
Fixed assets	4,000
Total assets	6,000
Current trade liabilities	1,000
Interest bearing debt	2,000
Total liabilities	3,000
Equity (300,000 shares @ $10)	3,000
Total liabilities & equity	6,000

If interest expense was not deductible for income tax purposes, Company R's income statement would appear as follows ($000):

EBIT	$1,000
Less: income tax @ 40%	(400)
Unlevered cash flows	600
Less: non-deductible interest (5% x $2 million)	(100)
Discretionary cash flows to equity holders	$ 500

Therefore, under the assumption that interest expense is not tax deductible, the real after tax return to equity holders increases from 12% to 16.67% ($500,000 / $3 million invested equity) due to the use of debt in Company R's capital structure. The levered return on equity under the scenario of non-tax-deductible interest expense could also be derived as follows:

FORMULA 7.2

$$K_L = K_U + (K_U - K_{DP}) \times (D/E) \times (1 - T)$$
$$= 12\% + (12\% - 5\%) \times (\$2 \text{ million}/\$3 \text{ million}) \times (1 - 0\%)$$
$$= 16.67\%$$

where:

K_L = the cost of levered equity;

K_U = the cost of unlevered equity;

K_{DP} = the cost of debt (pre tax);

D/E = the ratio of interest bearing debt to equity; and

T = the marginal income tax rate.

Notice that in the above calculation, the pretax cost of debt used (5%) is the real rate (net of inflation), consistent with the basis that the real unlevered return on equity (12%) is established. Further note that the tax rate is set at 0% where it is assumed that interest expense is not tax deductible.

Therefore, in circumstances where interest expense is not tax deductible, there is no impact on the value of Company R's equity (on a per share basis), since the higher rate of return only serves to compensate for the increased financial risk. Therefore, the leveraged value of Company R's equity remains at $3 million ($10 per share), and the enterprise value of Company R remains at $5 million (comprised of $3 million in equity and $2 million in debt).

However, interest expense usually is deductible for income tax purposes. Assuming this to be the case, the discretionary cash flows of Company R would appear as follows ($000):

EBIT	$1,000
Less: interest expense (5% x $2 million)	(100)
Earnings before tax	900
Less: income tax @ 40%	(360)
Discretionary cash flows to equity holders	$ 540

Consequently, from the viewpoint of Company R's shareholders, the claim by the debt-holders against the 'value' of Company R has effectively been reduced pursuant to the fact that the interest paid to the debt-holders is tax deductible. This increases the value of Company R's equity, as follows ($000):

Value of the underlying net assets	$ 5,000
Less: after-tax cost of debt ($2 million less 40%)	(1,200)
Value of levered equity	$ 3,800

Given the increase in the value of Company R's levered equity, the enterprise value of Company R has increased to $5.8 million, comprised of $3.8 million in equity and $2 million in debt. This result agrees with the Formula 7.1 presented earlier:

$$V_L = V_U + [T \times D]$$
$$= \$5.0 \text{ million} + 40\% \times \$2 \text{ million}$$
$$= \$5.8 \text{ million}$$

The required return on levered equity is now reduced to 14.21% ($540,000/$3.8 million) due to the tax deductibility of interest expense. Alternatively, using Formula 7.2 previously presented:

$$K_L = K_U + (K_U - K_{DP}) \times (D/E) \times (1 - T)$$
$$= 12\% + (12\% - 5\%) \times (\$2 \text{ million}/\$3.8 \text{ million}) \times (1 - 40\%)$$
$$= 14.21\%$$

Note that when applying this formula the debt to equity ratio (D/E) incorporates the increased value of the levered equity ($3.8 million), and that the income tax rate is set at 40%, assuming the tax deductibility of interest expense.

Stated another way, given the tax-deductibility of interest expense, at $3 million of equity value, the return to Company R's equity holders would increase from 16.67% ($500,000/$3 million) to 18% ($540,000/$3 million). However, the required rate of return on Company R's levered equity has declined to 14.21% given that the level of financial risk has decreased with the tax-deductibility of interest expense. As a result, the levered value of Company R's equity has increased from $3 million to $3.8 million, or from $10 to $12.67 ($3.8 million/300,000 shares) on a per share basis.

Finally, assuming that interest expense is tax deductible, Company R's weighted average cost of capital (WACC) can be calculated as the unlevered discretionary (after tax) cash flow stream of $600,000 divided by the enterprise value of $5.8 million to yield 10.34%. Alternatively, enterprise value could be determined by dividing the unlevered discretionary cash flow of $600,000 by the WACC of 10.34%, which equates to $5.8 million.

The theory of capital structure presented above is premised on the assumption that the operating risks of a business are independent of its financial risks. This may not always be the case. For example, a company that employs excessive amounts of financial leverage may:

- risk losing customers who fear the business will become insolvent and unable to honour its warranty obligations. The resultant decrease in revenues, or relative increase in the uncertainty of revenues, would increase operating risk;
- be placed on C.O.D. terms by its suppliers, thereby necessitating an increase in net trade working capital requirements. As explained in Chapter 4, (unlevered) discretionary cash flows are reduced by a business' net trade working capital requirements;
- have to forego required operating expenditures in favour of debt servicing costs (principal repayment and interest expense), thereby placing its prospective operating cash flows at greater risk; and
- have to forego growth opportunities due to its inability to raise capital at reasonable rates to finance said opportunities.

In each case, the prospective unlevered discretionary cash flows of the business either would decline, or become more volatile, resulting in a lower en bloc value of the business on an unlevered basis. *Consequently, a fundamental assumption underlying the basic theory of capital structure as presented above would not hold (i.e. that operating risk and financial risk are independent), in which case strict application of the theory would not be valid.*

As discussed in Chapter 2, the commonly accepted definition of Fair Market Value presumes that a vendor is neither disadvantaged in its negotiations, nor presumed to be under any 'compulsion to act' as a result of its existing capital structure. However, where a business is in financial difficulty due to, in whole or in part, excessive debt utilization at the valuation or pricing date, the issue might arise as to whether Fair Market Value, in its generally accepted meaning, is the appropriate valuation construct.

A strict interpretation of the preceding formulas suggests that for a given unlevered return on equity (K_U), the cost of levered equity (K_L) decreases as interest rates (K_{DP}) increase, and by extension that the cost of debt (K_{DP}) has no impact on WACC. However, this is not the case in practice. As interest rates rise, businesses tend to employ less debt financing, thereby decreasing the degree of financial leverage and generally increasing WACC. In addition, the cost of unlevered equity may increase with an increase in the cost of debt in circumstances where the:

- nominal cost of debt increases due to inflationary factors. Where the nominal interest rate increases, the nominal unlevered return on equity should (in theory) increase by the same amount. As a result, interest and inflation rates over the long term have a direct impact on WACC calculations; or
- real cost of debt increases due to incremental risk in the operating cash flows of the business (e.g. the volatility of unlevered discretionary cash flows). Where operating risk increases, this factor should also be reflected in the unlevered return on equity, and by extension, WACC.

However, an issue arises where the real cost of debt increases due to the use of 'excessive' amounts of debt in the business' capital structure (i.e. excessive financial risk). In this case, the cost of unlevered equity would not increase assuming no change in the operating risk of the business. However the incremental financial risk should be reflected in the levered cost of equity, and the WACC. The following example serves to illustrate this.

Assume that for Company R in the previous example, the real rate of interest increased from 5% to 7% due to the belief on the part of the Company's debt holders that the amount of debt utilized by Company R was excessive. Further assume that because there was no change in the operating risk of the business the unlevered rate of return on equity for Company R remained at 12%. A strict application of the financial leverage formula presented herein would result in the levered return on equity decreasing from 14.21% (previously computed) to:

$$K_L = K_U + (K_U - K_{DP}) \times (D/E) \times (1-T)$$
$$= 12\% + (12\% - 7\%) \times (\$2 \text{ million}/\$3.8 \text{ million}) \times (1 - 40\%)$$
$$= 13.58\%$$

Pursuant to this calculation, the financial risk component of the cost of levered equity would decline from 2.21% (14.21% less 12.0%) to 1.58% (13.58% less 12.0%), despite the increase in financial risk due to the higher real rate of interest. Clearly, this is counter-intuitive. The financial risk component of the cost of levered equity should be at least as high, and likely greater, with an increase in the real rate of interest due to incremental financial risk. It is clear that under these circumstances, the strict application of the conventional formulas for the levered cost of equity and WACC would be inappropriate.

Because, as a practical matter, the cost of both debt and equity financing escalate to higher levels until financing is unavailable at reasonable rates, formula 7.1 for the value of a firm can be expressed as:

FORMULA 7.3

$$V_L = V_U + [T \times D] - C$$

where:

C = bankruptcy costs, and generally is represented by a step function.

Therefore, where appropriate, an estimate should be made to reflect the incremental financial risk component in the cost of levered equity and WACC of a business that utilizes what is believed to be 'excessive financial leverage', unless an assumption is made that purchasers have the ability to refinance the acquisition at will.

In the end the capital structure decision becomes a tradeoff between financing through debt to increase equity value, and financing through equity to reduce the risk of insolvency. In practice, it rarely is possible to determine precisely an optimal mix of debt and equity. Most businesses operate within a target range believed appropriate.

Weighted Average Cost of Capital

Overview

Weighted average cost of capital ('WACC') is a finance concept that reflects what is believed to be an appropriate fact specific blend of the debt and equity financing and their respective costs. Weighted average cost of capital generally is determined as:

FORMULA 7.4

$$WACC = (K_D \times W_D) + (K_L \times W_E)$$

where:

K_D = the after tax cost of debt;

W_D = the relative weight of debt, (i.e. the ratio of: [interest bearing debt] to [interest bearing debt plus equity]);

K_L = the cost of levered equity; and

W_E = the relative weight of levered equity (i.e. the ratio of: [equity] to [interest bearing debt plus equity]).

The relative weight of debt and equity normally are determined by reference to their market values, not their book values, consistent with capital structure theory. Although the cost of capital of a business will change over time, its cost of capital or that of its industry should be relatively stable from period to period absent some dramatic structural reason that dictates change. It is the weighted average cost of capital, not the unlevered rate of return on equity, that is the appropriate discount rate to apply to discretionary cash flow that excludes debt servicing costs (after-tax interest expense and changes in debt principal outstanding).

The determination of the cost of each of the WACC components follows. The issue of appropriate relative weights for each of the components, which is the essence of the capital structure decision, is addressed later in this Chapter.

The Cost of Debt

The cost of debt that should be used in the WACC calculation is the after tax cost of interest expense. The appropriate tax rate is the marginal rate at which interest will be deducted for corporate income tax purposes. Importantly, the WACC derivation assumes interest expense is tax deductible. The cost of interest should be calculated at current market rates based on an 'appropriate' blend of short term and long term debt.

Most short-term debt is variable rate debt with the rate tied to the prime lending rate (for example, prime plus 2%). Accordingly, determining the current market rate of short term debt usually is a reasonably straight-forward exercise. It generally is based on analysis of existing banking agreements, with reference to the existing prime lending rate.

The cost of long term debt generally is more difficult to determine. For larger companies, an appropriate indication of the cost of long term debt may be reflected in a recent or prospective private or public placement, or by comparison to the yield on long term corporate debt of companies of similar size and business risk. For smaller companies, particularly those privately-held, direct comparables tend not to be available. In such cases, an analysis of the following may be helpful:

- existing or prospective term debt arrangements the company has with its banks or other lenders;
- prevailing long term government bond rates;
- prevailing long term mortgage rates;
- the implicit interest rate in recently negotiated capital leases; and
- the prevailing yield on so-called 'high yield debt' or 'junk bonds' of companies in the same industry and similar operating risks (generally regarded as bonds with a rating of BBB or lower).

When assessing the rate of return on long term debt, it is important to note that it is the current or prevailing rate which is being evaluated, and that rates on existing long term debt may not be indicative of current rates. Further, it is important that the long term debt rate be based on pure debt instruments. Stated differently, debt which includes conversion features, bonus interest, and so on likely does not bear a rate of interest which viewed in isolation is reflective of the return sought by a corporate lender whose only return will be interest income and principal repayment.

In theory, debt issue costs such as arrangement fees, legal fees, and so on should be considered in the determination of the effective rate on long term debt. Where significant, these costs have an impact on the effective cost of debt. For example, if a company were to issue $10 million of long term bonds at 9% and the issue costs were 3% of the gross proceeds, the effective cost of the debt would be 9.28%, determined as follows:

> Annual interest payment / (face value of debt − issue costs)
> = $900,000 / ($10,000,000 - $300,000)
> = 9.28%

This is the pre-tax cost of debt. The result would have to be multiplied by (1 − tax rate) to determine the after tax cost.

The Cost of Equity

As a general rule the 'cost of equity' refers to the 'cost of common share equity' in the context of both publicly and privately held companies where outstanding preferred shares are viewed by common shareholders as a form of debt. The derivation of the cost of equity is discussed in Chapter 8.

The cost of equity incorporated either in the WACC or adopted as a return on equity applied against cash flows determined net of after-tax debt costs should be a return on levered equity. Generally, the appropriate rate of unlevered equity is determined first, and that rate then is adjusted in accord with the WACC formula to account for financial risk attributable to the amount of financial leverage deemed appropriate. The cost of levered equity can be determined pursuant to Formula 7.2, presented earlier.

The Cost of Preferred Shares

As a practical matter, the cost of preferred shares normally is not a component of the determination of an appropriate WACC. However, where outstanding preferred shares are not retractable, and appropriately are valued based solely on their own attributes WACC is calculated as follows:

FORMULA 7.5

$$WACC = (K_D \times W_D) + (K_P \times W_P) + (K_E \times W_E)$$

where:

K_P = the cost of preferred shares; and

W_P = the relative market weight of preferred shares.

For companies whose non-retractable preferred shares are publicly traded, the cost of preferred shares generally is taken to be their prevailing market yield. In theory, issue costs should be deducted when determining the effective cost of such preferred shares. Therefore, if the prevailing market yield is 6% and issue costs are 5%, then the cost of preferred shares would be determined as:

= 6% / (1-5%)
= 6.32%

For privately held companies, the yield on preferred shares may not be indicative of current market rates. Therefore, adjustments may be necessary. If the preferred shares issued by a privately held company have a nominal stated value (such as those issued pursuant to an estate freeze), it may be preferable to determine an appropriate WACC using only debt and 'common equity equivalent' components. The en bloc value of the common equity would then be determined by effectively treating the value of the preferred shares as a debt equivalent. The valuation of preferred shares is addressed in Chapter 4.

As is the case with the cost of debt, when determining the cost of preferred shares care must be taken to ensure that the rate used is not distorted by retraction, redemption, conversion, or other features. Accordingly, if appropriate 'comparable' publicly traded preferred shares cannot be found, subjective adjustments may be required.

WACC Calculation Example

XYZ Limited ('XYZ') is a public company whose existing capital structure is as follows ($000):

	Book Value	Market Value
Short term debt	20,000	20,000
Long term debt	43,000	48,000
Preferred shares	10,000	12,000
Total debt and equivalents	73,000	80,000
Common shares	30,000	120,000
Retained earnings	60,000	included
Total equity	90,000	120,000
Enterprise value	163,000	200,000

Additional considerations regarding XYZ's capital structure are as follows:

- the short term debt bears an interest rate of prime plus 1.5%. The prevailing prime rate is 6.5%;
- the long term debt was issued at a rate of 10%. Current long term debt could be placed at a rate of 9%;
- the preferred shares are cumulative with a dividend of 6%. The current yield on comparable publicly traded preferred shares is 5%;
- the common shares are publicly traded. No dividend has ever been paid thereon. XYZ estimates that its nominal unlevered cost of equity is 15%; and
- XYZ's income tax rate is 40%.

Given this information, and ignoring issuance costs, WACC would be determined as follows (in nominal terms):

Cost of short term debt	20,000 / 200,000 x (6.5% + 1.5%) x (1-40%)	0.48%
Cost of long term debt	48,000 / 200,000 x 9% x (1-40%)	1.30%
Cost of preferred shares	12,000 / 200,000 x 6%	0.36%
Cost of equity (see below)	120,000 / 200,000 x 17.44%	10.46%
WACC		12.60%

The cost of equity is the cost of levered equity determined as follow (see Formula 7.2):

$$K_L = K_U + (K_U - K_{DP}) \times (D/E) \times (1 - T)$$
$$K_L = 15\% + (15\% - 8.9\%) \times (80,000/120,000) \times (1 - 40\%)$$
$$K_L = 17.44\%$$

The cost of unlevered equity (15%) represents the base rate as indicated. The pretax cost of debt adopted (8.9%) is a weighted average of the cost of short term debt, long term debt and the cost of preferred shares, all expressed on a pre-tax basis. That is:

Short term debt	20,000 / 80,000 x 8%	2.0%
Long term debt	48,000 / 80,000 x 9%	5.4%
Preferred shares	12,000 / 80,000 x 6%/(1-40%)	1.5%
		8.9%

Dividends on preferred shares are not tax deductible. Therefore, it is necessary to express the dividend yield as a pretax equivalent. The debt to equity ratio of $80,000 to $120,000 includes the sum of short term debt, long term debt and preferred shares in the numerator. This is because from a common share equity perspective all three sources represent a form of financial leverage.

This derivation of WACC is based on public equity market values. Due to important differences that may exist between public equity markets and the acquisition of a business 'en bloc', the rates of return used in the latter case may be different (higher or lower) than those implied by the former — see Chapter 8.

Alternative WACC Calculation

Rather than determining the cost of levered equity, and then applying the costs of debt and levered equity against their relative weights, WACC can be derived by the following formula[2]:

FORMULA 7.6

$$WACC = K_U \times (1 - T \times D)$$

where:

K_U = the unlevered rate of return on equity;

T = the marginal income tax rate; and

D = the ratio of interest bearing debt to the sum of interest bearing debt plus equity (i.e. enterprise value), based on market weightings

This WACC calculation uses the ratio of debt to enterprise value (debt plus equity), whereas the cost of levered equity calculation (K_L) uses the ratio of debt to equity.

Applying this formula where K_U = 15%, T = 40% and D = 40% [(20,000 + 48,000 + 12,000) / 200,000], WACC again is calculated to be 12.6%:

$$WACC = 15\% \times [1 - (40\% \times 40\%)]$$
$$= 12.6\%$$

This formula gives effect to the cost of both debt and levered equity through the interaction of the cost of unlevered equity, K_U, and the ratio of debt to equity where both are based on market weightings, D. Use of this formula does not require either an allocation among short term and long term debt and debt equivalents, or a separate conversion of unlevered to levered equity.

Determinants of Capital Structure

The Theory of Capital Structure

In theory there is an optimal capital structure for every business, being the mix of debt and equity that minimizes WACC. Accordingly, all other things equal, an unlevered firm can increase its enterprise value by employing an appropriate amount of debt in its capital structure in place of equity. As the percentage of debt in the capital structure increases the WACC decreases, which in turn has the effect of increasing enterprise value.

Figure 7.1 illustrates this. As leverage increases, the cost of both debt and equity increase because of the increase in financial risk. At comparatively low levels of leverage, the cost of debt increases very little as leverage increases. As a result, substituting debt for equity initially leads to a lower WACC. The savings resulting from substituting a cheaper source of funds (i.e. debt for equity) more than offsets the increase in the cost of equity capital. Beyond some fact specific finite point, which determines the point of the optimal capital structure in Figure 7.1, the increase in the cost of equity capital more than offsets the savings resulting from substituting debt for equity. In theory, by adopting the optimal capital structure, WACC is minimized and enterprise value is maximized.

FIGURE 7.1

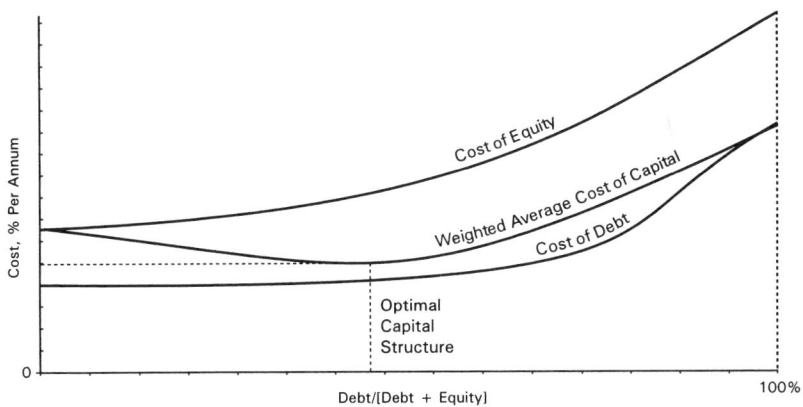

From a shareholder's point of view:

- an optimal capital structure results in the maximum share price; and
- additional debt beyond the point of optimal capital structure causes the increases in the cost of equity to exceed the benefit of using incremental debt, thereby resulting in declining shareholder value.

Stated differently, common share prices begin to decline when the present value of the expected tax advantages of incremental debt no longer are attractive enough to compensate investors for the additional financial risk associated with the incremental debt.

Although in theory the optimal capital structure can be found by balancing the tax-shield benefits of leverage against the financial distress and agency costs of leverage, in practice there are no set formulas or methodologies for determining the optimal capital structure for a particular business. Empirical evidence shows capital structures vary widely among businesses, even those in the same industry. It follows that informed judgement is a major component in capital structure decisions.

Employing Capital Structure Estimates in Valuation and Pricing Analysis

Estimating an appropriate capital structure for a business is a subjective exercise that generally requires consideration of a wide range of factors. However, where substantial tangible assets exist, potential purchasers normally conclude that an assumption of some amount of interest bearing debt is appropriate. Finance theory dictates that open market price determinations for a given business should include consideration of an appropriate amount of debt measured against invested equity. Whether or not debt exists as a component of the capital structure of a business at the valuation date, the market will reflect the capacity of the business to finance with debt. Stated differently, in transactions where businesses are sold, potential purchasers typically will reflect in their offering prices their respective abilities to utilize the debt capacity of the target business. Moreover, where a purchaser believes a target business is over-leveraged, and that as a result it has a negotiation advantage that can be exploited against the vendors, the purchaser normally will consider this in its pricing decision.

In a notional market valuation, it generally is assumed that the enterprise value of the business is not influenced by the basis by which the business is financed. As previously discussed, modern capital structure theory assumes that the operating risks of a business are distinct from its financial risks. Therefore, the impact of business financing mix is reflected in the allocation of enterprise value among the providers of capital to the business, first to the owners of interest bearing debt (and equivalents), with the residual amount accruing to the equity holders. This is consistent with the standard definition of fair market value, which assumes an 'open and unrestricted market' and that neither party is under 'compulsion to transact'. It follows that in most cases the definition of fair market value should assume a sufficient number of potential purchasers are interested in acquiring a business such that the vendors are not disadvantaged in their negotiations due to 'excessive' financial leverage. Stated another way, it would be normal to assume that although a business may be over-leveraged, prospective purchasers value the business (on a stand-alone basis) based on what they believed to be an 'appropriate' capital structure.

However, the usual assumption that the equity value of a business should not be discounted for excessive financial leverage may not (depending on prevailing facts) be appropriate in circumstances where the intrinsic value of a business is being determined, and where it is likely that the acquirer will be unable to refinance the acquisition based on what it believes to be an 'appropriate' capital structure. This may occur in circumstances where:

- the acquisition of all or a portion of the equity of the business will be funded, either wholly or in part, by post-acquisition cash flow generated by the business, and it is assumed that the acquirer will be 'disadvantaged' by such means of financing that consequently will be reflected in the price the buyer is willing or able to pay — see 'Internal v. External Financing' in Chapter 2. As previously discussed in this Chapter, such a disadvantage occurs where the operations of a business are negatively influenced by the basis by which it is financed, for example where:
  - the business must forego necessary operating expenditures or growth opportunities in favour of debt servicing requirements, or must raise financing at 'unreasonable' rates in order to maintain or grow its operations as planned, or
  - the revenues, costs, working capital requirements, and so on, of the business are negatively affected due to the reaction of customers, suppliers, and other parties to the perceived 'poor financial position' of the business; and
- a minority shareholding in the company is acquired, and as a non-controlling shareholder the acquirer is unable to meaningfully influence the capital structure of the business. The disadvantages relating to minority

shareholdings normally are accounted for as a 'minority discount' applied in valuing a particular equity interest as opposed to the en bloc value of the equity — see Chapter 13.

Where value is developed on an 'intrinsic' or 'stand-alone' basis, the appropriate relative weights and costs of debt and equity should reflect those for the business viewed in isolation, and not those of a notional acquirer, although they may be the same. If likely acquirers have more favourable costs of capital due to size, asset characteristics, and so on, this is indicative of post-acquisition synergy evidenced through capital structure advantage. The valuation of post-acquisition synergies is addressed in Chapter 11.

Factors Influencing Capital Structure

Literature available on capital structure is extensive and contradictory. In the end, the capital structure decision is one that involves thorough analysis and judgement. When estimating an appropriate capital structure for a business, the following factors normally should be taken into account:

- generally, determining an appropriate capital structure means determining an appropriate debt to common equity relationship. Capital structure analysis typically does not contemplate utilization of preference or other 'fixed income' shares unless such shares already are outstanding and are traded in an organized market;
- the quantum and nature of underlying tangible assets that can be securitized. Among other things, traditional lenders are interested in the level of security of their investment. In general, the greater the quantum of underlying tangible assets, the greater the debt capacity of the business. As previously noted, the ability to employ debt financing reduces the WACC and hence capitalization and discount rates, thereby increasing enterprise value. Businesses with potentially high financial distress costs, such as those whose value primarily is derived from 'goodwill' and other intangibles rather than from saleable tangible assets, tend to utilize lesser amounts of leverage;
- the nature of the underlying assets. In particular, traditional lenders normally lend against specific assets (based on the quality of the assets) according to pre-set formulas such as:
  — up to 75% of quality accounts receivable under 90 days;
  — up to 50% of book value of inventories, although this can vary widely depending on their composition;
  — up to 75% of the appraised value of real estate assets; and
  — up to 60% of the market value of other fixed assets;

- the estimated level of maintainable discretionary cash flows and potential variability thereof. Businesses with volatile unlevered discretionary cash flows, and hence substantive inherent risk, normally employ less debt than those whose unlevered discretionary cash flows are less volatile;
- the level of operating leverage measured by the relationship between fixed and variable operating costs. Businesses with higher operating leverage generally experience greater relative fluctuations in cash flow due to revenue fluctuation than do businesses that incorporate a greater variable component in their operating cost structure. As a result, they normally employ less debt than do those with relatively lower fixed operating costs;
- the nature of the industry. Over time, businesses in non-cyclical industries generally employ proportionately more debt than do those susceptible to economic cycles;
- the effective marginal income tax rate paid by the business. The greater the tax rate, the greater the benefit of using tax-deductible debt financing. Concurrently, it is necessary to consider the ability of the business to fully utilize the interest tax shield;
- the prevailing and prospective pre-tax cost of debt. The lower the cost of debt, the more attractive it is as a financing source;
- the near and long term strategy of the business. A business with aggressive expansion plans normally will employ proportionately more equity financing due to the greater risks attached to achieving growth, and hence the generally greater difficulty in obtaining debt at reasonable rates. Traditional lenders tend to prefer stable, slow to moderate growth businesses since they do not share in the upside returns from aggressive growth plans, and may find their security eroded if growth plans fail;
- the stage of the life cycle of the business. Companies in early or growth phases tend to employ proportionately more equity in their capital structures compared with stable or mature companies where a higher portion of debt is more common;
- existing banking agreements, which provide an indication as to current maximum borrowing capacity, security, rates, debt covenants, and so on; and
- the leverage employed by pubic companies believed reasonably 'comparable' in terms of size and business risk. Assessing 'comparability' is discussed in Chapter 9. In circumstances where believed useful, a review of 'comparable' public company financial information should address:
  — key debt ratios employed by those companies (debt to equity, times interest earned, debt serviceability, and so on) – see Appendix B;

— stock market reaction to capital structure changes in those companies; and
— reports from security analysts pertaining to those companies.

Where the business being valued or priced is a public company, additional information may be available to assist in determining an appropriate capital structure. This may include:

- debt rating agency reviews; and
- investment banker interest in placing new debt or restructuring existing debt.

The amount of debt used in privately held businesses often is a reflection of the personal views and personal financial position of the majority shareholder(s). Therefore, there may be a wide discrepancy between the amount of debt utilized and that considered 'appropriate' having regard to the nature of the business and the industry in which it operates. On the other hand, publicly held companies are more likely to employ a capital structure that management believes to be appropriate. Notwithstanding, notional adjustments to a public company's capital structure may be required where the company:

- is conservatively financed, both in absolute terms and in relation to other companies in its industry. This sometimes occurs where the public company is closely controlled and as a result is not at risk of being acquired; or
- employs excessive debt financing such that leverage is beyond what can reasonably be regarded as acceptable given the nature of the business and the industry in which it operates.

When determining an appropriate amount of debt for both private and public companies, it should be recognized that companies normally do not borrow to the maximum of their debt financing ability. Management groups typically prefer to be in a position where they can choose to borrow or pay off debt, as contrasted with being in the position of being compelled to borrow or pay off debt. Stated differently, managers generally use less debt than would maximize the near term value of their business because they want to maintain borrowing flexibility, thereby maximizing long term value. Moreover, because debt and equity offerings normally are executed in blocks and not small increments, businesses normally operate within a range of debt to equity ratios. The determination of weighted average cost of capital demonstrates a convex as opposed to linear relationship (see Figure 7.1). Therefore, minor deviations from the 'optimum' amount of debt generally have little impact on either the determination of weighed average cost of capital or resultant enterprise value.

Short Term v. Long Term Debt

When an appropriate overall level of debt has been determined it then may be segregated into long term and short term. Short term debt generally is variable, or 'floating' rate debt. The interest rate on short term debt at any point in time normally is less than the prevailing interest rate on long term debt. Therefore, consideration of the composition of short and long term debt may have an impact on the appropriate quantum of total debt, and therefore the appropriate debt to equity ratio. This in turn directly influences the weighted average cost of capital where it is determined independent of debt interest rates.

When determining the mix of short and long term debt, finance theory suggests that businesses follow the 'matching principle' pursuant to which short term assets should be financed with short term debt, and long term assets should be financed with long term debt. Accordingly, an estimate of the proportion to allocate between short and long term debt can be made by assessing:

- the relative short term and long term tangible assets, and using appropriate lending ratios in respect of each of them; and
- the financial ratios of what are believed to be meaningfully 'comparable' businesses.

It may be worthwhile to compile a notional balance sheet based on computations of 'appropriate' capital structure estimates (including long and short term debt), working capital and redundant assets in order to assess the reasonableness of assumptions and the overall value/price conclusions. In the end, the estimate of an appropriate capital structure must be plausible in light of the fact-specific circumstances of the business whose shares or net assets are being valued.

Capital Structure Estimation Example

Big Machines Limited (BML) is a manufacturer of heavy equipment used in resource extraction industries. BML is a private company. Mr. H is the sole shareholder. Mr. H wants to transfer ownership of the business to his children, and requires a business valuation for estate freeze purposes.

BML has been conservatively financed. Its balance sheet at November 30, 2000, is as follows:

SCHEDULE 7.1

Big Machines Limited
Balance Sheet
At November 30, 2000
($000)

Cash	23
Accounts receivable	1,656
Inventory	1,165
Current assets	2,844
Land and Building (net)	1,256
Production equipment (net)	652
Office furniture & equipment (net)	97
Net fixed assets	2,005
Total assets	4,849
Bank debt	0
Accounts payable & accruals	1,264
Current liabilities	1,264
Long term debt	0
Total liabilities	1,264
Shareholder equity	3,585
Total liabilities & equity	4,849

The heavy equipment industry is cyclical, and fluctuates with the level of capital spending in the economy. BML's performance over the past five years has been as follows:

SCHEDULE 7.2

Big Machines Limited
Statement of Income and Cash Flows
Fiscal Years Ending November 30
$(000)

	2000	1999	1998	1997	1996
Revenues	14,262	16,163	12,780	10,450	10,619
Expenses	13,123	14,415	11,799	9,726	9,761
Income before taxes	1,139	1,748	981	724	858
Income taxes	425	669	362	259	313
Net income	714	1,079	619	465	545
Cash flows:					
Net income per above	714	1,079	619	465	545
Depreciation	181	188	169	157	136
Capital investment	(267)	(204)	(181)	(123)	(158)
Change in non-cash working capital	238	(423)	(291)	21	20
Net cash flow	866	640	316	520	543

There are no unusual expenses. BML has always paid its employees, including Mr. H, market rates of compensation. Dividends were paid out in years of strong earnings. BML has never borrowed from arm's length lenders.

Analysis reveals that:

- accounts receivable are 80% current (under 90 days) and 20% holdback for performance (i.e. over 90 days);
- inventories primarily include supplies and work in progress;
- the replacement cost of the production equipment is estimated at $800,000;
- the current market value of the property (land and building) is $1,600,000;

- BML pays income taxes at a rate of 25% on its first $200,000 of taxable income and 40% on the excess; and
- a commercial bank has indicated that it will lend up to 75% against current accounts receivable, 25% against the book value of inventories, 50% against the market value of equipment, and 75% against the market value of real estate.

There are three public companies with operations similar to BML. These companies are much larger than BML both in terms of revenues and net assets. The average of selected ratios for these three companies is as follows:

Current ratio	1.5 to 1
Total debt to equity (at book)	3 to 1
Total debt to equity (at market)	1 to 1
EBIT to interest expense	5x

Capital Structure Determination

When determining an 'appropriate' capital structure for BML, consideration should be given to:

- BML's debt capacity based on its tangible assets;
- the estimated level of maintainable discretionary cash flows before debt servicing and income taxes, and the prospective likely variability thereof. In the past 5 years, pretax cash flows have been as follows (calculated as net cash flow plus income taxes):

Year	$000
2000	1,291
1999	1,309
1998	678
1997	779
1996	856

- long term investment opportunities BML may be considering, and how these would be financed;
- the estimated value of BML on an unlevered basis. If maintainable unlevered discretionary cash flows are estimated at $500,000 to $700,000 (based on the net cash flows indicated in Schedule 7.2), and real unlevered capi-

talization rates of 10% to 13% are believed appropriate, the unlevered enterprise value of BML would be estimated at approximately $5.0 million ($500,000/10%) to $5.4 million ($700,000/13%);
- the leverage ratios of 'comparable' firms, particularly the current ratio, interest bearing debt to equity, interest coverage ratio, and debt serviceability ratio. Because the 'comparable' companies identified are much larger than BML they are unlikely strong comparables. Therefore, less emphasis would be placed on this analysis;
- changes and developments in the industry; and
- prevailing economic conditions, including interest rates, projected economic growth impacting BML, and so on.

Using this information, an estimate of BML's borrowing capacity could be derived from analysis of underlying tangible assets, comparable ratios, and interest coverage as follows:

SCHEDULE 7.3

Big Machines Limited
Estimated Additional Debt Capacity
At November 30, 2000
($000)

Based on asset values:

	Book Value	Market Value	Maximum Lending	Borrowing Capacity
Accounts receivable	1,656	1,656	75% x 80% current	994
Inventory	1,165	1,165	25%	291
Total short term				1,285
Land and building	1,256	1,600	75%	1,200
Production equipment	652	800	50%	400
Total long term				1,600
Borrowing capacity based on tangible assets				2,885

Based on industry comparatives:

Ratio (see below)	Industry Average	BML Current	Additional Debt
Current ratio	1.5	2.25	632
Total debt to equity (book)	3.0	0.35	2,373
Borrowing capacity based on above ratios (higher amount)			2,373
Interest coverage ratio	5x	0	
Estimated maintainable EBIT, say		1,100	
Current interest rate (assume)		9%	
Borrowing capacity based on interest average			2,444

The above 'additional debt' estimates are computed as follows:

- in respect of the current ratio, BML has $2,844,000 in current assets. Therefore to derive a current ratio of 1.5 to 1, BML would require $1,896,000 ($2,844,000/1.5) of current liabilities. Since actual current liabilities are $1,264,000, this implies $632,000 of additional financing available ($1,896,000 less $1,264,000);
- in respect of the total debt to equity ratio at book value, BML has $1,264,000 of total debt and $3,585,000 of equity, a ratio of 0.35 to 1.0. Therefore, BML could borrow $2,373,000 of debt which would be paid to Mr. H. as a dividend. Consequently, BML's total liabilities would increase to $3,637,000 ($1,264,000 + $2,373,000), and its equity would decrease to $1,212,000 ($3,585,000 less $2,373,000). Accordingly, BML's total debt to equity ratio would become 3 to 1 ($3,637,000/$1,212,000); and
- in respect of the interest coverage ratio, an 'industry standard' of 5x implies that interest expense could be $220,000, assuming maintainable EBIT for BML (based on an analysis of Schedule 7.2) of $1,100,000 ($1,100,000/5=$220,000). Given the assumption of a 9% interest rate, interest bearing debt would then be $2,444,000 ($220,000/9%).

Based on this analysis, BML might conclude that an 'appropriate' level of debt to employ in the business is $2.0 million. While less than the maximum that might be available, it represents a balance of borrowing capacity based on asset values, invested capital, and interest coverage. In addition, the other variables noted earlier in this Chapter (including anticipated spending initiatives, and so on) should also be considered in determining an 'appropriate' capital structure.

If the unlevered enterprise value of BML is $5.0 million to $5.4 million and the 'appropriate' amount of debt is $2 million, the enterprise value of the levered business would increase to $5.8 million to $6.2 million using Formula 7.1. This implies an equity value in the range of $3.8 million to $4.2 million. Accordingly, BML would borrow $2 million which could be paid as a dividend to Mr. H, or alternatively retained in the business as a redundant asset or used to finance incremental growth opportunities. Of the $2 million in total debt, likely $0.6 million would be raised in the form of short term bank debt and the balance in longer term debt in order to maintain an acceptable current ratio. Schedule 7.4 summarizes the adjustments assuming the proceeds from debt financing are used to pay a special dividend to Mr. H.

SCHEDULE 7.4

Big Machines Limited
Notional Balance Sheet
At November 30, 2000
($000)

	Unadjusted	Restated
Current assets	2,844	2,844
Fixed assets (net)	2,005	2,005
Total assets	4,849	4,849
Bank debt	0	600
Accounts payable & accruals	1,264	1,264
Current liabilities	1,264	1,864
Long term debt	0	1,400
Total liabilities	1,264	3,264
Shareholder equity	3,585	1,585
Total liabilities & equity	4,849	4,849
Value of BLM's shares (mid-point) ($000)		
Enterprise value	$5,200	$6,000
Less: Interest bearing debt	Nil	2,000
Equity value	5,200	4,000
Add: dividend paid	Nil	2,000
Total value to shareholder	$5,200	$6,000
Ratios:		
Current ratio	2.25 : 1.0	1.53 : 1.0
Total debt to equity (at book)	0.35 : 1.0	2.06 : 1.0
Total debt to equity (at market)	0.24 : 1.0	0.82 : 1.0
Interest coverage (based on $1.1 million EBIT and 9% interest rate)	n/a	6.1 x

Summary

The determination of an 'appropriate' capital structure is an integral component of discount and capitalization rate determination. The theory of capital structure suggests that the value of a business, and in turn its overlying share value can be increased by replacing equity financing with tax-deductible interest bearing debt up to a point where the benefits of lower cost debt financing are outweighed by the incremental risks associated with excessive financial leverage. While in theory an optimal capital structure exists for a given firm, in practice it is difficult to determine precisely what that optimal point may be. As a result, both in theory and in practice, the capital structure decision becomes a subjective exercise based on a comprehensive analysis of the nature of the business, the industry in which it competes, and relevant economic factors.

NOTES

1 Modigliani, F. and M. Miller, 1958, the Cost of Capital Corporation Finance and the Theory of Investment, American Economic Review 48, 261-277.

2 The mathematical derivation of this formula is beyond the scope of this text.

Chapter 8
Discount and Capitalization Rates

Introduction

The term discount rate refers to the rate of return that a rational, prudent investor:

- requires in order to put capital at risk in expectation of realizing opportunities associated with a prospective stream of aggregate discretionary cash flows from a business; or alternately
- considers appropriate when converting a prospective stream of aggregate discretionary cash flows from a business to cash or cash equivalents.

A capitalization rate is determined by adjusting a discount rate for inflation, growth and differences in risk beyond the forecast period, as applicable.

The determination of an appropriate discount or capitalization rate inherently is a subjective exercise. When estimating an appropriate rate of return, consideration must be given to the important factors influencing the business, the industry in which the business operates, and economic conditions prevailing at the valuation date. This is not, and cannot be, a mechanical exercise. In the end, the discount or capitalization rate(s) selected should reflect an objective and comprehensive assessment of prevailing and prospective economic conditions, operating risk, financial risk, growth prospects, and overall expectations of the business.

This Chapter defines the terms discount rate and capitalization rate, discusses the underlying principles fundamental to their determination, and discusses the derivation of discount and capitalization rates using what commonly is referred to as a 'build-up approach'. Finally, the Capital Asset Pricing Model and its limitations are addressed.

Discount Rates vs. Capitalization Rates

The terms discount rate and capitalization rate are related, but are not interchangeable. A discount rate is the rate of return used in a discounted cash flow methodology to convert a series of forecasted discretionary cash flows to a present value — see Chapter 5. The discount rate is a function of the perceived risk related to whether the business being valued will underachieve, achieve, or overachieve projected levels of discretionary cash flows in comparison to the return on a benchmark 'risk-free' stream of cash flows (e.g. government debt).

A capitalization rate is the rate of return used to convert estimated maintainable discretionary cash flow to present value. There is an inherent assumption that the cash flow that is capitalized will be generated to perpetuity. The capitalization rate is derived when a growth factor is deducted from the discount rate. Depending on industry-specific and company-specific circumstances the growth factor normally is comprised of expected long term inflation, and may in some circumstances appropriately include an incremental real rate of growth or other adjustments. A capitalization rate is applied to an assumed perpetual discretionary cash flow in the capitalization of discretionary cash flow methodology, which also constitutes the 'terminal value' portion of a discounted cash flow valuation methodology. The inverse of the capitalization rate is referred to as a multiple, as in 'cash flow multiple', 'earnings multiple', and so on.

The discount rate is the rate of return required on the investment, whereas the capitalization rate is the required rate of return less a growth factor. The capitalization rate will only equal the discount rate when long term growth (including consideration of inflation) is expected to be non-existent and where no risk adjustments are considered appropriate.

Discount and capitalization rates usually are expressed either as a weighted average cost of capital or as a levered return on equity. A weighted average cost of capital is a function of the relative mix of debt and equity and the appropriate returns on each. A levered return on equity is the rate of return required by equity holders given the operating and financial risks of the business. Regardless of whether a weighted average cost of capital or a levered return on equity is adopted, an assessment of capital structure is an important determinant in discount and capitalization rate selection.

Underlying Principles of Discount and Capitalization Rate Determination

The following principles should be adhered to when deriving and applying discount and capitalization rates:

- discretionary cash flows are the appropriate earnings stream to be discounted or capitalized;
- there must be internal consistency between the derivation of the discount or capitalization rate and the cash flow stream to which it is applied;
- the fundamental tradeoff between risk and return should be considered in the derivation of a discount or capitalization rate;

- the discount or capitalization rate should reflect both operating risk and financial risk; and
- the discount or capitalization rate appropriately should consider market rates of return.

Discretionary Cash Flows

Discretionary cash flows are the appropriate income stream against which to apply the discount or capitalization rate. As discussed in Chapter 4, discretionary cash flow is the amount of cash available to the stakeholders of a business after providing for income taxes, capital investment, incremental net trade working capital, and other costs that must be incurred to generate (or maintain) projected net operating cash flows.

Where discretionary cash flows are determined before debt servicing costs (which normally is the case), the discount rate that is adopted should represent a weighted average cost of capital. Where discretionary cash flows are determined before debt servicing costs, direct stakeholders include debt holders and shareholders. Conversely, where interest expense (net of tax) and, where applicable, changes in debt principal outstanding are added or deducted when deriving discretionary cash flows, the discount rate that is adopted should represent a levered return on equity. The derivation and application of these rates is addressed in Chapter 7.

Pursuant to the discounted cash flow methodology the discount rate is applied to annual forecasted discretionary cash flows, and the capitalization rate is applied to estimated maintainable discretionary cash flows at the end of the forecast period to develop the terminal value component. The capitalization rate also is applied to the maintainable discretionary cash flows in the capitalization of discretionary cash flow methodology.

Internal Consistency

There must be consistency between the derivation of the discount or capitalization rate and the cash flow stream to which it is applied. For example:

- where pre-tax cash flows are projected, the discount or capitalization rate also should be determined on a pre-tax basis (although discretionary after-tax cash flows and after-tax rates of return almost always are preferable);

- the rate of inflation included in the discount rate should be consistent with the rate of inflation incorporated in the forecasted cash flows. Where inflation has been excluded from forecasted cash flows, it should also be excluded from the discount rate; and
- where expected real growth has been reflected in the estimate of maintainable discretionary cash flows, that same growth should not be accounted for again in the capitalization rate.

Risk – Return Tradeoff

There is an inverse relationship between perceived risk levels and required rates of return, commonly referred to as the 'risk-return tradeoff'. In simple terms, all other things equal the more aggressive the discretionary cash flow projections the higher should be the discount or capitalization rates and vice versa. The discount or capitalization rate and the discretionary cash flow stream to which they are applied are interdependent. In either valuation or acquisition analysis projected cash flows may include both those cash flows the business is believed capable of generating on a stand alone basis, and incremental cash flows a purchaser believes may accrue post-acquisition. Typically a higher degree of risk applies to the achieving the latter, thereby necessitating a higher rate of return applied to that component. Special purchaser value is discussed in Chapter 11.

Operating Risk and Financial Risk

The risks faced by any business can be broadly categorized as operating risk and financial risk. In the context of discount and capitalization rate determination, operating risk broadly may be thought of as the risk that projected unlevered discretionary cash flows will not materialize. Financial risk broadly may be thought of as the incremental risk assumed by equity holders resulting from employment of debt (and equivalents) in the capital structure of the business.

When determining a discount or capitalization rate, consideration must be given to both operating risk and financial risk, with each being segregated and addressed sequentially. That is, in theory the discount rate should first be derived pursuant to an assessment of operating risk (i.e. an unlevered rate of return). Financial risk (or 'financial leverage') should be superimposed on that rate. In most cases, financial risk is based on what is believed to be an 'appropriate' capital structure for the business. As a result, the capital structure decision forms an integral component of the rate of return derivation.

Market Rates of Return

Ultimately, at any given valuation date required rates of return are influenced by then prevailing general market rates of return and changes anticipated with respect to them. Accordingly, when adopting what are believed to be appropriate rates of return, consideration should be given to prevailing and prospective economic factors including the risk free rate of return, inflation rates, stock and money market conditions, and availability of capital.

Although market rates of return fluctuate on a daily basis, corporate acquirer expectations typically are influenced by the long term historic and prospective returns experienced in public financial markets, measured both in absolute terms and in relation to returns on risk free investments. This is not to suggest that discount and capitalization rates solely reflect stock market returns, but rather that corporate acquirers normally consider alternative investment opportunities and the comparative risks related thereto in their rate of return calculations.

Discount Rate Determination

Overview

As previously noted, a discount rate is the rate of return used to convert a series of projected discretionary cash flows to present value. The derivation of an appropriate discount rate or range of discount rates necessitates thorough analysis of the business being valued, the industry in which it operates, and macro and micro economic factors that influence rates of return in general.

The starting point in discount rate determination is to estimate an appropriate unlevered rate of return on equity. Appropriate unlevered rates of return on equity are 'point in time specific'. The unlevered rate of return on equity reflects the risks attached to achieving the projected discretionary cash flows, before consideration of debt servicing costs (interest expense and changes in debt principal outstanding). It follows that the unlevered rate of return on equity should appropriately reflect the degree of operating risk attached to the business and hence to any projection of its unlevered discretionary cash flows.

As set out in Figure 8.1 assuming a long term investment horizon the time specific unlevered return on equity employed when determining en bloc value typically is comprised of three principal components:

- a 'base rate' of return which is comprised of:
  – the prevailing long term risk free rate of return, which generally is derived from the pre-tax long term interest rate on government bonds,
  – a 'public market equity risk premium', which generally is taken to be equal to the average historic long term premium generated by common equity in the public markets over average risk free rates of return that prevailed over the same period,
  – a further, or 'incremental', 'equity risk premium' to compensate for the reduced liquidity that generally is available to an owner of 100% of the equity of a business as contrasted to that available to the owner of a liquid public market security, and
  – adjustments for industry-specific risks and opportunities, where it is believed that such factors are not adequately reflected in the equity risk premiums adopted.

  The resultant base rate of return, being a general market benchmark rate of return, often is referred to as a 'threshold' or 'hurdle' rate of return in the context of 'en bloc' equity investments. As a general rule, in both a notional and open market context there is an inherent assumption of long term investment objectives. *This is a fundamental factor which distinguishes valuation and pricing in an 'en bloc' or 'takeover' context from analysis and trading activity in normal sized minority share blocks in public companies in a securities market context where securities market participants have mixed short, mid, and long term investment strategies;* and

- where required, adjustments to the resultant base rate of return to account for:
  – business-specific risk factors and opportunities that are not reflected in the base rate of return (sometimes referred to as 'unsystematic risk'),
  – abnormal general, economic, money and securities market conditions, and
  – circumstances where the cash flow forecasts to which the discount rate is to be applied is believed to be aggressive or conservative, and the cash flows in that forecast have not been normalized or probabilized. Where this it the case, an adjustment to the discount rate otherwise determined is required to compensate for the increased or reduced level of risk of achieving the forecast results; and

- once an appropriate nominal unlevered rate of return on equity has been determined, a financial leverage adjustment is made to the discount rate to reflect what is believed to be an 'appropriate' level of financial risk. The result is either a nominal weighted average cost of capital (applied to discretionary cash flows before debt servicing costs), or a levered return on equity (applied to discretionary cash flows net of debt servicing costs).

Finally, in some cases, further adjustments are made to the weighted average cost of capital or levered return on equity to be consistent with the discretionary cash flow streams to which they are applied including:

- inflation rate assumptions in the cash flow projections; and
- corporate income tax assumptions in the cash flow projections.

In theory, the discount rate determined pursuant to the approach set out above should be applied to the intrinsic discretionary cash flows of the business determined on a consistent basis. Where anticipated post-acquisition net economic value added is considered in the value or price conclusion, further adjustments to the discount rate (weighted average cost of capital or levered return on equity) may be required for:

- risks related specifically to realization of expected incremental operating synergies incorporated in the projected discretionary cash flows, and
- purchaser-perceived strategic advantage and other advantages not accounted for in the prospective discretionary cash flows.

The components of a discount rate are set out in the following chart, which is followed by a discussion of each.

FIGURE 8.1

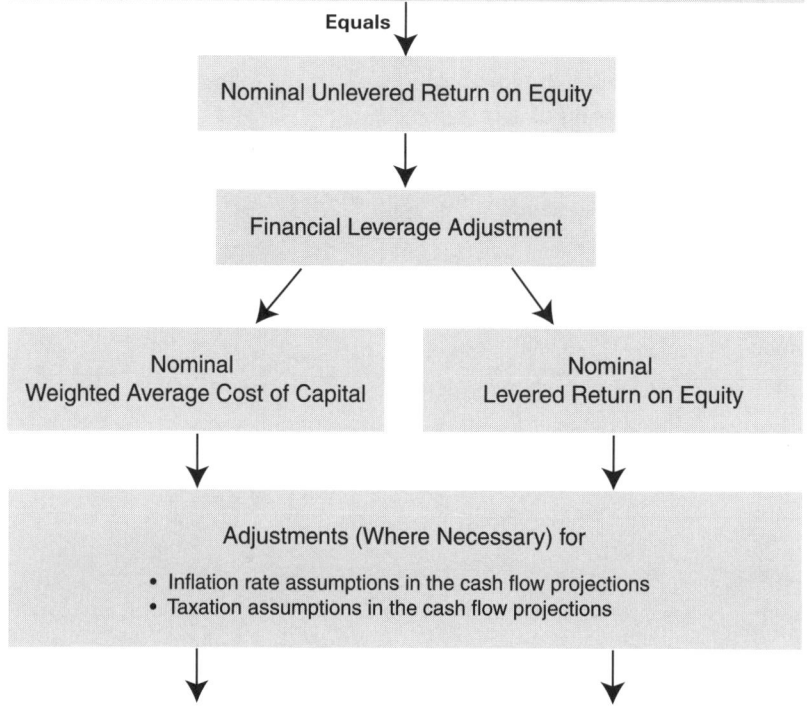

DISCOUNT AND CAPITALIZATION RATES

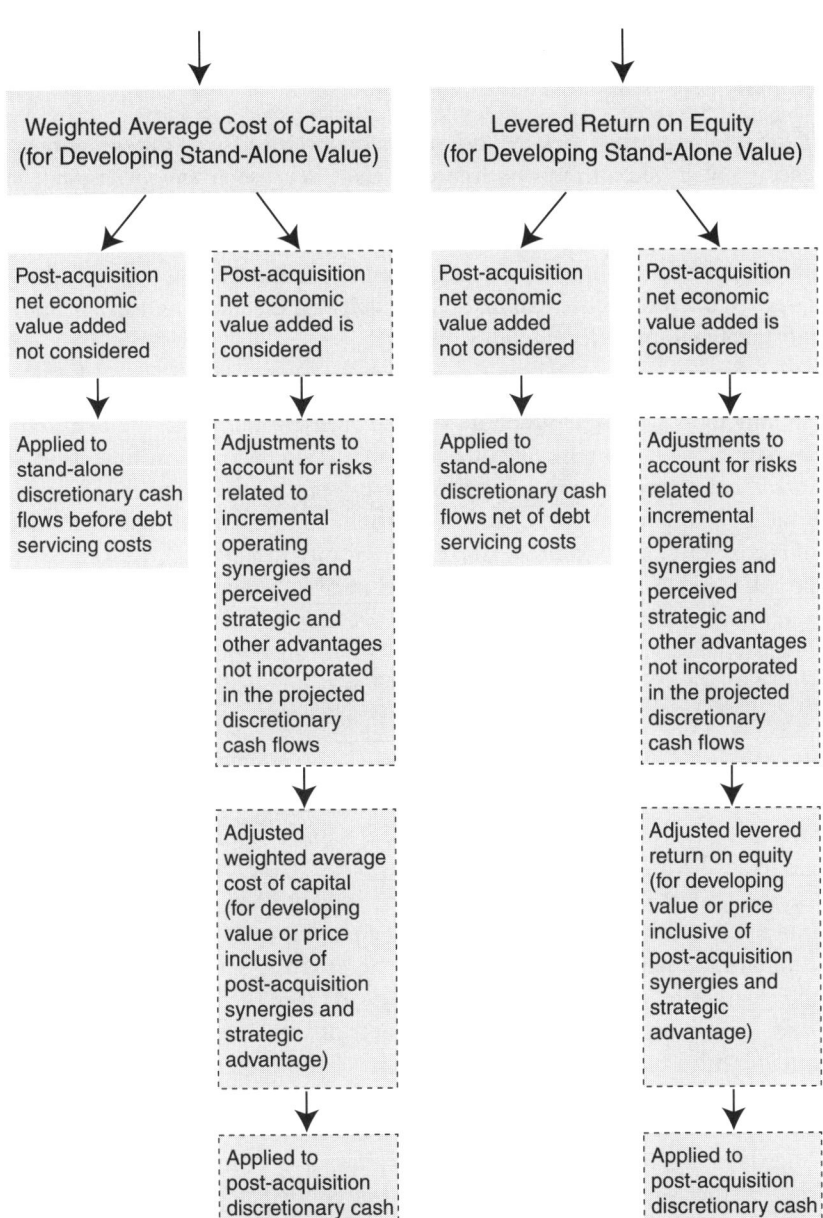

Base Rate of Return Components

Nominal risk-free rate

Time specific, market dictated, risk free rates of return are an important reference point in rate of return selection. This is because at any given point in time liquid investments are available that offer virtual certainty as to timing and quantum of stated cash flow returns. It follows that a risk premium must either explicitly or implicitly accrue beyond risk free rates either where risk attaches to the prospective realization of anticipated cash flow returns, or risk is attributable to imperfect liquidity.

The risk free rate normally used is taken to be the prevailing yield to maturity on long term government bonds. This is consistent both with the long term investment horizon normally attaching to en bloc equity investments, and with the determination of an appropriate capital structure. The risk free rate typically is a nominal rate, incorporating both an inflation rate and a real rate of return. Over the past fifty years, the major variant in the nominal composite risk free rate has been the inflation rate, in circumstances where the pre-tax real return component has fluctuated between approximately 2% and 4%. As discussed below, when adopting pre-tax risk free market rates of return as the base for rate of return selection, the inflation component of the risk free rate must be either appropriately integrated or eliminated.

The risk free rate of return typically is not adjusted for the impact of corporate income taxes. That is, where a corporate acquirer invests in a risk free debt instrument, the income on that investment is subject to corporate tax, thereby reducing the resultant discretionary cash flows. However, in the context of business valuation and acquisitions, corporate acquirers can be viewed as an intermediary between public equity market participants (individual investors, equity funds, pension funds, and so on), and the target company. Public equity market investors typically assess their returns before personal income taxes. Therefore, public equity market investors typically compare the gross rate of return on risk free debt instruments to the expected gross pre-tax returns from dividends and capital gains accruing from equity investments. In its role as an intermediary, to be successful a corporate acquirer must earn average long term rates of return on acquisition targets that are greater than or equal to the average long term rate of return required by public equity market investors. Failure to do so would result in a decline in the value of the acquirer's equity, measured on a per share basis. While not all acquirers are publicly held companies, the same theory extends to privately held businesses where individual investors are placing capital at risk (either directly or through a financial vehicle such as a pension fund), and therefore assess economic returns on a 'comparative' basis.

Public Market Equity Risk Premium

At any given point in time, the public market equity risk premium represents the consensus return that public equity market investors expect to realize in excess of risk free returns for placing capital into equity investments. This premium usually is quantified with reference to long term stock market rates of return in excess of risk free rates.

In the United States, a common source of stock market returns is the publication 'Stocks Bonds, Bills and Inflation' (SBBI) published annually by Ibbotson Associates. The 1998 SBBI Yearbook suggests that the equity risk premium from 1926 through 1997 (large company stock total returns minus long-term government bond income returns) was 5.8% on a geometric average basis. Other sources generally regard the equity risk premium for public stocks as being between 4% and 6%[1]. In Canada, a source of historic stock and money market returns can be found in the 'Report on Canadian Economic Statistics', published annually by the Canadian Institute of Actuaries. Studies have shown the return premiums in the Canadian and U.S. markets to be reasonably consistent[2].

As a general rule, stock market returns cannot be directly applied when deriving an appropriate discount rate for purposes of determining the en bloc value of the shares of a business. In particular, aggregate stock market data largely reflects returns on freely and readily tradable minority shareholdings in a diversified portfolio. Accordingly, further adjustments to the discount rate normally are required to reflect the comparatively lower degree of liquidity in en bloc equity investments, and to account for industry-specific and company-specific risk factors.

When adopting public equity market data as a proxy to assist in establishing a base rate of return, the following things should be kept in mind:

- the differences that generally exist between privately held businesses and large public companies. These may include critical mass related to size, differing access to financing and capital markets, management depth, and so on. Factors specific to the business being valued must be considered in the determination of time specific appropriate discount rates. These are addressed later in this Chapter;

- market rates of return inherently incorporate the impact of financial leverage by measuring returns on common equity, although generally it is not practical to segregate the financial leverage component of the market risk premium. As a result, if a discount or capitalization rate derived using public market data is adjusted to incorporate financial leverage, 'double counting' of financial leverage may occur; and
- due to differences in individual and corporate taxation rates, prevailing corporate law, and other factors affecting the composite returns in public equity markets, rates of return derived from public equity markets in the United States and other countries may not, without adjustment, reflect appropriate risk premium adjustments in Canada.

Some authors[3] have suggested that public equity market returns, being trades of normal sized minority interest shareholdings, inherently incorporate a 'minority discount'. Accordingly, those authors have suggested that when determining the en bloc equity value of a business a downward adjustment be applied to a public market equity risk premiums to reflect the benefits associated with control. For this view to be valid, one is required to assume:

- the en bloc value of all public companies expressed ratably on a per share basis at any given point in time will always exceed their respective prevailing public market trading prices. While valid in many specific circumstances, such an assumption is not valid stated as a generalization – see Chapter 13; and
- a comparison of prevailing public market trading prices to takeover prices where the former in a 'normal trading environment' generally do not include possible purchaser perceived synergies, and the latter almost always includes consideration of purchaser perceived synergies. Accordingly, to apply a downward adjustment to a public equity market risk premium to reflect a benefit associated with control would as a minimum in all probability result in the determination of an imputed 'takeover price' and not a stand-alone (or 'intrinsic') value.

In circumstances where the public market is reasonably informed and highly liquid with respect to a wide and diversified portfolio, and an individual investor can 'control' the timing of investment purchase and sale, the average price per share over such a widely diversified portfolio conceptually has characteristics in common with those upon which pro-rata 'stand-alone' en bloc value is premised. As a result, in most cases it follows that where 'en bloc' stand-alone value is being determined no adjustment should be made to the public market equity risk premium to account for a 'control benefit'. The concept of, and reasons for, discounts from en bloc value is discussed in Chapter 13.

Adjustments to the Public Market Equity Risk Premium to Account for Incremental En Bloc Illiquidity

The market for en bloc business equity investments (or a controlling interest therein) is subject to fundamentally different drivers than is the market for normal sized trading blocks in freely and (generally) immediately tradable publicly traded securities. The public equity markets entail a certain degree of risk — stock prices change every day and can sometimes be highly volatile. However, in most cases at any given point in time a public equity market participant dealing in 'normal sized' trading lots readily can convert public company shareholdings into cash at the prevailing market price with minimal cost. Absent unusual circumstances, even public equity market investors who claim to be 'in for the long term' almost always have the option of liquidating their positions if they so choose.

As a general rule, the greater the length of time required to market and sell an asset, the greater is the illiquidity attached to it. The divestiture of an en bloc or controlling interest in a business may take months or years to finalize, during which time significant events (both positive and negative) affecting the value of the business may transpire. The ultimate proceeds that a seller may realize typically are much less certain than are proceeds generated from the sale of freely tradable shares in a public equity market. Further, the costs involved in the disposition of an en bloc or controlling business interest can be significant as a percentage of the ultimate sale proceeds. Hence public market equity returns normally require an upward adjustment to account for this added degree of risk.

Quantifying the 'premium for illiquidity' for any given en bloc equity investment necessarily is a subjective exercise. However, where it is believed that an adjustment for incremental en bloc illiquidity differences is appropriate, the following factors normally should be considered:

- the nominal risk free rate and market equity risk premium at a given point in time, and the historical and prospective near-term volatility thereof;
- expected long term economic trends and developments;
- the known or stated objectives of likely identifiable purchasers. Where a purchaser expects to divest of the acquisition in a set period of time following acquisition, that may have a bearing on liquidity;
- the current and prospective status of the industry, vis-à-vis buyer interest, consolidation activity, number of competitors, degree of vertical and horizontal integration, and so on;

- the size of the business. Larger companies frequently have a larger number of potentially interested purchasers due to quantum of assets, market presence and so on, than do many small privately held companies; and
- the anticipated degree of integration with the identifiable purchasers. The more integrated a business becomes, generally the more difficult it is to segregate and divest.

Industry Specific Risk Factors

Industry-specific (or external) risk factors primarily address the risks faced by all companies in a particular industry. The public market equity risk premium applied in deriving a base rate of return normally reflects a composite rate of return, and may not be reflective of the particular risks and opportunities of a given industry. Accordingly, an adjustment may be required to increase or decrease the base discount rate depending on whether the industry is more or less risky than the level of risk implied in public market equity rates of return.

Where applicable, an adjustment for industry-specific risks necessarily is subjective. Having said that, it normally should consider:

- industry susceptibility to general economic conditions. Certain industries are more susceptible than others to fluctuations in the economy. For example, steel producers tend to experience greater cyclicality in their business than do manufacturers of non-durable necessities (e.g. food and drug producers);
- the regulatory or political environment. Where an industry is subject to government intervention and controls that are expected to continue at the same or increased levels, rates of return tend to be higher than otherwise would be the case. The exception to this is where government regulation effectively grants an exclusive or protective license to operate. In such circumstances, the resultant market protection generally contributes to comparatively reduced business risk, and therefore a lower required rate of return than otherwise would be the case;
- the social environment as it relates to the growth rate of existing and developing marketing areas, and levels of personal disposable income in specific geographic areas. In general, rates of return will vary directly with the risks and opportunities faced by a business when related to such factors. For example, rates of return lower than otherwise would be the case may appropriately be applied in the case of a consumer product business operating principally in an identifiable geographic area where high disposable incomes prevail. On the other hand, where such factors are reflected in pro-

jected discretionary cash flows the discount rate adopted for the forecast period would not be adjusted downward for this perceived advantage because to do so would be to double count;
- financial market psychology. At various times, some industries may go through so-called 'glamour' periods, an example being the technology industry where investments in internet related businesses were (and at the time of writing are) being made at imputed near term rates of return that are difficult, if not impossible, to rationalize in traditional economic terms;
- presence and importance of competitors, including industry ease of entry. It is axiomatic that unusually high discretionary cash flow generation and profitability attracts competition. This, in combination with considerations related to market share, cost structure, required capital investment, and existing competition's comparative positions with respect to those and other things all influence in rate of return selection. Where industry entry is costly, difficult, or regulated, existing businesses tend to be at less risk with the result that required rates of return generally are lower than otherwise would be the case. The converse is also true;
- sources, prices, and price trends of raw material supply. A protected supply of raw materials generally suggests lower risk and hence lower rates of return. Where there is dependence on relatively few suppliers, risk and hence rates of return generally are higher than otherwise would be the case. Further, where there has been a history of price fluctuations or price trends, this should be taken into account in assessing risk if not considered in maintainable or forecasted cash flows;
- industry rationalization. Historically, acquisition activity in a given industry has resulted in point in time downward adjustments to expected rates of return within those industries. The primary reason for this relates to the fact of there being a finite number of available viable acquisitions. Acquisition interest on the part of more than one purchaser typically results in a higher ultimate price being paid for the equity of a business than otherwise would be the case. Moreover, industry consolidation generally results in a greater degree of liquidity, which in turn has an upward influence on price;
- the impact and prospective impact on an industry and given business of changes in regional, Provincial, national and international trading patterns, manufacturing costs, transportation costs, and similar factors. Of particular importance is the issue of ongoing business change and viability in the face of such things;
- the impact and prospective impact of continually escalating technological change both from an:

- external point of view, being the basic question of how the business will be influenced by, and cope with, ongoing technological change, and
- internal point of view, being the ability of the business to keep up with such change from the point of view of prospective discretionary cash flow generation; and

• the prospective industry growth rate. Businesses participating in growing industries are more likely to experience long term growth in discretionary cash flows than are businesses participating in mature or declining industries where growth depends to a large extent on increasing market share which generally is a more costly and riskier process.

When making these adjustments to the base rate of return, it is important to avoid double-counting. Stated differently, many of the critical external and internal risk factors may already be considered in the cash flow forecast. For example, where a business is subject to environmental regulation, related capital and maintenance compliance costs typically will be included in a cash flow forecast and hence need not be further considered as an adjustment to the base rate of return. However, the direction of the regulatory process may indicate that although the business currently is in compliance, without incurring additional future costs business continuity may be at risk. These future costs, not being quantifiable, cannot be accounted for in the cash flow forecast. Accordingly, this incremental risk would be accounted for by increasing what otherwise would be the required rate of return.

Threshold Rates of Return

To ensure consistency in acquisition and internal capital spending analysis, rather than employing a build-up approach to determine a base rate of return, many corporations adopt pre-established, time adjusted, target rates of return in such analysis. These 'benchmark' or 'threshold' rates of return:

- generally are developed by senior management and approved by the Board of Directors;
- are time specific based principally on prevailing and forecasted money market conditions;
- typically are unlevered nominal (i.e. inclusive of inflation) rates of return on equity or a nominal weighted average cost of capital, and often are referred to as 'hurdle rates';

- adopted as 'benchmarks' or 'starting-points' in both corporate acquisition and capital spending analysis, with adjustments then being made in each instance to account for perceived fact specific risk assessment, strategic importance, near and long term real growth prospects, and so on; and
- may be higher for internal capital expenditure projects directed at operating cost savings (thought of as 'profit enhancement' projects) than for strategic internal growth projects or 'strategic' acquisitions.

Threshold rates of return typically are somewhat static over a period of time and tend not to be reflective of minor changes in prevailing market interest rates. They are influenced over the long term by alternate investment returns, corporate income tax rates, public stock market trends, and industry and economic developments. Accordingly, they tend to be adjusted as circumstances both internal and external to the acquirers' business change. Because threshold rates of return tend to be applied as benchmarks or guidelines, adjustments to them may be appropriate having regard to:

- the attributes of the specific business being valued, to the discretionary cash flow to which the rate of return is being applied, or both;
- particularly buoyant or depressed economic, financial market and money market conditions; and
- strategically important issues unique to the business being valued.

In circumstances where a corporation whose shares are publicly traded acquires outstanding shares of another corporation pursuant to a treasury share issue, different analysis may be required. This is because where a corporate acquirer uses treasury shares as 'acquisition currency', the 'value equation' becomes one of 'relative value' of the acquirer and the company acquired, as contrasted with 'absolute value' where the acquirer pays cash. The ability of such a corporation to use treasury shares as 'acquisition currency' typically is dependent on the:

- size of the securities market 'float' for the acquirer's shares, and
- extent of post-acquisition 'escrow' or other contractual obligations of those receiving the acquirer's shares that restrict the timing of their sale.

Where the acquirer's shares are widely traded and the vendors can immediately convert the acquirer's shares to cash, it can be argued that the acquirer paid, and the vendors received, a cash equivalent at the time of sale. However, it is important to recognize that in such circumstances the:

- cash accruing to the vendors effectively is akin to a 'primary offering' of the acquirer's treasury shares, and

- public market purchasers of those shares typically are driven by entirely different investment fundamentals and criteria than are corporate acquirers.

Adjustments to the Base Rate of Return

The base rate of return, being a return on unlevered equity, reflects a starting point when determining an appropriate rate of return to be adopted when valuing the en bloc equity in a given business. As previously noted, adjustments to the base rate of return may be required for:

- business-specific risk factors;
- abnormal market conditions; and
- aggressive or conservative prospective cash flows not probabilized or normalized in the projections.

Business Specific Risk Factors

Business specific (or internal) risk factors are those particular to a business not accounted for in an assessment of industry risk factors. An upward or downward adjustment in the rate of return may be required where a business faces more or less risk than does its industry in general. Where the base rate of return and the cash flow projections do not adequately reflect the specific risks or opportunities of the business that is being valued, adjustments should be made to the base rate of return. Identifying the critical factors influencing the direction, opportunities and potential of a business is essential to the determination of an appropriate discount rate. Each such factor viewed separately may have either a positive or a negative effect on the discount rate, and a melding of these positives and negatives will contribute to the selection of an appropriate discount rate.

The adjustment for business specific (or 'unsystematic') risk in the derivation of a discount rate is one of the fundamental differences between public market securities analysis and the derivation of discount rates pursuant to a long term en bloc equity investment. As a general rule, analysts of publicly traded securities do not adjust for business specific risks pursuant to the assumption that the purchaser holds a 'diversified portfolio' of publicly traded securities, and consequently in theory, the changes in the market value of any particular investment due to non-systematic (i.e. non market-related) factors has little bearing on the overall portfolio return. However, most corporate purchasers do not view en bloc equity investments as one component of a portfolio, and therefore normally will adjust for business specific risk factors where they believe that these are not adequately reflected in the base rate of return. Further, and as a practical matter, the perceived risk of an en bloc equity investment to a corporate acquirer normally is relatively greater compared to the purchase of a normal sized trading lot of securities from the standpoint of the holder of a diversified portfolio. This is so from the standpoint of the impact a failed acquisition has on the corporate acquirer's consolidated earnings, public equity market perceptions, and the personal implications to the business managers responsible for the 'poor' investment decision.

When determining an appropriate fact specific rate of return, business specific risk factors that should be considered normally include:

- the size of the business, both in absolute terms and in relation to other businesses in the industry. Smaller businesses normally have less market influence, less customer awareness, more restricted access to capital, less management depth, greater customer dependence, and so on. Each of these factors affects risk to varying degrees. Obviously, where the rate of return is adjusted for one or more of these factors separately, those factors should not be considered again in any composite risk adjustment made to account for size;
- management depth, including consideration of whether there is dependence on specific managers or other key personnel for business continuity. In general, greater management depth and continuity, particularly in the context of business size, implies a lower appropriate rate of return. Where business continuity is dependent on the personal involvement of one or more managers, as a general rule risk is greater and required rates of return are higher than they otherwise would be. A certain amount of management dependence is a factor common to most privately held companies. The important distinction to be made is that between dependence on management ability and dependence on existing management's personal contacts — see Chapter 2 for discussion of non-commercial goodwill and management and non-competition agreements;
- products and services offered. Product and service quality, measured by customer acceptance, market share, and otherwise, tends to have a direct bearing on risk. Further, where a product or service is protected by patent or copyright, or has brand name recognition, a lower rate of return generally would be expected than if no such protection existed;
- research and development. Where a business has an active research and development department with a proven record of success, thereby mitigating business risk, a lower rate of return typically would be expected than in circumstances where a business does not have such a program. Research and

development expenditures may relate to the enhancement of existing products, operating efficiencies, development of new products, and so on. Success in these areas may contribute to prospective discretionary cash flows or risk reduction which, when measured against ongoing research and development expenditure levels, incrementally contribute to the equity value of the business;

- plant facilities. If plant and equipment are well maintained, have suffered relatively little physical and technological obsolescence, would be costly, difficult, or impossible (for environmental related reasons, for example) to replace or relocate, rates of return typically would be lower than otherwise would be the case, and vice versa;
- labour force. Labour availability combined with historic and prospective labour relations affect risk assessment. In this regard, rates of return adopted for labour intensive businesses tend to be higher than those adopted for capital intensive businesses;
- contracts and leases. Where existing contracts and leases diminish risk or by themselves may influence open market value, rates of return tend to be lower than where such contracts and leases do not exist;
- customer dependence. In general, in 'non-commodity' businesses where a business is dependent on a few customers, rates of return are higher than in circumstances where a business has many customers and little or no customer dependence;
- ability to cope with, and react to change. Where a business has demonstrated an ability to cope successfully with changing economic, industry, business, social and other relevant factors, a lower rate of return generally would be selected than if the business had not demonstrated this ability;
- the degree of diversification in both product and service offerings, and geographic coverage. As a general rule, the wider the product and service offering and the wider the geographic coverage typically the lower will be the appropriate rate of return;
- historic operating results and projections. Typically lower rates of return than otherwise would be the case are adopted in circumstances where historic results have:
  - generally conformed with prior year's projections, or have deviated from them for non-recurring and explicable reasons; and
  - demonstrated an increasing trend and have not been unduly erratic;
- degree of operating leverage (as contrasted to financial leverage). A business that incorporates a higher degree of fixed operating costs (excluding depreciation) in its operating cost structure typically is subject to a higher

degree of risk than a business that employs a more variable-based cost structure. This is because by definition fixed costs cannot readily be reduced or eliminated in the event of a downturn in operating performance, or it may not be practical to do so;
- life cycles of the product offerings. Where product life cycles are short, and continuing investment in research and development is required, there is additional risk that a business' competitive position may erode, perhaps quickly, if such investments are diminished or curtailed; and
- the underlying net tangible assets to the extent their existence or absence are perceived to decrease or increase business risk.

As is the case with industry-specific risk factors, the discount rate would not be adjusted where business-specific risk factors were already quantified in the discretionary cash flow forecast.

General, Economic, Money, and Securities Market Conditions

The time-specific prevailing conditions and projected trends in the economy and financial markets influence the base rates of return. For example, where the:

- near-term and longer term outlook of the general economy is optimistic, this would tend to reduce base rates of return, and vice versa; and
- financial markets are buoyant at a particular point in time, this would tend to reduce base rates of return, and vice versa.

As previously discussed, as a general rule threshold rates of return are not adjusted for short term fluctuations in the economy or financial markets. However, adjustments may be considered appropriate where changes in the economy or financial markets are expected to prevail over the medium to longer term. Analysts of publicly traded securities often adjust the rates of return they employ in their analysis for small changes in interest rates and equity risk premiums, consistent with a short-term view of stock market investments. In theory, adjustments to the base rate of return for evaluating en bloc equity investments should be made only where the base rate of return is deemed not reflective of expected long term changes in general economic and financial conditions. Importantly, it is unlikely an adjustment to the base rate of return would be made where cash flow projections are thought to adequately account for these factors.

Aggressive or Conservative Cash Flow Projections

As previously discussed, appropriate rate of return selection is based on a risk-return tradeoff. Stated differently, it is a function of there being an appropriate interrelationship between the rate of return and the discretionary cash flow to which it is applied. All other things equal, an aggressive discretionary cash flow forecast should be subject to a higher discount rate and a conservative discretionary cash flow forecast should be subject to a lower discount rate. It bears repeating that it is important not to double-count rate of return adjustments made in respect of market, industry and business specific risk factors, and those specifically reflected in prospective discretionary cash flows. The degree to which a forecast is aggressive or conservative is a matter of judgement having regard to:

- the general economic and industry-specific outlook;
- the nature of the industry and the business;
- the assumptions used in the forecast regarding sales growth, cost savings, competitive developments, and so on; and
- the purpose for which the forecast was prepared, including consideration of the knowledge, experience and potential bias of those individuals who prepared it, the time and extent of analysis incorporated in it, and various other considerations influencing its credibility — see Chapter 5.

Generally, where the discretionary cash flow projections are believed optimistic or pessimistic, they should be probabilized or normalized to reflect what is believed to be a 'reasonable' projection. This can be done by:

- applying a probability factor to either:
  - the revenue projection or other forecast variable(s) and recalculating the discretionary cash flow, or
  - the discretionary cash flow projection itself, based on the estimated likelihood of achievement; or
- directly adjusting those revenue and expense items that are believed to be outside of a reasonable range.

The probabilized or normalized discretionary cash flow would then be discounted at appropriate unadjusted 'market dictated' discount rates.

It generally is preferable to adjust the forecast and to apply 'market dictated' discount rates rather than attempt to adjust the discount rate itself. This is because the cash flow forecast typically reflects specific variables that can be analyzed individually when determining whether adjustments are required. As a result, adjusting the cash flow forecast normally is a less subjective exercise than making an adjustment to the discount rate. However, where a forecast that is believed to be aggressive or conservative is not probabilized or normalized, it is necessary to reflect the risk in achieving the forecast through an upward or downward adjustment to the discount rate.

Financial Leverage Adjustment

The base rate of return, adjusted where necessary for business-specific risk factors, abnormal market conditions, and aggressive or conservative cash flow projections, represents a nominal unlevered return on equity. Again, an unlevered return on equity is a rate of return on equity assuming no interest bearing debt in the capital structure of the business. However, the rate of return applied to discretionary cash flows should reflect the financial risk of the business being valued, based on what is believed to be an 'appropriate' capital structure.

Where discretionary cash flows are projected before debt servicing costs, the unlevered rate of return should be converted to a weighted average cost of capital. The discounted or capitalized cash flows then represents the enterprise value (or aggregated debt and equity value of the business) and outstanding interest bearing debt is deducted to determine the en bloc value of the equity component. Where a weighted average cost of capital is adopted, income tax savings related to interest deductibility are inherently accounted for on the imputed debt portion of the appropriate optimal capital structure.

Where discretionary cash flows are projected after interest expense (net of the related income tax shield) and changes in debt principal outstanding, the unlevered discount rate should be increased by an appropriate financial risk factor to determine the levered return on equity. The discounted or capitalized cash flows then represent the en bloc equity value of the business. Pursuant to this methodology, where an adjustment is made to the notional amount of outstanding debt in the determination of an appropriate capital structure, a corresponding adjustment must be made to the en bloc equity value otherwise determined.

The derivation of a weighted average cost of capital and levered return on equity is discussed in Chapter 7.

Additional Adjustments to the Discount Rate

The derivation of the weighted average cost of capital or levered return on equity as explained above represents a nominal rate of return. As previously noted, there must be consistency between the rates of return and the cash flows to which they are applied. In this regard, further adjustments to the discount rate may be required for:

- inflation assumptions in the cash flow projections; and
- corporate income tax assumptions in the cash flow projections.

Inflation Assumptions in the Cash Flow Projections

Cash flow forecasts inherently assume either inclusion or exclusion of inflation and, where included, an inflation rate. The inflation rate incorporated in the discount rate adopted should be consistent with that used in the cash flow projection. Where the discount rate is 'built up' beginning with the rate of return on government bonds, an inflation expectation already is included therein. However, an adjustment may be necessary if the inflation rate in the cash flow forecast is different than the inflation rate implicitly incorporated in the risk free rate. General inflation forecasts typically are included as one component in pre-determined threshold rates of return. These must then be eliminated from the threshold rate of return adopted where inflation is not included in the cash flow forecast.

Corporate Income Tax Assumptions in the Cash Flow Projections

Discretionary cash flows are determined net of corporate income taxes. There must be consistency between the corporate income tax rates used when deriving the discretionary cash flows and those applied when deriving the discount rate. For example, if a corporate acquirer had a target weighted average cost of capital discount rate of 10% derived based on its blended corporate income tax rate of 40%, but was assessing a target business whose income was, and post-acquisition would continue to be, subject to taxation at a 35% rate, the discount rate should be adjusted to reflect the target company's 35% tax rate for the purpose of developing the intrinsic value of the vendor's business. Where a purchaser can take effectively take advantage of differing tax rates by employing debt in jurisdictions with higher income tax rates, that normally would be considered separately as a component of post-acquisition synergies.

In the event that the projected cash flows to be discounted are expressed on a pre-corporate income tax basis, the discount rate should be adjusted to be consistent with this. Where applicable, this is accomplished by 'grossing up' the discount rate using the appropriate corporate income tax rate. For example, if an appropriate after-tax discount rate was believed to be 15%, and corporate income taxes were paid at a rate of 40%, the equivalent pre-tax discount rate would be 15% / (1-40%) = 25%.

Whereas the result obtained by applying an after-tax discount rate to after-tax cash flows often will be the same as that obtained where a pre-tax discount rate is applied to pre-tax cash flows, the after-tax approach usually is preferable. Corporate acquirers typically analyze acquisition targets based on discretionary (after-tax) cash flow expectations. Moreover, in some cases, permanent and timing differences in corporate taxation sometimes can result in a different conclusion depending on whether a pre-tax or after-tax basis is used. Accordingly, both in theory and practice, forecast cash flows and discount rates typically should be determined on an after-tax basis.

Adjustment for Post-Acquisition Strategic Advantage

The weighted average cost of capital or levered return on equity derived pursuant to the methodology explained above does not incorporate the possible influence of purchaser-perceived net economic value added or strategic advantage. Accordingly, the discount rate so determined should be applied against the stand-alone discretionary cash flows of the target business to determine its intrinsic value.

As discussed in Chapter 11, the quantification of purchaser perceived post acquisition synergies can be segregated into three categories:

- tangible operating synergies, being those synergies that are inherently quantifiable – such as headcount reduction and identifiable incremental revenue opportunities;
- intangible operating synergies, being strategic advantages that are not inherently quantifiable, but contribute to an overall level of risk reduction or upside potential in prospective discretionary cash flows – such as the benefits of greater diversification; and
- financial synergies, being those related to post acquisition availability of a more efficient capital structure or lower cost financing.

Where post-acquisition tangible operating synergies are incorporated in cash flow projections or discounted separately, and a 'probability factor' is not applied to reflect the incremental risk attached to achieving those benefits, the discount rate should be adjusted to reflect this. Where a purchaser perceives post-acquisition intangible operating synergies and financial synergies, the benefit of these things often is reflected through a reduction in the discount rate otherwise determined.

Other adjustments to the discount rate might also be made in respect of a corporate acquirer's perception of:

- the level of competition for the acquisition of the target business; and
- other things not predictable beforehand but which arise in differing degrees during the course of open market negotiations.

As a practical matter, it is only in negotiation that these latter two things are quantified. The quantification of synergies, including adjustments to the discount rate, are discussed in Chapter 11.

Other Considerations

Mid-year Discount Rates

Where a discount rate is applied to annual discretionary cash flows, there is an inherent assumption that said cash flows accrue to the business at the end of each year. This may not be the case. Although not always done in practice, theoretically where discretionary cash flows accrue more or less evenly throughout the year an adjustment should be made to convert the end of year discount rate to a mid-year (or other interval) rate, consistent with the nature of the expected cash flows. A mid-year adjustment can be made by modifying the exponential function for the corresponding cash flow period. For example, a 12% discount rate (a present value factor of 0.8929 in year one and 0.7972 in year two, and so on) could be adjusted to:

$(1+.12)^{1/2} - 1 = 5.8\%$, or a discount factor of 0.9449 in year one;

$(1+.12)^{1\frac{1}{2}} - 1 = 18.5\%$, or a discount factor of 0.8437 in year two; and so on.

Accounting Earnings

As previously discussed, in both valuation theory and practice the prospective discretionary cash flow stream, and not reported or prospective after-tax accounting earnings, is the appropriate income stream to which rates of return are most meaningfully applied. Notwithstanding, if accounting earnings are used as the income stream to be discounted or capitalized further adjustments to the discount or capitalization rate may be necessary. Projected discretionary cash flows frequently are different than accounting earnings because (for example):

- capital expenditure requirements may be greater than depreciation in the near term, particularly in growing businesses, or may in some cases be less than depreciation;
- certain costs might be capitalized and amortized for accounting purposes in circumstances where they represent immediate cash outflows; and
- cash outflows due to incremental net trade working capital requirements are not considered an expense from an accounting standpoint.

As a result, the rate of return applied to after-tax accounting earnings may of necessity be greater or less than that applied to discretionary cash flows. In theory, the adjustment made should be based on the ratio of accounting income to discretionary cash flows - see Chapter 10.

Capitalization Rate Determination

Overview

A capitalization rate is applied in the capitalization of discretionary cash flow methodology and the terminal value component of the discounted cash flow methodology. A capitalization rate is derived by deducting a growth factor from the discount rate. The growth factor generally is comprised of an inflation factor and may incorporate an additional adjustment for real growth. In theory, the growth factor should be deducted from the discount rate on a geometric (as opposed to linear) basis. Finally, where a capitalization rate is used to develop the terminal value component in a discounted cash flow calculation, a further adjustment for business and time specific risk beyond the forecast period may be necessary to convert a discount rate to a capitalization rate.

The relationship between discount and capitalization rates can be summarized follows:

FIGURE 8.2

CAPITALIZATION RATE DETERMINATION

Nominal Discount Rate
(WACC or levered return on equity)

Less

Inflation

Less

Real long term growth (where applicable)

Add/deduct

Terminal value risk adjustment (DCF methodology)

Equals:

Capitalization Rate

↙ ↘

Weighted average cost of capital	Levered return on equity
↓	↓
Applied to discretionary cash flows *before* debt servicing costs	Applied to discretionary cash flows *net of* debt servicing costs

Inflation Adjustment

Where the discretionary cash flow is determined net of inflation the capitalization rate also must be expressed net of inflation. In such circumstances inflation should be deducted from the nominal discount rate (either WACC or levered return on equity). The inflation component deducted from the nominal discount rate should be reflective of the inflation rate included therein. Where the discount rate already is stated net of inflation no further inflation adjustment is necessary.

In theory, the inflation adjustment should be made on a geometric as opposed to a linear basis. For example, if the nominal discount rate is 15% and inflation is 3%, the real discount rate (or capitalization rate before further adjustments) is not 12%, but rather 11.65%. The applicable formula is:

FORMULA 8.1

$$[(1 + \text{nominal discount rate})/(1 + \text{inflation rate})] - 1$$

As a practical matter, the calculation normally is made on a linear basis for simplicity. The difference between the geometric and linear adjustment increases as the rate of inflation increases.

Using a real capitalization rate inherently assumes discretionary cash flows will continue to grow at the rate of inflation to perpetuity. Because this may not always be the case, an adjustment for real growth (or real decline where inflationary costs cannot be passed on to customers over the long term) may be required.

Finally, in theory an argument can be made that the adjustment for inflation should be applied to the nominal unlevered return on equity, and that financial risk then should be imputed to the real unlevered return on equity. This is because, due to the tax deductibility of interest expense, all things equal, a higher inflation rate will lead to a higher enterprise value and resultant higher equity value of the business. This may be counter-intuitive given the additional risks that may be perceived to exist in a high inflation environment. Notwithstanding, as a practical matter, the inflation adjustment normally is applied to the nominal WACC or nominal levered return on equity. The impact on value due to inflationary factors increases as the expected rate of inflation increases.

Real Growth

The real rate of growth does not include growth due to inflation, but rather growth due to sustained annual increases in real discretionary cash flows. Where real growth in after tax cash flows from operations is anticipated, perpetual annual increases in both net trade working capital and growth related capital expenditures normally are required to support the long term real growth assumption. Accordingly, such costs should be incorporated in the determination of discretionary cash flows.

There is an important distinction between business expansion and real growth. Most businesses generally intend to expand. However, in the context of business valuation, real growth translates into incremental value only where a business invests in projects that generate returns in excess of its required rate of return. Mathematically, this can be expressed as follows:

FORMULA 8.2

$$\frac{C \times (1 - g/r)}{k - g}$$

where:

C = discretionary cash flows

g = growth in discretionary cash flows

r = rate of return on new investment

k = required rate of return

Working through Formula 8.2, it can be shown that 'value' is only created where the rate of return on new investment (r) exceeds the rate of return required for the business as a whole (k). In competitive markets continual excess returns are unusual over the long run. Therefore, even if a business is expanding, it may be worth no more than its 'no-real-growth' equivalent value.

The real growth rate deducted from the real (net of inflation) discount rate to determine the capitalization rate (if any) should be a long term average growth rate. From a theoretical standpoint, it is required to be steady into perpetuity. Further, in theory the adjustment for real growth (where applicable), like the adjustment for inflation, should be made on a geometric basis.

It is important to assess the reasonableness of real growth projections in light of the nature of the industry and the business. The real rate of growth in discretionary cash flow may be greater than the real rate of growth in revenue if certain fixed costs can be leveraged over the long run. However, over the long term virtually all fixed costs will have to increase to accommodate higher revenues. Theoretically, in the long run, total growth cannot depart too far from inflation plus population growth. As noted above, if a business reasonably cannot be expected to pass on inflationary costs to its customers over the long term (as, for example, where businesses are in the decline stage of their product or life cycles), it may be necessary to build a 'real decline' into the rate of return (as contrasted with a 'real growth' rate).

The real rate of growth must be less than the discount rate. If this is not the case, the capitalization model will lose its validity. As the real rate of growth approaches the real rate of return, the capitalized value of a business increases exponentially. As a result, minor changes in assumptions can lead to substantially different value conclusions. This is illustrated as follows:

	Company X	Company Y
Discretionary cash flow, year 1	$1,000,000	$400,000
Real discount rate (net of inflation)	12%	12%
Real growth rate – low	2%	8%
– high	4%	10%
Capitalization rate – low value range	10%	4%
– high value range	8%	2%
Capitalized cash flow – low	$10,000,000	$10,000,000
– high	$12,500,000	$20,000,000
Range of value (high to low)	25%	100%

The prospect of a business sustaining high rates of real growth over the long term typically is unrealistic. Where a relatively high rate of real growth is expected in the near term, a discounted cash flow methodology should be adopted. This is because the discounted cash flow methodology considers all pertinent factors relevant to the achievement of growth, and enables a more informed assessment of whether such growth is sustainable beyond the forecast period. The terminal value determination (i.e. the capitalized discretionary cash flows at the end of the forecast period) should be made at the point in time where little, if any, real long term growth is anticipated. If the terminal value determination is made prior to that point in time, the capitalization rate should be adjusted to consider real long-term growth only for a plausible period following the point in time at which terminal value is determined.

Terminal Value Risk Adjustment

Pursuant to the discounted cash flow methodology forecasted discretionary cash flows are discounted for a given number of years (normally five to seven), and maintainable discretionary cash flows are estimated at the end of the forecast period for purposes of determining terminal value. Those maintainable discretionary cash flows may have a significantly different (typically higher) risk profile compared with forecast period discretionary cash flows. This may be the case where, for example:

- the industry is going through a period of rapid change, and the maintainable discretionary cash flows beyond the forecast period are highly unpredictable;
- the industry is subject to leaps in technology every few years and there is uncertainty associated with the resultant discretionary cash flows following same;
- the business has a license, patent, or some other strategic advantage that expires beyond the forecast period which may not be renewed; and
- the business is particularly sensitive to a political or regulatory environment that is subject to sudden change (e.g. due to an election or pending industry deregulation slated for some point in the future).

In such circumstances, the capitalization rate should be increased from that otherwise determined to recognize the greater uncertainty associated with the maintainable discretionary cash flow to which the rate is applied. In theory, such an adjustment should be applied to the unlevered return on equity component of the capitalization rate where the change in risk relates to the operating cash flows of the business. An adjustment for financial leverage then would be applied. However, as a practical matter, where a terminal value risk adjustment is made, it more commonly is made by adjusting the weighted average cost of capital or levered return on equity.

Other Adjustments

In theory, the capitalization rate derived by deducting real growth from the real discount rate should be applied to discretionary cash flow projected one year forward. Where current or indicated discretionary cash flows are being capitalized, the following adjustment to the capitalization rate may be necessary:

FORMULA 8.3

$$(d-g)/(1+g)$$

where:

    d = the nominal discount rate; and

    g = the growth rate (including both inflation and real growth, if any).

For example, assume discretionary cash flows in the fifth forecast year are $1 million, are expected to stabilize beyond that time, and that an appropriate nominal discount rate is 15% including 3% combined inflation and real growth. This suggests a capitalization rate of 12% (for simplicity based on a linear deduction for growth). If maintainable discretionary after-tax cash flows in year six and beyond are taken to be $1 million, adopting the above formula the capitalization rate should be adjusted from 12% to 11.65% [(15%-3%)/(1+3%)]. Alternatively, maintainable discretionary cash flow could be increased by the expected rate of growth, and that amount could be divided by the capitalization rate otherwise determined. In the example, this would entail increasing the maintainable discretionary after-tax cash flows in the terminal value calculation to $1.03 million, and not adjusting the capitalization rate from 12%. In practice, neither adjustment typically is made because it normally does not have a material impact on the value determination.

Discount and Capitalization Rate Example

XYZ Limited manufactures parts for the automotive industry. XYZ is contemplating the acquisition of Newparts Ltd., a small automotive parts manufacturer whose products are complimentary to those of XYZ. Newparts management has compiled the following unlevered discretionary cash flow projection in real dollars (excluding inflation) for its business (000's):

Fiscal Year	2001	2002	2003	2004	2005	Beyond
Discretionary cash flow	$650	$780	$805	$900	$950	$1,000

Management of XYZ is considering what discount and capitalization rates are appropriate to apply to this series of forecast discretionary cash flows. Other relevant information follows:

- XYZ adopts a threshold unlevered rate of return of 14% in its acquisition analysis, which includes 3% inflation;
- the auto parts industry historically has been cyclical, and XYZ management believes a downturn may be near after several years of growth;
- the major automotive manufacturers are becoming increasingly demanding and are entering into long term strategic partnerships with select parts manufacturers;
- Newparts has recently completed a major retooling and equipment upgrade program that is expected to generate significant improvements in cost efficiency;
- XYZ management considers Newparts' projections to be moderately optimistic, even in light of recent capital spending upgrades;
- no real growth is expected beyond the projection period;
- Newparts currently has $2 million of interest bearing debt outstanding and no redundant assets;
- an appropriate long term debt to total capital ratio for Newparts is 33%, and its effective income tax rate is 40%;
- approximately 50% of Newparts' gross revenues are generated from two customers. Newparts has supply contracts that extend to 2005 with both;
- XYZ management expects to achieve post-acquisition headcount reductions at Newparts. In addition, XYZ management believes it particularly important to acquire Newparts to enhance its long term opportunities in the market place. These benefits will be evaluated separately; and
- cash flows are expected to accrue mid-year.

Discount and Capitalization Rate Determination

Assuming the facts presented are the only relevant considerations, risk-adjusted discount and capitalization rates might be determined as follows:

Discount rate determination:

Starting point – nominal unlevered return on equity	14%
Adjustments for risks (benefits) relating to:	
Reliance two customers, say	2%
Retooling program (see following narrative)	nil
Aggressiveness of cash flow projections say,	1%
Risk-adjusted unlevered return on equity	17%
Converted to a nominal weighted average cost of capital = 17% x (1- 40% x 33%) (rounded)	15%
Deduct: inflation (linear basis)	(3%)
Real weighted average cost of capital for developing intrinsic value	12%

The starting point in discount rate determination is the nominal unlevered return on equity of 14%. Where the threshold rate is industry-specific, no further adjustments for industry risk should be made. However, adjustments for company specific risk (reliance on two customers, for example) are appropriate. It also is important to avoid double-counting. For example, although Newparts will benefit from its recent retooling program, these benefits have already been accounted for in the cash flow projections. Therefore, no further reduction in the discount rate to account for this should be made. However, an adjustment is made to account for aggressive cash flow projections that have not otherwise been normalized or probabilized. The target risk-adjusted nominal unlevered return on equity is estimated at 17%. This is converted to a nominal weighted average cost of capital based on a 40% income tax rate and 33% debt to total capital ratio. The nominal weighted average cost of capital is 15% (rounded) (see Chapter 7). Inflation is deducted to derive a real weighted average cost of capital of 12%, consistent with the discretionary cash flow projections that are stated in real dollars.

No adjustments to the discount rate were made for post-acquisition benefits or strategic advantage. Therefore, the discount rate as determined would be applied to derive the intrinsic value of Newparts. As a practical matter, XYZ may make further adjustments to its discount rate to account for the element of post-acquisition net economic value added in its pricing considerations.

Capitalization rate determination:

Discount rate (above)	12%
Less: inflation	n/a
Less: real growth beyond the forecast period	nil
Add: additional risk of contract renewal beyond 2005, say	2%
Equals capitalization rate (real WACC)	14%
Equivalent multiple (1/14%)	7 X

To determine the capitalization rate, no adjustment is required for inflation since the discount rate is expressed in real terms. No real long term growth is anticipated, as indicated. It is assumed that a risk premium of 2% beyond fiscal 2005 is appropriate given the nature of the contracts. Again, it may be more appropriate to adjust the unlevered return on equity (to which financial leverage subsequently would be imputed) rather than the weighted average cost of capital for this incremental risk element, given that it pertains to the operations of the business, and not its financing structure. Once again, post-acquisition synergies and strategic advantage have not been considered in the determination of the capitalization rate, and separate analysis incorporating these factors may be appropriate.

It follows that the intrinsic value of the shares of Newparts would be determined as follows ($000):

Fiscal Year	2001	2002	2003	2004	2005	Beyond
Discretionary cash flow	650	780	805	900	950	1,000
Terminal multiple						7X
Terminal value						7,000
Discount factor at 12%, based on mid-year rates	0.945	0.844	0.753	0.673	0.600	0.600
Discounted discretionary cash flow	614	658	606	606	570	4,200
Intrinsic value determination:						
Enterprise value	7,254					
Deduct: debt outstanding	(2,000)					
Add: redundant assets	0					
Intrinsic en bloc value of shares	5,254					

The Capital Asset Pricing Model

Overview

The Capital Asset Pricing Model (CAPM) is a theoretical comparative risk assessment model that relates risk and return for any asset. It is based on the concept that the required rate of return for an asset is directly related to the riskiness of the asset in comparison to other risky assets and the 'risk-free' rate of return. Greater risk requires a higher expected rate of return. CAPM measures risk in terms of the volatility of the asset price relative to a stock market index benchmark.

The Capital Market Theory, of which the Capital Asset Pricing Model is a component, divides risk into two types:

- systematic risk – being the uncertainty of future returns due to the sensitivity of the return on the asset (e.g. a particular business) to movements in the return for the market as a whole; and
- unsystematic risk – being related to the specific characteristics of the subject business, the industry, and the type of business interest.

The total risk to a particular business interest is the sum of its systematic and unsystematic risks. However, CAPM postulates that unsystematic risk can be eliminated by investors who choose to hold a totally risk diversified portfolio and accordingly, that the risk premium in CAPM relates solely to systematic risk.

The CAPM Methodology

The basic CAPM formula is expressed as follows:

FORMULA 8.3

$$R_e = R_f + B(R_m - R_f)$$

where:

- R_e is the rate of return on equity for a particular company;
- R_f is the risk free rate (normally taken as the rate on long term government bonds);
- B is Beta, a measure of relative risk (volatility); and
- R_m is the long term rate of return of the equity markets.

The CAPM formula essentially is a variation of the build-up methodology discussed previously. That is, an equity risk premium is added to the risk free rate. However, in the case of CAPM, industry risk factors are assumed to be incorporated through the use of the Beta factor and specific company risk is assumed to be eliminated pursuant to an assumption of a 'fully diversified' portfolio.

The equation ($R_m - R_f$) is a measure of the equity risk premium. That is, the additional return required over the risk free rate for investing in the public equity market. It is calculated by subtracting the historic risk-free rate (normally expressed as the return on long term government bonds) from the historical return on common stocks. The return on long term government bonds is a pre-tax return. The return on common stocks is a long term after corporate tax return, based on increases in market indices (such as the S&P 500 index), and normally includes notional income from dividend reinvestment. These statistics normally are obtained from publications such as 'Stocks, Bonds, Bills and Inflation'. Published annually by Ibbotson and Associates.

Beta is a measure of stock price volatility relative to the overall benchmark market index. Mathematically, Beta is equal to the covariance between the returns on a particular stock and those of the market portfolio. If a stock moves up or down proportionately to the overall market against which it is measured, it has a Beta of 1.0. If the stock movements are comparatively:

- greater than the overall market, the stock has a Beta greater than 1.0; and
- less than the overall market, the stock has a Beta less than 1.0.

In CAPM theory, Beta is a measure of risk. A stock with a Beta of 1.5 is considered riskier than a stock with a Beta of 1.0.

The Beta for a particular company usually is estimated based on some average of the Beta factors for to so-called 'comparable' public companies, as contained in stock market services reports. This presumes that there are closely comparable public companies in the same line of business, and that these companies have sufficient trading activity to permit a meaningful estimate of Beta. Where the equity risk premium is multiplied by Beta, the equity risk factor is adjusted for the price volatility of said so-called 'comparable' companies.

Interpreting CAPM Results

Because public stock market data is used, CAPM based rates of return represent those of freely tradable minority interests. Therefore, in the context of valuing a business 'en bloc', an adjustment may be required in respect of the reduced liquidity of an en bloc equity investment compared to a freely tradable and readily marketable security. In addition, CAPM-based rates of return represent capitalization rates, not discount rates. An adjustment for the growth factor implicitly built into the CAPM capitalization rate must be made in order to determine the discount rate suggested by CAPM. However, the growth factor implied in market rates of return is not readily identifiable, and an estimate thereof must be made.

CAPM rates of return are levered after-tax rates of return on equity or, stated differently, are after-tax returns on equity and not after-tax returns on enterprise value. Therefore, CAPM based rates of return should be applied to discretionary cash flows determined net of debt service costs. In addition, it should be recognized that the inherent financial leverage adjustment in the CAPM model is based on the 'comparables' used in the derivation of the Beta factor. Therefore, to be consistent the debt to equity ratio of the business being valued should be notionally adjusted to reflect the average debt to equity ratio of the group of companies adopted as 'comparable', thereby eliminating the need for any further adjustments for financial risk. Alternatively, the Betas of the 'comparable' companies can be unlevered to derive an average unlevered Beta. A leverage factor then can be applied to the business being valued to determine levered equity. The formula to derive unlevered Beta is:

FORMULA 8.4

$$\text{Beta (unlevered)} = \text{Beta (levered)} / [1 + (1-T) D/E]$$

and the formula to derive levered Beta is:

FORMULA 8.5

$$\text{Beta (levered)} = [1 + (1-T) D/E] \times \text{Beta (unlevered)}$$

where:

T = marginal corporate tax rate; and

D/E = the market value of debt to equity.

Adjustments to the Basic CAPM Model

As previously noted, CAPM postulates that company specific risk is irrelevant based on the assumption that it can be eliminated through a 'fully diversified' portfolio. Where it is believed that this assumption is not valid, to account for the unique characteristics of a particular business the CAPM formula can be modified to:

FORMULA 8.6

$$R_e = R_f + B (R_m - R_f) + R_c$$

where R_c is business specific risk.

Business specific risk factors represent additional risk not incorporated in Beta. Such factors were addressed as business specific risk adjustments as part of the rate of return build-up approach discussion. It is important to note that industry-specific adjustments are not required in the CAPM model because such influences are assumed to be addressed through the use of Beta. Therefore, in theory the CAPM method eliminates many of the risk differentials that are common to the build-up approach to rate of return development because the differences are presumed addressed in the Beta adjustment. Again, this approach to discount rate determination assumes that the 'comparable' companies adopted are in the same business as the business being valued, are closely comparable in so far as their respective business operations are concerned, and face largely similar market risks for their respective products and services.

Difficulties Inherent in CAPM

There are many difficulties inherent in the use of CAPM as a basis for determining appropriate discount and capitalization rates. In general terms:

- the identification of so-called 'comparable' public companies is a difficult and subjective task. As discussed in Chapter 9, true 'comparables' seldom exist;
- CAPM postulates that investors are 'price takers' which eliminates the negotiating element that occurs in open market transactions;
- Beta is a measure of the relationship between the stock of a particular company and a market portfolio. It is influenced by returns that are both better and worse than market performance. However, investors typically are more concerned with inadequate investment performance, and likely do not interpret excessive returns as 'risk'. Therefore, the semi-variance (i.e. returns below market) may be a more appropriate measure of investment risk;
- CAPM assumes that all investors have the same holding period, and does not recognize the incremental risks associated with longer term investment horizons. As previously discussed, en bloc equity investments typically are made by acquirers seeking to fulfill long term financial objectives;
- Beta figures for a given public company vary based on factors such as:
  — the 'market portfolio' (i.e. the 'R_m' component of CAPM) to which individual stock returns are compared. There are differences between the volatility of a particular equity market that is adopted in computing Beta for a particular business and the hypothetical market comprising all risky assets (which in theory is the relevant basis for measuring systematic risk). This sometimes is referred to as 'benchmark error';

— the time period covered. Beta examines historical data and assumes that the historical variability of the security, the market and the correlation between the two will persist. Where a company or the industry in which it operates have undergone significant changes in recent years, Betas calculated based on historical data typically do not account for this; and

— whether they are computed based on weekly or monthly data.

As a result, the Beta factor for a particular company can be different depending on the source of data and the way in which it is calculated. In the end, Beta factors are unstable;

- empirical evidence[5] indicates that actual returns do not match the theory of CAPM. Lower Beta stocks have been found to generate higher than projected returns and vice versa;
- CAPM ignores the fact that stock market prices are based on factors other than Beta;
- CAPM represents a capitalization rate, being a discount rate net of a growth rate implicitly incorporated therein, neither of which is separately identifiable. The general rate of growth in the securities markets may not be reflective of the growth rate for the business being valued. Further, any adjustment to that growth rate necessarily is subjective; and
- as a practical matter, Canadian public equity markets lack the broadness of the U.S stock markets and therefore the quantity of 'comparable' companies often is insufficient in Canada for the purposes of using the CAPM methodology. Proponents of CAPM in Canada often advocate the use of U.S. data to generate a greater number of 'comparables'. However, important differences between the two countries still exist (such as income tax rates and degree of market liquidity), which might have a significant impact on the application of U.S. data in Canada.

CAPM is commonly used by individual and institutional investors in public equity market security analysis and portfolio management, and the model lends itself reasonably well to that purpose. However, there are significant differences between these things and the valuation of a business interest pursuant to an en bloc equity investment decision. In particular:

- while the basic CAPM model considers broad market and industry risk, it ignores company specific risk. Although this may be acceptable for a portfolio manager or an adequately diversified individual investor, it is inconsistent with the basis upon which businesses typically are bought and sold en bloc;

- CAPM is based on public market data, which assumes liquidity. En bloc or controlling equity interests normally do not satisfy the strict definition of liquidity, which generally assumes the ability to readily realize a known price in a relatively short time frame;
- business owners typically have long term investment objectives. Although individual and institutional investors may also intend to hold marketable securities for the long term, the ability to readily liquidate their position typically results in a reduced level of risk;
- individual and institutional investors generally rely primarily on publicly available information when making investment decisions. Conversely, where the en bloc equity value of a business is determined, the due diligence and acquisition process in an open market transaction typically is much longer, more detailed, and based on a greater base of information – including so-called 'insider information' obtained pursuant to confidentiality and standstill agreements. It follows that in the latter case there generally is a larger base of information to assist in assessing the risks specific to a particular business entity. This difference in information availability is a fundamental difference between public equity market analysis and the acquisition of a business en bloc;
- individual and institutional investors can measure returns on public market investments almost immediately, and are able to continuously do so. Business owners typically measure returns on a monthly, quarterly or annual basis. This delay in return measurement capability may increase the perceived risk associated with such investments;
- Beta is meant to indicate prospective risk based on historical results. As Beta changes, an individual investor or portfolio manager can readily alter his or her portfolio to compensate for such changes. However, most business owners cannot readily change the composition of their of business; and
- as a practical matter the risk of acquiring of 100%, or control, of a business generally is much greater than is the risk attached to acquiring a portfolio investment. This is because the risk associated with a failed business acquisition (which risk may go beyond the failed acquisition itself) generally is significantly greater than the risk associated with a 'bad stock pick'.

As a practical matter, corporate acquirers tend to use pre-established threshold rates of return as opposed to short term models such as CAPM. This is not to suggest that CAPM has no relevance whatsoever to a corporate acquirer. As noted earlier in this Chapter, it generally is important to consider prevailing market rates of return when determining an appropriate discount or capitalization rate, and CAPM does accomplish that. Further, from the perspective of a public company acquirer, CAPM may be useful in measuring the 'minimum' rate of return a public company acquirer should seek at a given point in time. If the securities markets perceive an acquisition was completed at a rate of return below that suggested by CAPM, the acquirer's stock price may suffer following acquisition. Notwithstanding, the appropriate rate of return to use when evaluating a target company may be greater or less than that suggested by CAPM, depending on specific circumstances.

Comparable Data

Capitalization rates sometimes are derived through analysis of so-called 'comparable' public company stock prices and open market transactions involving similar businesses. While both things selectively can be of use in specific notional market valuation and open market pricing exercises, such analysis rarely by itself provides the basis for determining an appropriate capitalization rate. The use of comparable data and its limitations is discussed in Chapter 9.

Summary

A discount rate is the rate of return that converts a series of cash flows to present value. Pursuant to a build-up approach, the discount rate is derived by adjusting a base rate of return, being a nominal unlevered return on equity, for fact-specific risk factors to reflect specific operating risks, and subsequently applying a financial leverage adjustment to reflect financial risk. A capitalization rate converts a point estimate of cash flow into value. It is determined by adjusting the discount rate as applicable for each of inflation, growth, and differences in risk beyond the forecast period.

The Capital Asset Pricing Model relates risk and returns for assets based on the risk free rate, public equity market risk premiums, and a Beta factor, which is a measure of industry risk. CAPM often is used as a tool of public equity market analysts and portfolio managers, but generally is not an appropriate principal basis on which to develop rates of return for the purpose of evaluating long term en bloc equity investments.

NOTES

1 David W. King, The Equity Risk Premium for Cost of Capital Studies, Business Valuation Review, September 1994.

2 See, for example, 'Let's Get Objective', M. Dobner, The Business Valuator, No. 4, Vol. 16, September 1992.

3 See, for example, Pratt, Reilly, Schweihs, *Valuing a Business: The Analysis and Appraisal of Closely Held Companies*, 3rd ed., McGraw Hill, 1996.

4 G. Gilbert, Discount Rates and Capitalization Rates – Where are We?, Business Valuation Review, December 1990.

5 See, for example, Eugene F. Fama and Kenneth French, 'The Cross-Section of Expected Stock Returns', Journal of Finance 47, no. 2, June 1992.

Chapter 9
Comparative Analysis

Introduction

As this book is being written the ongoing well reported and widely discussed 'information revolution' is evolving and expanding rapidly. Detailed quantitative and qualitative information available today was not as readily available as only, say, three years ago. As the 'information age' develops increased public disclosure of business information, legislative actions, actions of securities regulators, and Court Decisions almost certainly will occur. As a result, there may come a time when available economic, industry, competitive, and transactional information will enable comparative analysis as discussed in this Chapter to be more useful and meaningful than, as a general rule, it is today.

Having said that, terms such as 'comparative analysis' and 'comparable companies' long have been encountered in both notional market valuations and open market pricing exercises. There are three basic types of comparative analysis that can be undertaken:

- 'benchmark analysis', whereby the objective is to establish 'normal' or 'industry-standard' performance indicators;
- analysis of public equity market data, being the multiples calculated for public companies in the same industry and for the industry as a whole. The objective is to provide an indication as to value and price relationships, and the rates of return sought by public market participants; and
- analysis of recent transactions that have taken place involving similar companies to provide some indication of rates of return required by corporate acquirers and, in some cases, the extent of post-acquisition synergies perceived in a given transaction and within a given industry.

Whether or not companies assessed as 'comparable' explicitly are used in a particular valuation, the state of public equity markets and their impact on companies in the same industry usually should be considered. This is because prevailing trends in the public equity markets reflect time-specific market conditions with respect to both general economic and industry-specific conditions. Specific public company data may assist in the valuation process, particularly in the context of analyzing the benchmark rate of return criteria targeted by corporate acquirers at any given point in time. Having said that, as a practical matter, and as a general rule, only in very limited circumstances can the results obtained from analyzing data of so-called 'comparable' companies be meaningfully applied when determining business value other than as a possible 'test of value' otherwise determined. The application of 'comparative' analysis normally is limited, at best, to providing a general understanding of the risk-reward dynamics of a given industry, and in assessing the overall reasonableness of valuation and pricing conclusions otherwise derived.

This Chapter discusses the factors relevant to assessing whether companies are 'comparable'. The various types of comparative analysis, their applications and their limitations are then addressed.

> While the term 'comparable' is used throughout this Chapter and elsewhere in this book, no two businesses are comparable in every respect. That factor must be considered in any analysis involving so-called 'comparable companies' and 'comparable industry transactions'.

Application of Comparative Analysis

Comparative analysis utilizes key operating ratios and multiples of what are perceived to be similar businesses. These indicators then are applied to the historical and projected financial relationships of the subject business when assessing value relationships, and to assist in determining appropriate rates of return when determining a reasoned value range for that business. The ratios and multiples generally are derived from available stock market data, from public financial disclosures of so-called comparable publicly traded companies, and from data from recent open market transactions involving similar companies. The key ratios and valuation multiples commonly reviewed include:

- financial operating ratios with respect to liquidity, financial and operating leverage, profitability and efficiency (see Appendix B);
- equity value compared with:
  - earnings,
  - discretionary cash flow,
  - book value,
  - net tangible assets,
- enterprise value compared with:
  - revenues,
  - EBIT-DA, and
  - EBIT; and

- for certain industries, ratios such as enterprise value per ton of capacity, per customer or some other performance or value indicator commonly used by acquirers or analysts in those industries.

Comparative analysis entails more than computing a myriad of ratios and multiples for businesses in the same industry, and applying some average of these amounts to the financial position and operating results of the business being valued. Careful analysis is required as to which businesses should be included as 'comparable' and to recognize the important differences that exist. In most cases, where comparative analysis is undertaken, its use is limited to assessing valuation conclusions derived pursuant to other valuation methodologies. Even where applied as tests of values otherwise derived, because of important differences existing between:

- the daily trading prices of publicly held companies;
- open market transactions; and
- the intrinsic en bloc value of the equity of a business,

the multiples developed from 'comparable' public company data and industry transactions may not be appropriate indicators of such intrinsic en bloc value. These differences are discussed in this Chapter.

Comparative Analysis in the United States

The use of comparative company data in notional market valuations in the past has been more common and perceived more credible in the United States than in Canada. This may be due in part to:

- U.S. Revenue Ruling 59-60, which is regarded as an important guideline for valuing closely held corporate interests for U.S. Income Tax purposes. This Revenue Ruling suggests that a measure of value can be found in the prices at which stocks of companies engaged in the same or in a similar line of business are selling in a free and open securities market;
- the extent of required public disclosure of corporate information often is greater in the United States than it is in Canada which at least in theory allows for a more informed assessment as to the degree of comparability; and
- for most industries, there normally are fewer Canadian companies whose shares are publicly traded to provide information that can be considered meaningful.

In some cases, data from U.S. (or other country) sources appropriately may be employed when conducting comparative analysis with respect to Canadian businesses. However, where employed it is important to recognize that there often are material differences that may impair the usefulness of such analysis. For example:

- U.S. public companies tend to be much larger than their Canadian counterparts. As a result, they may enjoy greater economies of scale and other benefits associated with greater size;
- depending on the industry, business, or products offered, there may be important differences based on markets covered due to the size of those markets, competitors, demographics, logistics, and so on;
- securities traded in U.S. public markets tend to be more liquid and active than those traded in Canada public markets. This may bear on comparability where so called 'small cap' and 'micro cap' stocks are adopted for comparison purposes;
- corporate income tax rates generally are lower in the U.S. than Canada. As a result, a U.S. company might trade at higher multiples of EBIT-DA and EBIT in recognition of the expectation that a relatively greater portion of its gross income will translate into discretionary cash flow;
- there may be important differences regarding the laws and regulations surrounding the products or services that the business offers; and
- accounting policies in the U.S. are different from those in Canada. For example, many U.S. companies use LIFO (last-in first-out) for inventory valuation because it is accepted for tax purposes in that country. By comparison, few Canadian companies use LIFO.

Adjusting for some of these differences in a meaningful way is difficult, and often not possible. This supports the proposition that comparative analysis should not be used as a primary valuation methodology.

Identifying 'Comparable' Companies

Factors to Consider

Comparative analysis generally is based on companies in the same industry, under the assumption that all firms within a given industry segment are faced with common risks. Due to the limited amount of public information typically available for privately-held businesses, the search for 'comparables' normally is restricted to public companies, supplemented by whatever 'private company' information is known to, and (pursuant to time and conditions of prevailing confidentiality agreements) able to be used by those undertaking value/pricing analysis.

In order to qualify as truly comparable, the 'comparable' must be in the same business and undertake the same and only the same business functions as the subject business. When selecting companies that are comparable, consideration should be given to factors such as:

- company size. Size should be assessed in terms of revenues, net assets, operating capacity, number of employees, and other meaningful measures. Larger companies tend to enjoy a greater degree of market presence, management depth, financial stability, financing options, economies of scale, and so on. These factors influence operating performance and importantly, rates of return required by prospective acquirers. As a result, companies of significantly different size are unlikely to be meaningful 'comparables';
- the nature of the products or services offered. Comparative analysis presumes that companies exist whose products and services are very similar to the business being valued or priced, and that the comparative mix of these business activities is similar both as to:
  — percentage of business by product and service, and
  — operating result by product and service.

  As a practical matter, the greater the level of diversification within a business, the less likely that a comparable company can be found. Further, where a company that might be comparable has operations in more than one industry segment, the amount of information publicly available for any particular segment normally is insufficient to form any basis of meaningful comparison. In any event, implied 'comparable' multiples typically are based on consolidated historical and prospective operating results;

- the degree of vertical integration. A vertically integrated business normally has different risk-return parameters compared with one that purchases its inputs or sells its outputs to an unrelated business. Not only does a vertically integrated company generally face less risk in the revenue or cost stream, but it may also enjoy economies of scale not available to a business that operates on a stand-alone basis;
- geographic coverage and market characteristics. For most businesses, the markets covered have a bearing on the degree of comparability. This is due to differences in customer base, logistics, cost to service a particular market,

local competition, and so on. In particular, there may be significant differences between the dynamics of domestic markets as compared with international markets;
- relative market share. Where the market share of two companies is significantly different, those companies unlikely will serve as a basis for direct comparison. Large differences in market share often will lead to a significant difference in size (revenues), which would provide another indication that comparability is impaired. Even where market share is similar, but where one company is the market leader, there may be important differences in terms of marketing strategy, market presence and other factors that might influence the relative degree of risk between the two;
- cost structure. The risk and return parameters of a business are influenced by the degree to which that business employs operating leverage (fixed costs) in its cost structure. In addition, it is important to consider whether a business is capital or labour intensive. In some industries, firms have the option of employing a manual or automated production process. Even though the finished product may be similar, the operating risks of a labour intensive business are different (normally greater) than those of a capital intensive business;
- level of net tangible assets and sustaining capital. In order to be considered comparable, underlying net tangible assets, the mix of these assets between current and fixed, the state of equipment technology, capacity and maintenance, and the required amount of sustaining capital must all be discernable and capable of comparison. Where a business has to invest significant amounts each year in sustaining capital (for example, due to changing technology), that will have a significant influence on prospective discretionary cash flows and therefore on business value. As a result, any 'comparable' company should be making and be required to make comparative annual capital investments;
- financial structure. As discussed in Chapter 7, in theory every business has an optimal capital structure. In practice, capital structure can vary significantly, even for businesses in the same industry. The extent to which a business employs debt in its capital structure is a key variable in determining the required return on invested (levered) equity. Where a 'comparable' has a different capital structure, adjustments generally are required to provide a more meaningful basis for comparison;
- profitability and operating measurements. These measures commonly include:

- profitability ratios such as gross profit, operating profit (EBIT-DA and EBIT) expressed as a percentage of sales, and operating profit expressed as a percentage of invested capital (shareholder's equity),
- turnover ratios such as gross revenues to total assets, and gross revenues to fixed assets,
- liquidity ratios such as current and quick ratios, and
- leverage ratios such as long term debt to invested capital and interest coverage.

Ratio analysis (see Appendix B) provides an indication of risk levels that influence comparability. Importantly, financial ratios are affected by the use of different accounting policies, which may have to be adjusted to provide meaningful comparisons;

- historic growth in profitability and discretionary cash flow. Where a business has demonstrated such growth, that normally influences the determination of appropriate rate(s) of return. Unless the 'comparables' have demonstrated similar growth patterns, they are unlikely to be meaningfully comparable;
- stability and potential growth in profitability and discretionary cash flow. Stability and potential growth in profitability and discretionary cash flow also influence appropriate rates of return. It seldom is possible to meaningfully determine the prospective discretionary cash flow of 'comparables'. Aside from this, unless the 'comparables' are expected to demonstrate similar stability and growth, they are unlikely to be meaningfully comparable;
- research and development ('R&D'). Businesses that spend significant amounts on R&D activities often are believed to have greater growth opportunities compared to those that do not. In this regard, it is important not only to compare the amounts invested in R&D (normally measured in terms of R&D expense to gross revenues) by 'comparables', but to assess the nature of R&D expenditures, the stage of development, and the product(s) being developed, all of which generally is not possible to do in a meaningful way; and
- strategic direction and focus. Although two companies may appear to have been similar in the past, a change in the strategic direction of either will affect comparability. A change in strategic direction can arise due to new opportunities, management change, a major acquisition or divestiture, and so on. Public companies may disclose strategic direction in a general way, but seldom disclose specifics with respect to overall long term strategic direction. All of these variables influence the degree of risk and, as a result, required rates of return.

No two companies are exactly alike and judgement must be exercised when determining whether a basis for meaningful comparison exists. As a practical matter, sufficient information usually is not available (even for public companies) to reach an informed conclusion as to the degree of meaningful comparability between two businesses. As a result, comparative analysis rarely is used as a primary valuation methodology, but rather is used to test value conclusions otherwise determined. Further, even where applied as a test methodology, such tests may not be meaningful. Having said that, some industries lend themselves better to comparative analysis than others. Subject to availability of meaningful detailed information, in theory:

- a greater degree of comparability may be possible in commodity type industries than may be possible in industries with a high degree of propriety in their products;
- industries that are better defined in terms of the products they offer or markets they serve provide a better basis for comparison than those that do not; and
- comparison may be more meaningful in mature industries than in emerging industries. The latter tend to have distorted operating ratios due to low or negative operating results. In addition, companies in emerging industries generally trade in the public equity markets on a greater degree on speculation than do companies in mature industries, and their resultant stock prices tend to be more volatile.

Comparability Adjustments

When companies that are considered appropriate for comparability purposes have been identified, adjustments to the stated financial results of those businesses may be appropriate to enhance comparability. For example, adjustments should be considered to account for:

- accounting policies where they differ between the subject company and the 'comparables' selected. Differences in accounting policies arise due to the fact that Canadian Generally Accepted Accounting Principles offer management various alternatives in how to account for certain items. Differences in accounting policies frequently relate to:
  - inventory costing (LIFO, FIFO, weighted average costing, and so on). Inventory costing affects both the inventory balance and cost of sales. As a result, inventory costing policies have an impact on all earnings indicators,

- depreciation. Both the method of depreciation, such as straight line, declining balance, and so on, as well as the estimated useful lives of the underlying assets should be compared,
- timing of revenue recognition, being the point at which revenue (and the resultant account receivable) is accrued,
- research and development expenditures, specifically whether such expenditures are capitalized or expensed and, where capitalized, the period of amortization,
- deferred income tax accounting, particularly where non-Canadian 'comparables' are being used,
- the classification of various expense items, such as what might qualify as an 'unusual' or 'extraordinary' item, and
- intangible assets, such as start-up costs and deferred charges;
• differing income tax rates when comparing ratios based on net income and discretionary cash flows. In addition, differences in income tax rates may partially explain why multiples such as enterprise value to EBIT-DA for one business are different from those of another business. Differences in income tax rates most commonly arise when comparisons are made between businesses whose operations are principally in different Provinces or countries;
• differing financial structures (i.e. mix of debt and equity). The amount of financial leverage used by various businesses within a given industry can vary substantially. In order to make meaningful comparisons between businesses using ratios or data influenced by financial structure, a notional adjustment to the amount of debt outstanding within the 'comparable' business should be made; and
• differing forecasted financial results where they are available for one or more 'comparables'. Where adopted, and where it is possible to do so, such forecasted data should be adjusted to conform to both normalization of applied 'Generally Accepted Accounting Principles', and consistencies in the financial positions and operating ratios of the businesses. As a practical matter, such forecasts often are taken from stock market service reports that are based on publicly available information. Where this is the case, such forecasts likely have been compiled based on incomplete information and lack of knowledge of the detailed strategic plans of the business. As a result, it seldom is possible to assess the reasonableness of forecasts for 'comparables' in a meaningful way.

In most cases, the detailed data required to make the appropriate adjustments (such as the impact of accounting policies or analysis of forecasts) is not available. Where the difference(s) could be significant, this further militates against meaningful comparability.

Where comparative data is used, it is not uncommon to compare the subject business with average ratios or multiples calculated from the group of 'comparables'. However, the use of a simple average may lead to inappropriate conclusions, particularly where there is a large variance in the performance indicators of the individual 'comparables'. Prior to finalizing a benchmark based on some sort of average it is important to analyze the data and, if possible, to adjust it for any outliers or anomalies.

Benchmark Analysis

Financial and operational data of so-called 'comparables' sometimes is used to assess how the performance of the subject business compares to 'normal' or 'industry-standard' measures. The applications of benchmark analysis may include:

- determining an 'appropriate' capital structure. A review of the debt to equity ratios of 'comparables' may assist in formulating a meaningful conclusion as to the amount of debt the subject business should have outstanding. In this respect, it is helpful to calculate relevant ratios such as debt to equity and debt serviceability. Importantly, capital structures may vary considerably among businesses within a particular industry, and a simple average of 'comparables' may not provide a sound basis for a conclusion — also see Chapter 7;
- evaluating the adequacy of net trade working capital. Where net trade working capital is much greater than industry norms, it may indicate the existence of a redundant asset that should be segregated for valuation purposes (such as non-trade receivables being grouped with trade accounts receivable). Conversely, where net trade working capital is below industry norms, a 'negative redundancy' may be indicated. When applying comparative analysis to assess net trade working capital, it is important to recognize possible differences in accounting policies, as well as to consider the impact of seasonality where comparisons are made based on year-end financial results and 'comparables' have different fiscal year-ends; and
- assessing the relative strengths and weaknesses of the subject business and the reasonableness of its projected operating results. When comparing ratios of the subject business to those of similar businesses in the same indus-

try, comparative advantages or disadvantages of the subject business may become evident. For example, where the business' inventory turnover is less than industry norms (adjusted for the impact of different accounting policies where necessary), inventory management difficulties may be indicated or it may become evident the business has obsolete or slow-moving items in its inventory. In addition, where prospective operating ratios are computed for forecast data, comparable analysis can help in assessing the probability of those results being realized. For example, where sales per employee are expected to rise well above industry norms, analysis may suggest sufficient headcount additions may not have been factored into the projections. While such analysis rarely by itself would provide conclusive evidence, it may assist in identifying areas for furthering investigation.

Public Equity Market Multiples

Applications and Limitations

As a general rule, at any given point in time public equity markets record public expectations of both general economic and specific industry conditions through both broad and industry specific market indices. Examples of such indices, which in some instances may be used as general indications or benchmarks against which to test values otherwise determined, include prevailing price to earnings and enterprise value to EBIT-DA multiples.

The use of so-called 'comparable' public market multiples is popular among stock market analysts preparing research reports and stock recommendations. These analysts tend to identify a public company's peer group of publicly traded companies and assess why the stock being analyzed should trade at a higher or lower multiple of earnings (or some other measure) than its peers. Public equity market data may lend itself relatively well to that purpose. However, there are numerous fundamental differences between the public equity markets and the market for all of the outstanding shares, the net operating assets, or control of a publicly-held or privately-held business. In particular:

- public market participants have a wide range of time horizon objectives (from a few minutes to many years), whereas purchasers of a controlling interest in either a public or private company tend to be long term holders. This has become all the more evident in the current (year 2000) volatile securities markets, where the internet has facilitated and may exacerbate:
  — rapid growth of 'day trading',

— a flow of investment monies from so-called 'old economy' companies to so-called 'new economy' (i.e. technology and 'e-commerce') companies, and
— so-called near term 'momentum trading'.

Investors with long term perspectives generally are less influenced by near-term fluctuations in money and securities markets compared to those with short term perspectives;

- stock prices can fluctuate erratically within a short time period based on investor sentiment. In general, value in a notional market sense and price in an open market transaction tend to reflect a greater level of stability;
- there may be significant differences in the degree of liquidity. Normal sized trading blocks of shares of a widely held public company enjoy a high level of liquidity, particularly in comparison to a thinly traded stock or a large block of shares that the market may not be able or willing to readily absorb. The liquidity of a controlling interest in a publicly held or privately held company can vary considerably depending on the nature of the industry and the company itself. Where a control position in a public or private company is believed to be less liquid compared with normal-sized trading lots of publicly held company shares, this reduced degree of liquidity may impact the perceived level of risk and resultant required rates of return – although the better view of this is that the market for a normal trading block in any given public company simply is different than is the market for 100% of the shares or control of either publicly held or privately held companies;
- public equity market data represents normal sized lots of public company share trading prices. As a result, public equity market transactions are those that take place between minority shareholders. As discussed in Chapter 13, whether or not such trading prices reflect a discount for either non-control or discount for illiquidity (in the case of thinly traded stocks) usually is not evident;
- where public market trading prices are believed to represent a ratable portion of en bloc intrinsic value at a point in time, resultant multiple of trailing EBIT-DA, multiple of trailing earnings, and so on, that are calculated based on that data generally would reflect 'stand-alone' valuation multiples. Accordingly, they may not be appropriate for comparison to a particular notional market value or open market price that incorporates an element of purchaser-perceived post-acquisition net economic value added (synergies);

- stock market transactions generally are based on available information that typically does not include important strategic and other 'insider' information not publicly disclosed. Typically, a greater amount of pertinent data is available where en bloc value is determined (e.g. detailed operating plans, company secrets, and so on) pursuant to detailed due diligence reviews. Such additional information usually has a significant bearing on risk assessment, business prospects, and required rates of return; and
- an open market transaction generally is characterized by lengthy negotiations between sophisticated parties, which negotiations influence price. This is not the case in a stock market transaction where parties seldom directly interact and, in the case of normal sized trading lots, rarely have a significant impact on price.

It is important to note that where price/earnings and price/cash flow ratios are used when assessing rates of return, their reciprocals represent the capitalization rate and not the discount rate. The capitalization rate converts a point estimate of cash flow to value assuming that it will be generated on an annual basis. The capitalization rate is determined by deducting a growth factor from the discount rate and adjusting for a terminal value risk factor, as applicable – see Chapter 8. The growth factor may incorporate both nominal and real growth. Therefore, while the capitalization rate of 'comparable' companies and industry transactions may be readily determinable, the underlying components (i.e. discount rate and growth factor) cannot readily be segregated. Given that the underlying components are among the key factors to consider in any valuation or pricing exercise, the usefulness of 'comparable' capitalization rates is diminished.

Compared to the use of 'comparable public equity market data', the discounted cash flow ('DCF') and capitalization of discretionary cash flow methodologies are the preferable approaches to business valuation for at least the following reasons:

- comparable equity market valuations are entirely dependent on there being direct comparables to the subject company being valued, and direct comparables almost never exist. The DCF methodology is dependent (in part) on the selection of an appropriate discount rate (normally a weighted average cost of capital) which typically is based on commonly recognized corporate acquirer 'benchmark' rates of return, adjusted as appropriate based on the risks and prospects of the target company;

- comparable equity market valuation generally uses 'earnings' and 'revenue' methodologies. As such, it is subject to the vagaries of the subjective application of Generally Accepted Accounting Principles. The DCF methodology, in contrast, utilizes forecasted (normally unlevered) discretionary cash flows, which are not subject to that sensitivity;
- utilization of public equity market data is in large part based upon an assumption and acceptance of the 'efficient market theory' (which postulates that all relevant information already is priced into the financial markets), and in any event is dependent on stock market prices at a point in time. As a result, it is influenced by stock market 'errors' in valuation. Specific stock market prices generally do not play a primary role in the DCF and capitalization methodologies, other than to the extent a public company acquirer is concerned with the amount of intangible value implied in a purchase price which it subsequently will have to amortize, and which may affect the post-acquisition market price of its own shares;
- stock market prices in part represent transaction prices between minority shareholders with relatively short investment time horizons. Corporate acquirers, in contrast, generally have long term investment time horizons, typically making the DCF methodology their valuation methodology of choice;
- because public equity market data largely is based on trades in small minority shareholdings, a simplistic view often is adopted that a 'control price' will exceed the value developed. This may or may not be true depending on the point in time of the analysis and the 'pre-control value' developed from it. The DCF and capitalization methodologies inherently develop 'en bloc' value;
- public equity market valuations rely on publicly available information, as contrasted with reliance on undisclosed (to the public) fact specific information known to management of the 'comparables'. In comparison, corporate acquirers complete detailed due diligence prior to closing a transaction. Through that process they develop their valuation models based on detailed information that is not all publicly available – both their own proprietary information, and information related to the target. As a result, the DCF and capitalization methodologies force detailed analysis of, and conclusions related thereto, fact specific variables which the comparative methodology does not do as specifically, if at all;
- as a result of lack of close comparability, public equity market valuations typically require subjective adjustments to be made either to the financial data of the 'comparables' or that of the subject business to account for differences in strategy, product offerings, financial structure, operating struc-

ture and so on. Fact specific information related to these things with respect to the subject business is available to a corporate acquirer who integrates them into its analysis. In particular, the DCF and capitalization methodologies segregate returns on debt and equity, and as a result deal with the financial structure of the subject business on a fact specific basis. Comparative analysis often does not do this;

- comparative public market analysis depends on market multiples to reflect forecasted revenue growth, gross margins, operating costs, income taxes, profit growth, capital expenditures, working capital requirements, redundant assets, and so on. In contrast, the DCF and capitalization methodologies segregate, analyze, and utilize an indicated or multiple year forecast of all of these things determined on a fact-specific basis; and
- comparative public market analysis typically does not segregate redundant assets from operating assets. These two asset categories typically face different risks and are dealt with separately pursuant to the DCF and capitalization methodologies.

The application of stock market data rarely is useful in the valuation of small, privately held businesses, and can often lead to inappropriate conclusions. Data based on 'comparables' may be of some use in the valuation of public companies and large privately owned businesses where meaningful or 'somewhat meaningful' 'comparables' can be identified. Even where this is the case, the application of public equity market data generally is limited, at best, to providing an understanding of the risk-reward dynamics of a given industry, and in assessing value conclusions derived pursuant to other valuation methodologies.

Application of Public Equity Market Data to Privately Held Businesses

As a practical matter, the usefulness of specific public company financial statistics and public market trading prices to assist in developing values for (particularly) small and medium sized private businesses – say, those with revenues under $50 million – generally varies directly with the size of the privately held business. Stated differently, the smaller the privately held business, the less likely it is that such information will prove useful. In addition, differences may relate to the fact that public companies generally are:

- larger, often significantly so, than businesses that are privately-held;

- either vertically or horizontally integrated, although this is not always the case. Small and medium sized privately-held businesses tend not to be vertically or horizontally integrated;
- spread over a broader geographical area than are small and medium privately-held businesses;
- more fully developed than most small and medium sized privately held businesses from the point of view of such things as management, financial stability, product development, and strategic planning;
- directed by management groups which:
  - emphasize accounting earnings given the influence of earnings on share price that in turn relates to the public market financing ability and cash flow. In contrast, small and medium sized private business management tends to focus principally on cash flow and relates earnings principally to income tax liability and satisfaction of banking covenants,
  - frequently have greater depth and strength than is the case with most small and medium sized privately held businesses, whose management generally tends to less regimented, more entrepreneurial, more direct 'personal reward' oriented, less strategic, and more personally identified with the business,
  - gear income tax planning corporately, and typically without consideration for the private tax planning of corporate shareholders. Owners of privately held businesses frequently gear income tax planning on a composite personal/corporate basis, with the prime consideration being to minimize income tax on a personal level. Therefore, as compared with public companies, privately held businesses may pursue accounting policies geared toward income minimization; and
- generally are capable of accessing a larger number of funding sources with greater resources than are small and medium sized privately held businesses. As a result, companies whose shares are publicly traded often have a lower cost of capital than do privately held businesses.

The degree to which 'comparables' are used will vary depending on the nature of the business being valued, and the benefits expected to be derived from comparative analysis. As a practical matter, for many small and medium sized private businesses it usually is difficult, if not impossible, to find meaningful 'comparables'. Notwithstanding, in some cases comparative analysis may be helpful as a 'reasonableness test' of a value conclusion.

Initial Public Offerings

Initial public offerings (IPO's) occur when a company whose shares previously were privately held elects to offer its securities to the public for the first time. The share price set in an IPO normally is at the low end of what is believed will be a 'market accepted' initial trading price in order to ensure that the offering is fully subscribed. Further, the price of many IPO's may be distorted by aggressive promotion by underwriters, securities dealers, and the company itself. This militates against comparability.

IPO offering memoranda often contain useful industry and company information that is otherwise unavailable (although in the U.S., 8-K and 10-K reports and other SEC filings frequently contain similar detail). Risk factors, competition, growth potential, customer base, and many other important elements typically are identified and discussed. This information helps not only in assessing 'comparability', but also can help in a general sense by identifying important factors that should be considered when deriving value.

Finally, where earnings multiples from recent IPO transactions are considered 'comparable', consideration must be afforded to the impact of monies flowing into the company itself, as opposed to between third parties (see Chapter 4 — 'Primary and Secondary Offerings').

Purchaser's or Vendor's Stock Price

Where the shares of corporate acquirers and acquisition targets trade in the public equity markets, from the standpoint of a:

- corporate acquirer:
  - the implicit public equity multiples may benchmark minimum rates of return that public equity participants expect on prospective acquisitions by the company at a point in time, and
  - as a practical matter, corporate acquirers are reluctant to consummate a transaction that likely will result in erosion of consolidated earnings per share that might depress their own share price beyond the near term; and
- vendor:
  - the public equity markets may provide (assuming an active, highly liquid security) an indication as to the relative and absolute degree of risk the public perceives for its business; and
  - the price at which the vendor's shares traded up to the date of the takeover offer represents a benchmark against which the company's management and its shareholders will evaluate the offer.

However, even when using the acquirers' or vendors' own stock prices, the previously noted caveats of using public market data still apply. In particular, public equity market participants usually are not aware of detailed long term forecasts that can have a significant influence on valuation conclusions. In addition, the prices at which a company's shares trade in the open market typically are representative of normal sized trading lots that may depending on share block size and trading volumes enjoy greater immediate liquidity as compared to an en bloc or controlling interest in a business.

Industry Transactions

Acquisition of Control of 'Comparable' Companies

It usually is beneficial to identify and analyze recent transactions where the acquired company is perceived to be a 'comparable' company. The identification and analysis of such transactions may provide insight as to the:

- relative degree of liquidity in a given industry. Where there have been numerous industry transactions and the industry is believed to be going through a consolidation phase, liquidity may be enhanced at that point in time which, all other things equal, may have an upward influence on open market price;
- perceived risks and rates of return of corporate acquirers. Depending on the parties involved, there may be sufficient information available with respect to transactions to enable some understanding of the valuation parameters employed in them;
- most likely buyers and post-acquisition synergies that might be expected — see Chapter 11; and
- price range competitors might bid for a business.

Although data derived from an analysis of transactions involving 'comparable companies' may provide such insights, its direct application to any particular en bloc valuation determination rarely is possible because:

- sufficient information normally is not available to fully understand the valuation dynamics of the business acquired. This includes the segregation of non-evident redundant assets, undisclosed liabilities, long range plans, and so on. As a result, the level of disclosure in open market transactions generally is insufficient to formulate concrete conclusions regarding rates of return that can be directly applied to a given business. The quantity and quality of disclosure is particularly restricted where both the vendor and purchaser are privately held;

- each open market transaction is unique. In the end the price and consideration paid are a function of purchaser and vendor knowledge, needs, negotiating skills, and bidding competition; and
- an open market transaction price normally is comprised (either implicitly or explicitly) of the perceived intrinsic value of the acquired business plus, in varying degrees, purchaser perceived post acquisition synergies. Therefore, even where sufficient information exists to compute earnings and cash flow multiples in an acquisition, in the absence of direct involvement with the purchaser it is unusual that the underlying value components can be meaningfully analyzed.

The application of open market transaction multiples is further complicated where all or part of the consideration paid involves a non-cash component such as shares of the acquirer, vendor take-backs, or so-called 'earnout' arrangements. Where this is the case, a cash equivalent price should be estimated for purposes of comparison. In many cases, insufficient detail regarding the fair market value of the non-cash components is available or determinable. Further, where open market transactions are stale-dated, important changes in industry, business, and economic factors during the interim period must be considered.

Where the business acquired was publicly held prior to the transaction, the following additional things generally should be considered:

- the transaction price per share generally is influenced by the market price of the target's shares prior to the takeover bid. In the acquisition of a publicly held company, premiums above market trading prices are the norm, although the magnitude of such premiums varies significantly. However, in the absence of direct knowledge of the transaction, it usually is not possible to determine what portion of the premium is attributable to anticipated post-acquisition synergies;
- the price paid may be distorted due to competitive bidding. This is less likely to be the case for a privately held business where the transaction generally is not announced until after it has been finalized;
- there may be some run-up in the price of the target's share price in the days or weeks immediately preceding the takeover transaction (due to speculation, inappropriately applied insider knowledge, and so on); and

- in an unsolicited public market takeover bid, the bidder seldom has free access to information with respect to the target company prior to making the bid. Rather, the bidder is forced to rely on publicly available information, plus whatever other information it has available to it. Further, the bidder does not have an opportunity to complete a pre-closing due diligence review.

Sometimes within an industry group there will be enough recent transactions and available information with respect to them that useful data is available. For example, in Canada at any given time, these circumstances may exist in government regulated industries such as the securities industry, the cable television industry, and the broadcast industry. However, even within such industry groups, reliance on 'comparable' transactions generally should be viewed with caution.

Each open market transaction involves a unique set of circumstances and vendor and purchaser motivations. Accordingly, in the absence of active participation in an industry transaction, it seldom is possible to obtain the detail necessary to formulate firm conclusions regarding the basis upon which the implicit multiples were derived. Again, as a result, the use of data derived from an analysis of comparable industry transactions generally is limited, at most, to assisting in:

- gaining an overview understanding of the risks and rates of return of a particular industry; and
- evaluating the reasonableness of a value determination derived pursuant to other valuation methodologies.

Acquisitions of Minority Interests in 'Comparable' Businesses

Privately Held Businesses

There is a general lack of knowledge of transactions pursuant to which minority shareholdings in privately held businesses are bought and sold in arm's length transactions. Unlike stock market transactions or purchases and sales of real estate, details of transactions involving equity interests in privately held businesses are not documented or compiled in any manner that permits them to be meaningfully researched and analyzed. More important than simply identifying 'comparable' private market transactions, the required understanding of the detailed background and motivations behind those transactions usually is missing. Accordingly, it usually is a meaningless exercise to attempt to identify and compare open market sales of minority interests in privately held businesses for purposes of assisting in developing the value of any given business interest.

Publicly Held Companies

Minority interest sales involving public companies typically involve normal sized trading lot stock market transactions, as previously discussed. However, on occasion public companies will offer an investor (typically a financial institution or fund management company) treasury shares pursuant to a private placement. Further, large blocks of shares in publicly traded companies trade pursuant to negotiated 'block trades'. Private placements or block trades normally involve significantly larger blocks of shares than those which trade on the open markets and may (although this is not usually the case) influence control of the company. Pursuant to private placements purchasers may be restricted from trading for a period of time. As a result, the degree of liquidity may be less than that of normal sized trading lots in public equity market transactions. Even where not restricted, liquidity may become an issue if the block of shares is sufficiently large that it cannot be readily absorbed in the market place. All of these things may have implications on comparability in a particular value determination.

When using private placement information it is necessary to understand the terms of the private placement such as the time period, restrictions on transfer, and so on. Adequate information may not be available to make a meaningful comparison. In addition, it is important to consider that the purchaser of a private placement typically is investing money into the company itself as opposed to purchasing an interest held by a third party. As a result, the injection of new capital creates incremental value in the company. This should be considered in any comparative analysis.

Transactions Involving Equity in the Subject Business

Acquisition of Control of the Subject Business

Occasionally 100% or control of the subject business recently may have been acquired. Where this is the case, details of the transaction should be analyzed to determine what the purchaser perceived to be the risks and potential of the business. The sophistication and depth of analysis of both purchaser and vendor, and comparative negotiating skill and strength should be assessed, as should the basis upon which the prior transaction price was established. When assessing comparability, such analysis must take into account changes during the interim period in:

- the economic environment, including changes to prevailing market rates of return;
- the industry. Following the transaction, there may have been significant developments regarding the competitive environment, advancements in technology, and so on; and
- the company. This might include changes in size, levels of profitability, products or services offered, and so on. In particular, following an acquisition, a business may experience changes in its management team and business strategy that would make any comparison less valid.

It also is important to consider whether the funds used in the acquisition came from internal or external financing sources.

Acquisitions of Minority Interests in the Subject Business (where Privately Held)

Where there have been recent transactions involving minority shareholdings in a privately held business, information from those transactions may aid in the determination of value of a minority shareholding in the same business. In such circumstances, at least the following things must be considered:

- the basis by which prior prices were established;
- the parties transacting, whether they were acting at arm's length, and what their motivations were when transacting;
- the percentage interest the minority shareholding(s) that was acquired represented;
- how informed the buyer and seller were as to the then current financial position of, and prospects for, the business;
- whether the transaction was funded by company funds or external funds, and whether there was an element of company-sponsored financial assistance present in any of the transactions;
- whether there were any contractual agreements governing the basis upon which the transactions were effected, particularly whether there was a Shareholder's Agreement that addressed 'value'; and
- changes that have occurred in the economy, the industry, and the prospects for the business between the dates of prior transactions and the valuation date.

Where such things are capable of analysis, it may be possible to adjust prior sales of minority shareholdings, thereby assisting in the determination of the current value of a given minority shareholding.

Acquisitions Undertaken by the Subject Business

Where the subject business has acquired other businesses, these transactions should be analyzed. In particular, such transactions might provide an indication as to the target rates of return of, and level of synergies anticipated by, the subject business. As in all cases, care is necessary when evaluating such transactions, particularly with respect to the degree of comparability between the purchaser and vendor. In particular, in comparison to the purchaser the vendor might:

- be considerably smaller in size, and not enjoy the same economies of scale;
- be subject to a different degree of financial risk;
- have one or more key employees who may or may not be retained pursuant to a management contract, or are subject to a non-competition agreement; and
- participate in different markets, with different products, and so on.

In addition, the purchaser may have succeeded in its acquisition bid because it overpaid. In circumstances where that was the case, it would not be appropriate to apply the same multiples when determining the en bloc value of the purchaser's outstanding shares or net assets.

Summary

The analysis of so-called 'comparable' companies and industry transactions generally forms part of a notional market valuation or open market pricing exercise. However, as a general rule, only in limited circumstances can comparative analysis be directly applied to develop a meaningful valuation conclusion in a particular situation. The use of 'comparables' generally is restricted, at best, to providing a general understanding of the risk-reward parameters of a given industry, and as a test of valuation conclusions derived pursuant to other valuation methodologies.

Chapter 10
Other Valuation Methodologies

Introduction

In most cases the appropriate methodology by which to value or price the shares or net assets of a business that is a going concern is either the discounted cash flow methodology or the capitalization of discretionary cash flow methodology. In limited circumstances, the value of the shares or net assets of a business can be determined by using the adjusted net book value methodology.

Other methodologies are also available for valuing a business that is a going concern, including the capitalization of maintainable earnings methodology, the dual capitalization of earnings methodology, and various operating multiples such as multiples of EBIT and multiples of EBIT-DA. While these methodologies generally are not adopted as a principal valuation approaches in en bloc value determinations, they sometimes can serve as a useful check on value conclusions derived pursuant to a cash flow based approach. Where a business is not a going concern, a liquidation value methodology is appropriate.

This Chapter discusses the capitalization of maintainable earnings and dual capitalization of earnings methodologies and their applications. This is followed by a discussion of other 'value test' methodologies including the caveats that should be observed where they are applied. The Chapter concludes with an explanation of the liquidation value methodology.

Capitalization of Maintainable Earnings Methodology

Overview

The capitalization of maintainable earnings methodology was widely adopted in the past as a principal valuation methodology. Over time, however, this methodology has given way to cash flow based methodologies as discretionary cash flows and not accounting earnings have become recognized as the principal value driver. As a result, the capitalization of maintainable earnings methodology now generally is restricted to circumstances where:

- a business has relatively stable earnings that approximate discretionary cash flows, and a capitalization of maintainable earnings methodology is adopted as a secondary technique to test the conclusions derived pursuant to a cash-flow based valuation methodology; and

- adopted by public company acquirers to test for post acquisition earnings accretion vs. dilution. This is a different exercise than a capitalization of maintainable earnings as discussed in this Chapter. As a general rule, public company acquirers are reluctant to consummate a transaction at a price that would result in a reduction in near term post-acquisition consolidated earnings per share.

Accounting earnings and discretionary cash flows of a business may differ significantly, particularly where:

- sustaining capital reinvestment does not approximate accounting depreciation;
- accounting policies include significant accruals, reserves, and cost deferrals, such as for warranties, development costs, pension expenses, and the like;
- depreciation and amortization for accounting purposes differs significantly from capital cost allowance (tax depreciation); and
- there are changes over time in a business' working capital requirements.

Notwithstanding the foregoing, an earnings based approach may provide insight into the reasonableness of a valuation conclusion determined pursuant to a cash flow based approach. In addition:

- given that the 'price/earnings multiple' remains a popular indicator in public market valuations, public company acquirers normally will consider the post-acquisition impact on their consolidated earnings per share when making an acquisition;
- use of an earnings based approach historically been accepted by the Courts[1], although recent Court Decisions increasingly have emphasized a discounted cash flow methodology[2]; and
- earnings-based valuations generally are less complex than those based on cash flows and in some cases can serve to provide a rough estimate of value.

The issue of post-acquisition consolidated earnings per share dilution is best explained by example. Assume that public Company A has 50 million shares outstanding, and that the current market price is $4.00 per share. Company A generates net income of $10 million per year, and therefore its earnings per share is $0.20. The implied price/earnings multiple is 20x.

Company A decides to acquire Company B for $40 million by issuing 10 million treasury shares of Company A in exchange for all of the outstanding shares of Company B. Company B generates net income of $2 million per year. In addition, the market value of Company B's net assets approximates their book value of $20 million. Therefore, for financial accounting purposes, goodwill of $20 million has been created in this transaction, which Company A will amortize over a period of 40 years.

Assuming that accounting earnings for each of Company A and B are expected to remain stable in the year following acquisition, and assuming that no synergies are generated in that year, the post-acquisition consolidated earnings per share of Company A in the year following acquisition would be:

Consolidated Net Income	
Company A	$10,000,000
Company B	2,000,000
	12,000,000
Less: amortization of goodwill ($20 million / 40 years)	(500,000)
Consolidated net income	$11,500,000
Shares of Company A outstanding after transaction	60,000,000
Earnings per share	$ 0.19
Change	-5%

The post-acquisition consolidated earnings per share of Company A have decreased. If stock market participants continue to value Company A at a price-earnings multiple of 20x, the price of Company A's shares would decline to $3.80 from $4.00.

The mechanics of the capitalization of maintainable earnings methodology are similar to those of the capitalization of maintainable discretionary cash flow methodology, except that the latter specifically addresses sustaining capital requirements and tax depreciation (capital cost allowance) which the former does not. Therefore, the capitalization of maintainable earnings methodology implicitly assumes that:

- depreciation expense approximates sustaining capital requirements;
- depreciation expense approximates the capital cost allowance tax shield;
- the amortization of deferred charges and deferred credits approximates the cash flow of those items; and
- income taxes for accounting purposes approximates the cash income tax liability.

Fundamentally, the capitalization of maintainable earnings methodology is premised on the assumption that a business will generate a certain amount of after tax earnings every year to perpetuity. Assumptions as to comparative financial risk, and whether earnings will grow or diminish from a constant annual rate are reflected in the capitalization rate adopted.

Components of the Capitalization of Maintainable Earnings Methodology

Overview

In the past, the capitalization of maintainable earnings methodology often was applied simply by dividing indicated or normalized net income (after interest expense) into a capitalization rate (a return on equity) to derive capitalized earnings, which was taken to be en bloc equity value (adjusting for redundant assets, where necessary). While this approach was attractive due to its simplicity, it did not specifically address (among other things) the impact of capital structure, prospective capital expenditures, or other prospective non-recurring items on the value of a business' equity. Consequently, the en bloc equity value derived may have been overstated or understated unless such things were appropriately accounted for in the capitalization rate adopted.

Having said this, the steps that normally should be followed where the capitalization of maintainable earnings methodology is adopted are as follows:

- an estimated range of maintainable earnings before interest and income taxes (EBIT) is determined;
- interest expense, based on an 'appropriate' level of debt, is deducted from EBIT to derive maintainable pre-tax earnings. In theory, the rate of interest applied in this calculation should be the real rate of interest for the business being valued, consistent with the capitalization rate, which is expressed in real terms. The balance sheet notionally is adjusted to reflect an 'appropriate' amount of debt;
- income taxes are applied against pre-tax income to derive after-tax maintainable earnings;
- a capitalization rate (being a levered return on equity) is estimated. The estimated after-tax maintainable earnings are divided by the capitalization rate (or multiplied by the price/earnings multiple) to derive capitalized earnings;

- where applicable, prospective non-recurring items are added to (deducted from) capitalized earnings. That is, maintainable earnings are assumed to be recurring (either stable or some average) with growth reflected in the capitalization rate adopted, where appropriate. If a non-recurring income or expenditure is anticipated, it should be accounted for separately (net of tax);
- the net realizable value of redundant assets is added to capitalized earnings and net non-recurring items to determine en bloc equity value; and
- where the 'appropriate' level of debt used in calculating interest expense differs from the actual amount of interest bearing debt outstanding, an adjustment is made to reflect the notional increase (decrease) in debt.

Alternatively, the capitalization of maintainable earnings calculation can be made on an 'enterprise value' basis where unlevered earnings are divided by a weighted average cost of capital based on an 'appropriate' capital structure, and the actual amount of debt outstanding is deducted to determine the en bloc equity value. As explained in Chapter 4, an 'enterprise value' approach eliminates the 'circularity' of an 'appropriate' capital structure determination.

Estimating Maintainable Earnings

An estimate of maintainable earnings begins with an estimate of maintainable earnings before interest and taxes (EBIT). The estimate of maintainable EBIT in a capitalization of maintainable earnings methodology entails a similar process to the estimation of maintainable EBIT-DA in a capitalization of discretionary cash flow methodology. The objective is to estimate a range of EBIT that the business reasonably can be expected to sustain over the long term. An informed, reasoned estimate of maintainable EBIT necessitates:

- an understanding of the nature of the business, the industry in which it operates, and prevailing economic conditions; and
- a detailed review and analysis of current, historic and projected operating and financial results.

When interpreting actual and projected operating and financial results, it is important to understand the accounting policies adopted, and to ensure that those accounting policies have been consistently applied. This is because judgement is inherent in the application of Generally Accepted Accounting Principles, and profits can be stated differently for identical accounting periods.

Interest expense is deducted based on the assumption of an 'appropriate' level of interest bearing debt with which to finance the business. In theory, the interest rate applied should be reflective of real interest rates for the business at the valuation date. The factors to consider in determining an 'appropriate' amount of debt are discussed in Chapter 7. EBIT less 'normalized' interest expense yields maintainable pretax income.

Income taxes are deducted from maintainable pretax income to derive after-tax maintainable earnings. The income tax rate used should be the financial accounting tax rate, which may include both a current and deferred income tax component.

Capitalization Rates

The selection of an appropriate capitalization rate is a complex and subjective task that requires a thorough analysis of the business, the industry and prevailing economic factors. Again, there is a direct interrelationship between the estimate of maintainable earnings and the capitalization rate applied thereto.

Where maintainable earnings are determined net of interest expense, the capitalization rate applied should be a real levered return on equity, determined consistent with the debt to equity assumptions used in calculating an 'appropriate' level of annual real interest expense. The derivation of levered cost of equity is discussed in Chapter 8. Importantly, the capitalization rate calculations set out in Chapter 8 represent the rate of return to apply to cash flows and not to accounting earnings. Accordingly, a further adjustment to the capitalization rate may be appropriate where maintainable after tax earnings are materially different from levered after tax discretionary cash flows. Where accounting earnings exceed discretionary cash flows an upward adjustment to the capitalization rate may be appropriate where a capitalization of maintainable earnings methodology is employed. As a practical matter, where the capitalization of earnings methodology is applied as a test of valuation conclusions derived pursuant to a cash flow based methodology, an adjustment to the capitalization rate seldom is made.

Non-recurring Revenue and Expense Adjustments

The capitalized earnings derived by dividing maintainable after-tax earnings by the capitalization rate represents the present value to perpetuity of that earnings stream from the business' principal operations. However, similar to the adjustments for non-recurring items made pursuant to a capitalization of discretionary cash flow methodology (see Chapter 4), certain adjustments to this value may be required for expected non-recurring revenues and expenses not reflected in estimated maintainable earnings. The benefit or cost of such non-recurring revenues and expenses should be tax effected, including the present value of the CCA tax shield where capital expenditures are involved. If the non-recurring revenues and expenses are not expected to occur immediately, or if there is uncertainty as to their quantification, it may be appropriate to discount them to present value at an appropriate rate. The discount rate selected should be reflective of the risk inherent in the realization of the non-recurring revenues and expenses, and may be different from the capitalization rate applied to maintainable earnings. The after-tax value of prospective non-recurring revenues and expenses (discounted where appropriate) is added to capitalized earnings.

Available Income Tax Losses

A business may have income tax losses available to be applied to future earnings. Since the income tax deducted from maintainable pre-tax earnings is the prospective rate, unless the value of available tax losses has been accounted for in the capitalization rate, they will not have been accounted for. As discussed in Chapter 4, the nature of the losses (capital vs. non-capital), and their quantum and expected timing of utilization must be understood. Where appropriate, the value of available income tax losses not otherwise considered should be added to capitalized earnings.

Redundant Assets

In a capitalization of earnings context, redundant assets are those that do not contribute to the generation of maintainable earnings. The net realizable value of redundant assets is added to the capitalized earnings of the business. In this context, the net realizable value of redundant assets is defined as value in exchange less disposition costs and corporate income tax, discounted where appropriate. The valuation of redundant assets is addressed in Chapter 4.

Financing Adjustment

As discussed above, the calculation of 'normalized' interest expense is based on an estimate of the amount of debt 'appropriate' to the business. Where this is different than the actual amount of interest bearing debt outstanding, the notional increase (decrease) in debt capacity is added to (deducted from) what otherwise would be en bloc equity value. This assumes that where a business is under-levered, the business would borrow funds and distribute them to the business owners. A under-levered business sometimes is referred to as having 'hidden redundancy'. Alternatively, where a business is over-levered, this adjustment assumes that the equity holders would inject capital into the business.

Example of the Capitalization of Maintainable Earnings Methodology

Eddie Electric Limited (EEL) is a wholesaler of electronic supplies and components used in electrical appliances. EEL purchases electrical components from manufacturers' outlets and in turn sells these to equipment assemblers who build electrical appliances, to electronic repair shops and to retailers (such as hardware stores). The founder is the company's sole shareholder, who has not been actively involved in the daily operations for many years. EEL is not dependent on his continued involvement.

EEL leases 20,000 square feet of office and warehouse space in Sudbury, Ontario, where it has operated for the past 20 years. EEL's premises are leased at $3 per square foot below market rates from the founder's nephew.

EEL's balance sheet for its most recent fiscal year ending July 31, 2000 is as follows ($000):

SCHEDULE 10.1

Eddie Electric Limited
Balance Sheet
At July 31, 2000
($000's)

Current assets	3,181
Fixed assets (net)	529
Total assets	3,710
Bank loan	258
Accounts payable & accruals	1,522
Total liabilities	1,780
Shareholder equity	1,930
Total liabilities & equity	3,710

Fixed assets are comprised of leasehold improvements, office furniture, and computers and warehouse equipment. In any given year, fixed asset additions approximate depreciation. EEL does not have any redundant assets.

EEL's historical and projected income statements are as follows:

SCHEDULE 10.2

Eddie Electric Limited
Income Statements
For the Fiscal Years Ending July 31
($000's)

	Budget			Actual		
	2001	2000	1999	1998	1997	1996
Sales	13,000	13,284	11,873	8,409	10,288	8,944
Cost of sales	9,750	9,764	8,845	6,559	7,819	6,976
Gross profit	3,250	3,520	3,028	1,850	2,469	1,968
Operating expenses	1,740	1,794	1,663	1,560	1,966	1,567
Bonuses	1,200	1,420	1,050	0	190	70
Depreciation	90	83	87	92	95	93
Interest expense	30	28	35	48	28	45
	3,060	3,325	2,835	1,700	2,279	1,775
Income before taxes	190	195	193	150	190	193
Income taxes	48	49	48	37	48	48
Net income	142	146	145	113	142	145

EEL's sales tend to fluctuate with the general local economic activity levels. Most operating expenses are fixed. In the 1997 fiscal year EEL made a one-time settlement of $250,000 to a former employee who sued for wrongful dismissal. The fiscal 2001 budget includes an anticipated property tax refund of $100,000 classified as part of 'operating expenses'. In order to minimize income taxes, the founder declares personal bonuses to reduce pretax income to the small business threshold of $200,000. The owner does not draw any other remuneration from the company.

The founder requires a valuation of the outstanding shares of EEL for estate freeze purposes. Analysis of EEL's business reveals:

- income taxes are paid at a rate of 23% on the first $200,000 of taxable income, and 45% thereafter;
- an appropriate amount of debt for EEL is estimated to be $1 million at a real interest rate of 5%;

- an appropriate capitalization rate for EEL is estimated in the range of 12% to 14%, being a real after-tax cost of equity including the impact of financial leverage;
- inflation has averaged 2% per annum over the past five years and this rate is expected to continue; and
- accounting earnings approximate discretionary cash flows.

Value Determination

The first step is to determination of maintainable EBIT. This is estimated in the range of $870,000 to $1,070,000, as follows:

SCHEDULE 10.3

Eddie Electric Limited
Estimated Normalized EBIT
For the Fiscal Years Ending July 31
($000's)

	Budget		Actual			
	2001	2000	1999	1998	1997	1996
Pretax income as reported	190	195	193	150	190	193
Adjustments:						
Interest expense	30	28	35	48	28	45
Bonuses	1,200	1,420	1,050	0	190	70
Settlement					250	
Property tax refund	(100)					
Rent expense	(60)	(60)	(60)	(60)	(60)	(60)
Adjusted EBIT	1,260	1,583	1,218	138	598	248
Inflation adjusted EBIT	1,260	1,615	1,267	146	647	273
Weighting factor	5	5	4	3	2	1
Weighted average	1,072					
Simple average	868					
	Low	High				
Range, say	870	1,070				

The starting point in this calculation is pretax income as reported for 1996 through 2000, and budget for 2001. To these figures, the following adjustments are made:

- interest expense is added back;
- bonuses to the founder are added back to income since these items are discretionary. Given that EEL would operate successfully without the founder, no third party manager bonus (or other remuneration) is reflected in the calculations pursuant to an assumption that none would be required;
- the wrongful dismissal settlement of $250,000 in 1997 is added back because it is a non-recurring item;
- the property tax refund projected for fiscal 2001 is deducted because this is also a non-recurring item. However, a subsequent adjustment for this anticipated income is made; and
- incremental rent expense is deducted to reflect arm's length lease rates. EEL's annual rental benefit is approximately $3 per square foot, or $60,000 for its 20,000 square foot premises.

The adjusted EBIT for 1996 through 2000 is then increased for inflation at a rate of 2% per annum since (although not always done in practice) maintainable EBIT in theory should be estimated beginning one year forward. All of the historical years from 1996, as well as the budget for fiscal 2001 have been considered when estimating maintainable EBIT. EEL's sales and profitability fluctuate with the general local economy, and therefore it is appropriate to reflect a full earnings cycle.

A weighted average and a simple average of the inflation-adjusted EBIT from 1996 through 2001 is calculated. When calculating the weighted average, the greatest weight (a factor of 5) was assigned to the 2000 actual results and 2001 budget. The weights decline each year back to 1996. This weighting scheme assumes that the most recent and prospective years are most indicative of future operating performance. Accordingly it places greater emphasis on the most recent fiscal years and the forecast year. The weighted average earnings for 1996 through 2001 is $1,072,000. The simple average of the inflation-adjusted EBIT from 1996 through 2001 is $868,000. The simple average places equal emphasis on each year. Maintainable EBIT is estimated in a range of $870,000 to $1,070,000. The low end of the range approximates the simple average of historical and projected results, whereas the high end is more consistent with the weighted average.

Interest expense is deducted from maintainable EBIT. Interest expense is taken to be $50,000 per annum ($1 million x 5% real rate of interest). Maintainable pretax income is then determined to be in the range of $820,000 to $1,020,000. Income taxes are deducted from pretax income at a rate of 23% on the first $200,000 of income, and 45% on the balance, resulting in maintainable after tax earnings of $495,000 to $605,000. (Note that the use of the small business tax rate was assumed to be appropriate for EEL, although this may not always be the case). The real levered capitalization rates of 12% to 14% are applied against estimated maintainable after-tax earnings to derive capitalized earnings of $4,125,000 to $4,321,000 (Schedule 10.4).

The property tax refund included in the 2001 budget is added to capitalized earnings since it has not been included in the estimate of maintainable earnings. The amount of $55,000 reflects the gross refund of $100,000, less income taxes at 45%. It may be appropriate to discount this anticipated refund to reflect both the time value of money, and the risk that the benefit proves to be less than expected.

Finally, an adjustment is made for the notional increase in EEL's debt capacity. Interest expense was calculated assuming an appropriate amount of interest bearing debt is $1 million. Given that EEL has $258,000 of interest bearing debt outstanding, it has a 'hidden redundancy' of $742,000. The sum of capitalized earnings, the adjustment for the prospective property tax refund and the financing adjustment results in an en bloc equity value estimated in the range of $4.9 million to $5.1 million.

SCHEDULE 10.4

Eddie Electric Limited
Estimated Fair Market Value
At July 31, 2000
($000's)

	Low	High
Estimated maintainable EBIT	$ 870	$1,070
Interest expense ($1 million @ 5%)	(50)	(50)
Earnings before income taxes	820	1,020
Income taxes @ 23% / 45%	(325)	(415)
Estimated maintainable after tax income	495	605
Capitalization rate	12%	14%
Capitalized earnings	4,125	4,321
Add: property tax refund (net of tax)	55	55
Add: financing adjustment	742	742
Estimated fair market value of equity	4,922	5,118
Say,	$4,900	$5,100

The Dual Capitalization of Earnings Methodology

The dual capitalization of earnings methodology (or excess earnings model) is a variation of the capitalization of maintainable earnings methodology. It recognizes and emphasizes that different risks may attach to the net tangible assets of a business than may attach to the value of the business represented by goodwill. In comparison with more conventional valuation methodologies, the dual capitalization of earnings methodology requires additional subjective estimates (such as the 'value in use' of underlying net tangible assets) and is highly theoretical. As such, it is infrequently used in practice, and then typically only in the case of smaller non-capital intensive businesses. Where it is adopted, it generally is applied as a test of the value determined pursuant to other going concern methodologies.

The dual capitalization of earnings methodology involves segregating the en bloc value of a business into two components:

- the value attributable to the return a business generates on its net tangible assets; and
- the value attributed to the ability of the business to generate returns in excess of appropriate levels of return on its net tangible assets.

Based on the presumption that risk attaching to goodwill is higher than the risk attaching to net tangible assets, capitalization rates attributed to returns on the former are taken to be higher (multiples lower) than those attributed to returns on the latter. Accordingly, the dual capitalization of earnings methodology requires an estimate of two capitalization rates. The first (lower) capitalization rate is applied to earnings presumed derived from net tangible assets, and the second is applied to earnings presumed derived from goodwill. As a result, the dual capitalization of earnings methodology often is found to be impractical due to the increased level of subjectivity and complexity involved.

By its nature, the dual capitalization of earnings methodology is a hybrid asset and earnings valuation methodology. After tax earnings selection and capitalization rate determination require the same considerations in the dual capitalization of earnings methodology as in the capitalization of maintainable earnings methodology. As with other going concern valuation methodologies, redundant assets are included in value as a separate component.

Importantly, as discussed in Chapter 6, while historically purchasers considered and weighted the underlying operating assets of a business being acquired in estimating value and price, emphasis on underlying assets generally has declined throughout the 1990's. At present, purchasers typically are most interested in the prospective discretionary cash flow generating ability of a target business, and often will not modify their valuation and pricing 'conclusions' based on what they believe to be acceptable deviations in 'value in use' estimates of its underlying operating assets. Accordingly, the dual capitalization of earnings methodology may be even less relevant today than it had been in the past.

Example of the Dual Capitalization of Earnings Methodology

Assume XYZ Limited ('XYZ') operates a chain of grocery stores, generates $400,000 after-tax income each year net of 'appropriate' interest expense, and has a book equity of $2 million including $300,000 of unamortized goodwill and $100,000 of deferred store-opening costs. XYZ's fair market value, adopting a real levered return on equity of 14%, is estimated at $2,857,000 (derived as $400,000/14%).

Assuming appropriate real after tax returns on net tangible and intangible assets to be 10% and 18% respectively, the fair market value of XYZ's equity would be estimated pursuant to the dual capitalization of earnings methodology as follows:

Maintainable after tax earnings	$ 400,000
Less return on net tangible assets $1,600,000 @ 10%	160,000
Return on intangible assets	240,000
Capitalized at	18%
Intangible value	1,333,000
Net tangible assets	1,600,000
Estimated fair market value	$2,933,000

XYZ's tangible assets are estimated at $1,600,000, taken in this example to be book equity of $2 million, less book value of goodwill ($300,000) and deferred store opening costs ($100,000), both of which are non-identifiable intangible assets. The after-tax income stream associated with XYZ's net tangible assets is 10% of $1.6 million, or $160,000. Therefore, of the $400,000 annual after-tax earnings generated by XYZ, $240,000 is attributable to 'goodwill'. Where goodwill faces greater risk than do net tangible assets, the return on investment in goodwill must be greater than the return on investment in net tangible assets, in this case taken to be 18%. The capitalized value of goodwill ($1,333,000) is added to the tangible assets of $1,600,000 to develop an estimated en bloc fair market value for the outstanding shares of XYZ of $2,933,000. The value derived using the dual capitalization of earnings technique appears to support the conclusion of $2,857,000 derived using the capitalization of maintainable earnings methodology. The implied rate of return in the dual capitalization of earnings technique is approximately 13.6% – being $400,000 after tax earnings divided by $2,933,000 estimated fair market value.

Where the dual capitalization of earnings methodology produces a value higher than determined pursuant to a single capitalization rate methodology, insufficient emphasis on underlying asset values when selecting a single capitalization rate may be indicated. Conversely, where the dual capitalization rate methodology produces a value lower than that determined pursuant to a single capitalization rate methodology, insufficient recognition to a comparatively high implied intangible value when selecting a single capitalization rate may be indicated.

A second application of the dual capitalization technique as a test method is to use it to 'force out' the implied rate of return on intangible value inherent in value otherwise determined. This is done by determining an appropriate rate of return on net tangible assets, and then determining the imputed rate of return on the implied intangible value component of the initial value determination. This imputed rate of return is then assessed for reasonableness on a stand-alone basis, and as compared to the selected return on net tangible assets.

For example, Interim Placements Inc. (IPI) is a placement agency which fills temporary and contract employment positions. IPI generates annual after-tax earnings of $400,000 and has net tangible assets of $1,500,000. The value of IPI's outstanding shares was estimated at $2,800,000 pursuant to the capitalization of maintainable earnings methodology, determined as 7 times (rate of return of 14.3%) maintainable after-tax earnings.

Assuming that an appropriate rate of return on net tangible assets is 12%, the implied return on intangible assets (goodwill) would be determined as follows:

Indicated after tax earnings	$ 400,000
Less return on net tangible assets $1,500,000 @ 12%	180,000
Return on intangible assets	$ 220,000
Intangible value $2,800,000 - $1,500,000	$1,300,000
Implied return on intangible value $220,000 / $1,300,000	16.9%

The reasonableness of the implied rate of return on intangible value of 16.9% must be assessed both relative to the 12% return required on net tangible assets and to the 14.3% composite return required as the selection of a single capitalization rate. If there had been an expectation that the rate of return on intangible value should have been 20%, the composite capitalization rate (and hence the value determination) would require reconsideration.

The foregoing describes the dual capitalization methodology as a variation of the capitalization of maintainable earnings methodology. The dual capitalization methodology has equal applicability as a variation of the capitalization of discretionary cash flow methodology, where discretionary cash flow forms the capitalization base.

To summarize, the dual capitalization of earnings methodology can assist in the assessment of the overall value/price conclusion determined using a single capitalization technique. In addition, it serves as a reminder of the integration of the various value components. However, it is not widely adopted, where adopted tends to be applied to smaller non-capital intensive businesses, and rarely is appropriate as a primary valuation methodology.

Operating Multiples

Multiple of Maintainable or Trailing EBIT

The multiple of earnings before interest and taxes (EBIT) methodology is a variation of the capitalization of earnings methodology. The multiple of EBIT methodology eliminates subjectivity related to the existing capital structure of the business. This is because since it is applied before interest expense, the multiple represents a weighted average cost of capital. In addition, because a pre-tax earnings measure is being used, the multiple also is determined on a pre-tax basis. The result obtained by multiplying maintainable or trailing EBIT by an EBIT multiple represents the enterprise value of the business. The value of the outstanding interest bearing debt is deducted to determine the en bloc value of the business equity. As is the case with the capitalization of maintainable earnings methodology, redundant assets and non-recurring items should be accounted for separately, although this is not always done.

Adopting data from the previous example of Eddie Electric Limited (EEL), the EBIT multiple methodology would be applied as follows ($000):

	Low	High
Maintainable EBIT (Schedule 10.3)	$ 870	$1,070
EBIT multiple	5.3x	4.5x
Enterprise value	4,611	4,815
Add: value of property tax refunds (net of tax)	55	55
Less: outstanding debt	(258)	(258)
Value of equity, en bloc	4,408	4,612
Say,	$4,400	$4,600

The maintainable EBIT of $870,000 to $1,070,000 (as previously determined) is multiplied by a multiple of 5.3 times and 4.5 times, respectively. These multiples are calculated as the inverse of pretax capitalization rates of approximately 19% and 22%, respectively. These rates are a pretax weighted average cost of capital (WACC), derived as follows — (see Chapter 7 Formula 7.4):

$$\text{After} - \text{tax WACC} = (K_L \times W_E) + (K_D \times W_D)$$

At the low end: $12\% \times 4,900/5,900 + 5\% \times (1-45\%) \times 1,000/5,900$
= 10.43% after tax

Gross – up for taxes: $10.43\%/(1-45\%)$
= 19% pretax

Multiple = 1/19% = 5.3×

At the high end: $14\% \times 5,100/6,100 + 5\% \times (1-45\%) \times 1,000/6,100$
= 12.16% after tax

Gross – up for taxes: $12.16\%/(1-45\%)$
= 22% pretax

Multiple = 1/22% = 4.5×

As before, the adjustment for the benefit of a one-time property tax refund is added on an after-tax basis. The amount of debt outstanding is deducted to derive the en bloc equity value. In this case, the en bloc fair market value of the shares of EEL derived pursuant to the multiple of EBIT methodology ($4.4 million to $4.6 million) is less than the conclusion derived pursuant to the capitalization of maintainable earnings methodology ($4.9 million to $5.1 million), as previously calculated. This is because the benefit of the small business income tax rate (23% on the first $200,000 of taxable income) was not reflected in the derivation of the EBIT multiples.

Although the multiple of EBIT methodology is attractive due to its simplicity, an after-tax approach is preferable. This is because tax rates are jurisdictionally and operationally different. In addition, like the capitalization of maintainable earnings methodology, a multiple of EBIT assumes that depreciation approximates sustaining capital reinvestment and capital cost allowance. Finally, where the multiple of EBIT methodology used is taken to be an 'industry standard', it likely reflects purchaser-perceived synergies that cannot be readily segregated. Therefore, the multiple of EBIT methodology normally should only be used in deriving a preliminary estimate as to value, or as a method to test the reasonableness of conclusions determined pursuant to other valuation methodologies.

Multiple of Maintainable or Trailing EBIT-DA

In most cases, the multiple of earnings before interest, taxes, depreciation and amortization (EBIT-DA) methodology is a variation of the capitalization of discretionary cash flow methodology, except that cash flows and net sustaining capital reinvestment are not specifically addressed.

Pursuant to the multiple of EBIT-DA methodology, EBIT-DA is multiplied by a multiple to derive an enterprise value for the business. Therefore, interest bearing debt and equivalents are deducted to derive equity value. Adjustments for non-recurring items and redundant assets technically should be made where material and believed appropriate, although this is not always done. Again, the multiple reflects a pre-tax weighted average cost of capital. The multiple used should take into account:

- the appropriate capital structure of the business. The greater the ability to utilize debt, the greater the EBIT-DA multiple;
- sustaining capital requirements. The greater the need for sustaining capital, the lower the EBIT-DA multiple; and
- growth and risk in maintaining EBIT-DA, the same factors affecting the determination of an unlevered return on equity.

The multiple of EBIT-DA methodology does not adequately address the valuation implications of income taxes and capital expenditure requirements, both of which are fundamental considerations for many businesses. As a practical matter, both the multiple of EBIT and multiple of EBIT-DA methodologies are little more than rules of thumb. As such, their use normally should be restricted to deriving a rough estimate as to value, or as methods to test in a general way the reasonableness of conclusions determined pursuant to other valuation methodologies. Where used to test value conclusions otherwise determined, 'comparative' EBIT an EBIT-DA multiples derived from public market proxies seldom, if ever, can be appropriately adjusted for one-time items and redundant assets. Since these things will (or should) have been adjusted for pursuant to application of one or more primary valuation methodologies, EBIT and EBIT-DA comparisons inherently may be flawed. Further, as is the case with other rules of thumb, 'industry standard' multiples of EBIT-DA likely include an element of purchaser-perceived synergies that cannot be readily segregated and analyzed.

Liquidation Value

Overview

Where it has been determined that a business is not viable as a going concern, it typically is valued on a liquidation value basis. Liquidation value may also be an appropriate basis in the infrequent circumstance where expected liquidation proceeds to the equity owners exceeds the en bloc value of the equity determined on a going concern basis. Liquidation value generally is described as the net amount available to the equity owners, if any, on the liquidation of all assets and liabilities of the business. Liquidation value can be determined under the scenario of a voluntary liquidation that assumes favourable circumstances to the business owners, or forced liquidation which assumes the business is forced into receivership by its creditors. As a practical matter, where a business is not viable as a going concern, the value of the net assets of the business frequently results in no residual value accruing to the equity owners.

Approaches to Determining Liquidation Value

The assumptions on which a liquidation value calculation is premised can have a significant impact on the conclusion. In this regard, two principal determinations must be made:

- whether the business is subject to a forced or voluntary liquidation; and
- the time frame of the liquidation. That is, whether an immediate liquidation or an extended liquidation period is assumed.

From a conceptual standpoint, liquidation value can be computed pursuant to one of four scenarios as follows:

	Immediate liquidation	Extended liquidation
Forced liquidation	Scenario 1	Scenario 2
Voluntary liquidation	Scenario 3	Scenario 4

Whether a forced or voluntary liquidation is assumed normally is dictated by prevailing circumstances. A failed or failing business typically will be valued pursuant to a forced liquidation assumption whereas a business being dissolved by its owners with no undue external influence to do so would be valued pursuant to a voluntary liquidation assumption.

As a rule, a receiver controls a forced liquidation after secured creditors have petitioned the business into bankruptcy. In Canada, the creditor payment process is governed by the Bankruptcy Act.

Where a business has petitioned the Court for protection under the Companies Creditors Arrangements Act (CCAA) while it works out a restructuring plan, a liquidation approach may or may not be appropriate. A successful restructuring plan requires the approval of a company's creditors. Presumably, such approval indicates that the creditors anticipate recovering a greater portion of the monies owed to them by allowing the business to continue operating rather than if the company was to be liquidated. As a result, a company under CCAA protection appropriately may be valued pursuant to a discounted cash flow methodology. In these circumstances there may or may not be residual value accruing to the equity holders.

In a voluntary liquidation scenario, the equity owners effectively control the liquidation process and seek to maximize their after tax net proceeds on dissolution of the business. A voluntary liquidation generally occurs under relatively favourable circumstances, generally with the expectation that some residual value will accrue to the equity holders. Presumably, the business' owners have determined that the net after tax proceeds from a voluntary liquidation will be greater than the net proceeds from a sale of the shares or net assets of the business. Residual value to the equity owners might also be anticipated in a Court-ordered windup.

Both a forced and orderly liquidation can occur quickly or over an extended period of time. Given the time value of money, the risk of adverse market developments during the liquidation period, and that liquidation over a period of time most often necessitates continuity of some overhead expenses, an immediate liquidation may yield greater net proceeds than a liquidation over time. The determination of whether an 'immediate' or 'extended' liquidation assumption is appropriate should be based on which is expected to generate greater proceeds net of all disposition costs, costs during the liquidation period, income taxes, and the time value of money.

When a receiver liquidates a business the choice of an immediate or extended liquidation time frame depends to a great extent upon the nature of the underlying assets. It is not possible to generalize as to the time required to complete a liquidation process. Certain smaller, simplistic businesses may be liquidated within a few months whereas others may require a year or more. The time span of a liquidation depends on many things, including the condition of the business and its records, whether any portion of the business can be sold as a going concern, whether the owners are cooperative in the liquidation process, the type of assets being sold, and so on. A voluntary liquidation scenario is more likely to take place over an extended time period, particularly where the business owners are involved in the wind-down of operations.

Liquidation Value Methodology

Overview

The mechanics of a liquidation value calculation are as follows:

- the balance sheet is adjusted to re-state assets to current net realizable values, being the amount that individual assets could be expected to fetch (i.e. value in exchange) at the valuation date, net of disposition costs;
- liabilities are deducted from the estimated net proceeds expected from the sale of the assets. Most liabilities are valued at their face value, although adjustments may be required for items such as long term debt and deferred income taxes;
- liquidation related costs are deducted to derive the net proceeds before income taxes;
- corporate income taxes are deducted based on the net proceeds expected from the sale of the assets measured against their respective tax base. Corporate income tax calculations must take into account liquidation costs, and the existing values in any tax pools at the valuation date. The net assets remaining (if any) after payment of liquidation costs, corporate income taxes (if any), and all liabilities is referred to as 'proceeds available for distribution' (i.e. net liquidation proceeds at the corporate level); and
- where the business is incorporated and is owned by one or more individual shareholders, personal income taxes are deducted to derive liquidation value at the owner level. Personal income taxes take into account the nature of the amounts being distributed and the components of the refundable income tax system, where applicable.

Each of these components is discussed in greater detail below. When preparing an estimate of liquidation value, it is important to be consistent in the application the underlying assumptions of either forced or orderly liquidation and immediate or extended time period.

The Valuation of Assets

All tangible assets and identifiable intangible assets (e.g. patents, licensing agreements, and so on) where separately saleable are valued at their net realizable values. Net realizable value is defined as the estimated proceeds such assets are expected to fetch, net of disposition costs based on their value in exchange (as contrasted with their value in continued use).

It is impossible to generalize either as to the likely net realizable value of the various types of assets held by operating businesses, or the likely costs of liquidation. Common bases of net realizable value estimation and issues that should be considered are as follows:

- marketable securities are valued at their present market values in the case of normal sized trading blocks of actively traded shares. When valuing marketable securities, disposition costs must be considered. If the business owns a large block of shares in a public company, a blockage discount may be appropriate – see Chapter 13;
- accounts receivable are estimated at the greater of expected net proceeds from factoring the entire receivables portfolio, and the amount that might reasonably be collected over the liquidation period. The profile of the customers owing money to the business often establishes the likelihood of accounts being collected following public disclosure of liquidation. Where there are numerous small accounts, a lower recovery rate may be more likely than if there are only a few large outstanding accounts. Creditors owing relatively small amounts sometimes will withhold payment assuming the receiver will not pursue small accounts. An added degree of complexity exists where there are long term holdbacks. In these circumstances, it normally is appropriate to discount the net amount expected to be received after consideration of the likely quantum of 'charge-back costs' to the business;
- raw material inventory valuations are based on the composition of the inventory and whether, on a category by category basis:
    - suppliers would buy back the materials and if so, at what price,
    - a sale at auction or through some other means is more likely, or

— all or part of the raw materials are so specialized that they would fetch only scrap value, and what scrap value is;
- work in progress inventory must be assessed in terms of whether greater proceeds would be realized if the inventory was sold on an 'as-is' basis, or if completion of the manufacturing process and sale of the work in progress inventory as finished goods would yield a greater net recovery. Careful consideration must be given to the cost of completion, which would include:
   — the cost and availability of any additional direct materials to be added,
   — the direct and indirect labour costs required to finish the inventory,
   — the overhead cost that would be incurred in maintaining production during the completion period, and
   — selling and administrative costs to be incurred during the completion process.

   Where a failed business is being liquidated and that failure is attributable to product problems, it is unlikely that finishing work in progress would maximize recovery. However, in circumstances of a favourable liquidation scenario, it would be usual to assume the work in progress to be worth at least book value;
- finished goods inventory generally should be considered in conjunction with the treatment of work in progress. Where it is assumed that work in progress will be completed, the sale of the finished goods inventory must include the additional product to be produced. Where finished goods are assumed to be sold immediately, it is necessary to establish whether higher proceeds would be realized by selling en bloc to a jobber or liquidator or by selling to existing customers, perhaps at a discounted price;
- prepaid expenses may be comprised of deposits for utilities and other services, and various amounts that have been paid for services not yet received such as insurance premiums, property and business taxes, and so on. Prepaid expenses should be analyzed on an item by item basis to determine whether any portion of each amount would be refunded in cash if the business were to cease;
- real estate assets, such as the land and building, are valued at their market values less disposition costs including legal fees and commissions. In addition, the likely timing of the sale should be considered, and the net proceeds discounted accordingly;
- machinery and equipment are valued at their value in exchange assuming piecemeal sale, or sale of groups of related assets. This requires considering the estimated quantum of gross proceeds, the commissions and fees involved in the sale, any expenses in preparing the equipment for sale, and

any transportation costs not paid for by the purchasers. For certain of these assets, there may be a significant difference between value in use and value in exchange;
- furniture and fixtures normally are valued based on the estimated net proceeds these assets likely would fetch if sold en bloc to a used furniture wholesaler or jobber. Frequently, net realizable value is less than net book value, particularly where the furniture is relatively new and has not been significantly depreciated;
- leasehold improvements are, as a practical matter, generally of no value. A liquidation calculation normally assumes the premises occupied by the business will be vacated in the near term. This is because leasehold improvements generally cannot be separated from the premises and sold individually. Leasehold improvements may have indirect value if they enable the business to sublet its leased premises sooner or at more favourable rates, thereby reducing any penalty suffered upon lease termination;
- identifiable intangible assets (such as patents, franchise agreements, licenses, royalty agreements, and so on) are valued at the estimated net proceeds such assets would fetch in the open market if sold on an individual basis. In a liquidation value context, these assets often have minimal or no value. For example, where a business is party to a licensing or franchising agreement, there usually are restrictions on the transfer of those rights. Further, most such agreements contain provisions automatically terminating them on the insolvency of one of the parties. Patents, copyrights or intellectual property may have specific value that can be transferred to a third party;
- non-identifiable intangible assets such as deferred charges, capitalized product development costs and goodwill are assigned a nil value since such assets are not commercially viable in and of themselves; and
- for those businesses with defined benefit pension plans, the market value of the pension assets may exceed the actuarial present value of the pension liabilities. Whether such a pension surplus belongs to the business or the employees is a legal issue, and may vary depending on the circumstances. If the amount of the pension surplus is significant, legal advice should be obtained as to what portion, if any, can be recovered by the business. As noted above, the book value of any deferred pension assets represent a non-identifiable intangible and should be assigned a nil value. Where the defined benefit pension plan is in a deficit position, it normally should be assumed that any shortfall will have to be funded. It may be necessary to obtain an actuarial valuation at the time of liquidation to determine the

quantum of pension surplus or deficiency, if any. Post-employment benefit obligations other than pensions (such as extended medical coverage after retirement) should also be considered.

The Valuation of Liabilities

Common bases of estimation and issues that should be considered are as follows:

- current liabilities usually are valued at their respective face values. The quantification of income taxes payable (if any) should be considered in light of the net tax liability or refund the business likely will incur or realize as a result of the liquidation;
- long term liabilities, which may include notes payable, bonds, debentures, and the current portions thereof should be analyzed individually, and valued at their estimated present values. Penalties for early retirement should be reflected, where appropriate. Any premium (or discount) which arose on the initial sale of long term debt and which has an unamortized value represents a non-identifiable intangible liability (asset) and would be assigned a nil value;
- lease obligations should be valued at their face amounts, with consideration given to any penalties for discontinuance. Penalties for both operating and capital leases must be considered;
- deferred income tax credits (or debits) are assigned a nil value since the tax consequences of the liquidation are separately determined;
- deferred revenues may exist where businesses invoice or collect monies from customers prior to revenue being earned for accounting purposes. Where such amounts represent deposits from customers and the goods or services are not to be provided as a result of the liquidation, the deferred revenues represent a liability and should be deducted when determining liquidation value. However, in circumstances of a liquidation where the business is expected to fulfill its order backlog, the portion of the deferred revenues that will be earned should not be included as a liability. The income tax consequences of the revenue recognition policy should be accounted for;
- reserve accounts often are established for product warranties, self-insurance, environmental liabilities, and so on. Where reserve accounts exist, they should be carefully scrutinized to determine the quantum of legitimate liabilities that exist, and to assess the sufficiency of the reserve. This particularly is the case where the business is being liquidated and product

liability issues are not adequately covered by insurance. Since reserve accounts usually are not allowed for Canadian income tax purposes until a liability actually is incurred, the expected settlement of such liabilities should also include consideration of any associated tax deductibility;

- contingent liabilities may exist where the business is party to a legal action or other matter where the outcome may not be known for some time. Where contingent liabilities exist, a reasonable estimate should be made regarding the likely outcome and the timing thereof. The existence of contingent liabilities generally is disclosed in a business' financial statements or in the notes thereto, but this may not always be the case. Consideration should be afforded to contingent liabilities that may not be disclosed, such as environmental and other social obligations. Where the business engages in any activity that may be hazardous to the environment, there may be an obligation for clean up or restoration at such time as the business vacates its premises. Such costs should be accounted for in the determination of liquidation value. The advice of legal counsel may be required where significant contingent liabilities are involved; and

- in recent years, many businesses have become party to financing arrangements or other obligations disclosed only in notes to the financial statements. These may include debt swap arrangements, debt securitization, forward currency exchange contracts, and so on. Therefore, it is important to carefully review the notes to the financial statements to assess whether such assets and liabilities do in fact exist and if they do, the value and appropriate treatment of each.

Liquidation Costs

The quantification of liquidation costs is dependant on whether a forced liquidation or voluntary liquidation is assumed. Under a voluntary liquidation, the owners of the business control the liquidation process, which normally reduces the fees and costs associated with the dissolution of the business. A forced liquidation necessitates additional expenses (such as the cost of a trustee-receiver) and may not have the co-operation of the business owners. Liquidation costs frequently include the following:

- receiver, legal, accounting and other professional fees that can be significant, even in a relatively small and simple liquidation. The quantum of professional fees should be related to the overall timeframe assumption, to the assumptions made as to the collection of receivables, the means of dealing with other assets, and so on;

- termination benefits and payment of vacation pay to discontinued employees, which may or may not have been accrued in the financial statements. When estimating employee termination costs, it is necessary to consider the time frame over which the employees would be terminated, and to quantify the business' legal and contractual obligations as to severance, vacation pay, and other leaving costs such as outplacement services. This typically involves reviewing each individual's employment history to establish remuneration levels, tenure, contractual obligations other than the applicable labour legislation, and so on;
- shutdown costs related to the termination of active operations. This may include equipment cleaning and safety procedures prior to storage. Care should be taken to ensure that double-counting of costs does not occur with disposal costs calculated as part of the net realizable value estimates for the equipment;
- outstanding commitments that must be satisfied. These may include minimum purchases from suppliers, forward sales contracts, futures contracts, and so on. Where an immediate liquidation is assumed and it is likely that the business will not satisfy its commitments, a provision for any penalties or damages must be accounted for where applicable. In addition, where premises are leased, leases should be reviewed to determine what early discharge penalties apply, as well as costs of removing signs, partitions and other alterations made to buildings. Capital and operating leases should be reviewed to establish responsibility for the costs of returning these items to the lessor, plus any applicable penalties;
- it is necessary to conceptualize the entire wind-down process, to estimate the period of time required, and to estimate the level of overhead costs to be incurred at each stage of the windup. The overhead costs estimate must consider whether an immediate or extended liquidation is assumed. An analysis of overhead costs is needed to understand the nature of each expense as to whether it is fixed or variable, whether contractual obligations impose any penalties for termination, and the like. It is also necessary to consider whether any overhead cost savings are possible during the liquidation period; and
- miscellaneous liquidation costs should be accounted for. These may include expenses such as the placement of newspaper notices, notification of affected parties, and so on.

Corporate Income Taxes

When determining the net amount available for distribution to owners, income taxes and recoveries that result on the disposition of the assets and liabilities must be accounted for. These include:

- capital gains or losses which may arise on the disposition of marketable securities;
- losses (gains) incurred where the estimated net proceeds of accounts receivable are less than (greater than) their net book values;
- losses incurred on inventories where they are disposed of at amounts less than their tax base. Alternatively, where an extended liquidation is assumed and inventories are expected to be completed and sold at amounts in excess of their tax base, the income taxes on any resultant taxable income should be considered;
- the value of prepaid expenses written off generally gives rise to a tax deduction;
- the estimated net proceeds of fixed asset dispositions (excluding land) must be compared with the cost base of the assets and undepreciated capital cost. Where the net proceeds exceed the original cost, a capital gain will result. Recapture (or a terminal loss) will result where the net proceeds are greater than (or less than) the undepreciated capital cost of the asset pool. The disposition of land normally will give rise to either a capital gain or a capital loss;
- the disposition of identifiable intangible assets may also give rise to a capital gain, recapture, or a terminal loss, depending on circumstances;
- where goodwill (eligible capital property) exists for tax purposes, a terminal loss will result where goodwill has no value in a liquidation scenario. Other non-identifiable intangibles (such as deferred charges) must be analyzed on an individual basis. In circumstances where cost deferrals have no cost base for tax purposes, no tax consequences will arise;
- reserves and contingencies generally are not allowable for Canadian income tax purposes until a liability actually is incurred. Therefore, the expected amount to be paid in respect of contingencies or from reserve funds generally gives rise to a tax deduction; and
- liquidation costs will give rise to an income tax deduction.

Several other considerations should be taken into account when estimating the appropriate amount of corporate income tax on liquidation. For example:

- as discussed below under the caption 'Personal Income Taxes' and in Chapter 14, qualifying companies are eligible for the capital dividend account ('CDA') and refundable dividend tax on hand ('RDTOH'). Where the value of the business is determined as the net proceeds to the individual shareholder, consideration must be given to whether these accounts are applicable in order to be consistent at both the personal and corporate levels;
- where a net capital loss or non-capital loss arises on the disposition of the net assets of the business, consideration must be given to whether those losses have any value. Since the business is being discontinued, capital losses may be of no value, except to the extent that they can be used to offset capital gains arising on liquidation. Non-capital losses can be carried back three years (and forward seven years, which usually is irrelevant in a liquidation scenario). Therefore, the quantum of previous income taxes paid which can be recovered through the carry-back of non-capital losses must be determined; and
- any existing income tax losses (i.e. losses which existed before the process of liquidating the business) must be considered, including the type of loss (net capital, non-capital, allowable business investment loss, and so on) and whether some or all of said losses can be utilized to reduce the income taxes otherwise payable on the disposition of the business' net assets.

Personal Income Taxes

Where a business is liquidated pursuant to a Court order or some other order pursuant to an insolvency proceeding, the net proceeds from the disposition of its underlying assets typically are less than its outstanding liabilities. Accordingly, in situations of a 'forced liquidation' there seldom is any residual after payment of debts that accrues to the equity holders. However, in situations of a voluntary liquidation, there sometimes is the expectation that the owners will receive a portion of the net proceeds, which may give rise to personal income tax considerations.

For an unincorporated business personal income taxes that arise on liquidation generally are taken into account in the liquidation calculation. Where the business is an unincorporated entity, the net proceeds available to its owner(s) (being the adjusted equity less liquidation costs) constitutes business income in the hands of the individual taxpayer and is taxed at the individual's marginal tax rate.

Where the business being liquidated is incorporated and the shareholder is a corporate entity, then:

- the subsidiary normally can be wound up into the parent on a tax-deferred basis where the parent owns at least 90% of the subsidiary's shares; or
- dividends normally can be paid from the subsidiary to the corporate shareholder on a tax-free basis.

Therefore, from the standpoint of a corporate shareholder no further income tax implications need to be considered.

Where the business being liquidated is a corporation with individual shareholders the net proceeds, if any, available to those individual shareholders in a liquidation or wind-up generally are comprised of the following:

- a return of paid up capital, which is tax free;
- a capital dividend account, which is only available to private companies. The capital dividend account represents that portion of capital gains which are not taxable (presently 50% in Canada) and certain other items, such as life insurance proceeds. Capital dividends are distributed to shareholders on a tax-free basis;
- for companies which were incorporated prior to 1972, there may be a balance available in the pre-1972 capital surplus on hand (CSOH) account. The pre-1972 CSOH is the accumulation of the capital gains net of losses that have been realized to December 31, 1971, and those gains (net of losses) which existed at December 31, 1971 which were realized subsequent to that date. Pre-1972 CSOH is only available on the wind-up of a company; and
- the balance, which represents a taxable dividend, and is eligible for the dividend tax credit at the personal shareholder level. In the case of Canadian Controlled Private Corporations any taxable dividend should be assessed to determine the impact on refundable dividend tax on hand.

The cash available for distribution less the paid up capital and taxable dividend represents the adjusted proceeds of distribution which, as a practical matter generally is equal to the amount of paid-up capital and pre-1972 CSOH, if any. Where the adjusted proceeds of distribution are greater or less than the individual's adjusted cost base for the shares, a capital gain or loss will arise. The tax consequences to the individual shareholder of the gain or loss must be considered in the determination of the net proceeds — see Chapter 14.

FIGURE 10.1

Determination of Deemed Dividend

Funds available for distribution
(including refundable dividend tax on hand)

Less

Paid up capital

Equals

Deemed dividend on wind-up

Less

Pre-1972 CSOH (if any)

Equals

Taxable dividend (post-1971)

Less

Capital dividend account (if any)

Equals

Deemed taxable dividend

FIGURE 10.2

Determination of Capital Gain or Loss

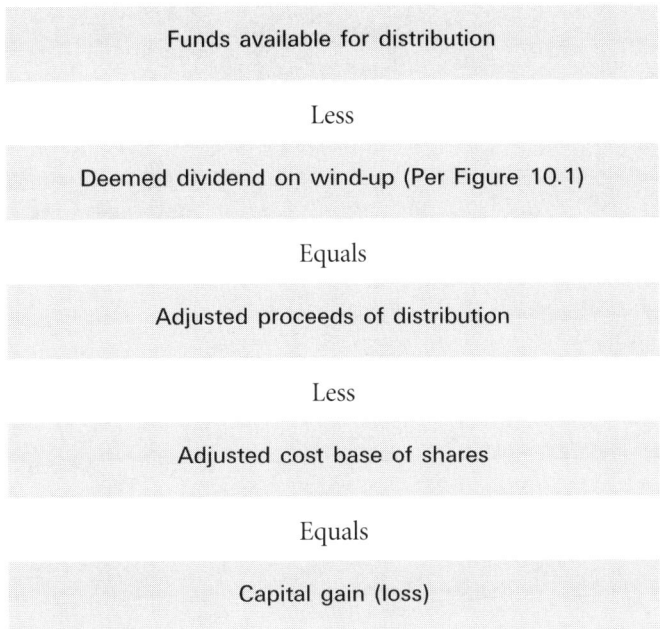

Example of Liquidation Value Calculation

XYZ Limited ('XYZ') operates a machine shop in Winnipeg, Manitoba. XYZ's outstanding shares are owned by John Steel. Mr. Steel has operated XYZ since its inception. Due to failing health, he has decided wind up XYZ immediately following its December 31, 2000 year-end.

XYZ's balance sheet at December 31, 2000 along with the tax base of the assets and their estimated market values is as follows:

SCHEDULE 10.5

XYZ Limited
Balance Sheet
December 31, 2000

	Net Book Value	Original Cost	Undepreciated Capital Cost	Estimated Market Value
Cash	73,000			73,000
Marketable securities	124,000	124,000		188,000
Accounts receivable	150,000	150,000		150,000
Inventories	125,000	125,000		110,000
Prepaid expenses	20,000	20,000		10,000
	492,000			
Land	146,000	146,000		250,000
Building	234,000	440,000	234,000	500,000
Production equipment	168,000	393,000	74,500	175,000
Furniture & other	48,000	79,000	36,000	20,000
	596,000			
Total assets	1,088,000			
Current liabilities	118,000			
Deferred income taxes	19,000			
Total liabilities	137,000			
Capital stock	1,000			
Retained earnings	950,000			
Total shareholder equity	951,000			
Total liabilities and equity	1,088,000			

Other information related to XYZ and to Mr. Steel follows:

- XYZ pays income tax at a rate of 22% on the first $200,000 of active business income and 40% on excess income which is eligible for the manufacturing and processing profits deduction. Non active business income is subject to income tax at a rate of 53%, which includes 6.67% of additional refundable tax;
- Mr. Steel's effective marginal personal income tax rates are 50% for employment income, 33% for dividend income and 25% for capital gains;
- as a Canadian Controlled Private Corporation, XYZ is eligible for dividend refunds at a rate of 26.67%. XYZ has no balance in its refundable dividend tax on hand account or capital dividend account at December 31, 2000;
- sales commissions equal to 5% of gross proceeds are payable on the disposition of the marketable securities, land and building. Disposition costs on production equipment and furniture and other assets are estimated at 10% of gross proceeds. There are no other disposition costs; and
- when winding up the corporation, Mr. Steel expects to incur $25,000 in overhead costs during the wind-up period and $20,000 in professional fees to dissolve the corporation.

Liquidation Value Determination

The after tax net proceeds to Mr. Steel are estimated at $819,711. This is determined as follows:

SCHEDULE 10.6

XYZ Limited
Estimated Net Proceeds
December 31, 2000

	Estimated Market Value	Disposition Costs	Net Realizable Value	Business Income (Loss)	Taxable Capital Gain	Capital Dividend Account	Refundable Dividend Tax on Hand
Cash	73,000		73,000				
Marketable securities	188,000	(9,400)	178,600		27,300	27,300	7,281
Accounts receivable	150,000		150,000		0		
Inventories	110,000		110,000	(15,000)			
Prepaid expenses	10,000		10,000	(10,000)			
Land	250,000	(12,500)	237,500		45,750	45,750	12,202
Building	500,000	(25,000)	475,000	206,000	17,500	17,500	4,667
Production equipment	175,000	(17,500)	157,500	83,000	0	0	0
Furniture & other	20,000	(2,000)	18,000	(18,000)	0	0	0
Total net proceeds			1,409,600	246,000	90,550	90,550	24,150
Current liabilities			(118,000)				
Adjusted equity			1,291,600				

SCHEDULE 10.7

XYZ Limited
Estimated Net Proceeds
December 31, 2000

	Estimated Market Value	Disposition Costs	Net Realizable Value
Adjusted equity (Schedule 10.6)			1,291,600
Liquidation costs:			
Overhead costs		25,000	
Professional fees		20,000	
Net liquidation costs			45,000
Net proceeds before taxes			1,246,600
Corporate income taxes:			
First $200,000 business income	22%	44,000	
Excess business income at	40%	18,400	
Taxable capital gains at	53%	47,992	
Liquidation costs	40%	(18,000)	
Refundable dividend tax	(Schedule 10.6)	(24,150)	
Net corporate tax			68,242
Proceeds available for distribution			1,178,358
Less: personal income taxes (Schedule 10.8)			(358,647)
Net proceeds after tax			$ 819,711

The market value of the assets less disposition costs amounts to $1,409,600.

Current liabilities of $118,000 are deducted from the total net proceeds at their respective face values to yield an adjusted equity amount of $1,291,600. Deferred income taxes are of 'nil' value since the income tax consequences arising on the disposition of the assets is separately considered.

Liquidation costs of $45,000 are deducted, including overhead costs of $25,000 and professional fees of $20,000. This results in net proceeds before income taxes of $1,246,600.

Income taxes at the corporate level are then deducted. The income taxes are estimated at $68,242, as follows:

- net active business income is estimated at $246,000. A loss of $15,000 and $10,000 is expected on the disposition of inventories and prepaid expenses respectively, being the difference between their estimated market values and tax cost. The building will generate recapture of $206,000, being the difference between its original cost of $440,000 (which is less than market value) and its undepreciated capital cost of $234,000. The production equipment will generate recapture of $83,000, being the difference between its net realizable value of $157,500 (which is less than original cost) and its undepreciated capital cost of $74,500. A terminal loss of $18,000 is realized on the disposition of the furniture, which represents the amount by which its undepreciated capital cost of $36,000 exceeds its net realizable value of $18,000;
- active business income is subject to income tax at a rate of 22% on the first $200,000 ($44,000 in tax) and 40% on the excess $46,000 ($18,400 in tax);
- capital gains are realized on the disposition of marketable securities, land and the building. One half of the capital gains ($90,550 in aggregate) are classified as taxable, while the balance is allocated to the capital dividend account. Taxable capital gains are subject to income taxes at a rate of 53%, including the refundable tax component;
- liquidation costs of $45,000 are deductible at a rate of 40% ($18,000 in total) since pretax income on dissolution was in excess of $200,000 (specifically, $246,000, as noted above); and
- there is refundable dividend tax (RDTOH) on the amount of taxable capital gains of $90,550 at a rate of 26.67%, or $24,150 in total. This reduces the amount of corporate taxes otherwise payable. It should be noted that the dividend refund accrues at a rate of 33 1/3% of deemed dividends, to a maximum of the balance in the RDTOH account. The refundable dividend tax calculation must take into account the total deemed dividend amount. In this case, the amount of deemed dividend is sufficient to provide for full recovery of RDTOH.

The net proceeds before taxes less corporate income taxes yields proceeds available for distribution of $1,178,358. From this amount, personal income taxes of $358,467 are deducted. The personal taxes are calculated as follows:

SCHEDULE 10.8

XYZ Limited
Personal Income Tax Calculation for John Steel
June 30, 2000

Deemed dividend

Proceeds available for distribution		$1,178,358
Less: paid-up capital		(1,000)
Deemed dividend on wind-up		1,177,358
Less: capital dividend account		(90,550)
Deemed taxable dividend		$1,086,808

Capital Gain (loss)

Proceeds available for distribution		$1,178,358
Less: deemed dividend		(1,177,358)
Adjusted proceeds of disposition		1,000
Less: adjusted cost base of the shares		(1,000)
Capital gain (loss)		$ 0

Income tax on deemed taxable dividend

Taxable dividend (above)		$1,086,808
Effective tax rate on dividends as provided	33%	$ 358,647

Mr. Steel receives a deemed taxable dividend of $1,086,808 on the wind-up. This is determined as the proceeds available for distribution of $1,178,358 less the paid up capital of $1,000 and the balance of the capital dividend account of $90,550. The return of paid up capital and capital dividends are paid to Mr. Steel tax free. Because the adjusted cost base of Mr. Steel's shares ($1,000) is equal to the paid up capital amount, there is no resulting capital gain or loss.

The amount of income tax on the deemed dividend equates to $358,647 given that Mr. Steel's tax rate in dividends of 33%. The proceeds available for distribution of $1,178,358 (i.e. the net assets less corporate taxes and net liquidation costs) less personal income taxes of $358,647 result in the net proceeds retained by Mr. Steel of $819,711.

Summary

The capitalization of maintainable earnings methodology is similar in many respects to the capitalization of discretionary cash flow methodology, except that it utilizes after-tax net income rather than discretionary cash flows. Given that discretionary cash flows typically are a key value driver from the perspective of a corporate acquirer, the application of the capitalization of maintainable earnings methodology generally is limited.

The dual capitalization of earnings methodology, being a variation of the capitalization of maintainable earnings methodology, in some circumstances may be helpful when assessing risks attaching to tangible and intangible assets. However, it is not frequently applied in practice. Operating multiples such as multiples of EBIT and multiples of EBIT-DA are simplifications of the capitalization of maintainable earnings and capitalization of discretionary cash flow methodologies. The application of such multiples generally is restricted to testing value conclusions reached by other methodologies. Finally, where a business is not expected to continue as a going concern, it should be valued using a liquidation approach.

NOTES

1 See, for example, Brant Investments v. Keeprite Inc., Domglas Inc. v. Jarislowsky, Neonex International Ltd. v. Kolasa, Redekop v. Robco., and re: Wall.

2 See, for example, Charles L. Grimes v. Vitalink Communications Corporation, C.A. No. 12334, Court of Chancery of Delaware, New Castle, 1997 Del. Ch. LEXIS 124.

Chapter 11
Business Pricing

Introduction

There may be a significant difference between fair market value determined in a notional market valuation and negotiated open market price. The many reasons for this include differing negotiating skills of buyer and seller, the form of consideration and, importantly, post-acquisition net economic value added (or 'synergies' or 'strategic advantage') perceived by potential open market acquirers of a particular business. Such acquirers anticipate that the value of an acquisition, defined in terms of the present value of its discretionary cash flows, extends beyond the intrinsic (or 'stand-alone') value of the target business. Fact-specific benefits accruing to each potential purchaser beyond a target business' intrinsic value might include anticipated incremental revenues, cost reductions, entry into a strategically important market, and so on.

This Chapter begins with an examination of the differences between notional fair market value and open market price determinations, and notional market valuation vs. open market pricing processes. Special interest purchaser issues including the identification and quantification of post-acquisition net economic value added then are addressed. The Chapter concludes with a discussion of the important elements of business pricing including the negotiation process, whether the shares or underlying assets of the business are being acquired, and various forms of consideration given and received.

Differences Between Notional Fair Market Value and Open Market Price

As discussed in Chapter 2, fair market value generally is defined as the highest price available in an open and unrestricted market between informed and prudent parties acting at arm's length under no compulsion to act, expressed in terms of cash. However, in an open market transaction, there inevitably are departures from this theoretical definition of fair market value that influence the price paid. For example:

- the 'highest price available' assumes that all potential acquirers have been solicited. This cannot be known with certainty in most open market transactions. Further, it is not always the case that a logical buyer is able to, or wishes to, submit a bid;

- in reality, markets are not 'open and unrestricted'. There may be external restrictions, such as government regulations (for example, the Competition Act, Investment Canada, and so on), or internal restrictions such as those imposed on a company by its Board of Directors or that exist pursuant to Shareholder's Agreements;
- parties to open market transactions seldom are fully 'informed'. Specifically, prospective purchasers, even following a thorough due diligence exercise, cannot expect to uncover all details about a prospective acquisition. Accordingly, they typically seek protection from material misrepresentations pursuant to vendor warranties and indemnities included in Agreements of Purchase and Sale. The vendor on the other hand typically is not aware of the details of a prospective (private company) purchaser's financial position nor the specific post-acquisition benefits and quantification thereof the purchaser expects to result from the acquisition;
- parties to open market transactions are not always 'prudent'. The level of due diligence undertaken varies considerably between purchasers and, as a result, important factors which might have a material impact on price are sometimes missed;
- parties do not always act at 'arm's length';
- the buyer or seller in an open market transaction may be 'compelled to act'. For example, a vendor may need to sell quickly in light of the deteriorating health of an owner-manager, or as a result of financial pressure. Alternatively, the purchaser might feel compelled to acquire a company to prevent the vendor from being acquired by a competitor; and
- the price may not always be 'in terms of cash'. Other forms of consideration often are used in an acquisition such as a vendor take-back, an earn-out or a share for share exchange. The conversion of non-cash consideration to a cash equivalent is subject to estimates and interpretation.

Notional Market Valuations

When determining fair market value in a notional market context, it is necessary to address the question of possible open market prices that might be paid by purchasers who perceive they can generate post-acquisition net economic value added by combining the acquired business with their existing operations. Unless qualified to the contrary, fair market value by definition incorporates the possibility of special interest purchasers as part of the 'highest price available' component. Court cases dealing with the issue of special interest purchasers in a notional market context generally have concluded that where such purchasers can be readily identified they should be considered in the determination of fair market value — see Appendix A for a listing of selected Court Decisions dealing with this issue.

Open market negotiations current to the date at which a notional valuation is required typically have not taken place. As a result it often is difficult to identify possible purchasers who might be interested in acquiring a given business at a given point in time. Further, where such possible purchasers are identified, it is difficult to determine which of them should be considered to be 'qualified' purchasers who have the financial capability to effect a purchase. Moreover, if and when 'qualified purchasers' can be identified it often is very difficult, if not impossible, to identify and meaningfully quantify post-acquisition value-added benefits each might enjoy. The purchaser typically is in a better position to identify and quantify what it perceives to be post-acquisition net economic value added. Importantly, the quantum of such benefits can vary significantly from one purchaser to the next. Finally, even if post-acquisition net economic value added can be identified and meaningfully quantified, it generally is difficult to ascertain the degree to which purchasers will negotiate to pay for some or all of those post-acquisition benefits.

It follows that in a notional market context there are four distinct scenarios – being where one or more potential open market purchasers who might enjoy post-acquisition net economic value added can:

- not be specifically identified, and it is believed that no such purchasers exist;
- not be specifically identified, but it is believed one or more such purchasers may exist;
- be identified, but their value to each prospective purchaser cannot be meaningfully quantified; and
- be identified, and the value of these things to each prospective purchaser can be meaningfully quantified.

In the first three instances, it is usual to state the parameters of the analysis that has been completed and the conclusions reached. In the third instance, it is usual to summarize those potential purchasers that have been identified, and to state that the value of post-acquisition net economic value-added cannot be meaningfully quantified and the reasons this is so. In each of the first three instances, notional market value determinations typically are based on intrinsic (or 'stand-alone') value, and are qualified to reflect the fact that an open market price might be different (and presumably higher) than the value determination made. In these circumstances, reports expressing notional value 'opinions' often are qualified in respect of the inability to reasonably quantify post-acquisition net economic value added, if it exists at all.

In the fourth instance, it is usual to attempt to quantify value inclusive of the post-acquisition net economic value-added that has been identified. In such cases, total 'value' sometimes is segregated between the value component reflective of 'stand-alone' value, and the value component reflective of estimated post-acquisition net economic value-added, with the latter usually being somewhat qualified.

Open Market Transactions

When dealing with 100% of the outstanding shares, 100% of the underlying net assets, or a control shareholding, there generally are two possible components that comprise open market price. These are:

- a price component reflective of the value of all of the outstanding shares or net operating assets of the business viewed on a stand-alone basis. That is, the value of the business interest assuming the business will continue to operate 'as is' absent a divestiture of all or part of it, and absent a combination or consolidation of the business with that of a purchaser or merger partner. This value component is referred to as intrinsic (or 'stand-alone') value; and

- an incremental value over intrinsic value perceived by the purchaser at the time of acquisition. The quantification of this incremental value is unique to each potential purchaser. Generally it is comprised of purchaser-perceived post-acquisition economies of scale and strategic advantages expected to accrue following acquisition. These are collectively referred as to either 'post-acquisition synergies' or 'post-acquisition net economic value-added'.

In virtually all open market transactions involving the purchase of a business of a reasonable size, some level of net economic value-added is perceived to exist by one or more potential purchasers. However, the extent to which said benefits are paid for varies significantly. Where not paid for, post-acquisition synergies act as a buffer against unexpected costs incurred as part of the acquisition.

Open market transactions involving small owner-managed businesses generally are less attractive to large corporate buyers who believe it is not economical to invest the time and effort required to consummate a transaction. Conversely, small businesses sometimes are of interest to one or more individuals who may undertake the acquisition for reasons such as:

- to act in the role of owner-manager of the business, thereby securing personal employment and realizing a return on both physical and invested capital in the form of salary, bonuses, dividends and other benefits; or
- as a personal investment with the objective of generating a return on capital pursuant to dividends or the eventual sale of the investment at a gain.

Where individual acquirers are involved, there seldom are purchaser-perceived post-acquisition synergies except to the extent that the prospective buyer believes he or she can operate the target business more efficiently or use their personal contacts to generate incremental revenues. Even if such opportunities do exist, they typically are not paid for. As a result, the basis for pricing a small owner-managed business generally is based on its intrinsic value. In addition, the acquirer of a small owner-managed business must be aware of the consequences of personal and individual goodwill that might exist — see Chapter 2.

In the end, no matter what the vendor's motivation for selling, it is purchaser-perceived opportunity that usually dictates the final negotiated price. Purchasers assess an acquisition candidate in light of the candidate's own operations on a stand-alone basis, combined with its perception of post-acquisition economies of scale and strategic advantage that might be available as a result of a business combination. Each potential purchaser typically brings unique opportunities to a combination of its own business and the one offered for sale. Accordingly, each such purchaser will perceive different opportunities, and hence will presume itself capable of generating different degrees of post-acquisition net economic advantage from the same acquisition opportunity. It follows that each purchaser can afford to, and likely will, pay a different price than every other purchaser for a particular pool of assets. Assuming disciplined purchasers, this price will be their so-called 'walk away' price. It defines the upper end of each purchaser's price range.

In theory, the purchaser who expects to realize the greatest level of post-acquisition synergies will pay the highest price for a particular business. However, in any given circumstance it may not be possible for a vendor to negotiate a potential corporate purchaser into paying more (or significantly more) than stand-alone value for at least the following reasons:

- a specific corporate purchaser may not be able to realize significant post-acquisition economic value-added, net of associated costs;

- some post-acquisition synergies cannot be readily identified or quantified. For example, entry into a new market may be highly valued by a prospective purchaser not presently in that market, but this may be unknown or not quantifiable from the vendor's perspective. Inevitably, the vendor and purchaser will differ in their perception of the post-acquisition benefits to be realized in any given transaction;
- the vendor may not have the negotiating strength necessary to extract a price reflecting some or all of the purchaser's perceived post-acquisition net economic value-added expectations;
- all prospective purchasers may not have been solicited, or may not be able or interested in making an acquisition at anything other than a 'bargain price'. For example, the target business may be outside of a prospective purchaser's size requirements, management may prefer to go the route of internal growth, or the prospective purchaser may not have the financial resources to fully pay for synergies; and
- the business may not want to fully pay for prospective synergies based on its historic and projected ability to actually realize anticipated benefits. Some companies may be willing to pay close to 100% for synergies whereas others may be willing to pay for little or none. The amount that a purchaser is willing to pay for post-acquisition synergies is dependent on the purchaser's perception of the importance of those benefits, risks of achieving same, and the purchaser's perception of the level of competition for the business being sold.

In general, the likelihood and quantum of post-acquisition synergies being 'paid for' increases when:

- there are a greater number of prospective purchasers involved. This increases the likelihood of one or more purchasers having the ability to realize considerable synergies and typically improves the negotiating position of the vendor. Conversely, by limiting market exposure and dealing only with one or a few purchasers, a vendor's ability to maximize price through the negotiation process generally is negatively affected, often materially so. Theoretically, in both an open market transaction and notional market context, and absent 'middle market' speculator considerations, where only one potential purchaser with a special interest in acquiring exists, that purchaser may pay only a nominal amount more than other purchasers. However, as a practical matter a single special interest purchaser's desire to complete a particular transaction combined with the purchaser's likely incomplete knowledge as to the existence of other possible purchasers may

result in such a purchaser being willing to pay a much higher price than others would pay;
- the target business has a unique competitive advantage that is attractive to, and can be readily transferred to, a corporate acquirer. This could include circumstances where the target business is of strategic importance due to brand name recognition, market coverage, technology, customer contracts, and so on;
- economies of scale are evident in the industry (for example, the elimination of 'back-office' operations in industries with a comparatively high administrative component);
- the industry is going through a consolidation phase. This normally increases the number of active purchasers. Corporate acquirers may be actively competing for acquisition candidates; and
- the relative and absolute size of the business in relation to its competitors. A larger business generally is more likely to realize a premium for strategic benefits than a smaller business due to its likely better competitive position, market clout, and general level of purchaser interest.

Even where a vendor has specific information with respect to the post-acquisition benefits perceived by one or more potential purchasers, it is only through the active marketing of a business and negotiations with specific purchasers that a vendor can do other than speculate as to the value to such purchasers of likely purchaser-perceived post-acquisition net economic value-added. Only when these things have been identified and quantified in economic terms by the vendor does the vendor have any opportunity to reflect them in a sale price. The purchaser has greater knowledge of its own business and the way it plans to integrate the acquisition than does the vendor. Hence the potential purchaser generally is in a far better position to quantify the value to it of the post-acquisition economies of scale and strategic advantages it perceives than is the vendor. Notwithstanding, the most meaningful open market pricing exercise from a prospective vendor's point of view must involve the most accurate possible assessment of purchaser-perceived post-acquisition net economic benefits that are expected to flow from the acquisition.

The more that is known by the purchaser and the vendor about the various elements that comprise purchaser-perceived post-acquisition net economic benefits, the better each will be able to quantify them. In turn, each of the components of perceived post-acquisition net economic value-added has yet to be proven at the date of transaction closing. Accordingly, the greater the value attributed to such things in relation to the aggregate purchase price the greater is the acquisition risk. As a result, the greater the purchaser's ability to analyze and quantify these things, typically the less risk-adverse the purchaser will be with respect to them.

Post-Acquisition Net Economic Value Added

Identifying Special Interest Purchasers

Generally, it is only through well researched, well executed, wide market exposure that a determination can be made as to whether there are in fact potential purchasers who:

- perceive potential economies of scale and/or strategic advantages;
- can identify and reasonably quantify the potential net economic value-added benefits that relate to those perceptions;
- are understood by the vendor to perceive such post-acquisition advantages to the degree they can be meaningfully quantified; and
- importantly, can be negotiated into a position of paying for some or all of that value-added component.

Where fair market value in a notional market valuation is not qualified to exclude special interest purchasers, the issue of special interest purchasers and the premium they might pay should not be readily dismissed or assumed not to be quantifiable without careful consideration. In an open market context, a primary vendor objective usually is maximization of selling price and hence after tax proceeds of sale. Accordingly, one would expect the vendor to attempt to identify those purchasers with the greatest apparent potential economic benefit from the acquisition, and the best possible 'fits' of his or her business with the businesses of those potential buyers. The more purchasers that believe they are not alone in being able to achieve post-acquisition economies of scale and strategic advantages, the greater the likelihood that one or more of them will be prepared to pay for some or all of the post-acquisition value-added component. Thus market liquidity, dictated by the number of potential purchasers in the market at any given time, usually plays a significant role in determining the price that a vendor can expect to receive.

The process of identifying the purchasers most likely to realize post-acquisition net economic value added normally includes:

- discussions with equity owners, management and industry analysts as to who they might expect the most logical buyers to be. In this regard, equity

owners and management may be aware of previous solicitations by potential corporate acquirers;
- review and analysis of competitors, suppliers and customers. Most open market transactions involve companies buying other businesses in the same or similar industry. This may include a competitive relationship, a buyer moving into a new geographic market, or a supplier relationship. Some industries are characterized by a few major players who commonly acquire smaller competitors; and
- a review of news releases and publications involving recent transactions involving similar businesses.

Identifying Post-acquisition Net Economic Value Added

Generally the purchaser is in a better position to identify and quantify post-acquisition synergies than is the vendor, who can only speculate on these things. Post-acquisition net economic value added includes all those things that increase the value of the combined business beyond the sum of its components resulting from:

- increases in the quantum of the aggregate prospective discretionary cash flows of the purchaser and the vendor from what they otherwise would be;
- reducing the risk of either the purchaser or the vendor or both achieving prospective discretionary cash flows; and
- creating growth opportunities and strategic advantage not otherwise available to either the purchaser or the vendor.

These benefits may accrue to the purchaser, the acquired business or a combination of the two.

Some post-acquisition synergies are more readily quantifiable than are others. Nonetheless, a critical step from the perspective of a buyer or seller in an open market transaction is the identification of likely post-acquisition benefits. From the vendor's perspective, this will assist in ascertaining which potential purchasers to canvass and the estimated price that each might pay. From the purchaser's standpoint, the identification of post-acquisition synergies is important from the perspective of determining all potential value components of the acquisition candidate, and in estimating the price others might pay.

Examples of post-acquisition benefits commonly anticipated are listed below. Although these benefits have been categorized as marketing, operating, financial and strategic, it is important to recognize that these classifications often overlap.

Marketing

- benefits associated with increased market share. Increased market share often lends itself to efficiencies in terms of general marketing expenses (advertising and promotion), administration and various other fixed costs. In addition, increased market share can help an acquirer in terms of the credibility associated with greater market presence and corporate awareness;
- the elimination of a competitor, thereby reducing price competition and the threat of new products being introduced by that competitor. From an economic standpoint, the primary determinant of price elasticity of demand is the availability of substitute products;
- improved market coverage resulting from the integration of product lines. This benefit most commonly occurs where complimentary products are acquired;
- gaining new customers to whom other products and services in the acquirer's portfolio can be sold, thereby generating incremental revenue. Incremental revenue opportunities may also arise for other reasons, such as cross-selling to existing customers or offering a more competitive basket of products or services by combining those of the acquired business and the acquirer; and
- improved distribution of products resulting from better utilization of the marketing organization and distribution channels of the combined entities, and more efficient marketing and sales cost per unit sold. This may include an overall reduction in the number of sales staff or distribution facilities.

Operating

- the ability to immediately transfer technology from the purchaser's business to the vendor's business and vice versa, thereby increasing profitability and eliminating the time that the vendor would otherwise require to develop the same capabilities internally;
- the ability to offset the seasonal/cyclical nature of the purchaser's existing market. This might lead to operating efficiencies where facilities have been underutilized for part of the year or industry cycle. Counter-cyclical products may also lead to a reduction in the risk related to the volatility of prospective discretionary cash flows;
- the benefits of improved capacity utilization. Where excess capacity exists, there may be an opportunity for incremental throughput, utilization of engineering and design services, and overall operating efficiencies;

- increased purchasing power. Where the acquirer significantly increases its size as a result of an acquisition, it often can realize post-acquisition purchasing efficiencies;
- access to employees with valuable technical skills and knowledge. This benefit is particularly important where such employees are in short supply or where the training period for new employees is lengthy; and
- headcount reductions. Reducing the total number of personnel is among the most common benefits anticipated following an acquisition, particularly where the acquirer is a competitor. Headcount reductions often include managerial and administrative functions, although reductions in sales and operations employees often also are expected.

Financial

- accelerated growth potential for the vendor's business through access to lower cost and greater and more varied financial resources;
- better utilization of capital structure. For example, enhanced financing capabilities for the purchaser by virtue of the demonstrated profitability and cash flow generation capability of the acquisition candidate; and
- for public companies, better stock analyst coverage due to an increase in consolidated business size, which might enhance the liquidity of the acquirer's stock, and increase its stock price.

Strategic

- acquisition of additional capacity and existing know-how, market presence, and market share on a 'buy' rather than 'build' basis;
- potential risk reduction resulting from upstream and downstream integration opportunities;
- entry into a new strategically important market, from either a product or geographic standpoint; and
- a reduction in risk through greater diversification of products, markets, and so on.

All of the foregoing may affect price to the extent that the purchaser believes that the potential benefits are realizable and is prepared pay for some or all of them. The benefits may be in the form of increased revenues, reduced costs, and a reduction of the risk from that which otherwise would exist. For example, the elimination of competition through acquisition may result in monetary benefits such as increased plant utilization, staff integration, and better market penetration. It may also reduce price competition. To the extent that such benefits are realized the cash flow volatility of the purchaser, and hence the risk associated with the acquisition, may be reduced. Pricing a business requires a careful examination of all such factors and a reasoned assessment of their likely realization and timing.

Transaction Costs

The quantification of potential benefits expected to accrue from an acquisition frequently is emphasized. Often adequate consideration is not given to the costs of integration, the capital expenditures required to meet post-acquisition growth expectations, the timing of the anticipated proceeds, and the probability factors related to the actual realization of the perceived benefits. In fact, post-acquisition costs often exceed purchaser expectations, thus reducing the net economic value-added from what had been anticipated. If transaction benefits concurrently have been overstated, the resultant cash flow shortfall from projections made by the purchaser when assessing price could be significant.

The purchaser incurs costs prior to, during and after the consummation of a transaction. Costs incurred up to and including the acquisition date often include:

- legal and advisory fees. These costs can vary significantly depending on the nature and size of the target business, and whether internal or external resources are used to fulfill these functions;
- management time. The successful purchase and integration of any acquisition generally involves a considerable amount of management time and effort. Larger companies often will employ one or more individuals whose primary function is corporate acquisitions; and
- incidental costs such as travel and accommodation, telephone expenses, and so on.

These costs normally are incurred as part of the acquisition process, including bid preparation, due diligence investigation, and finalization of the purchase and sale documentation. As a result, most of these expenses are incurred regardless of whether a transaction closes. In most open market transactions, such 'sunk costs' generally are not factored into the price paid. In notional market valuations, such costs generally are not deducted from the value otherwise determined.

After transaction closing, the purchaser typically will incur additional costs (either directly or through the acquired business) that should be considered and quantified when pricing the acquisition. These costs generally are associated with the post-acquisition integration of the target business. The necessary expenses to realize post-acquisition economic value added commonly include:

- severance costs associated with headcount reductions. These can represent a significant expense, and can be complicated if management and union contracts specify terms and conditions related to terminations and layoffs. Although anticipated headcount reductions may be achieved through attrition and working notice periods, severance payment quantification may necessitate legal advice;
- system integration costs. In many acquisitions, there is a need to integrate the accounting and reporting systems used by the purchaser and vendor so that reliable and timely financial and reporting information can be generated. Frequently the systems are not compatible, and considerable time and expense must be incurred to convert the acquired business' systems;
- employee training costs. This may include formal employee programs regarding the use of different technology, or training pertaining to reporting formats, procedures, and so on. The latter may not be readily quantifiable;
- lease termination payments and facilities disposition costs. Where economies of scale include the elimination of duplicate facilities, the costs of terminating occupation of existing premises must be determined. Where the premises are leased, lease termination payments may be required. Alternatively, if the acquired business owns the facilities to be disposed of, then that property likely should be regarded as a redundant asset. Disposition costs, including income taxes at the corporate level should be calculated. Relocation expenses should also be considered;
- general integration and monitoring costs. Where the target business is to be integrated with that of the purchaser, numerous integration costs arise. These may include expenses related to the implementation of policies and procedures, internal controls, administrative guidelines (e.g. forms and reports), changing signage, letterhead, and so on;
- quality standards - the product standards and operating standards of the purchaser may be considerably more rigorous than those of the acquired business. A detailed analysis of product quality, product standards, quality control, production systems, and so on must be undertaken by the purchaser in order to assess the changes that will likely be required subsequent to acquisition;

- income tax consequences. In virtually all cases, a corporate purchaser acquiring a privately held company does not have access to the small business deduction. Therefore, the stand-alone value of such a private company where it qualifies as a Canadian Controlled Private Corporation may be greater than the value to such a purchaser before consideration of synergies. Other income tax consequences must also be considered, including the potential impact on the manufacturing and processing profits deduction, the utilization of income tax losses, the impact on scientific research and experimental development (SR&ED) tax credits, and so on;
- management depth. In many businesses, particularly those that are small and privately-held, the management team is dominated by a single person, or only a few people. Where management personnel have not been groomed to provide for business continuity, purchasers often find it necessary to supplement management of the acquired business following acquisition;
- employee benefit and incentive plans. Where the employees of an acquired business have significantly different benefits and incentives compared with the employees of the purchaser, the transitional costs to deal with the differences must be considered. Where employees of the acquired business have a less favourable compensation package, it may be necessary to increase their compensation, particularly if the two companies will be highly integrated. Conversely, if the employees at the acquired business enjoy a significantly better compensation package than is offered by the purchaser, changes to the plans covering those employees may have to be made. For example, employees of the acquired business may be offered a one time cash payment in exchange for a reduced compensation plan to ensure consistency between the vendor's compensation plan and that of the purchaser;
- key personnel turnover. One of the consequences of acquisitions is that key employees may leave the acquired business due to uncertainty, differing management philosophies, or to seek other career opportunities. Where such employees perform a function that must be replaced, incidental costs may be incurred for hiring and training replacements. In addition, where the employees leaving possess important knowledge or abilities that cannot be readily replaced, the prospective discretionary cash flows of the acquired business may be at risk;
- deferred costs. Prior to sale, management of the target business may have deferred expenses in order to improve the business' reported financial results. Common such items include deferred equipment maintenance, a moratorium on new hires, reducing advertising and research expenditures,

and so on. During the pre-acquisition review, the purchaser must critically assess whether certain costs have been deferred and if so, what the short and long run impact on the acquired business will be;
- penalties for breaching minimum purchase or other commitments. Alternatively, if those commitments are fulfilled, the purchaser may incur an incremental cost; and
- the acquired business may have contingent liabilities that are not adequately reflected in its financial statements. These may include pending litigation where the outcome is uncertain, under-funded pension and post-retirement benefit liabilities, under-accrued warranty reserves, inadequate provisions for environmental and cleanup costs, and so on. A thorough due diligence program should detect most of these prospective expenses. However, costs inevitably arise subsequent to acquisition that were not identifiable before closing and are not recoverable pursuant to vendor representations and warranties.

Quantifying Post-acquisition Net Economic Value Added

The quantification of post-acquisition net economic value added (or synergies) should be a separate and distinct component of any business valuation or pricing exercise. Accordingly, the stand-alone (or intrinsic) value of the business should be estimated as the 'base value' and the value of synergies should be added to that base where applicable and appropriate. This segregation not only assists in evaluating the reasonableness of the components, but in an open market transaction enables the purchaser separately to consider the portion of the anticipated synergies it wants to 'pay for' in its pricing strategy. Where a purchaser does not pay for expected synergies, these serve to compensate for unanticipated shortfalls from expected post-acquisition discretionary cash flows. No acquisition review can be so complete as to eliminate all post-acquisition surprises. In many instances, a lower level of post-acquisition benefits and a higher level of costs materialize following acquisition than were anticipated during negotiations. Consequently, if the value-added component is fully paid for, the purchaser has eliminated all downside protection and the likelihood of post-acquisition success is reduced.

A proper quantification of post-acquisition net economic value added requires a balanced, realistic perspective of the potential benefits to be derived from the acquisition, as well as an assessment of the likely incremental costs to be incurred in their realization. In summary, the quantification of possible post-acquisition net economic value added in a given transaction generally requires at least the following:

- from the point of view of the vendor:
  - identification of the most logical purchaser(s) for the business,
  - an understanding of the motivations of each potential purchaser of the business,
  - a review of public information with respect to potential purchasers (financial statements, U.S. Security and Exchange Commission 8-K and 10-K reports, industry analysis, articles, and so on),
  - a determination of whether the acquisition falls within each potential purchaser's corporate strategy and whether each recently has been an active or interested acquirer; and
- from the point of view of the purchaser:
  - the estimated incremental discretionary cash flows the purchaser expects to realize beyond those expected to be generated by the vendor on a stand-alone basis,
  - the risks the purchaser perceives related to achieving said estimated incremental discretionary cash flows,
  - the expected timing of receipt of the perceived post-acquisition incremental discretionary cash flows,
  - the estimated costs associated with achieving the perceived post-acquisition incremental discretionary cash flows,
  - the purchaser's perception relative to competition for the acquisition, combined with the vendor's complacency or anxiety with respect to the transaction and the purchaser's level of interest with respect to completing the acquisition, and
  - the negotiating skills of the purchaser, vendor, and their respective advisors.

In most open market transactions involving medium and large sized businesses, one or more purchasers anticipate post-acquisition benefits. It is unusual for a vendor to be paid fully for all purchaser-perceived post-acquisition net economic benefits. However, pricing a business for open market purposes should always incorporate an effort to quantify the value-added potentially created by a transaction. Uncertainty as to the amount and likely realization of the value-added component should not prevent this.

The quantification of post-acquisition net economic value added generally can be segregated into three categories as follows:

- tangible operating synergies, being those that can be readily isolated and quantified in terms of incremental prospective discretionary cash flows. Tangible operating synergies typically relate to specific incremental revenue opportunities and cost reductions;

- intangible operating synergies, being those that cannot be readily segregated and analyzed on an individual basis. Intangible operating benefits typically relate to incremental growth opportunities or a reduction in business risk that has not been quantified as part of prospective discretionary cash flows; and
- financial synergies, being those related to a more efficient capital structure and lower cost financing. Financial synergies normally are reflected in the discount and capitalization rate(s) adopted.

Quantifying Tangible Operating Synergies

The quantification of tangible operating synergies generally involves:

- where applicable, determining the increase in EBIT-DA from incremental revenue opportunities, net of associated costs;
- determining the expected incremental EBIT-DA from cost savings;
- determining the costs of implementing and realizing the expected synergies. This should include both initial and ongoing costs, and may include operating expenses, capital expenditures and increased working capital requirements; and
- income tax affecting the expected net synergies.

The net incremental discretionary cash flows should be discounted (or capitalized) at a rate of return which appropriately reflects the risk of achieving the expected net synergies. In theory, in order to reflect incremental risk related to uncertainty of achievement, this should be a higher discount (capitalization) rate than is adopted when estimating the stand-alone value of the business. In addition, there may be circumstances where it is appropriate to apply a different discount (or capitalization) rate to different sources of synergies (i.e. cost reductions vs. incremental revenues) to properly reflect the different levels of risk of achieving each. Alternatively, the net synergies can be expressed net of 'contingency factors' related to the added risk of their realization. Where this is done, the expected net synergies typically would be discounted at more moderate 'market driven' rates of return, commonly the discount (capitalization) rate used in estimating the value of the target business on a stand-alone basis. This latter approach is more commonly adopted in practice.

The discounted cash flow methodology generally is the preferred approach to quantifying the impact of synergies. The discounted cash flow model explicitly considers all costs of realizing the expected net synergies, including the impact on working capital, capital additions (where applicable) and the timing of income tax loss utilization. Importantly, the discounted cash flow methodology normally should be used where significant up front costs are anticipated or where post-acquisition synergies are expected to emerge over time. This may be the case where:

- initial costs such as severance, lease termination, systems integration, and so on, are required in order to obtain cost reductions;
- incremental spending is required for new equipment, working capital, start-up costs and other expenses in order to generate incremental revenue opportunities; and
- the benefits are expected to phase in over time. This is particularly the case where the post-acquisition synergies relate to incremental revenue opportunities.

Quantifying Intangible Operating Synergies

Intangible operating synergies normally relate to one or both of:

- a reduced level of risk in achieving the prospective operating results. For example, the reduction in the risk of a critical manufacturing input through the acquisition of a supplier; and
- enhanced long term growth prospects or strategic advantages that have not been separately quantified. For example, the anticipated benefits related to the acquisition of new leading-edge technology.

Although the value of these post-acquisition synergies often is difficult to isolate, their quantification can be achieved through the application of lower discount or capitalization rates to the prospective discretionary cash flows of the target business than would otherwise be applied. In some cases, it may be appropriate to increase the value of tangible operating synergies otherwise quantified for such intangible factors as well. However, it is important to ensure that post-acquisition synergies are not double-counted.

In theory, the quantification of intangible operating synergies involves comparing the en bloc value of the target business based on discounting (capitalizing) the prospective discretionary cash flows at a discount (capitalization) rates that reflect:

- the risks and opportunities of the business in the absence of the intangible post-acquisition operating synergies; and
- adjustments to the risks and opportunities of the business given the expected intangible post-acquisition operating synergies.

The difference between the two resulting value determinations represents the value of intangible operating synergies. Again, it may be appropriate to apply a probability factor to that incremental value in recognition of the addition risks in its realization. As a practical matter, corporate acquirers often adjust their price upward in recognition of strategic importance and other intangible operating synergies. However, in many cases the quantification of such benefits is more influenced by a purchasers qualitative assessment of the level of importance and amount of competition for a target business than it is by a mathematical exercise.

In theory, a downward adjustment to the discount or capitalization rate resulting from the perceived reduction in the risk of realizing the projected post-acquisition unlevered discretionary cash flows should be made by reducing the unlevered return on equity before adjusting for financial leverage. In practice however, where the rate of return is adjusted downward to account for intangible operating synergies (both risk reduction and incremental growth opportunities), the reduction normally is directly applied to the discount or capitalization rate itself, being either a weighted average cost of capital or levered return on equity.

Quantifying Financial Synergies

Financial synergies are those related to the ability of the purchaser to obtain lower cost financing, or to employ a more efficient capital structure than the acquired business itself could. Financial synergies may arise due to:

- benefits related to the larger size of the combined entity, where the increased asset base provides greater security to debt and equity holders. Larger organizations typically are able to attract a greater number of interested lenders and prospective investors, which can also lead to reduced financing costs;
- existing relationships which the purchaser enjoys that can be extended to the target business resulting in a more efficient capital structure or lower cost financing than might otherwise be available to it;
- where both the vendor and the purchaser are privately held companies prior to a transaction and neither is of sufficient size in isolation to economically justify an initial public offering, but where the combined entity could offer its shares to the public resulting in a reduction in their respective costs of capital; and

- the ability to use more financial leverage in the capital structure of the combined entity due to greater stability of prospective discretionary cash flows or enhanced degree of lender interest.

As discussed in Chapter 8, the discount (or capitalization) rate normally should first be derived as an unlevered return on equity. Subsequently, the impact of financial leverage should be considered to express the discount or capitalization rate either as a weighted average cost of capital or a levered return on equity. Accordingly, in theory the value of financial synergies can be quantified by calculating the value of the target business pursuant to an 'appropriate' capital structure and rates of return that incorporate financial synergies, compared to the value of the business absent the benefits associated with those financial synergies. Once again, it may be appropriate to apply a probability factor to the value of financial synergies to reflect the risk related to their ultimate realization.

For example, assume the outstanding shares of Company S (which has no interest bearing debt or redundant assets) appropriately are valued on a standalone basis at $19 million, based on:

- $2 million of expected maintainable discretionary cash flow; and
- a real weighted average cost of capital of 10.5% determined by adopting a nominal unlevered return on equity of 14% (including 2% inflation), a debt to total capitalization ratio of 25%, and an income tax rate of 45%.

Management of Company P is contemplating acquiring the Company S's outstanding shares. It believes, based on Company P's more favourable access to debt financing, that it could reasonably increase Company S's debt to total capitalization ratio from 25% to 40%. Ignoring other possible sources of synergies, the benefit from that more efficient capital structure would be quantified as:

Company S's outstanding share value including financial synergies:

Discretionary cash flows	$ 2 million
Capitalization rate including financial synergies (see below)	9.5%
Equity value (rounded)	$21 million
Stand alone value	$19 million
Gross incremental value of financial synergies	$ 2 million

Where the capitalization rate of 9.5% is determined as (see Chapter 7):

$$14\% \times [1 - (45\% \times 40\%)] - 2\% \text{ inflation} = 9.5\%$$

Therefore, management of Company P believes that it can increase the en bloc value of the shares of Company S by up to $2 million through its ability to utilize a more efficient capital structure. Whether Company P 'pays for' all or part of this incremental value depends on other factors in the transaction, including comparative negotiating skills and the level of competition for Company S.

Where it is believed financial synergies will accrue to the purchaser's existing operations following acquisition, an estimate should be made of the incremental post transaction en bloc value of the purchaser's business that results from such synergies and should be considered by it in its pricing strategy. As is the case with intangible operating synergies, in practice the value of anticipated financial synergies often is quantified more by way of a subjective estimate than a purely mathematical exercise.

The quantification of post-acquisition synergies can be summarized as follows:

CHART 11.1

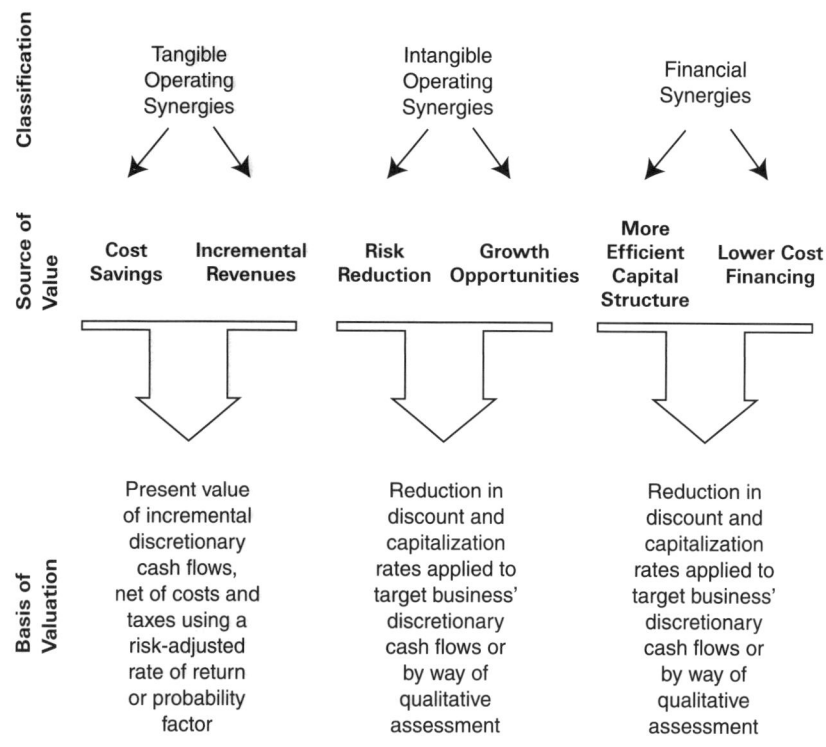

Industry Research

An analysis of open market transactions involving similar companies may provide (depending on the extent of public disclosure) some assistance in identifying possible purchaser-perceived post acquisition net economic value added and its quantification. From a notional market valuation perspective, where believed meaningful such an exercise may be undertaken as part of the valuation 'due diligence' exercise. From an open market vendor's perspective, where meaningful information is available an analysis of recent transactions may assist in the identification of special interest purchasers and ultimately in negotiating a sale price. From a prospective purchaser's standpoint, the analysis of such transactions may be helpful in assessing the likely level of interest in a particular acquisition opportunity, and in estimating what might be competitive bids for the target company. Notwithstanding, it is important to recognize that even where information is available that enables some quantification of synergies paid for, there is no assurance that all synergies were paid for or paid for fully.

Due to recent changes in U.S. statutory filing requirements, more information regarding so-called 'comparable' transactions generally is available when the purchaser, the vendor, or both, are public companies. Financial details generally are unavailable for most transactions that involve only privately-held companies. Sources of information which may provide quantitative data include:

- annual reports and accompanying audited annual financial statements, which disclose the acquisition activity undertaken by a public corporate acquirer. Disclosure requirements in Canada generally include the price paid, form of consideration, net assets acquired and quantum of goodwill;
- publications that provide a synopsis of acquisition activity of publicly traded companies. Although most such publications provide a limited amount of financial information with respect to each transaction, the reports often are organized by standard industrial classification ('SIC') code so that industry acquisition activity can be readily identified, and searches for additional information regarding the companies involved can be undertaken;
- statutory filings often provide useful information regarding acquisition activity involving publicly held companies. U.S. Securities and Exchange Commission Forms 8-K and 10-K often are useful in this regard, particularly in light of recent changes in the U.S. requiring greater disclosure as to anticipated post-acquisition synergies; and

- news releases often provide some, albeit limited, information regarding acquisition activity involving both public and medium to large size private companies.

In most cases, given the limitations on the availability of financial data and the lack of direct involvement in a particular acquisition, it is possible only to speculate as to how much of the price paid in any acquisition related to purchaser perceived synergies. Further, even if information regarding one or more particular transactions is available, each of those transactions was unique in some respects, and direct comparability to the subject business being valued or priced may be inappropriate. Nonetheless, a review of industry transactions may provide both the prospective vendor and acquirer with information that assists each of them to some degree in open market pricing analysis and the ensuing negotiations.

Business Pricing Example

Bigsnack Inc. ('Bigsnack') is a large manufacturer and distributor of a variety of snack foods. Bigsnack is interested in purchasing Cookie Co., a regional cookie manufacturer whose products enjoy strong brand name recognition. Cookie Co.'s financial performance has been relatively stable over the past few years, with annual revenues of approximately $25 million and annual maintainable discretionary cash flow estimated in the range of $2.2 million to $2.8 million. Cookie Co. has $6 million of interest bearing debt and has no redundant assets. On a stand-alone basis, management of Bigsnack estimates that Cookie Co. should be valued using a real weighted average cost of capital of 10% to 12%. In addition, the present value of Cookie Co.'s undepreciated capital cost allowance tax shield is estimated at $2 million.

Management of Bigsnack believes that the following post-acquisition benefits could be realized through the acquisition of Cookie Co.:

- headcount reductions in management and administration functions would amount to $500,000 per year. Average severance is estimated to be equal to six months wages;

- Bigsnack would integrate some of its warehousing operations that are in close proximity to those of Cookie Co. Facilities cost savings would amount to $100,000 per annum. The cost of terminating leases and relocating from existing facilities is estimated at $75,000;
- through its established national distribution system, Bigsnack expects to increase Cookie Co's sales by 15% over current levels. These incremental revenues would be realized gradually over 3 years. Direct costs, including manufacturing and selling, are estimated at 60% of sales. Since sufficient excess capacity exists at Cookie Co.'s plant, no incremental fixed costs or capital expenditures are anticipated. Net trade working capital requirements are estimated at 10% of revenues; and
- systems integration and other incidental expenses are estimated at $50,000.

In addition, Bigsnack views the acquisition of Cookie Co. as strategically important because it would enable Bigsnack to expand into the dessert category, which is outside Bigsnack's traditional snack food business, and which in turn could provide Bigsnack with a platform for greater expansion into the dessert category. Bigsnack typically prices its acquisition targets based on a 50% probability of achieving anticipated post-acquisition synergies. The effective income tax rate is 40%.

Price Determination

The price Bigsnack might pay for Cookie Co. is estimated as follows:

SCHEDULE 11.1

Cookie Co.
Estimated Price
($000's)

	Low	High
Estimated intrinsic or stand-alone value:		
Discretionary cash flows	$ 2,200	$ 2,800
Capitalization rate (real WACC)	10%	12%
Capitalized cash flow	22,000	23,333
Redundant assets	0	0
PV of existing UCC tax shield	2,000	2,000
Enterprise value	24,000	25,333
Less: debt outstanding	(6,000)	(6,000)
Intrinsic en bloc value of shares	18,000	19,333
Estimated value of tangible operating synergies Schedule 11.2	4,500	5,500
Estimated value of intangible operating synergies Schedule 11.3	1,000	1,200
Total estimated price	23,500	26,033
Say,	$23,000	$26,000

The stand-alone value of the outstanding shares of Cookie Co. is estimated at approximately $18.0 million to $19.3 million using the capitalization of discretionary cash flow methodology — see Chapter 4. That is obtained by dividing the estimated maintainable discretionary cash flow of $2.2 million to $2.8 million by the real WACC of 10% to 12%, and adding the present value of the undepreciated capital cost allowance tax shield to generate enterprise value. The outstanding interest bearing debt of $6 million is deducted to determine the stand-alone en bloc value of the shares of Cookie Co.

Post-acquisition benefits are segregated between tangible operating synergies and intangible operating synergies. It is assumed there are no financial synergies. Tangible operating synergies are detailed in Schedule 11.2 to include the:

- net contribution from incremental revenues phased in over three years, net of incremental costs and net trade working capital requirements; and
- annual cost savings from headcount reductions and warehousing.

A discounted cash flow methodology is used since the benefits are expected to phase in over time. The net benefits are tax-effected at a rate of 40%. A probability factor of 50% is applied to the net incremental discretionary cash flows. Since the cash flows are probabilized, and assuming the projections are stated in real and not nominal dollars, the discount rate used is the average real WACC of 11%, being the midpoint of 10% to 12% applied on a stand-alone basis. A terminal multiple of 9x (a real WACC of 11%) is assumed. Implementation costs such as severance, lease cancellation and system integration are deducted (net of tax) to determine the net value of tangible operating synergies in a range of $4 million to $6 million.

SCHEDULE 11.2

Cookie Co.
Estimated Value of Tangible Operating Synergies
($000)

	Year 1	Year 2	Year 3	Thereafter
Revenues				
Incremental revenues	1,250	2,500	3,750	3,750
Direct costs (60%)	(750)	(1,500)	(2,250)	(2,250)
Net contribution	500	1,000	1,500	1,500
Cost savings				
Headcount reductions	500	500	500	500
Facilities	100	100	100	100
Total cost savings	600	600	600	600
Operating cash flow, before tax	1,100	1,600	2,100	2,100
Income Tax (40%)	(440)	(640)	(840)	(840)
After tax operating cash flows	660	960	1,260	1,260
Required working capital (re: revenue increase)	(125)	(125)	(125)	0
Net incremental cash flows	535	835	1,135	1,260
Terminal multiple, assume				9x
Terminal value				11,340
Present value at 11%	482	678	830	8,292
Total – gross value	10,282			
Deduct costs:				
Severance	(250)			
Lease cancellation / moving	(75)			
Systems integration	(50)			
Less: tax savings on costs	150			
Net costs	(225)			
Net value of tangible operating synergies	10,057			
Probabilized at 50%	5,029			
	Low		High	
Range, say	4,500		5,500	

Rather than applying a probability factor, the incremental discretionary cash flows could have been discounted at a higher real WACC (say in the order of 23% with a terminal multiple of 4.3x) to reflect the risk in achieving same.

The incremental cash flows relating to 'strategic importance' cannot be readily isolated. For purposes of this example, it is assumed that Bigsnack estimates the value of strategic importance by reducing the rate of return applied to Cookie Co.'s stand-alone discretionary cash flows. In this case, a 1% reduction in real WACC is assumed (based on Bigsnack's subjective analysis) which generates capitalized cash flows of approximately $2.1 million to $2.4 million greater than was determined on a stand-alone basis. The incremental value is probabilized at a rate of 50%, which reflects Bigsnack's assessment that the benefits will materialize. The net amount of $1 million to $1.2 million represents the 'value' of strategic importance to Bigsnack.

SCHEDULE 11.3

Cookie Co.
Estimated Value of Intangible Operating Synergies
($000)

	Low	High
Annual discretionary cash flows	$ 2,200	$ 2,800
Capitalization rate (base rate WACC less 1%)	9%	11%
Capitalized cash flows – synergy adjusted	24,444	25,455
Less: capitalized cash flows as previously determined	(22,000)	(23,333)
Incremental value due to strategic importance	2,444	2,122
Probabilized at	50%	50%
Probabilized incremental value	1,222	1,061
Say,	$ 1,000	$ 1,200

The estimated price of Cookie Co., comprised of its stand-alone value plus the value of tangible operating synergies and intangible operating synergies, is estimated at $23 million to $26 million. However, this may or may not be the price actually negotiated and paid.

Additional Factors Influencing Price

Additional factors that play a role in determining the final price at which a transaction is consummated commonly include:

- whether the shares or underlying net assets of the business are acquired. As discussed in Chapter 4, absent consideration of non-capital loss carry forwards, as a general rule the sale of a pool of net assets that collectively comprise a going concern typically will fetch greater gross proceeds than the sale of all the outstanding shares of the company that owns the net asset pool;
- the form of consideration paid; and
- the negotiating abilities of the buyer and seller.

Where fair market value is determined in a notional market context, the issues of form of consideration and negotiating abilities of buyer and seller typically are assumed to have no impact on value. This is because fair market value contemplates a cash transaction where both buyer and seller are fully informed and are of equal negotiating strength. However, the consideration offered and prevailing negotiating abilities can have a significant influence on price in an open market transaction. The issue of the value of assets vs. shares is relevant in both a notional and open market value determinations.

Form of Consideration

Price and form of consideration are interdependent. In a notional market context, fair market value is determined on a cash or cash equivalent basis. In open market transactions, other forms of consideration (termed 'transaction structuring') frequently are used. It is beyond the scope of this book to deal with the intricacies of transaction structuring which tends to be specific to each negotiation. However, by way of general observation transaction structuring can be both necessary and desirable where:

- either the vendor, the purchaser, or both are in disagreement as to the prospective business risk or forecasts, or where there is a significant difference in value perception;
- a purchaser has an inability to close on a cash basis, but is prepared to compensate for this by offering cash alternatives, usually with an upward adjustment in apparent price;
- there are significant income tax advantages (usually tax-deferral related) to the vendor pursuant to receipt of non-cash consideration. In this regard, an understanding of available alternatives and the income tax implications of

each often is essential to bring vendors and purchasers to agreement to transact; and
- transactions likely would not be consummated were it not for the 'price' bridging potential of various forms of non-cash consideration.

Where a transaction involves a non-cash component, both the vendor and purchaser should attempt to determine the implied cash-equivalent price to provide a basis for comparison. Some of the common forms of non-cash consideration include:

- vendor take-backs. Where the vendor agrees to receive some or all of the payment over time, he or she effectively finances all or part of the transaction. Common forms of vendor take-backs include promissory notes and redeemable (or term) preferred shares. Where the rate of return on the vendor take-back is below (or above) market rates compared to financial instruments of similar risk, the difference can effectively be attributed to a price discount or premium as the case may be;
- earnouts. In some cases, a portion of the price is determined based on the prospective earnings, cash flow, or some other measurement related to the post-acquisition results of the acquired business. An earnout commonly is used to bridge a pricing gap between purchaser and vendor where the two disagree on the future prospects of the acquired business. An earnout effectively shifts the risk from purchaser to vendor since if prospective results are not realized, the buyer essentially pays a reduced price. Determining the cash equivalent of an earnout arrangement should consider the risk that the criteria for payment will not be satisfied. This becomes complicated where the vendor exercises little or no control over prospective operating results. Earnouts must be carefully structured to avoid unfavourable income tax consequences — see Chapter 14;
- share for share exchanges. A purchaser may offer its shares as currency to finance a transaction, leaving the vendor with an interest in the combined company after the transaction has taken place. In many respects, where a share for share exchange is contemplated the pricing negotiation becomes a relative valuation exercise. A Canadian vendor normally can defer income taxes arising on a gain on sale through a share for share exchange with a Canadian purchaser — see Chapter 14. Determining a cash equivalent price in a share exchange is complicated where the buyer is not a public company, or where public company shares are taken in exchange and either they are escrowed (i.e. where the vendor is restricted from selling the shares for some period of time) or of such quantity that they can not be sold into the public market without disrupting it;

- management and consulting contracts. Such contracts may provide for remuneration at greater than 'earned income' amounts to be paid to the vendor, usually for a fixed period subsequent to closing. In these circumstances the premium can be attributed to price. Management and consulting contracts are more common in privately-held businesses where the owner played an active role in the operations. In addition to bridging a price gap, such contracts also can assist in the transition of a business to the purchaser; and
- retention of a portion of the shares by the vendor, with an agreement between vendor and purchaser that the vendor can 'put' the withheld shares to the purchaser at a subsequent date at a set price or price determined at the date the 'put' is exercised (often based on a pre-established formula). This allows the purchaser to acquire control of the company without having to finance 100% of the price up front.

In addition, a vendor may be able to extract assets from a company on an income tax deferred basis prior to the sale of shares of a (typically privately-held) company. To the extent the vendor thereby defers income tax on capital gains, something of value is retained, and enhances what otherwise would be the net price received. Concurrently, as a rule there is no cost to the purchaser as a result of agreeing to this accommodation.

Negotiations

In a notional market context both buyer and seller are assumed to enjoy equal negotiating position and abilities. However, a key determinant of the ultimate price paid in an open market transaction is the comparative negotiating position and abilities of the purchaser, the vendor, and their respective advisors. As a general rule, the important things to consider when negotiating price in an open market context from the:

- vendor's perspective are the:
  - degree to which the vendor is willing, anxious, or required to sell,
  - vendor's ability to identify potential purchasers of the business interest,
  - number of interested, financially capable buyers for a given business at any particular point in time. This factor, commonly referred to as 'liquidity', usually has a significant influence on the price that ultimately will be negotiated in an open market transaction,
  - vendor's depth of knowledge of the businesses of each potential purchaser and the reasons each is motivated to buy. In particular, the ven-

dor's awareness of the possible post-acquisition economies of scale and strategic advantages that each potential purchaser perceives is important,
- uniqueness or lack thereof of the vendor's business operations and product offerings, and
- level of flexibility the vendor displays in terms of the purchaser's financing of the transaction. Where the vendor requires an all-cash deal, that may restrict the ability or interest of some prospective purchasers. Conversely, where the vendor will accept a vendor take-back, share for share exchange, or some other form of consideration, a higher price might be attainable; and

- purchaser's perspective are the:
  - ability to quantify the 'net economic value-added' potentially created as a consequence of an acquisition. In this regard, each purchaser's value-added perceptions can be assumed to be different and to change with changing circumstances,
  - reliance of the purchaser on non-cash forms of consideration. Where a purchaser has the ability to finance an acquisition either by cash or other means, it typically is in a better negotiating position than is a purchaser that requires a significant vendor take-back component,
  - purchaser's depth of knowledge with respect to both the business of the vendor and the reasons the vendor is motivated to sell,
  - purchaser's perception of likely competitive bids for the target business, including the number of potential bidders and estimated post-acquisition synergies each might enjoy,
  - other opportunities or alternatives that are available to the purchaser in order to attain its objectives, such as internal growth or the acquisition of another business, and
  - purchaser's threshold (or 'hurdle') rate of return and return on invested (or 'levered') equity criteria during the negotiating period, and the purchaser's flexibility with respect to that rate of return.

Other Factors

Every open market transaction is unique. Accordingly, it is not possible to provide an exhaustive list as to the factors that ultimately are reflected in the negotiated price. However, some of the more common considerations not previously discussed include:

- in the case of a public company purchaser, the public market performance of its shares during the negotiating period, and the expected impact that the contemplated acquisition would have on same. Public company acquirers normally consider the expected post-acquisition impact on consolidated earnings per share when contemplating a transaction, and generally look for them to be accretive in the near-term following acquisition. The price that a public company acquirer will pay generally is also influenced by its expectation as to how the acquisition will be viewed by stock market analysts and public equity market participants;

- where the vendor is a public company, the historic and prevailing market price per share around the transaction date. Shareholder approval of a sale of a publicly held company often poses interesting issues, and it is important to consider whether any large ownership blocks exist. Public company takeovers can also become complicated since there is often greater public awareness than there is in the case of private company acquisitions, which may serve to invite competing bids. Further issues may arise if the target company has a shareholder rights plan (or so-called 'poison pill'); and

- in the end, the purchaser should consider the price it is willing to pay for an existing business compared to the cost of a start-up, if the latter is practicable. Where a start-up is a practical alternative, this generally entails an analysis of the benefit of acquiring a business opportunity immediately, compared to the time required to create the comparable capability and 'value' through utilization of existing internal resources. In the case of the former, the purchaser also benefits from a reduction in competition that would otherwise exist. Further, the acquisition of another business may provide the purchaser with access to patents, licenses, and so on, which cannot be readily recreated.

Share for Share Exchanges

Overview

In many open market transactions, shares are exchanged in lieu of cash. This includes circumstances where:

- a corporation (normally a publicly held company) uses it own treasury shares as currency to acquire the shares of another company; and
- two or more corporations amalgamate.

Acquisition for Shares

With respect to acquisitions where the purchaser's shares are used as currency, there are at least three distinct scenarios:

- where both purchaser and vendor are publicly held companies;
- where the purchaser is a publicly held company and the vendor is a privately held company; and
- where both purchaser and vendor are privately held companies.

Where a publicly held corporation is acquired pursuant to an exchange of its shares for the shares of another publicly held company, benchmarks exist by which to measure both the value received and the value given up. In these cases, the principal issue often is the extent to which anticipated post-acquisition synergies are shared between purchaser and vendor. Synergies likely will be perceived to exist by both, as well as by market analysts and the investing public.

Where the vendor is a privately held company and the purchaser is a publicly held company, the vendor often can assess the value received if the shares taken in exchange are freely tradable. If there are restrictions on trading, or if trading in the shares is not sufficiently liquid to absorb the number of shares taken in exchange, the assessment of value must consider whether it is appropriate to apply a discount to prevailing stock market price to account for imperfect liquidity. Transactions involving a public company purchaser and private company vendor are further complicated by the dynamics of public and private market acquirers. Specifically, the purchaser's post-acquisition consolidated earnings per share will be affected as a result of the acquisition. The public equity markets may value those earnings more (or less) than a corporate acquirer would. That is, the multiples applied by the public markets to incremental earnings may be greater or less than those imputed pursuant to the acquisition of a privately held company. Therefore where it exists, the vendor may seek to extract a portion of the public market 'premium'.

Where both purchaser and vendor are privately-held companies, independent and non-subjective 'value' benchmarks for either rarely exist. Therefore, the vendor requires some indication as to the value of the purchaser's business en bloc, and the share for share exchange becomes a relative valuation exercise. Complications may arise pursuant to the vendor exchanging a controlling interest in a privately-held company for a minority interest position in a (likely larger) privately held company. As discussed in Chapters 12 and 13, absent a Shareholder's Agreement or some other agreement that dictates otherwise, a minority position in a privately-held company may be worth less than its pro-rata portion of en bloc value. Therefore, in a share for share exchange involving privately held companies, the provisions of such post-transaction agreements becomes critical.

As a practical matter, vendors normally are not interested in receiving shares of privately held companies as consideration unless there is some assurance as to the liquidity of the shares received. Liquidity may come in the form of a 'put' option or from the expectation (contractual or otherwise) that the purchaser will float an initial public offering or be sold en bloc to a third party in the near future.

Amalgamations

As discussed in Chapter 14, Section 87 of the Income Tax Act (Canada) allows two or more Canadian organizations to transfer their respective shares into a newly formed corporation on a tax deferred basis. In order to effect an income tax deferral all of the shares of each predecessor company must be transferred to the amalgamated company with the only consideration received being shares of the amalgamated company.

In an amalgamation, one of the predecessor parties might control the combined entity. Where one party emerges as the controlling shareholder, in many ways an amalgamation is not dissimilar to a share acquisition. Both privately held and publicly held companies may be involved. However, as a practical matter, amalgamations tend to take place among companies that are not too dissimilar in size, whereas acquisitions tend to be take place where a larger company acquires the outstanding shares or net assets of a smaller company.

Amalgamations sometimes are used to 'squeeze out' minority shareholders by issuing to them redeemable preferred shares for their common share interest and subsequently redeeming the preferred shares. As discussed in Chapter 12, amalgamations may give rise to a dissent remedy available to minority shareholders in most jurisdictions.

Where amalgamating entities are not dissimilar in size, there normally is the expectation of post-amalgamation net economic value added. Therefore, the valuation issues that arise not only include the relative value of the entities to be amalgamated on a stand-alone basis, but how the post-amalgamation synergies are to be divided. As a practical matter, smaller businesses sometimes enjoy a relatively greater portion of the overall synergies by combining with larger businesses. This is due to the relative increase in the value of the interest held by the previous shareholders of the smaller company subsequent to the amalgamation. That being said, amalgamation transactions often are facilitated where both parties agree that the interest held by each shareholder in the newly formed corporation will be a function of the relative stand-alone values of the companies prior to the transaction. The justification for this typically is that if the amalgamation does not proceed, the post-amalgamation synergies will not materialize. Whether or not parties agree in advance to 'put aside' post-amalgamation synergies for the purposes of amalgamation discussions depends on several factors, including:

- the alternatives available to each party in terms of other prospective purchasers who would purchase the outstanding shares or net assets of the vendor 'en bloc';
- the quantum of perceived net economic value added. Where post-amalgamation synergies are expected to be significant, the parties will recognize that the value of their respective business interests might be significantly enhanced regardless of what reasonable share ownership percentage they obtain in the combined entity; and
- other matters that are agreed by the parties in respect of the combined entity including management responsibility and the provisions of a post-amalgamation Shareholder's Agreement or other agreement.

Summary

Purchaser-perceived post-acquisition net economic value added often forms a significant component of acquisition price and, in some cases, is incorporated as part of notional fair market value. Post-acquisition synergies might be anticipated to accrue in many areas of a business following acquisition, including cost savings, incremental revenue opportunities, strategic advantage, and lower cost financing. Synergies that can be readily isolated generally are quantified in the forecasted post-acquisition discretionary cash flows, where the risk of achieving those synergies is reflected either by applying a probability factor to the net synergies anticipated, or in the discount and capitalization rates applied. Those synergies that are less quantifiable (such as strategic advantage) can be quantified by a reduction in the purchaser's required discount and capitalization rates, or by other subjective means.

Business pricing also is influenced by factors such as whether net assets or shares are being acquired, the form of consideration paid, the negotiating abilities of the parties involved, and other factors that may not be known until such time as negotiations with prospective purchasers commences. Where a share for share exchange (or partial share exchange) is the basis by which a transaction is consummated, the exercise all or in part becomes one of relative value between the businesses of the purchaser and vendor.

Chapter 12
Controlling and Minority Interests

Introduction

A controlling shareholder is defined as one that owns, either directly or indirectly, absolute (de jure) or effective (de facto) control of more than 50% of the votes cast at any meeting of shareholders of a company. A controlling shareholder normally is in a position to elect a majority of the Board of Directors and through them directly influence the risk/reward relationship of that investment. A minority shareholder is one who beneficially owns 50% or less of the outstanding voting shares of a company, and who at a given point in time does not enjoy de facto control. Minority shareholders generally do not enjoy all of the rights that accrue to a controlling interest.

It is not always apparent whether a particular shareholder has legal or, in particular, effective control of a company. The interpretation of whether or not control does exist may require the assistance of legal counsel. The valuation or pricing of a business 'en bloc' presumes an ability to control the business. Where the interest being valued does not enjoy the ability to control the company, a discount from ratable value may be appropriate.

The valuation (and pricing) of a minority interest requires an understanding of the important attributes associated with that interest in order to determine whether a discount should apply, and if so, to quantify such a discount. In this regard, it generally is important to understand the relevant terms and provisions that might be included in the applicable incorporating statutes, Articles of Incorporation, jurisprudence and any shareholder's or other relevant agreements that might exist.

This Chapter sets out a broad discussion of what constitutes control, which to a large degree requires an understanding of prevailing case law. This is followed by a discussion of the rights and obligations of both majority and minority shareholders, including shareholder dissent and oppression remedies. The Chapter concludes with an overview of provisions frequently found in Shareholder's Agreements which can influence the division of authority between controlling and minority shareholders.

The Valuation of Controlling and Minority Interests

Controlling Interests

En bloc value is the value of the equity ownership interest in a business viewed as a whole. Inherently, it includes the value associated with all of the risks and rewards of control. Said differently, en bloc value is equivalent to the value of a 100% controlling interest in the shares of a company. When en bloc value is divided by the number of common shares outstanding in circumstances where there are no other classes of shares, the resultant value per common share is said to be the ratable or pro rata portion thereof or 'value per common share'.

A controlling shareholder (normally defined as one having in excess of 50% of the voting shares of a company) typically is in a position to:

- elect the majority of the Board of Directors, thereby effectively controlling decisions that influence the strategic direction of the company, including its level of business risk and financial risk;
- determine the timing and quantum of dividend distributions, thereby influencing the return on investment;
- appoint themselves in a management position and thereby withdraw salaries and other forms of remuneration;
- determine the timing of the sale of control in the business and the form of consideration that would be acceptable, thereby maximizing 'price'; and
- liquidate the business and distribute the proceeds, thereby mitigating continued losses.

As a result, in a notional market context the value of a controlling interest on a per share basis generally is expressed as a pro-rata portion of en bloc value. For example, assume that the 'en bloc' fair market value of the shares of Company F is $10 million, and that there are 1 million shares outstanding. Further assume that there are two shareholders, one owning 80% of the outstanding shares and the other 20%. The pro-rata value of each share in Company F is $10 per share. Although there may be circumstances where a controlling interest appropriately is valued at an amount greater or less than pro-rata value, in most cases, the notional fair market value of the interest held by the 80% shareholder of Company F would be estimated at $8 million.

Minority Interests

The valuation of minority interests (whether in a notional or open market context) must consider that minority shareholders typically do not enjoy the same rights and privileges as a controlling shareholder. Further detracting from the value of a minority interest is the fact that in most privately held companies (and some publicly held companies) a less readily available market exists for a minority shareholding than for a controlling interest. As a result, a minority shareholder may be exposed to one or both of:

- a discount for the inability to unilaterally control the company (i.e. a 'discount for non-control'); and
- a discount for the absence of a ready market in which to sell the minority interest (i.e. a 'discount for illiquidity').

Extending the example above, the fair market value of the interest held by the 20% shareholder of Company F may not be its pro-rata value of $2 million. Rather, depending on the circumstances, the fair market value of that minority interest may be less, and possibly considerably less, than $2 million. Relevant factors to consider in determining the quantum of the discount include the nature of the business, the relationship between the shareholders, and provisions in the Articles of Incorporation, in the prevailing Shareholder's Agreement (if one exists) and in other relevant contractual agreements.

When arriving at the value of a particular shareholding, consideration must also be given to the restrictions, if any, placed on the transfer of shares in question. Such restrictions may be:

- in the contractual form of escrowed public shares or some form of limitations placed on the transfer of a corporate interest; or
- in the case of public company shareholdings may be in the form of practical restrictions having to do with the size of the minority shareholding vis a vis normal sized trading blocks (i.e. liquidity versus illiquidity issues).

Contractual restrictions typically are found in the incorporating documents or Shareholder's Agreements, if one exists. In the case of publicly held companies, restrictions on transfer may be found in agreements such as those pursuant to a share for share exchange. Factors to consider in quantifying discounts for non-control and illiquidity are discussed in Chapter 13.

Determinants of Control

Types of Control

In general terms, there are two types of control:

- legal control (or 'de jure' control) as exercised by means of majority ownership of the corporation's issued voting shares, or by a contractual right; and
- effective control (or 'de facto' control) which is less formal and occurs where the economic or other circumstances in which a corporation is placed allow control to be exercised by someone holding only a minority of shares, or perhaps none at all.

Effective control is a more elusive concept than legal control, but while it may be as effective as any form of legal control, it will always be overridden by legal control. Control of either variety is no less real even when it is infrequently exercised, because it is always available to the controlling shareholder whenever he or she chooses to use it.

Control is for most purposes said to exist when the shareholder holds shares which, taken together, carry more than 50% of the total votes which may be cast on an ordinary resolution at a shareholder's meeting. A shareholder with such voting power generally will be able to elect all or a majority of the Directors and, through them, to govern the company's business.

Although it is clear that legal control turns on ownership of voting shares, it is necessary to go further and examine the matters on which those shares may be voted. De jure control is keyed to a majority of the votes in the election of the Board of Directors. The power to elect Directors probably is the most important criterion with which to assess the importance of voting power because, in the usual situation, Directors are given broad authority to manage the corporation. Given this, the vesting of some specific and limited management authority elsewhere may not impair control. Nevertheless, the power to elect Directors does not determine de jure control in all situations.

The prominence of the power to elect Directors would apply only when the Directors had the 'usual' powers of Directors. Furthermore, consideration must be afforded to the circumstances where preferred shares and other company securities have the right to vote, as well as where different classes of common shares exist (e.g.; voting, non-voting and multiple voting). As always, the facts of each case must be carefully considered.

Finally, control may be subject to the specific and general restraints on the freedom of a controlling shareholder, such as minority shareholder rights legislation, which is discussed later in this Chapter. As a result, control comes in differing degrees. For example, a shareholder with 51% of the voting shares of a corporation may still be restricted in his or her ability to control the company pursuant to the inability to independently pass a 'special resolution' as set out in the Federal and Provincial Corporations Acts. These provisions set out the voting requirement to pass a special resolution, which usually is either two-thirds or three-quarters, depending on the prevailing Act. Special resolutions are required to enact a 'fundamental change' in the business, such as a major change in the direction of the business, a sale of most of the underlying assets, or a liquidation of the business. Specific requirements to abide by special resolution provisions and the terms thereof may also be set out in a company's incorporation documents or Unanimous Shareholder's Agreement.

If a shareholder owns 100% of the outstanding voting shares he or she may be said to have absolute control subject only to fetters on that control that may be found in the governing Corporations Act, a Shareholder's Agreement involving other classes of shares, or pursuant to corporate financing agreements. Issues arise in circumstances where a corporations' securities that do not possess the right to vote are given that right pursuant to corporations legislation. For example, in the Canada Business Corporations Act there are some matters in respect of which shares which ordinarily are non-voting can nevertheless vote so that a shareholder would have to own all the issued shares of all classes before he or she could be said to have absolute control.

A statute may define control in a particular way for the purposes of that statute, although, often, there is no statutory definition and the meaning of control must be found in the principles developed in the case law. Most of the case law in Canada involving the issue of control has arisen under income tax legislation. A list of selected Canadian cases dealing with the issue of control is presented in Appendix A. Although these cases must be read with an awareness of the context in which the question of control there arose, the principles enunciated in those Decisions are sufficiently general in their application to be useful for the purposes of determining whether control exists in most situations.

Means of Control

Control may not always be afforded by a shareholder having direct ownership of a majority of the voting shares. Circumstances arise, for example, where control might be exercised through a casting vote or through intermediary corporations, nominees and trustees, voting agreements and the like. Each of these is addressed below. Importantly, where such provisions exist and the determination of value could be significantly influenced by whether or not a shareholder is deemed to have control, it may be advisable to seek the assistance of legal counsel.

Control through a Casting Vote

In some cases, one shareholder has a casting vote that can be exercised in the event that shareholders are evenly divided on some issue. However, it is not necessarily correct to say that a casting vote affords the shareholder possessing that right with legal control. For example, if there are two shareholders, a casting vote will not prevail to give one of them control where both shareholders are necessary to constitute a meeting.

Casting vote provisions also have been characterized as techniques of de facto control not to be considered when determining de jure control. The Supreme Court of Canada has taken the view that a casting vote is not the property of a shareholder but an adjunct of the office of Chairman, and has no bearing on the question whether the shareholder possessing that right has control.

Control through Intermediate Corporations

It is well established that control may be exercised at one or more removed levels, or indirectly, in certain circumstances. Where, for example, the majority of a company's voting shares are held by another company, that other company's share register may be examined to discover the identity of those who control the first company through their control of the second company.

Control through Trustees and Nominees

In the case of a body corporate owning shares, the question is not whether the voice of that body corporate is affected by some external control, but which voice is heard, as a company has no voice of its own. With respect to shares held in trust, it appears that:

- in those cases in which the Courts have looked through a nominee shareholder or bare trustee (i.e. to find that control resides elsewhere) it was because the shareholder was found to be one who was prepared at all times to carry out the wishes and instructions of the person principally interested in the company;

- in those cases where the custodian trustee voted not with the voice of the management trustee(s) but with the voice of its own controlling shareholders, it was determined that control lay with the custodian trustee; and
- in the more complicated situation where there are joint trustees, it is the trustee or group of trustees who direct the voting of the shares held in trust who are said to have control (assuming that the joint trustees are not merely bare trustees).

The above summary simplifies the findings of several rather complex cases dealing with the issue of trustees and nominees. An in depth discussion of this topic, however, is beyond the scope of this book. Moreover, there are several Canadian cases which contradict the findings summarized above. For example, there are a substantial number of cases in which registered shareholders, even when they were acknowledged to be nominees or solicitors for someone else, have been said to be clothed with full and independent authority and the Courts have refused to look behind the share register to find the 'real' controller. Further complicating this issue is that some decisions include passages that imply that control includes de facto control.

Control through Voting Agreements

Voting and other agreements among shareholders are expressly authorized in section 146 of the Canada Business Corporations Act, and any such agreement may also be set out in the company's By-laws and, therefore, its Articles under subsections 103(1) and 6(2), respectively.

A Unanimous Agreement among shareholders pertaining to voting rights (such as unanimous consent or that a certain percentage of votes are required for specific decisions) may influence whether or not a majority shareholder has control in certain circumstances. However, some Court cases have come to the conclusion that a Unanimous Shareholder's Agreement is only effective if it is contained in the company's Articles or By-laws.

Proxies and Powers of Attorney

Canadian Courts have held that a vote cast under a proxy is a vote cast as agent for the owner of the share in question. That is, it is the principal who votes, not the agent. In any event, corporation law usually limits the life of a proxy, and both a proxy and a power of attorney may be revoked at any time. For these reasons it seems unlikely that a proxy-holder or an attorney could be said to have control of a corporation through such a temporary authority to vote shares in it.

Potential Control

A person is said to have a potential or future control over a corporation if he or she is in a position to trigger some future event giving rise to obtaining a position having legal control of the company. Control of this kind may sometimes be deemed to be legal control under a particular provision of a statute, including certain provisions of the Canadian Income Tax Act. Without such a statutory rule, however, potential control generally is considered to be no more than de facto control. Canadian Courts typically have concluded that the ability to obtain control through some course of conduct, in contrast to a presently existing ability to control the corporation by voting power (for example, the conversion of non-voting preference shares to common voting shares) will not be sufficient to give a person de jure control.

Group Control

When determining whether a particular shareholder controls a company or not, consideration should be given to the possibility that although the shareholder may not individually control the company, he or she might be part of a group which acts in concert to control the company. When no single person has legal control of a corporation it sometimes is necessary to investigate the circumstances in which two or more shareholders can be looked at collectively and treated as a group in control of the corporation.

Where shareholders are directly related, group control often is presumed to exist on the assumption that such shareholders will act in concert on important decisions involving the company and their respective interests therein. Circumstances may occur, however, where animosity arises among related shareholders and the presumption of goodwill among family members (or other normally cohesive group) may not be appropriate. This includes circumstances of marital dispute where the spouses collectively control a company.

Whether or not group control exists at a point in time clearly is a question of fact. If several minority shareholders act in concert to control a company, whether they have legally bound themselves to do so or not, a finding of group control may be appropriate. It is less certain whether facts showing that several persons are likely to act in concert are sufficient to establish control by these persons as a group. Even if a group of persons has historically acted in concert, there is no assurance (in the absence of a bona fide agreement between them) that they will continue to do so. Further, while a number of individuals may be thought to constitute a group on the basis of the de facto relationship existing among them, the principle that control of a company can only be satisfied by legal considerations is not diluted. A group may be established by factual circumstances but that group, once found, cannot, in law, control a company except through its power to vote a majority of the company's voting shares.

In this area more than any other, the Court Decisions in Canada have been influenced heavily by the fact that they arose in a tax avoidance setting. Therefore, caution must be exercised in applying these rulings in a particular business valuation exercise.

The Canada Customs and Revenue Agency and Control

Where minority shareholding interests are valued for income tax purposes, the guidelines for group and family control set out by the Canada Customs and Revenue Agency (formerly Revenue Canada) should be considered. It must be remembered that these guidelines could change, and in any event may have little relevance in an open market context.

Family Control

When referring to the valuation of an individual minority shareholding in a corporation collectively controlled by individuals with a familial relationship, the term 'family control' often is used. Family control, as group control, is a concept that is applied in connection with notional market valuation requirements for income tax purposes. The Canada Customs and Revenue Agency has accepted a premise that, barring family disputes, family members who collectively control may be presumed to act in concert to exercise some control over the economic direction and the liquidity of their investment. The rationale which underlies this theory is that related shareholders who hold in the aggregate more than 50% of the voting shares are in a position to realize proceeds not less than the ratable value of their respective shareholdings by acting in concert to sell a control shareholding. Canada Customs and Revenue Agency Information Circular 89-3 entitled 'Policy Statement on Business Equity Valuations' also includes discussion as to the considerations to be made in assessing whether family control exists.

The wording of Information Circular 89-3 seems to suggest that minority shareholders related to a family control group have the option of associating themselves with the family group. In other words, in those situations where such minority shareholders are desirous of establishing a lower notional value for their shares rather than a higher value, it would appear that the Canada Customs and Revenue Agency is offering the option of not claiming family control, or vice versa. Experience to date suggests that the Canada Customs and Revenue Agency primarily looks to consistent application of family control (or the lack thereof) at relevant valuation dates.

Group Control

Control may exist in a number of informal ways, such as in circumstances where no single person has de jure control, but where two or more shareholders own, in the aggregate, more than 50% of the issued voting shares. According to the Canada Customs and Revenue Agency, group control is deemed to exist where shareholders voting shares aggregating more than 50% of the votes cast at a general meeting of shareholders could demonstrate a pattern of acting in concert with respect to their shareholdings, and that they were:

- restricted in their right to sell their shares independently; and
- restricted in their right to vote their shares independently.

To satisfy the Canadian taxation authority, such evidence could be contained in the Articles of Incorporation, the By-laws, or in a Shareholder's Agreement. Information Circular 89-3 includes a discussion as to the considerations to be made in assessing whether group control exists. A strict reading of Information Circular 89-3 suggests that the Canada Customs and Revenue Agency is offering taxpayers the option of claiming group control. Again, experience to date suggests that the Canada Customs and Revenue Agency primarily looks to consistent application of group control (or the lack thereof) at relevant valuation dates.

Rights of Controlling and Minority Shareholders

Overview

In valuing a controlling or minority interest, it is important to be cognizant of the various factors that not only protect minority shareholders but may also place certain restraints on the ability of the majority shareholder to control the company. The value of either a controlling or minority interest in a corporation must be assessed in light of:

- the corporation's constitution, including its Articles, By-laws, and so on;
- the statute under which it is incorporated; and
- relevant case law.

At a given point in time, the provisions of the corporations legislation pursuant to which the company is incorporated, and the related body of jurisprudence, establish the basic rights and protections that universally are available in that jurisdiction. Minority shareholders in publicly traded companies can also look to the provisions of the prevailing securities legislation in the jurisdictions where a market for the shares is made. Further rights and/or restrictions that may affect the value of a shareholder's interest may be documented in the incorporating Articles and By-laws of the specific company or in a Shareholder's Agreement or Unanimous Shareholder's Agreement if one exists.

It is a culmination of the facts derived through an investigation of the above items (as they relate to each and every valuation exercise) which provide the necessary set of criteria to assess the appropriate discount, if any, to be applied to the ratable portion of en bloc value when valuing a minority interest.

Corporations Legislation

In Canada, both the Federal and Provincial governments have jurisdiction to incorporate companies. The Canada Business Corporations Act ('CBCA') incorporates companies by Articles of Incorporation, a 'registration' system that is also followed in Alberta, Manitoba, New Brunswick, Newfoundland, Ontario, Quebec, and Saskatchewan. The remaining Provinces provide for incorporation by Memorandums of Association. The two systems of incorporation differ mainly in that the powers and obligations of a registration company (i.e. incorporated by Articles of Incorporation) and related matters are defined by statute. Alternatively, in the case of a Memorandum company these matters largely are determined by the shareholders, subject to specific statutory requirements, and are documented in the incorporating Articles and By-laws.

The CBCA not only indicates the provisions which are most commonly used to strike a balance of interests different from that established by the law itself, but also provides further protection to minority shareholders in the form of, among others, dissent and oppression remedies. As such, these provisions may mitigate somewhat against the degree to which a minority shareholder is 'disadvantaged' than otherwise would be the case.

Each of the Federal and Provincial Corporations Acts sets out various shareholder's rights and related matters which may potentially affect the value of a minority shareholding in a company. Certain basic rights are accorded to both majority and minority shareholders by the provisions of the applicable corporations legislation. The interpretation and application of these rights is guided by judicial interpretation. Absent other considerations, the extent to which these rights are available generally affects the value of minority shareholding interests in a particular jurisdiction. Shareholder's rights that may be included in a particular Act include:

- distinguishing between widely-held and closely-held (or 'privately-held') companies (also termed public and private, or offering and non-offering companies), including restrictions and/or prohibitions on the offering of shares to the public by closely-held companies;
- specification of the rights and entitlements of each authorized class of shares;
- conditions and restrictions for the transfer of issued and outstanding share capital;
- the availability of shareholder's pre-emptive rights. That is, the requirement that new issues of treasury share capital first be offered to existing shareholders holding shares of that class, in proportion to their holdings of the shares of that class, and on the same terms as those shares are to be offered to others;
- shareholder's rights as to participation in corporate decisions, including:
  — procedural requirements related to the conduct of regular meetings,
  — specification of the types of transactions that require direct shareholder's approval, either by simple or special majority. These include specific matters such as the issuance or alteration of share capital, alteration of share rights and restrictions, amendment of the corporate charter, amendment to the stated capital amount, amalgamation, dissolution and wind-up of the company, and fundamental changes to the principal business of the company. Unless specifically provided by the incorporating statute or incorporating documents, corporate decisions taken in general or special meetings are decided by majority vote. In the absence of cumulative voting, the votes of a simple majority always will be sufficient to elect the entire Board of Directors,
  — provisions related to the requisitioning and content of extraordinary shareholders meetings, including the percentage shareholder's approval

required to effect so-called special resolutions (generally either 2/3rds or 3/4ths) and the availability of separate class voting provisions,
— the right to enter into Unanimous Shareholder's Agreements, being written agreements among all the shareholders, or among all the shareholders and a person(s) who is not a shareholder, to restrict all or some of the powers of the Board of Directors to manage the business of the corporation. Unless specifically provided by statute, shareholders may not contract to restrain the discretion of the Directors of the corporation, and
— entitlement to cumulative voting to determine the composition of the Board of Directors;

- those related to the election of the Board of Directors and the powers conferred on the members of the Board. This includes matters such as the number of Directors to be elected, the number of Directors constituting a quorum, the qualifications necessary for election, the powers of the Directors and any restrictions thereon, the duties and liabilities of the Directors, and whether the Chairman has a casting vote in the event of a tied vote;
- those regarding access to specified corporate information such as financial statements, corporate records, and listings of shareholders; and
- those which arise in the event of a takeover bid for the shares of the company. In some jurisdictions, a so-called compulsory acquisition provision gives an acquirer of at least 90% of the share capital of a corporation the right to acquire the remaining shares at the same price.

Further to the aforementioned shareholder's rights, the various corporations statutes may also provide other remedies, and hence protections for minority shareholders in specific circumstances. Where provided, these may include:

- a right to dissent in certain prescribed circumstances. This right enables a shareholder to require the company in which he or she holds shares to purchase them at 'fair value', where the company initiates certain 'fundamental changes' from which he or she dissents;
- the right of a minority shareholder (and sometimes other parties) to exercise a so-called oppression remedy where the affairs of the company have been conducted to the prejudice of that party's interest (the controlling shareholder is not in itself subject to the oppression remedy unless it happens to be a corporation and is therefore caught as an affiliate);
- the right to apply to a Court for an order liquidating or dissolving the company where the affairs of the company have been conducted to the prejudice of the minority's interest;

- the right to bring a derivative action, being a suit brought by a person in the name of, and on behalf of, the corporation to remedy a wrong done to the corporation. If the corporation has been wronged by the majority, a statutory derivative action allows the minority to seek leave (or permission) to prosecute or defend an action on behalf of the corporation;
- the right to apply to a Court for an investigation order to collect evidence where corporate wrongdoing is suspected; and
- the right to apply to a Court to compel the corporation to rectify its corporate register or records.

The availability in each Canadian jurisdiction of each of these remedies is summarized in the following chart.

CHART 12.1

Legislation	Federal (CBCA) Alberta Manitoba New Brunswick Newfoundland Ontario Saskatchewan	British Columbia	Nova Scotia	Prince Edward Island	Quebec
Dissent Right Available	Yes	Yes	Yes	No	No
Correction of Corporate Records	Add or Correct Name	Correct Registered Name Only	Correct Registered Name Only	Add or Correct Name	Add or Correct Name
Investigation Order	Yes	Yes	Yes	No	Yes
Who Can Apply	Any Shareholder Except N.B. – must hold 10% of shares	Must hold 20% of any class of shares	Must hold 10% of stock and be at least 1/5th of shareholders		Must hold sufficient interest to satisfy Inspector General
Derivative Action Available	Yes	Yes	Yes	No	No
Oppression Remedy Available	Yes	Yes	Yes	No	No
Can Apply for Court Ordered Windup	Yes	Yes	Yes	Yes	Yes

Further, the CBCA and various Provincial Acts also give the authority to shareholders to establish a Unanimous Shareholder's Agreement enabling the shareholders to agree upon and document their own variation of the division of authority granted to shareholders and Directors.

Dissent Remedy

Exercise of a dissent remedy enables minority shareholders to withdraw from the corporation rather than be subjected to 'fundamental changes' proposed by the majority. At the same time, the majority is permitted to carry out such changes if it is willing to risk that minority shareholders will exercise their right of dissent. In other words, the dissent remedy protects minority shareholders from fundamental changes not to their liking, while it simultaneously preserves flexibility within the enterprise. As such, the dissent remedy is intended to represent a balancing of interests between the majority and minority shareholders.

A statutory dissent remedy is available in all jurisdictions except Prince Edward Island and Quebec. The triggering events specified in the Federal legislation are set out in the CBCA, section 190. The same criteria have been adopted in the other jurisdictions which provide a dissent remedy (the British Columbia Companies Act contains additional provisions). Under these jurisdictions, the circumstances which create an appraisal right are:

- the passage of an amendment to the Articles to add, change, or remove any provisions restricting or constraining the issue, ownership, or transfer of shares or any restriction upon the business or businesses that the corporation may carry on;
- an amalgamation with a corporation other than its wholly owned subsidiary, its parent corporation if it is a wholly owned subsidiary, or its sister corporation, if both are wholly owned subsidiaries of the same corporation;
- the continuation of the corporation under the laws of another jurisdiction;
- a sale, lease, or exchange of all, or substantially all, of the corporation's property; and
- an amendment to the incorporating Articles or Memorandum which diminishes the rights or conditions attached to a class or series of shares, which amendment otherwise creates an entitlement to a class vote.

When a dissent remedy is activated, the corporation statutes in Canada require the shares of the dissenting party to be purchased for 'fair value'. As discussed in Chapter 2, the term fair value is not defined in the Federal or any of the Provincial Corporations Acts. Hence, the concept of fair value has been the subject matter of litigation both as to its interpretation as well as its quantification. In dealing with dissent cases under the CBCA, Canadian Courts generally have accepted the premise that it is the duty of the Court to determine what fair value is.

A list of selected Canadian cases dealing with the term fair value can be found in Appendix A. Although these cases indicate some disparity in the interpretation of fair value, Canadian Courts generally have found that:

- fair value and fair market value are not necessarily synonymous;
- the en bloc value of the outstanding shares of the subject company generally is to be determined under the assumption that the company is a going concern, rather than under the assumption of a liquidation of the company's assets;
- in circumstances where en bloc value is determined separate from stock market price, no minority discount generally is applied when determining the fair value of a minority shareholding;
- stock market price, generally being lower than stand-alone (or intrinsic) value, by itself is not representative of fair value, particularly where trading is thin or sporadic;
- post-amalgamation benefits may be taken into account where the dissenting party was forced out, and not given the opportunity to participate as a shareholder. Conversely, participation in post-amalgamation benefits is less likely where the dissenting party had the opportunity to continue with its participation but elected not to;
- a so-called 'premium for forcible taking' has seldom been found to be applicable; and
- the specific facts underlying a given dissenting shareholder appraisal action may influence the interpretation of the meaning of fair value pursuant to that action.

Oppression Remedies

Since a minority shareholder has no legal control over the affairs of a corporation, it is possible for the majority to act in a manner that is prejudicial to the interest of the minority. An oppression remedy permits an oppressed minority shareholder (and other specified parties) to request the Courts to intervene (or remedy a demonstrated unfairness) in the affairs of the corporation so as to protect the complaining shareholder's interest.

Oppression remedies are available in the same jurisdictions as are dissent remedies (that is, in every jurisdiction except Quebec and Prince Edward Island). Courts have broad discretion to make any interim or final order they see fit to deal with complaints, including ordering the corporation to purchase the minority shareholder's shares, and/or ordering the corporation to be wound up. Although the statutes do not specify the valuation basis pursuant to which a minority shareholder's shares are to be repurchased, the jurisprudence appears to support the application of a 'fair value' concept.

According to the CBCA, grounds for an oppression remedy application arise where:

- an act or an omission of the corporation; or
- the manner in which the business or affairs of the corporation is carried on; or
- the manner in which the powers of the Directors are exercised,

is oppressive, is unfairly prejudicial to, or unfairly disregards the interests of any security holder past and present, or any creditor, Director or Officer, former Director or Officer, or any other person who the Court decides is a proper person to make an application.

The oppression remedy is a comprehensive protection designed to provide relief for most kinds of corporate unfairness. However, it is only available in situations involving corporate acts or conduct of Directors and not shareholders acting in their capacity as shareholders. Although the oppression remedy is available in a very broad range of situations, in general terms jurisprudence indicates that the oppression remedy is available where it is shown that:

- the actions of the majority excluded the minority from participation in the management of a closely-held corporation;
- shares were issued for other than legitimate business reasons to the disadvantage of the minority;
- the majority treated the corporation as its own private company in a manner that unfairly disregarded the interests of the minority; and
- there was a denial of a legitimate expectation of the minority.

Where the Court has determined that oppression has occurred, it has broad statutory scope in making an interim or final order. In the various Canadian jurisdictions, the Courts generally have the power to make an order:

- restraining the conduct which gave rise to the complaint;
- appointing a receiver or receiver-manager;
- regulating a corporation's affairs by amending its Articles or By-laws or creating or amending a Unanimous Shareholder's Agreement;
- directing an issue or exchange of securities;
- appointing Directors in place of or in addition to all or any of the Directors then in office;
- directing a corporation, or any other person, to purchase securities of a security holder;

- directing a corporation, or any person, to pay a security holder any part of the monies paid by him or her for securities;
- varying or setting aside a transaction or contract to which a corporation is a party, and compensating the corporation or any other party to the transaction or contract;
- requiring a corporation to produce financial statements or an accounting in another form as specified by the Court;
- compensating an aggrieved person;
- directing rectification of the registers or other records of a corporation;
- liquidating and dissolving the corporation;
- directing an investigation to be made; and
- requiring the trial of any issue.

Pursuant to minority shareholder oppression remedies, Canadian Courts to date generally have determined fair value as a ratable portion of en bloc fair market value. However, the Courts appear to have left open the possibility of awarding a discounted amount where the actions of the minority warrants such treatment.

Articles of Incorporation and By-laws

A company's Articles of Incorporation (or Memorandum or Association), including any amendments thereto, may include provisions that impact the value of an equity interest in that company. Relevant provisions in the Articles might include:

- whether there is a maximum number of shares which may be issued;
- the existence of different classes of shares and their respective terms;
- the restrictions, if any, on the transfer of shares (closely-held corporations and widely-held corporations);
- the restrictions on the business or powers of the corporation;
- the restrictions on the corporation's right to purchase or redeem its shares; and
- whether there is a lien on the shares.

Special provisions may be embodied in the corporation's By-laws. If so, those provisions will then become subject to the statutory provisions regulating amendments to the Articles and By-laws respectively, subject again to any additional rules that the shareholders may want to add.

Shareholder resolutions (particularly where unanimous) may also contain provisions impacting the rights and obligations of controlling and minority shareholders.

Shareholder's Agreements

Types of Shareholder's Agreements

An important distinction must be made between a Unanimous Shareholder's Agreement and a Shareholder's Agreement. A Unanimous Shareholder's Agreement confers on the shareholders of a corporation who are party it the rights, duties, obligations and liabilities of the corporation's Directors as provided in the Agreement. A Unanimous Shareholder's Agreement effectively transfers Directors' responsibilities to the shareholders and may restrict in whole or in part the ability of the Directors to manage the company. A Unanimous Shareholder's Agreement is a governing document that supercedes the By-laws, Articles of Incorporation and other corporate documents or a corporate entity, except where not permitted under corporate law. A Unanimous Shareholder's Agreement becomes part of a corporation's constitution, and a purchaser of shares normally becomes subject to it.

Conversely, a Shareholder's Agreement that is not a Unanimous Shareholder's Agreement typically does not restrict the powers of the Directors but rather seeks to define the relationship and restrictions between shareholders in their role of owners of a corporation as opposed to its managers. A Shareholder's Agreement may provide for such things as restrictions on share transfer, share purchase and sale provisions, the valuation of the share interests and so forth. Such provisions may also be found in a Unanimous Shareholder's Agreement.

> In this book, unless otherwise specified, references to Shareholder's Agreements should be taken to mean ordinary Shareholder's Agreements and not Unanimous Shareholder's Agreements.

Purpose

A Shareholder's Agreement, or other agreement related to the ownership of shares, defines the privileges, protections, and obligations of the shareholders. In particular, such agreements frequently address the issue of, and sometimes ensure, minority shareholder liquidity. The specific provisions of an enforceable Shareholder's Agreement often are a significant determinant of minority shareholding value.

A Shareholder's Agreement attempts to define what is to occur in all subsequent transactions in a given company's shares. There are at least five (sometimes conflicting) interests that a Shareholder's Agreement usually is designed to:

- ensure a shareholder who is terminating his or her association with the corporation that there will be a market for his or her shares at a price he or she and all other shareholders believe to be fair. In this regard, the circumstances of a shareholder's departure can be a key determinant both of the price and of the terms of its payment;
- provide continuing shareholders with control over outside parties becoming shareholders;
- ensure all shareholders that on any acquisition or disposition of shares among themselves, they pay or receive a fair price for their respective shareholdings, and that the agreement adequately documents their collective intent in this regard. A Shareholder's Agreement can influence the fair market value of a minority shareholding by stipulating that 'fair market value' (or other value term adopted) will mean a ratable portion of en bloc value of the shares, or by specifying in some other fashion the basis of value determination. A specific definition of fair market value is required because that term in and of itself is too general;
- ensure that if an offer is received for all of the outstanding shares that is acceptable to shareholders who collectively own a prescribed number of shares (usually sufficient to constitute control), that all shareholders are obliged to tender to the offer (so-called 'mandatory sale' or 'drag-along' provisions). Such a provision protects the liquidity of a controlling shareholder(s) where a purchaser makes the acquisition of all outstanding shares a condition of the purchase offer; and
- ensure all shareholders of a so-called 'coattail' or 'tagalong' ability in the event an offer for less than all of the outstanding shares is received that is acceptable to shareholders who collectively own a prescribed number of shares (usually sufficient to constitute control). Such a provision protects the liquidity of all shareholders in the event of such an offer.

Shareholder's Agreements may also contain other provisions that may have an impact on value, such as non-competition provisions after shares are sold and restrictions on share transfer.

It is incumbent upon persons entering into a Shareholder's Agreement to ensure that it adequately documents their collective intent with respect to the terms and conditions of the transactions it provides for. As circumstances change over time, it is important to periodically review and modify, as necessary, the provisions of a Shareholder's Agreement prior to such time as it becomes the basis for an actual transaction.

Triggering Events

It is important for parties to a Shareholder's Agreement to understand and distinguish the various potential future events that might affect their shareholding interests and to consider these eventualities when structuring such an agreement. Further, shareholders must recognize the importance of ensuring the agreement clearly sets out their collective intent in dealing with any particular future circumstance.

Shareholder's Agreements contain provisions that either permit or require the sale of individual shareholdings in various circumstances. Such so-called 'triggering events' may include the:

- death of a shareholder;
- permanent disability of an employee/shareholder;
- retirement of an employee/shareholder;
- termination of a shareholder's employment;
- marriage breakdown of a shareholder; and
- insolvency or bankruptcy of a shareholder.

In most of these cases, it is important that the Shareholder's Agreement set out:

- whether the other shareholders will purchase the selling shareholder's interest, or whether the shares will be purchased for cancellation by the company;
- the method of determining the transaction price; and
- the payment terms.

When determining the en bloc fair market value (or some other defined value) of the shares, it is important to set out whether the value term adopted refers to the value of the shares on an intrinsic (i.e. stand-alone) basis, or whether special interest purchasers should be taken into account. In addition, it is important to set out whether a minority interest should be valued at its ratable portion of the en bloc value of the shares or on some other basis.

Where the shares of the selling shareholder are to be acquired by the company, it also is important to consider the implications of internal vs. external financing. As discussed in Chapter 2, the 'en bloc' value of the shares of a business (and consequently the pro-rata value of any interest therein) may be affected depending on whether a transaction is financed using funds within the company or from outside of the company. That is, where the business must forego necessary operating expenditures or growth opportunities in favour of payments to the departing shareholder, the en bloc value of the shares may suffer as a result. However, the remaining shareholder(s) subsequently might benefit to a larger extent than would otherwise have been the case if a prospective purchaser for the business can be found.

In addition, in cases where the departing shareholder was active in the business and enjoyed personal goodwill (which by definition is not transferable by contract or otherwise – see Chapter 2), the issue arises as to whether the value of the business should include or exclude that element of personal goodwill. As conventionally defined, fair market value does not incorporate an element of personal goodwill.

It also is important that careful consideration be given to the alternate income tax treatments that result from each of these 'triggering events'. Shareholders and their advisors should continually monitor amendments to the income tax law, and the significance of such amendments to the various buyout provisions set out in any given Shareholder's Agreement. Relevant tax implications are discussed in Chapter 14, and include such issues as capital gains reserves (where payment is made over time), the tax implications of earn-out arrangements (where used) and the use of the capital gains exemption where the company in which the shares are held meets the definition of a 'qualified small business corporation'.

Death of a Shareholder

Shareholder's Agreements commonly include an obligatory purchase and sale provision effective in the event of a shareholder's death. Such purchase requirements often are funded by life insurance proceeds thereby eliminating, or at least diminishing, what otherwise might prove to be direct or indirect changed financial obligations for the continuing shareholders. The Shareholder's Agreement must set out whether the corporation, or the other shareholders, will acquire the deceased's shares. It must also establish payment terms (including time period, applicable interest rate, security, and so on).

Where funding is provided all or in part by life insurance, the adequacy and availability of such insurance should be reviewed on a regular basis. Where life insurance is not used to fund such a purchase requirement, the source and availability of funds to satisfy it should continually be reviewed. If the source of such funds is the company itself, the agreement should stipulate whether the value of the shares is to be determined on either an internally or an externally financed basis as discussed above.

It also is important to specify whether the value of the shares should include or exclude the proceeds of corporate owned life insurance, irrespective of who the beneficiary is. For example, if all of the outstanding shares of a business with four equal shareholders have an en bloc value of $8 million, the pro-rata value of each shareholder's interest is $2 million. If one of the shareholders dies and the company, as beneficiary receives non-taxable insurance proceeds of $2 million immediately following death, then the en bloc value of the shares increases to $10 million. The issue arises as to whether or not the deceased shareholder's estate should participate in the increase in en bloc equity value. In addition, to avoid untimely disputes, the Shareholder's Agreement should specify how the proceeds of the life insurance (where the company is the beneficiary) are to be distributed to shareholders, since such proceeds flow through the capital dividend account of a privately-held company and the distribution thereof normally is tax-free (or virtually tax-free). This has the effect of converting a taxable gain (i.e. a taxable capital gain that would result if the business interest were sold to a third party) into a non-taxable gain.

Permanent Disability of an Employee/Shareholder

Shareholder's Agreement sometimes provide either for the optional, or required, sale of a shareholding in the event an employee/shareholder suffers permanent disability. Where it does, the Shareholder's Agreement should specify such details as:

- the circumstances that constitute permanent disability;
- how permanent disability is to be substantiated. This can require medical documentation, or simply the passage of a specified period of time;
- whether a disabled shareholder is entitled to draw income for a specified period of time. Shareholders often provide for long-term disability insurance coverage as a means of providing cash while they are disabled. How-

ever, there may be a waiting period for a disability to be classified as permanent, during which time insurance benefits usually are not payable; and
- the timing of a transaction triggered by the disability of a shareholder.

Retirement of a Shareholder

The retirement of an employee/shareholder often is addressed in a Shareholder's Agreement. Specific matters that should be covered include:

- whether retirement is mandatory at a prescribed age;
- whether a change (rather than cessation) in employment constitutes 'retirement';
- conditions pursuant to which a shareholder may be forced to retire;
- restrictions on retirement. For example, shareholders may agree not to retire for a fixed number of years following execution of the Shareholder's Agreement, or before reaching a certain age;
- penalties or disincentives for early retirement. These generally are reflected either in the determination of the purchase price or in the terms of payment;
- whether a retiring shareholder continues to draw remuneration, retain use of company assets, or receive other benefits for a specified period of time following retirement; and
- in some circumstances, a requirement that retiring shareholders execute non-competition agreements and non-disclosure agreements with respect to trade secrets and practices.

In the absence of a mandatory non-competition agreement pursuant to a Shareholder's Agreement, an employee being 'forced' to retire may, depending on factors such as health, financial ability and other factors, be able to compete with the business and impair its value as a result. From a valuation perspective the issue is whether that prospective diminution in value should be reflected in the en bloc value of the retiring shareholder's interest. From a practical perspective, in the absence of clearly established provisions, the retiring shareholder and the remaining shareholders may be able to negotiate an agreement whereby the retiring shareholder receives a price for his or her interest based on non-competition in exchange for agreeing to such.

Termination of a Shareholder's Employment

In the event of the termination of an employee-shareholder's employment, his or her shares should be acquired pursuant to prior agreement. This becomes an even more important issue as minority shareholder rights strengthen, because an adversarial minority shareholder increasingly may prove to be disruptive to ongoing business activities. In particular, a shareholder as a minimum is entitled to receive annual financial statements and to be invited to attend an annual meeting of shareholders. The resultant external flow of what otherwise would be confidential information typically is perceived to be undesirable. If the agreement contains such a provision, it generally is appropriate to distinguish whether employment is terminated by the employee/shareholder or by the company.

If employment is terminated by the employee-shareholder, the Shareholder's Agreement might stipulate a discount from a ratable value, thereby mitigating against an employee-shareholder 'cashing out' at a favourable price. As well, the continuing business should be protected, where necessary, by non-competition and non-disclosure agreements that become effective on voluntary termination.

Again, where a non-competition agreement is not required, the issue arises with respect to the departing shareholder's ability to compete. However, unlike cases involving a retiring shareholder, it is less likely that the respective parties could come to an agreement whereby higher proceeds are exchanged for agreeing to non-competition provisions, particularly where the dismissal of the employee-shareholder involved significant animosity or ill-will.

Where an employee/shareholder is terminated by the company, a further distinction should be made between termination without cause, and termination with just cause. Employee/shareholders will want protection against the corporation terminating their employment without cause in poor economic times, and buying their shares at a depressed price. When termination occurs with cause, the agreement should address the grounds that constitute just cause and, in specific situations, advance notice of impending termination.

Marriage Breakdown of a Shareholder

The marital situation of a privately-held company shareholder can directly affect the interests of all the shareholders and the company itself. For example:

- in most Provinces, privately-held corporation shares potentially are included among assets to be equalized on marriage breakdown;

- where corporate shares are included in the marital property pool, the non-titled spouse has the right upon marriage breakdown to obtain financial and other corporate information not usually made public;
- many jurisdictions give the Courts the discretion in specified instances to order the transfer of a spouse's assets to the other spouse; and
- the death of a spouse can be a triggering event for the equalization of assets in certain Provinces.

Accordingly, consideration should be given to marital related provisions in privately-held company Shareholder's Agreements. Canadian Family Law related jurisprudence provides little guidance as to the extent to which a Court is bound to consider the provisions of a Shareholder's Agreement in the event of marriage breakdown if a spouse is not a signatory to the agreement. However, where a Shareholder's Agreement is among unrelated parties, and has not been executed in contemplation of a marital dispute, it may provide persuasive evidence as to the value of a particular shareholding interest.

Where only one spouse is a shareholder in a privately-held company, the following provisions may be included in a Shareholder's Agreement:

- a requirement that all shareholders execute domestic contracts with their respective spouses excluding their shares from the marital asset pool for Family Law purposes. Alternatively, the Shareholder's Agreement could include such a provision, and the non-shareholder spouses could be parties to it. The jurisdiction of residence generally will determine how such a provision is best documented;
- a requirement that each shareholder enter into an agreement with their respective spouse stipulating that any Court order in a Family Law context will not be satisfied all or in part by the transfer of shares of the company to the non-titled spouse – which agreement could be ignored by the Court if a default in obligations to pay child support has occurred, or a default has occurred in fulfillment of a Court order; and
- failing an ability to get agreement with respect to the two previous points, consideration should be given to providing for specific buyout and related valuation provisions to be applied in the event of a shareholder's marriage breakdown.

Where both spouses are shareholders in a company, a Shareholder's Agreement might include the following provisions:

- where both spouses are active in the business, a right of first refusal between the spouses to purchase the other's shareholding in the event of death;

- where only one spouse is active in the business, a requirement that the non-active party also sell his or her shares upon the death or retirement of the active spouse; and
- in the event of marital breakdown, a mandatory buy/sell provision between the spouses. Where only one spouse is active in the business, that individual typically would be the purchaser. Where both spouses are active, the selection of the spouse that is to continue generally would require the concurrence of the other shareholders.

Insolvency or Bankruptcy of a Shareholder

When a shareholder becomes personally insolvent or bankrupt, a mandatory buyout of his or her interest may be desirable. Where the controlling shareholder is so affected, the control of the company ultimately could pass to a receiver or trustee in bankruptcy. This clearly would be an undesirable consequence. Similarly, the Shareholder's Agreement may restrain the ability of a shareholder to pledge his or her interest in the company as security, in case it was called.

The Shareholder's Agreement should specify the terms that constitute insolvency or bankruptcy and that the insolvent party's interest in the company be acquired before transfer to a third party. In this regard, it is important that the terms by which 'price' is established be perceived as fair so that the transaction is less likely to be contested.

Related Considerations

In drafting the buy/sell provisions of a Shareholder's Agreement, consideration also should be given to matters such as:

- the repayment of amounts owing to the company by the departing shareholder or members of his or her family, including credit card charges and similar current obligations;
- the return or purchase by the departing shareholder of 'personal use' corporate assets (for example, automobiles, cellular telephones, credit cards, computer equipment, and so on);
- the repayment of amounts owing to the departing shareholder;
- the release of a departing shareholder from any corporate guarantees; and
- the departing shareholder's resignation as an Officer and/or Director of the company.

Reciprocal Buy/Sell Provisions

A Shareholder's Agreement may provide for reciprocal buy/sell provisions, often called 'put-call', or 'shotgun' clauses. Such clauses provide that one party can offer to sell his or her shares to another party at a price per share and on terms specified in the offer. The other party is required to either accept the offer, or to make an identical binding offer to the shareholder making the initial offer. Whichever course of action is adopted by the second shareholder, it results in a binding agreement of purchase and sale between the two. Assuming the shareholders are of relatively equal financial strength, and that the personal or individual goodwill of one of the parties is not critical to the continued success of the business, a shotgun clause tends to ensure the liquidity of each shareholder's interest. Consequently, it establishes what the parties believe to be a fair price for the shares.

Issues may arise where both parties do not have an equal negotiating position. This might include circumstances where:

- one party is unable to obtain financing on reasonable terms and therefore potentially might be disadvantaged pursuant to having to sell at a low price;
- the parties have different proportionate equity interests, thereby creating a greater financial burden for the shareholder with the smaller interest;
- only one of the parties is active in the business, and therefore is presumably more knowledgeable about the operations and the future prospects of the business; and
- the personal goodwill enjoyed by one of the shareholders results in the en bloc value of the shares being greater to one shareholder than the other(s). The same may be true where individual goodwill exists if the transaction is not accompanied by a mandatory non-competition agreement.

Right of First Refusal

In privately-held companies, agreements among shareholders often include 'right of first refusal' provisions. Among other things, these provisions enable continuing shareholders to accept or reject proposed new shareholders. There are two distinct ways right of first refusal clauses can be drafted:

- in the first approach, sometimes referred to as a 'hard' right of first refusal, the shareholder wishing to sell solicits offers from third party purchasers. The shareholder holding the right of first refusal is then presented with the best third party offer received and is given the opportunity to purchase the selling shareholder's interest based on the price, terms, and conditions of that offer. If he or she elects not to purchase the shares within an agreed period of time, the vendor can then sell his or her interest to the party making the offer (on those same terms); and

- in the second approach, sometimes referred to as a 'soft' right of first refusal, the shareholder wishing to sell his or her interest establishes a price and terms of sale which is presented to the shareholder holding the right of first refusal. If the shareholder receiving the offer elects not to acquire the shares on those terms within an agreed time period, the prospective vendor is free to sell his or her interest in the open market at a price equal to or higher, and on terms no less favourable, than the price and terms offered to the shareholder holding the first refusal right.

The hard right of first refusal typically is far better from the point of view of the person holding the refusal right. Third party purchasers rarely will spend a significant amount of time assessing a potential share acquisition in the face of an overriding right of first refusal. The soft right of first refusal typically is better from the vendor's perspective. Although it forces the prospective vendor to be disciplined when establishing the initial price and terms offered to the shareholder holding the soft refusal right, in the event the shareholder to whom the shares are offered does not take them, the vendor is able to deal with open market purchasers unencumbered by a first refusal right.

Certain considerations should be kept in mind when drafting right of first refusal clauses. When drafting a hard right of first refusal, because some of the terms and conditions of the consideration offered by a third party could be particular to the offeror (e.g. shares of a offeror corporation), the remaining shareholder(s) should have the right to buy the shares on similar (as contrasted with the 'same') terms and conditions, and for consideration that is 'substantially equivalent' to that set out in the third party's offer. Further, if the right of first refusal is not exercised, the right of a shareholder to sell his or her shares to the third party should remain open for a specified period of time.

The terms of a hard or soft right of first refusal should specify that any third party purchaser must be one who deals at arm's length with the prospective vendor. Further, it should include a clause stating that if the right of first refusal is not exercised, one condition of selling to a third party is that the purchaser becomes a party to the original Shareholder's Agreement.

Mandatory Sale and 'Coattail' Provisions

Both controlling and minority shareholders may want to ensure the delivery of all outstanding shares pursuant to mandatory sale (or so-called 'drag-along') provisions. Many acquirers of privately-held company shares will close a transaction only if 100% share ownership is delivered. In such circumstances, the controlling shareholder will not want to have a transaction thwarted by the obstruction of one or more minority shareholders. Therefore, a Shareholder's Agreement often provides that all minority shareholders must tender their shares on the same terms and conditions as a specified majority of shareholders are prepared to do.

At the same time, a Shareholder's Agreement should ensure a minority shareholder the opportunity to sell into an offer at the same price, and on the same terms and conditions as accepted by the majority. These so-called 'coattail' (or 'tagalong') provisions protect the liquidity of a minority shareholder's interest in the event that a third party offer to acquire control of the company is received.

Restrictions on Share Transfer

In certain Shareholder's Agreements (or Articles of Incorporation), there are restrictions on the transfer of shares. Typically such provisions make reference to a requirement that approval be obtained from the Board of Directors or remaining shareholders of the company and that such approval is not to be unreasonably withheld.

In a notional market context, the 'open and unrestricted market' component of the definition of fair market value requires any restrictions on transfer contained in the Articles to be temporarily set aside, but nonetheless considered by an acquirer when price is finally determined. In an open market transaction, where Directors of a privately-held company refuse to approve the transfer of a minority shareholding, it still may be possible to transfer beneficial ownership pursuant to the establishment of a 'trust' arrangement between the vendor and the purchaser. However, as a practical matter this generally would prove to be an unwieldy relationship and hence is unlikely to occur.

As a general rule, in a notional market context share transfer restrictions are perceived to have a negative influence on the value of a specific minority shareholding. In actual transactions involving minority shareholdings, they tend to be of little practical consequence, since share transfers are approved as a condition of such transactions. Nonetheless, restriction on transfer can have a significant impact on the liquidity of a particular equity interest, and hence its value — see Chapter 13.

Value Terms in Shareholder's Agreements

The importance and implications of failing to adequately define value terms in Shareholder's Agreements sometimes are misunderstood by those who advise on them and draft them, and by those who execute them. For example, Shareholder's Agreements often state that an auditor or some other predetermined person is to determine the fair market value of a given shareholding interest in a closely-held company, but then fail to clearly define what is meant by 'fair market value' (i.e. intrinsic value, open market value or some other defined value). Accordingly, in such circumstances fair market value might be taken to mean either stand-alone value, or an amount that includes an open market net economic value-added component. Further, stand-alone value may be determined either on an internally financed or an externally financed basis, or as a pro-rata portion of en bloc value or otherwise.

The valuation provisions of Shareholder's Agreements sometimes refer to 'book value', 'net book value', or 'adjusted net book value'. These terms have generally accepted meanings. The use of such terms in Shareholder's Agreements may or may not satisfy the intent of the parties to such an agreement.

Although not an exhaustive list, the definition of value in a Shareholder's Agreement should clearly address whether:

- a minority interest should be subjected to a discount from ratable value (i.e. a 'minority discount') if found to be applicable, and if so, whether the discount should be predetermined or subject to interpretation at the time of a transaction;
- special interest purchasers are to be considered in determining en bloc value or whether the shares are to be valued on an intrinsic (or 'stand-alone') basis;
- the transaction is assumed to be financed internally or externally. If internal, it may be helpful to specify how the impact on 'value' should be affected (by a stated discount from pro-rata value for example) in light of the business having to forego operating expenditures or growth opportunities in order to finance the acquisition of the departing shareholder's interest;
- personal goodwill, where it exists, should form part of en bloc value and in what circumstances it should be considered;

- a selling shareholder is eligible to receive a portion of a premium for the subsequent sale of the shares or assets of the company en bloc and if so, to what extent and over what time period; and
- to what extent, in the event of the death of a shareholder, the proceeds from a corporate owned life insurance policy should be considered in the determination of value.

The Shareholder's Agreement also should address which basis of value and payment terms are applicable given the event which triggered the need for a valuation.

In summary, is critical that the parties to a Shareholder's Agreement ensure that the value terms adopted in the agreement are carefully defined, and that the definition(s) adopted reflect their collective intent in this regard. In the event that relevant value terms are not addressed in the Shareholder's Agreement, they are left to interpretation at the time a valuation is required. Depending on the situation, it may be beneficial for the valuer to request from the shareholders (separately, if each shareholder has a different bias with respect to the requested value) their reasoning as to which course of action they feel the valuer should take with respect to each of the aforementioned issues. In some cases, it may be appropriate to obtain a legal opinion as to the meaning of the wording in the agreement. The valuer can then consider all facts provided and subsequently make an informed decision.

Alternative Ways to Derive 'Value' Pursuant to Shareholder's Agreements

The determination of transaction pricing among shareholders may be dealt with in various ways. Shareholder's Agreements sometimes specify how fair market value (or some other definition of value) is to be determined. The most common are:

- value agreed annually by the shareholders;
- value agreed by formula;
- value determined by independent expert;
- value agreed by mediator or arbitrator; and
- a combination of the latter two where there is disagreement among experts.

Value Agreed Annually by the Shareholders

As a general rule, the best approach is for the shareholders periodically to agree upon the value (or values) of specific shareholdings for various purposes, and to stipulate it (or them) in writing. Where this is done, it is important that the values be updated on a regular basis, usually annually following receipt of year end financial statements. In practice, however, the following difficulties often are encountered with this approach:

- shareholders lack knowledge as to the value options available to them and/or lack understanding of their importance;
- getting agreement as to annual value among all shareholders, or the requisite majority if unanimity is not required;
- lack of discipline and diligence to systematically update values, such that the value becomes stale-dated; and
- shareholders may be biased where they anticipate that a transaction will be consummated in the near term at the determined value.

These difficulties may be overcome by providing for an annual independent valuation as the basis for transactions in the ensuing year. In practice, this approach is best suited to situations where there is significant value, the company has many shareholders, and frequent or periodic transactions are likely to occur.

Value Determined by Formula

In lieu of an annual value determination, shareholders sometimes set out a valuation formula in the Shareholder's Agreement. Formulas often are based on some predetermined multiple of historical accounting earnings or book value. While having the advantage of being comparatively simple once established, the use of predetermined formulas may result in inequities for at least the following reasons:

- given the various 'values' that shareholders may establish, or that may be required pursuant to different 'events' contemplated in the agreement, any single formula will of necessity result in a 'compromise' value that will satisfy the various required 'values' each to a greater or lesser degree at a given point in time;
- formulae, even if they do result in a reasonable 'value' at a particular point in time to satisfy a particular purpose, often will not yield equitable results over a lengthy period. This occurs because value is influenced by factors

both internal to and external to the business, including a (typically) constantly changing financial ability on the part of both the corporation and its shareholders; and
- the formula approach may yield a price different than any objective value calculation, perhaps resulting in severe income tax or other implications.

Having said that, in some circumstances (for example where employees are shareholders pursuant to an employee stock option plan) a well-conceived formula value may be the best overall basis of value determination for Shareholder's Agreement purposes given its ease of understanding and predictability.

Value Determined by Independent Expert

A Shareholder's Agreement sometimes will specify that an independent valuer is to determine the value of the company en bloc or an interest therein, either periodically or where a triggering event occurs. Parties to a Shareholder's Agreement should be satisfied that the independent expert selected is knowledgeable about the nature of the business and that he or she will consider all relevant factors in determining value. Shareholder's Agreements sometimes contain a list of valuation firms or individuals from which the shareholders can agree to select when required. The company's auditors often are precluded from acting in the role of independent valuation experts due to the real or perceived conflicts of interest they may have with one or more of the shareholders.

Often it is beneficial for the independent valuation expert to produce a draft report and to allow the shareholders to respond to the draft in terms of factual errors or omissions prior to finalizing the value conclusion. In some cases, an independent valuer produces a draft report that excludes the value conclusion so that the parties commenting on the draft focus on ensuring the accuracy and completeness of all relevant facts contained in the report rather than to become overly 'distracted' and adversarial by the draft conclusion. Once the independent valuer is satisfied that all of the relevant factors have been duly accounted for, he or she then formulates a value conclusion.

Value Determined by Mediation or Arbitration

Another alternative to the determination of value pursuant to a Shareholder's Agreement is to provide for binding or non-binding mediation or arbitration. Depending upon the availability of appeal from such a value determination, this can be an expensive process. Further, it often is difficult for the different parties to come to a consensus regarding which valuer to use, although in many cases the valuation firm or list of acceptable firms is set out in the Shareholder's Agreement.

Binding or non-binding mediation or arbitration can be established such that:

- each party retains an expert who provides their respective opinions in a Court-like environment to a single arbitrator or arbitration panel which reaches its own view based on the information presented to it; or
- each party retains an expert who provides their respective opinions to a single arbitrator or arbitration panel which, based on the information presented to it, selects one of the views presented to it without alteration (a so-called 'baseball arbitration').

In some cases, an arbitrator's decision may be quashed where it can be shown that he or she did not consider all of the relevant facts.

Summary

A minority shareholder generally is defined as one that owns 50% or less of the outstanding voting shares of a company, and absent a Shareholder's Agreement or other agreement may have little influence on how the company is run. Accordingly, a discount from pro-rata en bloc value may be applied in the valuation of a minority interest. However, minority shareholders are afforded certain statutory rights that normally preclude the controlling shareholder from treating them unfairly.

Shareholders in companies frequently enter into enforceable Shareholder's Agreements that set out their privileges, protections, and obligations as shareholders, and define what is to occur when certain triggering events take place. Shareholder's Agreements also may assist in protecting the liquidity of minority shareholders in particular. When drafting Shareholder's Agreements, it is important to ensure that the value terms adopted therein are carefully defined so as to avoid issues that arise due to differences in interpretation when various provisions calling for a determination of value are activated.

Chapter 13
Discounts for Non-Control and Illiquidity

Introduction

The determination of the en bloc value of a business inherently presumes the ability to both control the business pursuant to the election of the majority of the Board of Directors, and to be unrestricted in its disposition. Where a given shareholding is viewed in isolation and either the unilateral ability of the shareholder to:

- control absolutely the strategy and operations of a business on one hand; or
- deliver the shareholding free and clear of all encumbrances on the other

is fettered, a discount from a pro-rata portion of en bloc value to reflect one or both of these things may be warranted. A discount taken to account for an inability to unilaterally:

- control absolutely the strategy and operations of a business sometimes is referred to as a 'discount for non-control'; and
- deliver the investment free and clear of all encumbrances sometimes is referred to as a 'discount for illiquidity'.

In theory and practice, an individual shareholder who does not have the ability to control the strategy and operations of a business and to dictate the timing of the liquidity of the shareholding pursuant to a Shareholder's Agreement or otherwise, may face a discount from pro-rata per share value. In a notional market context, any discount taken from ratable value almost always must be subjectively determined. In the case of an open market price it must be established through negotiation.

Discounts for non-control and illiquidity in the context of individual shareholdings are relative concepts. Their quantification is dependent in the first instance on how en bloc value was determined. The factors that give rise to each of these discounts tend to be co-mingled, such that as a rule they are combined into one 'discount' amount or percentage (a 'minority discount' when referring to a minority shareholding, which typically is where such discounts apply). Having said that, discounts for non-control and illiquidity are distinct concepts. Control is a function of the relationship between the shareholders of a company, whereas liquidity is a function of external demand for a particular shareholding having regard to all of its attributes, including its degree of control over the business and the en bloc disposition of its outstanding shares.

Over the years, many studies have been undertaken regarding the quantification of discounts for non-control and illiquidity (and minority discounts). These studies have found a significant range (in percentage terms) in discounts applied by the Courts[1]. This indicates that each case must be assessed on its own facts and merits, with imposition of minority discounts being dependent on the relevant time specific facts. It is not possible to state unequivocally that minority shareholdings are consistently bought and sold at discounts from pro rata value. It also is not possible to state unequivocally that discounts where applied always fall in a range of X% to Y%.

This Chapter begins by distinguishing between the various types of discounts. This is followed by a discussion of the factors that normally should be taken into account when quantifying them.

Types of Discounts

Discounts for Non-Control and Discounts for Illiquidity

Conceptually, discounts for non-control relate to restrictions imposed by law, contract or circumstance on a shareholder that influence the risk and return parameters of his or her investment. Discounts for illiquidity relate to the inability of a shareholder to deliver to a purchaser an investment that is immediately liquid.

Discounts for non-control and illiquidity are not 'all or nothing' concepts. Rather, each moves along the following fact and circumstance dictated continuum:

FIGURE 13.1

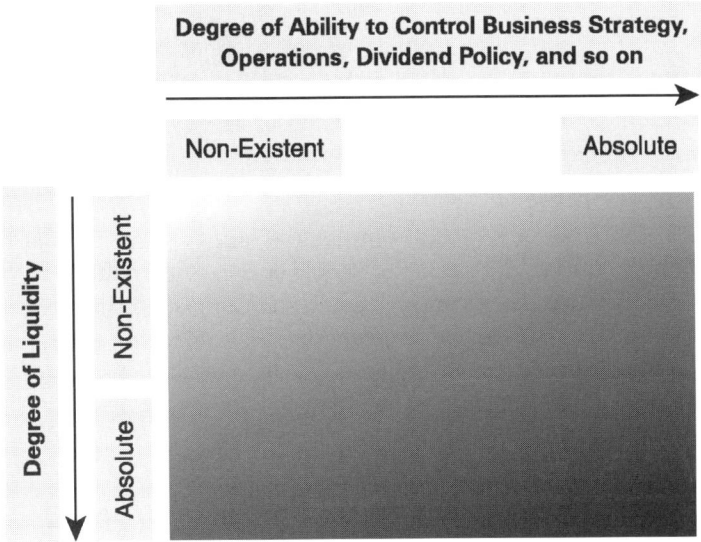

At the Absolute:

- control means the ability to do all those things normally associated with ownership. For example, the ownership of 100% of the common shares of a company typically allows the owner a free hand in strategizing and operating it, establishing a dividend policy, selling it, or liquidating it (i.e. 'absolute control'); and
- liquidity means the ability to readily convert an asset into known cash proceeds at any point in time, which may be, and likely in most cases is, influenced by the ability to control.

At the Non-Existent:

- from a control standpoint, the shareholder with 'no' control has virtually no influence on the strategic direction of the company, its operations, dividend payments, and so on, and is severely restricted in his or her ability to readily divest of his or her interest pursuant to restrictions imposed by the circumstances or the other shareholders; and
- from a liquidity standpoint the number of interested purchasers is expected to be few, or possibly none at all which may be, and likely is in most cases, influenced by an inability to control.

Although the concepts of a discount for non-control and discount for illiquidity are distinct, the line between them is blurred. Indeed, the factors giving rise to each frequently are common to each. The sale of a particular shareholding at an attractive price (except where a company is sold in bloc) is contingent upon finding another party willing to be subjected to the impediments of non-control. Therefore, separation of a discount for non-control and a discount for shareholding specific illiquidity arguably is somewhat circular.

In circumstances where both discounts are warranted and are thought to be separately quantifiable, the calculation should be done on a multiplicative and not an additive basis. For example, assume that Company X has an en bloc fair market value of $10 million. If circumstances dictated that a 25% minority shareholder should be subjected to a 20% discount for non-control and a 30% discount for illiquidity, the fair market value of the minority shareholder's interest would be $1.4 million. That is:

$10 million en bloc value $\times$ 25% ownership interest $\times$
$(1-20\%$ discount for non-control$) \times (1-30\%$ discount for illiquidity$)$.

Basis of En Bloc Value Determination

Discounts for non-control and illiquidity cannot be meaningfully quantified without first understanding the basis by which en bloc value was determined. In a notional market context, the en bloc value of a business can be determined based on different underlying assumptions. The principal assumptions are those surrounding:

- how the rates of return that were adopted when developing en bloc value were established. In this regard, where:
  - public market data is adopted as primary inputs to rate of return determination without adjustment, the resultant rate of return inherently may reflect an assumption of immediate liquidity or a greater degree of liquidity than is presumed by an acquirer who purchases all of the outstanding shares or net assets of a business;
  - the rate of return adopted already incorporates an element of illiquidity, this should be considered when applying a further discount for illiquidity at the shareholder level. For example, the established 'hurdle rates' used by corporate acquirers in assessing acquisition candidates normally presumes a long-term investment — see Chapter 8. Where this is the case, to apply a further discount for illiquidity of a particular shareholding may imply a 'double discount';

- whether the business was valued on a stand-alone basis or whether purchaser-perceived net economic value added has been quantified. In this regard:
  - unless the business operates in an industry where a value-added market clearly is evident, a notional market 'en bloc' value determination often may exclude value-added considerations. Where stand-alone value is adopted as the base of 'en bloc' value and purchasers who perceive post-acquisition net economic value-added exist at the date of valuation, as a practical matter to discount from stand-alone value may result in a 'double discount'. Mitigating against the perception of a 'double discount' is the inability of a minority shareholder, in isolation, to realize the synergistic value that might crystallize only in an en bloc sale of the shares of the business, and
  - where purchaser-perceived net economic value added is reflected in en bloc value, consideration must be given to the likely inability of a minority shareholder to extract a pro-rata portion of that value given the minority shareholder's inability to individually consummate an en bloc open market transaction;
- the assumptions regarding the capital structure (i.e. financial risk) of a business. A minority shareholder normally is unable to meaningfully influence the capital structure of the business. To the extent that 'en bloc' value was determined based on the assumption of an 'appropriate' capital structure, a discount from pro-rata value may be warranted where the company's actual capital structure is greater than or less than that amount; and
- the basis by which a notional transaction is assumed to be financed. That is, where stand-alone value has been determined, whether it has been determined on the basis of external or internal funding sources. Where en bloc value has been determined for a minority shareholding pursuant to the assumption of an internally financed transaction, the elements of non-control and illiquidity may be fully reflected in that minority interest value, and to apply further discounts might result in double-counting. As discussed in Chapter 2, an internally financed transaction might result in a lower en bloc value where operating or growth expenditures are foregone in favour of payments to a departing shareholder.

The quantification of discounts for non-control and illiquidity also may be dependent on the definition of value, be it fair market value, fair value, value to owner or price and so on. As noted in Chapter 2, fair value normally is defined as being the ratable portion of en bloc fair market value without the application of a minority discount.

In the end, the conclusion as to the value of a particular business interest net of discounts for non-control and illiquidity, where applicable, must be plausible in light of the specific prevailing facts and circumstances.

Discounts for Non-Control

When a business is valued en bloc, the presumption is made that a single owner of that business has the ability to directly influence the risk-reward relationship of his or her investment pursuant to:

- the election the Board of Directors which provides the ability to control the:
  - near term and long term business strategy,
  - level of business risk and financial risk assumed, and
  - return on investment pursuant to dividend payments or some other form of remuneration; and
- the ability to choose to discontinue his or her investment at any time pursuant to:
  - the en bloc sale of the business to a third party,
  - the sale of a portion of the business, either directly (pursuant to the sale of a division or subsidiary) or pursuant to an initial primary or combined primary and secondary public offering, or
  - the liquidation of the business, and distribution of the net proceeds.

Control in this context does not presume that the business interest is not exposed to risk, but that the controlling shareholder can, within the constraints of normal business practices (e.g. creditors rights, governmental legislation, and so on) unilaterally modify the risk-reward relationship of the business.

Importantly, the ability to divest of the business interest does not presume that a market for the acquisition of that business interest exists. Rather it refers to circumstances where there are no internal restrictions on the business owner from choosing the timing and nature (i.e. shares or assets, form of consideration, and so on) of the sale. As discussed subsequently, whether or not a market for the business interest exists relates to the separate issue of comparative liquidity.

Where a shareholder owns 100% of all the equity rights of a company, it is presumed that he or she enjoys absolute control. Where an equity interest constitutes less than 100% ownership of the voting shares in a business, a discount may be appropriate in recognition of impediments on control. Discounts for non-control (where applicable) typically are associated with minority interests. As discussed in Chapter 12, a minority shareholding is defined in general terms as any shareholding in either a publicly-held or privately-held company that is not a de jure, or de facto, control shareholding. A minority shareholder is not in a position to individually control business strategy, operations and financial risk, or the quantum or timing of dividends or other distributions.

In the absence of an agreement specifying otherwise, whether or not a discount for non-control should be applied pursuant to the inability of a shareholder to unilaterally control the company must be assessed in light of the degree of influence a shareholder enjoys relative to other shareholders in the company.

In some circumstances, a discount for non-control for a majority shareholder might be appropriate. For example, a majority shareholder with 51% of the voting shares of a company cannot unilaterally pass a special resolution requiring a two-thirds majority. Such a restriction may impair the controlling shareholder's ability to control business risk and financial risk, and to liquidate or sell the business en bloc. Where this is accompanied by restrictions on the ability to sell the majority interest pursuant to a Shareholder's Agreement or other contractual arrangement, a discount for non-control may be appropriate.

Finally, consideration should be afforded to circumstances where other outstanding securities (preferred shares, warrants, convertible debentures, and so on) might erode the level of control based on some future events or in certain circumstances (such as voting rights accruing to shares that normally are non-voting). Prevailing Shareholder's Agreements, Articles of Incorporation, By-laws and other agreements pertaining to any and all equity interests in the company and relevant corporate law provisions should be considered.

Quantifying Discounts for Non-Control

Minority Interests

The determination of minority interest value, which generally is a highly subjective undertaking, is required in a number of different circumstances including:

- notional market circumstances where an actual negotiated transaction does not occur. Examples include minority shareholding values in privately held companies determined for estate planning purposes, shareholder dispute purposes, and for income tax purposes such as deemed realizations. Such value determinations infrequently are tested by near-term subsequent actual sales;

- notional market circumstances where the value of minority shareholdings is determined by the Courts. For example, judicial determinations of fair value for purposes of dissenting shareholder appraisal remedies or oppression remedies fall into this category. A Family Law dispute brought before the Courts where the value of privately-held company shareholdings is at issue is similar. In these circumstances, the litigation process generally promotes a detailed discussion of the issues that influence the value of minority shareholdings. Accordingly, prior jurisprudence referable to the value of minority shareholdings tends to influence notional market value determinations;

- circumstances where actual transactions occur following negotiation or pursuant to dispute resolution, but where a true open market test of value is not made. Such transactions arise between privately-held company shareholders who are acting at arm's length, and in Family Law disputes; and

- transactions where, following open market negotiation, minority shareholdings in privately-held companies are sold to (generally) previously unassociated parties. Usually this occurs in circumstances where new capital is injected into treasury pursuant to a primary offering, and in arm's length sales of existing minority shareholdings (i.e. transactions pursuant to secondary offerings).

While there are general factors commonly considered, the value of a specific minority interest in the context of an actual transaction depends upon the time specific relevant facts and relative negotiating strengths of the parties to the transaction. In contrast, the valuation of minority shareholdings in a notional market context usually is based on a combination of fact and theory. In matters that are specifically income tax related, notional market values also are influenced by the published policies and the practices of the Canada Customs and Revenue Agency.

The quantification of a discount for non-control should be made having regard to:

- the provisions contained in a Shareholder's Agreement, where one exists. Relevant provisions influencing control might also be found in a company's Articles of Incorporation, By-laws, or other agreements; and

- where a Shareholder's Agreement (or other documentation with relevant provisions) does not exist, the specific circumstances surrounding the relationship among the shareholders that impact the minority shareholder's degree of influence in the affairs of the business.

Shareholder's Agreements

Where a Shareholder's Agreement exists, the specific provisions contained therein can have a significant impact on the quantum of discount, if any, for both non-control and illiquidity. Shareholder's Agreements that are Unanimous Shareholder's Agreements are distinguishable in that Unanimous Shareholder's Agreements override (to the extent allowed by corporate statutes) Corporate By-laws and Governance documents, whereas Shareholder's Agreements that are not Unanimous Shareholder's Agreements do not – see Chapter 12.

In some cases, a Shareholder's Agreement will specify that a majority shareholder is to receive a ratable portion of en bloc value, or stipulate the quantum of discount (if any) to be applied to minority shareholdings. Further, where a Shareholder's Agreement specifies no minority discount, that may only apply in circumstances of certain specified triggering events.

By definition, a minority shareholder does not have de jure or de facto control, and hence cannot elect a majority of the Board of Directors. However, the ability to exercise some degree of influence on the company as a whole may be provided for in a Shareholder's Agreement. For example, a Shareholder's Agreement might allow the minority shareholder(s) the ability to exercise some influence over the direction of the business pursuant to the requirement for shareholder approval for certain significant corporate decisions, or by way of representation on the company's Board of Directors. Accordingly, where a Shareholder's Agreement exists, a minority shareholder might enjoy elements of 'negative control' pursuant to his or her ability to block other shareholders from making certain changes to the business that are undesirable from the minority shareholder's perspective. Where such provisions exist, it is important that they be carefully scrutinized to assess in what circumstances that influence can be brought to bear and the degree of influence that accrues to individual shareholders.

Shareholder's Agreements (and Articles of Incorporation) often contain provisions regarding restrictions on the transfer of shares. Such restrictions might include:

- the requirement for approval from other shareholders or the Board of Directors; or

- a right(s) of first refusal.

Restrictions on transfer often impair the ability of the shareholder to control the risk-reward parameters of his or her investment because he or she cannot freely choose to divest of that business interest. As a result, in the absence of the ability to control the risk and return of the corporation itself (which control is rare for a minority shareholder), a discount for non-control may be warranted. Again, the restrictions on transfer discussed in this context relate to control (i.e. the ability to sell at will) and not liquidity (i.e. the likely number of interested purchasers and timing of sale). Whether or not a market exists for a particular minority shareholding is a separate issue. In many cases, restrictions on transfer also impair the liquidity of a business interest and, as discussed below, a separate discount for illiquidity may be required.

When assessing the impact of a Shareholder's Agreement on the value of a minority shareholding, it is important to determine whether or not a new shareholder would be subject to the existing agreement. Where this is not the case (which would be rare), and an external transaction is assumed, the provisions contained in the Shareholder's Agreement may not be applicable, and that factor should be considered in the valuation.

Where No Shareholder's Agreement Exists

Where no Shareholder's Agreement exists, in quantifying a discount for non-control, (and a discount for illiquidity – as subsequently discussed) consideration must be given to the fact and time-specific relationship among the shareholders. The relevant factors that should be considered in such circumstances include:

- the applicable corporations and securities legislation, jurisprudence and trends related thereto;
- the prevailing relationships between and among the shareholders;
- the size of the particular business interest, both in absolute and relative terms;
- the shareholder's level of involvement in the business;
- the historic and prospective dividend yield on the investment; and
- whether the shareholding has, or may have, 'nuisance value'.

Corporations Legislation and Jurisprudence

As discussed in Chapter 12, at any point in time a minority shareholder has legal entitlements established by Federal and Provincial Corporations Acts, and in jurisprudence relating to shareholder interests. It is important to be cognizant of the jurisdiction in which a corporation was formed and the prevailing rights pursuant to the governing legislation. From a valuation standpoint, the impact of these rights generally is to reduce the discounts for non-control and shareholding specific illiquidity from what they otherwise might have been. However, such rights in and of themselves normally do not eliminate altogether the appropriateness of a discount in a given fact situation.

Shareholder Relationships

Personal and familial relationships between and among shareholders and shareholder groups who collectively control may affect the degree of influence and liquidity of their respective shareholdings, and therefore may affect the value of same at a particular point in time. Barring disputes between and among them, two or more shareholders often act in concert to exercise control over the economic direction and the liquidity of their investment. However, because interpersonal relationships can change over time, absent a written Shareholder's Agreement there is no assurance if so-called 'group' or 'family' control in fact exists at a given point in time that it will continue indefinitely. Because value is specific point in time related, the value of a minority interest in relation to en bloc value can be influenced by changes in relationships – also see commentary under heading 'the Position of the Canada Customs and Revenue Agency' in this Chapter.

Where two shareholders of a company are married to each other, their relationship as shareholders generally is a direct reflection of their marital situation. A valuation issue that often arises in Family Law matters has to do with the determination of the value of a minority shareholding interest in a corporation controlled by the shareholder's estranged spouse. Where both spouses retain their shareholding interests following a division of assets and no Shareholder's Agreement exists, the minority may have to resort to statutory oppression remedies in the event of unfair treatment by the majority.

Size of Shareholding

The absolute size of a shareholding and its size relative to other shareholdings in the company are important considerations when assessing both control and shareholding specific illiquidity. The relevant incorporating statutes establish four significant shareholding percentage levels within a particular class of shares:

- 10% or less. As noted in Chapter 12, in most jurisdictions minority interests representing 10% or less of the issued shares of a particular class are subject to compulsory acquisition provisions[2]. These provisions entitle a purchaser, pursuant to a takeover bid, of at least 90% of that class of shares which it did not previously own to acquire the remaining shares of the class from those shareholders who did not tender at a price equal to that paid to the other shareholder(s). While the shareholder owning 10% or less of the class of shares cannot prevent a takeover, the opportunity to receive a pro rata portion of en bloc value may ease any disadvantage this might create;
- greater than 10% and up to 33 1/3% (25% in some jurisdictions[3]). A minority shareholder who is in a position to prevent the sale of his or her shares into a takeover bid (i.e. greater than 10% of the class) can prevent a takeover where a prospective purchaser makes the acquisition of 100% a condition of its offer. As a result, that shareholder may positively influence the value of his or her shareholding at the time of the bid. However, the restrictions and limitations attaching to a minority shareholding can be severe where it represents 33 1/3% or less (25% or less in some jurisdictions) of the issued shares entitled to vote on a specific special resolution. In such circumstances the minority shareholder has no power to prevent the passing of such special resolution. Subject to statutory and common law limitations, a controlling shareholder owning 66 2/3% or more of the voting shares (75% or more in some jurisdictions) may amend the Articles of Incorporation virtually at will. However, this disadvantage to a minority shareholder is tempered in most jurisdictions by dissent rights and related appraisal remedies available to minority shareholders. It is also tempered by voting privileges which accrue to all classes of shares directly affected by any such changes, regardless of whether they ordinarily are entitled to vote;
- greater than 33 1/3% (25% in some jurisdictions) and up to 50%. A minority shareholder who can unilaterally prevent the passing of special resolutions arguably is less disadvantaged than one who cannot. Accordingly, the value of such a shareholding may be positively influenced by this compared to where such influence did not exist; and
- 50%. Where a shareholder owns a 50% voting interest, he or she is a minority shareholder from a legal standpoint, but may have effective control. This will largely depend upon the size and interrelationship of the other shareholdings in the company. Where two shareholders each own 50%,

typically both are regarded as minority shareholders. However, in such circumstances the two shareholders often ensure each other's liquidity, although this is not always the case.

While the absolute size of a particular shareholding is important from the standpoint of statutory rights, the size of the shareholding in relative terms also has a significant impact on control and liquidity. For example, the appropriate quantum of discount(s) for a shareholder with a 33 1/3% interest could be significantly different in circumstances where the remaining shares were held by one other shareholder (with 66 2/3%) or by two other shareholders each holding a one third interest as well. In the former case, absent a Shareholder's Agreement, in theory (although generally not in practice) the minority shareholder essentially is subjected to the whims of the majority, and likely has little influence on the strategic direction of the company. Moreover, the market for a one third interest in circumstances where one individual owns the remaining two-thirds in theory likely is limited where no provision for liquidity exists. Conversely, where a company is owned by three equal shareholders, generally two of the three are required to make most significant business decisions. In theory, there is a natural market for any particular one-third interest since each of the other two shareholders likely would acquire his or her pro-rata share so as not to be disadvantaged.

Level of Shareholder Involvement

The value of a particular business interest might be affected by whether or not the shareholder in question is actively involved in the business. This might include circumstances where the shareholder is:

- a senior manager or Director of the corporation, and can influence the risk level of the corporation pursuant to business decisions under his or her control;
- another corporation, and there is a supplier-customer relationship or some other form of dependence (such as pursuant to a licensing or technology agreement); and
- also a key employee (possibly possessing personal and individual goodwill) and where a non-competition agreement is not in place. In that case, the shareholder might be able to manipulate the decisions of the majority pursuant to his or her threat of departing from the company.

Historic and Prospective Dividend Yield

A minority shareholder in a company generally cannot unilaterally dictate the quantum or timing of dividend payments or other shareholder distributions. In reality, dividend yield seldom plays a significant part in privately held company share valuation because the (typically) close ownership of a private company permits broad discretion in the distribution of corporate funds to the shareholders. The personal requirements and motives of the controlling shareholders, combined with income tax planning and proposed or contemplated changes to the income tax laws, frequently dictate the timing and amount of dividend payments. Notwithstanding, some privately held corporations have a history of regular dividend payments at rates approximating market returns, or a history of bonus payments pro-rata to participating shareholders at comparable levels. In the absence of a contractual commitment, a minority shareholder generally cannot ensure the continuation of such policies. Fact-specific circumstances will determine whether this has any effect on the value of a minority interest.

In public company share valuations, dividend continuity is more commonly a shareholder expectation. As a result, dividend yield often forms a significant consideration in the valuation of such interests.

Nuisance Value

The term 'nuisance' sometimes is used in reference to a situation where the existence of one or more minority shareholdings forms an obstacle to the strategies of the controlling interest. These strategies often relate to the disposition of said controlling interest. However, they may also affect the management of the business. Where minority shareholdings are viewed to be a 'nuisance' by the majority shareholder(s) at a point in time, they may be more valuable than they otherwise might be.

'Nuisance value' describes the incremental amount that a purchaser (often a controlling shareholder) would pay over what otherwise would be the value of a minority shareholding to remove the minority from ownership of the company. Where it exists, it is but one component of the value of the particular minority shareholding. Nuisance value typically results from facts and circumstances that arise at a particular point in time. For example, a controlling shareholder may be prepared to pay a 'nuisance value' price in order to remove a specific minority shareholder from future participation in the ownership of the company, either where:

- the minority shareholder is taking an absurd position. For example, a minority shareholder that misapplies or abuses the statutory remedies available to such shareholders can divert significant management time from the business and cause unnecessary expenses to be incurred. In such circumstances, it may be desirable to remove the minority shareholder from the company, even at a 'nuisance value' price;
- the minority interest is acting responsibly, but the continued ownership of his or her shareholding stands in the way of corporate reorganization or business changes contemplated by the controlling shareholder(s). The 'nuisance value' element arises from the special interests of the controlling shareholder(s) at the time. In some instances, it may also stem from conflicts in the personalities of the individual shareholders involved; or
- the minority shareholder is blocking the sale of the business pursuant to the purchaser's stipulation of 100% ownership.

Controlling Interests

The valuation of a controlling interest that is less than 100% of the voting shares of a business usually is determined as the ratable portion of en bloc value. As previously discussed, control generally is defined as the ability to directly influence the risk-reward parameters of an investment. Therefore, where the ability of a controlling shareholder to control the business is restricted, the issue arises as to whether or not there should be a discount from the pro-rata value of that controlling interest. A controlling shareholder's ability to unilaterally control the business might be impaired where:

- the controlling shareholder does not own a sufficient percentage to individually pass a special resolution, generally requiring a two-thirds majority (three-quarters in some jurisdictions). Special resolutions relate to fundamental changes in a business;
- decisions cannot be made unilaterally given the rights afforded to minority shareholders pursuant to legislation and jurisprudence — see Chapter 12;
- there are specific provisions in the Articles of Incorporation, By-laws or Shareholder's Agreement (where one exists) that impair the degree of control. In particular, the rights granted to minority shareholders in respect of:
  - a minimum percentage of votes (or unanimous agreement) being required for certain decisions,
  - the ability to block a sale of the controlling shareholder's interest either directly (pursuant to approval or acceptance) or by virtue of the absence of a mandatory sale provision in a Shareholder's Agreement that would

force the sale of 100% of the business to a prospective purchaser who would not execute a transaction in the absence of absolute ownership; and

- where the minority shareholding has nuisance value (as previously discussed), that could take away from the value of a controlling shareholder's interest otherwise determined.

As a practical matter, a discount for non-control from the pro rata value of a controlling interest seldom, if ever is applied. Even though minority shareholders are afforded certain rights pursuant to governing legislation, Shareholder's Agreements, and so on, these should not impair the control of the majority shareholder(s) acting reasonably. Further, in the case of a dissent and appraisal remedy, the Courts generally have recognized that a balance must be struck between the rights of the minority and those of the majority. Therefore, a discount for non-control likely would only be applied to a majority ownership position in the very unusual circumstances where control was restricted beyond the reasonable expectations of a prospective purchaser.

In addition, any discount for non-control in the context of a controlling interest must take into account that a majority shareholder might be viewed as benefiting from the fact that he or she enjoys a controlling position in a company without having to expend the financial resources to acquire 100% ownership. This sometimes is referred to as a 'premium for control', and is discussed below. In some cases, the benefit of obtaining control of a company without having to finance 100% of the price of the shares may offset any limitations of control that arise by virtue of the rights afforded to the remaining minority shareholders.

Premium for Control

The term 'premium for control' often is cited in transactions involving the takeover of publicly traded companies. Historical studies have suggested that when takeovers of companies whose shares are publicly traded occurs, average takeover prices often are in the order of 30% greater than the trading prices prior to a takeover announcement, although the range of premiums varies significantly[4]. So-called 'premiums for control' most often relate to the crystallization of purchaser-perceived post-acquisition net economic value added (i.e. synergies).

The quantification of minority discounts with respect to shareholdings in privately held companies sometimes is estimated based on the reciprocal of this so-called premium for control. That is, if a premium for control is taken on a 'rule of thumb' basis to be in the order of 40%, then the minority discount is taken to be approximately 29% (determined as: [1-1/(1 + 40%)]. However, quantification of a minority discount in this manner may lead to an inappropriate conclusion given that:

- importantly, where the shares of the acquired public company were actively traded prior to the bid on widely disseminated information, premiums to pre-bid market prices typically relate all or in part to purchaser perceived synergies;
- such a methodology presumes that daily trading prices of shares of publicly held companies incorporate a minority discount, which may be measured from a takeover price per share;
- where the shares of some publicly held companies are not widely traded, the 'premium' might reflect the elimination of a 'stock market' discount for illiquidity referable to that;
- when a public company is 'in play', competitive bidding for the acquisition sometimes occurs, which in turn may distort the calculated premium;
- public company trading prices in some cases may gravitate upward on speculation of a takeover announcement. This effectively reduces the calculated premium in percentage terms;
- the premium for control normally is based on an average of the premiums of open market transactions. However, the actual premiums paid vary significantly, and in some cases are even negative amounts. Further, published statistics summarizing the premiums over stock market prices paid in open market transactions may not be reflective of appropriate fact specific control premiums for reasons such as[5]:
  – negative premiums may not be considered, which inflates the computed average, and
  – the statistics include both cash transactions and non-cash transactions (e.g. share for share exchanges). The latter may include certain restrictions on behalf of the vendor and therefore may not be reflective of a cash equivalent price;
- importantly, studies of 'takeover premiums' are specific to point in time prices, and reflect only transactions that are completed, and not those considered but not pursued. In this regard, transactions normally are not pursued where economic analysis does not support the price that would have to be paid to consummate a successful takeover bid. Accordingly, the average 'takeover premium to market' statistics reflect only those transactions where takeovers are completed, and accordingly represent a skewed sample of the population of all transactions both contemplated and completed. Be-

cause information with respect to transactions that are contemplated but abandoned generally is not available, 'takeover premiums to market statistics' are incomplete and accordingly, likely are not as meaningful as they frequently are represented to be;
- takeovers of publicly traded companies occur at the price the purchaser believes it needs to offer to complete the transaction. That 'offer price' (on which the 'premium to market calculation' is based) may be less than the purchaser would have been prepared to pay based on its own internal analysis; and
- takeovers of publicly traded companies may reflect circumstances where the purchaser believes that the target company's shares are trading in the market at a 'bargain price'. As a result, quoted takeover 'premium to market statistics' likely are, on average, greater than they otherwise might be.

Therefore, where a minority discount is determined by taking the reciprocal of the 'rule of thumb' premium for control, the quantum of discount likewise would be distorted. It is important to take into account the specific facts of each situation when determining a minority discount. Furthermore, where practical, the segregation of that discount into its components of non-control and illiquidity (as discussed herein) may ultimately result in a more reasoned and supportable conclusion.

As discussed in the previous section, a 'premium for control' might be perceived to exist pursuant to the ability of the controlling shareholder to leverage the investment made by the minority shareholder. For example, a purchaser could acquire 51% of a business valued at $10 million en bloc and, pursuant to the ability to elect a majority of the Board of Directors, exercise control of that business. Therefore, a purchaser might pay more than the pro-rata value of that interest ($5.1 million) in light of the fact that the purchaser can achieve its objectives at a significantly reduced cost. However, any such premium attributed solely to the ability of a controlling shareholder to leverage off minority shareholdings must be conditioned by the legal and contractual fetters on control available to those minority shareholders — see previous discussion.

Discounts for Illiquidity

A discount for illiquidity (sometimes referred to as a 'marketability discount') is a reduction in the pro-rata portion of en bloc value attributable to an equity interest due to lack of an immediately available market in which it can be sold in the short term at a predictable price. It is the absence of an immediately available market for a particular shareholding that leads to a discount for illiquidity over and above that already reflected in the determination of en bloc value.

Liquidity may be defined as the ability to convert a non-cash asset into cash in a short period of time with relative certainty as to the net proceeds that will be received. In theory, a discount for illiquidity does not relate to the ability of the owner to choose whether or not to sell – which is an element of a discount for non-control. Rather, once the decision to sell has been made the discount for illiquidity pertains only to:

- the time required to consummate a transaction (viewed in terms of when cash or other consideration is received); and
- the uncertainty surrounding the net proceeds that ultimately will be received.

Stated another way, a business interest (or any asset for that matter) that is not readily marketable may experience some level of discount resulting from having to:

- reduce the agreed price from what might otherwise have been contemplated in order to attract prospective purchasers and to consummate a near term sale; or
- expose the business interest for sale in the open market for an unusually long period of time, thereby receiving lower proceeds in present value terms. Further, if it is necessary to expose a business interest for sale over an unusually long period of time, its value may fluctuate due to changes in the business itself, the industry, and prevailing economic and market factors. This in turn results in uncertainty as to the ultimate net proceeds. Although the quantum of net proceeds might be greater than anticipated, finance theory equates 'uncertainty' with risk.

Many of the factors that may give rise to a discount for non-control may also give rise to a discount for illiquidity. For example, absent provisions in a Shareholder's Agreement (or other agreement) to the contrary, a minority interest in a privately held company where there are restrictions on the sale of that interest often is subject to a discount for non-control. In addition, the market for business interests with restrictions on control usually is not as liquid as the market for business interests where no such restrictions exist. Therefore, either separate discounts for both non-control and illiquidity, or a combined discount to reflect both (i.e. a 'minority discount'), might be warranted. As previously noted, when both a discount for non-control and a discount for illiquidity are to be applied, and an attempt is made to quantify each of them separately, the calculation should be made on a multiplicative basis rather than on an additive basis.

Quantifying Discounts for Illiquidity

Overview

In theory, a discount for illiquidity is related to the time value of money and the risk of adverse events that negatively affect price occurring while waiting to consummate the sale of a business or interest therein. Whether to adopt, and if so quantify, a discount for illiquidity are both matters of judgement having regard to fact specific circumstances. Factors that normally should be considered in this regard include:

- whether a controlling interest or a minority interest is being valued. In the absence of a Shareholder's Agreement or other agreement which provides liquidity, for reasons of both non-control and comparative illiquidity a minority position in a closely held company generally is less marketable than is a controlling interest therein;
- general economic conditions. During good economic times, there generally is more disposable income available combined with a general increase in the level of merger and acquisition activity *across all industries*. As a general rule, a more favourable economic environment normally contributes to an increase in liquidity. However, in a private company context as a practical matter this generally would not be as important to the liquidity of a minority shareholding as it would be to the comparative liquidity of an en bloc or control shareholding;
- the level of merger and acquisition activity *within a given industry*. Certain industries go through periods of very active acquisition activity and consolidation. Where this is the case, corporate acquirers are more actively seeking investment opportunities and may provide a ready market, particularly for an en bloc or control shareholding. Again, in a private company context as a practical matter this generally would not be as important to the comparative liquidity of a minority shareholding;
- the size of the company in which the interest is held. Larger companies normally are more liquid simply as a result of the general interest in the market place and the likelihood of a larger number of competing bids. In addition, a larger company more likely has the financial resources to em-

ploy an intermediary to conduct an active search for prospective purchasers. Conversely, a small privately held company may not be of interest to many corporate acquirers who may view the costs involved in acquiring and integrating a small company as exceeding the benefits to be derived therefrom. Again, in a privately held company context this generally would not be as important to the liquidity of a minority shareholding as it would be to the liquidity of an en bloc or control shareholding;

- post-acquisition synergies. Where a company offers a potential purchaser significant post-acquisition net economic value added and strategic advantage by virtue of certain patents, territories covered, customer base, and so on, it more likely will be of interest to one or more corporate acquirers, thereby enhancing its marketability. While this generally would be relevant in a private company context to the valuation of an en bloc or control shareholding, unless a 'strategic purchaser' acquired a minority shareholding as part of a long term strategy to acquire control of, or all of the outstanding shares of, a private company, as a practical matter this generally would not be as important to the liquidity of a minority shareholding as it would be to the liquidity of an en bloc or control shareholding; and

- the shareholding structure of the company. As a general rule, where no one shareholding controls, and depending on the comparative size of the existing shareholdings, there may be greater liquidity attached to a particular minority shareholding than otherwise would be the case. Stated another way, purchasers of a minority interest in a privately held company may be less interested in consummating a transaction where one or more shareholders control the company as contrasted to circumstances where no one shareholder or defined group has a controlling interest.

Minority Interests

For most widely held publicly traded companies, there exists a ready market for normal sized trading lots, allowing a shareholder to convert his or her interest into cash at a known price very quickly (sometimes within minutes). Such securities therefore are not subject to a discount for illiquidity. Having said that, a discount for illiquidity for publicly held stocks might apply where the stock is thinly traded or where a disproportionately large trading block is being valued. The following discussion focuses on discounts for illiquidity pertaining to minority shareholdings in privately held companies.

When determining whether a discount for illiquidity is appropriate for a minority interest in a privately held company, and if so quantifying it, the following factors normally should be considered:

- the provisions of a Shareholder's Agreement, where one exists;
- whether an organized market for the shares exists;
- the relative degree of influence the shareholding has vis a vis the other existing shareholdings;
- the likelihood of a near term en bloc sale; and
- the likelihood of a statutory-related triggering event.

Again, when quantifying a discount for illiquidity, consideration must be given to the basis by which en bloc value was determined. Any illiquidity discount in respect of a specific minority shareholding should reflect only incremental illiquidity perceived appropriate for that shareholding over and above illiquidity that has been considered (typically in the discount or capitalization rate employed) in the determination of en bloc value — see Chapter 8.

Shareholder's Agreements

Shareholder's Agreements typically include provisions relating to both control and liquidity. The concept of a discount for non-control in the context of prevailing Shareholder's Agreements was discussed earlier in this Chapter. In theory, it may be appropriate to consider a discount for illiquidity that is incremental to a discount for 'non-control' where the latter is viewed in isolation. An incremental discount for illiquidity may relate to such things as:

- restrictions on transfer, such as the requirement for approval from the Board of Directors or other shareholders. In an open market context a minority shareholding with restrictions on transfer typically has a limited market from the prospective of both limitations on eligible buyers (e.g. competitors typically would be excluded purchasers) and the fact of the restrictions themselves. In a notional market context, even though such restrictions typically are considered momentarily to be lifted for the purpose of determining 'fair market value', the acquirer of the shares is assumed to be subject to them. Accordingly, where restrictions on share transfer exist they typically impair the liquidity of the business interest. For example, where the sale of the shares requires approval from the Board of Directors or other shareholders, there usually is a requirement that such approval not be unreasonably withheld. Having said that, a successful purchaser generally will be subjected to the same restrictions on transfer, in particular where the purchaser is required to execute the existing Shareholder's Agreement, which typically is the case. As a practical matter, a purchaser may discount the price from what they otherwise might have been willing to pay in recognition of the risk that restrictions on transfer may impose;

- existence or lack of a right of first refusal in a Shareholder's Agreement. Where there is no right of first refusal a minority shareholding typically is less liquid than it otherwise might be. Having said that, where there is a right of first refusal pursuant to which existing shareholders have the opportunity to match the price and terms offered by a third party (sometimes referred to as a 'hard' right of first refusal — see Chapter 12), the liquidity of the offering shareholder's shareholding often is impaired. This is because few purchasers are willing to invest the time and effort required to prepare an offer to purchase shares in circumstances where it likely will not be accepted. As a result, the number of prospective purchasers willing to do this typically is significantly reduced, thereby reducing the degree of liquidity. The impact on liquidity pursuant to a right of first refusal where the shares can be offered to third parties on the same terms as those offered to, but refused by, existing shareholders (i.e. a 'soft' right of first refusal) is not as severe, but still may have some impact;
- existence or lack of a 'coattail' (or 'tag-along') provision in a Shareholder's Agreement. A coattail provision is one that ensures that in the event of a takeover bid all shareholders are entitled to sell into the bid — see Chapter 12. Accordingly, at least in theory where a coattail provision exists any discount for illiquidity believed appropriate normally would be somewhat reduced from what it would be where such a provision did not exist; and
- existence or lack of a 'put option' provision in a Shareholder's Agreement. A Shareholder's Agreement may protect a minority shareholder pursuant to a put option. That is, where the shareholder has the right to sell his or her interest to the other shareholder(s) at a predetermined price, a price to be agreed upon, or a price independently determined. In such circumstances, the liquidity of that interest all or in part is protected pursuant to the fact that a 'put' market exists. In some cases, particularly where there are two equal shareholders, the Shareholder's Agreement incorporates a buy/sell or 'shotgun' clause – see Chapter 12. In both theory and practice, where the liquidity of a business interest is protected pursuant to a put option or buy/sell clause, no discount for illiquidity normally is applied. However, where a Shareholder's Agreement requires that a business interest be purchased by the other shareholders, the issue of internal vs. external financing should be addressed — see Chapter 2.

Organized Market

Although it occurs infrequently, in some privately held companies minority share transactions between employees or others follow a recognizable pattern.

Where such transactions occur, prices paid may be (but are not necessarily) a reliable indicator of minority share values, particularly where a given minority shareholding is of a size comparable to that normally traded.

Where similar sized minority shareholdings in the same company have been sold in the near term prior to the valuation date, careful analysis of such transactions should be made before relying on them. It is necessary to have full knowledge of the circumstances surrounding such transactions, including:

- the dates on which the transactions were negotiated, and the indicated en bloc value of the outstanding shares of the company at each of those dates and at the valuation date;
- the reasons why the transactions took place;
- the knowledge levels of the participants at the time of the transactions with respect to the business, its opportunities, ongoing or prospective negotiations with respect to an en bloc sale, and so on;
- the terms of any Shareholder's Agreement or other contracts which may have dictated the transaction prices;
- the payments terms; and
- whether there was any familial or business relationship between buyer and seller that influenced the price, terms or conditions of the transaction.

Size of the Ownership Interest

Where a Shareholder's Agreement does not exist, the factors previously discussed with respect to a possible discount for non-control related to the absolute and relative size of a minority shareholding also have an impact on liquidity. As previously discussed, specific statutory rights pertain to various sizes of shareholdings. Further, the relative size of a specific minority shareholding compared with other shareholdings is an important consideration. For example, all other things equal, a 30% minority interest typically is a more attractive investment if the remaining 70% is held by 7 shareholders each with 10%, rather than if the entire remaining 70% is held by one shareholder. In the former case, the 30% minority shareholder may enjoy de facto control. In the latter case, where no Shareholder's Agreement exists or depending on its terms where one does, and subject to the provisions of prevailing legislation, the minority shareholder typically is subject to the whims of the majority.

The Likelihood of an En Bloc Sale

A minority interest in a business may become highly liquid in the event that the entire business is sold. Because a minority shareholder is not in a position to dictate whether or not a sale takes place, consideration must be given both to where such influence lies, and to the likely timing of such an event. With respect to the latter, it is necessary to ascertain whether either the controlling shareholder or control group (if either exists) is considering the possibility of offering the company for sale. Where there is evidence of activity leading towards such a sale, in both a notional and open market context where a discount for illiquidity otherwise is thought appropriate, this would tend to reduce or eliminate any such discount.

In theory, absent other considerations the value of a minority shareholding increases as the probability of a near term en bloc sale of the outstanding shares increases. When assessing the likelihood and timing of an en bloc sale, consideration normally should be given to matters such as:

- the prevailing general economic conditions and market availability of funds;
- the prevailing conditions within the industry in which the company functions vis-a-vis evident purchaser perceived net economic value-added, completed open market transactions, trends in business consolidation, and so on;
- circumstances which might promote a sale. These can be external to the business, such as a growing inability to effectively compete against larger competitors, or internal to the business, such as a requirement for financing growth;
- whether the outstanding shares and net operating assets of the company have significantly increased in value during the time period they have been owned by the current owners;
- the length of time the current controlling shareholder(s) have owned their investment;
- the current profitability and future outlook for the business relative to other times during which the controlling shareholder(s) held its investment. In the absence of a distress situation, vendors of shares of both publicly traded and privately held companies generally time the sale of their interest so as to maximize the proceeds to be obtained. In the case of privately-held companies, the controlling shareholder(s) typically would be more likely to sell when the company is in an upward stage of its business cycle rather than during depressed economic times;

- where the controlling shareholder is an individual(s), the age(s) of the controlling shareholder(s), their health, their interest in selling in the near term, other relevant issues personal to them, and their other business interests; and
- whether the controlling shareholder(s) or the minority shareholder(s) as individuals contribute either personal or individual goodwill to the company, and the likelihood of such individuals continuing with the company for a period of time in order to transfer 'individual goodwill' accruing to them. In some instances, an en bloc sale may only be possible where a contractual management continuity commitment by individual(s) contributing individual goodwill forms an integral part of such sale. Where a minority shareholder contributes individual goodwill, this may enhance his or her negotiating position.

It also is important to consider whether or not a prospective purchaser is likely to be interested only in purchasing the company en bloc, or is prepared to purchase only a controlling interest. In this regard it normally is important to consider:

- the provisions of a prevailing Shareholder's Agreement, particularly to determine whether there are mandatory sale (or 'drag-along') rights that force a minority shareholder to sell his or her shares to a prospective purchaser on the same terms as a controlling shareholder;
- the size of the shareholding. As previously discussed, where a shareholder has more than 10% of the voting shares, absent compulsory sale provisions he or she can prevent the acquisition of 100% of the shares of the company; and
- whether or not the shares have nuisance value.

Liquidity may also be created pursuant to an initial primary or joint primary and secondary offering. However, the degree to which liquidity is created by such an event normally is dependent upon:

- the restrictions (if any) placed on trading the minority interest being valued. That is, where a shareholder is identified as an insider pursuant to securities legislation, some or all of those shares may be restricted from being freely traded for some period of time;
- whether a block discount or premium is applicable — see following discussion; and

- whether the shares, once publicly traded, are thinly traded or widely held. A large block of thinly traded shares may face a (possibly significant) discount for illiquidity.

Finally, where a single shareholder controls a company and there is no Shareholder's Agreement in place, at any given point in time the controlling shareholder's intent with respect to prospectively dealing with minority shareholdings is an important consideration. In such circumstances, the prior pattern of conduct of the controlling shareholder often will provide evidence as to how the minority shareholder(s) will be treated.

The Probability of a Statutory-Related Triggering Event

As a general rule, absent consideration of other factors that influence the liquidity of a minority shareholding, the greater the opportunity for a minority shareholder to successfully trigger a dissent or oppression remedy, the greater will be the likely liquidity of that shareholding. Accordingly, at a given point in time, the probability of a statutory-related triggering event that would give rise to either a dissent remedy or an oppression remedy should be considered when determining the fair market, or other value, of a minority shareholding.

Block Premiums and Discounts

Whether a discount for illiquidity is applicable for normal sized trading lots of publicly traded shares generally is a function of how actively those shares are traded. However, at issue is whether or not a discount for illiquidity should be applied where value must be determined for a block of shares larger than a normal sized trading lot. Rationale for such a discount might be based on the fact that:

- a large block of shares sometimes creates an imbalance in the normal supply/demand equation. Where supply is greater than demand, that typically has a downward influence on price and vice versa; and
- it may take some time for the market to fully absorb a large share block if it were sold off in traunches, if indeed the market could absorb it – which has implications with respect to the time value of money and the risk of adverse price fluctuations in the interim period.

Alternatively, in some cases a premium might accrue to a block of shares pursuant to advantages that block enjoys with respect to the ability to exercise a greater degree of influence than normal sized trading lots. Whether or not a premium is applicable and if so, the quantum thereof, generally should be derived in consideration of such factors as:

- the size (both in relative and absolute terms) of the block of shares;
- whether the shareholder enjoys Board representation and the impact of cumulative voting rights of the shares, if any;
- whether there is influence pursuant to a managerial or operational relationship;
- whether other blocks of shares are held by related persons; and
- whether and to what extent the daily trading prices are believed to incorporate a discount for non-control or a discount for illiquidity.

Controlling Interest

While the owner of control normally can decide the timing of offering that controlling interest for sale, it generally takes several months to actually sell the business. During that time the value of the controlling interest may fluctuate significantly. At the same time the controlling shareholder may benefit from ongoing income from the business during that interim period.

In practice, a discount for illiquidity rarely is applied to a controlling interest. In theory, such a discount would only be considered when:

- the controlling shareholder was a party to an agreement with the minority shareholder(s) that restricted the sale of the formers' shareholding;
- circumstances were such that the identifiable purchasers unlikely would consummate a transaction for less than 100% share ownership, and the controlling shareholder did not have a contractual ability to dictate the concurrent sale by the minorities; and
- one or more minority shareholdings has 'nuisance value', and it is believed that such 'nuisance value' detracts from the pro-rata value of the controlling interest.

The Position of the Canada Customs and Revenue Agency

While the relatively few Canadian Court Decisions dealing with minority interest values for income tax purposes limits analysis, those Decisions generally have held that in a notional market context minority shareholdings in privately held companies for income tax purposes have a fair market value somewhat lower than their ratable value.

When determining the value of minority shareholdings for Canadian income tax purposes, the Canada Customs and Revenue Agency's attitudes and practices must be considered. The Canada Customs and Revenue Agency imposes a general requirement of consistency over time in reviewing notional market values of privately held company shares. In most circumstances, share values for income tax purposes are determined to measure capital gains or losses. As a result, values at two different dates commonly are compared to measure the base on which any applicable income tax will be calculated. Unless there have been demonstrable changes between the two measurement dates, the Canada Customs and Revenue Agency generally will insist that comparable valuation principles be applied, particularly with respect to matters such as group or family control.

Historically, the Canada Customs and Revenue Agency has combined the concepts of non-control and illiquidity into an all-encompassing 'minority discount'. With respect to the quantum of minority discounts, in the absence of an enforceable Shareholder's Agreement over the past many years the Canada Customs and Revenue Agency has tended to accept discounts from ratable value as follows:

- where there are two 50% shareholdings, discounts in the range of 10% to 20%; and
- where a shareholding is less than 50% of the outstanding voting shares, discounts in the range of 20% to 40%.

Summary

A discount for non-control relates to the inability of a particular shareholder to elect a majority of the Board of Directors and through them to effectively influence the risk-return trade-off of a company, and to dictate the timing of an en bloc sale or liquidation of the business. A discount for illiquidity relates to the absence of a ready market in which to sell a particular shareholding in the near term at a relatively predictable price, which in particular is a function of the number of interested purchasers. Discounts for non-control and illiquidity, melded or not melded, typically are associated with minority shareholdings.

The quantification of discounts for non-control and illiquidity is a subjective exercise. The specific facts of each case must be carefully considered, including the terms of any existing Shareholder's Agreement and the basis by which en bloc value was determined. The factors giving rise to discounts for non-control and illiquidity overlap, and they often are combined into an all-inclusive 'minority discount'.

NOTES

1. See, for example, Minority Discounts Revisited, Joel Adelstein, Journal of Business Valuation, 1993.
2. All Canadian jurisdictions except Prince Edward Island have compulsory acquisition provisions.
3. Specifically, British Columbia and Nova Scotia. In addition, voting provisions are determined by the company's incorporating Charter in Prince Edward Island.
4. See, for example, statistics published in Mergerstat Review, published annually.
5. For further discussion on this topic, see Z. C. Mercer, A Brief Review of Control Premiums and Minority Interest Discounts, Journal of Business Valuation, 1997.

Chapter 14
Income Tax Considerations

> The discussion of the Canadian income tax issues in this Chapter is included only for information and general guidance. Because the specific facts of each business transaction may lead to different interpretations or applications of the Income Tax Act (Canada) (the 'Act'), no commercial transaction should be entered into without seeking advice of tax counsel.

Introduction

This Chapter briefly summarizes certain provisions of the Act as at January 1, 2000 that have application for business valuations. Changes to some of these provisions were proposed in the February 2000 and October 2000 Federal Budgets, as noted herein, although these changes had not been enacted at the time of writing. This Chapter is not intended to be an exhaustive discussion of the many specific detailed provisions of the Act which can affect calculations of value. Interested readers should consult income tax texts such as Hogg and Magee, *Principles of Canadian Income Tax Law*, Krishna, *The Fundamentals of Canadian Income Tax* or *The Canadian Master Tax Guide*.

Valuations often are done at a non-current date and the provisions of the Act in force at those dates should be considered. A detailed discussion of changes to income tax legislation over the past decades is beyond the scope of this book. Accordingly, readers are encouraged to obtain professional tax advice whenever a valuation is done at a non-current date.

This Chapter begins with a look at the importance of fair market value and where relevant tax provisions apply, followed by an overview of corporate restructuring mechanisms that sometimes are utilized in open market transactions and on occasion are a factor in a notional market valuation. The Chapter then addresses the taxation implications of assets vs. shares, including the relevant considerations of both purchaser and vendor. Finally, the Chapter examines specific taxation issues of privately held companies, anti-avoidance provisions and various other topics in taxation that sometimes arise in a business valuation or pricing exercise.

Taxation and Fair Market Value

The term 'fair market value', although undefined in the Act, is nevertheless used throughout the Act. Many types of transactions are deemed to occur on the basis of fair market value and generally there are adverse tax consequences if such transactions are completed on any basis other than at fair market value.

Section 69 of the Act prevents a taxpayer in certain circumstances from recognizing consideration in excess of fair market value paid to persons with whom the taxpayer is not dealing at arm's length, or from failing to account for the full value of anything disposed of in similar circumstances. The meaning of 'arm's-length' is defined in section 251 of the Act and the administrative position of the Canada Customs and Revenue Agency (the "Agency", formerly Revenue Canada) is discussed in the current version of Interpretation Bulletin IT-419. In general, individuals connected by blood relationship, marriage, or adoption do not deal with each other at arm's length, nor do a corporation and the individual who controls that corporation. If non-arm's length transactions are carried out on a basis that is other than at fair market value, there is potential for double taxation as will be demonstrated below.

There are numerous circumstances where a business valuation might be required for purposes of the Act (for example, on the death of a taxpayer or in a capital reorganization) and business people should be aware of the potential adverse consequences of effecting transactions on any basis other than at fair market value. Occasionally, even where a bona fide attempt is made to arrive at fair market value, the Agency may not agree with the conclusion, particularly where the parties are not acting at arm's length. Price adjustment clauses typically are inserted into agreements in such situations to protect the parties involved.

Acquisition of Property

Except in special circumstances, a taxpayer who acquires anything from a non-arm's length person for a consideration greater than the fair market value of the property received will be deemed to have acquired it at its fair market value (paragraph 69(1)(a)).

For example, assume that Individuals A and B do not deal with each other at arm's-length and that A owns 100 shares of Company X. On June 1, 1999, A sells these shares to B for cash consideration of $200,000, however, the fair market value of the shares at that date is $100,000. The cost to A of those shares (acquired in an arm's-length transaction in 1995) is $50,000.

In this situation, paragraph 69(1)(a) will deem B to have acquired the shares for $100,000 despite the fact that $200,000 was paid for them. If B subsequently sold these shares in an arm's length transaction for say, $150,000, B would have a capital gain of $50,000 ($150,000 less the deemed adjusted cost base of the shares of $100,000). Individual A in computing the capital gain on the sale will still have deemed proceeds equal to the actual proceeds of $200,000 resulting in a capital gain of $150,000 ($200,000 less the adjusted cost base of the shares of $50,000). Individual B has effectively lost $100,000 of cost base (which will be subject to tax). Double taxation results because the proceeds to the vendor are greater than the adjusted cost base of the purchaser and the difference between these two amounts is effectively taxed twice, in the hands of the vendor and in the hands of the purchaser.

Except in special circumstances, a taxpayer who has acquired property by way of gift, bequest, or inheritance is deemed to have acquired such property at its fair market value at the time of acquisition (paragraph 69(1)(c)). The donor is also deemed to have disposed of the property and to have received proceeds equal to fair market value. There is no distinction between arm's length and non-arm's lengths parties to transactions covered by this section of the Act. The provisions of section 69(1)(b) and (c) do not apply, however, to dispositions and acquisitions on death.

Disposition of Property

Except in special circumstances, a taxpayer who disposes of anything for no proceeds or for proceeds less than fair market value to a non-arm's length person, or by way of an inter vivos gift whether at arm's length or not, is deemed to have received proceeds equal to its fair market value (paragraph 69(1)(b)).

For example, assume that Individuals A and B do not deal with each other at arm's length and that A owns 100 shares of Company X. On June 1, 1999 A sells these shares to B for cash consideration of $75,000, however, the fair market value of the shares is $100,000. The cost to A of those shares (acquired in an arm's-length transaction in 1995) is $50,000.

In this situation, paragraph 69(1)(b) will deem A to have received proceeds of $100,000 despite the fact that only $75,000 was actually received, resulting in a capital gain of $50,000 ($100,000 less the deemed adjusted cost base of the shares of $50,000). Individual B will have a cost base for the shares of $75,000. Individual A will effectively have to pay tax on $25,000 of capital gains which was not received. Again double taxation will eventually result because the cost base of the shares to the purchaser is not equal to the deemed proceeds on the sale of the shares to the vendor.

Subsection 70(5) of the Act deems a person to have disposed of certain assets immediately before death including capital property, depreciable property, eligible capital property, resource property and land inventory. The fair market value of such assets must be determined in order to calculate any resulting tax liability. The jurisprudence suggests that the words 'immediately before his death' do not make it necessary to take into account the imminence of death in valuing assets though subsection 70(5.3) provides a specific exception. Subsection 73(1) provides rollovers which permit recognition of a gain (or loss) to be deferred in certain circumstances when property is transferred upon death of a taxpayer to a resident spouse or spouse trust.

Certain trusts, on the 21st anniversary of their creation, are deemed to have disposed of each capital property, resource property or land included in the inventory of a business of the trust for proceeds equal to their fair market value and to have immediately re-acquired them at a cost equal to that amount. This deemed disposition at fair market value is then repeated on each 21st anniversary of the first deemed disposition.

Each capital property owned by the taxpayer is deemed to be disposed of, immediately before death, for an amount equal to its fair market value and result in a capital gain or loss or in the case of depreciable property, recaptured capital cost allowance or a terminal loss, (subparagraph 70(5)(a)) to the deceased taxpayer. When the deemed proceeds of depreciable property exceed the capital cost to the taxpayer of the property, the transferee inherits the deceased taxpayer's capital cost and the excess is deemed to have been allowed to the transferee as capital cost allowance (paragraph 70(5)(c)). Special rules in subsections 13(2)(a) and 13(2)(d) apply where the depreciable property is a building which is disposed of together with the land on which it is located.

Subsection 69(5) deals with situations in which a corporation appropriates property on winding-up to shareholders. In such cases the corporation will be deemed to have sold the property immediately before the winding-up and to have received proceeds equal to the fair market value of the property at that time. There is no restriction on creating a loss as a result of the deemed disposition.

Eligible Capital Property

Where a taxpayer has died, and by reason of the death, another person has acquired a particular eligible capital property of the taxpayer, the taxpayer generally is deemed to have disposed of the eligible capital property immediately before death. The deceased taxpayer is deemed to have received proceeds of disposition and for such eligible capital property in respect of a business carried on by the deceased equal to four/thirds the cumulative eligible capital in respect of the business at that time. The effect of this rule is that the deemed proceeds will be offset by the deceased's undeducted eligible capital expenditures and no amount is added to the deceased's income in the year of death.

The person who has acquired the particular eligible capital property is deemed to have acquired a capital property at the time of the taxpayer's death at a cost equal to the deceased's deemed proceeds of disposition. If, however, the transferee continues to carry on the business previously carried on by the taxpayer, the transferee is deemed to have acquired an eligible capital property (rather than a capital property) and to have made an eligible capital expenditure at a cost equal to the proceeds. The net effect of these rules is that if the business is carried on by the transferee, the deceased's cumulative eligible capital in respect to the business will become the transferee's cumulative eligible capital in respect of the business and the transferee can continue to deduct such cumulative eligible capital on a declining balance basis of 7% annually. If the business is not carried on by the transferee, the transferee will have a capital property which cannot be written off on any basis and when the property is sold the beneficiary will have a capital gain or a capital loss. Subsection 24(2) of the Act provides special rules where an individual has ceased to carry on a business and thereafter the spouse, or a corporation controlled by, the deceased, has carried on the business.

Becoming or Ceasing to be a Resident of Canada

Section 128.1 of the Act contains rules which apply when a taxpayer becomes, or ceases to be, a resident of Canada. In general, they are designed to ensure that gains which accrue on property while a person (individual, trust or corporation) is a resident of Canada are subject to Canadian tax. A taxpayer who becomes a resident of Canada is therefore deemed to acquire each property at a cost equal to its fair market value at that time and, on ceasing to be a resident of Canada, is deemed to dispose of each property for proceeds equal to its fair market value at that time. Certain property is excluded from these dispositions and acquisitions including "taxable Canadian property" (that is, property, the gains on which, if it were held by a non-resident, would be taxable in Canada), inventory and eligible capital used in a business carried on in Canada and property in respect of which the taxpayer had elected not to realize the deemed disposition on an earlier immigration from Canada. In October of 1996, the Minister of Finance announced proposed changes to these rules which would substantially reduce the class of properties excluded from the deemed disposition. Draft legislation enacting these proposed changes, (which were to be effective as of October 2, 1996) was released in December, 1999 but has not yet been enacted.

Corporate Restructuring

Transfers to a Corporation

Subsection 85(1) provides for a tax-deferred rollover in respect of a transfer of certain types of property (including capital property, depreciable property, eligible capital property, and inventory) by a taxpayer to a taxable Canadian corporation. The rollover provisions of 85(1) often are used in a business valuation context where:

- an estate freeze is being executed following a notional market valuation of a business interest;
- redundant assets are removed from a corporation prior to an open market transaction; and
- a corporation reorganizes into two or more separate entities in contemplation of a divestiture of one or more of the new entities.

A joint election must be made by the taxpayer and the corporation and the consideration received for the transfer must include shares in the capital stock of the corporation. Similar provisions are contained for rollovers by partnerships in subsection 85(2). The amount which may be elected on the transfer is limited by the following rules:

- the elected amount cannot be less than the value of any non-share consideration received;
- the elected amount cannot be greater than the fair market value of the property transferred;
- depreciable property cannot be transferred at less than the least of the capital cost of the particular property, fair market value of the property, and undepreciated capital cost of all the property of the class;
- inventory, non-depreciable capital property and securities or debt obligations used in an insurance or money-lending business cannot be transferred at less than the lesser of their cost amount and fair market value; and
- eligible capital property cannot be transferred at less than the least of its cost, fair market value and four/thirds the undepreciated amount of its cost.

The elected transfer price is important because it serves as the proceeds of disposition to the transferor, the cost of the property to the corporation, and is relevant in determining the cost of shares taken by the transferor from the corporation in return for the assets transferred to the corporation. The taxpayer is deemed to have acquired any non-share consideration at a cost equal to its fair market value. Preferred shares acquired by the taxpayer are deemed to be acquired at the lesser of the fair market value of such shares and the amount by which the elected amount exceeds the value of the non-share consideration. The common shares are deemed to be acquired at a cost equal to the difference between the elected amount and the total of the value of non-share consideration and the cost of the preferred shares.

In addition to fair market value considerations, further care must be exercised in using section 85 as there are a number of anti-avoidance provisions in the Act (including subsection 84.1 and subsections 55(2) to (5)) which can result in adverse consequences to the taxpayer. A more complete discussion of anti-avoidance provisions is contained later in this Chapter.

Where a subsection 85(1) election is made and where immediately before it is transferred to the corporation, the fair market value of the property exceeds the greater of the fair market value immediately after the transfer of all consideration received by the corporation and the elected amount, and it is reasonable to consider the excess to be a benefit conferred on a related person, the amount of such benefit may be converted into an immediate capital gain to the vendor by paragraph 85(1)(e.2). Accordingly, care must be taken to ensure that property, and particularly shares, received on a subsection 85(1) are valued appropriately. Where there are shareholders in the transferee corporation other than the transferor, it is usual to use preferred shares for this purpose, redeemable at the option of the shareholder (i.e. 'retractable') with a redemption amount equal to the desired fair market value.

Share Capital Reorganizations

Section 86 of the Act provides for a tax-deferred rollover on the disposition by a taxpayer of shares that represent capital property to the taxpayer in the course of a reorganization of the capital of a corporation. The rollover applies where the taxpayer has disposed of all of the shares of a particular class and where new shares of the same corporation, with or without non-share consideration, are received. The provisions of section 86 of the Act are commonly used in estate freezes where the common shares of a parent might be converted into preference shares and new common shares would be issued to children in whom equity growth was to vest.

As with the other forms of corporate reorganizations, there are fair market value considerations. The taxpayer is deemed to have acquired the new shares at a cost equal to the adjusted cost base of his old shares, less the fair market value of any non-share consideration receivable in the reorganization, and is deemed to have disposed of his old shares for proceeds of disposition equal to the cost of the new shares and the fair market value of any non-share consideration.

Generally, no immediate tax liability will result from the application of section 86 as long as the paid-up capital of any shares received by the shareholder in the course of the reorganization is no greater than the paid-up capital of the shares which the taxpayer turned over to the corporation, the non-share consideration does not exceed the adjusted cost base of the shares disposed of and there is no 'indirect gift' conferred on a related party to the taxpayer as a result of the transaction. An indirect gift can result if the fair market value of the shares disposed of by the taxpayer exceeds the fair market value of non-share consideration (such as debt) and the fair market value of the new shares acquired. The amount of the indirect gift is added to the adjusted cost base of the shares exchanged and the deemed proceeds will result in an immediate capital gain.

Price Adjustment Clauses

There are several situations in which it may be appropriate to insert a price adjustment clause into a sale agreement to avoid adverse tax consequences resulting from the Agency assessing a different fair market value than arrived at by the parties to the agreement, including non-arm's length transactions and the situation where parties to a sale agreement make an election under subsection 85(1) of the Act in respect of the sale (as discussed below) and the Agency determines that the fair market value of the property sold is greater than the value of the consideration paid.

Interpretation Bulletin IT-169 (dated August 6, 1974) sets out the Agency's position that price adjustment clauses will be accepted if a bona fide effort was made to arrive at fair market value, both vendor and purchaser inform the Agency of the clause, and both are willing to accept the Agency's valuation as binding. Although there have been no court cases dealing with such clauses since IT-169 was issued, the previous jurisprudence suggests that price adjustment clauses will be accepted by a Court of law as long as a bona fide attempt is made by the parties to effect the sale at fair market value, notwithstanding that the Agency's requirements as contained in IT-169 have not been fully complied with.

There is only one Canadian income tax decision dealing with a price adjustment clause (Guilder News Co. v MNR). The taxpayers entered into a transaction and included a price adjustment clause in the sale agreement. The Court found that the transaction price indicated that no reasonable attempt was made to estimate fair market value and therefore the price adjustment clause was not recognized. It would therefore appear that a Court will recognize a price adjustment clause as long as the parties to the sale, reasonably and in good faith, attempt to transact at a sale price that approximates fair market value and that it would be unacceptable to artificially lower the price until an adjustment is required by the Agency.

Amalgamation

Amalgamations are commonly used in leveraged buy-out situations and in 'going private' transactions. A business combination can be effected by the use of the appropriate corporate law provisions and relying on section 87 statutory amalgamation provisions. This will, in general, result in the following:

- all the properties and liabilities of the predecessor corporations become those of the amalgamated company;
- all the shareholders, except predecessor corporations, become shareholders of the amalgamated company;
- all tax bases are rolled over from the predecessor corporations to the amalgamated corporation; and
- all loss carry-forward balances of predecessor corporations become loss carry-forward balances of the amalgamated corporation subject only to the change in control rules.

There are, however, numerous detailed rules in section 87 and care must be taken to review thoroughly any proposed amalgamation.

Fair market value is an issue when there is more than one class of shares acquired in the amalgamated corporation or where an indirect benefit has been conferred. Where shares of more than one class of the amalgamated corporation are acquired, the cost of the old shares is prorated among the classes in proportion to their respective fair market values. Indirect benefit provisions, similar to that described in the previous section on share capital reorganizations, apply if the fair market value of the shares of a shareholder in a predecessor corporation exceeds the fair market value of the shares received in the amalgamated corporation, and it is reasonable to regard any portion of the excess as a benefit which the taxpayer desired to confer on a related person.

Winding Up of a 90% Subsidiary

Section 88(1) of the Act provides for a tax-deferred rollover on the winding-up of a subsidiary corporation in which the parent corporation owns at least 90% of the shares of each class. Both corporations must be taxable Canadian corporations, and shares of the subsidiary not owned by the parent must be owned by persons dealing at arm's length with the parent. Section 88(1) windups are most commonly used in corporate restructuring and where a subsidiary is determined to no longer be a going concern.

One of the disadvantages of buying shares of a corporation is that the purchaser generally is left with the historic tax values of the target corporation's assets. Some relief is available through the use of a paragraph 88(1)(d) 'bump'. In general, upon the winding-up of the subsidiary, the parent can increase the cost of any of the target's non-depreciable capital property to its fair market value. However, the amount of the increase is restricted to the difference between the adjusted cost base of the purchaser's shares in the subsidiary and the cost amount of the subsidiary's assets (net of liabilities). The amount of available increase is also decreased to the extent of any taxable and capital dividends received by the parent corporation from the subsidiary prior to winding-up. Special rules limit the 'bump' with respect to property transferred to the corporation by a parent corporation or other non-arm's length person or in 'butterfly' transactions.

Fair market value is a consideration if property is distributed to minority shareholders as part of the transaction. Subsection 69(5) deems such property to have been sold by the subsidiary for proceeds equal to fair market value and acquired by the shareholder at a cost equal to that amount.

Section 88(2) Winding Up

Section 88(2) of the Act applies to the winding-up of a Canadian corporation in circumstances where the rules in section 88(1) do not apply. Where section 88(2) applies, the corporation is deemed to have disposed of each property distributed by it on the winding-up for proceeds equal to its fair market value so that any accrued gains or losses are realized at that time. To the extent that the value of the property distributed by the corporation on the winding-up exceeds the paid-up capital of its shares, section 84(2) deems the corporation to have paid a dividend at the time equal to the excess. This winding-up dividend is deemed to be paid first out of the capital dividend account as a tax-free capital dividend and, to the extent of the corporation's 1972 capital surplus on hand, is deemed not to be a dividend. This allows these amounts to be removed from the corporation free of tax. Any remaining portion of the winding-up dividend is deemed to be a separate taxable dividend received ratably by the shareholders of the corporation at that time.

The effect of a winding-up under section 88(2) is illustrated below under 'Assets vs. Shares – Comparison of Purchaser's and Vendor's Positions'.

Share for Share Exchange

Where, in an open market transaction, the acquirers' shares are used as its 'currency' in lieu of cash, a rollover may be available under section 85.1 of the Act where a shareholder sells shares of a corporation to another corporation and receives treasury shares of the purchasing corporation as consideration. For a section 85.1 rollover to apply, the purchasing corporation must be a Canadian corporation and the shareholder must hold the shares as capital property. If those considerations are met, the capital gain or loss to the vendor shareholder is deferred automatically unless the taxpayer specifically chooses not to have the provisions of this section of the Act apply (i.e. a joint election is not required by both the vendor and the purchaser of shares).

Fair market value is a consideration to the purchaser corporation as the cost of the shares acquired are deemed to be the lesser of their fair market value or their paid-up capital. In most situations, the paid-up capital of shares would be less than their fair market value. Where it is not, it may be preferable to use subsection 85(1) to transfer the shares rather than section 85.1 because the purchaser can elect the adjusted cost base of the vendor as its cost base.

Assets vs. Shares

Overview

A business carried on by a corporation may be acquired either by purchasing the assets from the corporation or purchasing the shares of the corporation itself. Income tax considerations are important in making this choice and will likely influence the final determination of the price, its allocation and the way in which it is satisfied (see Chapter 4 — Assets vs. Shares).

A conflict exists between the vendor and purchaser in structuring the sale of a business due to the differing positions of each under the Act. It is usually advantageous for the purchaser to purchase assets rather than shares because it enables the purchaser to write up assets to their fair market value to get the full advantage of the tax shield from depreciable assets, whereas for the vendor it has been more advantageous to sell shares due to simplicity and generally favourable capital gains treatment. Where there is a contingency with respect to the purchase price, as in an earn-out arrangement, the transaction must be designed as to avoid certain adverse tax consequences (see Other Taxation Topics – Earn-outs) whether a sale of shares or assets is contemplated.

Whenever the assets of a business are sold or purchased, section 68 of the Act requires the total purchase or sale price to be allocated among the assets purchased or sold on a reasonable basis. The amount so allocated to each asset is then deemed to be the proceeds of disposition of the property to the vendor and the cost of the property to the purchaser. Often this allocation is included in the purchase agreement and is a result of genuine bargaining on the part of the vendor and purchaser acting at arm's length. Where this is not the case and the allocation is grossly at variance with the fair market value of the assets, an allocation will be made on some reasonable basis, which frequently is the fair market value of the various assets.

It is particularly advantageous to the vendor to sell shares of a small business corporation because the taxpayer may be entitled to the $500,000 lifetime capital gain 'super' exemption in respect of the sale. If all of the payment for the sale of shares is not received in the year of sale and part of the purchase price is to be deferred, the vendor is entitled to deduct a reasonable reserve in computing his or her capital gain. Generally, the maximum deferral period of capital gains using reserves is five years and a minimum of 20% of the total gain must be recognized in the first year (40% in the second year, 60% in the third year, and so on).

The purchaser of shares generally is left with the historic income tax values in the assets of the acquired corporation. Interest on debt incurred to acquire the subject corporation generally is deductible (see Other Taxation Topics — Interest Deductibility). Tax advisors should be consulted to determine the deductibility of any losses of the acquired corporation that are available for carry forward (see Other Taxation Topics — Loss Carry Forwards).

Whenever a sale of assets is contemplated, the shareholder of the corporate vendor will have to calculate the resulting tax liability of the corporation and, once the proceeds and tax liability are known, the tax arising on the distribution of the resultant corporate surplus to the shareholder. The vendor corporation will wish to allocate as much of the sale price as possible to nondepreciable capital property or eligible capital property since this minimizes recapture of capital cost allowance.

A corporate purchaser of assets by contrast would like to allocate as much of the purchase price as possible to inventory or to other depreciable assets, and particularly to those classes of assets which have higher capital cost allowance rates. Consideration should be given to making an election under section 22 of the Act (a joint election of the purchaser and vendor) with respect to accounts receivable, to ensure that the vendor is entitled to deduct the difference between the face value of the accounts receivable (other than the accounts already deducted as bad debts) and the consideration received for the accounts receivable. This amount of difference between the face value and the consideration received for the receivables is included in the purchaser's income but, to the extent that the accounts prove doubtful or bad, the purchaser will be entitled to a deduction.

Comparison of Purchaser's and Vendor's Positions

Assume that the following represents the tax cost and fair market value of the various assets of Company A, a Canadian-controlled private corporation ('CCPC') for purposes of the Act:

SCHEDULE 10.1

	Tax Cost (000)	Fair Market Value (000)
Net Current Assets	$200	$200
Land	100	200
Building (see below)	300	500
Goodwill	Nil	200
Total	$ 600	$1,100
Represented By:		
Capital Stock	$ 50	
Retained Earnings	550	
	$ 600	

Assume that:

- the original cost of the building was $500,000 and there is undepreciated capital cost of $300,000 (i.e. $200,000 has been claimed as CCA since acquisition);
- the shareholder's adjusted cost base of the shares is $150,000 and that the paid-up capital of the shares is $1,000;
- Company B, also a CCPC, wishes to purchase the business of Company A and has assessed the fair market value of the assets as being $1,100,000 as indicated above; and
- the October 2000 Budget proposal to reduce the capital gains inclusion rate from 75% to 50% has been enacted and there is a corresponding reduction in the rates applicable to the sale of goodwill. (At the time of writing, the acquisition of goodwill remains subject to a 75% inclusion rate).

Purchaser's Perspective

Company B would be willing to pay less for the shares as it would lose the step-up on the depreciable assets to fair market value. The tax shield from the lost step-up is calculated (assuming a corporate tax rate of 45% and a required rate of return of 10%) as follows:

- Building. The step-up lost would be $200,000 and the present value of the tax shield associated with it (noting that capital cost allowance on buildings is calculated at 4% on a declining balance basis). The formula used to calculate the CCA tax shield foregone where shares are purchased instead of assets is as follows (see also Formula 4.1):

FORMULA 10.1

$$\frac{\text{Appraised value} \times D \times T}{(K+D)} \times \frac{(1+0.5 \times K)}{(1+K)} \text{ less } \frac{\text{existing UCC} \times D \times T}{(K+D)}$$

where:

    Appraised value = $500,000;

    UCC = $300,000

    D = CCA rate (4% in this case);

    T = tax rate (45% in this case); and

    K = the weighted average cost of capital (10% in this case).

Substituting these values into the formula, the calculation yields:

$$\frac{\$500{,}000 \times 4\% \times 45\%}{(10\% + 4\%)} \times \frac{(1 + 0.5 \times 10\%)}{(1 + 10\%)} \text{ less } \frac{\$300{,}000 \times 4\% \times 45\%}{(10\% + 4\%)}$$

$$= 22{,}792 \text{ (say \$23,000)}$$

- Goodwill. Three-quarters of the goodwill amount will be tax deductible on a declining balance basis of 7% per annum (noting that there is no half year rule associated with eligible capital expenditures) and is calculated as:

$$\frac{\$200{,}000 \times 75\% \times 45\% \times 7\%}{(10\% + 7\%)}$$

$$= 27{,}794 \text{ (say, \$28,000)}$$

Accordingly, Company B would be willing to pay $1,100,000 less $51,000 ($23,000 + $28,000) for the shares of Company A (as opposed to the assets) or $1,049,000. Assume that Company B offers to the shareholder of Company A $1,050,000 for the shares or $1,100,000 for the assets of Company A, being indifferent to the form of purchase at the offered prices.

Vendor's Perspective

Assume that the vendor needs cash and will sell the shares outright or, alternatively, will wind-up Company A after the sale of the assets in order to cash out his investment. If the vendor sells the shares, the net return (ignoring any capital gains exemptions) would be as follows (see also Chapter 10 — Liquidation Value):

SCHEDULE 10.2

Proceeds on sale of shares	$1,050,000
Adjusted cost base	150,000
Capital Gain	$ 900,000
Tax ($900,000 x 1/2 x 50% marginal personal rate)	$ 225,000
Net Cash Return to Vendor	$ 825,000

If Company A sold its assets and then immediately afterward wound-up, the shareholder's after tax position would be determined as follows:

SCHEDULE 10.3

Proceeds from current assets		$ 200,000
Proceeds from sale of land	$ 200,000	
Less tax on sale ($100,000 x 1/2 x 51 2/3%) (including the refundable tax component)	25,830	174,170
Proceeds on sale of building	500,000	
less recapture ($200,000 x 45%)	90,000	410,000
Proceeds on sale of goodwill	200,000	
less tax ($200,000 x 1/2 x 45%)	45,000	155,000
Refundable Taxes re capital gain on land ($100,000 x 1/2 x 26 2/3%)		13,330
Total Cash Available for Distribution		$952,500

The sale of the assets results in the following additions to the capital dividend account:

From sale of land (1/2 of $100,000)	$ 50,000	
From sale of goodwill (1/2 of $200,000)	100,000	
		$150,000

The tax cost of winding-up Company A would then be as follows:

SCHEDULE 10.4

Cash available for distribution	$952,500
Less paid-up capital of the shares	1,000
Deemed Dividend	951,500
Less Capital Dividend	150,000
Deemed Taxable Dividend	$801,500
Taxable Capital Gain:	
Actual Proceeds	$952,500
Less Deemed Dividend (above)	801,500
Proceeds of Disposition	151,000
Cost	150,000
Capital Gain	$ 1,000
Tax ($1,000 x 50% x 50% marginal personal rate)	$ 250

Taxes on Deemed Taxable Dividend When Distributed to Shareholder:

SCHEDULE 10.5

Deemed Taxable Dividend	$ 801,500	
Grossed Up 25%	$1,001,875	
Combined Federal and Provincial Taxes @50% of $1,001,875		$500,937
Less Dividend Tax Credit		200,375
Total Tax Payable		$300,562
Total Net of Tax Proceeds on Sale of Assets ($952,500 less $300,562)		$651,938

It would therefore by advantageous for the shareholder of Company A to sell shares given that the after tax return would be higher ($825,000) than on a sale of assets ($651,938).

Income Tax Loss Carry-Forwards

To a potential purchaser of shares of the corporation, the benefit of income tax loss carry-forwards could be an important consideration in the determination of a purchase price that can be offered. Generally, non-capital losses can be carried back three years and forward seven years, while net capital losses can be carried back three years and carried forward indefinitely. However, there are restrictions on the deductibility of loss carry forwards where there has been a change in control of a corporation.

Paragraphs 111(4)(a) and (b) provide that net capital losses realized before the change in control are not deductible in computing taxable income or subsequent taxation years and cannot be carried back to years prior to the change in control. In addition, paragraphs 111(4)(c) and (d) provide that, to the extent that the adjusted cost base of any capital property (other than depreciable property) exceeds the fair market value of such capital property, the adjusted cost base of the property will be reduced to fair market value and the reduction considered a capital loss of the taxation year immediately prior to the change in control. The corporation is allowed to elect (paragraph 111(4)(e)) to have disposed of in the year prior to the change of control any capital properties it so elects at proceeds of disposition in excess of the adjusted cost base of properties up to fair market value (this has the effect of triggering capital gains to utilize the capital losses triggered on the change of control in paragraph 111(4)(d) and step-up the cost base of these assets).

Net capital losses include allowable business investment losses which have not been utilized within the maximum seven year carry-forward period. On a change of control, such losses expire at the end of the carry-forward period and are not included in net capital losses (paragraph 111(8)(a)(ii)).

Non-capital losses can only be carried forward or back to the extent of the corporation's income from the business in which the losses arose, where the business of the corporation in which the losses arose was carried on continuously since the change of control for profit or with reasonable expectation of profit (paragraphs 111 (5)(a) and (b)). In addition, where the undepreciated capital cost of a class of depreciable property exceeds the fair market value of that class at the date of the change of control, the undepreciated capital cost is deemed to be reduced to fair market value and the difference treated as capital cost allowance claimed for the year immediately preceding the change in control. There are similar provisions under which the excess of the cumulative eligible capital balance over its fair market value becomes a non-capital loss of the prior year. Non-capital losses from a business, therefore, can be carried back or forward on a change of control and only under certain circumstances. Losses from property and allowable business investment losses cannot be carried forward or back under any circumstances. Importantly, a change in control will trigger a deemed year-end which must be considered in relation to the expiry dates of the losses.

Capital Gains Exemption and Reserves

Section 110.6 of the Act provides for a lifetime exemption for an individual from tax on up to $500,000 of capital gains realized on the disposition of certain types of property. Section 110.6 as originally enacted also included a general exemption in respect of any capital gains of up to $100,000 but the general exemption was repealed in 1994. Any portion of the general exemption used by an individual will reduce the $500,000 exemption.

Property eligible for the exemption consists of various interests in family farms, including shares in a corporation or interest in a partnership more than 50% of the property which was used in carrying on a family farm business in

Canada or property used directly in carrying on such a business. The exemption also extends to a 'qualified small business corporation share'. To qualify, a share must be a share of a 'small business corporation'. This is a corporation which is a:

- Canadian-controlled private corporation; and
- 90% of the property of which is used in carrying on a small business primarily in Canada or shares or debt of one or more connected small business corporations.

In general, a shareholder must have held a share for at least 24 months and a complex definition is used to prevent the 'stacking' of corporations to avoid the asset test described above.

Section 110.6 contains a number of specific anti-avoidance provisions relating to the capital gains exemption and a careful review is required in any case to ensure that the exemption is available. Because the exemption is only available to individuals, consideration must be given to the form of a transaction for the sale of a business if access to the exemption is desired.

When the sale price for a capital property is payable in instalments, recognition of the gain for tax purposes may be deferred over a five year period providing that at least 20% of the gain is recognized in each year.

Proposed Capital Gains Rollover

The February 2000 Federal Budget proposed a limited rollover where an individual (other than a trust) disposes of shares that are an 'eligible small business investment' and uses the proceeds to re-invest in shares that are also an 'eligible small business investment'. In general, shares which qualify for rollover treatment will be shares eligible for the capital gains exemption except that the total carrying value of the assets of the corporation invested in cannot exceed $2.5 million immediately before the shares are issued and $10 million immediately after the shares are issued. The initial investment need only be held for six months prior to the time of disposition and the replacement investment shares must be purchased after the commencement of the taxation year in which the initial investment was disposed of but within the earlier of 120 days following the disposition and 60 days following the end of the taxation year. Where the rollover applies, the cost base of the new shares will be reduced by the amount of capital gain deferred.

Section 22 Election

Section 22 applies where there has been a sale of accounts receivable in connection with the sale of all or substantially all of the property of a business. Section 22 allows the vendor and purchaser to make an election which allows consistent and symmetrical treatment of the receivables by both vendor and purchaser. Where the election is made:

- the vendor deducts in computing income any difference between the face value of the receivables and the sale price; and
- this amount is included in computing the purchaser's income and the receivables purchased are deemed to have been included in computing the purchaser's income for the purpose of the doubtful and bad debt deduction provisions of paragraphs 20(l)(p) of the Act.

The effect of a Section 22 election is to allow the purchaser to claim doubtful or bad debt provisions in respect of the receivables as if the purchaser had originally acquired them in the course of business.

Earn-outs

In negotiations for the sale of a business, a vendor and purchaser often cannot agree on the value of goodwill attributable to that business and may resort to an 'earn-out' arrangement as part of the sale price whereby a formula is applied to value goodwill based on the results from the business for a fixed period of time in the future.

Future payments made under such earn-out arrangements may be considered part of the proceeds of sale or as income under the Act, depending on the terms of the agreement. The Agency has stated its views on earn-outs in Interpretation Bulletin IT-426. If the amount received by the vendor in respect of the purchase price is dependent on the use of, or production from, property, the amounts received by the vendor in respect of the purchase price will be included in income under paragraph 12(1)(g), even if the assets which have been disposed of are capital property. Generally, 12(1)(g) will not apply if the purchase price is dependent on the earnings of the corporation, although IT-426 indicates that this section of the Act may still apply when an earn-out is designed in this way in certain circumstances.

When shares are sold in an earn-out arrangement, the tax treatment is not entirely clear. As payments are made over a number of years, there may be a series of partial dispositions under section 43 of the Act, with the potential realization of both capital gains and losses depending on the amount of the payment under the earn-out. Alternatively, the 'cost recovery' method of determining gains realized on a sale of shares is acceptable to the Agency as set out in IT-426 if:

- the vendor and purchaser act at arm's length;
- the shares are capital property of the vendor;
- it is reasonable to assume that the earn-out relates to the value of goodwill, which cannot be easily valued at the time of sale;
- the earn-out period does not exceed 5 years; and
- the vendor undertakes to follow the cost recovery procedure.

If the earn-out arrangement is in accordance with these conditions, the proceeds of disposition will be first considered to reduce the adjusted cost base of the shares and only when total proceeds exceed such adjusted cost base will any gains be recognized. No capital losses may be realized until the ultimate proceeds are determined.

When assets are sold as part of an earn-out arrangement, the vendor may wish to design the transaction as a reverse earn-out, setting the purchase price for the assets at a reasonable maximum, subject to reduction if the performance guidelines set out in the earn-out arrangement are not met. In Interpretation Bulletin IT-462, the Agency states that paragraph 12(1)(g) will not apply if the asset sale is structured as a reverse earn-out as defined in this paragraph. However, paragraph 12(1)(g) may be applied to the entire purchase price in circumstances where the price is set at a minimum subject to increase by the formula in the earn-out arrangement. Therefore, any asset sale based in whole or in part on an earn-out arrangement should be structured as a reverse earn-out.

Private Corporations

In valuations, consideration must be given to the income tax impact of the capital dividend account ('CDA') which is available to a private corporation and refundable dividend tax on hand account ('RDTOH') which is available to a Canadian-controlled private corporation (CCPC). It should be noted that the benefits associated with these accounts would be lost if control of the private corporation was acquired by a public corporation or by non-residents of Canada such that private corporation or CCPC status were lost.

The CDA and RDTOH tax accounts are the mechanism for the integration of the taxation of investment income of Canadian-controlled private corporations with that of their individual shareholders. This integration system is designed to insure that investment income earned by an individual through such a corporation will be taxed in the same manner as if it had been earned by the individual directly.

Capital Dividend Account ('CDA')

The CDA operates by allowing a corporation to distribute on a tax-free basis the 50% non-taxable portion of capital gains. The CDA involves complex calculations, however, it is essentially composed of the following amounts:

- the portion of net capital gains not recognized in computing income (one-half of net capital gains before 1988, one-third of net capital gains after 1987 and before 1990, one quarter of net capital gains after 1989 and before February 2000, one third of net capital gains from February 2000 to October 2000, and one-half after October 2000);
- capital dividends received;
- the portion of proceeds not recognized on the disposition of eligible capital property; and
- life insurance proceeds received upon the death of the insured to the extent they exceed original cost,

minus:

- capital dividends paid.

Dividends deemed to have been paid from CDA (on making an appropriate election pursuant to subsection 83(2)) are received tax free by the taxpayer. It often is prudent to pay out capital dividends prior to the sale of a corporation because the ability to do so may subsequently be lost on change in control. However, anti-avoidance provisions may disallow the capital dividend and declare it a taxable dividend if the sole purpose of the sale transaction is for the purchaser to acquire the right to the capital dividend.

On the sale of a corporation, if a corporation has a balance in its CDA and also accrued but as yet unrealized capital losses, it may be good planning to distribute the capital dividend account and then realize the capital losses. By doing so, the capital dividend account will not be reduced on realization of the capital losses.

Refundable Dividend Tax on Hand ('RDTOH')

The RDTOH account operates to allow an eligible corporation a refund of a portion of its tax paid on investment income on the payment of sufficient dividends to the shareholder. If the shareholder is another private corporation, the refunded tax will be paid by the recipient corporation. If the recipient is an individual shareholder, the corporation receives the refund and the individual includes the income in computing his or her income in the normal manner. The availability of the dividend tax credit for an individual will then adjust the amount of tax paid at the individual level to integrate the overall taxation.

A CCPC pays corporate income tax on investment income at ordinary corporation tax rates plus a 6 2/3% tax on investment income under section 123.3. An amount equal to 26 2/3% of investment income is added to the corporation's RDTOH. For every $3 of dividends paid, $1 of taxes is refunded from this account. On the sale of a CCPC consideration should also be given to paying dividends prior to the sale in order to trigger refundable taxes from RDTOH. An existing balance in the RDTOH account might mitigate from a decline in the en bloc value of the shares of a corporation where dividends are to be paid to shareholders prior to a sale of shares. Attention must be paid to the timing of the sale of shares to ensure that CCPC's receive the full benefit of refundable dividends from RDTOH.

Small Business Deduction

A deduction in computing tax payable is available to Canadian-controlled private corporations which earn active business income. A Canadian-controlled private corporation is a private corporation resident in Canada that is not controlled directly or indirectly by one or more non-residents or public corporations. An active business is any business other than the provision of services by an 'incorporated employee' or a business of earning income from property such as rents, interest or dividends, except in either case, where the corporation employs more than five full-time employees in the business. Qualifying corporations are entitled to a tax credit which effectively reduces the Federal tax rate by 16 percentage points on the first $200,000 of active business income in any year (in addition to lower Provincial rates). Special rules apply to require the credit to be shared among a group of associated corporations and to 'claw back' the deduction for larger, otherwise eligible corporations.

In the context of a business valuation, the issue sometimes arises as to whether or not to include the benefit of the small business deduction in calculating the discretionary cash flow of a company that normally qualifies for that deduction. Although the specific facts of each case must be considered, as a general rule:

- in a notional market valuation:
  - depending on the circumstances, the small business deduction may be factored into the discretionary cash flow calculations where fair market value is determined on a stand-alone or intrinsic basis,
  - the small business deduction normally is not taken into account where fair market value includes a component of post-acquisition net economic value added given that the acquirer likely would not enjoy such a benefit; and
- in an open market context:
  - where a small business is being acquired by an individual and the company is expected to prospectively continue to qualify for the small business deduction, then said deduction normally is taken into account, and
  - for medium and large sized businesses, where the acquirer will likely be another corporation, the small business deduction normally is not considered pursuant to the expectation that the prospective taxable income of the acquiree will not qualify for that deduction.

Tax Avoidance Provisions

Arm's Length Disposition to Obtain Tax Benefits

Subsection 69(11) of the Act contains an anti-avoidance rule which applies where a person or partnership disposes of property at arm's length as part of a series of transactions for proceeds of disposition less than fair market value and it may reasonably be considered that one of the main purposes of the transactions was to obtain the benefit of the tax deductions or entitlements of a person not 'affiliated' with the taxpayer, or the tax exemptions available to any person on a subsequent disposition of the property. The definition of 'affiliated' persons is contained in section 251.1 of the Act and generally is similar to, but somewhat more restricted than, the concept of 'related persons' contained in subsection 251(2) of the Act.

The provision is intended to address the situation where taxpayer transfers property with an accrued gain to an unrelated party on a tax-free rollover basis so that, on a subsequent disposition of the property, the transferor may offset the accrued profit with losses or other available deductions, such as unclaimed undepreciated capital cost, undeducted scientific research and development costs or balances in resource expenditure pools. When subsection 69(11) applies, the taxpayer is deemed to have disposed of the property for proceeds of disposition equal to its fair market value at the time. For the purposes of determining whether subsection 69(11) applies to a merger or amalgamation of corporations, subsection 69(13) deems each corporation to have disposed of Canadian and foreign resource properties for nil proceeds and any other property for proceeds equal to its cost amount.

Dividend Stripping Sections 84.1 and 212.1

Section 84.1 of the Act applies to a transferor who is a Canadian resident individual or trust and deals with so-called 'dividend stripping'. The provisions of this section of the Act are best demonstrated by way of example. Assume that Individual A owns 100% of the shares of an operating company ('Opco') that have a paid-up capital and an adjusted cost base of $10,000, and fair market value of $100,000. A sets up a holding company ('Holdco') and transfers his shares of Opco to Holdco using the provisions of section 85, taking as consideration on the transfer $10,000 cash and shares of Holdco with a fair market value and paid-up capital of $90,000. Holdco could then borrow $90,000 and pay it to A as a tax-free reduction of paid-up capital.

The net result (absent section 84.1) would be that A would 'strip' out his accrued gain of $90,000. Section 84.1 operates to reduce the paid up capital of the shares issued by Holdco to the adjusted cost base of the transferred shares, resulting in a deemed dividend to Individual A of $90,000. The paid-up capital of the shares issued of Holdco to Individual A and the fair market value of any non-share consideration is compared with the greater of the paid-up capital of the shares transferred to Holdco and the adjusted cost base of such shares. Where the former exceeds the latter, section 84.1 operates to effect a reduction in the paid-up capital of the shares of Holdco, and depending on the circumstances, a deemed dividend to the transferor. Special rules determine adjusted cost base where the shares were held before 1972 or acquired after 1971 in a non-arm's length transaction.

Section 212.1 applies to non-resident transferors and contains rules similar to section 84.1, except that under section 212.1 only the paid-up capital of the shares transferred is taken into account in determining any deemed dividend or reduction in paid-up capital of shares of the holding corporation.

Generally, to avoid the application of sections 84.1 and 212.1, only shares should be taken back as consideration and their paid-up capital should be limited to the paid-up capital of the shares transferred (or, if section 84.1 applies, the adjusted cost base of the shares transferred determined under the rules in section 84.1). Where neither sections 84.1 nor 212.1 apply (for example, an intercorporate transfer), subsection 85(1.2) will apply to reduce the paid-up capital of the shares when the paid-up capital of the shares exceeds the amount which can be withdrawn on a tax-free basis as a result of the transaction.

Capital Gains Strips (Section 55) and Safe Income

Section 55 prevents a Canadian-resident corporate shareholder from converting a capital gain on the disposition of shares held in another corporation into a dividend that would not be taxable under the Act. For example, assume Individual A owns shares of Holdco, which in turn owns shares of Opco. Further assume that Individual A wishes to dispose of the Opco shares, which have an adjusted cost base of $10,000 and a fair market value of $100,000. One method to accomplish such a disposition would be for Opco to pay Holdco a $90,000 dividend and then sell the Opco shares for $10,000 being remaining fair market value of the shares. There would be no immediate tax consequence because Holdco would receive the dividend on the shares tax free and there would be no capital gain on the disposition of the shares of Opco because the adjusted cost base of the shares would be equal to the proceeds. Under subsection 55(2), to the extent that the dividend of $90,000 is deemed to have been paid from anything other than the after tax earnings of the corporation after 1971, the amount of the dividend paid to Holdco generally will be added to the proceeds of disposition on the sale of the Opco shares thereby resulting in a deemed capital gain.

Another way in which the capital gain can be stripped is to have Holdco transfer its shares of Opco to a purchaser corporation ('Purchaser') in return for treasury shares of Purchaser issued at a fair market value of $100,000 and paid up capital of $10,000. Purchaser could then redeem the shares issued to Holdco for $100,000, which would result in a $90,000 deemed dividend to Holdco which would be received tax free (the transaction would be designed as to make Holdco and Purchaser 'connected' by definition of the Act). Again, subsection 55(2) of the Act may deem the vendor's dividend to be a taxable gain to the extent that such dividend is deemed to have been paid from anything other than after tax earnings of Opco after 1971.

Safe Income

The after tax undistributed earnings of a corporation earned after 1971 is commonly referred to as 'safe income'. Where the amount of an actual or deemed dividend paid to Holdco exceeds the 'safe income', the entire dividend may become tainted for the purposes of subsection 55(2). A special designation can be filed under paragraph 55(5)(f) whereby the taxpayer can designate the appropriate portion of the dividend as being paid out of safe income so as not to taint the entire amount of the dividend.

'Safe income' is not a defined term, but is the term generally used to describe the dividend which can be safely paid. In general, this is the after-tax undistributed income of a corporation calculated in respect of a particular share from the time the share was acquired by its current owner. The calculation of safe income is governed to a significant extent by complex Agency administrative rules and any calculation of safe income requires a careful review of those rules. The ability of a corporation to pay a safe income dividend which will reduce the capital gain realized on the disposition of the shares of the corporation may be a significant factor in determining the structure for the sale of a business.

General Anti-Avoidance Rule ('GAAR')

In addition to specific anti-avoidance provisions contained in the Act, there is a general anti-avoidance provision (the 'GAAR') in section 245. For GAAR not to apply to a transaction, it must have a bona fide purpose other than solely to obtain a tax benefit and must not result in a misuse or abuse of the provisions of the Act taken as a whole. Information Circular 88-2 and supplements discuss how the Agency would apply GAAR in specific situations. To date there is little jurisprudence considering GAAR. However, the possibility of enacting GAAR provisions should be considered in any business restructuring exercise.

Other Taxation Issues

Transfer Pricing

Section 247 of the Act contains transfer pricing rules which were enacted to ensure that cross border non-arm's length transactions in goods and services are accounted for as if they had occurred at arm's length which, by definition, is at fair market value prices. Section 247 does not contain any definition of fair market value but is intended to provide a statutory base for application of the transaction-based methods of determining arm's length prices approved by the OECD. The OECD views and the Agency's related administrative policy are described in Information Circular 87-2R, dated September 27, 1999.

The transfer pricing rules in section 247 apply to transactions between a person resident in Canada or carrying on business in Canada (or a partnership of which such a person is a member) or any non-arm's length non-resident. If any of the terms or conditions in the transactions are different from those that would have been made between arm's length persons or the transaction would not have been entered into by arm's length persons and was not entered into primarily for a *bona fide* purpose other than to obtain a 'tax benefit', the results of the transaction for Canadian tax purposes may be adjusted or re-characterized.

'Tax benefit' is defined in the same manner as for the general anti-avoidance rule under section 245 of the Act, as a reduction, avoidance or deferral of tax or income or a refund. The adjustments will be made so that the results of the transaction reflect the terms and conditions which would have been made had the transaction been at arm's length. If the transaction in question would not have been entered into by arm's length persons, the results are re-characterized on the basis of the hypothetical transaction that would have been entered into by arm's length persons.

There is no protection for taxpayers who establish that transactions do not constitute an abuse of the Act. The provisions of section 247 override the more general provisions of subsections 69(1)(1.2). The rules apply not only to transfers of goods and services but also to transfers of depreciable and non-depreciable capital property and extend to cross-border guarantees. Section 247 contains provision for substantial penalties for failure to respect the transfer pricing rules by not making reasonable efforts to determine arm's length prices or allocations. The taxpayer is deemed not to have made such reasonable efforts if detailed and extensive documentation of transactions is not made by the taxpayer.

Corporate Owned Life Insurance

As previously noted, on the death of a taxpayer there is a deemed disposition of shares owned at the time of his death at fair market value. Sometimes the corporation in which the deceased taxpayer owned shares may own life insurance policies on the life of the deceased taxpayer. The determination of the fair market value of the shares is made on the basis that the fair market value of the life insurance policy is its cash surrender value at the time immediately before the taxpayer's death (subsection 70(5.3)).

The cash surrender value of life insurance policies is computed without regard to policy loans, policy dividends (other than paid-up additions) payable under the policy or interest payable on such dividends. Subsection 70(5.3) probably does not apply where the deceased owned shares of a holding corporation and the beneficiary of the policy was an operating corporation owned by the holding corporation. This subsection of the Act applies to deaths occurring after December 1, 1982 and reflects the decision of the Federal Court of Appeal in *Mastronardi v. MNR*.

In the *Mastronardi* case, a deceased taxpayer was a major shareholder in a corporation that owned a policy on his life and upon the taxpayer's death, the corporation received the proceeds from the policy. The Minister of National Revenue argued that the phrase 'immediately before death' was the equivalent to the instant of death and that, accordingly, the proceeds of the life insurance policy should be considered in the valuation of the deceased taxpayer's shares due to the imminence of death. The Court rejected the Minister's arguments and held that the amount of the insurance proceeds did not have to be taken into account in valuing the shares of the corporation for determining capital gains of the deceased taxpayer.

Where death occurred prior to December 2, 1982, The Agency has taken the position (Interpretation Bulletin IT-416R3) that the *Mastronardi* decision is limited to the situation where the death of a taxpayer was sudden or unexpected. In the situation where it was known that the taxpayer had a terminal illness or was critically injured and would not recover, the amount of insurance proceeds could properly be taken into account in valuing shares.

Interest Deductibility

In general, interest expense on money borrowed to purchase shares of a corporation or in connection with the purchase of assets of a business is deductible under paragraph 20(1)(c) of the Act. The use of the borrowed funds is the key determinant as to whether interest will be deductible.

The decision of the Supreme Court of Canada in *The Queen v Bronfman Trust* has raised doubt about the deductibility of interest on money borrowed to purchase shares where there is no reasonable expectation of income from the shares at least equal to the interest expense. A Notice of Ways and Means Motion to amend the Act tabled on June 2, 1987 generally would allow the deduction of interest on borrowed money used to pay dividends, make partnership distributions (in each case to the extent of accumulated profits), or to return capital to shareholders or partners. The Notice of Ways and Means Motion essentially confirmed that present assessing rules of the Agency with respect to the deductibility of interest will be followed for money borrowed prior to 1990. This includes the position taken by the Agency in Interpretation Bulletin IT-474R that, where an acquiring corporation borrows funds to purchase the shares of, and subsequently amalgamates with, a target corporation (a 'leveraged buy-out'), the amalgamated corporation will be able to continue deducting interest paid on the money borrowed to fund the takeover. While the legislation promised in the Ways and Means Motion has never been introduced, the Agency has maintained these assessing practices.

Scientific Research and Experimental Development ('SR&ED') Tax Credits

In general, expenditures on scientific research and development, both current and capital in nature, are deductible in computing income of a taxpayer from a business in a year under sections 37(1)(a) and 20(1)(t) of the Act, providing the expenditures are made in Canada and the research and development is carried out in Canada. The Agency's administrative guidelines for what constitutes scientific research and experimental development are complex and are set out in detail in Interpretation Bulletin IT-151R4, dated August 16, 1993.

In the alternative, a taxpayer may claim an investment tax credit in respect of qualified scientific research and development expenditures to reduce tax otherwise payable under section 127, or a refundable tax credit under section 127.1, in respect of such expenditures. The refundable investment tax credit under section 127.1 is available only for a CCPC with a taxable income which does not exceed its business limit for purposes of the small business deduction for the year. The general investment tax credit rate under section 127 is 20%. Higher rates apply for scientific research performed in certain economically depressed areas and on certain scientific research expenditures incurred by small businesses.

In valuing a company, whether or not SR&ED tax credits should be taken into account in computing discretionary cash flow sometimes is at issue. Where EBIT-DA prospectively to be generated includes an amount in respect of research and development activities and it is likely that those research and development activities will qualify for SR&ED tax credits, such benefit normally should be taken into account.

Summary

The Income Tax Act (Canada) normally specifies that fair market value is the value definition to be adopted when dealing with issues that require arm's length equivalent value to be established. In an open market transaction the tax treatment of assets vs. shares, the special tax accounts of privately held companies, and corporate restructuring possibilities all ultimately may affect the price that is paid and received. The income tax considerations of each valuation and pricing exercise are unique, and professional advice should be obtained where necessary.

Appendix A
Table of Selected Court Decisions

Overview

This Appendix lists selected Court Decisions that have involved matters related to the valuation and pricing of business interests. It is not intended to be an exhaustive list. The categorization of these cases is meant for convenience of reference only and should not be taken to mean that a particular case or cases serves as jurisprudence in any particular circumstance. Legal advice should be obtained where litigious matters are involved.

Appraisal Remedy – General

Arthur v. Signum Communications Ltd., [1993] O.J. No. 1928

Baniuk v. Carpenter (1991), 1 B.L.R. (2d) 300

Re Brant Investments et al. and KeepRite Inc. et al. (1987), 60 O.R. (2d) 737

Re Domglas Inc.; Domglas Inc. v. Jarislowsky et al. (1981), 13 B.L.R. 135; affd (1983), 138 D.L.R. (3d) 521

Re Fraser Inc. and Sarah J. Aitken et al. (1989), 41 B.L.R. 87

Goguen v. Metro Oil (1989), 42 B.L.R. 30

Hermitage v. Kruger Inc., [1995] A.Q. No. 294, [1993] Q.J. No. 600

Jakobson v. Aggasiz Enterprises Ltd. (1988), 49 Man. R. (2d) 270

Lajoie v. Lajoie Brothers Contracting (1990), 45 B.L.R. 113

Les Investissements Mont-Soleil Inc. v. National Drug Ltd. (1983), 22 B.L.R. 139

LoCicero v. B.A.C.M. Industries Ltd. (1985), 31 Man. R. (2d) 208; (1986), 25 D.L.R. (4th) 269, 38 Man. R. (2d) 134 (Man. CA); [1988] 1 S.C.R. 399, [1988] 4 W.W.R. 671, 49 D.L.R. (4th) 159

Manning v. Harris Steel Group Inc., [1987] 1 W.W.R. 86, 7 B.C.L.R. (2d) 69 [1990] 1 W.W.R. 346 (C.A.), 63 D.L.R. (4th) 125 (C.A.)

MICA Management Centre Inc. v. Lockett (1988), 37 B.L.R. 209

New Quebec Raglan Mines Ltd. v. Blok-Andersen et al. (1993), 9 B.L.R. (2d) 93

Nunachiaq Inc. v. Chow (1993), 8 B.L.R. (2d) 109 (B.C.S.C.); affd [1994] B.C.J. No. 608

Safarik v. Ocean Fisheries Ltd., [1995] B.C.J. No. 76, Vancouver Registry number CA17791/CA018274/CA018007; (1994)10 B.L.R. (2d) 246

Second Shirley Rubin Family Trust (Trustee of) v. Revenue Properties Co., [1992] O.J. No. 1028

Frank C. Smeenk v. Dexleigh Corporation (1991), 49 B.L.R. 1

Ultramar Canada Inc. v. Montreal Pipe Line Ltd. (1991), 49 B.L.R. 279

Westfair Foods Ltd. v. Watt (1992), 5 B.L.R. (2d) 179

Arbitrator

Arenson v. Arenson, [1973] 2 All E.R. 235

Arenson v. Casson Beckman Rutley & Co, [1972] 2 All E.R. 939; affd [1973] 2 All E.R. 235; revd [1975] 3 All E.R. 901

Bottomly v. Ambler (1877), 38 L.T. 545

Finnegan v. Allen, [1943] 1 All E.R. 493

Re Hopper (1867), LR 2 Q.B. 367

Muskoka & Parry Sound Telephone Co. Ltd. v. Ontario Telephone Development Corp. (1984), 32 L.C.R. 154 (O.M.B.); (1985), 32 L.C.R. 238 (O.M.B.)

Parrot v. Shellard (1868), 15 W.R. 928

Re Portnoy, [1949] 3 D.L.R. 449

Taylor v. Yielding (1912), 56 Sol. Jo. 253

Turner v. Goulden (1873). L.R. 9 C.P. 57

Buy-Sell Agreements

Irwin v. D.W. Coates Enterprises Ltd., [1985] 3 W.W.R. 765

TABLE OF SELECTED COURT DECISIONS

Capitalization Rates

Footitt v. Gleason, [1995] O.J. No. 2662, Commercial List No. B177/95

Ivesleigh Holdings Inc. et al. v. M.N.R., (1978) 32 D.T.C. 1716

R. G. Mersereau v. M.N.R., [1977] C.T.C. 2412

Seto Holdings Ltd. v. M.N.R. (1975), 29 D.T.C. 1

Cash Consideration

J.C. Adam v. M.N.R., [1952] C.T.C. 400, 7 D.T.C. 1001

Henfrey Samson Belair v. Wedgewood Village and Skalbania, 59 C.B.R. 38 (B.C.S.C.); (1987), 14 B.C.L.R. (2d) 1 (B.C.C.A.)

Estate of Umberto Mastronardi v. The Queen (1977), 31 D.T.C. 5217, [1977] C.T.C. 355

Schroder Estate v. M.N.R., [1955] C.T.C. 290, 9 D.T.C. 1128

Compulsion to Act

Crane Estate v. FC of T, 75 A.T.C. 4001

Findlay's Trustees v. IRC (1938), 22 A.T.C. 437

Village of South Orange v. Alden Corp., 365 A. 2d 469

Control

Barclays Bank Ltd. v. IRC, [1961] A.C. 509, [1960] 2 All E.R. 817

Fairgreen Investments Ltd. v. M.N.R., [1972] C.T.C. 2446, 26 D.T.C. 1374

IRC v. Harten Coal Co. Ltd., [1960] 3 All E.R. 48

New Hamburg Mills Ltd. v. M.N.R. (1965), 40 Tax A.B.C. 89, 20 D.T.C. 53

Sheldon's Engineering Ltd. v. M.N.R., (1955), 9 D.T.C. 1110; (1954), 8 D.T.C. 1106; (1953), 7 D.T.C. 11

Vineland Quarries and Crushed Stone Ltd. v. M.N.R., [1966] Ex. CR 417, [1966] C.T.C. 69, 20 D.T.C. 5092; affd without written reasons (1967), 21 D.T.C. 5283 (S.C.C.)

Control Premium

Dean v. Prince, [1953] 1 Ch. 590

Re Domglas Inc.; Domglas Inc. v. Jarislowsky et al. (1981), 13 B.L.R. 135; affd (1982), 138 D.L.R. (3d) 521

Gold Coast Section Trust Ltd. v. Humphrey, [1948] 2 All E.R. 379 (H.L.); affg in part [1946] 2 All E.R. 742 (C.A.)

Minister of Finance v. Mann Estate, [1972] 5 W.W.R. 23 at 27; affd [1973] C.T.C. 561 (C.A.); affd [1974] C.T.C. 222 (S.C.C.)

Short v. Treasury Commissioners, [1948] A.C. 534, [1948] 2 All E.R. 509

Winram Estate v. M.N.R., [1972] F.C. 463, [1972] C.T.C. 193, 26 D.T.C. 6187

Control Through Casting Vote

Allied Business Supervisions Ltd. v. M.N.R., [1967] 1 Ex. C.R. 21, [1966] C.T.C. 330, 20 D.T.C. 5244

Alpine Drywall & Decorating Ltd. v. M.N.R., [1966] Ex. C.R. 1148, [1966] C.T.C. 359, 20 D.T.C. 5263

Bert Robbins Excavating Ltd. v. M.N.R., [1966] Ex. C.R. 1160, [1966] C.T.C. 371, 20 D.T.C. 5269

CJOY Ltd. v. M.N.R. (1966), 42 Tax A.B.C. 364, 21 D.T.C. 6

Dealers Acceptance Corp. Ltd. v. M.N.R. (1964), 37 Tax A.B.C. 33, 18 D.T.C. 771

Dominion Fibre Drum Corp. v. M.N.R. (1965), 40 Tax A.B.C. 79, 20 D.T.C. 46

M.N.R. v. M. F. Esson & Sons Ltd. et al., [1967] S.C.R. 223, [1967] C.T.C. 50, 21 D.T.C. 5035

IRC v. Monnick Ltd. (1949), 29 T.C. 379

B.W. Noble Ltd. v. IRC (1926), 12 T.C. 911

Pender Enterprises Ltd. v. M.N.R., [1965] Ex. C.R. 180, [1965] C.T.C. 343, 19 D.T.C. 5202

Control Through Intermediate Corporations

Bert Robbins Excavating Ltd. v. M.N.R., [1966] Ex. C.R. 1160, [1966] C.T.C. 371, 20 D.T.C. 5269

British American Tobacco Ltd. v. IRC, [1943] A.C. 335, [1943] 1 All E.R. 13

IRC v. F.A. Clark & Sons Ltd., [1941] 2 K.B. 270, 29 T.C. 49

Glaspie v. M.N.R. (1963), 33 Tax A.B.C. 274, 17 D.T.C. 828

Vancouver Towing Co. Ltd. v. M.N.R., [1946] Ex. C.R. 623, [1947] C.T.C. 18, 2 D.T.C. 706

Vineland Quarries and Crushed Stone Ltd. v. M.N.R., [1966] Ex. CR 417, [1966] C.T.C. 69, 20 D.T.C. 5092; affd without written reasons 21 D.T.C. 5283 (S.C.C.)

Yarmouth Industrial Leasing Ltd. v. The Queen, (1985), 39 D.T.C. 5401 (F.C.T.D.)

Control Through Trustees and Nominees

Anglo-B.C. Distributors Ltd. v. M.N.R., [1970] C.T.C. 138, 24 D.T.C. 6105

The Queen v. Ann-Gus Holdings Ltd. (1984), 38 D.T.C. 6363 (F.C.A.)

R. M. Ballantyne Co. Ltd. v. M.N.R. (1952), 6 Tax A.B.C. 71, 6 D.T.C. 115

Barclays Bank Ltd. v. IRC, [1961] A.C. 509, [1960] 2 All E.R. 817

Benaby Realties Ltd. v. M.N.R. (1961), 28 Tax A.B.C. 176, 19 D.T.C. 5761; (1967), 21 D.T.C. 5275 (S.C.C.)

Berendsen Ltd. v. I.R.C., [1958] 1 Ch. 1, [1957] 2 All E.R. 612

IRC v. J. Bibby and Sons Ltd., [1945] 1 All E.R. 667, 29 T.C. 167

The Canada Trust Company v. The Queen, [1981] C.T.C. 319, 35 D.T.C. 5248 (F.C.T.D.)

Career Girl Store Ltd. v. M.N.R., [1967] 1 Ex. C.R. 21, [1966] C.T.C. 330, 20 D.T.C. 5244

M.N.R. v. Consolidated Holdings Co. Ltd., [1972] C.T.C. 18, 26 D.T.C. 6007 (S.C.C.)

C. A. de Fehr & Sons Ltd. v. M.N.R. (1954), 11 Tax A.B.C. 190, 8 D.T.C. 390

Deshaies & Raymond Inc. v. M.N.R., [1970] Tax A.B.C. 725, 24 D.T.C. 1466,

M.N.R. v. Dworkin Furs (Pembroke) Ltd. et al., [1967] S.C.R. 223, [1967] C.T.C. 50, 21 D.T.C. 5035

Edison Wholesale Ltd. v. M.N.R. (1963), 32 Tax A.B.C. 307, 17 D.T.C. 583

H. A. Fawcett & Sons, Ltd. v. The Queen, (1980), 34 D.T.C. 6195 (F.C.A.)

Finley v. M.N.R., (1984), 38 D.T.C. 1536 (T.C.C.)

M.N.R. v. Kirby Maurice Co. Ltd., [1958] Ex. C.R. 77, [1958] C.T.C. 41, 12 D.T.C. 1033

The Queen v. Lusita Holdings Ltd., (1984), 38 D.T.C. 6346

The Queen v. Ans, [1983] C.T.C. 8, 37 D.T.C. 5038 (F.C.T.D.)

W. Ralston & Co. (Canada) Ltd. v. M.N.R., [1982] C.T.C. 2108, 36 D.T.C. 1128 (T.R.B.)

Rolka v. M.N.R., [1963] Ex. C.R. 138, [1962] C.T.C. 637, 16 D.T.C. 1394

Rubenstein v. M.N.R. (1965), 39 Tax A.B.C. 7, 19 D.T.C. 494

Scandia Plate Ltd. v. R., [1983] 1 F.C. 51, [1982] C.T.C. 431, 37 D.T.C. 5009 (T.D.)

M.N.R. v. Sheldons Engineering Ltd., [1955] S.C.R. 637, [1955] C.T.C. 174, 9 D.T.C. 1110

John Shields & Co. (Perth) Ltd. v. IRC, [1950] S.C. 441, 29 T.C. 475

IRC v. Silverts Ltd., [1951] 1 Ch. 521, [1951] 1 All E.R. 703, 29 T.C. 491

Special Risks Holdings Inc. v. The Queen, [1984] C.T.C. 553, 38 D.T.C. 6505 (F.C.T.D.); affd, 40 D.T.C. 6035, 63 N.R. 390 (F.C.A.)

Taylor Lumber Co. Ltd. and Matheson Lumber Ltd. v. M.N.R., [1967] Tax A.B.C. 875, 21 D.T.C. 593

R. Truax Son & Co. Ltd. v. M.N.R. (1954), 12 Tax A.B.C. 12, 8 D.T.C. 562

Wynndel Logging Co. Ltd. v. M.N.R., [1980] C.T.C. 2141, 34 D.T.C. 1125 (T.R.B.)

Control Through Voting Agreements

Aaron's Ladies Apparel Ltd. v. M.N.R., [1967] 1 Ex. C.R. 21, [1966] C.T.C. 330, 20 D.T.C. 5244; [1967] S.C.R. 223, [1967] C.T.C. 50, 21 D.T.C. 5035

Credit La Verendrye Ltee v. M.N.R., [1972] C.T.C. 2404, 26 D.T.C. 1344

IRC v. James Hodgkinson (Salford) Ltd. (1949), 29 T.C. 395

International Iron & Metal Co. Ltd. v. M.N.R., [1969] C.T.C. 668, 23 D.T.C. 5445; affd [1974] S.C.R. 898, 27 D.L.R. (3d) 1, [1972] C.T.C. 242, 26 D.T.C. 6205

Lou's Service (Sault) Ltd. v. M.N.R., [1967] C.T.C. 315, 21 D.T.C. 5201

Rubenstein v. M.N.R. (1965), 39 Tax A.B.C. 7, 19 D.T.C. 494

De Facto Control

Buckerfield's Ltd. et al. v. M.N.R., [1965] 1 Ex. C.R. 299, [1964] C.T.C. 504, 18 D.T.C. 5301

M.N.R. v. Dworkin Furs (Pembroke) Ltd. et al., [1967] S.C.R. 223, [1967] C.T.C. 50, 21 D.T.C. 5035

Vina-Rug (Canada) Ltd. v. M.N.R., [1968] S.C.R. 193, [1968] C.T.C. 1

De Jure Control

British American Tobacco Ltd. v. IRC, [1943] A.C. 335, [1943] 1 All E.R. 13

Buckerfield's Ltd. et al. v. M.N.R., [1965] 1 Ex. C.R. 299, [1964] C.T.C. 504, 18 D.T.C. 5301

Donald Applicators Ltd. et al. v. M.N.R., [1969] C.T.C. 98, 23 D.T.C. 5122; affd [1971] C.T.C. 402, 25 D.T.C. 5202

M.N.R. v. Dworkin Furs (Pembroke) Ltd. et al., [1967] S.C.R. 223, [1967] C.T.C. 50, 21 D.T.C. 5035

Glasgow Expanded Metal Co. Ltd. v. IRC, [1923] S.C. 365, 12 T.C. 573

The Queen v. Imperial General Properties Ltd., [1985] 2 S.C.R. 288, [1985] 5 D.T.C. 5500, [1985] 2 C.T.C. 299

B.W. Noble Ltd. v. IRC (1926), 12 T.C. 911

Oakfield Developments (Toronto) Ltd. v. M.N.R., [1971] S.C.R. 1032, [1971] C.T.C. 283, 25 D.T.C. 5175

Vancouver Towing Co. Ltd. v. M.N.R., [1946] Ex. C.R. 623, [1947] C.T.C. 18, 2 D.T.C. 706

M.N.R. v. Wrights' Canadian Ropes Ltd., [1947] A.C. 109, [1947] C.T.C. 1, 2 D.T.C. 927

Degree of Care and Skill

Jenkins v. Betham (1855), 15 C.B. 168, 139 E.R. 384

Directors' Powers

Donald Applicators Ltd. et al. v. M.N.R., [1969] C.T.C. 98, 23 D.T.C. 5122; affd [1971] C.T.C. 402, 25 D.T.C. 5202

Dividends

Winram Estate v. M.N.R., [1972] F.C. 463, [1972] C.T.C. 193, 26 D.T.C. 6187

Employment Contract

Crutchfield v. Crutchfield (1987), 10 R.F.L. (3d) 247 (Ont. H.C.J.)

Expert Evidence

Re Brant Investments et al. and KeepRite Inc. et al. (1987), 60 O.R. (2d) 737

Re Fraser Inc. and Sarah J. Aitken et al. (1989), 41 B.L.R. 87

Footitt v. Gleason, [1995] O.J. No. 2662 Commercial List No. B177/95

Schaefer Brothers Inc. v. M.N.R., 33 D.T.C. 288

G. Trepanier v. M.N.R., 33 D.T.C. 924

Fair Market Value

Re Brant Investments et al. and KeepRite Inc. et al. (1987), 60 O.R. (2d) 737

Dibbley v. Dibbley and Liddle (1987), 5 R.F.L. (3d) 381

Re Domglas Inc.; Domglas Inc. v. Jarislowsky et al. (1981), 13 B.L.R. 135; affd (1983), 138 D.L.R. (3d) 521

Heon v. Heon (1989), 22 R.F.L. (3d) 273 (Ont. H.C.J.)

Jackh v. Jackh, 22 B.C.L.R. 182 (S.C.)

Minister of Finance v. Mann Estate, [1972] 5 W.W.R. 23 at 27; affd [1973] C.T.C. 561 (C.A.); affd [1974] C.T.C. 222 (S.C.C.)

Menage v. Hedges (1987), 8 R.F.L. (3d) 225

Re Wall and Redekop Corp et al. (1974), 50 D.L.R. (3d) 733 (B.C.S.C.)

Winter v. The Queen (1989), F.C.T.D., court file T-1711-86

Fair Value

Baniuk v. Carpenter (1991), 1 B.L.R. (2d) 300

Re Brant Investments et al. and KeepRite Inc. et al. (1987), 60 O.R. (2d) 737

Calmont Leasing Ltd. v. Kredl, [1996] A.J. No. 283

Cyprus Anvil Mining Corp. v. Dickson et al. (1983), 20 B.L.R. 21, 40 B.C.L.R. 180; (1987), 8 B.C.L.R. (2d) 145

Diligenti v. RMWD Operations Kelowna Ltd. (1978), 4 B.C.L.R. 134

Re Domglas Inc.; Domglas Inc. v. Jarislowsky et al. (1981), 13 B.L.R. 135; affd (1982), 138 D.L.R. (3d) 521

Re Fraser Inc. and Sarah J. Aitken et al. (1988), 41 B.L.R. 87

Footitt v. Gleason, [1995] O.J. No. 2662, Commercial List No. B177/95

Hermitage v. Kruger Inc., [1995] A.Q. No. 294, [1993] Q.J. No. 600

Jakobson v. Aggasiz Enterprises Ltd. (1988), 49 Man. R. (2d) 270

Lajoie v. Lajoie Brothers Contracting (1990), 45 B.L.R. 113

Les Investissements Mont-Soleil Inc. v. National Drug Ltd. (1983), 22 B.L.R. 139

LoCicero v. B.A.C.M Industries Ltd. (1985), 31 Man. R. (2d) 208, (1986), 25 D.L.R. (4th) 269, 38 Man. R. (2d) 134 (Man. C.A.); [1988] 1 S.C.R. 399, [1988] 4 W.W.R. 671, 49 D.L.R. (4th) 159

Lough v. Canadian Natural Resources Ltd. (1983), 45 B.C.L.R. 335

Manning v. Harris Steel Group Inc. [1987] 1 W.W.R. 86, 7 B.C.L.R. (2d) 69; [1990] 1 W.W.R. 346, 63 D.L.R. (4th) 125 (C.A.)

Montgomery et al. v. Shell Canada Ltd. (1980), 5 W.W.R. 443, 111 D.L.R. (3d) 116

Morrison v. United Westburne Industries Ltd. (April 15, 1988), Toronto RE 1926/87

Neonex International Ltd. v. Kolasa et al. (1978), 84 D.L.R. (3d) 446, [1978] 2 W.W.R. 593, 3 B.L.R. 1

New Quebec Raglan Mines Ltd. v. Blok-Andersen (1993), 9 B.L.R. (2d) 93

Nunachiaq Inc. v. Chow (1993), 8 B.L.R. (2d) 109 (B.C.S.C.); affd [1994] B.C.J. No. 608

Robertson et al. v. Canadian Canners Ltd. (1979), 4 B.L.R. 290

Safarik v. Ocean Fisheries Ltd., [1996] B.C.J. No. 76, Vancouver Registry No. CA17791/CA018274/CA018007; (1994), 10 B.L.R. (2d) 246

Second Shirley Rubin Family Trust (Trustee of) v. Revenue Properties Co., [1992] O.J. No. 1028

Frank C. Smeenk v. Dexleigh Corporation (1990), 49 B.L.R. 1

Ultramar Canada Inc. v. Montreal Pipe Line Ltd. (1991), 49 B.L.R. 279

Re VCS Holdings and Helliwell (1979), 5 B.L.R. 265

Re Wall and Redekop Corp et al. (1975), 50 D.L.R. (3d) 733 (B.C.S.C.)

Westfair Foods Ltd. v. Watt (1992), 5 B.L.R. (2d) 179

Re Whitehorse Copper Mines Ltd.; Hudson Bay Mining and Smelting Co. Ltd. v. Lueck et al. (1980), 10 B.L.R. 113

Fiduciary Responsibility

Bell et al. v. Source Data Control and Hood et al., 14581/81, (1988), 29 OA.C. 134

Percival v. Wright, [1902] 2 Ch. 421

Ervin L. Dusik v. John F. Newton et al. (1984), 50 B.C.L.R. 321

Trimac Ltd. v. CIL Inc., [1990] 1 W.W.R. 133; (1989), 69 A.L.R. (2d) 113

Forcing Out Premium

Re Fraser Inc. and Sarah J. Aitken et al. (1989), 41 B.L.R. 87

Re Brant Investments et al. and KeepRite Inc. et al. (1987), 60 O.R. (2d) 737

Re Domglas Inc.; Domglas Inc. v. Jarislowsky et al. (1981), 13 B.L.R. 135; affd (1982), 138 D.L.R. (3d) 521

Jakobson v. Aggasiz Enterprises Ltd. (1988), 49 Man. R. (2d) 270

Les Investissements Mont-Soleil Inc. v. National Drug Ltd. (1983), 22 B.L.R. 139

LoCicero v. B.A.C.M Industries Ltd. (1985), 31 Man. R. (2d) 208; (1986), 25 D.L.R. (4th) 269, 38 Man. R. (2d) 134 (Man. C.A.); [1988] 1 S.C.R. 399, [1988] 4 W.W.R. 671, 49 D.L.R. (4th) 159

Manning v. Harris Steel Group Inc., [1987] 1 W.W.R. 86, [1990] 1 W.W.R. 346 (C.A.)

New Quebec Raglan Mines Ltd. v. Blok-Andersen et al. (1993), 9 B.L.R. (2d) 93

Second Shirley Rubin Family Trust (Trustee of) v. Revenue Properties Co., [1992] O.J. No. 1028

Westfair Foods Ltd. v. Watt (1992), 5 B.L.R. (2d) 179

Going Concern Value and Fair Value

Diligenti v. RMWD Operations Kelowna Ltd. (No. 2) (1978), 4 B.C.L.R. 134

Re VCS Holdings and Helliwell (1979), 5 B.L.R. 265

Re Wall and Redekop Corp et al. (1975), 50 D.L.R. (3d) 733 (B.C.S.C.)

Goodwill – Valuation

U.S.M. Canada Ltd. v. The Queen, [1996] 2 C.T.C. 2289

Group Control

Adelaide Motors Ltd. v. FCT (1942), 66 C.L.R. 436, 7 A.T.D. 147

Ancaster Development Co. Ltd. v. M.N.R., [1961] Ex. C.R. 201, [1961] C.T.C. 9, 15 D.T.C. 1047

Atomic Truck Cartage Ltd. v. The Queen, [1985] 2 C.T.C. 21, 40 D.T.C. 6032 (F.C.T.D.)

Thomas J. Baxter et al. v. Biotech Electronics Ltd. et al. District of Montreal, No. 500-05-003585-856, February 15, 1990

Commissioner of Income Tax v. Bjordal, [1955] A.C. 309, [1955] 1 All E.R. 401 (P.C.)

Buckerfield's Ltd. et al. v. M.N.R., [1965] 1 Ex. C.R. 299, [1964] C.T.C. 504, 18 D.T.C. 5301

M.N.R. v. Consolidated Holdings Co. Ltd., [1972] C.T.C. 18, 26 D.T.C. 6007 (S.C.C.)

Dad's Cookie Co. (Ontario) Ltd. v. M.N.R. (1965), 39 Tax A.B.C. 73, 19 D.T.C. 535

Express Cable Television Ltd. v. M.N.R., [1982] C.T.C. 2447, 36 D.T.C. 1431 (T.R.B.)

The Queen v. B.B. Fast & Sons Distributors Ltd. (1986), 64 N.R. 297, [1986] 1 C.T.C. 299, 40 D.T.C. 6106 (F.C.A.)

Golden Arrow Sprayers Ltd. v. M.N.R., [1961] Ex. C.R. 432, [1961] C.T.C. 318, 15 D.T.C. 1185

King George Hotels Ltd. v. M.N.R., [1968] Tax A.B.C. 785, 22 D.T.C. 635

Lundberg Explorations Ltd. v. M.N.R. (1958), 19 Tax A.B.C. 208, 12 D.T.C. 291

S. Madill Ltd. v. M.N.R., [1972] C.T.C. 47, 26 D.T.C. 6027

Jacob Mayer & Sons Ltd. v. M.N.R., [1954] Ex. C.R. 310, [1954] C.T.C. 141, 8 D.T.C. 1075

McMillan Hotel Co. Ltd. v. M.N.R. (1953), 8 Tax A.B.C. 334, 7 D.T.C. 231

Les Messageries de Presse Periodique Ltee et al. v. M.N.R., [1968] Tax A.B.C. 881

Miron & Freres Ltd. v. M.N.R., [1955] S.C.R. 679, [1955] C.T.C. 182, 9 D.T.C. 1109

New Hamburg Mills Ltd. v. M.N.R. (1965), 40 Tax A.B.C. 89, 20 D.T.C. 53

No. 60 v. M.N.R. (1952), 6 Tax A.B.C. 412, 6 D.T.C. 268

No. 264 v. M.N.R. (1955), 13 Tax A.B.C. 46, 9 D.T.C. 300

No. 324 v. M.N.R. (1956), 14 Tax A.B.C. 391, 10 D.T.C. 133

Radio CFUN Ltd. Wellport Broadcasting Ltd. v. M.N.R., [1969] Tax A.B.C. 565, 23 D.T.C. 420

Ronda Holdings Ltd. v. M.N.R., [1984] C.T.C. 2357, 38 D.T.C. 1331 (T.C.C.)

Southside Car Market Ltd. v. The Queen, [1982] 2 F.C. 755, [1982] C.T.C. 214, 36 D.T.C. 6179 at 6186 (T.D.)

Vina-Rug (Canada) Ltd. v. M.N.R., [1968] S.C.R. 193, [1968] C.T.C. 1

Maurice J. Walsh Ltd. v. M.N.R. (1955), 14 Tax A.B.C. 69, 9 D.T.C. 593

FCT v. West Australian Tanners & Fellmongers Ltd. (1945), 70 C.L.R. 623, 8 A.T.D. 25

Yardley Plastics of Canada Ltd. v. M.N.R., [1966] Ex. C.R. 1027, [1966] C.T.C. 215, 20 D.T.C. 5183

Highest Price

IRC v. Clay, [1914] 3 K.B. 466 (C.A.)

Hindsight

Wallace R. Brunelle v. M.N.R., [1977] C.T.C. 2506, 31 D.T.C. 326

J. Allen Carr v. M.N.R., [1993] 2 C.T.C. 3018

W. H. Crandall v. M.N.R., [1974] C.T.C. 2289, 28 D.T.C. 1204

Cyprus Anvil Mining Corp. v. Dickson et al. (1983), 20 B.L.R. 21, 40 B.C.L.R. 180; (1987), 8 B.C.L.R. (2d) 145

Diligenti v. RMWD Operations Kelowna Ltd. (1978), 4 B.C.L.R. 134

Re Domglas Inc.; Domglas Inc. v. Jarislowsky et al. (1981), 13 B.L.R. 135; affd (1982), 138 D.L.R. 521

Fischer v. Fischer (1993), 109 D.L.R. (4th) p. 189

Ganson v. Ganson (1996), 66 A.C.WS (3d) 706

Holt v. IRC, [1953] 2 All E.R. 1499

Re Lohn Estate, [1997] B.C.J. No. 1367

Manning v. Harris Steel Group Inc., [1987] 1 W.W.R. 86, [1990] 1 W.W.R. 346 (C.A.)

National System of Baking of Alberta Ltd. v. The Queen, [1978] C.T.C. 30, 32 D.T.C. 6018; affd [1980] C.T.C. 237, 34 D.T.C. 6178

New Quebec Raglan Mines Ltd. v. Blok-Andersen (1993), 9 B.L.R. (2d) 93

Nunachiaq Inc. v. Chow (1993), 8 B.L.R. (2d) 109 (B.C.S.C.); affd [1994] B.C.J. No. 608

Produits LDG Ltd. v. M.N.R., [1973] C.T.C. 273, 27 D.T.C. 5222 (F.C.)

S.G. & S. Investments (1972) Ltd. v. Golden Boy Foods Inc. (1992), 3 B.L.R. (2d) 80

Joseph Simard & Cie, Ltee v. M.N.R., [1964] C.T.C. 461, 18 D.T.C. 5289

Frank C. Smeenk v. Dexleigh Corporation (1990), 49 B.L.R. 1

Taylor Estate v. M.N.R., [1967] Tax A.B.C. 555, 21 D.T.C. 405

H. Taylor Estate v. M.N.R., [1990] 2 C.T.C. 2304

Woeller v. Woeller (1988), 15 R.F.L. (3d) 120

Imminence of Death

Estate of Umberto Mastronardi v. The Queen, (1977), 31 D.T.C. 5217, [1976] C.T.C. 355

Industry Knowledge

Re Fraser Inc. and Sarah J. Aitken et al. (1989), 41 B.L.R. 87

Information Disclosure

Holt v. IRC, [1953] 2 All E.R. 1499

Re Lynall, [1969] 3 All E.R. 984 at 990 (C.A.)

National System of Baking of Alberta Ltd. v. The Queen, [1978] C.T.C. 30, 32 D.T.C. 6018; affd [1980] C.T.C. 237, 34 D.T.C. 6178

No. 179 v. M.N.R. (1954), 11 Tax A.B.C. 78, 8 D.T.C. 336

Insider Knowledge

National System of Baking of Alberta Ltd. v. The Queen, [1978] C.T.C. 30, 32 D.T.C. 6018; affd [1980] C.T.C. 237, 34 D.T.C. 6178

Insurance – Life

Estate of Umberto Mastronardi v. The Queen, (1977) 31 D.T.C. 5217, [1976] C.T.C. 572

Interest Deductibility

The Queen v. Bronfman Trust, [1987] C.T.C. 117, 41 D.T.C. 5059

Minority Discount

Louie Allred Executrix of the Estate of Carl M. Allred v. M.N.R. (1986), 86 D.T.C. 1479, 83-886 (IT)

Baniuk v. Carpenter (1991), 1 B.L.R. (2d) 300

Calmont Leasing Ltd. v. Kredl, [1996] A.J. No. 283

Khoury v. Khoury (1993), 122 N.B.R. (2d) 150; 306 A.P.R. 150 (Q.B.)

William C. Krafve v. M.N.R., (1984), 38 D.T.C. 1002

Diligenti v. RMWD Operations Kelowna Ltd. (1978), 4 B.C.L.R. 134

Re Domglas Inc.; Domglas Inc. v. Jarislowsky et al. (1981), 13 B.L.R. 135; affd (1982), 138 D.L.R. (3d) 521

Henfrey Samson Belair v. Wedgewood Village and Skalbania, 59 C.B.R. 38 (B.C.S.C.); (1987), 14 B.C.L.R. (2d) 1 (B.C.C.A.)

Hermitage v. Kruger Inc., [1995] A.Q. No. 294, [1993] Q.J. No. 600

Irwin v. D.W. Coates Enterprises Ltd., [1985] 3 W.W.R. 765

Les Investissements Mont-Soleil Inc. v. National Drug Ltd. (1983), 22 B.L.R. 139

Mathers v. Mathers (1992), 113 NSR (2d) 284, 309 A.P.R. 284 (T.D.); (1993), 123 NSR (2d) 14, 340 A.P.R. 14 (C.A.)

Naneff v. Con-Crete Holdings Ltd. (1995), 23 O.R. (3d) 481

Nunachiaq Inc. v. Chow (1993), 8 B.L.R. (2d) 109 (B.C.S.C.); affd [1994] B.C.J. No. 608

O' Conner v. Winchester Oil & Gas Inc. et al. (1986), 69 B.C.L.R. 330, [1986] 2 W.W.R. 737

Roberts v. Pelling (1982), 16 B.L.R. 150 (B.C.S.C.)

William Russel Steen v. The Queen, [1986] 2 C.T.C. 394

Safarik v. Ocean Fisheries Ltd., [1996] B.C.J. No. 76, Vancouver Registry No. CA17791/CA018274/CA018007; (1993)10 B.L.R. (2d) 246

Minority Shareholdings

J.A. Carruthers v. M.N.R. (1982), 36 D.T.C. 6009; (1979) 33 D.T.C. 906

H. Johansen v. M.N.R. (1972), 26 D.T.C. 1528

Meszaros et al. v. M.N.R., [1982] C.T.C. 2509

William L. Moynihan v. M.N.R., [1962] 28 Tax A.B.C. 293, 16 D.T.C. 64

Helen I. New and Riley J. New v. M.N.R., [1971] Tax A.B.C. 583, 25 D.T.C. 379

Lawson v. Proirier Estate, [1998] NBJ No. 154

No. 179 v. M.N.R. (1954), 11 Tax A.B.C. 78, 8 D.T.C. 336

No. 513 v. M.N.R., [1958] 19 Tax A.B.C. 243, 12 D.T.C. 301

Taylor Estate v. M.N.R., [1967] Tax A.B.C. 555, 21 D.T.C. 405

A. Yager v. The Queen, [1985] 1 C.T.C. 89

Non-Competition Agreements

Annabelle Candy Co. v. Commissioner, 314 F 2nd 1, 7-8 (9th Cir. 1962)

Better Beverages, Inc. v. U.S., 80-2 UST.C. Para 9516

Crutchfield v. Crutchfield (1988), 10 R.F.L. (3d) 247 (Ont. H.C.J.)

Deguire v. Deguire (1998), 34 R.F.L. (4th) 164

Forward Communications Corp. v. U.S., 78-2 UST.C. Para. 9542 (Ct Cl Trial Div 1978); affd in part and revd in part 608 F 2nd 485 (Ct Cl 1979)

General Insurance Agency Inc. v. Commissioner 17 BTA 1213 (1929)

Golden State Towel and Linen Service v. U.S., 67-1 UST.C. Para 9302, 179 Ct Cl 300, 373 F 2nd 938 (1967)

Katz v. Katz, June 27, 1989, Ontario U.F.Ct. (unreported)

Michaels v. Commissioner 12 T.C. 17, 19 (1949)

Morrison v. Rathmell, 650 SW 2nd 145

Visador Co. v. Commissioner T.C. Memo 1973-173

Oppression Remedy

Re Abraham and Inter Wide Investments Ltd. et al. (1985), 51 O.R. (2d) 460

Arthur v. Signum Communications Ltd., [1993] O.J. No. 1928

Camroux v. Armstrong (1990), 47 B.L.R. 302

Diligenti v. RMWD Operations Kelowna Ltd. (1978), 4 B.C.L.R. 134

Re Ferguson and Imax Systems Corp. (1983), 43 O.R. (2d) 128 (C.A.), leave to appeal to S.C.C. refused 52 N.R. 317n

Fulmer v. Peter D Fulmer Holdings Inc., [1997] O.J. No. 4121

Re Gandalman Investments Inc. et al. and Fogle et al. (1985), 52 O.R. (2d) 614

Johnston v. West Fraser Timber Co. Ltd. (1982), 17 B.L.R. 16, 19 B.L.R. 193 (C.A.)

Frances Mason v. Intercity Properties (1987), 59 O.R. (2d) 631 (Ont. C.A.)

Mathers v. Mathers (1992), 113 NSR (2d) 284, 309 A.P.R. 284 (T.D.); (1993), 123 NSR (2d) 14, 340 A.P.R. 14 (C.A.)

Michalak v. Biotech Electronics (1987), 35 B.L.R. 1

Naneff v. Con-Crete Holdings Ltd. (1995), 23 O.R. (3d) 481

Oakly v. McDouball (No.2) (1988), 37 B.L.R. 47

O' Conner v. Winchester Oil & Gas Inc. et al. (1986), 69 B.C.L.R. 330, 2 W.W.R. 737

Trimac Ltd. v. CIL Inc., [1990] 1 W.W.R. 133, (1989), 69 A.L.R. (2d) 113

Vedova et al. v. Garden House Inn Ltd. et al. (1985), 29 B.L.R. 236

Xerox Canada Inc. v. OMER (1992), 3 B.L.R. (2d) 68

Personal Goodwill

Adair v. M.N.R. (1962), 29 Tax A.B.C. 324, 16 D.T.C. 356

G-H Couture v. M.N.R. (1978), 32 D.T.C. 1511

W. H. Crandall v. M.N.R., [1974] C.T.C. 2289, 28 D.T.C. 1204

Croteau v. M.N.R. (1964), 36 Tax A.B.C. 299, 18 D.T.C. 643

Lecompte (J.) et al. v. M.N.R. (T.R.B.), [1976] C.T.C. 2127, 30 D.T.C. 1104

W.J. Legere v. M.N.R. [1980] C.T.C. 2202, 34 D.T.C. 1171

Losey v. M.N.R., [1957] C.T.C. 146, 11 D.T.C. 1098

Marentette v. M.N.R., [1977] C.T.C. 2147, 31 D.T.C. 97

Majean Investments Ltd. v. The Queen, [1994] 2 C.T.C. 2578

Nail v. Nail (1972), 477 SW (2d) 395

Rabow v. M.N.R., 26 Tax A.B.C. 445

A & N Robitaille Inc. v. M.N.R., [1996] 1 96 C.T.C. 2141

Samila v. Samila (1989), 32 B.C.L.R. (2d) 25

Thomas v. M.N.R. (1975), 29 D.T.C. 37

Young v. M.N.R. (1965), 38 Tax A.B.C. 73, 19 D.T.C. 242

1860-3043 Quebec Inc. v. The Queen (1995), 1 C.T.C. 2793

Point in Time

Dominion Metal & Refining Works Ltd. v. M.N.R., [1983] C.T.C. 2386

Lakehouse Enterprises Ltd. et al. v. M.N.R., [1983] C.T.C. 2431

Potential Control

The Queen v. Ann-Gus Holdings Ltd. (1984), 38 D.T.C. 6363 (F.C.A.)

Arctic Geophysical Ltd. v. M.N.R., [1967] C.T.C. 571, 22 D.T.C. 5013

Himley Estates Ltd. and Humble Investments Ltd. v. IRC, [1933] 1 K.B. 472, 17 T.C. 367

W.P. Leigherly Proprietary Ltd. v. FCT (1957), 100 C.L.R. 66, 11 A.T.D. 359

The Queen v. Lusita Holdings Ltd. (1984), 38 D.T.C. 6346

Renown Steel & Service Ltd. v. M.N.R., [1969] Tax A.B.C. 678, 23 D.T.C. 497

Rous & Mann Press Ltd. v. M.N.R. (1953), 9 Tax A.B.C. 56, 7 D.T.C. 326

John Shields & Co. (Perth) Ltd. v. IRC, [1950] S.C. 441, 29 T.C. 475

Fritz Werner Ltd. v. M.N.R., [1971] Tax A.B.C. 209, 25 D.T.C. 189

MFCT v. Sidney Williams (Holdings) Ltd. (1957), 100 C.L.R. 95, 11 A.T.D. 368

Prescribed Price

Lomb v. Sugden, [1936] 82 F 2d 166

J.J. West Estate v. Minister of Finance (B.C.), [1976] C.T.C. 313

Price Adjustment Clause

Guilder News Co. (1963) Ltd. et al. v. M.N.R., [1973] C.T.C. 1, 27 D.T.C. 5048 (F.C.A.)

Property in Control

Re Brant Investments et al. and KeepRite Inc. et al. (1987), 60 O.R. (2d) 737

Farnham v. Fingold, [1973] 2 O.R. 132 (C.A.)

Jones v. H.F. Ahmanson & Co., [1969] 1 Cal 3d 93, 460 P 2d 464

Re R.J. Jowsey Mining Co. Ltd., [1969] 2 O.R. 549, 6 D.L.R. (3d) 97

Perlman v. Feldman, 219 F 2d 173; cert. denied 349 U.S. 952 (1955); 154 F. Supp. 436 (1957)

Short v. Treasury Commissioners, [1948] A.C. 534; [1948] 2 All E.R. 509

Purchasers Considered

Salomon v. Commissioners of Customs and Excise, [1966] 3 W.L.R. 36

J.J. West Estate v. Minister of Finance (B.C.), [1976] C.T.C. 313

Purchase Price Allocation

Demco Management Ltd. v. The Queen, [1986] 1 C.T.C. 92

Franciss Enderes and IEM Management Ltd. v. M.N.R. (1980), 34 D.T.C. 1523

Rateable Value

Diligenti v. RMWD Operations Kelowna Ltd. (1978), 4 B.C.L.R. 134

Neonex International Ltd. v. Kolasa et al. (1978), 84 D.L.R. (3d) 446, [1978] 2 W.W.R. 593, 3 B.L.R. 1

Re Whitehorse Copper Mines Ltd.; Hudson Bay Mining and Smelting Co. Ltd. v. Lueck et al. (1980), 10 B.L.R. 113

Restrictions on Shares

Beament Estate v. M.N.R., [1970] S.C.R. 680

Groupe D' Investissement Savoie, Lavoie Inc. v. M.N.R., [1992] 1 C.T.C. 2355

Harold P. Connor v. The Queen, [1978] C.T.C. 669, affd [1979] C.T.C. 365

IRC v. Crossman, [1937] A.C. 26 at 34 (H.L.), [1936] 1 All E.R. 762 (H.L.)

Attorney General for Ireland v. Jameson, [1904] 2 IR 644 (upheld on appeal [1905] 2 IR 218)

Salvesen's Trustees v. IRC, [1930] S.L.T. 387

Trimac Ltd. v. CIL Inc., [1990] 1 W.W.R. 133, (1989), 69 A.L.R. (2d) 113

J.J. West Estate v. Minister of Finance (B.C.), [1976] C.T.C. 313

Shareholder Remedies

Foss v. Harbottle (1843), 2 Hare 461, 67 E.R. 189

Special Interest Purchaser

Cyprus Anvil Mining Corp. v. Dickson et al. (1983), 20 B.L.R. 21, 40 B.C.L.R. 180; (1987), 8 B.C.L.R. (2d) 145

Glass v. IRC, [1915] 52 S.C. LR 414

Holt v. IRC, [1953] 2 All E.R. 1499

Levitt v. M.N.R., [1976] C.T.C. 2307, 30 D.T.C. 1047

Edmund Littler Sr. v. M.N.R., [1976] C.T.C. 379; affd [1978] C.T.C. 235

IRC v. Clay, [1914] 3 K.B. 466 (C.A.)

IRC v. Crossman, [1937] A.C. 26 at 34 (H.L.), [1936] 1 All E.R. 762 (H.L.)

Re Lynall, [1969] 3 All E.R. 984 (C.A.)

Milne v. The Queen, [1994] 2 C.T.C. 2190

New Quebec Raglan Mines Ltd. v. Blok-Andersen (1993), 9 B.L.R. (2d) 93

Untermyer Estate v. Attorney General (B.C.), 1929 S.C.R. 84

Hugh Waddell Ltd. v. The Queen, [1982] C.T.C. 24

Second Shirley Rubin Family Trust (Trustee of) v. Revenue Properties Co., [1992] O.J. No. 1028

Verdun v. Verdun (1995), 9 R.F.L. (4th) 54

Westfair Foods Ltd. v. Watt (1992), 5 B.L.R. (2d) 179

Stock Market Data

Estate of Victor P. Clarke, 35 T.C.M 1482 (1976)

Re Libby, McNeill & Libby, 406 A. 2d 54 (Maine), revd August 16, 1979

Tallichet v. Commissioner, 33 T.C.M 1133 (1974)

Ivesleigh Holdings Inc. et al. v. M.N.R. (1978), 32 D.T.C. 1716

Stock Market Price and Fair Value/Fair Market Value

Estate of A.M. Collings Henderson v. M.N.R. (1975), 29 D.T.C. 5332; (1973), 27 D.T.C. 5471

Dairy Queen v. Queen (1995), 2 C.T.C. 2543

Re Domglas Inc.; Domglas Inc. v. Jarislowsky et al. (1981), 13 B.L.R. 135; affd (1982), 138 D.L.R. (3d) 521

Re Fraser Inc. and Sarah J. Aitken et al. (1989), 41 B.L.R. 87

Lough v. Canadian Natural Resources Ltd. (1983), 45 B.C.L.R. 335

Manning v. Harris Steel Group Inc., [1987] 1 W.W.R. 86, [1990] 1 W.W.R. 346 (C.A.)

Montgomery et al. v. Shell Canada Ltd. (1980), 5 W.W.R. 443, 111 D.L.R. (3d) 116

Morrison v. United Westburne Industries Ltd. (April 15, 1988), Toronto RE 1926/87

Neonex International Ltd. v. Kolasa et al. (1978), 84 D.L.R. (3d) 446, [1978] 2 W.W.R. 593, 3 B.L.R. 1

New Quebec Raglan Mines Ltd. v. Blok-Andersen (1993), 9 B.L.R. (2d) 93

Nunachiaq Inc. v. Chow (1993), 8 B.L.R. (2d) 109 (B.C.S.C.); affd [1994] B.C.J. No. 608

Frank C. Smeenk v. Dexleigh Corporation (1991), 49 B.L.R. 1

Re Wall and Redekop Corp et al. (1974), 50 D.L.R. (3d) 733 (B.C.S.C.)

Westfair Foods Ltd. v. Watt (1992), 5 B.L.R. (2d) 179

Xerox Canada v. OMERS (1992), 3 B.L.R. (2d) 68

TABLE OF SELECTED COURT DECISIONS 561

Tax and Disposition Costs

Ganson v. Ganson (1996), 66 A.C.WS (3d) 706

Goodfield v. Goodfield (1990), 71 O.R. (2d) 457

Heon v. Heon (1989), 22 R.F.L. (3d) 273 (Ont. H.C.J.)

85956 Holdings Lt. v. Fayerman Brothers Ltd. (1987), 57 Sask. R. 141, [1986] 2 W.W.R. 754

Kelly v. Kelly (1986), 50 R.F.L. (2d) 360

Khoury v. Khoury (1993), 122 N.B.R. (2d) 150, 306 A.P.R. 150 (Q.B.)

McPherson v. Mcpherson (1988), 48 D.L.R. (4th) 577

Sengmueller v. Sengmueller (1994), 17 O.R. (3d) 208 (C.A.)

Transaction Causing Dissent

Re Brant Investments et al. and KeepRite Inc. et al. (1989), 60 O.R. (2d) 737

Re Fraser Inc. and Sarah J. Aitken et al. (1989), 41 B.L.R. 87

Les Investissements Mont-Soleil Inc. v. National Drug Ltd. (1983), 22 B.L.R. 139

Re Ripley International Ltd. (1977), 1 B.L.R. 269

Valuation Approach/Methodology

Baniuk v. Carpenter (1991), 1 B.L.R. (2d) 300

British Columbia v. MacMillan Bloedel Ltd. (1995), 127 D.L.R. (4th)

Cyprus Anvil Mining Corp. v. Dickson et al. (1983), 20 B.L.R. 21, 40 B.C.L.R. 180; (1987), 8 B.C.L.R. (2d) 145

Re Domglas Inc.; Domglas Inc. v. Jarislowsky et al. (1981), 13 B.L.R. 135; affd (1982), 138 D.L.R. 521

Gilvesy Enterprises Inc. v. The Queen, [1997] 1 C.T.C. 2410

Glenex Industries Inc. v. R., [1997] 3 C.T.C. 2217

Gregoric v. Gregoric (1991), 4 O.R. (3d) 588

Jakobson v. Aggasiz Enterprises Ltd. (1988), 49 Man. R. (2d) 270

Kelvin Energy Ltd. v. Bahan et al. (1987), 52 Alta. L.R. (2d) 71

Khoury v. Khoury (1993), 122 N.B.R. (2d) 150, 306 A.P.R. 150 (Q.B.)

Lessany v. Lessany (1989), 17 R.F.L. (3d) 433

LoCicero v. B.A.C.M Industries Ltd. (1985), 31 Man. R. (2d) 208; (1986) 25 D.L.R. (4th) 269, 38 Man. R. (2d) 134 (Man. C.A.); [1988] 1 S.C.R. 399, [1988] 4 W.W.R. 671, 49 D.L.R. (4th) 159

Manning v. Harris Steel Group Inc., [1987] 1 W.W.R. 86, [1990] 1 W.W.R. 346 (C.A.)

MICA Management Centre Inc. v. Lockett (1988), 37 B.L.R. 209

Moase Produce v. Royal Bank of Canada (1987), 64 C.B.R. (NS) 191

Muskoka & Parry Sound Telephone Co. Ltd. v. Ontario Telephone Development Corp. (1984), 32 L.C.R. 154 (O.M.B.); (1985), 32 L.C.R. 238 (O.M.B.)

Nunachiaq Inc. v. Chow (1993), 8 B.L.R. (2d) 109 (B.C.S.C.); affd [1994] B.C.J. No. 608

Pocklington Foods Inc. v. Alberta (Provincial Treasurer), [1998] A.J. No. 364

Samila v. Samila (1989), 32 B.C.L.R. (2d) 25

S.G. & S. Investments (1972) Ltd. v. Golden Boy Foods Inc. (1992), 3 B.L.R. (2d) 80

Shepp v. R., [1999] 1 C.T.C. 2889

Frank C. Smeenk v. Dexleigh Corporation (1991), 49 B.L.R. 1

G. D. Stanfield v. M.N.R. (1979), 3 D.T.C. 128

Starkman v. Starkman (1991), 75 O.R. (2d) 19

Stan Steevs & Sons Ltd. v. R., [1996] 1 C.T.C. 2818

H. Taylor Estate v. M.N.R., [1990] 2 C.T.C. 2304

Westfair Foods Ltd. v. Watt (1992), 5 B.L.R. (2d) 179

Value

Caratun v. Caratun (1992), 42 R.F.L. (3d) 113

Re Corless and Corless (1987), 8 O.R. (2d) 19

Dibbley v. Dibbley and Liddle (1987), 5 R.F.L. (3d) 381

Heon v. Heon (1989), 22 R.F.L. (3d), 273 (Ont. H.C.J.)

Jackh v. Jackh (1981), 22 B.C.L.R. 182 (S.C.)

Menage v. Hedges (1987), 8 R.F.L. (3d) 225

Montague v. Montague (1992), 37 A.C.WS (3d) 520 (Ont. Ct. (Gen. Div.)), affd (1996), 23 R.F.L. (4th) (Ont. C.A.)

Pocklington Foods Inc. v. Alberta (Provincial Treasurer), [1998] A.J. No. 364

Rawluk v. Rawluk (1986), 55 O.R. (2d) 704, 3 R.F.L. (3d) 113 (H.C.J.); affd 10 R.F.L. (3d) 113 (Ont. C.A.); January 25, 1990, S.C.C.

Sartori v. Sartori (1993), 13 O.R. (3d) 710

Value Based on Prospects

Cyprus Anvil Mining Corp. v. Dickson et al. (1983), 20 B.L.R. 21, 40 B.C.L.R. 180; (1987), 8 B.C.L.R. (2d) 145

Value-to-Owner

Brinkos v. Brinkos (1986), 4 R.F.L. (3d) 381; revd (1989), 20 R.F.L. (3d) 445 (C.A.)

LoCicero v. B.A.C.M Industries Ltd. (1985), 31 Man. R. (2d) 208; (1986), 25 D.L.R. (4th) 269, 38 Man. R. (2d) 134 (Man. C.A.); [1988] 4 W.W.R. 671, 49 D.L.R. (4th) 159

Montague v. Montague (1992), 37 A.C.WS (3d) 520 (Ont. Ct. (Gen. Div.)); affd (1997), 23 R.F.L. (4th) 62 (Ont. C.A.)

Windup – Court Ordered

Frances Mason v. Intercity Properties (1987), 59 O.R. (2d) 631 (Ont. C.A.)

Appendix B
Selected Financial Ratios

Overview

Ratio analysis frequently is used in both notional market valuations and open market pricing transactions to assist in understanding important trends and relationships for the business being valued, and to help in detecting issues that should be further investigated during the course of the valuation assignment. However, the computation of a myriad of financial ratios and other ratios should not be taken to provide an all-encompassing view of a particular business, and the caveats in the application of ratio analysis should be kept in mind – see Chapter 3.

This Appendix provides an overview of some of the more common financial ratios applied in business valuation. It is not intended to be an exhaustive discussion. More details can be found in many available textbooks on financial management.

Financial ratios generally can be categorized as relating to:

- liquidity;
- financial leverage;
- efficiency;
- profitability; and
- return on investment.

Liquidity Ratios

Liquidity ratios are a measure of the short term financial strength of the business and generally focus on:

- the ability of the business to meet its short term obligations as they are due;
- the general degree of risk associated with the types of assets held by the business;
- the possible existence of redundant assets; and
- the ability of the business to withstand short term fluctuations in cash flow.

Commonly used measures for assessing short term liquidity are the current ratio, quick (or 'acid test') ratio, and the cash cycle of a business.

$$\text{Current Ratio} = \frac{\text{Current Assets}}{\text{Current Liabilities}}$$

Sometimes referred to as the working capital ratio, the current ratio indicates the extent to which short term creditors' claims are covered by assets expected to be converted to cash in the normal operating cycle of the business, usually one year. When compared to the current ratio of prior periods and industry averages, the short term strength of the operations can be assessed and, if apparently stronger than normal in the industry, may be an indicator of excess working capital, which in turn, may be a redundant asset. Alternatively, if a company's current ratio is consistently high relative to the industry norm (for example, due to excessive overdue accounts receivable or inventory levels), this ratio may indicate financial mismanagement. Care must be taken to analyze the composition of the current assets, having regard to the quality of each asset in terms of its convertibility into cash during the normal operating cycle of a business.

$$\text{Quick Ratio} = \frac{\text{Cash \& Equivalents} + \text{Accounts Receivable}}{\text{Current Liabilities}}$$

This ratio, when analyzed in conjunction with the current ratio, assists in the assessment of short term strength, and may reveal current asset composition differences from industry averages. The relative strength or weakness of liquidity in the company and the existence of excess working capital or redundant assets may be determined through inter-period comparisons, industry average comparisons, and possibly examination of the company's present bank financing ratios.

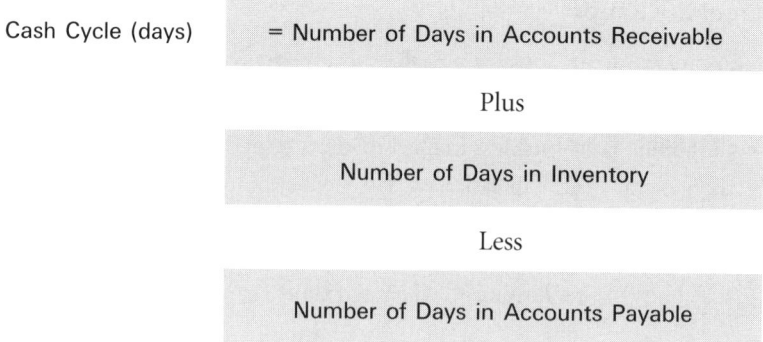

The cash cycle of a business is the length of time it takes for a business to convert its investment in inventories and accounts receivable into cash (including a 'gross profit' component). This calculation generally applies to traditional 'product' businesses that purchase inventory for resale. For credit sales, there normally is a time period (sometimes significant) between recording a sale for accounting purposes and cash collection. Offsetting the need for cash in many cases is that all or part of the funds required to finance the inventory may be absorbed by trade credit. The longer the cash cycle, the greater the need for 'net trade working capital', which reduces what otherwise would be discretionary cash flow of the business. The calculation of number of days in accounts receivable is discussed subsequently in this Appendix, and the calculations for number of days in inventory and accounts payable are calculated in a similar fashion.

Financial Leverage Ratios

Financial leverage is the degree to which a business is financed by interest bearing debt. Higher financial leverage generally means higher financial risk. In an economic downturn, a highly-levered business might not be able to earn a return in excess of the cost of borrowed capital. Accordingly, borrowing decisions must balance higher relative return on capital invested by equity participants against higher risk. The assessment of the degree of leverage in a business provides an indication of:

- the inherent financial risk of the business; and
- so-called 'hidden redundancy' due to an under-levered financial position.

There are several ratios which indicate the degree of financial leverage of an enterprise, such as assets to net worth, debt to total capital, interest coverage, and debt serviceability.

$$\text{Assets to Net Worth} = \frac{\text{Total Assets}}{\text{Shareholders Equity}}$$

The assets to net worth ratio reflects the degree to which the assets of a business are financed by equity as opposed to debt (including trade debt and borrowed funds). A higher ratio indicates a higher degree of financial leverage. A refinement to this calculation is to deduct current (trade) liabilities from total assets. A ratio of 1.0 would be reflective of an 'all equity (i.e. 'unlevered') firm'.

$$\text{Debt to Total Capital} = \frac{\text{Interest Bearing Debt and Equivalents}}{\text{Total Capitalization}}$$

Interest bearing debt and equivalents normally includes short term and long term interest bearing debt such as bank loans, capital leases, mortgages, and so on. Interest bearing debt equivalents refers to items such as interest-free loans from shareholders. Total capitalization reflects the sum of interest bearing debt and equity of the firm, ideally measured at market values – i.e. the 'enterprise value' of the business. Accordingly, the debt to total capital ratio frequently is adopted as the basis upon which an 'appropriate' capital structure is measured in valuing a business. A variation to this ratio is a 'debt to equity' calculation whereby the market value of the equity in the business forms the denominator.

$$\text{Interest Coverage} = \frac{\text{Earnings Before Interest and Taxes (EBIT)}}{\text{Interest Charges}}$$

This ratio is used as a measurement of safety, or risk in a business financed by debt and helps assess long term solvency from an income statement rather than from a balance sheet perspective. Interest coverage helps to measure the extent that a business' operating income can decline before the business may be unable to meet its financial (interest expense) obligations.

$$\text{Debt Serviceability} = \frac{\text{Unlevered Discretionary Cash Flow}}{\text{Principal Repayments} + \text{Interest Charges Net of Tax}}$$

This ratio measures the ability of a business to service its debt based on its operating cash flows, prior to relying on financing from equity, new debt, or other sources. When considering the financial risk inherent in the prevailing debt structure, or attempting to assess the degree of leverage available in the business, the ability to service the debt must be considered along with the capacity to secure it. Unlevered discretionary cash flows represent 'free' cash flows before debt servicing costs – see Chapter 4. Accordingly, those free cash flows must first be applied to satisfy the debt service obligations of a business before its equity holders can realize an economic return. Interest charges are measured net of tax where such payments are deductible for income tax purposes. Where the debt serviceability ratio is less than 1, the business must either secure additional external financing (debt or equity), or increase unlevered discretionary cash flows by such means as forgoing necessary operating or capital expenditures in favour of debt servicing payments. The latter approach may negatively influence the 'enterprise value' of the business.

Efficiency Ratios

Efficiency ratios may be used to assess asset productivity, and sometimes assist in detecting uneconomic management practices or redundant assets within a business. Commonly-used efficiency ratios include average accounts receivable collection period (or 'days in accounts receivable'), inventory turnover, net trade working capital to sales, and total asset turnover.

$$\text{Average Collection Period (days)} = \frac{\text{Average Accounts Receivable}}{\text{Credit Sales per Day}}$$

This ratio reflects the efficiency of management in collecting accounts receivable, particularly when measured against the company's credit terms and industry averages. The denominator, credit sales per day, normally is calculated as net revenues excluding cash sales divided by 365 days. Business, industry, and economic conditions must be evaluated in order to assess control over collections versus a restrictive element in sales growth due to tight credit policies.

$$\text{Inventory Turnover} = \frac{\text{Cost of Goods Sold}}{\text{Average Inventory}}$$

This ratio indicates how often during an accounting cycle the inventory available for sale is sold. Generally a high turnover ratio would suggest reduced risk as relatively large sums of money are not tied up in inventories, and management appears efficient in its inventory control. However, a high inventory turnover ratio must also be considered for its effects on inventory shortages and possible resultant lost sales or production problems. A low turnover may indicate obsolete or slow-moving inventories.

$$\text{Net Trade Working Capital to Sales} = \frac{\text{Net Trade Working Capital}}{\text{Revenues}}$$

The ratio of net trade working capital to sales assists in measuring the amount of working capital (excluding interest bearing debt, cash, and current assets and current liabilities that are not of a 'trade' nature) that a business needs to support existing and prospective revenue levels. Net trade working capital normally is defined as accounts payable plus inventories less accounts payable, accrued liabilities, and income taxes payable. In many businesses, as revenues grow, a portion of the cash flow must be used to finance increases in net trade working capital requirements, and hence is not 'discretionary' cash flow.

$$\text{Asset Turnover} = \frac{\text{Revenues}}{\text{Average Total Assets}}$$

This ratio measures the ability of a business to generate revenues using its existing asset base. A higher ratio implies greater efficiency. As is the case with other financial ratios, the asset turnover ratio is sensitive to the accounting policy choices of a business. In particular, accounting policies affecting depreciation, asset capitalization, and operating vs. capital leases can have a significant impact on the calculated asset turnover. Therefore, care must be taken in comparing the asset turnover ratio to industry averages or other benchmarks.

Profitability Ratios

Profitability ratios help in assessing what proportion of revenues is retained by the business at some level. As such, profitability ratios focus on the income statement of a business. Common profitability ratios include gross profit margin, EBIT-DA margin, and net profit margin.

$$\text{Gross Profit Margin} = \frac{\text{Gross Profit}}{\text{Revenues}}$$

This ratio is useful in determining the relationship between direct costs and selling prices over a period of time. When compared to industry averages and in light of changing business conditions, it may give some insight into the effectiveness of management in coping with change. The relationship of each of the components of cost of goods sold to revenues will also assist in the analysis of the changes in the gross profit margin ratio. That is, it may become apparent that one or more of direct labour, materials, or overhead has had a significant effect on the gross profit margin. If the information is available, an attempt should be made to assess gross profit margins by product line, geographic area, division, or such other basis as may be appropriate in order to better assess the risks and returns comprising the business results.

$$\text{EBIT - DA Margin} = \frac{\text{EBIT - DA}}{\text{Revenues}}$$

EBIT-DA (earnings before interest, taxes, depreciation, and amortization) is a measure of cash flow from the operations of a business, before working capital, capital investment, and income taxes. It therefore avoids distortions due to the classification of expense items for financial accounting purposes. Variations of this ratio include [EBIT-DA less capital expenditures] to sales, and EBIT (earnings before interest and taxes) to sales.

$$\text{Net Profit Margin} = \frac{\text{Net Profit}}{\text{Revenues}}$$

When compared to industry averages, this ratio may assist in measuring management's ability to operate successfully from an equity holder's perspective. The net profit measure is determined after income taxes, and should exclude extraordinary items. The risk inherent in falling selling prices or increases in costs may be more readily comprehended when considered in relation to this ratio. The net profit margin ratio should be compared with the gross profit margin and EBIT-DA margin, and their trends analyzed over time. A variation of this ratio is to divide discretionary cash flows (net of debt servicing costs) into revenues.

Return on Investment

Ratios that focus on return on investment are those that help measure whether a business is generating income at levels that produce an 'adequate' return given the resources that are employed by it. Return on investment ratios principally focus on return on assets and return on equity (or return on invested capital).

$$\text{Return on Assets} = \frac{\text{EBIT}}{\text{Average Total Assets}}$$

The return on assets ratio measures the ability of a business' asset base to generate income. The income measure normally used is earnings before interest and taxes (EBIT), so that the measure of profitability is not distorted by how those assets are financed. EBIT is a pre-tax return. A variation of this ratio is to use [EBIT x (1 – tax rate)] in the numerator to generate an unlevered net income measure. Alternatively, unlevered discretionary cash flow sometimes is used in the numerator in lieu of after-tax EBIT. Another common variation is to use net assets in the denominator, being total assets less current trade liabilities. Since the return on assets measure is a function of the profit level of a business and the efficiency in which assets are employed, return on assets also can be derived as the product of EBIT margin and asset turnover.

$$\text{Return on Equity} = \frac{\text{Net Income}}{\text{Shareholders Equity}}$$

This ratio determines the rate of return on the owners' investment in the business and may be compared with industry averages (recognizing important differences in accounting policies and other differences that might exist). Ideally, shareholder's equity is measured at market rates rather than based on historical accounting data. A refinement of this calculation is the computation of a net return on common equity such that the net income would be reduced by preferred dividends and the denominator would become the average common equity outstanding during the period. The ability of a business to generate a return on equity is a function of its operating profitability, financial leverage, and operating efficiency. Accordingly, in what commonly is referred to as the 'Dupont Formula', the return on equity can be derived as follows:

Return on Equity = Net Profit Margin × Asset Turnover × Assets to Net Worth

Bibliography

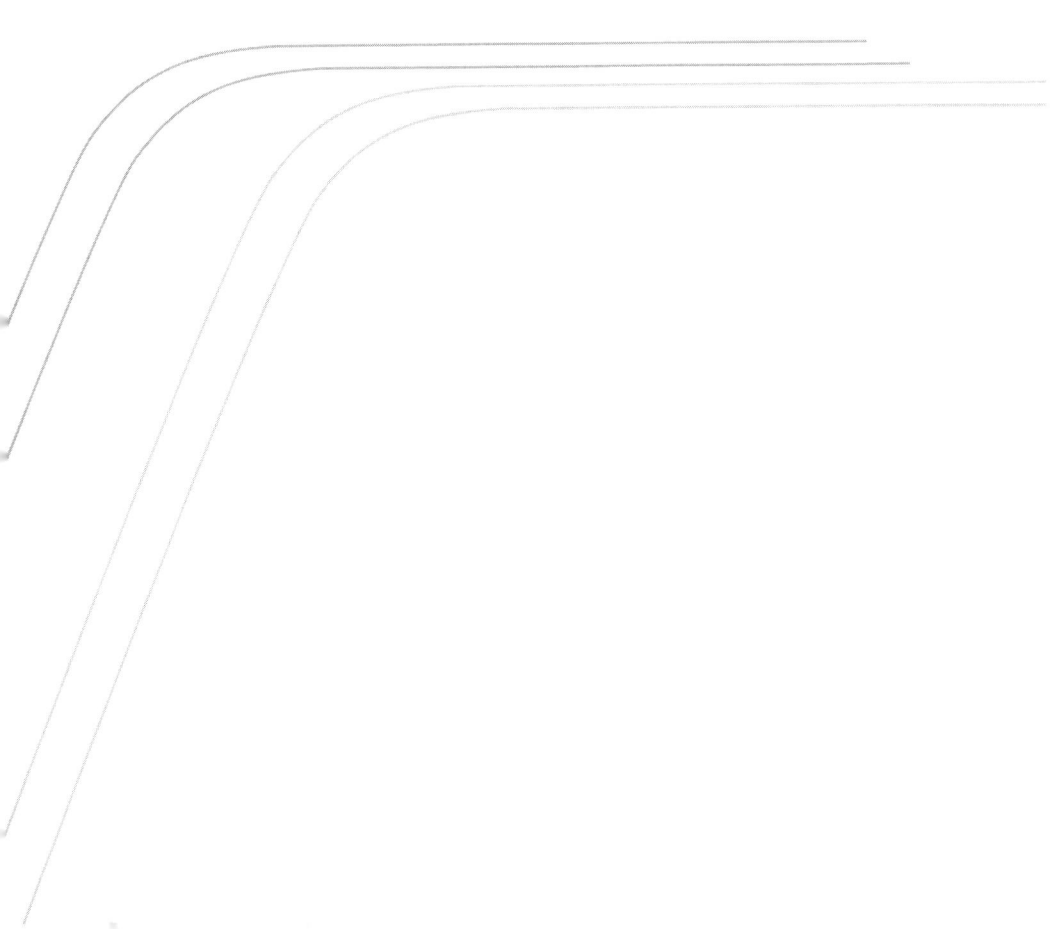

Articles

Abrams, Jay B. "Discount For Lack of Marketability: A Theoretical Model." *Business Valuation Review*, September 1994, pp. 132-139.

Adelstein, Joel A. "Minority Discounts Revisited." *Journal of Business Valuation*, 1993, pp. 413-432.

Anderson, Ronald C. and Groth, John C. "Capital Structure: Perspectives for Managers." *Management Decision*, July 1997, pp. 552-562.

Anderson, Simon J. "Valuing High Technology Business – Fact vs. Fantasy." *Journal of Business Valuation*, 1999, pp. 115-132.

Annin, Michael. "Fama-French and Small Company Cost of Equity Calculations." *Business Valuation Review*, March 1997, pp. 3-13.

Annin, Michael. "Understanding and Quantifying Control Premiums: The Value of Control vs. Synergies or Strategic Advantages. Part I." *Journal of Business Valuation*, 1999, pp. 31-35.

Anson, Weston. "Establishing Market Values for Brands, Trademarks and Marketing Tangibles." *Business Valuation Review*, June 1996, pp. 47-56.

Baarenbaum, Dr. Lester. "Utilizing the Gordon Model: Discounting Net Income vs. Available Cash Flow." *Journal of Business Valuation*, 1987, pp. 119-127.

Banister Financial, Inc. "Discounts for Lack of Marketability: A Highly Abbreviated Overview." www.cris.com/~Banniste/Mktdisco.htm, *Fair Value*, September 1994, pp. 1-4.

Barron, Robert A. "Some Comments on the Discount Valuation of Publicly Traded Stock for Federal Estate, Gift, and Income Tax Purposes." *Securities Regulation Law Journal*, Summer 1996, pp. 199-207.

Blair, Vernon A. "The Use and Abuse of Cash Flows." *Journal of Business Valuation*, 1985, pp. 67-78.

Bowlin, Oswald D. and Dukes, William P. "A Comparison of Valuation Techniques for Closely Held Firms." *Business Valuation Review*, June 1993, pp. 80-91.

Bowlin, Oswald D., Dukes, William P., and Ma, Christopher K. "Valuation of Closely-Held Firms: A Survey." *Journal of Business Finance and Accounting*, April 1996, pp. 419-439.

Booth, Dr. Lawrence. "The Capital Asset Pricing Model + Equity Risk Premiums and the Privately-Held Business." *The 1998 CICBV/ASA Joint Business Valuation Conference*, September 1998, pp. 1-36.

Carlson, Severin C. "Using The Capital Asset Pricing Model To Determine Capitalization Rates: Adjusting For Differences In Financial Structure." *Business Valuation Review*, June 1991, pp. 58-66.

Chaganti, Rajeswararao, Deeds, David and DeCarolis, Dona. "Predictors of Capital Structure in Small Ventures." *Entrepreneurship: Theory and Practice*, Winter 1995, pp. 7-19.

Chu, Franklin J. "Optimal Capital Structure Revisited." *The Bankers Magazine*, September-October 1996, pp. 9-14.

Dobner, Michael. "Let's Get Objective." *The Business Valuator*, 1992, No.4 Vol.16, pp. 7-8.

Dobner, Michael. "Are We Using the Right Discount Rates?" *The Business Valuator*, 1990, No.2 Vol.14, pp. 5-6.

Eastman, Kent. "EBITDA; An Overrated Tool for Cash Flow Analysis." *Commercial Lending Review*, Spring 1997, pp. 64-72.

Eber, Victor I. "Statements in Quotes." *Journal of Accountancy*, June 1984, pp. 103-118.

Emory, John D. "The Value of Marketability As Illustrated In Initial Public Offerings of Common Stock." *Business Valuation Review*, December 1995, pp. 155-160.

Fairchild, Keith VM. and Woodley, Thomas T. "Valuation of Privately-Held Companies: A Survey of Investment Banking Firms." *Business Valuation Review*, September 1990, pp. 81-87.

Firth, Michael. "The Impact of Institutional Stockholders and Managerial Interests on the Capital Structure of Firms." *Managerial & Decision Economics*, March-April 1995, pp. 167-176.

Fitchett, Gary. "Financing Closely-Held Businesses." *Journal of Business Valuation*, 1989, pp. 11-20.

Fowler, Bradley A. "Venture Capital Rates of Return Revisited." *Business Valuation Review*, March 1996, pp. 13-16.

Gilbert, Gregory A. "Discount Rates and Capitalization Rates – Where are We?" *Business Valuation Review*, December 1990, pp. 108-113.

Greer, Willis R. "The Growth Rate Term in the Capitalization Model." *Business Valuation Review*, June 1996, pp. 72-79.

Guthrie, Art and Harry, Glen. "Establishing Multiples for Business Valuations." *The Journal of Business Valuation*, 1985, pp. 19-44.

Hawkins, George B. "Critically Assessing a Business Valuation: Is the Capitalization Rate Used Reasonable?" *Banister Financial, Inc.*, June 1998, pp. 1-6.

Hawkins, George B. "Public & Private Company Differences Can Have Major Valuation Implications." *Banister Financial, Inc.*, February 1998, pp. 1-5.

Hawkins, George B., Public and Private Company Differences Have Major Valuation Implications." *Business Valuation Digest*, November 1997, pp. 1-5.

Howitt, Idelle A. "Valuing Closely Held Stock. High Net Worth: The Accouterments of Success." *The CPA Journal Online*, September 1993.

King, David W. "The Equity Risk Premium for Cost of Capital Studies: Alternatives to Ibbotson." *Business Valuation Review*, September 1994, pp. 123-129.

Kish, Richard J., Ryen, Glen T. and Vasconcellos, Geraldo M. "Capital Structure Decisions: What Have I Learned?" *Business Horizons*, September-October 1997, pp. 41-51.

Krishnan, V. Sivarama and Moyer, R. Charles. "Determinants of Capital Structure: An Empirical Analysis of Firms in Industrialized Countries." *Managerial Finance*, February 1996, pp. 39-56.

Lauzon, Bernard and St-Amour Jacques. "Discounting Cash Flows . . . But Which Ones?" *Journal of Business Valuation*, 1987, pp. 195-225.

Leland, Hayne E. and Toft, Klaus Bjerre. "Optimal Capital Structure, Endogenous Bankruptcy, and the Term Structure of Credit Spreads." *Journal of Finance*, July 1996, pp. 987-1020.

Leonard, Gary B. "Business Valuations: Capitalization Rates; Risk Free Rates of Return." *The Business Valuator*, 1991, pp. 4-5.

Leung, Tony T.S. "Myths about Capitalization Rate and Risk Premium." *Business Valuation News*, March 1996, pp.6-10.

Lippitt, Jeffrey W. and Mastracchio, Nicholas J. "A Comparison of the Earnings Capitalization and the Excess Earnings Models in the Valuation of Closely-Held Businesses." *Journal of Small Business Management*, January 1996, pp. 1-12.

Lippitt, Jeffrey W. and Mastracchio Jr., Nicholas J. "Developing Capitalization Rates for Valuing a Business." *The CPA Journal*, November 1995, pp. 24-28.

Macdonnel, Ian. "Understanding How IPO's are Valued: The Nuts and Bolts." *Insight Information Inc. Conference Report Going Public*, 1997, pp. 147-168.

McDougall, Craig and Taylor, Richard. "Capital Asset Pricing Model Practical Applications." *Arthur Anderson*, February 1997, pp. 1-20.

Mercer, Z. Christopher. "The Adjusted Capital Asset Pricing Model for Developing Capitalization Rates: An Extension of Previous 'Build-Up' Methodologies Based Upon the Capital Asset Pricing Model." *Business Valuation Review*, December 1989, pp. 147-156.

Mercer, Z. Christopher. "Understanding And Quantifying Control Premiums: The Value of Control vs. Synergies or Strategic Advantages." Part II. *Journal of Business Valuation*, 1999.

Mercer, Z. Christopher, and Brown, Terry S. "Fair Market Value vs. The Real World". *Business Valuation Review*, March 1999, pp. 16-25.

Mercer, Z. Christopher. "A Brief Review of Control Premiums and Minority Interest Discounts". *Journal of Business Valuation*, 1997, pp. 365-387.

Mullen, Maggie. "Critical Valuation Issues in International Mergers and Acquisitions". *Journal of Business Valuation*, 1997, pp. 399-414.

Nath, Eric W. "How Public Guideline Companies Represent 'Control' Value for a Private Company". *Business Valuation Review*, December 1997, pp. 167-171.

Pratt, Shannon P. "Developing the Valuation Model – Comparisons, Approaches, and Sources." *Journal of Business Valuation*, 1985, pp. 7-18.

Rajan, Raghuram G. and Zingales, Luigi. "What Do We Know About Capital Structure? Some Evidence from International Data." *Journal of Finance*, December 1995, pp. 1421-1461.

Razaire, Christopher. "How to Figure Odds in Forecasting Acquisition Results." *Mergers & Acquisitions*, November-December 1995, pp. 6-12.

Rees, William P. "The Impact of Dividends, Debt and Investment on Valuation Models." *Journal of Business Finance and Accounting*, September 1997, pp. 1111-1141.

Revisuisse Price Waterhouse, Switzerland. "Appendix I (B): Additional Guidance Material on the Discounted Cash Flow Method." www.rpw.ch/appb.htm, April 21, 1998, pp. 1-2.

Richman, Tom. "Capital Structure: What Matters, What Doesn't." *Harvard Business Review*, September-October 1995, p.15.

Saunders, Philip Jr. "Control Premiums And Minority Discounts." www.philipsaunders.com Philip Saunders Associates Economics and Finance, 1998.

Schilt, James H. "Selection of Capitalization Rules For Valuing a Closely-Held Business." *Business Valuation News*, June 1982, pp. 2-4.

Schilt, James H. "Selection of Capitalization Rates – Revisited." *Business Valuation Review*, June 1991, pp. 51-52.

Schmidt, Richard M. "Valuing the Assets of a Manufacturing Company." *Appraisal Journal*, April 1997, pp. 120-124.

Swad, Randy. "Discount and Capitalization Rates in Business Valuations." *The CPA Journal Online*, October 1994, pp. 1-12.

Swad, Randy. "Discount and Capitalization Rates in Business Valuations." *Business Valuation Digest*, July 1995, pp. 1-7.

Taub, Maxwell J. "Some Thoughts on the Lack of Marketability Discount." *Business Valuation Review*, September 1994, pp. 113-114.

Ward, David G. "Financing Alternatives and Impact on Value." *Journal of Business Valuation*, 1995, pp. 103-115.

Wise, Richard M. "Multiple-of-Revenues as a Valuation Method." *Business Valuation Digest*, October 1996, pp.1-4.

Zemanovich, John. "Price is What You Pay, Intrinsic Value is What You Get." *Investor's Digest*, August 14, 1998, pp.480.

Books

Albo, Wayne, Bryk, Adam, and Pigott, Andrew. *The Purchase and Sale of Privately-Held Businesses, 3rd ed.* Toronto, Ontario. CICA, 2000.

Beam, R.E., Laiken, S.N. "Introduction to Federal Income Taxation in Canada" 19th ed. 1998-1999, CCH Canada Ltd.

Copeland, Tom, Koller, Tim and Murrin, Jack. *Valuation: Measuring and Managing the Value of Companies, Second Edition.* New York, New York. John Wiley & Sons, 1995.

Fishman, Jay E., Pratt, Shannon P., Griffith, J. Clifford and Wilson, D. Keith. "Capitalized and Discounted Returns Methods." *Guide to Business Valuations,* March 1998, pp. 5.1-5.72.

Mercer, Z. Christopher. *Quantifying Marketability Discounts.* Memphis, Tennessee: Peabody Publishing, LP, 1997.

Parr, Russell L. and Smith, Gordon V. *Valuation of Intellectual Property and Intangible Assets.* New York, New York. John Wiley & Sons, 1994.

Pratt, Shannon P., Reilly, Robert F. and Schweihs, Robert P. *Valuing a Business: The Analysis and Appraisal of Closely Held Companies.* McGraw Hill, 1996.

Reilly, Frank K, Brown, Keith C., *Investment Analysis and Portfolio Management, 5th ed.,* Dryden Press, 1997.

Topical Index

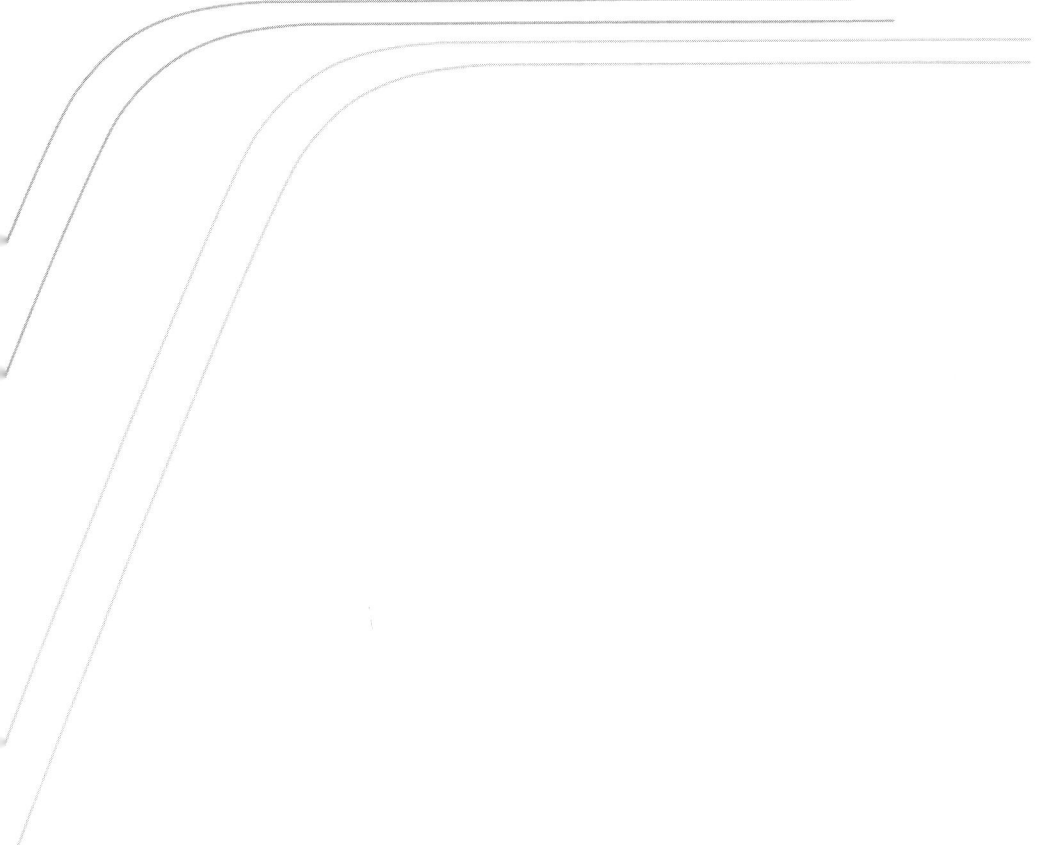

A

Absolute risk, xiii
Accounting earnings, 342, 305, 353
Accounting policies, 330, 334, 354, 357
Accounts receivable, 375
Acquisition
    date, xiii, 64
    for shares, 428
    of property, 506
Active business, 528
Additional refundable tax, 236
Adjusted cost base, xiii, 128, 236, 383, 385, 391, 507, 512, 514, 515, 518, 519, 522, 523, 526, 530, 531
Adjusted net book value, xiii, 213, 214, 233
    methodology, 213, 235
Allowable business investment losses, 523
Amalgamation, xiii, 430, 450, 513
Amortization, xiii, 24, 114, 118, 124, 128, 135, 182, 335, 354, 355, 371, 572
Apportionment between land and building, 231
Appraisal, xiii, 12, 40 - 43, 47, 58, 219, 225, 237, 323, 450, 451, 480, 484, 488, 539
    date, xiii
    remedies, xiv, 40
Arm's length, 37, 396, 506
    disposition, 529
Articles of Incorporation, 441, 445, 453 - 454, 465, 480, 484, 487
Assets
    excess net, 141
    intangible, 216, 335
        identifiable, 217, 375, 377
        non-identifiable, 24, 377
    net tangible, 50, 63, 332, 365
    non-operating, 97
    ratio to net worth, 569
    real estate, 238, 376

redundant, xxxii, 26, 75, 81, 85, 92 - 99, 101 - 104, 107, 110, 114 - 117, 119, 137, 139 - 141, 147 - 149, 166, 172, 175, 178, 179, 186, 190, 197, 208, 209, 224, 235, 245, 267, 312, 341, 344, 356, 357, 359, 360, 366, 369, 371, 414, 418, 420, 510, 567, 570
    transaction, xiv, 165, 224
    vs. shares, 60, 204, 515
Averaging results, 122

B

Bankruptcy Act, 373
Bankruptcy
    costs, 253
    of shareholder, 462
Bare trustees, 441
Base rate of return, xiv, 284, 289, 296
Benchmark
    analysis, xiv, 336
    error, 319
Beta factor, 316, 318
Blockage discount, xiv, 375
Block premiums and discounts, 499
Block trades, 347
Business specific risk, 318
    factors, 284, 296, 318
Buy/sell
    agreement, xv
    clause, 495
    provisions, 462
    reciprocal provisions, 463
By-laws, 445, 453 - 454, 480, 487

C

Canada Business Corporations Act, 439, 441, 445
Canada Customs and Revenue Agency, 443, 500
Canada, resident of, becoming or ceasing to be, 509

Canadian controlled private corporation (CCPC), xv, 236, 238, 383, 408, 528
Capital Asset Pricing Model (CAPM), xv, 9, 315, 318 - 319
Capital cost allowance (CCA), xv
    tax shield, 128, 214
Capital cost, undepreciated, 135
Capital dividend account, xv, 382, 383, 458, 515, 527
Capital expenditures, 308, 356
Capital gains, 381, 383, 426, 516
    exemption, 457, 523
        'super' exemption, 516
    reserves, 457, 523
    rollover, 524
    strips, 531
Capital intensive business, xv, 66, 298, 332, 365, 369
Capital investment, 177, 189
Capital market theory, 316
Capital structure, 207, 261 - 262, 264, 266 - 267, 282, 332, 336, 356, 405, 413, 477, 570
    determinants, 261
Capital surplus on hand, 515, 383
Capitalization, 244, 264, 371
Capitalization of
    discretionary cash flow methodology, 113, 114, 177, 280 - 281, 369
    earnings methodology, dual, 365
    maintainable earnings methodology, 353, 356, 369
Capitalization rate, xvi, 114, 132, 195, 230, 279, 305, 317, 320, 339, 356, 358, 366
    discount rate, 195, 411 - 412, 415
CAPM. *See* Capital Asset Pricing Model
Cash
    price in terms of, 38, 396
Cash cycle, 568
Cash flow
    capitalized, xvi, 115, 149, 301, 309, 400, 423
    discounted, 339
        methodology, 113 - 114, 175, 177, 217, 279, 281, 354, 411

discretionary, xix, 25 - 26, 61, 113, 115, 131, 175, 195, 205, 217, 244,
   251, 265, 280, 281, 283, 293, 300, 307, 332, 353, 403, 411, 414
      methodology, 371
      normalized, 300
      probabilized, 300
   from operations, 114, 177, 186
   real estate valuation methodologies, 229
CCAA. *See* Companies Creditors Arrangement Act
CCPC. *See* Canadian controlled private corporation
Classes of common shares, 157
Coattail provision, xvi, 455, 465, 495
Common size financial statements, 84, 85
Companies Creditors Arrangements Act (CCAA), 373
Company management, 17
Comparability adjustments, 334
Comparable, 231, 265, 267, 318, 320, 330, 333, 336, 340
   Companies, 330
   data, 322
   transactions, 417
Comparative analysis, 328
Compulsion
   to act, 37, 252, 396
   to transact, 176, 263
Compulsory
   acquisition provisions, 484
   sale, xvi, 498
Confidential information memorandum, xvi
Conglomerate, xvii, 145
Consideration
   form of, 424
   non-cash, 38
Consulting contracts, 426
Contingencies, 381
Contingent liabilities, 379

Control
    absolute, 439, 475, 478
    de facto, xvii, 438, 442
    de jure, xvii, 438, 442
    effective, 438, 484
    family, 443, 483
    group, xxii, 442 - 444, Appendix A
    negative, 481
    potential, 442
    premium for, xvii, 8, 488 - 489
    price, 340
    shareholder's, 7, 435 - 437, 444, 486
Control through
    casting vote, 440
    intermediate corporations, 440
    trustees and nominees, 440
    voting agreements, 441
Controlling interest, xvii, 69, 337, 429, 487, 498, 500
Controlling shareholder, 7, 435 - 437, 444, 486
Convertible preferred shares, 152
Convertible securities, 159
Corporate acquirers, 7, 15
Corporations
    associated, xiv, 528
Capital
    legislation, 483
    jurisprudence, 483
Cost of
    debt, 254
    equity, 261
        levered, 254
        unlevered, 260
    preferred shares, 256
Costs
    bankruptcy, 253
    disposition, 49, 374
    equity, 256
    head office, 169
    income tax, 236

    issue, 256 - 257
    liquidation, 379
    overhead, 123
    replacement, 232
    transaction, 406
Cost structure, 332
Cumulative eligible capital, 137
Cumulative preferred share, 155
Cumulative voting, 446
Current liabilities, 378
Current operating results, 120

D
Death, 508, 533
    of shareholder, 457, 467
    of taxpayer, 508
Debt
    cost of, xvii, 254
    interest bearing, 101, 116, 142, 178, 197
        equivalents, 144, 178
    long term interest bearing, 143
    ratio to equity, 250, 266, 267, 318, 570
    short term interest bearing debt, 142
Debt to equity ratio, 250, 266, 267, 318, 570
Deemed dividend, 530 - 532
Deferred
    income tax, 218, 335, 378
    revenues, 217, 378
Defined benefit pension plans, 377
Depreciated replacement cost, 232
        methodology, 226
Depreciated replacement value, xviii, 214, 216, 225
Depreciation, xviii, 335, 354
Derivative action, 448
Dilutive securities, xviii, 159, 172
Direct comparison methodology, 228

Discount
    blockage, 375
    block premiums and, 499
    capitalization rate, 195, 411 - 412, 415
    cash flow. *See* Cash flow
    marketability, 490
    minority, 8, 10, 41, 47, 70, 264, 290, 451, 466, 473, 477, 488, 489 - 491, 501
    rate, xviii, 25, 195, 244, 264, 279, 283, 302, 317, 320, 339, 411 - 412, 415
        mid-year, 304
Discount for
    illiquidity, xviii, 437, 473, 474, 476, 482, 489, 490, 492
    non-control, xviii, 437, 473, 474, 476, 478 - 479, 488, 491
Discount
Discounted cash flow. *See* cash flow
Discretionary cash flow. *See* cash flow
Disposition, 236
    costs, 49, 374
    of property, 507
Dissent, 447
    remedy, xix, 430, 445, 449, 499
Diversification, 298, 331, 405
Diversified portfolio, 316, 318
Dividend
    stripping, 530
    yield, 486
Divisions, 122 - 123, 170, 235, 236
Divorce Act, 11
Drag-along, 455, 498
    provisions, 465
Due diligence, 5 - 6, 321, 396, 406, 417

E

Earnings before interest and income taxes (EBIT), xix, 356, 357
    multiple of maintainable or trailing, 369

Earnings before interest, income taxes, depreciation and amortization (EBIT-DA), xix, 114, 186
    maintainable, 115, 118, 123, 194
    maintainable annual, 194
    multiple of maintainable or trailing, 371

Earnings per share, 16, 343, 354, 428

Earn-out, xix, 55, 345, 396, 425, 525
    arrangements, 457

EBIT. *See* Earnings before interest and income taxes

EBIT-DA. *See* Earnings before interest, income taxes, depreciation and amortization

Economic
    analysis, 90
    conditions,
        general, 62, 292, 337
        securities market conditions, 299
    life, xix

Economies of scale, xx, 398, 401 - 402

Effective control, 438, 484

Efficiency ratios, 570

Efficient market theory, 9, 340

Eligible capital property, 164, 166, 508

Employee stock option plan, 469

En bloc value, xx, 436, 476

Enterprise value, xx, 116, 142, 186, 243, 244, 246, 251, 261 - 262, 264, 301, 328, 357, 371

Equalization, 461
    payment, 44, 46, 48, 49

Equity,
    value, xx, 144, 243, 244, 246, 301, 328, 356
    cost of, 256, 261
        invested, xxiv
        levered, xxiv, 254

    levered return on, 413
    ratio to debt, 250, 266, 267, 318, 570
    return on, 114
    risk premium, 284, 316
        unlevered, 249, 260
    value, 144, 243, 244, 246, 301, 328, 356
Escrowed, 425
Estate freeze, 510, 511
Expropriations Acts, 11
Extended liquidation, 372
External funding, 477
Externally financed transaction, xx, 59
Extraordinary
    item, 335
    shareholders meetings, 446

F

Fair market value, xx, 12, 23, 31, 38, 176, 252, 263, 395, 396, 402, 424, 437, 451, 453, 455 - 457, 465 - 466, 494, 505, 506 - 509, 511 - 512, 513, 529
Fair value, xx, 40, 450 - 451, 480
Fairness opinions, 11
Family control, xxi, 443, 483
Family Law, 11, 44, 46, 461, 480, 483
Financed internally or externally, 466
Financial
    analysis, 81
        business plans and forecasts, 83
        historic and current, 81
    buyers, 17
    intermediaries, 19
    investors, 7
    leverage, xxi, xxiv, 93, 246, 263, 282, 290, 335, 413 - 414
        adjustment, 284, 301, 318
        ratios, 569
    markets, 283
    redundancies, 105
    risk, xxi, 243, 246, 251, 253, 263, 282, 284, 318, 569

structure, 332, 335
synergies, xxi, 303, 411, 413
Financing adjustment, 359
Finished goods inventory, 376
First refusal, right of, xxxiii, 463, 482
hard right of, xxii, 463, 495
soft right of, xxxv, 464, 495
Forced liquidation, xxi, 233, 372, 382
Forecast, 180, 185
period, 180
Fundamental changes, 449
Furniture and fixtures, 377

G

Generally Accepted Accounting Principles (GAAP), 16, 357
General Anti-Avoidance Rule (GAAR), 532
Going concern, xxi, 372, 374, 451
approach, 23
assumption, 215
risk, 50, 213
value, xxii, 22, 24, 50, 63
Goodwill, xxii, 21, 51, 54, 166, 216, 235, 297, 355, 365, 377, 381
commercial, 51
individual, xxiii, 52, 54, 399, 485, 498
personal, xxix, 52, 67, 399, 457, 463, 466, 485, 498

H

Hidden redundancy, 93, 360, 569
Highest and best use
property, 225
Highest price available, 32, 395 - 396
High growth businesses, 205
Hindsight, 61
Historic operating results, 118
Holding company, xxii, 169, 213, 235

Horizontal analysis, xxiii
Hurdle rates, xxiii, 294, 476

I
Identifiable intangible assets, xxiii, 217, 375, 377
Illiquidity, 291
    discount, 437, 473, 474, 476, 482, 489, 490, 492
Income properties, 238
Income tax, 49, 124, 171, 177, 186, 194, 218, 302, 335, 356, 358, 381 - 382, 424
    advisors, 20
    costs, 236
    losses, 359, 408
        carried forward, 137
    pools, 115, 134
Individual goodwill, xxiii, 52, 54, 399, 485, 498
Industry
    analysis, 89
    research, 417
    specific risks, 284
    specific activity ratios, xxiii
        factors, 292
    transactions, 344
Inflation, 184, 196, 282, 285, 294, 302, 307
Information
    availability, 4, 9
    base, 75
    circular 89, 443
    inside, 5, 339
    publicly available, 331
Informed, 396
Informed parties, 35
Initial public offering, 343, 13
Inside information, 5, 339
Insolvency, xxiii
    of a shareholder, 462

Insured values, 232
Intangible
    assets, 216, 335
    operating synergies xxiv, 303, 411, 412
    value, 21, 50
Integration, 405
    horizontal, 342
    vertical, 331, 342
Interest bearing debt, 101, 116, 142, 178, 197
    equivalents, 144, 178
Interest deductibility, 534
Intermediaries, xxiv, 18
Internal analysis, 79
Internal financing, 48
    vs. external financing, 57, 263, 457
Internal rate of return (IRR), xxiv
Internally financed transaction, xxiv, 477
Intrinsic value, xxiv, 21, 58, 290, 395, 397 - 398, 399, 456, 466
    en bloc, 329
Inventory
    costing, 334
    finished goods, 376
Investigation order, 448
Investment
    in operating companies, 236
    return on, 573
    tax credits, 138

L

Lease obligations, 378
Leasehold improvements, 377
Legal advisors, 20
Legal control, 438
Leverage, xxiv
Leveraged buyout, xxv, 17, 58, 62

Levered equity, xxv, 249
    return on, 132
    cost, 243
    return, 280 - 281, 285, 301, 356, 358, 414
Life insurance, 458, 467, 533
Liquidation, xxv, 23, 61
    costs, 379
    extended, 372
    forced, 233, 372, 382
    immediate, 372
    liquidation value, 64, 232 - 233, 372
    orderly, 233
    preferred shares premiums, 154
    value, xxv, 64, 232 - 233, 372
    voluntary, 372
Liquidity, xxv, 5, 68, 284, 289, 317, 321, 338, 344, 347, 402, 430, 473, 475 - 476, 485, 491, 495, 498
    ratios, 567
Long term liabilities, 378
Loss carry forwards, 186, 522

M

Machinery and equipment, 376
Maintainable after tax earnings from operations, xxv
Maintainable earnings before interest, taxes, depreciation and amortization, 115, 118, 123, 194
Management agreement, xxv, 53, 56, 297
    non-competition agreements, 297
Management contract, 349, 426
Mandatory sale, 455, 465, 498
Manufacturing and processing profits deduction, 124, 408
Market prices, 9, 43
Market value, 214, 216, 225
Marketability discount, xxvi, 90
Marketable securities, 235, 375
Matching principle, 267
Memorandum of association, 445, 453

Minority
    discount, xxvi, 8, 10, 41, 47, 70, 264, 290, 451, 466, 473, 477, 488, 489 - 491, 501
    interest, 69, 346, 429, 437, 457, 478, 479, 493, 497
    shareholder, xxvi, 7, 8, 435, 437, 449, 453, 477, 481, 484
Multi-divisional business, 169, 171
Multiples, xxvi, 115, 280, 328, 336, 343, 355, 366, 429

N

Negative redundancy, xxvi, 96, 97, 336
Negotiations, 424, 426
Net capital loss, 236, 382, 522
    carry forwards, 186
Net economic value-added, 181
    purchaser perceived, xxxi, 303, 477, 497
Net family property, 49
Net income (loss), xxvii
Net realizable value, xxvii, 374, 375
Net tangible asset backing, xxxvi, 213 - 214
Net trade working capital, xxvii, 98, 115, 130, 177, 190, 308, 336, 569
    requirements, 190
Nominee shareholder, 440
Non-arm's length transactions, 11, 119, 506 - 507, 512, 532
Non-capital
    loss, 187, 197, 382, 424, 522
Non-cash consideration, 38
Non-competition, 53, 455, 459 - 460
    agreement, xxvii, 54 - 55, 349, 460, 463
    contracts, 52
Non-identifiable intangible assets, xxviii, 24, 3
Non-recurring, 119, 229
    items, 357 - 358, 369, 371
    expense adjustments, 358
    revenue adjustments, 358
Notional leverage adjustments, 97

Notional market, xxviii, 31, 396, 424, 479
    valuation, 11, 32, 402
Notional value, 397
Nuisance value, 486, 488, 498, 500

O

One-time items, 371
Open market, xxviii, 33, 263, 396, 465
    transaction, 11, 329, 344, 396, 398
Operating
    cash balance, 190
    cash requirements, 99
    leverage, xxviii, 265, 298, 332
    prospective results, 121
    risks, 246, 251, 263, 282
Opportunity cost, xxviii, 6, 52
Oppression remedy, xxviii, 40, 445, 447, 451, 499
Options, 162
Overhead costs
    common, 123
Over-the-counter market, xxviii
Owner-managed businesses, 398

P

Paid up capital, 383
Participating preferred shares, 156
Partnership, xxix, 3, 312, 510, 523, 529, 533, 535
Past-acquisition net economic value added, 493
Pension surplus, 217, 378
Permanent disability of an employee/shareholder, 458
Perpetual growth, 115
    real growth, 194, 208
Post-acquisition
    economies of scale, 15, 21
    net economic value added, xxix, 8, 33, 123, 338, 397, 398, 403, 409
    synergies, 493

Post-amalgamation benefits, 42, 451
Powers of attorney, 441
Pre-emptive rights, 446
Preferred shares, 151, 511, 512
    liquidation premiums, 154
    valuation based on dividend yield, 155
Premium for
    control, xxix, 8, 488 - 489
    forcible taking, 42, 451
    subsequent sale of shares, 467
Prepaid expenses, 376
Price, xxix, 6, 21, 38, 395, 398, 402, 424
    adjustment clauses, 512
    control, 340
Price/earnings multiple, xxix, 354, 356
Primary offering, xxx, 158, 295
Private placement, 347
Privately held businesses, xxx, 16
Probability factor, 300, 304
Profitability ratios, 572
Pro-forma, xxx, 191
Proposal to creditors, xxx
Proprietorship, xxx, 3
Proxies, 441
Prudent, 396
    parties, 37
Public equity market
    multiples, 337
    risk premium, 284, 289, 290, 291, 292
Public vs. private companies, 8
Publicly held companies, xxxi, 15
Purchase and sale
    agreements, 396
Put option, 426
    provision, 495
Put-call, 463

R

Ratable value, xxxi, 58, 59, 435, 443, 460, 466, 473 500, 501

Rateable or pro rata, 436

Rate of return, xxxi, 62, 206, 344, 476
    base, xiv, 284, 289, 296
    hurdle, 321, 427
    levered
        on equity, xxxi
    nominal, xxvii, 184
    real, xxxii, 184, 288, 309
    risk free, 284, 288, 291, 315, 316
    threshold, 321, 427
    unlevered
        on equity, 283 - 284, 301, 413

Ratio analysis, 84, 96, 567

Ratios, 98, 191, 207, 265, 328, 333, 336 - 337

Raw material inventory, 375

RDTOH. *See* Refundable dividend tax on hand

Real estate, xxxi
    assets, 238, 376
    valuation, 223

Real growth, 127, 308

Real property, xxxi, 19, 226, 228

Recapture, xxxii, 381

Receivership, xxxii, 372

Redeemable preferred shares, 154, 425

Redundant assets, xxxii, 26, 75, 81, 85, 92 - 99, 101 - 104, 107, 110, 114 - 117, 119, 137, 139 - 141, 147 - 149, 166, 172, 175, 178, 179, 186, 190, 197, 208, 209, 224, 235, 245, 267, 312, 341, 344, 356, 357, 359, 360, 366, 369, 371, 414, 418, 420, 510, 567, 570

Refundable dividend tax on hand (RDTOH), xxxii, 382, 528

Refundable tax, 238
    income taxes, 236

Replacement cost, 232

Reproduction cost (new), xxxii

Research and development, 333, 335
    scientific, tax credits, 138, 408, 535

Reserve accounts, 378
Residual value, 177, 194, 373
Restrictions, 498
    on share transfer, 437, 455, 465, 481
    on transfer, 494
Retractable preferred shares, 153
Revenue recognition, 335
Risk
    absolute, xiii
    assessment, 103
    business, xiv, 140, 155, 175, 182, 235, 255, 265, 292, 297, 299, 411, 424, 436, 478, 479
    business specific, 318
        factors, 284, 296, 318
    premium, 284, 316
    financial, 243, 246, 251, 253, 263, 282, 284, 318, 569
    going concern, risk, 50, 213
    industry specific risks, 284
    operating, 246, 251, 263, 282
    public equity market
        premium, 284, 289, 290, 291, 292
    return, 300
    return tradeoff, 282
    return assessment, 7
    systematic, 316
    terminal value adjustment, 310
    unsystematic risk, 296, 316
Risk free rate of return, xxxiii, 284, 288, 291, 315, 316
Risk-return, 300
Rollover provisions, xxxiii, 510
Rules of thumb, xxxiii, 207, 371

S

Safe income, xxxiii, 237, 531 - 532
Salvage value, 234
Scrap value, 234
Seasonality, 336

Secondary offerings, xxxiii, 159
Section 22 election, 517, 525
Security analysis, xxxiii, 4
Sensitivity analysis, 183
Share capital reorganizations, 511
Share for share exchange, xxxiv, 396, 425, 428, 515
Shareholder
    controlling, 7, 435 - 437, 444, 486
    minority, 8, 435, 437, 449, 453, 477, 481, 484
    nominee, 440
Shareholder's
    Agreement, xxxiv, 8, 34, 348, 396, 445, 454, 456, 466 - 467, 480, 481, 487, 494
        Unanimous, 439, 441, 445, 447, 449, 454, 481
    bankruptcy/insolvency, 462
    control, 7, 435 - 437, 444, 486
    death, 457, 467
    equity, xxxiv, 215, 333
    extraordinary meetings, 446
    marriage breakdown, 460
    permanent disability, 458
    relationships, 483
    retirement, 459
    rights, 446
    termination of employment, 460
Shares vs. assets, 164
Share transaction, xxxiv, 165, 224, 495
Shotgun clauses, xxxiv, 463, 495
Size of shareholding, 483
Small business deduction, xxxiv, 124, 528
Special interest purchaser, xxxv, 23, 32, 50, 69, 396, 400, 402, 456, 466
    price, 22
Special resolution, 439, 484, 487
Special use value, 225
Squeeze out, xxxv, 430
Stand-alone
    basis, 398, 477
    value, xxxv, 395, 397 - 398, 409, 430

Standard industrial classification code, 417
Start-up businesses, 205
Statutory-related triggering event, 499
Stock market
    investors, 7
    price, 451
Stock exchange, xxxv, 5, 32
Strategic advantage, xxxv, 21, 285, 303, 398, 402, 403, 412
Strategic importance, 295, 401
Sustaining capital, 332
    reinvestment, xxxv, 115, 125, 189, 194, 354
        adjusted net book value, 232
S.W.O.T. analysis, xxxvi, 91
synergies, xxxvi, 8, 10, 21, 32, 59, 181, 285, 302, 344 - 345, 372, 398, 403, 409, 411, 417, 429, 430, 489
    financial, 303, 411, 413
    post-acquisition, 493
    intangible operating, 303, 411, 412
    tangible operating, 303, 410, 411
Systematic risk, 316

T

Tagalong provision, xxxvi, 455, 465, 495
Takeover, 13, 428, 447, 488
    bid, 345, 484
    premiums, 489
    prices, 290
Tangible operating synergies, xxxvi, 303, 410, 411
Tax avoidance provisions, 529
Tax pools, 177, 196
Tax shield, xxxvi, 128
Taxable dividend, 383, 515
Terminal
    loss, 381
    value, 113, 114, 177, 194 - 195, 280, 305, 309
        risk adjustment, 310

Threshold rates of return, xxxvii, 294, 321, 427
Trade working capital, 98
Tradeoff, 300
Transfer pricing, 532
Transfers to a corporation, 510
Trend analysis, 84, 85
Triggering Events, 456
Trustee, 441

U

Undepreciated capital cost (UCC), xxxvii, 135
Unlevered
    equity, 249
    rate of return on equity, xxxvii, 283 - 284, 301, 413
Unrestricted market, 34
Unsystematic risk, 296, 316
Unusual
    items, 120
    revenues and expenses, 229

V

Vacant land, 239
Valuation, xxxvii
    based on dividend yield, 155
    business, xv
    date, xxxvii, 47
    notional market, 11, 32, 402
    principles, 60
    real estate, 223
        methodologies, 229
Value, xxxvii, 467
    agreed annually by the shareholders, 468
    en bloc, 329, 436, 476
    enterprise, 116, 142, 186, 243, 244, 246, 251, 261 - 262, 264, 301, 328, 357, 371
    equity, 144, 243, 244, 246, 301, 328, 356

determined by
    formula, 468
    independent expert, 469
    mediation or arbitration, 469
fair, 40, 450 - 451, 480
fair market, 12, 23, 31, 38, 176, 252, 263, 395, 396, 402, 424, 437, 451, 453, 455 - 457, 465 - 466, 494, 505, 506 - 509, 511 - 512, 513, 529
going concern, 22, 24, 50, 63
in exchange, xxxvii, 215, 225, 374 - 376
insured, 232
intangible, 21, 50
intangible assets, 216, 335
intangible operating synergies, 303, 411, 412
intrinsic, 21, 58, 290, 395, 397 - 398, 399, 456, 466
in use, xxxvii, 50, 214, 216, 225, 232, 377
liquidation, 64, 232 - 233, 372
market, 214, 216, 225
net book, xxvi
    adjusted, 213, 214, 232, 233
        methodology, 213, 235
net realizable, 374, 375
notional, 397
nuisance, 486, 488, 498, 500
pro-rata, xxx, 58, 59, 71, 158, 161, 163, 164, 204, 436, 437, 457, 458, 466, 477, 487, 490, 500
rateable, xxxi, 58, 59, 435, 443, 460, 466, 473, 500, 501
replacement, xxxii, 232
    depreciated, 214, 216, 225
residual, 177, 194, 373
salvage, 234
scrap, 234
special use, 225
stand-alone, 395, 397 - 398, 409, 430
to owner, xxxviii, 43, 46, 67
Vendor take-back, xxxviii, 345, 396, 425
Vendors, 14
Vertical analysis, xxxviii
Voluntary liquidation, xxxviii, 372

W

WACC. *See* weighted average cost of capital

Warrants, 162

Weighted average cost of capital (WACC), xxxviii, 114, 122, 131 - 132, 176, 244, 246, 251, 254, 261, 264, 266, 280 - 281, 285, 301, 357, 369, 371, 413, 414

Widely held corporation, xxxviii

Winding-up, xxxix, 514

Work in progress, 376

Working capital, xxxix, 96, 97, 101, 194, 267
    requirements, 354